D1266623

A HISTORY OF
ELY CATHEDRAL

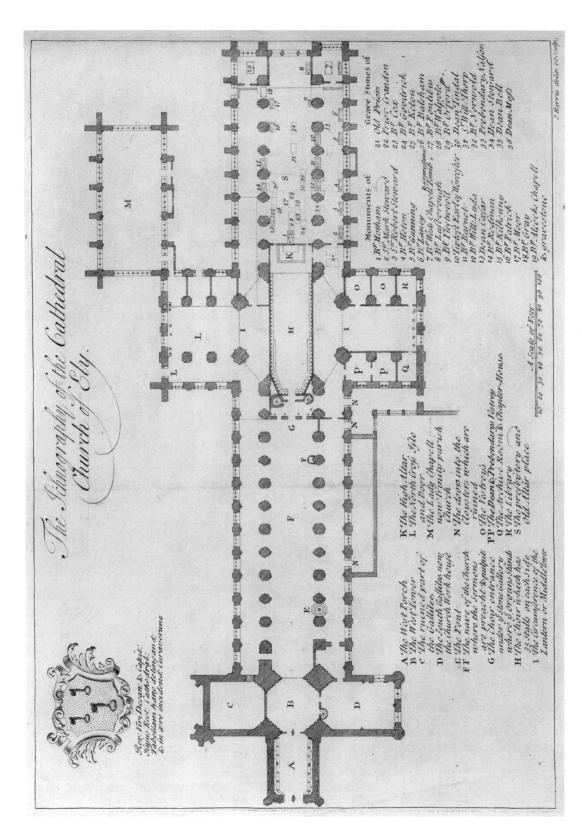

J. Harris, ground-plan of Ely Cathedral Church, for Browne Willis, *Survey of Ely* (1730)

A HISTORY OF
ELY CATHEDRAL

EDITED BY
PETER MEADOWS AND NIGEL RAMSAY

THE BOYDELL PRESS

First published 2003
The Boydell Press, Woodbridge

ISBN 0 85115 945 1

The Boydell Press is an imprint of Boydell & Brewer Ltd
PO Box 9, Woodbridge, Suffolk IP12 3DF, UK
and of Boydell & Brewer Inc.
PO Box 41026, Rochester, NY 14604–4126, USA
website: www.boydell.co.uk

A catalogue record for this book is available
from the British Library

Library of Congress Cataloging-in-Publication Data
A history of Ely Cathedral / edited by Peter Meadows and Nigel Ramsay.
    p. cm.
Includes bibliographical references and index.
    ISBN 0–85115–945–1 (alk. paper)
1. Ely Cathedral – History.   2. Ely (England) – Church history.
I. Meadows, Peter, 1958– II. Ramsay, Nigel.
    BX5195.E5H57 2003
    283′.42656 – dc21   2002156576

This publication is printed on acid-free paper

Typeset by Joshua Associates Ltd, Oxford
Printed in Great Britain by
Cromwell Press Ltd, Trowbridge, Wilts

Contents

Ely Abbey 672–1109

Ely Priory 1109–1539

Foreword by HRH The Duke of Edinburgh

Ely Cathedral is one of the most spectacular examples of church architecture in this country. Its setting on the Isle of Ely allows it to dominate the fen landscape and it has a very special place in the affections of the people of East Anglia.

With a history dating back to 673, there is ample scope for the contributors to this splendid book to put together a fascinating account of the many triumphs and vicissitudes in the long story of this great Cathedral. Quite apart from the sheer technical challenges in constructing such an immense building, it is a reflection of the strength of the dedication of its designers and builders to their Christian faith. The skills, efforts and time devoted to the building and rebuilding of its fabric are their own reward.

This same devotion has also allowed it to become a very important cultural focus. Music, scholarship and the arts have flourished in its shadow and continue to inspire and encourage their further development.

Thanks to generous contributions, largely from the people of East Anglia, the Cathedral has just emerged from a major programme of repair and maintenance. This has ensured that many future generations will continue to be able to stand in awe and wonder of this unique building.

Foreword by the Rt Revd Dr Anthony Russell, Bishop of Ely

Ely Cathedral, with the Lantern illuminated at night and visible for miles around, dominates both this small town and large Diocese. Its beauty, history and continuing life of prayer make it one of the most loved and magnificent cathedrals in England.

Long regarded as an ecclesiastical backwater, cathedrals have undergone a renaissance in recent years, and Ely has been at the forefront of this renewal of their life and witness.

Ely Cathedral is a complex and many-layered place. It is a building of sublime magnificence which continues to speak powerfully of the majesty and glory of God; a sacred place and a sacrament in stone. It is above all else a house of prayer, where the daily rhythm of worship has continued since the time of its foundress, St Etheldreda, in 673. It is a place of pilgrimage and attracts tens of thousands of visitors. It is a community of people who serve God, and whose love and dedication make possible the continuing life of the Cathedral.

This book records the fascinating history of the Cathedral's development, from the time that Etheldreda established her monastic community on this island amidst the mists and marshes of the undrained fens. It is a worthy successor to James Bentham's famous history of the Cathedral, published in 1771, and complements John Maddison's contemporary account of its architectural development. The history of Ely Cathedral is a story of varying fortunes, of times of prosperity and times of neglect, that culminates in the glories of the recently restored fabric and the energetic and robust life of the Cathedral today.

Cathedrals are about prayer and people, and the dedication of generations who have served God in this place. This book is a memorial to their work and an encouragement to us, who have the privilege of serving God and his Church in this place today.

+ Anthony Ely

Foreword by the Revd Canon Dr John Inge, Vice-Dean

This is the most significant book about Ely Cathedral since James Bentham published his *History* in 1771, and I should like, on behalf of the Chapter, to express thanks to the many people who have made its publication possible. First, the contributors, who gave freely of their time and expertise to produce some outstanding essays. Second, the editors Peter Meadows and Dr Nigel Ramsay, who have worked unstintingly to ensure that it would be of a very high standard. Third, Professor Derek Brewer, who chaired both the Steering and Editorial Committees and whose commitment to the undertaking has been invaluable. Fourth, the members of those committees: Dr Hugh Richmond, Miss Jane Kennedy, Professor Jacques Heyman, Miss Pam Blakeman, Miss Ella Thurmott, Mr Sam Lawrence, Dr Philip Dixon, Miss Joyce Whale and Dr Thomas Cocke. I have personally appreciated working with all the above on what has been a very fascinating project. Finally, we are most grateful to those who have given financial assistance towards the publication of the volume. Particular thanks are due to the Dulverton Trust for providing us with a large sum. Other generous assistance was given by Boydell & Brewer, Mrs L.D. Rope's Second Charitable Settlement, the John Jarrold Trust, the Aurelius Charitable Trust, and the Friends of Ely Cathedral.

Editors' Preface

In the preface to his *History*, James Bentham wrote: 'I should willingly hope, that the CHURCH OF ELY will be allowed to be one of the most curious monuments of ecclesiastical antiquities in this Kingdom: and therefore meriting some kind of distinction.' In the same spirit the authors of these essays have expanded and reinterpreted Bentham's account, introduced new aspects of scholarly research, and carried the story forward to the present day. We should like to thank them for their enthusiastic response to the task of writing their chapters. We are much indebted to the members of the Editorial Committee, and especially Professor Derek Brewer, for their judicious guidance; to the staff of Ely Cathedral, particularly the former Bursar, David Smout, for much unseen and therefore unsung help; and to the Dean and Chapter, who never wavered in their backing for this project.

Peter Meadows
Nigel Ramsay

Black and White Plates

1 (a) *Liber Eliensis* (EDC 1): Cnut's song, Book II, chapter 85, 'Merrily sung the monks of Ely' (indicated by arrow).

  (b) Land charter, AD 973: King Edgar grants land at West Wratting to his servant Ælfhelm (EDC 1B/1A)

2 (a) Regulations of the thegns' guild at Cambridge, in an 8th-century gospel-book from Ely (BL, MS Cott. Tib. B. v, vol. I, fo. 75)

  (b) Ely farming memoranda: lists of goods supplied to Thorney Abbey, pigs on Ely estates, details of fen rents, *etc.*, preserved as sewing guards in 17th-century bindings (BL, Add. MS 61735)

  (c) Ely titulus: commemoration of King Edgar and several abbots, priors and sacrists of Ely Abbey, in the mortuary roll of Abbot Vitalis of Savigny (d.1122) (L. Delisle, *Rouleau mortuaire* (Paris, 1909), pl. XLV)

3 (a) Plan of the 'chapter house' (monastic kitchen) (Stevenson, *Supplement*, pl. L, figure III)

  (b) Robert Willis, plan of the Cathedral's Norman apse and east end, sketched for D.J. Stewart's *Ely*, 1868 (EDC 14/36/1/49)

  (c) W. St John Hope, reconstruction of the elevation of the Norman nave pulpitum, destroyed in 1770 (*PCAS*, xxi (1919), pl. 1, facing p. 19)

4 (a) The Prior's Door, opening into the former cloister on the south side of the nave.

  (b) The Monks' Door and the south transept door, both partly blocked by a buttress supporting the Octagon (John Maddison)

  (c) West tower interior, looking upward: angle squinches built to support a spire (John Maddison)

  (d) Norman capitals in the south transept (John Maddison)

5 (a) South-west transept restored (*Illustrated London News*, 27 Sept. 1845)

  (b) South-west transept, west front and lower part of turret (John Maddison)

  (c) West tower, south-west transept; St Catherine's Chapel as restored by Robert Willis (Crown copyright. NMR)

  (d) St Catherine's Chapel, interior (A.F. Kersting)

6 (a) Galilee Porch, exterior (Philip Dixon)

  (b) Galilee upper chamber, unroofed *c.*1800 (Philip Dixon)

  (c) Galilee Porch, interior and west portal

7 (a) Bishop Northwold's presbytery, looking south, drawn by E. Mackenzie, engraved by F.J. Havell (George Millers, *Ely*, 3rd edn (1834), pl. IX)

  (b) Bishop Hotham's presbytery bays, looking north (Millers, *Ely*, 3rd edn (1834), pl. VIII)

  (c–e) Wall brackets in presbytery: (c) Bishop Northwold, east end; (d) Bishop Hotham, south side; (e) Bishop Hotham, north side (Philip Dixon)

8 (a) Remains of 13th-century choir stalls, in the cathedral wood store

  (b) 14th-century choir stalls, with 19th century carved panels

  (c) Photomontage of the stalls relocated in the Octagon space, showing the arrangements which lasted until 1770 (Edward Maddison)

Colour Plates

Text Figures

Acknowledgements

The editors wish to thank those who have given permission to reproduce illustrations: The Dean and Chapter of Ely; the Dean and Chapter of Canterbury; the Chapter of Gloucester Cathedral; the British Library; the Bodleian Library, Oxford; Cambridgeshire Libraries; the Master and Fellows of Corpus Christi College, Cambridge; the Master and Fellows of Emmanuel College, Cambridge; the Master and Fellows of Downing College, Cambridge; the Master and Fellows of Jesus College, Cambridge; the Master and Fellows of Peterhouse, Cambridge; the Master and Fellows of Pembroke College, Cambridge; the Victoria and Albert Museum, London; the Fitzwilliam Museum, Cambridge; the Ashmolean Museum, Oxford; Aberdeen Art Gallery and Museums Collections; the National Portrait Gallery, London; the National Monuments Record; the Society of Antiquaries of London; the Royal College of Music, London; the Victoria County History; Cambridge University Collection of Air Photographs; the City of Ely Council; A.F. Kersting; Nigel Bloxham; Lord Burton; Christopher Sparke; T. Fenton; Geoff Newman (Images of England); Roy Hallett; Reeve Photography; and Cambridge University Library (especially Les Goody and Nancy Allen of the Photography Department, and Iain Burke). They are also indebted to Philip Dixon, John Maddison and Edward Maddison for much specially commissioned photography.

Abbreviations

Abp	Archbishop
AJ	*Archaeological Journal*
ASC	*Anglo-Saxon Chronicle*
Atkinson, *Ely Monastery*	T.D. Atkinson, *An Architectural History of the Benedictine Monastery of Saint Etheldreda at Ely* (Cambridge, 1933)
BAACT	British Archaeological Association Conference Transactions
Bede, *HE*	B. Colgrave and R.A.B. Mynors (ed.), Bede's *Ecclesiastical History of the English People* (Oxford, 1969) (citations are to book and chapter, followed by page in the edition)
Bentham, *Ely*	James Bentham, *The History and Antiquities of the Conventual and Cathedral Church of Ely: from the Foundation of the Monastery, A.D. 673, to the Year 1771*, 2nd edn (Norwich, 1812)
Bodl.	Bodleian Library, Oxford
Bp	Bishop
BL	British Library, London
cal.	calendar
CAS	Cambridge Antiquarian Society
CCCC	Corpus Christi College, Cambridge
Chapman, *Sacrist Rolls*	F.R. Chapman, *Sacrist Rolls of Ely*, 2 vols. (Ely, 1907)
CPL	*Calendar of Entries in the Papal Registers relating to Great Britain*, 17 vols. (London and Dublin, 1893–)
CPR	*Calendar of Patent Rolls*, 60 vols. (London, 1901–)
CUL	Cambridge University Library
CYS	Canterbury and York Society
DNB	*Dictionary of National Biography*
EDC	Ely Dean & Chapter Archives, Cambridge University Library
EDR	Ely Diocesan Records, Cambridge University Library
Emden, *Register*	A.B. Emden, *A Biographical Register of the University of Cambridge to 1500* (Cambridge, 1963)
Eng. Hist. Rev.	*English Historical Review*

Evans, *Ordinances*	S.J.A. Evans (ed.), 'Ely Chapter Ordinances and Visitation Records 1241–1515', *Camden Miscellany XVII*, Camden 3rd series, lxiv (Royal Historical Society, 1940)
fo., fos.	folio, folios (citations are of rectos, unless otherwise indicated)
Goodwin, *Ely Gossip*	Harvey Goodwin, *Ely Gossip, A.D. 1858–1869* (Ely, 1892)
Greatrex, *BRECP*	Joan Greatrex, *Biographical Register of the English Cathedral Priories of the Province of Canterbury c.1066 to 1540* (Oxford, 1997)
HMC	Historical Manuscripts Commission
JBAA	*Journal of the British Archaeological Association*
JEH	*Journal of Ecclesiastical History*
LE	see *Liber Eliensis* below
Le Neve, *Fasti*	J. Le Neve, *Fasti Ecclesiae Anglicanae*, revised edn (Institute of Historical Research, University of London, 1962–)
Liber Eliensis (ed. Blake)	E.O. Blake (ed.), *Liber Eliensis*, Camden 3rd series, xcii (Royal Historical Soc., 1962) (first citation in a chapter; subsequent citations are *LE*, followed by book and chapter, and the page(s) in Blake's edition)
LP Henry VIII	J. Brewer, J. Gairdner and R.H. Brodie (eds.), *Letters and Papers, Foreign and Domestic, of the Reign of Henry VIII*, 22 vols. in 37 pts. (London, 1864–1932)
LPL	Lambeth Palace Library
Maddison, *Ely Cathedral*	John Maddison, *Ely Cathedral: Design and Meaning* (Ely, 2000)
Miller, *Abbey & Bishopric*	Edward Miller, *The Abbey and Bishopric of Ely* (Cambridge, 1951)
NRO	Norfolk Record Office
Owen & Thurley, *King's School*	D.M. Owen and Dorothea Thurley (eds.), *The King's School, Ely*, Cambridge Antiquarian Records Society, 5 (1982)
Payne, *Provision and Practice*	I. Payne, *The Provision and Practice of Sacred Music at Cambridge Colleges and Selected Cathedrals c.1547–c.1646: A Comparative Study of the Archival Evidence* (New York, 1993)
PCAS	*Proceedings of Cambridge Antiquarian Society*
PRO	Public Record Office, London
Proc.	*Proceedings*
Reg.	Register
Ridyard, *Royal Saints*	Susan J. Ridyard, *The Royal Saints of Anglo-Saxon England. A Study of West Saxon and East Anglian Cults* (Cambridge, 1988)
Robertson, *Anglo-Saxon Charters*	A.J. Robertson (ed.), *Anglo-Saxon Charters*, 2nd edn (Cambridge, 1956)

S 1844 (*etc.*)	Peter Hayes Sawyer, *Anglo-Saxon Charters: An Annotated List and Bibliography* (London: Royal Historical Society, 1968) (citrations are by charter no.)
s.a.	*sub anno* (for the year)
ser.	series
Shaw, *Succession of Organists*	H. Watkins Shaw, *The Succession of Organists at the Chapel Royal and the Cathedrals of England and Wales from c.1538* (Oxford, 1991)
Stevenson, *Supplement*	William Stevenson, *A Supplement to the Second Edition of Mr. Bentham's History and Antiquities of the Cathedral and Conventual Church of Ely* (Norwich, 1817)
Stewart, *Ely*	D.J. Stewart, *On the Architectural History of Ely Cathedral* (London, 1868)
TCC	Trinity College, Cambridge
UA	University Archives, Cambridge University Library
VCH	The Victoria History of the Counties of England
Venn, *Alumni*	John Venn and J.A. Venn, *Alumni Cantabrigienses*, 10 vols. (Cambridge, 1922–54)
Wharton, *Anglia Sacra*	H. Wharton (ed.), *Anglia Sacra, sive collectio Historiarum, partim recenter scriptarum, de Archiepiscopis et Episcopis Angliae, a prima Fidei Christianae susceptione ad Annum MDXL*, 2 vols. (London, 1691)
Wulfstan, *VSÆ*	M. Lapidge and M. Winterbottom (eds.), *Wulfstan of Winchester: The Life of St Æthelwold* (Oxford, 1991)

Dates

Dates before 1752 are given in Old Style, but the year has been taken to begin on 1 January, not 25 March.

A HISTORY OF ELY CATHEDRAL

Figure 1. The Fenlands before the mid-17th-century drainage (Jan Blaeu, *Regiones Inundatae*, 1648). South is to the left, north to the right. Ely was approached by roads and causeways from east and west.

Ely Abbey 672–1109

Simon Keynes

> Ely [*Elge*] is a district of about 600 hides in the kingdom of the East Angles and resembles an island in that it is surrounded by marshes or by water. It derives its name from the large number of eels which are caught in the marshes.

Writing in 731, from the vantage-point of his monastery at Jarrow, in Northumbria, the Venerable Bede fastened upon the natural features which for so long gave Ely its distinctive identity.[1] The name (*El-ge*) originally signified 'eel-district', and a glance at a map representing the general appearance of the area before the draining of the fens in the seventeenth century (Figure 1) shows with what good reason the name came to be altered in the eighth or ninth century to *El-eg* ('eel-island'). It was, moreover, a place well suited to those who wished to devote themselves to the worship of God: relatively inaccessible, remote from worldly distractions, yet blessed with the natural resources necessary for sustaining the life of a religious community. The place now owes its distinction not so much to its eels as to St Æthelthryth, who founded a monastery at Ely in the early 670s; and not so much to Æthelthryth herself as to the veneration in the tenth and eleventh centuries of one who in the manner of her life had come to be regarded as a symbol of sanctity in the early English church.[2]

The sources of information

Ely Abbey was one of the many religious houses which flourished in Anglo-Saxon England, but it stands apart from the rest for the quality, quantity and variety of source material available for its study.[3] We are dependant for our knowledge and understanding

---

[1] Bede, *HE*, iv. 19: p. 396.

[2] The following account of Anglo-Saxon and Anglo-Norman Ely draws on material prepared in collaboration with Alan Kennedy for our projected *Anglo-Saxon Ely: Records of Ely Abbey and its Benefactors in the 10th and 11th Centuries*, commenced in the late 1980s. Some parts of this work will now be published separately, pending an opportunity to bring them together in consolidated form. I am otherwise indebted for help of one kind and another to Tethys Carpenter, Janet Fairweather, John Inge, Rosalind Love, Peter Meadows and Nigel Ramsay.

[3] The standard account of Anglo-Saxon and Anglo-Norman Ely remains E. Miller, *The Abbey and Bishopric of Ely* (Cambridge, 1951); see also VCH, *Cambs.*, II, pp. 199–210, and S. Keynes, 'Ely Abbey', in M. Lapidge *et al.* (eds.), *The Blackwell Encyclopaedia of Anglo-Saxon England* (Oxford, 1999), pp. 166–7. There is much useful information in Bentham, *Ely*, published in 1771, based largely on the *Liber Eliensis* and other local histories. The notebooks and letter-book kept by Bentham are CUL, MSS Add. 2944–62; a copy of Bentham's 1771 book, annotated by him with material for a new edition, is in the Fitzwilliam Museum, Cambridge (13.2.F.11).

of the original foundation on the various manifestations of the cult of St Æthelthryth (and other members of her family) produced from the eighth century onwards.[4] Bede's *Historia ecclesiastica gentis Anglorum* is the main source of authoritative information on the life of St Æthelthryth herself and on the early history of her community at Ely.[5] The story was retold in the ninth century, in the *Old English Martyrology* and in the vernacular translation of Bede's *History*, though without adding anything to the story.[6] Our attention is next directed towards the *Liber miraculorum beate virginis*, which provides an account of events which took place at Ely in the mid tenth century (following the Abbey's destruction by the Danes, *c*.870), written ostensibly by a certain Ælfhelm, who was one of the priests serving the church at that time and who would appear to have become a monk there after the refoundation of the Abbey *c*.970.[7] There is reason to believe that a more substantial 'Life' of St Æthelthryth was composed at Ely some time between the late tenth and the end of the eleventh century, embroidering the basic story as told by Bede with additional details (and miracles) derived from local tradition, imagination, or wishful thinking; for it is necessary in this way to explain some of the similarities between the various 'Lives' of St Æthelthryth produced in the late eleventh and early twelfth centuries.[8] It should be noted in the same connection that a 'booklet written in English' on St Æthelthryth existed at Ely in the twelfth century, as well as a vernacular account of her sister Seaxburh;[9] but it is difficult to guess what they might have contained. Lost or hypothetical sources of this kind lie behind the consolidation of the hagiography of this family of saints in the late eleventh and early twelfth centuries, represented by the contents of a manuscript produced at Ely probably in the 1120s.[10] The collection begins with a short account of Æthelthryth's sister St Æthelburh (Abbess of Faremoûtier-en-Brie), based on Bede,[11] and continues with a 'Life' of Æthelthryth herself, in rhyming prose, accompanied by a book of

---

The 2nd edn, edited by James Bentham (the younger) and published in 1812, contains a valuable section of Addenda. The supplement, edited by W. Stevenson and published in 1817, contains some further material on the old church; see below, n. 103.

[4] For recent work on St Æthelthryth and her cult, see C.E. Fell, 'Saint Æthelthryth: a Historical-Hagiographical Dichotomy Revisited', *Nottingham Medieval Studies*, 38 (1994), pp. 18–34; P.A. Thompson, 'St Æthelthryth: the Making of History from Hagiography', in M.J. Toswell and E.M. Tyler (eds.), *Studies in English Language and Literature* (London, 1996), pp. 475–92; S. Rosser, 'Æthelthryth: a Conventional Saint?', *Bulletin of the John Rylands University Library of Manchester*, 79 (1997), pp. 15–24; and V. Blanton-Whetsell, '*Tota integra, tota incorrupta*: the Shrine of St Æthelthryth as Symbol of Monastic Identity', *Journal of Medieval and Early Modern Studies*, 32 (2002), pp. 227–67.

[5] Bede, *HE*, iv. 19–20: pp. 390–400. The only other authoritative source is Stephen's *Life of St Wilfrid*, chs. 19, 22: B. Colgrave, *The Life of Bishop Wilfrid by Eddius Stephanus* (Cambridge, 1927), pp. 40 and 44.

[6] See further below, p. 15.

[7] See further below, pp. 8 and 16–17.

[8] For further discussion, see *Liber Eliensis*, ed. Blake, pp. xxx–xxxi; S.J. Ridyard, *The Royal Saints of Anglo-Saxon England: a Study of West Saxon and East Anglian Cults* (Cambridge, 1988), pp. 53–6; M. Lapidge and R.C. Love, 'England and Wales (600–1550)', in G. Philippart (ed.), *Hagiographies: histoire internationale de la littérature hagiographique latine et vernaculaire, en Occident, des origines à 1500* (Turnhout, 2001), III, pp. 1–120, at pp. 41–2; and *Goscelin of Saint-Bertin: the Female Saints of Ely*, ed. R.C. Love (Oxford Medieval Texts, forthcoming).

[9] *LE*, i. Prol., i. 33, and i. 36: pp. 6, 48 and 51.

[10] CCCC, MS 393: M.R. James, *A Descriptive Catalogue of the Manuscripts in the Library of Corpus Christi College Cambridge*, 2 vols. (Cambridge, 1909–13), II, pp. 251–3, and *Saints of Ely*, ed. Love (cit. in n. 8).

[11] Bede, *HE*, iii. 8: pp. 238–40.

Miracles (of different and more complex origin); this is followed by a versification of the 'Life' and Miracles of Æthelthryth, attributed to Gregory, monk of Ely (writing probably in the 1120s), and the collection concludes with separate 'Lives' of Æthelthryth's sister Wihtburh, her sister Seaxburh (second Abbess of Ely), her niece Eormenhild (third Abbess), and Eormenhild's daughter Werburh (of Chester).[12]

For the history of the monastery refounded at Ely in the late tenth century, we have what amounts (for the period) to an extraordinarily wide range of documentation. A number of royal charters recording grants of land or privileges were preserved as title-deeds in the Abbey's archives, and survive to this day either in their original form or as copies entered in Ely cartularies (Plate 1b).[13] These charters are complemented by a small but important set of vernacular records entered on the blank leaves of an eighth-century Northumbrian gospel-book which was evidently at Ely in the late tenth century:[14] the record of Ælfhelm Polga's grant of land at Potton, Bedfordshire, to Leofsige, his goldsmith;[15] the regulations of the thegns' guild at Cambridge (Plate 2a);[16]

---

[12] For all this material, see *Saints of Ely*, ed. Love. The 'Lives' of Æthelthryth and Wihtburh are of uncertain date and authorship; the 'Lives' of Seaxburh, Eormenhild and Werburh are probably the work of Goscelin of Saint-Bertin. For the poem, see P.A. Thompson and E. Stevens, 'Gregory of Ely's Verse Life and Miracles of St. Æthelthryth', *Analecta Bollandiana*, 106 (1988), pp. 333–90. The book of miracles is based on Ælfhelm's work, supplemented by a group of miracles belonging to the time of Bishop Hervey (1109–31). There is some related material in Dublin, Trinity College, MS B.2.7. The information about Ely's saints in William of Malmesbury's *Gesta Pontificum* was presumably derived from a collection of this nature; see WM, *GP* iv. 183–5 (*Willelmi Malmesbiriensis Monachi De Gestis Pontificum Anglorum Libri Quinque*, ed. N.E.S.A. Hamilton, Rolls Series, 52 (1870), pp. 322–6); D. Preest, *William of Malmesbury: The Deeds of the Bishops of England (Gesta Pontificum Anglorum)* (Woodbridge, 2002), pp. 218–20. A new edn of *GP*, ed. R. Thomson with translation and commentary, is forthcoming).

[13] For the history of the Abbey's muniments, see Ramsay, below, pp. 161–72. A charter by which King Edgar granted land at Bishampton (Worcs.) to Ely, dated 970, was transferred sooner or later to Worcester, and was still preserved there in the 17th century (S 1844). According to Humfrey Wanley's annotated copy of Tanner's *Notitia Monastica* (1695), now BL, Add. MS 47842, at least two single-sheet charters from the Ely archive came into the hands of John Moore (Bishop, 1707–14). One was King Edgar's supposed foundation charter, dated 970 (S 779); see further below, p. 21. The other was a charter by which King Eadwig granted land *æt Helig* to Archbishop Oda in 957 (S 646: S. Keynes, *Facsimiles of Anglo-Saxon Charters* (London, 1991), no. 5); see further below, p. 17. Both were noticed, when in Bishop Moore's possession, in BL, MS Lansdowne 969, fo. 111 (and BL, MS Harl. 7045, fo. 184). The two charters are known to have belonged subsequently to Charles Mason (1699–1771), Fellow of Trinity College, Cambridge. Both were copied, when in Mason's possession, by Bentham (CUL, MS Add. 2945, fos. 96ᵛ–102ʳ), again in 1773, after Mason's death, by William Cole (BL, Add. MS 5819, fos. 3–5ʳ), and then went their separate ways. Only one purportedly pre-Conquest single sheet – King Edgar's charter for Ælfhelm dated 974 (S 794: Keynes, *Facsimiles of Anglo-Saxon Charters*, no. 25) – remains to this day among the Ely muniments (Plate 1b). The principal cartulary is TCC, MS O.2.41, which contains copies of seven pre-Conquest charters (S 779–81, 907, 958, 1051, 1100); the texts in another Ely cartulary, in BL, MS Cotton Tiberius A. vi, are derived from TCC, MS O.2.41.

[14] For the gospel-book itself (now CUL, MS Kk.1.24), see E.A. Lowe, *Codices Latini Antiquiores*, II, 2nd edn (Oxford, 1972), no. 138. The two leaves containing the documents were cut out of the MS, probably in the 16th century, and are now mounted separately in BL, MS Cotton Tiberius B. v, vol. I, fos. 74 and 76; see N.R. Ker, *Catalogue of Manuscripts Containing Anglo-Saxon* (Oxford, 1957), no. 22. The MS is rejected from the list of surviving Ely books in *Medieval Libraries of Great Britain: a List of Surviving Books*, ed. N.R. Ker, *Supplement to the Second Edition*, ed. A.G. Watson (London, 1987), p. 35, on the grounds that it contains 'Ramsey Abbey, not Ely, documents'; see also below, p. 32. There can be no doubt, however, that it is an Ely book.

[15] Robertson, *Anglo-Saxon Charters*, pp. 144–5 (no. 71) and 388–9.

[16] Bodl., MS Twyne 2, fo. 82 (script-facsimile); G. Hickes and H. Wanley, *Antiquæ Literaturæ Septentrionalis Libri Duo*, 2 vols. (Oxford, 1703–5), I, 'Dissertatio Epistolaris', pp. 20–1 (text); B. Thorpe, *Diplomatarium Anglicum Ævi Saxonici* (London, 1865), pp. 610–13 (text and translation); and D. Whitelock (ed.), *English Historical Documents c.500–1042*, 2nd edn (London, 1979), pp. 603–5 (no. 136) (translation).

and a register of serfs on the Abbey's major estate at Hatfield, in Hertfordshire.[17] Of special interest, not least for the miraculous story of their survival, are the so-called 'Ely farming memoranda', also in the vernacular, which were entered on both sides of a leaf of parchment serving as a flyleaf in a book, kept presumably in the Abbey's library[18] (Plate 2*b*). The memoranda comprise various lists of goods supplied by Ely Abbey to Thorney Abbey, a list of pigs on Ely estates, a list of payments out of money given by a certain Æthelflæd, a list of livestock at Hatfield when a certain Ælfnoth took office, and details of the rent of the fen at Fordham and Hilgay (Norfolk). The memoranda are significant precisely because they take us down to ground level, affording a glimpse of rural estate management in eleventh-century East Anglia, and demonstrating at the same time how the written word could be used for such utterly mundane purposes. The community itself is brought to life, in a manner of speaking, by the list of monks of Ely entered in the *Liber Vitae* of the New Minster, Winchester,[19] giving us names of those who belonged to the community in the late tenth and early eleventh centuries (Colour pl. 18*a*), and this material is in turn complemented by a collection of obits entered in an Ely calendar, commemorating the Abbey's friends and benefactors (often with details of their benefactions) as well as the monks themselves.[20] The status achieved by Ely within a century of its refoundation, as a major land-owning institution and therefore as a considerable social and economic (as well as religious) force in eastern England, is symbolised by the detailed record of its endowment *tempore regis Eadwardi* (that is to say, in 1066), contained in Great and Little Domesday Book.[21] Documents bearing on the losses suffered by the Abbey in the late 1060s and early 1070s, and on the measures

[17] Thorpe, *Diplomatarium*, pp. 649–51 (text and translation); J. Earle, *A Hand-Book to the Land-Charters, and Other Saxonic Documents* (Oxford, 1888), pp. 275–7; and D. Pelteret, 'Two Old English Lists of Serfs', *Mediaeval Studies*, 48 (1986), pp. 470–513, at pp. 471–92 (text and translation, with commentary). The document was amusingly misunderstood by Sharon Turner (*The History of the Anglo-Saxons*, 7th edn, 3 vols. (London, 1852) III, p. 11 n. 18) to refer to the Hatte family, whence Lewis Carroll's name (Hatta) for one of his Anglo-Saxon messengers.

[18] At some point, probably in the late 16th or early 17th century, the leaf was removed from the book and cut in half vertically. One half was cut again into two vertical strips, which were used as sewing guards in a copy of Diophantus, *Rerum arithmeticarum libri sex* (Basel, 1575). The book was given to Queens' College, Cambridge, in 1626; but the two strips did not come to light until 1902, and were soon afterwards published by W.W. Skeat, 'Two Anglo-Saxon Fragments of the 11th Century', *Proc., Cambridge Philological Soc.* 63 (1903), pp. 12–16. The other half of the leaf, which had been used in a book-binding, was identified in 1925 by Sir Frank Stenton, in the collection of Capt. W.R. Cragg of Threekingham House, Lincolnshire; it was placed on deposit at Queens' College in 1954, and was bought by the College in 1978. The re-united leaf was sold by the College in the following year (Sotheby's, 11 Dec. 1979, lot 25), and was acquired by the BL for £52,000; it is now BL, Add. MS 61735. See Ker, *Catalogue*, no. 80; Robertson, *Anglo-Saxon Charters*, Appx II, no. 9 (text and translation); and J. Backhouse *et al.* (eds.), *The Golden Age of Anglo-Saxon Art* (London, 1984), no. 150 (with plate).

[19] BL, MS Stowe 944, fo. 27: see *The Liber Vitae of the New Minster and Hyde Abbey, Winchester*, ed. S. Keynes, Early English Manuscripts in Facsimile, 26 (Copenhagen, 1996), p. 96.

[20] The obits were copied from an 11th-century source into a 12th-century Ely calendar at the beginning of one of the MSS of *LE* (below, n. 26): TCC, MS O.2.1, fos. K1-K13. See B. Dickins, 'The Day of Byrhtnoth's Death and other Obits from a Twelfth-Century Ely Kalendar', *Leeds Studies in English*, 6 (1937), pp. 14–24; J. Gerchow, *Die Gedenküberlieferung der Angelsachsen*, Arbeiten zur Frühmittelalterforschung, 20 (Berlin, 1988), pp. 280–9 and 343–50 (no. 24); and *Liber Vitae*, ed. Keynes, p. 60.

[21] For modern facsimile-editions of the two main manuscripts, with translation and maps, see *Great Domesday*, ed. R.W.H. Erskine (London, 1986), and *Little Domesday Book*, ed. G.H. Martin and A. Williams (London, 2001). For separate editions of each county survey, with translation, see *Domesday Book*, ed. J. Morris, 35 vols. (Chichester, 1975–86).

taken in the 1070s and 1080s to recover its former position, were preserved in the Abbey's archives.[22] And as if this were not enough, it is the case that one of the most important and substantial of the 'satellites' generated by the Domesday survey itself – the *Inquisitio Comitatus Cantabrigiensis* – was preserved at Ely, together with copies of the Abbey's consolidated survey of its own estates, known as the *Inquisitio Eliensis*.[23]

The variety of documentary material surviving from Ely Abbey demonstrates if nothing else that respect for the written record flourished there in the late tenth and eleventh centuries, yet what survives to this day is but a pale reflection of what is known to have existed at Ely in the Middle Ages. The community had occasion, in the twelfth century, to produce various works concerning different aspects of the history of its own house, and these works are replete with information derived directly from documentation then available in the Abbey's library or archives. The short work known at Ely as the *Libellus Æthelwoldi episcopi*, compiled in the early twelfth century at the instigation of Hervey, first Bishop of Ely (1109–31), was intended by its compiler to advertise the involvement of Æthelwold, Bishop of Winchester (963–84), in the Abbey's refoundation and endowment.[24] It has no obvious connection with contentious matters such as the division of the Abbey's lands between the monks and the bishop, and seems symbolic of their *common* interests.[25] The *Libellus* is essentially an early manifestation of the house chronicle, of interest in part because it arises not so much from the cultivation of St Æthelthryth as from the commemoration of St Æthelwold, but principally because it was based on vernacular documentation generated at Ely in the 970s and now lost. There is nothing comparable from any other religious house founded or refounded in the late tenth century, and nothing else which affords such a detailed view of the process of endowment and its impact on local society. The more substantial work known as the *Liber Eliensis*, probably compiled at Ely in the 1170s, is self-evidently a work intended to

---

[22] For texts, translations and analysis of the 'Ely land pleas', see *LE*, pp. 426–32; R.C. van Caenegem (ed.), *English Lawsuits from William I to Richard I*, 2 vols., Selden Soc. 106–7 (London, 1990–1) I, pp. 43–50 (no. 18); and D. Bates (ed.), *Regesta Regum Anglo-Normannorum: the Acta of William I (1066–1087)* (Oxford, 1998), pp. 410–39.

[23] The 'ICC' is preserved as part of the Ely cartulary in BL, MS Cotton Tiberius A. vi; the 'IE' is with the cartularies in TCC, MS O.2.41, and BL, MS Cotton Tiberius A. vi. For both texts, see N.E.S.A. Hamilton (ed.), *Inquisitio Comitatus Cantabrigiensis . . . Inquisitio Eliensis* (Cambridge, 1876). For a translation of the ICC, see VCH, *Cambs.*, I, pp. 400–27; see also D.C. Douglas and G.W. Greenaway (eds.), *English Historical Documents 1042–1189*, 2nd edn (London, 1981), pp. 943–50 (nos. 214–15).

[24] The text of the *Libellus* is preserved in two 12th-century Ely MSS (TCC, MS O.2.41, pp. 1–64, and BL, MS Cotton Vespasian A. xix, fos. 2–27), which appear to be independent copies of a lost original. The former also contains an Ely cartulary and a text of the *Inquisitio Eliensis*: see S. Keynes, *Anglo-Saxon Manuscripts and other items of related interest in the Library of Trinity College, Cambridge*, Old English Newsletter, Subsidia, 18 (Binghamton, NY, 1992), pp. 41–3 (no. 27). The latter is the earliest part of a composite book otherwise containing later material from Ely. The *Libellus* was printed by Thomas Gale in 1691, but is better known in the form in which it was incorporated in *LE* (below, n. 93). For an edition and translation of the *Libellus*, with commentary, see *The Book of Bishop Æthelwold ('Libellus Æthelwoldi episcopi'), on the Refoundation and Endowment of Ely Abbey in the 970s*, ed. S. Keynes and A. Kennedy (forthcoming). The *Libellus* incorporates some verses on St Æthelwold which have been attributed on stylistic grounds to Gregory, monk of Ely, who is otherwise known to have composed a poem on St Æthelthryth (above, n. 12); see *Wulfstan of Winchester: The Life of St Æthelwold*, ed. M. Lapidge and M. Winterbottom (Oxford, 1991), pp. 81–6. The compiler of the *Libellus* may have been Gregory himself, or one of his colleagues.

[25] On Bishop Hervey's division of estates, see *LE*, iii. 25–6: pp. 261–3, with Miller, *Abbey & Bishopric*, pp. 75–7 and 282–3 (charter of Bishop Hervey). For further discussion, see E. Crosby, *Bishop and Chapter in Twelfth-Century England: a Study of the Mensa Episcopalis* (Cambridge, 1994), pp. 151–74.

exalt the standing of the monks and to protect their interests against the reality or threat of episcopal interference (Plate 1a).[26] Nigel, second Bishop of Ely (1133–69), was an operator of the first order, never averse to drawing on the resources of his church in pursuit of his political ends. The monks now had especially good reason for creating an historical identity for themselves which would give them strength in resisting the demands of their own bishop, emphasising the Abbey's great antiquity, showing how the community had long enjoyed the special protection of St Æthelthryth, and providing plentiful evidence of her thaumaturgical powers. The *Liber Eliensis* is by any standards a work of outstanding interest. As might be expected, the compiler made effective use of local traditions,[27] and of various written works (including the *Libellus Æthelwoldi episcopi*) which survive in their own right. Yet, as in the case of the *Libellus*, the *Liber Eliensis* is of special value because it contains information on the Abbey's history in the tenth and eleventh centuries derived from written material which does not otherwise survive. Embedded in Book One (covering the period from the first foundation of the Abbey by St Æthelthryth to the eve of its refoundation) is material derived from Ælfhelm's *Liber miraculorum beate virginis*, providing a view of Ely in the late ninth and tenth centuries and showing at the same time how those who partook in the reform movement regarded the immediate past.[28] Incorporated in Book Two (covering the period from the refoundation of Ely (*c.*970) to the establishment of the bishopric in the early twelfth century) is a quantity of detailed information on donations made to the Abbey by lay men and women in the late tenth and early eleventh centuries, derived for the most part from vernacular documentation which had accumulated in the Abbey's archives, in the form of wills, chirographs, and other such records.[29] Also incorporated in Book Two is information derived from a mid-twelfth-century work commemorating a

---

[26] There are two principal MSS. One (designated E) is TCC, MS O.2.1, for which see Keynes, *Anglo-Saxon Manuscripts*, pp. 43–5 (no. 28). The other (F) is the property of the Dean & Chapter of Ely, and is now CUL, EDC 1. The definitive edition is *Liber Eliensis*, ed. E.O. Blake, which follows the later and 'most complete' (p. lviii) of the principal MSS (F). A translation, by Janet Fairweather, commissioned by the Dean and Chapter, will be published in due course. For extracts in translation, see J. Paxton, 'The Book of Ely', in T. Head (ed.), *Medieval Hagiography: an Anthology* (New York, 2000), pp. 459–94 (*LE*, iii. 60, 92–4, 115–22 and 137–8). On the authorship of the work, see *LE*, pp. xlvi–xlix, and R. Sharpe, *A Handlist of the Latin Writers of Great Britain and Ireland before 1540* (Toronto, 1997), pp. 467–8 (Richard) and 654 (Thomas). See also J. Paxton, 'Charter and Chronicle in 12th-Century England: the House-Histories of the Fenland Abbeys', PhD thesis, Harvard University (1999), esp. pp. 157–214.

[27] Especially notable are the chapters on Abbot Byrhtnoth (*LE*, ii. 6, 52–3, 56), Abbot Leofwine and Abbot Leofric (*LE*, ii. 80), Abbot Leofsige (*LE*, ii. 74, 84), Abbot Wulfric (*LE*, ii. 94, 96–7), and Abbot Thurstan (*LE*, ii. 105, 109, 112). Also important are the chapters on King Æthelred (*LE*, ii. 78), King Cnut (*LE*, ii. 85), Alfred the Atheling (*LE*, ii. 90), and Edward the Confessor (*LE*, ii. 91). For tales of Ely and Hereward the Wake, see below, p. 00.

[28] *LE*, i. 41–9: pp. 56–61. See further below, pp. 16–17.

[29] The chapters drawing on vernacular documentation in the archives are as follows. **Abbot Byrhtnoth**: *LE*, ii. 29 (Leofric and Leofflæd), from a tripartite chirograph; **Abbot Ælfsige**: *LE*, ii. 59 (Æthelgifu of Thaxted), from her will [*testamentum*]; *LE*, ii. 60 (Leofwine, son of Æthulf), from a chirograph, and from a will [*testamentum*]; *LE*, ii. 61 (Ælfwaru of Bridgham), from her will [*scriptum*]; *LE*, ii. 64 (Æthelflæd, sister of Ælfflæd and wife of Ealdorman Æthelstan), from her will [*testamentum*]; *LE*, ii. 66 (Uvi of Willingham), from his will [*testamentum*] in the form of a chirograph; *LE*, ii. 67 (Oswig, brother of Uvi), from a document [*scriptum*]; *LE*, ii. 68 (Æthelric, brother of Uvi), from his will [*testamentum*]; *LE*, ii. 69 (Godwine of Hoo), from a chirograph; *LE*, ii. 70 (Ælfmær, brother of Godwine), from a chirograph. **Abbot Leofric**: *LE*, ii. 81 (Godgifu), from a will [*testamentum*]; *LE*, ii. 83 (Godgifu, as before), from a writ. **Abbot Leofsige**: *LE*, ii. 88 (Leofflæd, wife of Oswig), being a Latin translation of a letter to [Æthelred or Cnut] and Emma, in the form of a tripartite chirograph; *LE*, ii. 89 (Lustwine and Leofwaru), from their will [*testamentum*]. See further below, pp. 32–3 n. 152, 37 and n. 179.

group of seven 'Confessors of Christ' who had been buried at Ely in the late tenth and eleventh centuries, and whose bones were translated by Prior Alexander, probably in the mid-1150s, from their original resting-places into the northern part of the new Cathedral.[30] The 'confessors' comprised Ealdorman Byrhtnoth, Archbishop Wulfstan, and five other pre-Conquest bishops.[31] Elsewhere in the *Liber Eliensis* we find three inventories of the treasures which had accumulated in the church during the later tenth, eleventh, and early twelfth centuries, conveying a vivid sense of the provision at Ely of reliquaries, vestments, church plate, images, and other furnishings.[32] Collectively, these are riches indeed.[33] It may be 'a sad epitaph on the industry and good intentions of the compiler that his history is most useful where his own work can be altogether undone and the compilation be dissolved into its component parts';[34] but there is much for which he must be thanked.

Students of this period are not accustomed to working with such extensive and varied material bearing on the history of a single religious house; yet while all of the material for Ely is well enough known, there is still much to be done in bringing the different parts of it into relationship with each other, and in exploiting all of the opportunities which it affords for understanding the history of Ely Abbey and the surrounding region in the Anglo-Saxon and Anglo-Norman periods. We can observe and attempt to understand the development of a saint's cult in its local and its larger settings, and we can examine the unfolding relationship between hagiography and historiography. At a more mundane level, we can trace the stages and the processes by which a major religious house accumulated its landed endowment in the tenth and eleventh centuries, and examine the impact which the processes had on local society. We can look closely at the conduct of transactions involving the transfer of land and other property, and we can investigate the Abbey's management of its large estate. There is scope here for analysis of the place of a religious house in its wider region, and of its relationship with other houses, with high-ranking persons, and with particular families. We can pursue such matters against the background of national events: in isolation during the dark years of the eighth and ninth centuries, within the context of the 'Anglo-Danish' society which emerged in eastern England in the tenth and eleventh centuries, and as the Abbey tried to recover its position in the wake of the Norman Conquest. We may not be able to

---

[30] The date of the translation (1154) depends on the inscription placed above the bones when they were subsequently removed, in 1771, to their present resting-place in Bishop West's Chapel; see Bentham, *Ely*, Addenda, p. 24, and below, p. 58.

[31] The accounts of these men were dispersed in *LE*, ii. 62 (Ealdorman Byrhtnoth, d.991), ii. 65 (Æthelstan, Bishop of Elmham, d.1001), ii. 71 (Eadnoth, Bishop of Dorchester, d.1016), ii. 72 (Ælfgar, Bishop of Elmham, d.1012 × 16), ii. 75 and 86 (Ælfwine, Bishop of Elmham, d.1023 × 29), ii. 87 (Wulfstan, Archbishop of York, d.1023), and ii. 99 (Bishop Osmund, d. ?1067). See *LE*, pp. xxxviii, 136 n. 1, and 156 n. 2.

[32] The three inventories are as follows: (A) an inventory made soon after the death of Abbot Theodwine, in 1075, augmented by Eudo c.1081, in *LE*, ii. 114: pp. 196–7; (B) an inventory made by Ranulf Flambard, c.1093, in *LE*, ii. 139: pp. 223–4; (C) an inventory made by Bishop Nigel in 1134, updated in the 1140s, in *LE*, iii. 50: pp. 288–94. Texts and translations of the inventories, with comparison and analysis, will be provided in S. Keynes and A. Kennedy, *The Treasures of Ely Abbey* (Cambridge, forthcoming).

[33] There is a later (14th-century) Ely chronicle (with continuations), preserved (*e.g.*) in BL, MS Cotton Nero A. xv–xvi, well known by virtue of its publication in Wharton, *Anglia Sacra*, I, pp. 591–688; but although the chronicle contains valuable information for the 13th and 14th centuries, it is not clear that it has any independent authority for the earlier period. For discussion, see *LE*, pp. xxv–xxvii and 410–14.

[34] *LE*, p. lviii. The comment does not, of course, apply to the compiler's coverage of the 12th century.

get much sense of the scale or external appearance of the pre-Conquest church at Ely, and we cannot hear the services conducted within it, yet we can build up a picture of a place stuffed with holy relics, full to the brim with costly treasures, and served by a flourishing monastic community which was deeply conscious of its past, instinctively protective of its position, and eager to claim a place at the centre of the nation's affairs. We can also observe the process by which churchmen newly arrived from the continent came to realise what had fallen into their hands, and began to work out how best to match their reforming zeal with a natural instinct to protect and extend their interests; and the very healthy competition which ensued not only with predatory laymen but also with other religious houses. Given the nature and extent of all the opportunities for further study of Anglo-Saxon and Anglo-Norman Ely, it would be rash to suggest that anything can yet be reduced to simplicity and order. What follows, therefore, is essentially an exercise in exploring the parameters of a subject; for while the massive Norman arches in the transepts and nave of the present Cathedral may be the earliest parts of the standing structure, it needs only a little exercise of the historical imagination to see on what foundations they stand.

Æthelthryth and her sisters

The kingdom of the East Angles extended in the mid-seventh century from its heartland in Norfolk and Suffolk westwards into the fenlands of the Middle Angles, which separated and to some extent protected the East Angles from the Mercians in the north-west midlands and from other Anglian peoples of northern and midland England. Anna, King of the East Angles (d.654), is described variously by Bede as 'a good man, blessed with a good and saintly family', 'an excellent man of royal descent and the father of a distinguished family', and 'a very religious man, noble both in mind and deed'.[35] His eldest daughter was Seaxburh, who married Eorcenberht, King of Kent, and subsequently became second Abbess of Ely; her sister Æthelthryth was married to Tondberht, ruler of the South Gyrwe, and, after Tondberht's death, to Ecgfrith, King of the Northumbrians, before becoming the first Abbess of Ely; a third sister, Æthelburh, seems to have entered the religious life from the outset, but chose to do so in Frankia, becoming Abbess of Faremoûtier-en-Brie. Long associated with the three daughters of Anna mentioned by Bede (and with Anna's step-daughter, Sæthryth, who also became Abbess of Faremoûtier-en-Brie) is Wihtburh, said to have been found in 798 'all sound and undecayed in Dereham (Norfolk), 55 years after she departed from this life [in 743]'.[36] Nearly two hundred years later Wihtburh was removed from Dereham to Ely, but whether she was genuinely a sister of Seaxburh, Æthelthryth and Æthelburh, and a daughter of King Anna, is perhaps another matter.[37]

Æthelthryth (a common name for a girl, meaning literally 'noble-glory') is perhaps better known as 'Etheldreda' (a later latinized form of her English name) or as 'Audrey' (the product of further corruption). Bede was already aware of the essential details of

[35] Bede, *HE*, iii. 7: p. 234, iii. 18: p. 268, and iv. 19: p. 390.
[36] *ASC*, MS F, *s.a.* 798.
[37] See further below, pp. 24–5.

the life of St Æthelthryth when he wrote his hymn on the subject of virginity ('many years' before he wrote the *Historia ecclesiastica*), and when he wrote his *Chronica Maiora* in 725;[38] but it was in the *Historia ecclesiastica*, written in 731, that he took the opportunity to tell the whole story as it was known to him.[39]

> King Ecgfrith [of the Northumbrians] married a wife named Æthelthryth, the daughter of Anna, King of the East Angles, who has often been referred to, a very religious man and noble both in mind and deed. She had previously been married to the chief (*princeps*) of the South Gyrwe, named Tondberht. But he died shortly after the marriage and on his death she was given to King Ecgfrith. Though she lived with him for twelve years she still preserved the glory of perfect virginity.

Æthelthryth would appear to have travelled north to Northumbria *c.*660, during the reign of King Oswiu (642–70), a decade or so before the accession of Oswiu's son Ecgfrith as King of the Northumbrians (670–85). Bede tells us elsewhere that she was accompanied from East Anglia by a certain Owine, who was 'the chief of her officers and the head of her household';[40] we learn in another context that the Northumbrian thegn Imma, captured at the battle of the river Trent in 679, had been one of Æthelthryth's thegns before becoming a thegn of Ecgfrith's brother Ælfwine.[41] Æthelthryth and her husband are said to have been obedient to Wilfrid, bishop of the Northumbrians, in all things, and it was she who gave Wilfrid the land at Hexham, where he built a church.[42] Sooner or later Ecgfrith asked Wilfrid to persuade Æthelthryth to consummate their marriage, without any success; and since Bede informs his readers that he had been told this by Bishop Wilfrid, he writes as a monk who had conversed with a bishop who had conversed with the queen herself. After twelve years Æthelthryth prevailed upon her husband to allow her to enter the monastery at Coldingham, in northern Northumbria, where she is said to have received the veil and habit of a nun from Bishop Wilfrid; but she did not stay there for long.

---

[38] For Bede's poem on virginity, see *HE*, iv. 20: pp. 396–400. For Bede's *Chronica Maiora*, see C.W. Jones (ed.), *Bedae Venerabilis Opera*, VI: *Opera Didascalica 2*, Corpus Christianorum Series Latina 123B (Turnholt, 1977), pp. 463–544, at pp. 528–9, and F. Wallis, *Bede: the Reckoning of Time* (Liverpool, 1999), pp. 157–249, at p. 232; see also J. McClure and R. Collins (eds.), *Bede: The Ecclesiastical History of the English People; The Greater Chronicle; Bede's Letter to Egbert* (Oxford, 1994), pp. 307–40, at pp. 335–6.

[39] Bede, *HE*, iv. 19: pp. 390–6.

[40] Bede, *HE*, iv. 3: pp. 338–42. Owine ended his life at Lastingham (*ibid.*) The inscription 'O Lord, grant your light and peace to Ouin, Amen' is inscribed (in Latin) on an ancient stone which was used in the early 18th century at Haddenham (Cambs.), as part of a horse-block. The stone, regarded not unreasonably as a memorial to Æthelthryth's steward Owine, was first published by William Stukeley in 1724; see also correspondence between Stukeley and Bentham, 1756, in CUL, MS Add. 2960, 5–6ᵛ. It was brought to Ely in 1770: 'Memd. March 18, 1770. Having by favour of my friend Mr Thomas Gotobed of Ely Gent., procured this curious & valuable stone; – I have, with leave of the Dean & Chapter, placed it in the Cathedral Church of Ely, under an arch at the West end of the North Side-Isle of the Body or Nave of the Church, – there to remain, I hope, for Ages to come! James Bentham' (CUL, MS Add. 2956, fo. 1ᵛ). See also Bentham, *Ely*, pp. 50–1, with *Addenda*, p. 28; whence it has come to be known as 'Ovin's Stone'. Unfortunately, the connection between the stone and Æthelthryth's Owine is the product of little more than a wishful thought; see E. Okasha, *Hand-list of Anglo-Saxon Non-Runic Inscriptions* (Cambridge, 1971), pp. 74–5 (no. 43).

[41] Bede, *HE*, iv. 22: p. 404.

[42] Stephen, *Vita S. Wilfridi*, chs. 19 and 22 (ed. Colgrave, pp. 40 and 44).

A year afterwards she was herself appointed Abbess in the district called Ely, where she built a monastery and became, by the example of her heavenly life and teaching, the virgin mother of many virgins dedicated to God.

Although the date is not given by Bede, the monastery at Ely would appear to have been founded in 672.[43] Little is known of Æthelthryth's activities as Abbess, beyond the familiar details of her personal life, though it is apparent from Bede's narrative that she presided over a mixed community of men as well as women.[44] She died of plague, after seven years as Abbess, on 23 June 679,[45] and was buried in a wooden coffin.

It is probably as well to keep these facts about Æthelthryth, attested by authoritative sources, quite separate from the other details of her life, derived from later hagiographical writing. We learn, for example, from these later sources that Æthelthryth was born at Exning, near Newmarket,[46] that she had received the Isle of Ely from Tondberht, as her marriage-gift,[47] and that she had established herself there for a short while after Tondberht's death, not on the older settlement at *Cratendune* (a mile or so south of the present Cathedral) but on the higher ground.[48] We also learn that she was a skilled embroideress, and had made a stole and maniple for St Cuthbert, which could still be seen at Durham in the twelfth century;[49] that she was forced to flee from Coldingham, accompanied by Sewenna and Sewara, who followed her south back to Ely, via Winteringham (Lincolnshire) and other places;[50] and that she was joined at Ely by a priest called Huna, who retreated after her death to a smaller island in the fens.[51] If

---

[43] Bede placed the story of Æthelthryth between his accounts of the council of Hatfield in 679 (*HE*, iv. 17) and the battle of the Trent in the same year (*HE*, iv. 21), which is most naturally taken to suggest that to the best of his knowledge she died in 679; in which case Ely was founded seven years previously, in 672. The West Saxon chronicler made a slightly different calculation (below, n. 65).

[44] For the institution of the double house, see S. Foot, *Veiled Women, I: The Disappearance of Nuns from Anglo-Saxon England* (Aldershot, 2000), pp. 49–56. Bede did not approve of the institution; hence his account of the fate of Coldingham, in *HE*, iv. 25: pp. 420–6.

[45] 23 June is the day given for the feast of St Æthelthryth in the 9th-century *Old English Martyrology* (below, n. 63), and in the majority of pre-Conquest calendars, as registered by R. Rushforth, *An Atlas of Saints in Anglo-Saxon Calendars*, ASNC Guides, Texts and Studies 6 (Cambridge, 2002).

[46] *LE*, i. 3: p. 13.

[47] *LE*, i. 4: p. 15, adding that they were married for almost three years.

[48] *LE*, Prol., pp. 3–4 and i. 8: p. 20. According to the Ely legend, an earlier church founded at Ely by St Augustine (no less) had been destroyed by Penda; see *LE*, Prol., and i. 15: pp. 4 and 32. It seems reasonable to assume that the site of Æthelthryth's monastery was on the hill where the Cathedral now stands (below, p. 23). It has been suggested, on the other hand, that Æthelthryth's monastery stood in West End, where later stood the hospitals of St Mary Magdalene and St John Baptist, and that the importance of this site in the Middle Saxon period is indicated by the settlement excavated in 1999 at the west end of West Fen Road, which appears to have flourished from the early 8th to the late 12th century. For the local topography, see E.M. Hampson and T.D. Atkinson, 'City of Ely', *VCH, Cambs.*, IV, pp. 28–89, at pp. 28–30. See also D. Gibson, *Excavations at West Fen Road, Ely, Cambs.*, Cambridge Archaeological Unit Report 160 (1996), and A. Holton-Krayenbuhl, 'Ely', in T. Kirby and S. Oosthuizen (eds.), *An Atlas of Cambridgeshire and Huntingdonshire History* (Cambridge, 2000), no. 79.

[49] *LE*, i. 9: p. 24.

[50] *LE*, i. 11: p. 27 and i. 13: pp. 29–30. Æthelthryth is said to have founded a church at *Alftham*, often identified as West Halton, near Winteringham, which has a church dedicated to St Etheldreda. For the suggestion that the site of the church was in fact at Whitton, also near Winteringham, see D. Hadley, in *The Daily Mail*, 16 Aug. 2001, pp. 22–3.

[51] *LE*, i. 15, 18 and 22: pp. 32, 36 and 40–1. Huna's retreat was at *Huneia* (probably Honey Hill, Chatteris), but his relics were later translated to Thorney.

we are to believe the legend, Æthelthryth was able to secure for her Abbey freedom of interference from king, bishop, or tax official, and with Wilfrid's help managed to get a privilege to the same effect from the Pope.[52]

According to Bede, Æthelthryth was succeeded as Abbess of Ely by her elder sister Seaxburh, widow of Eorcenberht, King of Kent (d.664). Sixteen years after Æthelthryth's death (that is to say, some time after 23 June 695), Seaxburh decided to remove her sister's body from its original burial-place, and to place it in a new coffin in the church. She instructed some monks to look for stone for the purpose; so they went by boat 'to a certain small deserted fortress', called Cambridge (*Grantacaestir*),[53] where they found a white marble coffin with a close-fitting lid, which they took with them back to Ely. Æthelthryth's body was raised, and found to be 'as uncorrupt as if she had died and been buried that very day', a phenomenon duly verified by a doctor (*medicus*) called Cynefrith who had been present at her death-bed and who was also present at her elevation. The nuns of Ely washed Æthelthryth's body, 'wrapped it in new robes, carried it into the church, and placed it in the sarcophagus which they had brought, where it is held in great veneration to this day'.[54] Bede does not specify the actual day of Æthelthryth's Translation, but it was commemorated in the liturgy on 17 October, and so it presumably took place on that day in 695.[55]

Bede does not take his own account of Ely beyond the times of the first two abbesses (Æthelthryth and Seaxburh), so we are dependent on later traditions for any continuation of their story. The version of events current at Ely in the twelfth century was that Seaxburh's daughter Eormenhild, widow of Wulfhere, King of the Mercians (d.675), succeeded her mother as the third Abbess of Ely, and was herself succeeded by her daughter Werburh.[56] If this was indeed the case, Ely takes on the appearance of a house serving the particular interests of a royal family, in a way which might not have met entirely with Bede's approval. He clearly found much to admire in the story of Æthelthryth, as a woman who had enjoyed all the trappings of worldly status yet had shunned them for the simplicity of the religious life, and as one whose purity elevated her to the level of the Virgin Mary, mother of Christ, as was so clearly demonstrated by her incorruptible body. Seaxburh was inseparable from the story, since she had presided over the Translation in 695. Perhaps that was as far as Bede was prepared to go. Like

[52] *LE*, i. 15 and 19: pp. 33 and 37.

[53] The natural but erroneous presumption that Bede's *Grantacaestir* denotes modern Grantchester, as opposed to Cambridge, remains firmly embedded in the literature. *Grantacaestir* means 'the (Roman) fort on the (river) Granta', with reference to the Roman town on Castle Hill, Cambridge. By the late 9th century *Grantacaestir* had come to be known as *Grantabrycg*, 'the bridge over the (river) Granta' (*ASC, s.a.* 875). Under Norman influence, *Grante-* became *Cante-*, and this presently gave rise to the modern form Cambridge. The river, originally known as the Granta, thus came to be known, by back-formation, as the Cam. The nearby village of Grantchester is called *Granteseta* ('the dwellers on the (river) Granta') in Domesday Book; *Grancestre* is recorded in the 13th century, and *Granchester* in the 17th.

[54] *HE*, iv. 19: pp. 392–4. *LE*, i. 25–8: pp. 42–7, adds little of any substance. On the re-use of Roman sarcophagi, see C.R. Dodwell, *Anglo-Saxon Art: a New Perspective* (Manchester, 1982), pp. 125–6; C. Neuman de Vegvar, 'The Value of Recycling: Conversion and the Early Anglo-Saxon Use of Roman Materials', *Haskins Society Journal*, 9 (2001 for 1997), pp. 123–35, at p. 130; and J. Crook, *The Architectural Setting of the Cults of Saints in the Early Christian West c.300–1200* (Oxford, 2000), pp. 77–8.

[55] *Cf.* his poem on virginity, in *HE*, iv. 20: p. 398. The date (17 October) is recorded in several pre-Conquest calendars; see Rushforth, *Atlas of Saints*, under October.

[56] *LE*, i. 36–7: pp. 51–2. The story told earlier in Goscelin's *Vita S. Werburge* is rather different; see *Saints of Ely*, ed. Love.

Æthelthryth (in Northumbria) and Seaxburh (in Kent), Eormenhild had been a queen, but a queen in Mercia. We are simply not in any position to gauge the potential significance of her presence at Ely in the early eighth century, at a time when the Mercians were seeking to develop their interests in the east, whether at Crowland, *Medeshamstede* (Peterborough) or elsewhere. It is the case, however, that appearances of undimmed sanctity, especially when constructed in retrospect, should not be allowed to distract us from contemplating the less wholesome realities of social, economic and political life.

Ely Abbey in the eighth and ninth centuries

The history of Ely Abbey from the early eighth to the late ninth century is all but lost from view. Excavations at West Fen have revealed evidence of settlement and economic activity in the Middle Saxon period, from which we may infer that the resources on the Isle of Ely continued to be exploited all the while.[57] There is reason to believe that the fenlands were still under the notional control of the king of the East Angles in the first half of the eighth century, but sooner or later the whole area, including East Anglia, was brought within the extended sphere of influence of the Mercian kings. The community would doubtless have been affected in one way or another by these shifts in the balance of political power, although it is not clear that the abbess of a double house such as Ely would ever have been as well placed as, say, the abbot of a monastery such as *Medeshamstede* to play a leading part on the larger stage.[58] In 794 Æthelberht, King of the East Angles, was beheaded when on a visit to the Mercian court; and by the time the East Angles were able to reassert their independence from Mercian overlordship, in the 820s, they may already have been suffering from the disruption caused by Viking raids. In 866 a 'great heathen army' came to England and 'took up winter quarters in East Anglia'; after excursions elsewhere the army returned to East Anglia in 869, 'and that winter King Edmund fought against them, and the Danes had the victory, and killed the King and conquered all the land'.[59] It is generally assumed that the Viking 'conquest' of East Anglia in 869–70 was attended by widespread destruction of the religious houses in the area, but it has to be admitted that there is no hard evidence for whatever may have happened at Ely.[60] The compiler of the *Liber Eliensis* gives an account of desperate resistance on the Isle, ending with the slaughter of the inhabitants, the massacre of the community (monks as well as nuns), and the general destruction of

---

[57] See above, n. 48.

[58] Abbesses seem to be conspicuous only by their absence from the records of church councils in the late 8th and early 9th centuries; see S. Keynes, *The Councils of Clofesho* [Brixworth Lecture 1993], Vaughan Paper 38 (Leicester, 1994), pp. 19–21, and C. Cubitt, *Anglo-Saxon Church Councils c.650–c.850* (London, 1995), pp. 42–4. The notion that the late 8th-century Gandersheim Casket had some association with Ely, perpetuated in James Campbell (ed.), *The Anglo-Saxons* (Oxford, 1982), p. 128, has no basis, and is rightly dismissed in L. Webster and J. Backhouse (eds.), *The Making of England: Anglo-Saxon Art and Culture AD 600–900* (London, 1991), pp. 177–8.

[59] *ASC, s.a.* 867–70.

[60] For Alfred's remarks on the devastation caused by the Vikings, in his prefatory letter to his translation of Gregory's *Pastoral Care*, see S. Keynes and M. Lapidge, *Alfred the Great: Asser's 'Life of King Alfred' and Other Contemporary Sources* (Harmondsworth, 1983), p. 125. See also D.N. Dumville, 'Ecclesiastical Lands and the Defence of Wessex in the First Viking-Age', in his *Wessex and England from Alfred to Edgar* (Woodbridge, 1992), pp. 29–54, at p. 34, n. 20.

the church and all its contents.[61] The story is also told of a particularly nasty Viking who raised an axe with his blood-stained hands and attempted to break into St Æthelthryth's marble tomb, in order to steal the money which he thought it would contain; but as soon as he had made a hole in the tomb, his eyes were torn out of his head by act of divine vengeance, and Æthelthryth was thereafter left alone.[62]

The presumed destruction of Ely Abbey, c.870, can perhaps be invoked to account for the loss of all documentation relating to the history of Æthelthryth's foundation, and it may be that it was difficult to sustain organised religious life in the kind of circumstances which prevailed in the fenlands in the late ninth century; for while there was some advantage in being relatively inaccessible, communities needed to be part of larger social, political and ecclesiastical networks if they were to prosper. Yet if Ely's institutional memory was disrupted in the late ninth century, there was no danger whatsoever to the cult of St Æthelthryth. The wide dissemination of Bede's *Ecclesiastical History*, not to mention its popularity in high places, ensured that knowledge of Æthelthryth's qualities would endure, and that Ely would always be venerated as the place where she had passed the last years of her life in the 670s. A work known to modern scholarship as the *Old English Martyrology*, composed probably by a Mercian scholar some time in the ninth century, gives a short account of Æthelthryth, based squarely on Bede though adding the day of her feast (23 June).[63] The story was told again in the vernacular translation of Bede's *Ecclesiastical History*, made probably by another Mercian scholar in the late ninth century.[64] It is also striking that a West Saxon chronicler, active c.890, took the trouble to incorporate two references to St Æthelthryth at the appropriate points in his work, registering her foundation of the Abbey in '673' and her death in 679.[65] There was already some East Anglian competition for St Æthelthryth in the nascent cult of Edmund, King and Martyr, but nothing could take away from her the place that she had been given by Bede, as a Virgin Mother for the English people of his own age.[66]

Ely in the tenth century

The question arises whether there was any degree of continuity from the community of monks and nuns at Ely in the second half of the ninth century to the body of priests who would appear to have served the church there in the first half of the tenth. An important source of information bearing on precisely this period, ostensibly written some time in

---

[61] *LE*, i. 40: pp. 54–5. For some effective discussion of the fate of religious houses for women (and men) in the 9th century, see Foot, *Veiled Women* (cit. in n. 44), I, pp. 71–84.

[62] *LE*, i. 41: pp. 55–6. The story was presumably developed by the compiler from Ælfhelm's *Liber miraculorum beate virginis*, and recurs in Ælfhelm's simpler and more restrained form in *LE*, i. 49: p. 60.

[63] G. Herzfeld (ed.), *An Old English Martyrology*, Early English Text Society, o.s. 116 (London, 1900), p. 102; see also Lapidge, *Encyclopaedia of ASE* (cit. in n. 3), pp. 303–4.

[64] *The Old English Version of Bede's Ecclesiastical History of the English People*, ed. T. Miller, 4 pts, Early English Text Society, o.s. 95–6 and 110–11 (London, 1890–8), I, pt 2, pp. 316–24.

[65] *ASC*, s.a. 673: 'and St Æthelthryth began the monastery at Ely.' *ASC*, s.a. 679: 'In this year Ælfwine was slain, and St Æthelthryth died.' The date of Æthelthryth's death was probably inferred from Bede (above, n. 43). The date of the foundation of Ely was presumably worked out by subtracting seven years from 679, which could have given 673 or 672: if Æthelthryth had completed seven years as Abbess before her death, on 23 June 679, she became Abbess in early 672; but if 679 is regarded as her seventh year, 673 might be reckoned as her first.

[66] Bede, *HE*, iv. 20: pp. 396–400.

the second half of the tenth century, is incorporated in the first book of the *Liber Eliensis*.[67] It would appear that the compiler of the *Liber Eliensis* had come across the *Liber miraculorum beate virginis* in the course of his research at Ely, and found reason to believe that it was written by a certain Ælfhelm, who featured in it as one of the priests at Ely in the mid-tenth century. The purpose of the *Liber miraculorum* was not only to exalt the saint, but to do so at the expense of those who had then had custody of her tomb. The narrative is set in the reign of King Eadred (946–55), when the church at Ely is said to have been occupied by *canonici* of both sexes. On Æthelthryth's feast-day, the Archpriest summoned the priests and clerics and announced his intention to investigate whether Bede was right, and whether there was anything in Æthelthryth's tomb. One of the priests protested that the Archpriest, as an outsider, could have no knowledge of the miracles worked by the saint, and said he would apprise him of some of the miracles which she had worked there most recently. The priest told of a woman suffering from paralysis, who had derived no benefit from doctors but who was cured during a vigil at Ely; of a young man from *Bradeford* (possibly Bradford Farm, in Stuntney), who had been dumb for seven years and who, on being brought to the church, found himself able to speak again; of a ten-year-old girl, blind from birth, who on coming into the church suddenly recovered her sight; and of a young man who came to Æthelthryth's tomb and recovered the use of his withered hand. He told also of a certain priest who when visiting Ely had instructed his servant-girl to pick some vegetables from the garden. The stake she was using for this illicit purpose stuck to her hand; but when, five years later, some of the priests of Ely happened to be visiting her master, they took her into her master's church and appealed to St Æthelthryth, whereupon the stake was released from her hand. The priest who told of these miracles (having witnessed the fourth and fifth ones himself) urged the Archpriest to abandon the proposed investigation of Æthelthryth's tomb, warning him of the punishments that awaited him if he chose to persist. Unimpressed by the warning, the Archpriest summoned four young men from among the clerics, and approached the tomb. At this point the author of the *Liber miraculorum* interjects the cautionary tale of what had happened when the 'Northmen' ravaged the Isle of Ely [in 869–70]: how one of their number, on making a small hole in the tomb, had promptly lost his eyes and his life; and how eight of the clerics who had been driven from Ely by the Vikings afterwards returned, one of whom as an old man [c.900] related the events to a younger man, who lived on to become the elderly priest who took the stand against the Archpriest [c.950]. The point is, of course, that the priest who gave the warning knew exactly what happened to those who had the audacity to desecrate St Æthelthryth's tomb. The Archpriest began by poking a stalk through the small opening in the tomb (that is to say, the hole made by the Viking in 870), and then subjected the relics within to further indignities. The outcome was predictable enough. The Archpriest's wife and children promptly died of plague. The Archpriest himself left the area, but soon contracted the plague and went to Hell. Two of his four accomplices died a sudden death. The third priest, though said to be 'proficient in the scribal duties pertaining to the church and to priests', forgot all that he knew and went mad. The

---

[67] *LE*, i. 43–9: pp. 57–61. The *Miracula S. Ætheldrethe*, preserved with Ely's hagiographical material in CCCC 393 (above, n. 12), appears to represent a later (early 12th-century) reworking and elaboration of the 10th-century work; see *Saints of Ely*, ed. Love.

fourth was Ælfhelm, author of the *Liber miraculorum*, who fell seriously ill for about eight months but was then brought by his parents to St Æthelthryth's tomb and, in happy extension of the earlier sequence of miracles, recovered his health through her intervention. In other words, Ælfhelm had been a young man when these events took place, in the mid tenth century; and since the tale that he told was evidently intended to expose the unworthiness of the priests who had formerly looked after Æthelthryth's shrine, it seems most likely that he had remained at Ely, becoming a monk when Ely was re-founded in *c*.970,[68] and that he was then moved or prevailed upon to write his account of the earlier period in the interests of the new regime.

We learn more about the church at Ely in the mid-tenth century from the *Libellus Æthelwoldi episcopi*. It emerges, for example, that grants of land to the shrine of St Æthelthryth were being made at least fifteen years *before* the Abbey's re-foundation, in *c*.970, and that the church was served at that time by a group of secular clerics (as is apparent from the story above); it also emerges that a layman called Wulfstan of Dalham was active in promoting St Æthelthryth's interests.[69] This Wulfstan, who took his name from Dalham in Suffolk, appears to have held office as a reeve in Cambridgeshire, and it could be that he enjoyed the patronage of King Eadred himself.[70] It is possible, however, that following the death of King Eadred and the accession of his nephew King Eadwig (955–9) changes took place which might have left a person like Wulfstan of Dalham at a disadvantage (at least for the time being), and a place like Ely not unaffected.[71] On 9 May 957 King Eadwig granted 40 hides of land *æt Helig* to Oda, Archbishop of Canterbury.[72] The charter survives to this day in its original single-sheet form; and there seems little doubt that it represents a grant of a substantial estate on the Isle of Ely to the Archbishop of Canterbury.[73] There is, however, no hint in other Ely records of this seemingly important stage in the Abbey's history, and it is far from clear what it might signify; but it could be, for example, that it had been Eadwig's purpose to set the church on a new footing, and perhaps to transfer it from local to outside control. Yet such was the pace of change in the 950s that this arrangement did not last for long, if indeed it was ever implemented. Soon after the charter was issued, the kingdom was divided between Eadwig and his younger brother

---

[68] At Winchester, the secular clerics were given the choice of leaving, or taking monastic vows and staying: Wulfstan, *VSÆ*, ch. 18: ed. Lapidge and Winterbottom, p. 32. The compiler of *LE* believed that the same choice had been given to the secular clerics at Ely: *LE*, ii. 3: pp. 74–5.

[69] *Libellus Æthelwoldi*, ch. 27 and 34 (*LE*, pp. 93–4, 97–8).

[70] S 572 (*LE*, p. 102) appears to be based on a charter of King Eadred granting land at Stapleford (Cambs.), to Wulfstan, styled the King's *sequipedus* (follower, or household official). There is no sign in Eadred's charters that Wulfstan was at this stage of sufficient importance in the King's circle to warrant regular inclusion in the witness-lists; *cf.* below, n. 78.

[71] For an account of political developments in the 950s, see S. Keynes, 'England, 900–1016', in *The New Cambridge Medieval History*, III: *c.900–c.1024*, ed. T. Reuter (Cambridge, 1999), pp. 456–84, at 474–9.

[72] S 646 (BCS 1347): Keynes (ed.), *Facsimiles of Anglo-Saxon Charters* (cit. in n. 13), no. 5 (face and dorse). For an account of Oda's career, see Lapidge, in *Encyclopaedia of ASE* (cit. in n. 3), pp. 339–40.

[73] Any lingering doubt that Eadwig's charter relates to Ely should be dispelled by the clear indications that it came from the Ely archives (above, n. 13); see also J.A. Robinson, *The Times of Saint Dunstan* (Oxford, 1923), pp. 118–20. Unfortunately (and perhaps significantly) the charter does not contain a boundary clause, rendering it impossible to locate the 40 hides in question; but the hidage suggests that it would represent a substantial part of the Isle. The estate at Abingdon given by King Eadred to Æthelwold was also assessed at 40 hides (Wulfstan, *VSÆ*, ch. 11: pp. 18–20), suggesting the possibility that Eadwig was in some respect following his uncle's example.

Edgar. Edgar became King of the Mercians, controlling the land north of the river Thames, and it is apparent that East Anglia and the east midlands fell within his share of the realm. At about the same time Archbishop Oda 'separated King Eadwig and Ælfgifu [his wife], because they were too closely related',[74] as if the ecclesiastical establishment was no longer inclined to indulge the King as he had been indulged before. When Archbishop Oda died, on 2 June 958, he was succeeded first by Ælfsige (958–9), then briefly by Byrhthelm (959), and then by Dunstan (959–88); and following Eadwig's death, on 1 October 959, Edgar succeeded to the kingdom of the English. In one way or another the estate at Ely reverted into royal control, and one can imagine that various parties might have taken a close interest in its fate.

The re-foundation of Ely Abbey

The origins of the monastic reform movement in England can be traced back to the growing familiarity at King Æthelstan's court with the renewed enthusiasm on the continent for the strict observance of the Rule of St Benedict.[75] This led in time to the refoundation of Glastonbury, under Abbot Dunstan, c.940, and to the refoundation of Abingdon, under Abbot Æthelwold, c.954, as expressions of a determination to combine monastic reform with a reaffirmation of the traditions of the ancient English church. It was not, however, until the protagonists gained the support and protection of King Edgar, and until the King (for his part) saw what could be gained from extending his support to them, that separate initiatives were brought together as an organised movement. Our understanding of these matters depends largely on sources written by or about the protagonists themselves, and we know rather less than we should like of the contexts in which the movement progressed in the 960s. Analysis of the attestations of abbots in the corpus of surviving charters affords at least some indication of the position which one abbot enjoyed in the periodic meetings of the King's councillors, in relation to other abbots, and by extension a sense of an Abbey's importance, at one time or another, in the kingdom as a whole.[76] We see in this way the high standing which Abbot Æthelwold enjoyed in the entourage of King Edgar (959–75), and his distinctive position at court in the early 960s, prior to his consecration as bishop of Winchester on 29 November 963. Barely three months later, in February 964, King Edgar 'drove the priests in the city [of Winchester] from the Old Minster and from the New Minster, and from Chertsey [in Surrey] and from Milton (Abbas) [in Dorset], and replaced them with monks.'[77] This was the act which demonstrated to all parties that monastic reform was firmly on the King's

---

[74] *ASC*, MS D, *s.a.* 958 (*The Anglo-Saxon Chronicle: a Collaborative Edition*, VI: *MS D*, ed. G.P. Cubbin (Cambridge, 1996), p. 45).

[75] For various manifestations of the movement, see *The Golden Age of Anglo-Saxon Art 966–1066* (cit. in n. 18); for the abbots, see D. Knowles *et al.* (eds.), *The Heads of Religious Houses England and Wales*, I: *940–1216*, 2nd edn (Cambridge, 2001). For a review of recent work in the field, see C. Cubitt, 'The Tenth-Century Benedictine Reform in England', *Early Medieval Europe*, 6 (1997), pp. 77–94. For a new assessment of the role of Bishop Æthelwold, see M. Gretsch, *The Intellectual Foundations of the English Benedictine Reform* (Cambridge, 1999).

[76] The evidence is assembled, in tabular form, in S. Keynes, *An Atlas of Attestations in Anglo-Saxon Charters c.670–1066*, I: *Tables*, ASNC Guides, Texts and Studies 5 (Cambridge, 2002), Table LV ('Attestations of abbots during the reign of King Edgar'). For the succession of Abbots of Ely, see *Heads of Religious Houses*, pp. 44–6 and 247–8.

[77] *ASC*, MS A, *s.a.* 964.

agenda, and it is a matter of particular significance for present purposes that King Edgar's chosen agent in lending the force of royal authority to Bishop Æthelwold for his action in 964 was none other than Wulfstan of Dalham, described as one of the King's most notable thegns and certainly by this stage in regular attendance at the King's court.[78] From 964 onwards the King's charters were often attested by at least five or six abbots, and before the decade was out charters were sometimes attested by as many as nine.

The Isle of Ely remained all the while in King Edgar's hands; but it was only a matter of time before monastic life would be revived there in honour of St Æthelthryth. We learn from Byrhtferth of Ramsey, writing c.1000, that when Oswald, bishop of Worcester (961–71), had asked the King for a monastery where he might gather together a group of monks, Edgar had given him a choice between that of St Alban (in Hertfordshire), that of St Æthelthryth (at Ely), and Benfleet (in Essex); Oswald went off to inspect the three places, but in the event managed to secure what he regarded as a more suitable home for his monks, on the island of Ramsey.[79] A rather different impression of the circumstances leading up to the refoundation of Ely Abbey is given by Wulfstan of Winchester, in his 'Life of St Æthelwold', also written c.1000:

> There is a well-known spot in East Anglia, surrounded like an island by swamps and water. From the quantity of eels taken in these marshes it has been given the name Ely. Here there is a place held to deserve all reverence, for it is made glorious by the relics and miracles of St Æthelthryth, queen and perpetual virgin, and her sisters. But at this time it was abandoned and pertained to the royal fisc. The servant of Christ [Æthelwold] began to reverence this place greatly, out of his love for the distinguished virgins, and he paid a large sum of money to buy it from King Edgar. In it he established a large group of monks, ordaining his prior Byrhtnoth as Abbot. He renovated the place as it deserved, giving it monastic buildings, and enriched it lavishly with possessions in land. He confirmed this grant with a privilege conferring perpetual liberty; and dedicated it to the Almighty Lord.[80]

A somewhat later but seemingly authoritative account of the re-foundation of Ely Abbey, given in the Libellus Æthelwoldi episcopi, introduces another dimension. The place was coveted (presumably in the 960s) by two of King Edgar's leading men: a certain Bishop Sigewold (said to be Greek by birth) and a certain Thurstan (said to be a Dane). We are not told why either person wanted the place, though it is possible that their conflicting claims arose in some way from the fact that Ely had recently been in the hands of Archbishop Oda.[81] Anyway, as the argument raged between them

[78] Wulfstan, VSÆ, ch. 18: p. 32. Attestations of thegns in charters of Eadred, Eadwig and Edgar suggest a basic distinction between a thegn Wulfstan at Eadwig's court in 957 (who received a grant of land at Conington (Hunts), in that year), a thegn Wulfstan who was one of Edgar's leading thegns from 962 until the end of the reign (but not thereafter), and a lesser thegn Wulfstan at Edgar's court in the late 960s. The second of these men was quite probably Wulfstan of Dalham, which suggests that he did not achieve his full status in the royal household until the early 960s.

[79] Byrhtferth, Vita S. Oswaldi, iii. 12 (J. Raine (ed.), Historians of the Church of York, 4 vols., Rolls Series, 71 (1879–94), I, p. 427).

[80] Wulfstan, VSÆ, ch. 23: pp. 38–40.

[81] Unfortunately, nothing more is known of either person. There is no other trace of a Bishop Sigewold in the 10th century; but there is no reason to doubt that he may have held office as some form of assistant bishop in

Wulfstan of Dalham stepped in and apprised the King of Ely's particular fame and distinction, whereupon the King, inflamed by a divine passion, rejected their claims and resolved to take measures of his own.[82] We are left wondering whether the initiative should be attributed to Bishop Æthelwold, to King Edgar, or to Wulfstan of Dalham; but whatever the case we need not doubt that responsibility for restoring regular observance at Ely fell largely upon Æthelwold himself.

The question arises why Ely was refounded as a house for monks. The monastic reformers would not have countenanced the revival of the double house, preferring separate communities for men and for women; yet one might have supposed that Æthelthryth's credentials would have affected the choice. Of course it was not as simple as that. Responsibility for nunneries rested with Queen Ælfthryth, who had married Edgar in 964; and there were several ancient or more recently re-founded nunneries, at Wilton (Wilts.), Horton (Dorset), Shaftesbury (Dorset), Winchester (Hants), and Romsey (Hants) – all in the heartland of Wessex, where daughters of the nobility could be kept out of harm's or temptation's way.[83] The intensity of Bishop Æthelwold's devotion to St Æthelthryth was doubtless fuelled by his knowledge of Bede's *Historia ecclesiastica*, and finds due reflection in the prominence accorded to her in the 'Benedictional of St Æthelwold', a manuscript produced for Æthelwold by the monk Godeman, at the Old Minster, Winchester, probably in the early 970s.[84] Æthelthryth is included, and explicitly identified, in the 'Choir of Virgins' at the beginning of the book.[85] The first of two openings for the blessing for the Feast of St Æthelthryth (23 June), on fos. 90^v–91^r, bears on the left a full-page image of the saint (Colour pl. 17a), complemented on the right by an image of Christ enclosed in the initial O; and in the text which follows, on fos. 91^v–92^r, Æthelthryth is held up as a shining example of virtuous life and as one who had adopted the 'strict life of monasticism'.[86] The full-page images of St Swithun and St Benedict, which occur at

---

England, or that he was of Greek origin. For the suggestion that his name represents a 'translation' into English of the Greek name Nicephorus, see M. Lapidge, 'Byzantium, Rome and England in the Early Middle Ages', *Roma fra oriente e occidente*, Settimane di studio del centro italiano di studi sull'alto medioevo 49 (Spoleto, 2002), pp. 363–400, at pp. 386–99. The only attestation of a Thurstan in Edgar's charters occurs among the thegns in S 779 (Ely, 970); a Wistan, son of Thurstan, is mentioned in the *Battle of Maldon*, line 298.

[82] *Libellus Æthelwoldi*, ch. 2 (*LE*, pp. 396–7); see also *LE*, ii. 2: p. 73.

[83] For the nunneries which flourished in the 10th century, see Foot, *Veiled Women*, I, pp. 85–96, and Map 4 (p. 90). Others were founded sooner or later at Horton (Dorset), Amesbury (Wilts.) and Wherwell (Hants.). The only nunneries outside Wessex were at Barking (Essex) and at Chatteris (Cambs.).

[84] BL, Add. MS 49598. For a complete facsimile in colour, see A. Prescott, *The Benedictional of Saint Æthelwold: a Masterpiece of Anglo-Saxon Art: a Facsimile* (London, 2002). See also *Golden Age of Anglo-Saxon Art* (cit. in n. 18), no. 37, with plate VI, and R. Deshman, *The Benedictional of Æthelwold*, Studies in Manuscript Illumination 9 (Princeton, NJ, 1995). The date of the Benedictional remains controversial. It is generally presumed to have been produced after the Translation of St Swithun in 971 and before Bishop Æthelwold's death in 984; and if the monk Godeman is identified as Bishop Æthelwold's chaplain of that name, who was probably still at Winchester in the early 970s before his move to Thorney, it may be that it was produced at about the time of King Edgar's second coronation, at Bath, in 973 (*ibid.*, esp. pp. 213–14 and 260–1). For further discussion, see M. Biddle (ed.), *The Anglo-Saxon Minsters of Winchester*, I: *The Anglo-Saxon Minsters*, Winchester Studies 4. i (Oxford, forthcoming), and M. Lapidge (ed.), *The Anglo-Saxon Minsters of Winchester*, II: *The Cult of St Swithun*, Winchester Studies 4. ii (Oxford, 2003); see also *Liber Vitae*, ed. Keynes (cit. in n. 19), p. 88.

[85] BL, Add. MS 49598, fos. 1^v–2^r, at 2 (Æthelthryth on the left): see Deshman, *Benedictional of Æthelwold*, p. 151, and Prescott, *Benedictional of Saint Æthelwold*, p. 10.

[86] BL, Add. MS 49598, fos. 90–92: see Deshman, *Benedictional of Æthelwold*, pp. 121–4, 172, 173, 184, and 206–7,

the appropriate liturgical points later on in the same manuscript, symbolised different aspects of Æthelwold's programme, representing his office as bishop of Winchester and the essence of his own monastic vocation. The image of St Æthelthryth would naturally evoke the comparison which Bede had made between her and the Virgin Mary, yet it seems that she stood more generally for the perfection of monastic life in the early English church, and that Bishop Æthelwold took up her cause as an example for emulation by all.

The reasons which led King Edgar to lend his support to Bishop Æthelwold at Ely are more difficult to fathom. It is possible that the King was eager, quite simply, to restore the institutions of the English church which had flourished in the seventh century. Or perhaps his motivation was to do good in the eyes of God, or at least in the eyes of those who were guiding his actions in the 960s. He may even have calculated that the establishment of a major land-owning institution in the fenlands, controlled by a community conscious of what they owed to the King, would promote his own interests in an area where he might well have felt in need of friends.[87] Whatever the case, King Edgar endowed the Abbey with lands and confirmed his grant 'with a privilege conferring perpetual liberty'.[88] The expression is so vague as to be effectively meaningless; but if Wulfstan had a single charter in mind, it has to be said that there is no demonstrably or even putatively authentic document which might answer to this description. It is disconcerting in such circumstances that a religious community should have been so careless as to lose its foundation charter, although monks could generally be relied upon to produce such documents for themselves, some years after the event, when things had begun to fall into place. An imposing bilingual document which purports to have been issued from a royal council held at Woolmer (Hants), at Easter (27 March) in 970, and which survives in the form of a single sheet of parchment written probably in the late eleventh century, suggests that sooner or later the monks of Ely found reason to provide themselves with something calculated to impress.[89] The basic message conveyed by the charter is that Edgar granted the land at Ely to Bishop Æthelwold in exchange for a large estate at Harting, in Sussex, to which he added estates at Melbourn and Armingford (Cambs.) and at Northwold (Norfolk), together with the jurisdiction of the Two Hundreds of the Isle of Ely and the Five Hundreds of 'Wicklow' (in south-east Suffolk); to which the

with pl. 28, and Prescott, *Benedictional of Saint Æthelwold*, pp. 16–17. It would be interesting to know whether the image of St Æthelthryth in the Benedictional was related in any way to the images of virgins on the back covering of the gospel-book which King Edgar gave to Ely, as described in Inventory C (above, n. 32), or indeed to the tenth gospel-book in the same inventory, which is said to have been 'covered in silver plate, and gilded throughout, with figures of St Æthelthryth, which Ælfric Cantor made'. For both, see *LE*, iii. 50: pp. 290–1.

[87] The political ('West Saxon') associations of the reformed monastery at Ely are stressed by Ridyard, *Royal Saints*, pp. 189–90 and 196, but can be overstated.

[88] Wulfstan, *VSÆ*, ch. 23: pp. 38–40.

[89] S 779. For further discussion, see *LE*, pp. 414–15. For the Old English version, see Robertson, *Anglo-Saxon Charters*, pp. 98–103; see also J. Pope, 'Ælfric and the Old English Version of the Ely Privilege', in P. Clemoes and K. Hughes (eds.), *England before the Conquest: Studies in Primary Sources presented to Dorothy Whitelock* (Cambridge, 1971), pp. 84–113. S 776 is another form of the transaction represented by S 779; perhaps significantly, it is not found in the Abbey's 12th-century cartularies. It seems to have been only under exceptional circumstances that the foundation of a religious house was marked, in Anglo-Saxon England, by the drawing-up of a foundation charter; so it became common practice, in the 12th century and thereafter, for the deficiency to be met by fabrication.

Libellus Æthelwoldi adds that Æthelwold also gave Edgar a payment of 100 pounds with (or in the form of) 'a golden cross furbished with marvellous workmanship and stuffed with relics'.[90]

It is accepted that the origins of the medieval liberty of Ely Abbey are more likely to be found in the circumstances of the Abbey's refoundation, in the late tenth century, than in any earlier arrangements which might have dated back to the late seventh century;[91] yet it has to be admitted that the diplomatic form of Edgar's charter renders it wide open to suspicion, and that privileges of the kind which it conveys are more likely to have developed in the late tenth and eleventh centuries than to have been granted *de novo* by King Edgar in 970.[92] There is also an important contrast to be drawn between the Woolmer charter and some other charters of King Edgar, dated 970, which have every appearance of authenticity and which represent early stages in the process by which Bishop Æthelwold secured an endowment for the Abbey.[93] These charters show that the abbey was a fully functioning institution by that date; but if we discount the supposed foundation charter itself (the date of which was perhaps suggested by that of the others), the possibility arises that a community had in fact been set up at Ely in the late 960s, and that it was not until 970 that the process of endowment began in earnest, with a series of complex transactions involving local landowners. Perhaps one should add that King Edgar's initial act of foundation seems to have been commemorated at Ely in ways which may have taken the place of a foundation charter. Among the treasures still preserved at the Abbey in the 1130s was 'a cross, on the front side entirely of gold with three golden figures and precious stones, and on the other sides of silver gilded all over, which King Edgar gave to St Æthelthryth in testimony of his gifts', and a gospel-book 'which King Edgar gave to St Æthelthryth with the golden cross mentioned above, when confirming the liberties of the church' (said to have 'a Christ in Majesty, four angels and twelve apostles in silver on the front, on a golden surface with precious and enamelled stones', and covered in silver on the back, 'with figures of virgins').[94] The King gave a number of other things to the Abbey, including a cloak of

---

[90] *Libellus Æthelwoldi*, ch. 4 (*LE*, pp. 75–6); *LE* added that Æthelwold had acquired the estate at Harting from his lord King Æthelstan.

[91] For the view that the liberty of Ely originated in King Edgar's charter of 970, see Miller, *Abbey & Bishopric*, pp. 15 and 25–35, and E. Miller, 'The Liberty of Ely', in VCH, *Cambs.*, IV, pp. 1–27, esp. 4–5; see also F.E. Harmer, *Anglo-Saxon Writs* (Manchester, 1952), pp. 222–4.

[92] On the nature of privileges actually granted to ecclesiastics in the late 10th century, as opposed to the nature of the privileges subsequently claimed by them, see P. Wormald, 'Oswaldslow: an "Immunity"?', in N. Brooks and C. Cubitt (eds.), *St Oswald of Worcester: Life and Influence* (London, 1996), pp. 117–28. For a 12th-century view of the privileges, see *LE*, ii. 54: pp. 124–6.

[93] The charters are not quite what they seem. S 780, by which King Edgar granted 10 hides at Linden (Isle of Ely) to Ely, and S 1844, formerly preserved at Worcester (above, n. 13), both dated 970, have to be understood in relation to *Libellus Æthelwoldi*, ch. 6 (*LE*, pp. 80–1); it emerges that the charters do not represent straightforward grants of land by the King to the Abbey, but were part of the means by which a more complex transaction was effected. S 781, by which Edgar granted 10 hides at Stoke (Suffolk) to Ely (at the instigation of his wife Ælfthryth), also dated 970, has to be understood in relation to *Libellus Æthelwoldi*, ch. 51 (*LE*, pp. 111–12), which reveals that Æthelwold bought the land from the King.

[94] The cross and the gospel-book are duly registered and described in 'Inventory C' (above, n. 32); see *LE*, iii. 50: pp. 290–1. The gold cross which Bishop Æthelwold had given to King Edgar in part-payment for the land at Ely is said to have been given by Edgar to Ely, with the gospel-book (*LE*, ii. 4, p. 76). Bishop Nigel subsequently sold the cross and the gospel-book to the Jews of Cambridge, whereupon Prior William and the monks gave 200 marks presumably to get them back (*LE*, iii. 92, p. 339). The cross was among treasures stolen from Ely in 1322, though soon afterwards recovered in London (Wharton, *Anglia Sacra*, I, p. 645).

fine *purpura* [shot-silk taffeta][95] (which was made into a chasuble), a *cingulum* [belt] (which was made into a *baltheus* [belt]), and some *caligae* [stockings] (which were made into an alb), as well as various caskets and reliquaries from his chapel, filled with relics.[96]

The factor which determined progress at Ely in the years immediately following its re-foundation, *c*.970, was the close collaboration between Bishop Æthelwold and Abbot Byrhtnoth. As a former prior of the Old Minster, Byrhtnoth would have been closely involved with Æthelwold in the establishment at Winchester of a regular monastic community, following the ejection of the secular clergy in 964; and just as at Winchester some of the clergy were allowed to stay on as monks, so too at Ely may there have been scope for members of the older community to embrace the Rule of St Benedict, if they were prepared to do so with the required degree of zeal.[97] It would then have been necessary to set in hand the re-equipping and refurbishment of the Abbey, by the acquisition of books and other necessities of the monastic life (vestments, objects for display and decoration, and items needed for divine service). No doubt Æthelwold himself was as generous to Ely as he was to his other foundations, notably at Abingdon and Peterborough;[98] and while much of any silver and gold would appear to have been lost in the aftermath of the Norman Conquest, many other items associated with Æthelwold were still preserved and used at Ely in the mid-twelfth century.[99] We may also assume that Byrhtnoth set about other aspects of the task in hand: undertaking whatever building work was deemed to be necessary for the purposes of the new community, tending to the shrine of St Æthelthryth and her sisters, and developing the resources of the monastery, whether in relics, estates, or manpower. Byrhtnoth delegated responsibility for the management of the Abbey's estates to his prior (*praepositus*) Leo, who seems to have been instrumental in establishing the boundaries of the Isle of Ely and whose green fingers earned him a special place in the Abbey's communal memory.[100]

The priority must have been to ensure that the church at Ely offered a fitting place of rest for such a potent group of saints. Little is known of the external appearance or indeed the precise location of the tenth-century church, beyond the indications that the work of its construction involved respect for whatever remained of the old (seventh-century) church on what is necessarily presumed to be the same site,[101] that it had (or

---

[95] On the nature of *purpura*, see Dodwell, *Anglo-Saxon Art* (cit. in n. 54), pp. 145–50.

[96] The items made from Edgar's clothing were described as such in the third inventory, *c*.1140; see *LE*, iii. 50: p. 293. For a later and more circumstantial account of these gifts, see *LE*, ii. 50: pp. 117–18. Edgar's cloak and belt are also recorded among treasures entrusted as security to the Bishop of Lincoln; see *LE*, iii. 92: p. 339.

[97] *LE*, ii. 3: pp. 74–5, with Blake's comment, p. 75 n. 1; see also above, p. 18, and *LE*, ii. 86: p. 155, for Bishop Ælfwine at Holme.

[98] For Æthelwold's gifts to Abingdon, see B. Yorke, 'Introduction', in B. Yorke (ed.), *Bishop Æthelwold: his Career and Influence* (Woodbridge, 1988), pp. 1–12, at pp. 7–8, and A. Thacker, 'Æthelwold and Abingdon', *ibid.*, pp. 43–64, at pp. 57–8. For Æthelwold's gifts to Peterborough, see Robertson, *Anglo-Saxon Charters*, no. 39.

[99] For Æthelwold's gifts to Ely, see *LE*, ii. 3: p. 75. The items registered in 'Inventory C' (above, n. 32) as having formerly belonged to St Æthelwold include banners, albs, copes, dalmatics, tunics, palls, and an ancient cloak, as well as woollen curtains, embroideries, seat covers, silk pillows, and silk mantles. Against this background, the absence of anything in gold or silver is all the more striking.

[100] *LE*, ii. 54: pp. 123–6. For Leo's gift to the Abbey of a silver cross containing relics of SS Vedast and Amand, see also *LE*, iii. 50: p. 290. The reeve Leofwine who is to be found acting on Ely's behalf in the 970s (*Libellus Æthelwoldi episcopi*, chs. 10, 20, 46) may or may not have been the same person.

[101] For the 7th-century church, see above, p. 12 and n. 48.

soon acquired) a tower or steeple at the west end and side chapels or towers further east,[102] and that some part of the church lay underneath the northern arm of the present Cathedral.[103] The building operations appear to have involved both Bishop Æthelwold and Abbot Byrhtnoth.[104] Æthelwold is said to have found St Æthelthryth's tomb 'beside the high altar', where it had been placed by Seaxburh in 695, and left it untouched, 'not lying hidden under the earth but raised above it'. Indeed, Æthelthryth was resplendent 'in a tower (*in turre*), entombed at her own altar on the south side', while Seaxburh, 'buried directly opposite (*e regione*) in the same place', shone forth 'from the north' (*ab aquilone*). Æthelwold is also said to have sealed the tombs of St Seaxburh and St Eormenhild with lead, leaving the latter as he had found her 'on the bare floor of the sepulchre without any covering'. It would appear to follow that Æthelthryth and Seaxburh lay respectively south and north of the high altar, in raised tombs, and that Eormenhild lay underneath the flagstones, somewhere near her own mother. Meanwhile, Byrhtnoth pressed on with the building. The restored church was dedicated on the day following the feast of the Purification of St Mary (2 February), with much ceremony; unfortunately, no year is given.

Byrhtnoth was otherwise instrumental, in the early 970s, in consolidating the collective identity of Ely's saints. As we have seen, only Æthelthryth and her sister Seaxburh were central to the story as told by Bede; Seaxburh's daughter Eormenhild, and the third sister Wihtburh, seem in one way or another to have been later additions. To judge from the range of feasts entered in pre-Conquest calendars, the cults of Æthelthryth (23 June, 17 October), Seaxburh (6 July) and Eormenhild (13 February) were already part of a common ecclesiastical tradition before the end of the tenth century;[105] so it would appear that Eormenhild had managed to join her aunt and mother as part of the local tradition. The cult of Wihtburh (17 March), on the other hand, seems to have been a separate development. According to an eleventh-century entry in a Canterbury manuscript of the *Anglo-Saxon Chronicle*, for 798, 'the body of Wihtburh was found all sound and undecayed in Dereham, 55 years after she departed from this life'.[106] It follows that she died *c*.743, a date which is difficult enough to reconcile with the notion that she was a sister of Æthelthryth (who died in 679), let alone a daughter of King Anna (who died in 654). The tale of her life as a

---

[102] See below, pp. 37 and 42. For discussion of the form of the 10th-century church, see A.W. Clapham, *English Romanesque Architecture*, 2 vols. (Oxford, 1930–4), I, pp. 89–90; D. Purcell, *The Building of Ely Cathedral* (Ely, 1973), p. 3; and E. Fernie, *The Architecture of the Anglo-Saxons* (London, 1983), pp. 114–15.

[103] This is suggested by the fact that the tombs of Archbishop Wulfstan and St Wihtburh had to be moved in order to make way for the new building: *LE*, ii. 87: p. 157 and ii. 146: p. 231, and below, pp. 34–5, 54–5. See also Hampson and Atkinson, 'City of Ely' (cit. in n. 48), p. 50; and Maddison, *Ely Cathedral*, pp. 9–11, 16 and 23. It was the opinion of Bentham and Essex (*Ely*, pp. 24–5, 29 and 289, with pls. IV and XLIX, and Addenda, pp. 9–10; also Stevenson, *Supplement*, pp. 41–7) that the 'Old Conventual Church' lay to the south-east of the present Cathedral; the building which they had in mind was, however, subsequently identified as the hall and chapel of the late 12th-century monastic infirmary. See T. Cocke, 'The "Old Conventual Church" at Ely: a False Trail in Romanesque Studies', in S. Macready and F.H. Thompson (eds.), *Art and Patronage in the English Romanesque*, Soc. of Antiquaries Occasional Papers, n.s. 8 (London, 1986), pp. 77–86.

[104] *LE*, ii. 52: p. 120 and ii. 144–5: pp. 229–31. For *LE*, ii. 144–7, describing the translations in 1102 and 1106, with allusions to the earlier activities of Bishop Æthelwold, see E.M. Goulburn and H. Symonds, *The Life, Letters, and Sermons of Bishop Herbert de Losinga*, 2 vols. (Oxford, 1878), I, pp. 212–21.

[105] For details, see Rushforth, *Atlas of Saints*; and *Saints of Ely*, ed. Love; see also Ridyard, *Royal Saints*, p. 185 n. 46.

[106] *ASC*, MS F, *s.a.* 799 (*Anglo-Saxon Chronicle*, VIII: *MS F*, ed. P.S. Baker (Cambridge, 2000), p. 58).

solitary at (East) Dereham (in Norfolk), is told in hagiographical material which probably originated at Ely in the eleventh century, but which reached its present form in the early twelfth century; to which must be added a later twelfth-century account of her childhood at Holkham (also in Norfolk).[107] Most remarkable is the story of how Abbot Byrhtnoth came with a large force, in 974, to his estate at Dereham (given to Ely by King Edgar), and how, while the villagers slept off the effects of food and drink, he stealthily removed Wihtburh's body from its tomb, and set off with it back home, pursued for much of the way by the infuriated men of Dereham until greeted at Ely on 8 July by SS Æthelthryth, Seaxburh, and Eormenhild.[108] As we shall see, it seems likely that Wihtburh was buried beyond the high altar, perhaps on a raised floor at the eastern extremity of the church itself.[109] Byrhtnoth would have had every reason to concentrate his best relics at Ely; but one does wonder at the same time whether he might have considered this a reasonable pretext for attaching Wihtburh, with all her undoubted merits, to the same most holy and royal family.[110] We know very little about the appearance of the shrine which might have stood over the tomb of St Æthelthryth in the late tenth century,[111] though we may be sure that Abbot Byrhtnoth was concerned to ensure that she, her sisters and her niece made their impact as a group. He had images made of all four of the blessed virgins (of wood overlaid with gold and silver, studded with jewels), placing two to the left and two to the right of the high altar, where 'they presented a great spectacle to the populace in magnification of the glory of the temple of God'.[112] An uncritical mind in search of a telling analogy wanders across the channel to the reliquary statue of St Foy, kept in the church at Conques in south-western France, and wheeled out by the monks in solemn procession whenever they needed her aid in asserting their rights to one of their estates.[113] No doubt the effigies of Ely's saints made quite an impression on all those who came into the church; and there they remained for nearly one hundred years,

---

[107] For the *Vita S. Wihtburge*, in CCCC 393 and in TCC, MS O.2.1, see *Saints of Ely*, ed. Love. The *Life* in CCCC 393 (possibly by Goscelin) covers Wihtburh's life at Dereham (chs. 2–7), her removal to Ely (chs. 8–14), and her translation into the new church at Ely in 1106 (chs. 15–24). The version of the *Life* in TCC O.2.1, which seems to be an elaboration of the earlier work, adds the story of how in her childhood Wihtburh and her friends made piles of stones on the sandy beach near Holkham, and how the stones were miraculously reformed into a landmark on higher ground inland, represented by the church built in her memory at *Withburgsstowe*, in Holkham. For the cult of Wihtburh at Ely, see also Ridyard, *Royal Saints*, pp. 59 and 185.

[108] *Vita S. Wihtburge*, chs. 10–14 (*Saints of Ely*, ed. Love); *LE*, ii. 53: pp. 120–3.

[109] For the translation of her body in 1106, see above, n. 104, and below, pp. 54–5, following *Vita S. Wihtburge*, chs. 15–24 (*Saints of Ely*, ed. Love), and *LE*, ii. 146–8: pp. 231–4.

[110] For the extension of what may have been the same process in the 12th century, see Ridyard, *Royal Saints*, pp. 185 n. 46 and 209 n. 151 (with reference to the cult of Werburh). Doubts about Wihtburh's relationship with the other Ely saints were being raised already in the 12th century, on the grounds that she is not mentioned by Bede, and were countered by the author of the version of the *Vita S. Wihtburge* in TCC, O.2.1; see *Saints of Ely*, ed. Love.

[111] For descriptions of 10th- and 11th-century reliquaries and shrines, see Dodwell, *Anglo-Saxon Art*, pp. 196–201, and J. Crook, 'King Edgar's Reliquary of St Swithun', *Anglo-Saxon England*, 21 (1992), pp. 177–202. For the appearance of the shrine in the early 12th century, some part of which may have been of pre-Conquest origin, see below, pp. 54–5.

[112] *LE*, ii. 6: pp. 78–9; for their size and form, see Dodwell, *Anglo-Saxon Art*, pp. 213–15.

[113] For the reliquary statue of St Foy, and the uses to which it was put in the 10th and 11th centuries, see P. Sheingorn, *The Book of Sainte Foy* (Philadelphia, 1995), pp. 16–17, 120–1 and 247–8; see also D. Gaborit-Chopin and É. Taburet-Delahaye, *Le trésor de Conques*, exhibition catalogue (Paris, 2001). For effigies of the Madonna and Child, see below, n. 135.

until stripped of their metal, and thereby reduced to powerless wooden manikins, during the reign of King William I.

If a religious house was to prosper in the late tenth century an abundance of relics and other treasures was essential, but so too was a sufficiency of manpower and land. A significant aspect of Ely's history in the early 970s was thus its rapid accumulation of a landed endowment, not only in the two hundreds of Ely but also in the southern half of Cambridgeshire and further afield.[114] The details of this process can be reconstructed in remarkable detail from the *Libellus Æthelwoldi episcopi*, which shows what agency was acting for the Abbey in each case, from whom the land was acquired, and often at what price. The process was by no means a simple matter of the community gratefully receiving gifts from the more pious members of the local landowning classes, anxious to earn credit at the Last Judgement, but a matter which entailed the Bishop and the Abbot seizing whatever initiatives they could and taking advantage of whatever opportunities came their way, followed by some hard-headed bargaining and leading eventually to the standard procedures of purchase and exchange. It emerges from the *Libellus* that Bishop Æthelwold himself played the leading part, and that his expenditure on Ely's behalf amounted to about 375 pounds (or over 90,000 silver pence). He also worked for the cause in other ways. Most significantly, he translated the Rule of St Benedict into English; and having received an estate at Sudbourne (Suffolk) from King Edgar and Queen Ælfthryth in payment for his work, he gave the land to Ely with its charter.[115] It was a process, however, which often antagonised those with expectations or designs of their own, resulting in a build-up of resentment towards the community so recently established in their midst. It is perhaps no surprise, therefore, that when King Edgar died, still only in his early thirties, on 8 July 975, precipitating a disputed succession which compromised the maintenance of law and order, many of the affected or aggrieved parties took advantage of the circumstances in an attempt to undo what had been done under the previous regime. The result was a short but intense outbreak of claim and counter-claim, regarded by some contemporaries (and modern commentators) as an 'anti-monastic reaction' but better characterised as an expression of feelings (in some cases second thoughts) which had previously been suppressed or contained. The singular interest of the *Libellus Æthelwoldi episcopi*, in this connection, is that much of it was based on vernacular records generated in the course of all this litigation in the later 970s; for it transports us into the heart of the society around the Abbey, and provides an insight into the realities of life at this local level.[116] The men of Cambridgeshire and the surrounding region would have come to know in the early 970s what it meant to be a neighbour of St Æthelthryth;[117] and if some among their number tried to take

---

[114] Miller, *Abbey & Bishopric*, pp. 16–21.

[115] *Libellus Æthelwoldi*, ch. 49 (*LE*, p. 111). The land had formerly belonged to Earl Scule, who flourished in the 930s. For further discussion, see M. Gretsch, 'The Benedictine Rule in Old English: a Document of Bishop Æthelwold's Reform Politics', in M. Korhammer (ed.), *Words, Texts and Manuscripts* (Cambridge, 1992), pp. 131–58.

[116] See A. Kennedy, 'Law and Litigation in the *Libellus Æthelwoldi episcopi*', *Anglo-Saxon England*, 24 (1995), pp. 131–83, and Keynes, 'England, 900–1016', pp. 482–3; see also *Book of Bishop Æthelwold*, ed. Keynes and Kennedy.

[117] The expression is borrowed from B.H. Rosenwein, *To be a Neighbor of St Peter: the Social Meaning of Cluny's Property, 909–1049* (Ithaca, NY, 1989).

advantage of her good nature in 975, they would soon have found that if one had to be her neighbour it was best to be her friend.

The heyday of Ely Abbey

After such intense activity in the 970s, when Ely Abbey first accumulated a substantial landed endowment and then found itself immersed in litigation, the Abbot and community might have looked forward to a period of relative peace and quiet. The reign of King Æthelred the Unready (978–1016) is, of course, characterised in received historical tradition as a period of chaos, proceeding from the incompetence of the King himself and leading inexorably to military and political catastrophe; so the question arises whether the Abbey suffered during this period with the rest of the country, or whether impressions formed from a local perspective should encourage us to put a different construction on the course of national events. As we move out of the period covered by the *Libellus Æthelwoldi episcopi*, we move into the period for which the *Liber Eliensis* comes into its own, providing us with a wealth of material based on local traditions, lost vernacular documentation, and much else besides.[118] It should always be remembered, of course, that there were many other religious houses in the landscape. Among other fenland houses, the major establishments were Peterborough, Crowland, Thorney, and Ramsey, joined sooner or later by lesser houses at Eynesbury (St Neots), *Slepe* (St Ives), and Chatteris; while to the east were Bury St Edmunds (Suffolk) and Holme (Norfolk). Each of these houses was founded under circumstances peculiar to itself; each had or soon developed its own associations, fortunes and identity; and while there was co-operation between some houses, there was also rivalry between others, as they competed in the same market for patronage, land, resources, and holy relics.[119]

Abbot Byrhtnoth had attested the charters of King Edgar somewhat infrequently, and without any obvious indication that he was a significant figure at the King's court.[120] In Æthelred's reign he is to be found among the witnesses in 980–2, yet is conspicuous only by his absence during the rest of the 980s; but he 'returns' to court *c*.990, and occurs regularly thereafter until his death on 5 May in ?996.[121] The pattern overall is intriguing, and might be taken to suggest that it was not until the 990s that Abbot Byrhtnoth began to make his presence felt at meetings of the King's council. It could be significant in this connection that Æthelwine, Ealdorman of East Anglia, and patron of Ramsey Abbey, was the leading ealdorman at court from 983 until his death in 992;[122] for there are

---

[118] Above, pp. 7–9.

[119] For Abbot Byrhtnoth's involvement in the establishment of a priory at Eynesbury, *c*.980, see *LE*, ii. 29: pp. 102–4; for its later appropriation from Ely, see below, p. 48. For Bishop Eadnoth and the establishment of a church at *Slepe*, and for his foundation of a nunnery at Chatteris, see below, p. 31. In his *Vita S. Oswaldi*, v. 2 (ed. Raine, pp. 453–4), Byrhtferth of Ramsey tells how, on a visit to Ramsey, St Oswald was told of the death of a monk of Ely called Huna, and ordered prayers to be said for 30 days; the monks appeared to Oswald one night, and gave thanks to him for his salvation. The obit of a monk called Huna was kept at Ely on 12 September (above, n. 20).

[120] Keynes, *Atlas of Attestations*, table LV.

[121] *Ibid.*, table LXI.

[122] *Ibid.*, table LXII; see also S. Keynes, *The Diplomas of King Æthelred 'the Unready' 978–1016* (Cambridge, 1980), pp. 157–8. For a survey of Ealdorman Æthelwine's career, see C. Hart, 'Æthelstan "Half-King" and his Family' [1973], reprinted in *The Danelaw* (London, 1992), pp. 569–604, at pp. 591–7.

various signs in the *Libellus* of the tension that existed between Æthelwine and Abbot Byrhtnoth in the 970s, which might have had further repercussions.[123] The better friend of Ely Abbey was Ealdorman Byrhtnoth, who in the 980s was next in the hierarchy after Æthelwine. This Byrhtnoth, not to be confused with his namesake the Abbot, features in the *Libellus* as one who had often been seen in the 970s to protect the Abbey's interests.[124] There is much that is erroneous, or delightfully contrived, about the later twelfth-century tradition describing the ealdorman's dealings first with the Abbot of Ramsey and then with the Abbot of Ely, as he marched past their abbeys on his way to his fateful encounter with the Vikings at Maldon (Essex) in August 991;[125] yet it was all a good way of showing that Ramsey received its come-uppance, and by extension Ealdorman Æthelwine his just deserts, when Ealdorman Byrhtnoth decided to bequeath a large quantity of his land to the monks of Ely.[126] We are also told that on hearing of Ealdorman Byrhtnoth's death the Abbot despatched some of his monks to Maldon, where they found the ealdorman's decapitated body and brought it back to Ely for burial (a round mass of wax being substituted for the head);[127] and it was at this time that Ealdorman Byrhtnoth's widow, Ælfflæd, gave Ely 'a hanging embroidered and decorated with the deeds of her husband'.[128] Of course it can be no more than a pleasant thought that Abbot Byrhtnoth's 'return' to court, c.990, was a reflection of his increasing stature as Abbot of Ely, and perhaps also of Ealdorman Æthelwine's declining powers; but it is a thought which prompts us to wonder in addition what then passed between Byrhtnoth and King Edgar's widow, Ælfthryth, who was also back at court in the 990s. For something must lie behind the extraordinary tale, told in the *Liber Eliensis*, of Abbot Byrhtnoth's death, c.996. When passing through the New Forest on his way to King Æthelred's court, 'on church business', Abbot Byrhtnoth needed to relieve himself; when searching for a suitable place, he encountered the queen, making her potions and cavorting with horses; when they met again at court, she tried at first to draw the Abbot into her wicked ways, and then, when he refused, had him killed; and only later, at Wherwell (where she had founded a nunnery in expiation of her role in the death of King Edward the Martyr), did she confess to her part in Byrhtnoth's murder.[129]

The importance of Ely Abbey was maintained and perhaps extended by Byrhtnoth's successor, Ælfsige (996 × 99–1012 × 16). An abbot of Ely always started from a good

---

[123] See, *e.g.*, *Libellus Æthelwoldi episcopi*, chs. 5 (*LE*, pp. 79–80), 14 (pp. 90–1), 38–9 (pp. 100–1 and 104), 46 (p. 110), 60 (p. 116). See also *LE*, ii. 55: pp. 126–7, for Æthelwine's special place among the malefactors.

[124] See, *e.g.*, *Libellus Æthelwoldi episcopi*, chs. 35 (*LE*, pp. 98–9), 38 (pp. 100–1), 44 (p. 108).

[125] *LE*, ii. 62: pp. 133–6, from the tract commemorating the translation of the bones by Prior Alexander in the 1150s (above, p. 9). See also A. Kennedy, 'Byrhtnoth's Obits and 12th-Century Accounts of the Battle of Maldon', in D. Scragg (ed.), *The Battle of Maldon AD 991* (Oxford, 1991), pp. 59–78.

[126] For the estates given by Byrhtnoth to Ely, see M.A.L. Locherbie-Cameron, 'Byrhtnoth and his Family', in *Battle of Maldon AD 991*, pp. 253–62.

[127] *LE*, ii. 62: p. 136. Byrhtnoth's head was missing when his tomb was opened in 1769; see further below, p. 58.

[128] *LE*, ii. 63: p. 136, reproduced from *LE*, MS E (above, n. 26), in Kennedy, 'Byrhtnoth's Obits', p. 66. For further discussion, see Dodwell, *Anglo-Saxon Art*, pp. 134–6 (challenging the presumption that the hanging would have depicted Byrhtnoth's death at Maldon), and M. Budny, 'The Byrhtnoth Tapestry or Embroidery', in *Battle of Maldon AD 991*, pp. 263–78 (re-opening the possibilities). For the possibility that the hanging was stolen in 1093, see below, p. 51.

[129] *LE*, ii. 56: pp. 127–8. For further discussion, see C.E. Wright, *The Cultivation of Saga in Anglo-Saxon England* (Edinburgh, 1939), pp. 158–61, and R.M. Wilson, *The Lost Literature of Medieval England* (London, 1952), pp. 46–7. For the method of murder, see K. Sisam, 'A Secret Murder', *Medium Ævum*, 22 (1953), p. 24.

base, for the cult of St Æthelthryth had lost none of its appeal, and her story was retold at about this time by Ælfric of Cerne, in his 'Lives of the Saints',[130] and (sooner or later) also in the charter of Ely Abbey.[131] It is significant nonetheless that the (admittedly crude) index of activity provided by a pattern of attestations in Anglo-Saxon charters suggests that Ælfsige was accorded some prominence at King Æthelred's court from the moment of his appointment in the late 990s, and that he continued to enjoy this position until his death towards the end of Æthelred's reign.[132] The *Liber Eliensis* gives him a general stamp of approval,[133] and otherwise records his role in bringing the relics of the mysterious St Wendred to Ely, from their resting-place at March (Cambs.), and placing them in a fine reliquary.[134] It was during Ælfsige's period of office that some further building work was undertaken, at the expense of a certain Leofwine, son of Æthulf. The walls of the church were in some way enlarged and extended on the south side, and a new altar was set up to St Mary, above which was a throne 'as high as man', with an effigy of the Madonna and Child, 'superbly made from gold and silver and gems'.[135] The effigy was broken up in 1071 when the monks had to raise additional sums of money in order to induce King William to raise his siege of Ely; and in this connection we are informed that the effigy had been made by Abbot Ælfsige.[136] Remarkably, no fewer than five of the seventeen gospel-books separately registered among the Abbey's treasures in 1134 are said to have had covers made by Abbot Ælfsige: the third, 'silver-plated on one side and well gilded, with a crucifix and cast figures with cut stones throughout, which Abbot Ælfsige made'; the sixth, 'covered in silver plate, with a crucifix and cast figures, and gilded, which Abbot Ælfsige made'; the seventh, 'covered in silver plate, with a small crucifix and with 2 cast angels, and well gilded, which the same Abbot made'; the eleventh, 'covered in silver plate, and partly gilded, with a crucifix and unadorned figures, with a band around it, which Abbot Ælfsige made'; and the fourteenth, 'covered in silver plate, with a crucifix and embossed figures, gilded throughout through the efforts of Abbot Ælfsige, which the bishop lost at Wareham'.[137] Among other treasures registered in 1134, we find '3 staffs with well-made feet of gilded silver, which Abbot Ælfsige of blessed memory made', as well as nine precious stoles (of

---

[130] *Ælfric's Lives of Saints*, ed. W.W. Skeat, 4 pts, Early English Text Society o.s. 76, 82, 94 and 114 (Oxford, 1881–1900), I, pt 2, pp. 432–40; for a translation, see L.A. Donovan, *Women Saints' Lives in Old English Prose* (Cambridge, 1999), pp. 32–5. For a recent study, see P. Jackson, 'Ælfric and the Purpose of Christian Marriage: a Reconsideration of the *Life of Æthelthryth*, Lines 120–30', *Anglo-Saxon England*, 29 (2000), pp. 235–60, with further references.

[131] Pope, 'Ælfric and the Old English Version of the Ely Privilege' (cit. in n. 89).

[132] Keynes, *Atlas of Attestations*, Table LXI. Ælfsige of Ely took up his place behind Ælfsige of the New Minster, Winchester, who died in 1007; they are carefully distinguished from each other in S 896 (issued in 999).

[133] *LE*, ii. 57: pp. 128–9.

[134] *LE*, ii. 76: p. 145. The Abbey had acquired land at March from Oswig: *LE*, ii. 67: p. 139. According to *LE*, ii. 79: p. 148, the monks of Ely took some of their relics into battle at Ashingdon (1016), as was the custom of the church, but they were laid low, and the relics of St Wendred were taken away – allegedly by Cnut, who gave them to Canterbury.

[135] *LE*, ii. 60: pp. 131–2; according to *LE*, ii. 52: p. 120, the south part of the church was dedicated to Mary. For a contemporary ivory book-cover representing the Madonna and Child, which might suggest what the effigy looked like, see Dodwell, *Anglo-Saxon Art*, pp. 214–15. See also I.H. Forsyth, *The Throne of Wisdom: Wood Sculptures of the Madonna in Romanesque France* (Princeton, NJ, 1972), esp. pp. 100–2 and 112–15 (describing the golden Madonna at Essen).

[136] *LE*, ii. 111: pp. 193–5.

[137] *LE*, iii. 50: p. 291. *Cf.* Dodwell, *Anglo-Saxon Art*, pp. 108, 202–3, on book-bindings.

which four had belonged to Ælfsige), two well-made linen albs (of which one had been Ælfsige's), 94 vestments with gold fringes (of which eight had been Ælfsige's), and 29 undecorated copes (of which two had been Ælfsige's).[138]

It is apparent that Abbot Ælfsige enjoyed the patronage of King Æthelred, and that in the early eleventh century Ely Abbey attained the kind of distinction which put it among the leading religious houses in the land. Æthelred had first visited Ely during his childhood, when Bishop Æthelwold had taken him there during the reign of Edward the Martyr (975–8);[139] and he was at Ely again during the abbacy of Ælfsige, when he and Queen Emma are said to have presented their eldest son, Edward, at the holy altar, and entrusted him to the community for upbringing with the boys.[140] These facts establish a context of some kind for the story, also told in the *Liber Eliensis*, about King Æthelred's granting of a special privilege to the church of Ely:

> He indeed laid down and granted how long the church of Ely both then and always would perform the office of chancellor in the royal court, which he also established for . . . St Augustine's and Glastonbury, so that the abbots of these communities might divide the year into three . . . in succession . . . for administration of the reliquaries and the other accoutrements of the altar. The Abbot of . . . Ely moreover would always proceed to the work of administration on the day of the purification of St Mary, at the beginning of . . . February, and thus the Abbot . . . would complete that work . . . in four months, namely a third part of the year.[141]

If we may take this story at face value, it indicates that the Abbot of Ely discharged a special function at court, here described or dignified as the office of chancellor, for four months each year; and since the period of service began on the day of the Purification of the Blessed Virgin Mary (2 February, being the day before the re-dedication of the church at Ely), it would extend each year thence until the end of May. No other trace of this arrangement is be found at St Augustine's, Canterbury, or at Glastonbury, whose abbots presumably took over for their stints in June–September and October–January, and it is not clear what construction should be put upon it. It may be that the abbots held an office at court which gave them responsibility, in turn, for the safe-keeping of the royal collection of holy relics, a task which of its nature would not be expected to have left any trace; and it may be that the compiler of *Liber Eliensis* put his own construction on the facts, and presumed, with his twelfth-century mind-set, that the privilege approximated to the office of 'chancellor'.[142]

---

[138] *LE*, iii. 50: pp. 292–4. See also *LE*, iii. 78: p. 325 for other items which had belonged to Ælfsige and which were lost at Wareham.

[139] *LE*, ii. 78: p. 146.

[140] *LE*, ii. 91: pp. 160–1; the gown worn by the infant Edward, 'edged with small circles, largely in green colouring', was still preserved at Ely in the mid-12th century. *LE* may well have misrepresented the nature and duration of Edward's time at Ely; see F. Barlow, *Edward the Confessor* (London, 1970), pp. 32–4.

[141] *LE*, ii. 78: pp. 146–7; and *LE*, ii. 85: p. 153, indicating that the arrangements persisted into Cnut's reign.

[142] For further discussion, see Keynes, *Diplomas of King Æthelred*, pp. 151–2, and S.E. Kelly (ed.), *Charters of St Augustine's Abbey, Canterbury, and Minster-in-Thanet*, Anglo-Saxon Charters, 4 (Oxford, 1995), pp. 215–16. There is reason to believe that the abbey of Glastonbury had enjoyed special privileges of some kind in the mid-10th century, which extended to the production of royal charters (S. Keynes, 'The "Dunstan B" Charters', *Anglo-Saxon England*, 23 (1994), pp. 165–93); but it may be more to the point that Abbot Dunstan at Glastonbury was among those to whom King Eadred had entrusted some of his finest 'treasures' for safe-keeping (B, *Vita S. Dunstani*, chs. 19–20; W. Stubbs (ed.), *Memorials of Saint Dunstan*, Rolls Series, 63 (1874), pp. 29–31).

A significant aspect of Ely's history during the abbacy of Ælfsige is the close relationship which appears to have developed between Ely and successive bishops of the East Angles, at (North) Elmham in Norfolk. The Abbey fell within the large diocese of Dorchester-on-Thames (before the removal of the see to Lincoln in 1072), and would have been pleased to maintain good relations with its bishop, but it also had strong interests in Norfolk and Suffolk, and might have enjoyed playing the bishops off against each other. Æscwig, bishop of Dorchester (975 × 9–23 Apr. 1002), had been present c.980 at the dedication of the church founded at Eynesbury (later known as St Neots) in Huntingdonshire, and was party to the agreement which had placed the priory under Ely's control;[143] he is known to have given a well-embroidered chasuble of *purpura* to the Abbey, and also owned a stole which fetched up among the abbey's treasures.[144] The question arises whether this harmonious relationship persisted further into the eleventh century, or whether other factors came into play. Of the three prelates who were buried at Ely in the early eleventh century, and who were subsequently numbered among the Abbey's seven Anglo-Saxon 'confessors', two were bishops of Elmham and the third, of Dorchester, was (as we shall see) a special case. Æthelstan, Bishop of Elmham (995 × 7– 7 Oct. 1001), is said to have negotiated his burial at Ely some time in advance of his death, with Abbot Byrhtnoth and Ælfsige, and seems from that time forth (? c.996) to have been accorded the privilege of receiving the professions of the monks, and the granting of holy orders. The author of the account of Æthelstan's life incorporated in the *Liber Eliensis* cannot resist adducing this fact (said to be demonstrated by the preservation in the Abbey's archives of written professions, made in Bishop Æthelstan's presence) as evidence of the abbey's freedom from interference by the bishop 'of Lincoln' (that is, Dorchester); and as if to drive home the point, we are told that Æthelstan gave the Abbey his symbols of episcopal office, later destroyed by Bishop Nigel.[145] Æthelstan's successor Ælfgar, Bishop of Elmham (1001–1012 × 16), had been priest and confessor of St Dunstan (d.988) before his elevation to episcopal office, and as bishop maintained Æthelstan's devotion towards Ely; eventually he resigned his office and retired to Ely (probably before the end of Æthelred's reign), where he died and was buried a few years later (during the reign of Cnut).[146] The presence at Ely of the mortal remains of Eadnoth, Bishop of Dorchester (1007 × 9–18 Oct. 1016), is more of a surprise. He was a protégé of Bishop Oswald and Ealdorman Æthelwine, by whom he was appointed Abbot of Ramsey. He translated the relics of St Ive to his own abbey, and later built a church at *Slepe* (St Ives, Hunts.), where they had been found. As bishop, he founded a nunnery at Chatteris (Cambs.) for his sister Ælfwynn, and was instrumental in moving the body of the martyred Archbishop Ælfheah from Greenwich to St Paul's in London. He died at the battle of Ashingdon in 1016, alongside Wulfsige, Abbot of Ramsey. Yet while there is no sign here of a particular connection with Ely, it proves to have been Ælfgar, the former Bishop of Elmham (by 1016 in retirement at Ely), who effectively hijacked Eadnoth's body when it was being taken from Ashingdon

---

[143] *LE*, ii. 29: pp. 102–4; see also below, p. 48.

[144] *LE*, iii. 50: p. 293; the gift of the chasuble is duly registered in the Ely obits, under 23 April (above, n. 20).

[145] *LE*, ii. 65: pp. 137–8. The date of Æthelstan's death was given as 'c.996' in the inscription placed above his tomb in 1771.

[146] *LE*, ii. 72: pp. 142–3. The date of Ælfgar's death was given as '1021' in the inscription placed above his tomb in 1771.

back to Ramsey, via Ely, and buried it secretly in the Abbey, believing that Eadnoth was a martyr.[147] The truth is that Ely instinctively looked east, into East Anglia, rather than south-west, into Mercia.

The quality of documentation preserved at Ely means that we are able to form a good impression of the process of endowment in what was effectively its second stage, covering the late tenth and early eleventh centuries (*c*.980–1020). The Abbey was no longer immersed in litigation, as it had been in the later 970s, and was able to enjoy a period of relative calm and prosperity.[148] The miscellaneous records kept in an eighth-century gospel-book at Ely testify in their different ways to the manner in which the Abbey conducted its routine business, and discharged its role within society at large. The record of Ælfhelm Polga's grant of half a hide of land at Potton, Beds., to his goldsmith Leofsige (witnessed by Abbot Byrhtnoth and others) shows how such records of private transactions were often kept; the later addition of the detailed regulations of the thegns' guild of Cambridge (Plate 2*a*) reflects Ely's role in relation to the principal secular organisation of the borough; and the register of serfs on the Abbey's estate at Hatfield, Herts., shows how the Abbey kept a watchful eye on the movements of its work force. Records of this kind are remarkable survivals in their own right; and when one bears in mind that this gospel-book was presumably but one of the seventeen gospel-books known to have been at Ely in the twelfth century, one begins to wonder what else might have been lost. Reflections of much the same kind are prompted by the Ely farming memoranda (Plate 2*b*), which afford a view from the ground of the Abbey's management of its own resources, and of its mundane dealings with one of the other religious houses in the fenlands.[149] To all this should be added the material in the *Liber Eliensis* explicitly based on vernacular documentation in the Abbey's archives. The Latin terminology – *testamentum* (will), *scriptum* (written document), and *cyrographum* (chirograph) – reflects the various forms in which vernacular documents were drawn up, and it turns out that much of it was generated during the abbacy of Ælfsige.[150] Yet while his predecessor Byrhtnoth had been actively involved in the land market, Ælfsige was seemingly able to sit back and let the benefactions roll in. Local landholders (individually, or as members of families) had many reasons of their own for giving or bequeathing land to the Abbey, and it is apparent that Ely benefitted, in the early eleventh century, from the practice of child oblation, whereby young children were handed over to the community by their parents, often accompanied by a substantial gift of land. Leofwine, son of Æthulf, was a wealthy man who had accidentally killed his mother with a log. In order to make amends he went to Rome, gave his first-born son Æthelmær to the Abbey, with a large amount of land, and then made further arrangements for the improvement of the church (including provision of the life-size effigy of the Madonna and Child).[151] Æthelflæd, widow of King Edmund and of Ealdorman Æthelstan, and her younger sister Ælfflæd, widow of Ealdorman

---

[147] *LE*, ii. 71: pp. 140–2. The date of Eadnoth's death was given as '1016' in the inscription placed above his tomb in 1771. As we have seen, the monks of Ely had taken the relics of St Wendred to Ashingdon, and lost them (above, n. 134); so perhaps they were taking revenge.

[148] Miller, *Abbey & Bishopric*, pp. 21–4.

[149] Above, nn. 13–18.

[150] Above, n. 29.

[151] *LE*, ii. 60: pp. 131–2.

Byrhtnoth, were the daughters of Ealdorman Ælfgar. The wills of all three were preserved at Bury St Edmunds, and suggest that their focus of attention was a church at Stoke-by-Nayland in Suffolk;[152] but it is interesting to see how the two daughters developed an additional interest in Ely, and how Ælfflæd, in particular, expressed her bequest as one 'to St Peter and St Æthelthryth and St Wihtburh and St Sexburh and St Eormenhild', showing that the Ely Four had by now assumed their collective identity. It is apparent, furthermore, that the veneration of St Æthelthryth could prove contagious. A certain Uvi of Willingham bequeathed land in Cambridge-shire to Ely, c.1000.[153] At about the same time Uvi's brother Oswig, and Oswig's wife Leofflæd (daughter of Ealdorman Byrhtnoth and Ælfflæd), gave their son Ælfwine to Ely as a monk, with further lands in Cambridgeshire.[154] Whereupon Æthelric, brother of Uvi and Oswig, was inspired by his brothers' example to give his own son Æthelmær to Ely as a monk, with land in Suffolk.[155] We hear also of Godwine of Hoo, who fell ill and was admitted to Ely as a monk by Abbot Ælfsige, with his land, and of his brother Ælfmær, who gave part of his own inheritance to the Abbey for Abbot Ælfsige and the monks to use as they pleased.[156] Ælfsige did take some initiatives, for in 1008 he paid the King nine pounds of the purest gold, 'according to the great measure of the Northmen', for land at Hadstock (Essex), Stretley (in Littlebury, Essex) and Linton (Cambs.).[157] The net result of the spate of random benefactions in the late tenth and early eleventh centuries was a more widely scattered estate, adding greatly to the Abbey's resources of all kinds, and raising its profile even further as a social, economic and political force in the region. It should also be noted that when King Æthelred's eldest son, Æthelstan, drew up his will, in 1014, he bequeathed his (unnamed) estates in East Anglia to his brother Edmund (Ironside), making elaborate arrangements for the performance of charitable works at Ely 'on the mass-day of St Æthelthryth', for as long as Christianity should last (with reversion of the estates to Ely if the charitable works were ever neglected).[158] One cannot escape the feeling that when Abbot Ælfsige died, some time between 1012 and 1016, the Abbey's associations were firmly in East Anglia;[159] and woe betide a bishop of Dorchester who would have had it another way.

Ælfsige was succeeded as Abbot of Ely by Leofwine, also known as Oscytel, who is said to have been consecrated by Ælfwine, Bishop of Elmham (? × 1019–1023 × 9). The compiler of the *Liber Eliensis* knew of him only that he had been driven from Ely 'by his own people', went to Rome with Archbishop Æthelnoth (in September/October 1022),

---

[152] Will of Ælfgar: S 1483 (D. Whitelock (ed.), *Anglo-Saxon Wills* (Cambridge, 1930), no. 2). Æthelflæd: S 1494 (*ibid.*, no. 14); see also *LE*, ii. 64: pp. 136–7. Ælfflæd: S 1486 (*Wills*, no. 15); see also *LE*, ii. 63: p. 136. Ælfflæd asked that (Ealdorman) Æthelmær should be, after her death, 'a true friend and advocate of the holy foundation at Stoke . . . and its property'; and it may be that Æthelmær's apparent discomfiture in 1006 undermined her intentions (S. Keynes, 'A Tale of Two Kings: Alfred the Great and Æthelred the Unready', *Trans. Royal Historical Soc.*, 5th ser. 36 (1986), pp. 195–217, at p. 207 n. 43).

[153] *LE*, ii. 66: p. 138.

[154] *LE*, ii. 67: p. 139. Oswig was later killed in battle against the Vikings at Ringmere, on 5 May 1010.

[155] *LE*, ii. 68: pp. 139–40.

[156] *LE*, ii. 69–70: p. 140.

[157] S 919 (*LE*, pp. 145–6). It is not entirely clear what was meant by 'the great measure of the Northmen'; cf. P. Nightingale, 'The Ora, the Mark, and the Mancus: Weight-Standards and the Coinage in 11th-Century England', *Numismatic Chronicle*, 143 (1983), pp. 248–57, and 144 (1984), pp. 234–48.

[158] S 1503 (Whitelock (ed.), *Anglo-Saxon Wills*, no. 20).

[159] For Ælfsige's death and burial at Ely, see *LE*, ii. 80: p. 149.

and cleared himself before Pope Benedict VIII of all the charges which had been brought against him.[160] We have no idea what lay behind this local difficulty, but it is apparent that Leofwine had been driven out by the summer of 1022, and already succeeded by Abbot Leofric, formerly prior, who was also consecrated by Bishop Ælfwine. In 1022 King Cnut, at the instigation of Bishop Ælfwine and Abbot Leofric, granted land at (Wood) Ditton (Cambs.) to the monastery at Ely, in exchange for some woodland at Cheveley (Cambs.).[161] The charter was issued 'on the day of the feast of St Æthelthryth queen and virgin [23 June], who for her saintly merits acts as patron of and rules over that monastery, with her sisters, namely Wihtburh, Sexburh, and Sexburh's daughter Eormenhild'; and it must have been soon afterwards that Leofwine set off for Rome with the archbishop. The consequence of Leofwine's vindication in Rome appears to have been that Ely had two abbots in the 1020s, and the compiler of the *Liber Eliensis* appears to suggest that they took turns discharging their office.[162] This puts an interesting complexion on the list of members of the community of Ely incorporated in the 'Liber Vitae' of the New Minster, Winchester (Colour pl. 18*a*). The list is headed by three successive Abbots, Byrhtnoth, Ælfsige, and Leofric, followed by several priests (with Leofsige, evidently the next Abbot, in first position); so it looks as if the list had been supplied from Ely to Winchester by Abbot Leofric in the mid-1020s, and that Leofwine himself was pointedly suppressed.[163]

In most other respects it was business as usual. Benefactors known to have patronised the Abbey in the 1020s included a certain Godgifu, who gave estates in Essex and in Suffolk.[164] Other friends of Ely at this time included two more prelates who chose the Abbey as their place of burial. First and foremost was Wulfstan, Archbishop of York (1002–23), said to have been a monk and then an abbot before he became a bishop, who developed a great affection for the Abbey and resolved to be buried there when his time should come.[165] He died on 28 May 1023, after a distinguished career as homilist, legislator and statesman, responsible above all for easing the transition from an English to an Anglo-Danish regime. Some time during the course of the construction of the new church at Ely, in the late eleventh or early twelfth century, Wulfstan's body had to be removed from its first resting-place, in the old church, to a place 'outside the church, near the chancel, in the monks' cemetery'; and it seems to have been in this connection, amid

---

[160] *LE*, ii. 80: pp. 149–50, citing an 'English chronicle', evidently with reference to the annal in *ASC*, MSS EF, *s.a.* 1022.

[161] S 958 (*LE*, pp. 150–1), attested by (among others) Gerbrand, Bishop of Roskilde. For further discussion, see S. Keynes, 'Cnut's Earls', in A.R. Rumble (ed.), *The Reign of Cnut: King of England, Denmark and Norway* (London, 1994), pp. 43–88, at p. 49 and n. 38.

[162] *LE*, ii. 80: pp. 149–50. Attestations in the names of abbots called Leofric and Leofwine in charters of the early 1020s might reflect this curious situation; see Keynes, *Atlas of Attestations*, Table LXVII, and Knowles (ed.), *Heads of Religious Houses*, pp. 44 and 247.

[163] The obit of Abbot Leofwine was not registered in the Ely calendar (above, n. 20); but nor too was that of Abbot Ælfsige.

[164] *LE*, ii. 81 and 83: pp. 150, 151). Both grants were made by Godgifu during the abbacy of Leofric.

[165] *LE*, ii. 87: pp. 155–7. Wulfstan is said to have 'adorned it [Ely] with decorations'; a processional cross of gilded silver, given by Wulfstan to Ely, was still preserved among the Abbey's treasures in the mid-12th century, as was a chasuble which had belonged to him (*LE*, iii. 50: pp. 290, 293). He is also said to have 'confirmed our many charters with his signature first among the leading men'. It is true that Wulfstan is often first among the witnesses in charters of Æthelred and Cnut, whether in the absence of an Archbishop of Canterbury or because he took precedence (under certain circumstances) over the Archbishop of Canterbury.

reports of miracles, that his tomb was first opened. His body was decayed; but his chasuble and pallium, 'affixed with gilded pins', and his stole and maniple, were miraculously well preserved. In the mid-1150s Wulfstan's body was reburied in the northern part of the new church, taking its place with the six other 'confessors', and as one of that group it was moved again in the mid-fourteenth century, to a place in the Choir. Remarkably, when Wulfstan's tomb was opened in 1769, it was found to contain not only his skull, still intact, but also a small gilded bronze pin (Plate 15a).[166] The second of the prelates in question, who chose to be buried at Ely, was Ælfwine, Bishop of Elmham (? × 1019–1023 × 9), who had been a monk of Ely from boyhood (joining the community with an extensive portfolio of real estate, provided by his parents), and who is said to have been appointed bishop by King Æthelred. He was involved in the refoundation of Bury St Edmunds, c.1020, filling it with monks from Ely and from Holme (Norfolk), and appointing Uvi as their abbot, before resigning his see in order to spend his last years back at Ely.[167]

Ely Abbey had long been a place where St Æthelthryth and other saints were venerated, and was now fast becoming a place seen to be worth cultivating in its own right. Under Wulfstan's guidance, King Cnut (1016–35) had embraced the principle that his regime was a continuation of King Edgar's (and in effect, therefore, also of King Æthelred's), which meant that Ely had little to fear and much to gain from the Anglo-Danish king.[168] For her part, Queen Emma was always eager for opportunities to display her powers of patronage, and it may be that her gifts to Ely, which included a pall of *purpura*, for St Æthelthryth, and several altar cloths, were for the most part given to the Abbey during Cnut's reign.[169] An abbot appointed at the height of the Anglo-Danish regime is likely to have moved with ease in the new political landscape. Leofsige, who succeeded Leofric as Abbot in the late 1020s, had been given over to the community as a boy, accompanied as usual by a substantial quantity of land.[170] According to the *Liber Eliensis*, it was some time before Leofsige was formally blessed as Abbot,[171] but eventually he was consecrated on Cnut's orders by Archbishop Æthelnoth, at *Walewich* (unidentified). Whatever his status, Leofsige was remembered at Ely as one who insisted that all those received into the community should be intelligent and well-born, laying down stringent arrangements for the proper sharing of all goods which came to the Abbey with them. With the King's approval he also devised a system for the effective management of the Abbey's estates, by stipulating which estates should provide for the sustenance of the monks in strict rotation throughout the

[166] See below, p. 58. The pin was given by James Bentham to the Society of Antiquaries of London in 1777; see A. Way, *Catalogue of Antiquities . . . in . . . the Society of Antiquaries of London* (London, 1847), pp. 21–2.

[167] *LE*, ii. 75 and 86: pp. 144–5 and 155). The date of Ælfwine's death was given as '1029' in the inscription placed above his tomb in 1771. For other evidence of Ælfwine's involvement in the refoundation of Bury, see the mid 11th-century note in the Bury Psalter, cited in Keynes, 'Cnut's Earls', p. 56 n. 65; and *cf.* A. Gransden, 'Legends and Traditions Concerning the Origins of the Abbey of Bury St Edmunds' [1985], in her *Legends, Traditions and History in Medieval England* (London, 1992), pp. 81–104, at pp. 93–4.

[168] A remark in *LE*, ii. 109: p. 109 suggests that Cnut had once had occasion to lay siege to Ely, presumably in 1016, though to no avail.

[169] *LE*, ii. 79: p. 149. The fate of the pall is told in *LE*, iii. 122: p. 372–3, transl. Paxton, 'The Book of Ely' (cit. in n. 26), pp. 487–8. For Emma's gifts to Ely and other houses, see S. Keynes, 'Queen Emma and the *Encomium Emmae Reginae*', in A. Campbell (ed.), *Encomium Emmae Reginae*, Camden Classic Reprints 4 (Cambridge, 1998), pp. xi–lxxxvii, at lxxvi–lxxviii.

[170] *LE*, ii. 74: pp. 143–4, with p. 424.

[171] It may be significant that there is no trace of Leofsige among the abbots attesting charters in the 1030s.

year.[172] The abbacy of Leofsige otherwise provides the apparent historical context for one of the more memorable tales of the Anglo-Saxon past, which deserves to take its place beside Alfred and the burning cakes, Cnut and the incoming tide, and Harold with the arrow in his eye. The story is told of an occasion when King Cnut and Queen Emma visited Ely in order to celebrate the Purification of St Mary (2 February), 'when the Abbots of Ely beginning in their turn are accustomed to have service in the royal court'. It is interesting that Ely should have retained the special privilege accorded to its Abbot by King Æthelred the Unready, but that is not here the point at issue. The King's party was approaching the Abbey by boat. As they neared the land, Cnut stood up and looked towards the church, which stood out on a hill, for he thought he could hear singing. He soon realised that it was the monks of Ely, singing the divine office, whereupon he urged his men to gather round and sing praise with him. The King was moved by the occasion to compose his own song in English, of which we are given just the beginning (Plate 1*a*):

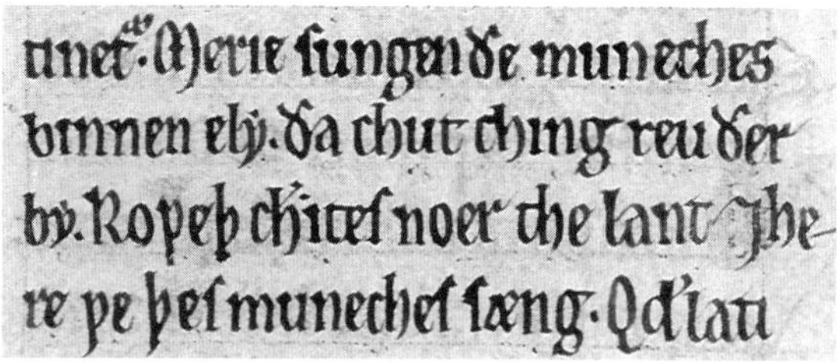
tunes. Merie sungen ðe muneches
binnen ely. ða cnut ching reu ðer
by. Roweþ cnites noer the lant and here we þes muneches sæng. Qd' lau

How sweetly sang the monks of Ely
when Cnut the king rowed by:
'Row, lads, nearer the land,
and let us hear the monks' song.'

Figure 2. 'Merie sungen' from EDC 1: *Liber Eliensis* ii. 85

On reaching land, the King was greeted by the monks, who led him in procession to the church, where by his own charter he confirmed the Abbey's lands as given by previous kings of the English, and where, standing in front of the high altar, he solemnly ratified its privileges. The tale of Cnut and the singing monks of Ely passed quickly into local legend, for the King's song was still sung publicly in the mid-twelfth century and the story was remembered in old sayings.[173] Linguistic analysis of the opening verse, as preserved in the *Liber Eliensis*, suggests that it may well have originated in the eleventh century;[174] but of course the tale remains no more than a charming story. The compiler of the *Liber Eliensis* tells how on another occasion Cnut was unable to reach Ely because of ice, and how a certain islander called Brihtmær *Budde* ('beetle', so called on account of his bulk) had bravely led the way across the frozen marsh; as a reward the King granted Brihtmær an estate of his own, 'in consequence of which the sons of his sons survive free and immune by virtue of that grant down to the present day'.[175]

The documentation for this period otherwise suggests that Ely remained firmly locked

[172] *LE*, ii. 84: pp. 152–3. For discussion of the farming arrangements introduced by Leofsige, see Miller, *Abbey & Bishopric*, pp. 37–9; and for his leasing of estates to Stigand, see below, n. 199.

[173] *LE*, ii. 85: pp. 153–4; see also Wright, *Cultivation of Saga* (cit. in n. 129), pp. 36–8, and Wilson, *Lost Literature of Medieval England* (cit. *ibid.*), p. 159. Charles Stubbs published some verses based in part on Cnut's song, in his book *In a Minster Garden* (London, 1901). These verses subsequently formed the basis of a carol, with music by Arthur Wills (Organist, 1958–90), often sung in the Cathedral at Christmas. The carol was published by Novello & Company Ltd. in 1967 (Carols 690).

[174] W.W. Skeat, in C.W. Stubbs, *Historical Memorials of Ely Cathedral* (London, 1897), pp. 49–52.

[175] *LE*, ii. 85: p. 154. For Brihtmær's name, see G. Tengvik, *Old English Bynames*, Nomina Germanica 4 (Uppsala, 1938), pp. 296–7; for occurrences in Domesday Book, see *LE*, p. 154 n. 4.

into the affection of local society. Leofflæd, much given to charitable works at Ely, had lost her father Byrhtnoth at the battle of Maldon in 991 and her husband Oswig at the battle of Ringmere in 1010. She made known her own will in a document addressed to the King and his Queen, in terms which suggest that she may once have been in their service; and after her death her body was brought to Ely for burial in the monks' cemetery.[176] Her daughter Æthelswith was established on a small island immediately to the west of Ely, at Coveney, where she and a group of other young women worked on embroidery.[177] Her daughter Leofwaru, on the other hand, seems to have been more of a swinger; yet even so Leofwaru, and her husband Lustwine, were both devoted to the Abbey, and made arrangements to be buried there.[178] Their son Thurstan, in the third generation after Ealdorman Byrhtnoth, did not forget his maternal connections with Ely, but it is clear that he also had interests much further afield.[179] Documentation of this quality enables us to appreciate the extent of Ely's involvement with East Anglian society in the eleventh century, and thereby to understand why the Abbey occupied such an important place in the social and economic landscape. The relationship which appears to have existed between Abbot Leofsige and the Anglo-Danish regime also helps to prepare us for Ely's involvement in the political developments of 1035–42. In 1036 the athelings Edward and Alfred, sons of King Æthelred and Queen Emma, came from Normandy to England in an attempt to advance their own political interests in the immediate aftermath of Cnut's death. Edward soon turned back whence he came, to wait for a better opportunity; but Alfred was captured by forces sympathetic to the perpetuation of the Anglo-Danish regime, as now represented by Harold Harefoot and Earl Godwine, and had to be put somewhere out of the way. Interestingly, Alfred was taken to Ely, where he was blinded by his captors on board ship, 'and thus blind was brought to the monks, and he dwelt there as long as he lived'. He died at Ely on 5 February, probably in 1037, and was buried at Ely 'in the south chapel at the west end, full close to the steeple'.[180] Within five years of his death miracles were being reported at his tomb;[181] but there is little further sign of an emergent cult of Alfred at Ely,[182] and it

---

[176] *LE*, ii. 88: pp. 157–8, also registered as S 1520 (dated 1017 × 35). *LE* presumed that the king was Cnut; but the expression of thanks for granting permission to make her bequest 'when my husband was taken from me' (*i.e.* at Ringmere in 1010), suggests that the king might in fact have been Æthelred. There were three copies of the will: one at Ely, one in the King's treasury, and one with Leofflæd herself.

[177] See Foot, *Veiled Women*, II, pp. 79–81.

[178] *LE*, ii. 89: p. 158.

[179] *LE* cannot be relied upon to give a full account of the bequests, and thus gives a misleadingly simplified impression of the often elaborate arrangements made by laymen for the disposal of their property in the 11th century. Among the estates said to have been left by Lustwine and Leofwaru to Ely was Wimbish (Essex), which seems in fact to have passed in the first instance to their son Thurstan. S 1530, MS 1, is part of a tripartite chirograph recording Thurstan's bequest of Wimbish to Christ Church, Canterbury; S 1530, MS 2, is part of a tripartite chirograph recording a slightly modified version of the same bequest. S 1531 is the will of Thurstan, incorporating the modified arrangement, also issued in triplicate, with copies for Bury St Edmunds, Ely, and Thurstan himself. An addition to the will suggests that Ely was given an interest in land at Henham (Essex); but more impressive now is the wide range of Thurstan's interests (the beneficiaries including Christ Church and St Augustine's in Canterbury, as well as Bury St Edmunds, Ely, Ramsey, Holme, Barking, and several parish churches).

[180] *ASC*, MSS CD, *s.a.* 1036, adding 'His soul is with Christ'.

[181] *Encomium Emmae Reginae*, iii. 6 (ed. A. Campbell, Camden 3rd ser. 72 (London, 1949), pp. 44–6); see also Keynes 'Queen Emma and the *Encomium Emmae Reginae*' (cit. in n. 169), p. lxv.

[182] The account of Alfred in *LE*, ii. 90: pp. 158–60 is based on John of Worcester and William of Poitiers, though the compiler adds that some wonderful things had happened at his burial place.

may be that under the conditions which prevailed in the 1040s, during the ascendancy of Earl Godwine, his memory was quite effectively suppressed.[183]

Whatever may have been the feelings of Abbot Leofsige and the community in being used in this way by the political establishment of the day, it was not long before the native dynasty was restored in the person of King Edward the Confessor (1042–66). As we have seen, Edward had been brought up at Ely as a boy, and now the Abbey was also the resting-place of his younger brother Alfred. Abbot Leofsige seems to have died within two or three years of the beginning of Edward's reign,[184] giving Edward the opportunity to appoint as Leofsige's successor a kinsman of his own called Wulfric, who may have come from outside the community.[185] King Edward's writ announcing Wulfric's appointment was addressed 'to all my bishops and my earls and my sheriffs and all my thegns in the shires in which the lands belonging to Ely are situated', a formulation which in its very lack of precision reflects the wide extent of the Abbey's interests in the mid-eleventh century.[186] It is fitting, therefore, that we now encounter signs that Ely was experiencing the kind of difficulties which often arose in connection with the management of widely dispersed estates, whether in dealing with powerful men who appropriated the Abbey's property or in failing to resist the temptation to use church land for improper purposes. Part of the land at (High and Good) Easter in Essex which had been given to the Abbey by Godgifu, during the abbacy of Leofric,[187] was subsequently appropriated by Asgar the Staller, who was by any account one of the principal thegns in Edward's kingdom, with special interests in London.[188] Abbot Wulfric and the monks of Ely tried unsuccessfully to get the land back, but managed eventually to establish their claim by showing Godgifu's will (*testamentum*) and the King's charter (*regis privilegium*). Asgar was given a life interest in the estate, with reversion to Ely after his death, as recorded in a vernacular document attested by King Edward, his Queen, and the leading men of the kingdom.[189] In another context, the compiler of the *Liber Eliensis* gave Abbot Wulfric all due credit for having purchased an estate at Barham (Suffolk) from Earl Ælfgar,[190] but only in order to provide a contrast with the failure of judgement which later cost Wulfric his reputation. Wulfric's brother Guthmund had somewhat less than the forty hides of land required to give him high

---

[183] S. Keynes, 'Alfred the Ætheling', in N. Higham and D. Hill (eds.), *Harold I Harefoot and Harthacnut* (forthcoming).

[184] The suggestion that Leofsige survived into the mid-1050s (Robertson, *Anglo-Saxon Charters*, p. 467; Harmer, *Anglo-Saxon Writs*, pp. 566 and 578) depends essentially on a charter (S 1478: Robertson, *Anglo-Saxon Charters*, p. 214) which shows that two abbots of that name were active in the early 1050s (either or neither of whom may have been Abbot of Ely); see also Keynes, *Atlas of Attestations*, Table LXXIII. But the tradition at Ely was clearly that its own Leofsige died *c*.1045; and it is probably best, with *LE*, p. 412, and *Heads of Religious Houses*, pp. 44–5, to follow it in good faith.

[185] *LE*, ii. 94: p. 164. For what it may be worth, Wulfric is not to be found in the list of Ely monks (*c*.1025) incorporated in the *Liber Vitae* of the New Minster, Winchester (above, p. 6).

[186] S 1100: Harmer, *Anglo-Saxon Writs*, pp. 222–5 (no. 47); *LE*, ii. 95: p. 164.

[187] *LE*, ii. 81: p. 150.

[188] For Asgar the Staller, renowned as the wealthiest of the Confessor's thegns, see F. Barlow (ed.), *The 'Carmen de Hastingae Proelio' of Guy Bishop of Amiens* (Oxford, 1999), pp. 40–2. See also S. Keynes, 'Regenbald the Chancellor (*sic*)', *Anglo-Norman Studies*, 10 (1988), pp. 185–222, at p. 205; R. Fleming, *Kings and Lords in Conquest England* (Cambridge, 1991), pp. 63, 114–15; and P.A. Clarke, *The English Nobility under Edward the Confessor* (Oxford, 1994), pp. 243–9.

[189] *LE*, ii. 96: pp. 165–6.

[190] *LE*, ii. 97: p. 166.

standing among the King's thegns, and could not, therefore, be counted among the leading men (*procere*); for which reason his chosen bride rejected him.[191] Guthmund sought help from Wulfric, who secretly loaned him several of the Abbey's estates 'without title or witness', so that Guthmund might appear a better prospect. After a while the monks discovered their Abbot's deceit, and Wulfric had to retire in his shame to Occold in Suffolk (an estate given to Ely by Ealdorman Byrhtnoth, and one of the estates secretly loaned by Wulfric to his brother). Guthmund held on to the estates after Wulfric's death, and subsequently came to an agreement with Abbot Thurstan, securing a life interest in them; but all were lost after the Conquest when appropriated by Hugh de Montfort.[192] There is reason to suppose that the Abbey managed, in the mid-1050s, to secure a general privilege for itself from Pope Victor II;[193] and while there is rather little to recommend the authenticity (in its received form) of the associated charter of King Edward, confirming the Abbey in its possession of a long list of estates and granting it a very useful set of privileges, the charter is precisely the kind of document that would have helped to comfort the monks whenever they felt under pressure from outside.[194]

It was during the time of Abbot Wulfric that an elderly bishop called Osmund is said to have come from Sweden to England, attaching himself at first to the court of King Edward before retiring to Ely.[195] He was evidently as much liked as he was well remembered, although it may have been fortunate for him that little if anything was known at Ely of his earlier career. According to Adam of Bremen, writing in the 1070s, Osmund had dropped out of school at Bremen (in north Germany), was refused consecration in Rome, and had eventually secured consecration from an archbishop in *Polonia*; whereupon he went to Sweden, claiming to have been consecrated as archbishop for that people, and fetched up with King Emund Gamular, corrupting the heathen with his unsound teaching and driving away accredited legates from Bremen, including the rightful bishop of the Swedes.[196] At Ely Bishop Osmund is said to have performed all episcopal functions for the community (like Æthelstan before him); and when he died, in the late 1060s (during the time of Abbot Thurstan), he bequeathed to the community 'the episcopal adornments granted here while he lived'.[197]

For a brief period after the death of Abbot Wulfric, probably in the mid-1060s, Ely passed into the control of Stigand, archbishop of Canterbury (1052–70). It was a fate which befell other religious houses at the time, and appears to have been a mixed blessing.[198] On the one hand Stigand took over and then retained some of the best of the

[191] *LE*, ii. 97: pp. 166–7. See also *LE*, pp. xvii and 424–5.
[192] *LE*, ii. 97: pp. 166–7. See also Clarke, *English Nobility* (cit. in n. 188), pp. 119–20 and 312–14.
[193] *LE*, ii. 93: pp. 163–4, with comment, p. 418.
[194] S 1051 (*LE*, pp. 161–3, with comment, pp. 417–18).
[195] *LE*, ii. 99: pp. 168–9.
[196] Adam of Bremen, *Gesta Hammaburgensis ecclesiae pontificum*, iii. 15 (transl. F.J. Tschan, *Adam of Bremen: History of the Archbishops of Hamburg-Bremen* (New York, 1959), pp. 125–6). For further discussion of his career, see L. Abrams, 'The Anglo-Saxons and the Christianization of Scandinavia', *Anglo-Saxon England*, 24 (1995), pp. 213–49, at pp. 234–6. The older notion that Osmund should be identified as the prolific Swedish rune-master called Asmund is for good reason no longer taken seriously: see C.W. Thompson, 'A Swedish Runographer and a Headless Bishop', *Mediaeval Scandinavia*, 3 (1970), pp. 50–62, and C.W. Thompson, *Studies in Upplandic Runography* (Austin, Texas, 1975), pp. 162–7.
[197] For vestments which had belonged to Bishop Osmund, see *LE*, iii. 50: p. 293.
[198] M.F. Smith, 'Archbishop Stigand and the Eye of the Needle', *Anglo-Norman Studies*, 16 (1994), pp. 199–219.

Abbey's estates, apparently for his own use;[199] on the other hand he was renowned for his gifts of treasures to the houses with which he was associated or which came into his hands. Ely was favoured by Stigand with the gift of a silver Crucifix bearing a life-size figure of Christ, with associated figures of Mary and John, all mounted on a wooden base and presumably accorded a prominent place near (or above) the high altar.[200] It was not long, however, before King Harold (1066) appointed a monk of Ely called Thurstan as the next Abbot in succession to Wulfric (or perhaps he allowed the monks to make their own choice). Thurstan is said to have been born of a distinguished English family at Witchford (a place described as 'the head of the two hundreds of the Isle'),[201] and had been educated in the Abbey, from his boyhood, in both English and Latin.[202] Clearly he was too young for inclusion in the list of Ely monks c.1025, in the *Liber Vitae* of the New Minster, but he features in one of the Ely inventories as maker of a censer and silver ewer, and as the former owner of several vestments.[203] So far as one can tell, he was the kind of person who would have been steeped in the traditions of his house, wholly integrated into the social structures of the region, and perhaps above all one to whom others would look for guidance in an hour of need.

A religious house in Anglo-Saxon England can be assessed in many different ways, not all of which may be applicable in a given case: the fame of its relics, the extent of its lands, the quantity of its treasures, and the quality of its book-production, as well as the distinction of its members and the range of its social contacts and political connections. By whatever criteria it may be judged, Ely Abbey in the late tenth and eleventh centuries was without question one of the most successful foundations of the Benedictine reform movement. The fame of its relics was never in doubt. It managed a vast rural estate scattered across the whole of East Anglia, giving it control of economic resources which would put it second only to Glastonbury in a league table of the wealth of monastic houses in the country by 1066.[204] It had accumulated a considerable store of treasure; and while all that survives from before the Norman Conquest is a single bronze pin (Plate 15a), what still counted so much about so many of the treasures in the twelfth century were the carefully remembered associations, of makers, donors, and former owners. The second of the three post-Conquest inventories accounted for the Abbey's library as if as an afterthought ('and 287 books . . .'), and although its compiler had taken the trouble to count the service books among them ('. . . of which 19 are missals, 8 lectionaries, 2 benedictionals, 22 psalters, 7 breviaries, 9 antiphoners, and 12 graduals') it is unfortunate that he should have said nothing of the

---

[199]   *LE*, ii. 98: p. 168; see also *LE*, p. 425, and Smith, 'Archbishop Stigand', pp. 207–8 and 213–14. The origins of Stigand's interests in Ely estates can be traced back to his days as Bishop of Elmham in the early 1040s, when he leased some land from Abbot Leofsige (GDB 199ᵛ: *DB Cambs.* 26.2). *LE* cites a *Liber terrarum* as evidence of his retention of the Abbey's estates. If the reference is not to an Ely satellite of Domesday Book (*e.g.* the *Inquisitio Eliensis*), it could be to a cartulary not unlike Archbishop Wulfstan's part of the Worcester cartulary in BL, MS Cotton Tiberius A. xiii.

[200]   *LE*, ii. 98: p. 168, subsequently broken up by Bishop Nigel; also described in 'Inventory C', in *LE*, iii. 50: p. 290, when it stood on a beam above the high altar, and, among objects vandalised by Nigel, in *LE*, iii. 89: p. 335. For references to other objects of similar form and kind, see Dodwell, *Anglo-Saxon Art*, pp. 211–12.

[201]   *LE*, ii. 105: p. 180, a passage derived by *LE* from Richard of Ely's *De gestis Herwardi* (below, n. 224).

[202]   *LE*, ii. 100: p. 169.

[203]   *LE*, iii. 50: pp. 292–4.

[204]   For the figures in 1086, see D. Knowles, *The Monastic Order in England*, 2nd edn (Cambridge, 1963), pp. 702–3.

208 books which remained, a great many of which would doubtless have been at Ely since before the Conquest.[205]

Yet Ely had much to gain in the eleventh and twelfth centuries from the careful cultivation of its historical identity, and this is where it comes into its own. The material embedded in the *Liber Eliensis* demonstrates the extent to which the Abbey was integrated into East Anglian society, and what role it must have played, by virtue of its standing, in the politics of the region. The Latin digests of the lost vernacular documentation doubtless conceal more complex provisions, but they still give us a good impression of the interaction between church and lay society, and of the dependence of each on the other; and while the traditions about Ely's Abbots represent only part of the story, the Abbots emerge as more than a succession of stereotypes, subsumed in the dignity of their office, since each has his own distinctive profile. Ely was, moreover, an institution which took care to respect the memory of its members, its benefactors, and its friends. It was not simply a matter of preserving the records which provided evidence of entitlement to land. Among the products of the various forms of liturgical commemoration practised at the Abbey in the late tenth and eleventh centuries, Ely's extensive collection of obits shows how its friends and benefactors were remembered, among the monks, in the company of saints;[206] and while we may lack a *Liber Vitae* of Ely, to set beside the *Liber Vitae* of the New Minster, Winchester, or the *Liber Vitae* of Thorney, there is every reason to believe that one was kept at the Abbey during this period.[207] The memories so carefully kept at Ely were as long as its traditions were old and its estates were wide; but for the time being the Abbey would have greater need of its natural defences.

The Norman Conquest of Ely

A member of the thegns' guild of Cambridge entering the church of St Peter and St Mary at Ely in the spring or summer of 1066 would have found himself surrounded by an extraordinary array of artefacts and other furnishings, many of them shimmering with silver and gold against a more sombre architectural background. If he had entered through the west door, underneath the tower, he would have noticed to his right, in a chapel on the south side of the church, the tomb where Alfred the Ætheling had been buried nearly thirty years before. In another chapel, probably on the same side of the church, he might have noticed an altar dedicated to the Blessed Virgin Mary, above

---

[205] *LE*, ii. 139: p. 224. For pre-Conquest books from Ely, see R. Sharpe, J.P. Carley, R.M. Thomson and A.G. Watson (eds.), *English Benedictine Libraries: the Shorter Catalogues*, Corpus of British Medieval Library Catalogues 4 (London, 1996), pp. 127–31, at p. 127; but the rejected gospel-book should be reinstated (above, n. 14). The apparent lack of a pontifical (unless included among the benedictionals) may be noteworthy; for the suggestion that a surviving 11th-century pontifical (CCCC 44) was given to Ely by Archbishop Stigand, see M. Budny, *Insular, Anglo-Saxon, and Early Anglo-Norman Manuscript Art at Corpus Christi College, Cambridge: an Illustrated Catalogue*, 2 vols. (Kalamazoo, Missouri, 1997), pp. 675–85 (no. 46).

[206] Above, n. 20. For an illustration of TCC, MS O.2.1, fo. K8ᵛ (for August), see Kennedy, 'Byrhtnoth's Obits' (cit. in n. 125), p. 61, and Keynes, *Anglo-Saxon Manuscripts*, pl. XXVIII.

[207] For the practices of liturgical commemoration, see Lapidge, *Encyclopaedia of ASE* (cit. in n. 3), pp. 291–2. According to *LE*, ii. 61: pp. 132–3, the body of Ælfwaru of Bridgham was brought for burial to Ely, 'and her name, inscribed above the holy altar with the names of the brothers, has perpetual memory in the church'. When Ealdorman Byrhtnoth visited Ely in 991, he is said to have come into the chapter-house in the morning, 'for the purpose of receiving the brotherhood'; see *LE*, ii. 62: p. 135.

which was a life-size effigy of the enthroned Madonna and Child, commissioned by Leofwine, son of Æthulf, and made by Abbot Ælfsige in the early eleventh century. His attention would soon have been drawn towards the four life-size images of Ely's principal saints (in wood, inlaid with gold, silver, and precious stones), two placed to the left of the high altar and two to the right. Somewhere near this altar, on the south side, stood the shrine of St Æthelthryth, in her 'tower', and in the same part of the church, but to the north, stood the tomb of her sister St Seaxburh. If the thegn had chosen to visit the church on a feast day, the altars and shrines would have been covered with sumptuous textiles, doubtless including the magnificent covering for the tomb of St Æthelthryth, and the others of lesser quality for the tombs of her sisters and niece, given to the church by Queen Emma. On the altar, perhaps, stood the golden reliquary cross given by King Edgar, and the gospel-book, in its beautifully decorated cover, by which the same King had confirmed the Abbey's privileges nearly one hunded years before. Above the altar, perhaps, was Archbishop Stigand's altar screen, comprising life-size figures of the crucified Christ and Mary and John. In the vicinity lay St Eormenhild, awaiting the resurrection from underneath the flagstones; while elsewhere, probably further to the east and up a flight of steps, lay the tomb of St Wihtburh. The thegn might have registered the presence not only of some former Abbots of Ely but also of Ealdorman Byrhtnoth, three Bishops of Elmham, a Bishop of Dorchester, and Wulfstan, Archbishop of York. There were no kings here, as there were at Canterbury, York, Sherborne, Winchester, Malmesbury, Glastonbury, Shaftesbury, London, and Westminster; but there was quite enough to stir the heart of a web-footed thegn from the fenlands, and to evoke what an Englishman held most dear.

In the aftermath of the Norman Conquest, a basic distinction can be recognised between the response of the bishops and the response of the abbots. Many of the bishops who held office in 1066 had been appointed by Edward, and might have been predisposed to accept William as Edward's successor.[208] Abbots and their communities, on the other hand, were instinctively protective of the traditions of their respective houses, and particularly conscious of their place in local society, making them a natural focus of resistance to the incomers.[209] Several ancient abbeys of Anglo-Saxon England became sanctuaries for the defeated and disconsolate English. Prominent among those who took refuge at Ely, probably soon after the Conquest, was Archbishop Stigand, who came with a store of treasures and then instructed Ecgfrith, Abbot of St Albans, to join him there with relics and treasures of his own. Ecgfrith brought with him the relics of St Alban, and placed them in a small church; and, once he had abandoned hope of ever returning to St Albans, arrangements were made to lay the relics at Ely for good. By an ingenious arrangement with Abbot Thurstan, the relics of St Alban were ceremonially placed beside those of St Æthelthryth, and by further agreement secretly removed, soon afterwards, to a safer place at Ely, so that other bones could be sent to St Albans when the inevitable demand came to give the relics back.[210] For his part King William can have had few delusions about the abbeys, and would have looked at them

[208] For an episcopal perspective, see S. Keynes, 'Giso, Bishop of Wells (1061–88)', *Anglo-Norman Studies*, 19 (1997), pp. 203–71, at p. 241.

[209] For resistance among the abbeys, see Knowles, *Monastic Order* (cit. in n. 204), pp. 103–6.

[210] *LE*, ii. 103: pp. 176–7. For discussion, see *LE*, pp. xxxvii–xxxviii and 425–6. Unsurprisingly, the story as told at St Albans was quite different.

not only as centres of potential trouble until safely in new hands, but also as repositories of some of the moveable wealth of Anglo-Saxon England. He had already taken treasures back to Normandy, for distribution during the course of his triumphal progress in 1067.[211] On a subsequent occasion, in 1070, the King 'had all the monasteries that were in England plundered';[212] and no doubt he took some of the proceeds to Normandy in the winter of 1070–1. It is apparent, however, that those who plundered monasteries in the immediate aftermath of the Conquest were not just the Normans, but also disaffected Englishmen, eager to strike back at their conquerors once a monastery had fallen under Norman control.

In 1071 the Isle of Ely, in the Cambridgeshire fens, provided for the English the kind of refuge which the Isle of Athelney, in the Somerset marshes, had provided for the West Saxons in 878. A near-contemporary entry in the *Anglo-Saxon Chronicle* is the closest that we can come to the events:[213]

> In this year Earl Eadwine and Earl Morcar fled away and travelled aimlessly in woods and moors until Eadwine was killed by his own men and Morcar went to Ely by ship. And Bishop Æthelwine and Siweard Bearn came there, and many hundred men with them. But when King William found out about this, he called out a naval force and a land force, and invested that part of the country from outside, and made a bridge and placed a naval force on the seaward side. And they then all surrendered to the King, that is to say Bishop Æthelwine and Earl Morcar and all who were with them except Hereward alone and those who could escape with him, and he led them out valiantly. And the King took their ships and weapons and plenty of money, and he took all the men prisoner and did as he pleased with them: Bishop Æthelwine he sent to Abingdon, and there he died.

We need not presume that Abbot Thurstan had been ready to countenance the presence of the English forces on the Isle of Ely, and that he had necessarily been willing, therefore, to be projected into the forefront of organised and overt opposition to the Normans;[214] but the fact that William responded by laying siege to the Isle shows how seriously he was inclined to take the situation. A rather different story is told by Orderic Vitalis, following the (lost) closing part of William of Poitiers' *Deeds of Duke William* (written in the early 1070s), but putting constructions upon it which probably reflect an attitude of his own.[215] Earl Morcar was enticed out of his impregnable position by promises of safe conduct, only to be tricked by the King and thrown promptly into prison; no one else at Ely is mentioned, though Orderic goes on to provide an account of

[211] See *The 'Gesta Guillelmi' of William of Poitiers*, ed. R.H.C. Davis and M. Chibnall (Oxford, 1998), pp. 152–4, 174, 176, and 180, and *The Ecclesiastical History of Orderic Vitalis*, ed. M. Chibnall, 6 vols. (Oxford, 1968–80), II, p. 196; see also D.N. Dumville, 'Anglo-Saxon Books: Treasure in Norman Hands?', *Anglo-Norman Studies*, 16 (1994), pp. 83–99.

[212] *ASC*, MS D, *s.a.* 1070 (ed. Cubbin, pp. 84–5). John of Worcester implies that William was eager to lay his hands on the treasures which rich Englishman had deposited in the monasteries for safe-keeping.

[213] *ASC*, MS D, *s.a.* 1071 (ed. Cubbin, p. 85); trans. *ASC*, ed. Whitelock, p. 154.

[214] A letter from Archbishop Lanfranc to an Abbot Thurstan gives him support in his adversity, and urges him to offer satisfaction to the King 'through friends and loyal intermediaries': H. Clover and M. Gibson (eds.), *The Letters of Lanfranc Archbishop of Canterbury* (Oxford, 1979), pp. 172–3 (no. 57). It is not clear whether the recipient was the English Abbot of Ely or the Norman Abbot of Glastonbury; if the former, as seems likely, it suggests that Thurstan found himself in a difficult position which was not exactly of his own making.

[215] *Orderic*, ed. Chibnall, II, pp. 256–8.

the circumstances leading up to Earl Eadwine's death, suggesting that he had managed to stay free for some while longer. As one might expect, Ely preserved its own memories or traditions of the siege, rich in details of local topography although far from easy to follow as a sequence of events.[216] The most we can say with any certainty is that Morcar and others took refuge at Ely in 1071, prompting William to lay siege to the Isle, and that matters came to an end, apparently in late October, when the King at last made his entrance into the church. Abbot Thurstan and his monks are said to have made terms with the King at Warwick, though it is not clear when, or under what circumstances.[217] It was at Witchford, on the Isle of Ely, in late October 1071, that they handed over a great quantity and variety of treasures, to a value of 700 marks of silver; but when it turned out that the payment was light by one eighth of an ounce, the King was enraged, and upheavals and depradations followed. In order to secure their lands and privileges the monks were subsequently obliged to promise a further 300 marks of silver, making 1000 in all; and in order to raise the extra money they had to break up the life-size image of the Madonna and Child, which had been made by Abbot Ælfsige, and to strip bare the images of the holy virgins, made by Abbot Byrhtnoth.[218] It may also have been at about this time that the monks secreted 'a great weight of silver and gold' at Wentworth, on the Isle, intending to use it to make good their losses; but the hoard was discovered, and taken to King William's treasury at Winchester.[219]

Our understanding of events in 1070–1 is complicated by the legends which developed subsequently, at Peterborough and at Ely, about the person known to posterity as Hereward the Wake.[220] Hereward came to be for the English what Arthur had once been for the Welsh; but he never achieved quite the same of fame, perhaps because he laboured under the disadvantage of a genuine historical identity, as a minor landowner in Lincolnshire and a tenant of both the abbots of Peterborough and Crowland.[221]

---

[216] *LE* brought together three separate but overlapping accounts of the siege, and attempted to turn them them into a sequential narrative, with very confusing results: *LE*, ii. 102: pp. 173–6, dated '1069', from an *opusculum* on the siege which seems to have had a separate origin and existence; *LE*, ii. 104–7: pp. 177–88, from material related to *Gesta Herwardi*; and *LE*, ii. 109–11: pp. 189–95, representing a 'Norman' point of view, in a mixture of local tradition and other written sources. For further discussion, see *LE*, pp. xxxiv–xxxvi, liv–lvii and 173–95 (esp. 178 n. 3).

[217] *LE*, ii. 109: pp. 189–91.

[218] *LE*, ii. 111: pp. 194–5.

[219] *LE*, ii. 113: pp. 195–6; see also *LE*, iii. 50: p. 289. For William's bridge and castle at Ely, see Henry of Huntingdon, *HA* vi. 33 (*Henry, Archdeacon of Huntingdon: Historia Anglorum (History of the English People)*, ed. D. Greenway, Oxford Medieval Texts (Oxford, 1996), pp. xliv and 396–8).

[220] For modern discussion of the Hereward legend, see *LE*, p. 178 n. 3; C.R. Hart, 'Hereward "the Wake" and his Companions' [1974], reprinted in his *The Danelaw* (London, 1992), pp. 625–48; Ridyard, *Royal Saints*, pp. 196–8; V. Head, *Hereward* (Stroud, 1995); and E. van Houts, 'Hereward and Flanders', *Anglo-Saxon England*, 28 (1999), pp. 201–23. For Hereward's alleged association with the Wake family, see J.H. Round, *Feudal England* (London, 1895), p. 161, and E. King, 'The Origins of the Wake Family', *Northamptonshire Past and Present*, 5 (1973–7), pp. 167–77.

[221] Hereward's identity is established from the combination of several entries in Domesday Book. His 'Peterborough' holding comprised Witham (on the Hill), Manthorpe, Toft and Lound, with berewicks at Barholme and Stowe and with further bovates at Stowe, as a soke of Witham (Great Domesday Book, fo. 346: *Domesday Book, Lincs.* (both cit. in n. 21), 8.34–5 and 37, under the fief of Peterborough. His more northerly holding, held jointly with a certain Toli, comprised land at Laughton, with a berewick at Aslackby and Avethorpe (GDB 364[v]: *DB Li* 42.9–10, under the fief of Ordger the Breton). Hereward had leased a more substantial property at Rippingale, nearby, from the Abbot of Crowland (GDB 377[rv]: *DB Li* Kesteven 48). Two entries in the section of claims in Kesteven suggest that some dispute had arisen in connection with the

There can be no doubt that Hereward played a conspicuously heroic part in the events of 1071. He would have had good cause, with many others, to regard the arrival of (the Norman) Abbot Turold at Peterborough, in 1070, with considerable alarm, and was perhaps among those who are known to have plundered the monastery in that year. It may have been by a connection with Earl Morcar, at Bourne, that he joined the English resistance at Ely in 1071. Hereward need not at this stage have been a leader of the resistance, and it was perhaps only in the circumstances of his escape from the Isle that he first came into prominence. Orderic, following William of Poitiers, knew nothing of Hereward, presenting the siege of Ely as a confrontation between William and Morcar. Yet the annal in the *Chronicle* (quoted above) shows that Hereward was renowned already in the 1070s for the manner in which he had made good his escape, and the references in *Domesday Book* to Hereward as one who 'fled from the country' also reflect awareness of his disappearance into oblivion (in 1071). By the early twelfth century Hereward had gained even greater fame and glory. The tradition at Peterborough, represented by a clumsy twelfth-century interpolation into the E manuscript of the *Anglo-Saxon Chronicle*, and the later twelfth-century chronicle of Hugh Candidus, sets the story in the context of a supposed Danish invasion in 1070, which, when judged in relation to other sources, looks like a complete invention,[222] involving some high level negotiation between King William and King Swein, and featuring Ely's hero quite pointedly as Peterborough's villain.[223] The tradition at Ely is represented by the *Gesta Herwardi*[224] and the *Liber Eliensis*. Hereward's fame was now projected backwards in order to turn him into a far more significant and heroic figure *before* the Conquest; but it difficult to take much of it very seriously. The growth of the legend is, however, a sign that the monks of Ely wished, in the twelfth century, to bathe in Hereward's reflected glory. Now it was *they*

---

succession to Hereward's lands: Asfrothr seems to have acquired Hereward's Peterborough holdings although Hereward was not in possession of all of them 'on the day he fled' (GDB 376^v: *DB Li* K 4); and Ordger the Breton, who acquired his more northerly holdings, gained an interest in Rippingale as well, despite the fact that the Abbot had repossessed the land 'before Hereward fled from the country' (GDB 364^v: *DB Li* 42.13; and GDB 377: *DB Li* K 48). Although the legend connects Hereward with Bourne (which lies between his two parcels of land), neither he nor his (alleged) father Leofric of Bourne is mentioned in that connection in Domesday Book; Bourne was held by Earl Morcar, and passed into the hands of Ordger the Breton (GDB 364^v: *DB Li* 42.1).

222 *The Peterborough Chronicle 1070–1154*, ed. C. Clark, 2nd edn (Oxford, 1970), pp. 1–4; *The Peterborough Chronicle of Hugh Candidus*, ed. W.T. Mellows (Oxford, 1949), pp. 77–83 (text), and C. Mellows and W.T. Mellows, *The Peterborough Chronicle of Hugh Candidus*, 2nd edn (Peterborough, 1966), pp. 40–3 (translation).

223 The Peterborough legend has infected even the most authoritative of the modern accounts of the events of these years: *e.g.* F.M. Stenton, *Anglo-Saxon England*, 3rd edn (Oxford, 1971), pp. 605–6; D.C. Douglas, *William the Conqueror* (London, 1964; new edn., 1999), pp. 221–2; D. Bates, *William the Conqueror* (London, 1989), p. 83; M. Bennett, *Campaigns of the Norman Conquest* (Botley, 2001), pp. 57–60. See also *LE*, pp. lv–lvi, and Hart, 'Hereward "the Wake"', pp. 627–30.

224 The (anonymous) *Gesta Herwardi incliti militis* ('Deeds of the renowned knight Hereward'), although written at Ely, is preserved uniquely in a mid 13th-century Peterborough Abbey register: CUL, Peterborough MS 1, fos. 320–39. The text is edited in *Lestorie des Engles solum la Translacion Maistre Geffrei Gaimar*, ed. T.D. Hardy and C.T. Martin, 2 vols., Rolls Series (1888–9), I, pp. 339–404, and (with parallel translation) in S.H. Miller and W.D. Sweeting, *De Gestis Herwardi Saxonis* (Peterborough, 1895), issued as part of *Fenland Notes & Queries*, 3 (1895–7). For more recent translations, see T.A. Bevis, *Hereward: the Siege of the Isle of Ely and Involvement of Peterborough and Ely Monasteries, together with 'De Gestis Herwardi Saxonis'* (March, 1982), and M. Swanton, *Three Lives of the Last Englishmen*, Garland Library of Medieval Literature (Series B), 10 (New York and London, 1984), pp. 45–88, reprinted in T.H. Ohlgren (ed.), *Medieval Outlaws: Ten Tales in Modern English* (Stroud, 1998), pp. 12–60.

who had invited the renowned Hereward to lead them in defence of liberty, though it was as well for them to show that he later came to terms with the Norman establishment. The danger lies in conflating the Peterborough and Ely traditions, and in putting the interpolated (Peterborough) annal for 1070, in MS E, on a par with the contemporary annal for 1071, in MS D. There is much to be learnt from close analysis of the 'local' accounts of events at Ely in 1071, and from some other sources,[225] but the received tale of Hereward, with its farrago of improbable adventures and romantic interludes set in purportedly historical contexts, is best regarded with a degree of circumspection.[226]

A small object known to have been on the Isle of Ely in the eleventh century gives us a flavour of the material culture of the age. A lead casket found in ploughing at Sutton, Isle of Ely, in April 1694, contained a silver disc brooch, five gold rings, and about 100 coins of William I, of which only the disc brooch is known to survive (Figure 3).[227] The design incised on the face of the brooch comprises four overlapping circles, each containing a zoomorphic motif (a pair of interlaced snakes, a quadruped, another snake, and another quadruped). On the back of the brooch, incised round the outer edge, is an inscription in Old English verse: '+ Ædvwen owns me, may the Lord own her. May the Lord curse him who takes me from her, unless she gives me of her own will'.[228] The coins were dispersed before they were properly recorded, so we have no idea whether the hoard was deposited near the beginning, in the middle, or nearer the end of William's reign.[229] It could have been deposited at the time of the siege of Ely in 1071, or at any other time in William's reign; whatever the case, the Anglo-Saxon curse would appear to have had its desired effect.

Ely and the Normans

Norman barons moving into the region in the late 1060s and early 1070s would not necessarily have been much impressed by the prospect of becoming neighbours of

---

[225] An apparently independent tradition of Hereward's escape from Ely is reported by Geffrei Gaimar, who is known to have had access to traditions current in Lincolnshire: see *L'Estoire des Engleis by Geffrei Gaimar*, ed. A. Bell, Anglo-Norman Texts, 14–16 (Oxford, 1960), pp. 173–81 (lines 5457–704); transl. *Gaimar*, ed. Hardy and Martin, II, pp. 173–80 (lines 5463–710). For discussion of Gaimar on Hereward, see *ibid.*, II, pp. xxxiii–xxxv, and *Gaimar*, ed. Bell, pp. xiv and 269–71.

[226] The historical contexts are not improbable in themselves (as shown by van Houts, 'Hereward and Flanders'), but the question is whether the Lincolnshire Hereward was active within them. Unlike many of the best legends in English history, the tale of Hereward, though originating in 11th- and 12th-century sources, was not popularised for modern readers until the 19th century: Charles Macfarlane, *The Camp of Refuge*, 2 vols. (London, 1844); Charles Kingsley, *Hereward the Wake: Last of the English* (London, 1866); Art-Union of London, *Illustrations by H.C. Selous of 'Hereward the Wake' by Charles Kingsley* (London, 1870).

[227] The earliest account of the finding of the brooch is in a letter to Thomas Turner, 22 May 1694 (Bodl., MS Rawlinson lett. 91, fo. 236ᵛ). The brooch was first published in Hickes and Wanley, *Antiquæ Literaturæ Septentrionalis Libri Duo* (cit. in n. 16), I, 'Dissertatio Epistolaris', pp. 187–8 (with line drawings); see R.L. Harris (ed.), *A Chorus of Grammars: the Correspondence of George Hickes and his Collaborators on the Thesaurus linguarum septentrionalium*, Publications of the Dictionary of Old English, 4 (Toronto, 1992), pp. 84, 391–2 and 405. For the brooch itself, which was acquired by the British Museum in 1951, see D.M. Wilson, *Anglo-Saxon Ornamental Metalwork 700–1100 in the British Museum* (London, 1964), pp. 174–7 (no. 83), with pls. XXXI–XXXII.

[228] Okasha, *Anglo-Saxon Non-Runic Inscriptions* (cit. in n. 40), pp. 116–17 (no. 114); see also E.V. Thornbury, 'The Genre of the Sutton Brooch Verses', *Notes and Queries*, ccxlvi (2001), pp. 375–7.

[229] J.D.A. Thompson, *Inventory of British Coin Hoards A.D. 600–1500*, Royal Numismatic Society Special Publications, 1 (London, 1956), p. 131 (no. 346).

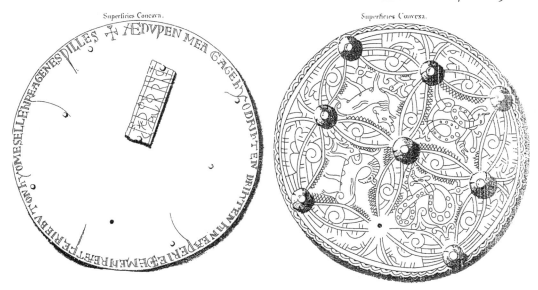

Superficies Concava.   Superficies Convexa.

Figure 3. The Sutton brooch, 11th century, found during ploughing in 1694 (G. Hickes and H. Wanley, *Antiquae Literaturae Septentrionalis Libri Duo* (Oxford, 1705), I, 'Dissertatio Epistolaris', p. 188. It is now in the British Museum.

St Æthelthryth, and it is apparent that Ely suffered serious losses during this period in its far-flung estates. The Abbey was able at least for the time being to maintain control of its interests in the two hundreds of Ely, but even Æthelthryth found it difficult to extend her protection to *all* of her property in southern Cambridgeshire, Essex, Suffolk, and Norfolk. Prominent among the predators was Picot, sheriff of Cambridgeshire, likened by the *Liber Eliensis* to 'a ravenous lion, a rampaging wolf, a cunning fox, a filthy pig, a shameless dog', devouring the county as if it were the carcass of a dead animal. Many were quick to warn Picot of the danger of antagonising the Abbey's patron saint, but he replied: 'Who is this Æthelthryth, whose lands you say I have seized? I have never heard of Æthelthryth, and I shall not give them up.' There appears to have been no evidence that Picot suffered the end which he so plainly deserved; so instead the *Liber Eliensis* sentenced him to death by rhetoric, and presumed damnation.[230] Yet if Picot had managed to avoid any worse fate than this, the same could not be said of his henchman, Gervase, who seems to have specialised in giving the monks and their agents a hard time. On the eve of a lawsuit against the Abbot, Æthelthryth appeared to Gervase in a dream, and, having first verified his identity, stabbed him through the heart with her staff; at which point her sisters Wihtburh and Seaxburh came up behind her, and impaled him on staffs of their own. Gervase had the presence of mind to inform his servants that he had just been attacked by the three sisters, and then announced that Æthelthryth was returning to finish him off, which she did. The news spread quickly through the country, and men were the more disinclined thereafter to mess with Æthelthryth, since it was seen that she protected her possessions in the approved manner, wherever they were.[231] Oppression of a rather different kind is

---

[230] *LE*, ii. 131: pp. 210–11; Ridyard, *Royal Saints*, pp. 204–5.
[231] *LE*, ii. 132: pp. 212–13; Ridyard, *Royal Saints*, pp. 205–6.

represented by 'Gilbert de Clare', *i.e.* Richard Fitz Gilbert, who appropriated from Ely the monastery of Eynesbury (St Neots), and placed it under monks whom he imported from Bec.[232]

The Abbey's cause had not been helped by its involvement with the English resistance, but it was not long before it developed its defensive mechanisms. The beloved Abbot Thurstan appears not to have been in a position to do much more than remonstrate against the predators;[233] and following his death, in 1072, the Abbey passed into 'foreign' hands. At once we see the friction that was bound to arise between representatives of the new regime. Theodwine, monk of Jumièges, appointed Abbot of Ely in 1073, only accepted the appointment on the understanding that the Abbey's treasures would be restored;[234] and when he died, *c.*1075, having held office for two and a half years, the King's agents quickly made an inventory of all that could be found in the treasury.[235] It is an impressive list, especially when the separate entries are interpreted in the light of additional information given in the twelfth-century inventory, identifying makers, owners, and donors, making it easier to appreciate how much of the material was of pre-Conquest origin.[236] Theodwine's close associate Godfrey, monk of Ely, took over the running of the Abbey until appointed Abbot of Malmesbury in 1082.[237] Little is known of their activities at Ely, yet there can be no doubt that they were responsible for initiating the process of litigation by which the Abbey sought to recover the lands which it had lost in the immediate aftermath of the Conquest and to prevent further losses of lands or privileges.[238] The earliest stage in the process is represented by a document which reports the outcome of a hearing convened on the King's orders in the early 1070s, to which is appended a list of lands lost in the first four or five years after the Conquest and still held 'unjustly' by others.[239] It is not clear that the Abbey was able to do much, in the later 1070s, to prevent further losses, though further hearings appear to have taken place during Godfrey's administration, including a meeting of three shires convened at Kentford (Suffolk) on 2 April 1080.[240] Thereafter, the pace quickened. Simeon, previously Prior of Winchester (and brother of Bishop Walchelin), was appointed Abbot of Ely in 1082, when he was already in his late eighties, and held office for about ten years. A sequence of royal writs carefully preserved in the Abbey's archives, and also incorporated in the *Liber Eliensis*, reflects intense lobbying activity throughout the 1080s by Simeon himself, doubtless taking advantage of his good connections at court. Initially, King William ordered Bishop Geoffrey and Robert of Mortain to convene a

---

[232] *LE*, ii. 108: pp. 188–9. Richard Fitz Gilbert was the father of Richard, Abbot of Ely: below, p. 51.

[233] *LE*, ii. 112: p. 195. Thurstan was remembered at Ely as the 'beloved lord Abbot Thurstan': see *LE*, iii.50: p. 289.

[234] *LE*, ii. 113: pp. 195–6. Theodwine was able to use the treasure found at Wentworth for making the *tabula* described in *LE*, ii. 113: p. 196 and iii. 50: p. 289.

[235] *LE*, ii. 114: pp. 196–7.

[236] *LE*, iii. 50: pp. 288–94.

[237] *LE*, ii. 115: p. 197.

[238] For the Ely land pleas, see above, p. 7, n. 22.

[239] *Acta of William I*, ed. Bates, pp. 410–17 (no. 117), from TCC, MS O.2.1, fos. 210ᵛ–213ᵛ.

[240] *Acta of William I*, pp. 419–20 (no. 118), transl. *English Historical Documents* (cit in n. 16), II, no. 51; see also *LE*, ii. 116: pp. 198–9. For King William's purported charter of confirmation, referring back to the proceedings at Kentford, see *Acta of William I*, pp. 428–30 (no. 122), transl. *EHD*, II, no. 51; see also *LE*, ii. 117: pp. 199–200.

meeting of all those who held land of the demesne of Ely, and to ensure that Abbot Simeon had all things that properly belonged to him.[241] The King then demanded a second meeting, at which all matters would be sorted out, adding that the causeway at Ely should be properly maintained as before.[242] The outcome is perhaps represented by a writ ordering that certain lands and privileges should be restored to the Abbot.[243] At some point the King ordered that the Abbot should be consecrated without delay, insisting that he should have his lands and customs as ordered in previous writs.[244] When Remigius, Bishop of Lincoln, began to assert what he might reasonably have considered to be *his* rights over the Abbot of Ely, the King fired off a writ ordering the Bishop to be prevented from claiming 'new customs' within the Isle, and ordering yet again that other disputes should be settled;[245] and since one of the customs in question was evidently the right to consecrate the Abbot of Ely, the King ordered a special investigation of the matter, with insistence again that other things should be done.[246] The King was also concerned to ensure that Simeon enjoyed the rights which pertained to the Abbot in Suffolk.[247] In what appears to be one of his last writs for Ely, William ordered Archbishop Lanfranc to consecrate the Abbot if that could be seen to be the proper practice, to ensure that the causeway was kept in good repair, and to provide a full written account of the Abbey's lands.[248] Two other lists of alienated lands, evidently compiled at Ely and preserved in the Abbey's archives, bring us closer to the tenurial situation reached by the time of the Domesday survey in 1086.[249] All of this material testifies to an extraordinary burst of activity under Abbot Simeon, as he sought, probably in the early to mid-1080s, to set his house in order; and it is striking how the campaign was driven at every stage by a determination to restore those customs and entitlements which had obtained during the reign of King Edward the Confessor. At one level, twenty years of semi-organised chaos associated with the establishment of the Normans in England, whether as churchmen or as laymen, produced the untidy result which was reduced to order in the Domesday survey; at another level, we see in the case of Ely how much this must have had to do with the energies of the incumbent Abbot, Simeon, in pressing for his rights, and perhaps in ensuring that all the associated documentation was carefully preserved for posterity.

It is clear that Abbot Simeon did a great deal to restore the Abbey's fortunes in the aftermath of the Norman Conquest. It may have been difficult for the monks of Ely to forget that he had brought ten monks from Winchester, to act as examples of the

---

[241] *Acta of William I*, pp. 421–2 (no. 119); see also *LE*, ii. 121: p. 204.

[242] *Acta of William I*, pp. 423–5 (no. 120); see also *LE*, ii. 120: p. 203.

[243] *Acta of William I*, pp. 426–7 (no. 121); see also *LE*, ii. 122: pp. 204–5.

[244] *Acta of William I*, pp. 434–5 (no. 125); see also *LE*, ii. 126: p. 207.

[245] *Acta of William I*, pp. 431–2 (no. 123); see also *LE*, ii. 124: p. 206, and D.M. Stenton, *English Justice between the Norman Conquest and the Great Charter 1066–1215* (London, 1965), pp. 17–18.

[246] *Acta of William I*, pp. 436–7 (no. 126); see also *LE*, ii. 127: p. 207.

[247] *Acta of William I*, p. 433 (no. 124); see also *LE*, ii. 123: p. 205.

[248] *Acta of William I*, pp. 438–9 (no. 127); see also *LE*, ii. 125: p. 207.

[249] Hamilton (ed.), *Inquisitio Comitatus Cantabrigiensis* (cit. in n. 23), pp. 175–83 and 184–9. These lists were characterised as a 'Schedule of Claims' and treated as a single document by R.W. Finn, 'The Inquisitio Eliensis Re-considered', *Eng. Hist. Rev.*, 75 (1960), pp. 385–409, at pp. 398–405, and R.W. Finn, *Domesday Studies: the Eastern Counties* (London, 1967), pp. 87–91; but the relationship between them, and their relationship with Domesday Book, require further consideration.

religious life (and to help him run the Abbey's administration),[250] that he allowed royal officials to conduct legal proceedings on the Isle,[251] and that he had allowed himself to be consecrated Abbot by Remigius, bishop of Lincoln, thereby jeopardising the Abbey's independence.[252] And although he had derived much benefit from royal support, he found out at what cost when King William demanded military service from all his bishops and abbots, in respect of their lands, and instructed him to maintain a garrison of forty knights on the Isle of Ely. According to the *Liber Eliensis*, the Abbot was urged by the monks to remind the King that no-one oppressed the Abbey without incurring the vengeful wrath of St Æthelthryth; but although the Abbot promised treasure as well as prayers, it was all to no avail. The forty knights were given their sustenance in the Abbey's hall; and as if this indignity was not bad enough, some of the Abbey's lands had to be leased to laymen in return for knight-service, so that some of the worst of the Abbey's predators (including Picot) ended up as its tenants.[253] In the late 1080s and early 1090s several unscrupulous men seem to have been able to take advantage of Abbot Simeon's great age. William Rufus made even greater demands in respect of knight-service; lesser men, such as William *Peregrinus*, took some of the Abbey's estates into their own hands; and when the Abbot sent for help from outside, matters only went from bad to worse.[254] A certain Ælfwine *Retheresgut* ('cow's paunch') besmirched the good name of the former Abbot Thurstan, and managed at the same time to antagonise the King's agent, Ranulf Flambard, who helped himself to some of the contents of the treasury. These unhappy times also saw the introduction of an annual allowance for the monks, evidently considered to be rather stingy.[255] Yet in spite of it all, Simeon was afterwards regarded with affection, as one who had done his best to stabilise and to improve the quality of the religious life at Ely, after so much disruption, and gave back to the community its sense of identity, purpose, and direction. It had only been a matter of time before Æthelthryth would work her magic on one of the incoming abbots, and before the Abbot in question would turn to her for protection against his own kind. We may have hereabouts the context for the manufacture of the charter in the name of King Edgar.[256] Simeon certainly identified himself wholeheartedly with Ely's cause. He had once in his slumbering heard demons carrying off the soul of one of the Abbey's oppressors, Earl William de Warenne, and announced it in chapter the next morning, three or four days before news of the Earl's death reached Ely by more conventional means;[257] and it may be no coincidence that during Simeon's abbacy Goscelin, the itinerant hagiographer of Anglo-Norman England, spent time at Ely working on the Abbey's saints.[258]

---

[250] *LE*, ii. 129: pp. 208–9, ii. 133: pp. 213–16, on the good one among them (Godric) who had a vision of all four of the holy virgins, ii. 137: pp. 220–1, and ii. 138: pp. 221–2, showing how eventually the monks of Winchester got their just deserts.

[251] *LE*, ii. 135: pp. 218–19, with reference to Ranulf Flambard, and ii. 137: pp. 221.

[252] *LE*, ii. 118: pp. 200–2, ii. 133: p. 213 and ii. 137: pp. 220–1. Of course the story seems different when told from a different perspective: see D. Bates, *Bishop Remigius of Lincoln 1067–1092* (Lincoln, 1992), esp. pp. 28–9.

[253] *LE*, ii. 134: pp. 216–17, with comment; see also R.A. Brown, *The Norman Conquest* (London, 1984), pp. 118–20, with translation, and Miller, *Abbey & Bishopric*, pp. 66–8. It is evidently this story which underlies the tale of the forty knights billeted at Ely in the early 1070s, on which see below, p. 57.

[254] *LE*, ii. 135: pp. 218–19; see also Brown, *Norman Conquest*, pp. 119–20.

[255] *LE*, ii. 136: p. 220, with comment.

[256] See above, p. 22.

[257] *LE*, ii. 119: pp. 202–3.

[258] *LE*, ii. 133: p. 215. For Goscelin's work at Ely, see *Saints of Ely*, ed. Love.

Abbot Simeon died, in his hundredth year, on 21 November 1093.[259] The tale was told of the wicked monks who had come to Ely from Winchester, with Simeon, and who after his death appropriated all manner of precious things from the Abbey, including 'an especially valuable and famous hanging', and relics of St Botulph; and the *Liber Eliensis* delighted in telling how they got their come-uppance at Guildford.[260] For the rest of the 1090s, the Abbey appears to have remained under the control of Ranulf Flambard. It is to this period that we must assign the second of the Abbey's inventories, compiled apparently by Ranulf himself in the aftermath of Abbot Simeon's death, in the presence (most interestingly) of the entire community of 72 monks.[261] Since the successive inventories were compiled in accordance with different principles, it is not always easy to match entries in one with entries in another; but while there are signs of the losses inflicted by Simeon's departing monks, there is also evidence of the way in which the Abbey had acquired new treasures and the necessities for divine service during Simeon's period of office. The *Liber Eliensis* was as hostile to Ranulf as to all other outsiders, though in fact there is little basis on which to judge the impact of his regime.[262] In August 1100, following the death of William Rufus and the accession of Henry I, the Abbey received a new Abbot in the person of Richard, monk of Bec, son of Richard de Bienfaite (Fitz Gilbert, founder of the priory of St Neots).[263] Abbot Richard was highly regarded at Ely, not least because he adamantly refused to be consecrated by Robert, Bishop of Lincoln, and sought instead to affirm Ely's independence by making it an episcopal see. It was his misfortune, however, to be rather grand and well connected, for he soon found himself embroiled in the politics of the royal court and suddenly out of favour with the King. Richard appealed to Rome, and was eventually reinstated. He was astute enough during these troubled years to continue work on Abbot Simeon's new church, and, in particular, to take the necessary measures to ensure that the distinction of Ely's saints would not pass unnoticed; for it is clear that he hoped in this way to strengthen his case for what was always his grand plan, to free Ely from the clutches of Lincoln by raising its own status to that of an episcopal see.[264] The *Liber Eliensis* took pleasure in relating the story of Richard's recovery of the Abbey's estate at (Little) Hadham (Herts.), from Ranulf Flambard; and – a master stroke, at the end of book II – how St Wihtburh appeared to Richard on his deathbed, and received him into her care.[265]

Abbot Richard died on 16 June 1107. He was succeeded, in effect, by Hervey, a Breton who had served as a chaplain of William Rufus before his appointment as Bishop of Bangor in 1092, but who had made himself so unpopular in Wales that Henry I thought it better to despatch him to Ely, where indeed he fared rather better.[266] Hervey was naturally eager to pursue the possibility of raising Ely to episcopal status, and in

[259] *LE*, ii. 137: p. 221.

[260] *LE*, ii. 138: pp. 221–2.

[261] *LE*, ii. 139: pp. 223–4.

[262] *LE*, ii. 140: pp. 224–5.

[263] *LE*, ii. 141–3: pp. 224–8. For Richard Fitz Gilbert and St Neots, see above, p. 48. For a genealogical table, see Round, *Feudal England* (cit. in n. 220), opp. p. 473. The compiler used a book about him: *LE*, ii. 141: p. 225.

[264] *LE*, ii. 148: pp. 233–4.

[265] *LE*, ii. 149 and 150: pp. 234–6.

[266] *LE*, iii. 1: pp. 245–6. See also William of Malmesbury, *GP* iv. 185 (ed. Hamilton, pp. 325–6).

November 1108 managed to obtain mandates from Pope Paschal II to that end.[267] The new see was duly established by charter of King Henry I, issued at Nottingham on 17 October 1109, 'in die translationis beate Ætheldrethe virginis'.[268]

The new church at Ely

The story which has been set out above constitutes an essential part of the foundations of Ely Cathedral. Without St Æthelthryth, there would have been no cult to lend its special associations to the place and to serve as a focus for religious observances in the region; without Bishop Æthelwold, Abbot Byrhtnoth and a host of others there might have been no church and endowment at Ely in the eleventh century, and none of the resources which gave it such potential for further development; and without King William, Picot the sheriff and their friends there would have been less incentive in the aftermath of the Conquest for successive Abbots, notably Simeon and Richard, to wrap themselves in Æthelthryth's mantle. A modern historian is impressed by the sheer quality of the available evidence, and grateful for the opportunities which it affords for observing much that is fundamental to our understanding of the eleventh century; but, unsurprisingly, the monks of Ely in the twelfth century had rather different concerns. The driving force behind the Liber Eliensis is a demonstration of the power and determination of St Æthelthryth to defend the interests of her church. An important sub-text is the relationship between the Abbey or Priory and episcopal power, drawing a deliberate contrast between the friendly relations which the Abbey had enjoyed with bishops of Elmham, before the Conquest, and the attempted interference by successive bishops of Lincoln, thereafter. Yet the lesson to be learnt from it all was that the saints of Ely eventually effected their own conquest of the Norman conquerors.

The incomers may have been taught to hold the English Church in scorn,[269] and it may be true, to some extent, that Archbishop Lanfranc was sceptical about the Anglo-Saxon saints and concerned to eradicate them from liturgical calendars.[270] For all we know, Anglo-Norman attitudes at Ely in the mid-1070s were no more deferential to native traditions; but it cannot have been long before the incomers came to realise what they stood to gain from the continued veneration of the local saints,[271] and began to vie with each other in promoting their respective causes.[272] The most effective form of

---

[267] LE, iii. 2–5: pp. 246–9, all dated 21 November 1108.

[268] LE, iii. 6: pp. 249–50. For Henry's charter (BL, Harl. Ch. 43. C. 11), see C. Johnson and H.A. Cronne (eds.), Regesta Regum Anglo-Normannorum 1066–1154, II: Regesta Henrici Primi 1100–1135 (Oxford, 1956), pp. 87–8 (no. 919), with LE, p. 249, n. 2.

[269] William of Malmesbury, Gesta Regum iii. 245 (William of Malmesbury: Gesta Regum Anglorum / The History of the English Kings, ed. R.A.B. Mynors, R.M. Thomson and M. Winterbottom (Oxford, 1998), I, pp. 456–60).

[270] Knowles, Monastic Order (cit. in n. 204), pp. 118–19. For more recent discussion, see D. Rollason, Saints and Relics in Anglo-Saxon England (Oxford, 1989), pp. 223–8, and T.A. Heslop, 'The Canterbury Calendars and the Norman Conquest', in R. Eales and R. Sharpe (eds.), Canterbury and the Norman Conquest: Churches, Saints and Scholars 1066–1109 (London, 1995), pp. 53–86.

[271] E. Fernie, The Architecture of Norman England (Oxford, 2000), p. 33, makes the interesting observation that churches rebuilt in the 1070s had biblical or Roman dedications, 'while Winchester, Ely, and Bury after 1079 were dedicated to the Saxon saints Swithun, Edmund, and Etheldreda'. For the apparent suppression of St Swithun's Day at Winchester, and its return, see Miracula S. Swithuni, ch. 52 (M. Lapidge, The Cult of St Swithun (cit. in n. 84), pp. 684–7, at p. 686 n. 44).

[272] It is now acknowledged that is difficult to reconcile the notion of Norman scepticism with the obvious vitality in Anglo-Norman England of a wide range of pre-Conquest cults. See S.J. Ridyard, 'Condigna Veneratio:

expression was always the building of a new church, which in symbolising the glory of God also advertised the wealth and power of those who identified with local ecclesiastical interests. It was Abbot Simeon, probably in the mid-1080s, who laid the foundations of a new church at Ely, with associated monastic buildings,[273] and it is apparent that he drew his inspiration from his brother's work at Winchester.[274] For all his troubles, and his great old age, Simeon persisted in his work, completing the domestic buildings of the monks and laying foundations for the church, which, however, remained unfinished at his death in 1093.[275] It seems that building work was suspended during the interregnum in the later 1090s, when Ranulf Flambard had charge of the Abbey, but the appointment of Abbot Richard, in August 1100, put matters back into the hands of one determined to make Ely stand out in comparison with the church of any episcopal see. The *Liber Eliensis* avers that Richard gave all his attention to the work, endeavouring to complete what Simeon had started 'in as fitting a shape and on as fitting a scale as possible', so that it would deserve to be regarded as the finest church in the land.[276]

The apsidal east end of the new church appears to have been placed a short distance to the south-east of the standing Anglo-Saxon church; so as the work progressed westwards, the builders had to deal with the older structures that lay in their path.[277] In 1102 the tomb containing the body of St Wihtburh was moved from wherever it had been buried in 974 and placed 'elsewhere in the church', in order to make way for the new building works; so presumably Wihtburh, as a more recent arrival, lay somewhere to the east of her sisters, and thus had to be moved first. As her sarcophagus was being taken down some steps, the lower part of it cracked; but for the time being it was left in that condition.[278] The mortal remains of St Eormenhild do not appear to have been moved on this occasion;[279] nor was there any need at this stage to move St Æthelthryth and St Seaxburh, who appear to have lain either side of the high altar (the former to the south, in a 'tower', with her own altar, and the latter to the north).[280] Four years later, in

Post-Conquest Attitudes to the Saints of the Anglo-Saxons', *Anglo-Norman Studies*, 9 (1987), pp. 179–206; see also Ridyard, *Royal Saints*, pp. 200–6.

[273] *LE*, ii. 118: p. 200. See above, p. 51.

[274] For recent accounts of the building of the Norman church at Ely, see Maddison, *Ely Cathedral*, pp. 12–24, and Fernie, *Architecture of Norman England*, pp. 124–8; see also below, pp. 95–6.

[275] *LE*, ii. 135: pp. 218–19.

[276] *LE*, ii. 143: pp. 227–8.

[277] Fernie, *Architecture of Norman England*, esp. p. 126, recognises a distinction between the early Norman work at Ely, under Simeon (Abbot, 1082–93), and later Norman work under Abbot Richard and his successors, after 1100. The east wall of the north transept and the whole of the south transept were part of the first phase of construction. This would accord with the supposition that the east end of the old church, with the tombs of the four saints, lay in the path of the projected north transept of the new church, and that it was not until Abbot Richard set about the completion of the north transept, in the early 1100s, that it was necessary to disturb them. Thus the nave of the new church would have lain alongside and to the south of the nave of the old church, explaining how the bones of the Abbey's 'confessors' could be translated from the old church into the new as late as the mid-12th century (above, p. 35). In a typescript headed 'St Etheldreda's Church at Ely' [Nov. 1970], of which there is a copy in CUL, EDC 14/35/2, Donovan Purcell notes that the presence of old foundations under the north transept might have contributed to the collapse of the north-west corner in 1699.

[278] *LE*, ii. 146: p. 231; Goulburn and Symonds, *Herbert de Losinga* (cit. in n. 104), I, pp. 218–19. No reference is made to this earlier translation in the *Vita S. Wihtburge* (*Saints of Ely*, ed. Love), though it is said (ch. 19) that the old coffin had been broken for a long while.

[279] The statement apparently to the effect that Eormenhild was moved in 1102 (*LE*, ii. 146) is contradicted by the more explicit indication that she was moved in 1106 (*LE*, ii. 145).

[280] *LE*, ii. 146: p. 231.

1106, the time came to move Æthelthryth herself 'from the old church into the new one, from a church of moderate size into one greater and more beautiful'. Abbot Richard appointed the propitious day (17 October), and invited a distinguished company to participate in the proceedings. The marble sarcophagus containing the body of St Æthelthryth remained where Bishop Æthelwold had left it, c.970, and indeed where it had been placed originally by Æthelthryth's sister Seaxburh in 695; now perforce it was removed from its position in the old church, taken thence into the new church, and placed 'in a special chamber behind the high altar'. Bishop Herbert preached a moving sermon, and Æthelthryth used the natural elements to make known her displeasure at being disturbed.[281] Abbot Richard and his men then opened up the tombs of St Seaxburh and St Eormenhild (which had been sealed with lead by Bishop Æthelwold). Seaxburh's body, contained in a wooden casket underneath a stone monument, was found to be decayed, though well wrapped in silk and muslin; she was reburied at Æthelthryth's feet, looking east. Eormenhild's body, also decayed, remained where Bishop Æthelwold had left it, in a plain tomb underneath the flagstones; she was reburied on Æthelthryth's right.[282] Meanwhile, Abbot Richard had prepared a new tomb for St Wihtburh. It was intended to be exactly the same size as the one that had been broken, but when measured it turned out to be too short by a foot. The broken tomb was opened, and the saint's body was found to be whole and incorrupt; and suddenly the tomb mended itself, indicating that Wihtburh in fact had no wish for a new one. So in the event Wihtburh's tomb was moved from wherever it had been put in the old church, in 1102, and reburied in its appointed place in the new church, on Æthelthryth's left.[283]

The translation of the Abbey's saints was prompted, of course, by practical considerations, but there is no mistaking that Abbot Richard would have regarded the ceremonial in 1106 as an opportunity both to consolidate and to proclaim Ely's identity as the resting-place of four famous saints. It may have been at about the same time that a shrine was prepared for the tomb of St Æthelthryth, described in remarkable detail in the inventory compiled at Ely in the second quarter of the twelfth century:[284]

> There is a shrine, under which is enclosed the marble sarcophagus holding the virgin body of St Æthelthryth, facing her own altar, just as the distinguished lady, entirely whole, entirely incorrupt, rests in the tomb which had been prepared for her at God's command, as we believe, by the hands of angels, just as Bede, the most learned of the English, tells in the history of his people. The side of this shrine which faces the altar [*i.e.* the west side, facing the high altar] is of silver with embossed figures well worked in gold. Around the 'Christ in Majesty' are 7 beryls and crystals, 2 onyxes, 2 garnets, and 26 pearls; and in the crown of this 'Christ in Majesty' are an amethyst, 2 carnelians, 6 pearls, and 8 translucent stones; and in the 4 corners [of the crown], 4 large crystals; and

[281] *LE*, ii. 144: pp. 228–30; Goulburn and Symonds, *Herbert de Losinga*, I, pp. 212–17.

[282] *LE*, ii. 145: pp. 230–1; Goulburn and Symonds, *Herbert de Losinga*, I, pp. 217–18.

[283] *Vita S. Wihtburge*, chs. 19–24 (*Saints of Ely*, ed. Love), and *LE*, ii. 147: p. 233; Goulburn and Symonds, *Herbert de Losinga*, I, pp. 219–21. The tombs would have been placed in the Norman apse, which was itself replaced by a square east end in the late 12th century. The disposition of the tombs of Seaxburh, Eormenhild, and Wihtburh, in relation to Æthelthryth, is confirmed by the account of the shrine in *LE*, iii. 50: p. 290. See also Henry of Huntingdon, *Historia Anglorum*, ix. 33 (ed. Greenway, pp. xliv, 662).

[284] *LE*, iii. 50: p. 289.

around it 9 crystals. And in the southern corner of this side [of the shrine], a golden collar affixed with a topaz, 3 emeralds and 3 sardonyxes. In the crown of the upper figure are 7 precious stones and 11 pearls. There is a knob bearing a cross of well gilded copper, with 12 crystals. On the left-hand side of this shrine [*i.e.* the northern side], the whole side is of well gilded silver with sixteen embossed figures with 94 large crystals and 149 small crystal and translucent stones. The eastern side of this shrine is of silver with gilding in places with embossed figures. There are 2 crystal lions with 32 crystal and 3 translucent stones and 8 enamelled and 7 ordinary buckles. There is a 'Christ in Majesty' which belongs to the altar frontal [*i.e.* the frontal of Æthelthryth's own altar]. On the southern side [of the shrine] there are 16 silver figures without gilding and, beneath, bands of gilded silver. In this part there are 26 crystals. There is a another copper knob, holding up a cross of well gilded copper with 12 crystals.

In front of the altar [the high altar, or Æthelthryth's altar] there is a *tabula* of silver well worked in gold with embossed figures, which Abbot Theodwine made from money which had been found at Wentworth during the time of the beloved Lord Abbot Thurstan. On this there are around the 'Christ in Majesty' 2 chalcedonies, 10 crystals and beryls, 3 enamels and 42 pearls, and 10 enamels, 3 stones and 5 pearls are missing; and to the right of the 'Christ in Majesty' are 12, and similarly to the left 12 crystals and beryls; and in the circle of the 2 courses of the sun and moon there are 8 beryls and crystals, and 8 stones are missing and 16 pearls are missing; and around the 'Christ in Majesty' are 4 ivory figures of angels. And on the outside edge of this *tabula* in ungilded silver 28 stones are missing, and on the inside gilded edge 24 stones are missing.

The shrine of St Æthelthryth, placed behind the high altar in the new church at Ely, must have made a strong impression on all those who saw it.[285] It might be visualised as a house-shaped structure, large enough to enclose the saint's sarcophagus. The western end of the shrine, visible from the high altar, was of silver, bearing a crowned figure above a Christ in Majesty, studded all over with an extraordinary variety of precious stones. The eastern end of the shrine, also of silver, bore two 'crystal lions', interspersed with crystals, glass, and enamels. Each of the two sides was decorated with sixteen embossed images, worked in silver and gold, again interspersed with crystals and other translucent stones. There were also two knobs surmounted by crosses, perhaps on the apexes at each end of the structure.[286] It is possible that the twelfth-century shrine, which was already missing some of its decorative elements when described in the 1130s, incorporated some eleventh-century or even earlier work, if only to judge from the comparable elaboration of Abbot Theodwine's *tabula*, which must have been made in the mid-1070s;[287] but this can be no more than a wishful thought, since the structure was stripped bare of its decoration later in the twelfth century, by the wicked Bishop Nigel.[288]

---

[285] For the shrine of St Æthelthryth in the context of shrines in general, see J.C. Wall, *Shrines of British Saints* (London, 1905), pp. 55–60, and B. Nilson, *Cathedral Shrines of Medieval England* (Woodbridge, 1998), pp. 35–42 (at pp. 37 and 39).

[286] For an imaginative but plausible reconstruction of the general appearance of the shrine, see Bentham, *Ely*, pl. XLVIII (Figure 4, p. 67); a folded sheet preserved among the papers of James Essex (BL, Add. MS 6772, fos. 195–6) bears pencil and ink sketches of the shrine, and of the disposition of the tombs in 1106, evidently made for these purposes. For the shrine and pilgrimages in the medieval period, see below, pp. 67–70.

[287] On the nature of a *tabula*, see Nilson, *Cathedral Shrines of Medieval England*, p. 52.

[288] *LE*, iii. 50: p. 289: 'Bishop Nigel afterwards broke up this *tabula* and also the shrine of St Æthelthryth at the

When so much was held to begin in 1066, it is reassuring (for an Anglo-Saxonist) that Ely retained a clear consciousness of its pre-Conquest origins. Æthelthryth soon gave way to Etheldreda, but her cult continued to prosper, not least in competition with the cults of other saints elsewhere. The shrine was at the centre of the great works undertaken by Bishop Northwold (1229–54) towards the middle of the thirteenth century;[289] the fourteenth-century Octagon was conceived in her honour, as shown by the sculptured corbels (Plate 10c–d);[290] and in the mid fifteenth century the shrine altar was provided with wooden panels illustrated with scenes from her life (Colour pl. 20a). Needless to say, the monks of Ely showed respect for their past in many other ways. They took care to commemorate King Edgar in the Priory's *titulus* entered on a mortuary roll in the early 1120s (Plate 2c);[291] a variety of pre-Conquest documentation was preserved in the Priory's archives, some of which was included in its cartularies; and when the time came to consolidate Ely's historical identity, in the form of the *Liber Eliensis*, it was naturally a history which began in the seventh century. Somewhat more remarkable was the treatment accorded to Ealdorman Byrhtnoth and the six other worthies who had been buried at Ely in the eleventh century. In the mid-1150s the bones of the seven 'confessors' were ceremonially translated by Prior Alexander and Bishop Nigel from their resting-places in or around the old conventual church into the 'northern part' of the new Cathedral,[292] perhaps marking the completion of another significant stage in its construction.[293] Many years later, in course of work undertaken after the collapse of the Norman crossing tower in 1322, the bones were immured in the north wall of the rebuilt Choir (in the Octagon);[294] and their presence was advertised on the outer face of the said wall by a row of seven painted 'effigies' set in an elaborate architectural arcade, over a row of seven arches which framed the tombs themselves. These fourteenth-century wall-paintings do not survive, but they are known from drawings made by William Stukeley in the 1730s or 1740s and by Michael Tyson a fortnight before their eventual destruction on 18 May 1769 (Colour pl. 22c).[295]

A rather different manifestation of historical awareness at Ely is represented by the seemingly ancient tradition that after the proceedings at Warwick King William lodged

---

urging of evil men who hated peace, and took and broke up all the gold and silver which was in them.' See also *LE*, ii. 113: p. 196 and iii. 89: p. 335.

[289] P. Draper, 'Bishop Northwold and the Cult of Saint Etheldreda', in P. Draper (ed.), *Medieval Art and Architecture at Ely Cathedral*, BAACT, 2 (London, 1979), pp. 8–27, at pp. 16–21; see also Maddison, *Ely Cathedral*, pp. 46–7.

[290] For the corbels, see Bentham, *Ely*, pls. IX–XII; Stubbs, *Historical Memorials of Ely* (cit. in n. 174), pp. 70–84; and Maddison, *Ely Cathedral*, pp. 65–6.

[291] 'Titulus Sancti Petri Apostolorum principis et sancte Ætheldrethe virginis', in the obituary roll of Vitalis, Abbot of Savigny (d.1122): L. Delisle, *Rouleau Mortuaire du B. Vital. Abbé de Savigni* (Paris, 1909), pl. XLV, no. 191.

[292] *LE*, ii. 87: pp. 155–6, and above, p. 35. Archbishop Wulfstan had been moved from the old church into the monks' cemetery in the late 11th or early 12th century (above, pp. 34–5), but it is not said that any of the other six 'confessors' had been moved at the same time. According to *LE*, ii. 87, they were removed 'from their old graves', which were very deep and could be found only with great difficulty, though each was in fact clearly marked.

[293] As suggested by Maddison, *Ely Cathedral*, pp. 32–3.

[294] See the late 14th-century note inscribed at the beginning of *LE*, MS F (CUL, EDC 1), copied by Bentham in CUL, MS Add. 2947, fo. 135, and cited by Bentham, *Ely*, p. 85 n., with Addenda, pp. 23–4; see also *LE*, pp. xxiv and xxxviii.

[295] For further details of the drawings, see below, Appendix, pp. 401–4. See also Bentham, *Ely*, pp. 285–6 [written in 1770], and Addenda, p. 23, and Stevenson, *Supplement*, pp. 69 and 144, with pl. opp. p. 69 (from Gough).

forty of his knights at Ely, in order to prevent any further rebellion; for, according to this story, so strong was the friendship that developed between each knight and the monk designated as his host that the monks were sorry to see them go, and commemorated them by painting their arms on the refectory walls. The story has travelled some distance from its apparent origin,[296] and in its medieval form was perhaps no more than an expression of the genealogical and heraldic pretensions of those who wished to claim a distinguished ancestry for themselves, among the followers of William the Conqueror;[297] but it is more familiar in the form of the sixteenth-century 'Tabula Eliensis', which hangs in the Cathedral (Colour pl. 22a), conveying its message that relations between the monks and the secular powers had long been harmonious.[298]

The relics and shrines of Ely's saints were lost at the time of the Reformation, and in that sense the Cathedral now lacks what it was built to contain. It was perhaps for this reason that when the tombs of the Abbey's seven Anglo-Saxon 'confessors' were opened, in 1769, the bones were accorded the kind of treatment previously reserved for holy relics, culminating with their solemn reburial two years later in the place where they remain to the present day. The fourteenth-century paintings advertised the exact location of the tombs; so, when the walls of the old Choir were demolished, on 18 May 1769, prior to the construction of the new Choir in the eastern arm of the Cathedral,[299] an expectant company of learned men had gathered to see what would be revealed.[300] The fact that Ealdorman Byrhtnoth lacked his head was regarded as reassuring evidence of the authenticity of the other bones in his tomb. Archbishop Wulfstan's skull was 'quite whole', though his teeth 'were all rotten, & crumbled like loose chalk'; a gilded bronze pin said to have been found with his bones was presented by Bentham, some years later, to the Society of Antiquaries.[301] The bones of Ealdorman Byrhtnoth were

---

[296] The notion of the 40 knights at Ely was evidently suggested by references in *LE*, to the imposition of knight-service by William I, regarded at Ely as a most oppressive measure: see above, p. 50.

[297] The story is best told in copies of what was perhaps an early 14th-century roll of arms: *e.g.* BL, Add. MS 38164 (which formerly belonged to the Norfolk antiquary Francis Blomefield), made in the 16th century. The roll gave the name and coat of arms of each one of the forty knights, naming the monk to whom each was assigned, and incorporated an explanatory text in Latin; there is a translation of this text (headed 'Storie found in the Isle of Ely') in an early 17th-century collection of genealogical and historical material, from Ely, now BL, MS Royal 18 C. 1, fos. 14–15ᵛ, copied by Bentham in CUL, MS Add. 2948, fos. 5–7, and printed (in part), *Ely*, Appendix, p. 4*.

[298] The 'Tabula' incorporates imaginary portraits of each knight and monk. It may have been copied from an older picture, but the style suggests that it cannot have been much earlier than the 15th century. A fine engraving was published by Bentham, *Ely*, pl. XIII. Several letters about the 'Tablet' are scattered among the papers of Cole, Bentham, Essex and others in the BL; see, *e.g.*, Bentham to Cole, 7 Jan. 1762, in BL, Add. MS 33491, fos. 73–4, with Cole's detailed response printed in Bentham, *Ely*, Appendix, pp. 5*–9*.

[299] For the debate surrounding James Essex's proposed alterations to the choir, see correspondence copied by Bentham in CUL, MS Add. 2960 (Bentham to Nichols, 20 Oct. 1758; circular letter, 18 Dec. 1759) and Add. 2957 (Essex to Dean & Chapter, 12 June 1759; proposal, dated May 1761; Essex to Nichols, 10 May 1761). See also T. Cocke, 'The Architectural History of Ely Cathedral from 1540–1840', *Medieval Art and Architecture at Ely Cathedral*, BAACT, 2 (London, 1979), pp. 71–7, at 75; G. Cobb, *English Cathedrals: the Forgotten Centuries. Restoration and Change from 1530 to the Present Day* (London, 1980), pp. 77–8; P. Lindley, 'The Imagery of the Octagon at Ely' [1985], reprinted in his *Gothic to Renaissance: Essays on Sculpture in England* (Stamford, 1995), pp. 113–46, at 128–30; and Cocke, below, pp. 218–19.

[300] The fullest account of the proceedings is to be found in the notebooks of William Cole (1714–82), who was present both when the tombs were opened, in 1769, and when the bones were reburied, in 1771: see Appendix 3 below, pp. 401–4. Bentham's account in *Ely*, Addenda, pp. 23–4, is an extract from a letter to the Society of Antiquaries; the full text, dated 16 Nov. 1771, is in Bentham's letter-book (CUL, MS Add. 2960, pp. 72–4). See also Gough, *Sepulchral Monuments*, pt 1, p. clvi.

[301] Above, n. 166.

examined that evening, over dinner, by a passing apothecary called Mr Tooky, who estimated the ealdorman's height at between 6 and 7 feet; Bentham himself sent his measurements to the celebrated anatomist Dr John Hunter (1728–93), who calculated that all the prelates stood over 6 feet and that Byrhtnoth stood a towering 6 feet 9 inches.[302] For over two years the bones lay in one of the prebendal houses, but presently it was decided to place them elsewhere, and in a formal ceremony conducted on 31 July 1771 they were immured in a row of Gothic niches under the arch of the tomb of Bishop West (d.1533), in the south-eastern corner of the east end, underneath inscriptions recording their identities and the supposed dates of their deaths (Plate 13c).[303] So here lie the mortal remains of an Anglo-Saxon ealdorman slain by the Vikings at the Battle of Maldon in 991, of a Bishop of Dorchester who also died in defence of his country, at the battle of Ashingdon in 1016, and of a renowned Archbishop of York who most famously lamented the current state of affairs in his 'Sermon of the Wolf to the English' (first preached in 1014), and who died in 1023. Here too lie the remains of three Bishops of Elmham, all good friends of Ely, their presence testifying to the Abbey's East Anglian inclinations in the eleventh century.

The magnificent structure which dominates the Isle of Ely and the surrounding countryside stands to the glory of God and in honour of St Æthelthryth upon foundations laid by Bishop Æthelwold, Abbot Byrhtnoth, and Abbot Ælfsige. It bears silent witness to the faith and good will of successive generations of East Anglian folk, in the tenth and eleventh centuries, who had looked to the saints of Ely for intercession in times of distress and for the redemption of their souls. Wulfstan of Dalham, Ælfhelm Polga, Ælfwaru of Bridgham and so many others like them have long since passed into oblivion; but all had their day on the Isle of Ely, and in their different ways helped to determine the shape of what was to come.

---

[302] Modern science has revised the estimates downwards, though Byrhtnoth's stature remains impressive by the standards of his day: see M. Deegan and S. Rubin, 'Byrhtnoth's Remains: a Reassessment of his Stature', in Scragg (ed.), *Battle of Maldon AD 991* (cit. in n. 125), pp. 289–93, at pp. 290–1.

[303] Again, William Cole gives the fullest account: below, pp. 401–4. Bentham, *Ely*, Addenda, pp. 23–4, gives the text of the 18th-century inscriptions; both are reproduced in Deegan and Rubin, 'Byrhtnoth's Remains'. See also E. Coatsworth, 'Byrhtnoth's Tomb', *Battle of Maldon AD 991*, pp. 279–88, at p. 280 (showing the main inscription) and p. 285 (showing the row of niches above Bishop West's tomb).

Ely 1109–1539:
Priory, Community and Town

DOROTHY OWEN

The site of the monastic settlement[1]

The original site of the monastery of Ely, founded by St Etheldreda, is the 'island' described by the author of the *Liber Eliensis* in the twelfth century, copying from Bede and other earlier writers, 'inaccessible to boats because of the changing surface of the marshes until causeways of rushes had been made. The island is seven miles long from *Cotingelade* to Littleport or *Abbotsdelf* . . . and four miles wide from *Chirchewere* to Stretham mere'[2] (Colour pl. 2a). This island formed the basis of the Ely establishment from its earliest days, and the site of the monastic enclosure, on the eastern escarpment of the island, above the marsh, has remained relatively unchanged and for a long time was relatively isolated from the world (Figure 1, p. 2).

It was pointed out by A.K. Astbury that when the body of St Wihtburga was brought from Dereham to Ely, in 974, it came by water to Turbutsey (near Queen Adelaide) and was then carried overland, presumably because the south-eastern Ouse and Cam did not then flow by Ely.[3] Professor Darby, using the work of Gordon Fowler on extinct waterways of the fens,[4] concluded that the 'Ely cut', which brought the river close to the eastern margin of the Isle at Ely, had perhaps been made by the time that King Cnut, travelling to Ely by boat, heard from across the water the monastic choir singing the service in their church.[5] Cnut died in 1035, and if this deduction is valid it seems clear that by this date Ely was linked directly by water with Cambridge to the south and Littleport to the north. From Littleport the onward connection to the sea was via Welney and Wisbech to the Nene outfall, and it is not clear when a direct cut was made from Littleport to Lynn.[6] However, Lynn was fully established as a port before 1180,[7]

---

[1] This section is abridged from part of D.M. Owen, *The Medieval Development of the Town of Ely* (Ely, 1993).

[2] Translated from *Liber Eliensis* (ed. Blake), *'Incipit de situ Elyensis insule'*, pp. 2–3.

[3] A.K. Astbury, *The Black Fens* (Cambridge, 1958), p. 159.

[4] Gordon Fowler, 'The Extinct Waterways of the Fens', *Geographical Journal*, lxxxiii (1934), pp. 30–9.

[5] *LE*, ii.85: pp. 153–4; C.E. Wright, *The Cultivation of Saga in Anglo-Saxon England* (Edinburgh, 1939), pp. 36–8 and App. no. 5, pp. 251–2.

[6] H.C. Darby, *The Medieval Fenland* (Cambridge, 1940), pp. 96–7.

[7] D.M. Owen, *The Making of King's Lynn. A Documentary Survey*, British Academy, Records of Social and Economic History New Series IX (1984).

Wiggenhall had become a flourishing multiple settlement, presumably on the new cut, by the second quarter of the twelfth century,[8] and a number of citizens of Lynn had before 1200 colonised a new area of mercantile settlement in Ely, in Broad Street, behind the quays.[9] It seems certain then, that before 1180 the Littleport cut had been made, and Ely assumed its medieval economic importance as an ancillary port for Lynn and Cambridge.

At the time of the Domesday Survey none of these developments was apparent, for the community described there, and in the *Inquisitio Eliensis* which followed on it,[10] was a purely agricultural one, with forty villeins, twenty-eight cottars and twenty slaves, arable land, meadow and pasture and three *arpents*[11] of vineyard. No mention is made of mills, fairs, or other economic resources, except for the single fishery which produced 3750 eels. It is almost certain, nevertheless, that a market was already meeting before the monastery gate – that is, in the present market-place.

Obedientiaries

A feature of Benedictine life which had taken firm root at Ely by the middle years of the thirteenth century was the departmentalisation of the administration of the house. Under the Prior and subprior were the departmental officers – the obedientiaries, whom T.D. Atkinson described in four 'divisions', the Prior's (subprior, treasurer, steward of estates, and steward of the Prior's hospice), 'church' (sacrist, precentor, shrine-keeper or feretrar, and keeper of the Lady Chapel), 'domestic' (chamberlain, cellarer, granator, pittancer, infirmarer, and keeper of rushes), and 'hospitality' (hosteller, almoner).[12]

All these officers except the subprior and the steward of estates kept account rolls, which have survived to a greater or lesser extent:[13] these acounts were needed for the regular audit of departmental accounts. The surviving cartularies provide some additional evidence for the systematic endowment of the departments.

The earliest officer to have a separate department was undoubtedly the sacrist. He was, and remained until the Dissolution, the monastic officer in charge of the monastic church, its ornaments and fittings. The sacrist's responsibility became much wider after the twelfth century, as his account rolls reveal.[14] The office of sacrist was endowed with a series of rents payable from lands in the Isle, the receipts of five churches, and the offerings made at the shrines.[15] To ensure the suitable upkeep of the Cathedral fabric, the sacrist maintained a staff of building craftsmen and other specified craftsmen and labourers (including goldsmiths and other metalworkers) and was aided by a monk known variously as his vicar or deputy.

[8] BL, MS Harl. 2100 (Castleacre cartulary), fo. 123ᵛ.

[9] Owen, *King's Lynn*, p. 50.

[10] N.E.S.A. Hamilton (ed.), *Inquisitio Comitatus Cantabrigiensis . . . Inquisitio Eliensis* (London, 1876), from BL, MS Cotton Tiberius A. vi.

[11] Roughly 3 acres.

[12] Atkinson, *Ely Monastery*, p. 10, n. 1.

[13] There are for example 53 granator's rolls, 45 sacrist's rolls and about 40 cellarer's rolls; but only 1 surviving infirmarer's roll, and 8 each of the hosteller's and of the steward of the Prior's hospice.

[14] Chapman, *Sacrist Rolls*, I, p. 3 (provision of candles for altars), p. 9 (multifarious activities and duties); the rolls are EDC 1/F/10/1–45.

[15] Chapman, *Sacrist Rolls*, I, pp. 111–12.

The next official to appear in the records (c.1330) seems to have been the precentor, whose duty was the care of liturgical celebration, and especially of the manuscripts used for the liturgy. For the provision of the books, the precentory was endowed with the church of Impington. He paid organists and choirmen, and provided altar cloths, books and crosses. The books included missals, tropers, antiphoners and processionals, for use at all the consecrated altars within the Cathedral; hardly more than a few fragments of them have survived.[16] Duty-tables were set out for the readings of the week and special groups of singers, boys and adults, were engaged during the fifteenth century. At least one singer seems to have come from across the Scottish border.[17] Similarly, special organs were bought, chiefly it seems from East Anglia (Walsingham provided instruments decorated with paintings). The precentor was also responsible for the care and safety of books in the monastic library, and a few notes of loans of books to neighbouring scholars appear in his account rolls.[18]

Perhaps the busiest of the monastic departments was that of the chamberlain, who clothed and fed the community, and arranged for its blood-letting and for the instruction and teaching of novice recruits, besides the bathing and shaving which prepared the monks to receive the regular tonsure as the proof of their ordination. The chamberlain's department was in the very centre of the Priory to the south of the dormitory, and it included ponds for the provision of fresh fish, departments for the barber and shoemaker, and decidedly most important, a large and well-equipped tailor's shop. It is clear that the chamberlain's office was a busy and thriving department with responsibility for a variety of offices, wells, cloths for the refectory, bath houses, soap, sponges and fuel for water heating, cobbler's equipment, and leather for shoe repairs. The chamberlain had also general supervision over the monastic buildings other than the church, including their repairs and equipment: it is clear that institutions such as the bath house and the special heating were called for by the Maundy celebrations and the laundering of bed linen and habits, and by the blood-letting.[19]

More limited and specific duties were required of the shrine-keeper, whose special responsibility was the shrine of St Etheldreda and the management of the appeal to pilgrims for funds, especially at times when special indulgences were granted by the Pope. It was necessary on these occasions to hire secular priests to celebrate for the pilgrims, to pay the clerks administering the sale of indulgences, and to renew or refresh the various statues in the sanctuary, the altar cloths (of horse hair) and altar frontals, banners for the processions, and to provide a solemn parade of wax lights for the same purpose. It seems certain that some of the rents which formed the endowment of the charitable distributions were normally paid in wax.

After about 1300 the shrine keeper appears among the monk officers to whom the treasurer issued annual funds. He seems to have received some of the offerings made at the shrine of St Etheldreda and to have expended them on wax and banners for the feast of the dedication of St Etheldreda's altars, and for the purchase of cloth for altar

---

[16] See N.R. Ker (ed.), *Medieval Libraries of Great Britain. A List of Surviving Books*, 2nd edn (Royal Historical Society, 1964), pp. 77–9, for titles and locations of Ely books.

[17] EDC 1/F/9/8, precentor's roll 1465–6: John Rede of Scotland was paid 4s. as a singer. The precentor's rolls are EDC 1/F/9/1–13.

[18] See also Nigel Ramsay, below, p. 162, n. 33.

[19] The chamberlain's account rolls are EDC 1/F/3/1–34.

hangings, and a tailor to stitch them, for the same occasion. Some at least of the cloth was provided by the merchants who came specifically for the annual fair of St Etheldreda in July.[20]

Similar expenditure was called for when the Lady Chapel replaced the Lady altar in the early fourteenth century, and it was at about this time that a keeper of the Lady Chapel began to keep accounts.[21] He maintained the chapel, paid for its stained glass, and had his chamber over the processional way from the north choir aisle to the chapel.

The duties of the other obedientiaries were perhaps more specific. The cellarer provisioned the monastery, the granator provided corn and malt and was in charge of baking bread and brewing beer, and the pittancer had charge of providing extra allowances of food, 'treats' and meat on certain days.[22] The rush-keeper provided not only rushes for floors and thatched roofs but also peat for fuel. The infirmarer cared for sick and aged monks. The duties were not all so clearly defined, however, for the almoner not only supported the poor with food and second-hand clothing; he also kept a school for a few boys. The hosteller received the ordinary guests of the house; the steward of the Prior's hospice ran the Prior's household and received the higher-class guests.

Most of the departments, especially those established later in the medieval period, drew their funds for the upkeep of their buildings, maintenance of the monks, and the purchase of food and of habits from the monastic treasurer.

The community

The Priory's income had to provide for the physical needs of the professed religious as well as the many laymen who also lived in the community and who at times, especially in the fifteenth and sixteenth centuries, were a heavy charge on the funds. The obedientiaries were obliged by episcopal mandate to produce regular accounts to be audited annually in chapter, and these, although incomplete, provide our principal source of information about the life of the community.[23] They include mention of dramatic players of metropolitan origin and the plays they produced, of sculptors and craftsmen coming to provide monuments, relatives of members of the community, and distinguished representatives of the Priory's tenants. From time to time, leading members of the Benedictine order were entertained, often in connection with a visitation of the house. Then also there were singers and other musicians hired to perform at the special celebrations of St Etheldreda's feast, or at the times when a papal indulgence was granted in support of the fabric of the shrine. The entertainment of these varied guests was the responsibility for the most part of the prior's household, and it is in the accounts of his household that most information is to be gleaned about the regular diet of the community and also of special 'treats' given to the monks and the lay inhabitants of the house at special seasons such as Christmas. The formal responsibility for the entertain-

---

[20] For shrines and pilgrimages at Ely, see below, pp. 67–70.

[21] The earliest surviving roll (EDC 1/F/5/7/1) is 1356.

[22] Pittances were 'allowances of food, wine, beer, or money, issued in compliance with customs or bequests, and so frequently that at the close of the thirteenth century there were about three pittance days in every month': Stewart, *Ely*, p. 223. On pp. 224–7 is a list of pittance days, and by whom they were bestowed, derived from LPL, MS 448.

[23] See Evans, *Ordinances*.

ment of less distinguished guests lay with the hosteller; and the almoner arranged a daily distribution to paupers of the broken meats of the convent and also provided for the schoolmaster and pupils of the almonry school. One particular source of special foods was the funds administered by the pittancer, who from at least the thirteenth century controlled the proceeds of funds bequeathed by testators to provide for memorial feasts. This led to the distribution of such special 'treats' as pastry and confectionery. In order to perform their duties, each of the obedientiaries had servants in varying degree, all wearing uniform clothes by which they could be identified; none of these uniforms were to be distributed to the poor at the almonry.

For all practical purposes the history of the monastic community in the latter half of the medieval period is obscure. It is marked by changes to the buildings, and particularly by the fall of the tower and its replacement, which is treated elsewhere in this work. It is not even possible to establish clearly the way in which the landed endowment evolved. A few clues can be gained from the visitation documents published by Seiriol Evans, in which certain outstanding hints of changes in the community can be discerned.[24] Several monitions (directives) issued during the first half of the fourteenth century show that minor irregularities had been detected. In 1314, for example, the books issued to brothers were to be returned to the library at the beginning of Lent, and the spoons of deceased members were to be given to the refectorer. There was trouble about clothes money in 1403, privately procured beds in 1466, and there are ominous words in this latter year about breaking out to visit houses of ill fame.[25] Nevertheless there is no very clear indication of serious harm: the keeping of dogs in the cloister seems to have been the worst fault.

It is not clear how many professed monks there were in Ely at any one time. Numbers certainly fluctuated, especially during the plague times of the fourteenth and early fifteenth centuries, and it seems likely that the population of 70 monks which is mentioned in the early years of the medieval period was never again reached.[26] Following the division of property at the foundation of the bishopric in 1109, the convent complained that its resources allowed provision for only 40 men. Listings of the community are not often found in its early years. After the Black Death in 1349 there were only 28 monks including the Prior.[27] A full list of the entire community appears in the clerical subsidy roll of 1379, and lists the Prior and 45 professed monks.[28] At the Dissolution, the deed of surrender was signed on 18 November 1539 by 22 monks, the Prior and sub-prior. At times the account rolls of the chamberlain of the house record, among the graces (pocket money), payments made for the funeral expenses of monks dying through the previous year, and it is possible to calculate the rate of losses by death from the community, so far as the chamberlain's rolls have been preserved; but no clear pattern can be established.

---

[24] See also Evans's *Medieval Estate of the Cathedral Priory of Ely. A Preliminary Survey* (Ely, 1973).
[25] Evans, *Ordinances*, p. 61.
[26] *Ibid.*, p. x, 'an inventory of the possessions of the house in 1093 shows seventy-two monks among the witnesses'; p. 1, 'The ordinances of 1241–54 state that the monks anciently numbered 70.'
[27] Stewart, *Ely*, p. 207.
[28] PRO, E179/23/1. See also W.M. Palmer, 'A List of Cambridgeshire Subsidy Rolls. Appendix No. XII. The Clerical Poll Tax of 1378 [*recte* 1379] in Cambridgeshire', *The East Anglian; or, Notes and Queries on Subjects connected with the Counties of Suffolk, Cambridge, Essex and Norfolk*, 4th ser., xiii (1909–10), pp. 101–2.

Monastic life

Many of the young men joining the Ely religious community came from the Priory's own estates in eastern England.[29] There is evidence too of vacancies in the community being filled up by the existing monks nominating relatives or dependants. Such young men may well have been trained in the almoner's school which flourished under a master and usher appointed and licensed by the bishop.[30] Those seeking admission to the Benedictine order were examined by senior monks. On completion of the scholastic course they entered the novitiate, bringing with them from home an appropriate outfit:

> Necessary items to be provided by novices newly entering the religious life. Two shirts, a mattress, two pairs of blankets, two pairs of bed covers, three coverlets, a fur coverlet, a blue cloth of wool, a cowl and frock, a black tunic, furred, and another plain one, two white tunics, a black furred hood, and another, plain, a belt and pouch containing a knife, writing tablets, a comb, needle and thread, a small night belt, three shirts, four pairs of breeches with waistband and thongs, two pairs of stockings, four pairs of socks, two pairs of day boots and one pair for night, a leather jacket, three pairs of handkerchiefs, three pillows, a white night cap, two towels, a bag for dirty clothes, a shaving cloth, a bowl, a glass cup, and a silver spoon.[31]

Judging by the visitation documents published by Seiriol Evans, it is clear that the whole convent, laymen as well as monks, lived according to the Benedictine rule. There are several repetitions of the need for silence to be observed at all times, except in the parlour which was specifically set aside for conversation, and for which a keeper was responsible. Visitors, and especially females, were excluded from the community. The life of the house was regulated by the sound of the bell of the convent clock, which was certainly in existence from the mid-thirteenth century. There were some servants permanently resident in the house, distinguished from the professed religious by their dress, which was provided for them by the chamberlain. While the monks wore black, the servants had clothes of deep or light green, with blue for pages; they wore black at funerals. These house-servants were, as far as can be determined, three bell-ringers, three clerks who kept the three altars within the church, two servants in the kitchen, two others in the bakery, a doorkeeper of the parlour, a bath keeper, a barber, a brewer, a janitor, a tailor, a stabler, the master of the almonry boys and a launderer. There were also unspecified numbers of clerks and gentlemen attending on the Prior, and they too wore their convent's green and blue livery. Those going out of the house on official convent business were provided by the chamberlain with a horse, horse trappings, bridle and spurs. It is not clear how many assistants were called for by such departments as the kitchens and tailor shops, but they were obviously fairly numerous, and so, too, must have been the assistants in such labour-intensive areas as the laundry, the brewery and the bakery.

---

[29] See Greatrex, below, p. 78.

[30] R. Bowers, 'The Almonry Schools of the English Monasteries *c.*1265–1540', in Benjamin Thompson (ed.), *Monasteries and Society in Medieval Britain. Proceedings of the 1994 Harlaxton Symposium*, Harlaxton Medieval Studies, 6 (Stamford, 1999), pp. 177–222.

[31] Stewart, *Ely*, p. 232, quoting from LPL, MS 448, fo. 106ᵛ.

The visitation injunctions make it clear that the nightly awakening of the convent for service was accomplished in the dark and in silence. A cresset light and service books were kept in the choir, to fortify the memory of the forgetful, but the persistent chatterers were to be punished by a diet of bread and water, or bread and pottage. There was to be no ribald conversation with the pilgrims who came to St Audrey's feast or to the fair. Conversation with females (called invariably 'suspect') was forbidden, and so too were private drinking parties. All the monks were to sleep in the dormitory in separate beds.[32]

A regular break in the routine was provided by the bloodlettings (*minuciones*), which were organised by the senior officials of the house at five-weekly intervals.[33] They seem in some cases to have taken place in one or other of the nearby granges such as Turbutsey, but in the later medieval period they appear to have been held on the convent's own site, in a building specially provided, now known as Powcher's Hall. For these occasions special food was bought in: salt fish, oysters, eels, rabbits, pigeons, beef, veal, geese, eggs, cheese and butter. As in other religious houses the rule of silence, enforced especially in the refectory, was slightly mitigated by a series of signs, parts of which have survived in a manuscript once in the convent library. The sign-language portion of this has been transcribed by David Sherlock and William Zajac.[34] Signs were provided for such things as service books, food and drink, personal clothing and items from the dormitory. Mr Sherlock concludes from his detailed study of the list that the novices learned the signs from their novicemasters.

Clearly, many of the signs that are listed were for use in the refectory and the kitchen. In the earlier days of the community each of the obedientiary households seems to have had its own kitchen and refectory, but after Archbishop Arundel's visitation injunctions of 1403[35] the cellarer was required to provide for the refectory, the Prior's household, the guests, the bloodlettings, and the *recreaciones* of the house. These departments were on the south and east sides of the Cathedral; the sacristy and the almonry, to the north, were allowed to keep their separate kitchens.[36] Guests were all to be accommodated in the Prior's house, the Prior's hall or in the guest chamber, and relatives of the members of the community were to be housed similarly. Equally the old customary measures of bread and ale provided for the brethren were to be adjusted so that a sufficiency was available for all. All distributions of food and clothes and clothes money, and the giving of clothes as alms to relatives and friends, were forbidden.

There were throughout the convent's existence statutory provisions for servants. The numbers of servants who were part of the establishment, and who were not professed religious, were approximately as follows: twenty-one in the Prior's household, seven in the almonry, with schoolboys, six in the hostelry, three in the church (provided by the sacrist), six in the sacrist's office and six in his hospice. The cellarer had four servants, the chamberlain had one, the precentor two, and the infirmarian three.[37]

---

[32] *Ibid.*

[33] For an account of Ely Priory blood-letting practices see J.W. Clark (ed.), *The Observances in Use at the Augustinian Priory of S. Giles and S. Andrew at Barnwell, Cambridgeshire* (Cambridge, 1897), pp. lxiv–lxv.

[34] D. Sherlock, *Signs for Silence: The Sign Language of the Monks of Ely in the Middle Ages* (Ely, 1992); from LPL, MS 448, fos. 103ᵛ–105ᵛ.

[35] Evans, *Ordinances*, pp. 52–6, from Archbishop Arundel's register, Lambeth Palace Library.

[36] *Ibid.*, pp. xiv–xv.

[37] *Ibid.*, p. xi, an estimate by Evans based on a study of the account rolls.

Visitors to the house, apart from high-status individuals with political or economic business with the Prior or other higher officials, were sometimes relatives of the monks, sometimes merchants who had business with the house. Or they might be players or singers hired to provide entertainment at the greater festivals or to commemorate the installation of a prior or subprior. To provide these potential visitors with food was the business of the principal kitchen of the Priory, for which purchases were made by the Prior's servants.

It is also fairly easy to find some information about the food consumed in the refectory, chiefly from the accounts of purchases made for the kitchen by the cellarer, pittancer and infirmarian.[38] The Benedictine rule prescribed just one or at most two meals per day, with two separate main dishes, neither to include flesh. To these might be added such seasonal fruit and fresh vegetables as were available. The number of kitchens maintained was sharply reduced after 1401 when the establishments of the cellarer and the infirmarer were combined with those of the steward and hosteller.[39] Each kitchen retained a cook and a pottager, who supplied the basic soup or stew which all consumed, and each bought its own supplies, many of which came from the Priory's own resources. Grains and pulses were organised and cooked by the granator, who was also the baker of bread and pastry. Milk, eggs and cheese came from the nearby granges. Fresh fish was bought from the weirs on the Ouse, or was caught in the Priory's fish ponds which lay to the south of the cellarer's establishment, in the centre of the precinct. Dried and salted fish was procured annually from Lynn or from the Norfolk fishing ports, especially Cromer. No vegetables, except occasionally onions and garlic, were bought, and the convent's pottage was plainly supplied from the monastic gardens. Daily, except in Lent, a snack of bread and a warm drink was served in the morning or at night.

Wednesday, Friday and often Saturday were fish days; meat could in practice be produced on other days. There was always a choice of two main dishes: these included dishes made of pulse, milk, cheese or eggs. It was for this course that milk puddings called tansies, and also cheese cakes or flauns, were regularly made. Pottage, from a vegetable or perhaps a meat base with black peas in Lent, white peas or beans, was regularly served, with leeks and cabbage as principal ingredients. In one week in 1352 the provisions used in the refectory can be seen from the cellarer's accounts, and were as follows:

> Sunday: dinner, meat (rissoles and pancakes) or eggs; supper, fresh fish or eggs.
> Monday: dinner and supper, turbot or eggs.
> Tuesday: meat and eggs for batter and fresh fish.
> Wednesday: whelks, eggs; supper, milk and fresh fish.
> Thursday: rissoles, eggs.
> Friday: white herrings, eggs.
> Saturday: eels with pepper, cumin and saffron.

Varieties of fish mentioned in the accounts are dried cod, salted herrings, dried salmon, sturgeon, turbot, porpoise, plaice, haddock, oysters, crabs and whelks, and they seem to have been fried, baked with spices or frumenty, or dressed raw with verjuice.[40]

---

[38] Their account rolls are EDC 1/F/2, 1/F/8 and 1/F/14.
[39] Evans, *Ordinances*, p. 54, Archbishop Arundel's visitation 1401.
[40] EDC 1/F/2/14, cellarer's accounts, 1352.

Figure 4. T.D. Atkinson, reconstruction of the shrine of St Etheldreda (VCH, *Cambs.*, IV, p. 71)

The cult of St Etheldreda[41]

Ely was fortunate among English cathedrals in having a saint of such renown as Etheldreda, and her shrine in the eastern arm of the Cathedral was an object of veneration and a source of income for the Priory throughout the medieval period. The care and upkeep of the shrine or *feretrum* was the particular responsibility of the feretrar, who kept separate accounts, although they were subsidiary to those of the sacrist, who had overall control of the Cathedral church, its fabric and finances, and who entered the feretrar's accounts in his own.[42]

The shrine stood in the centre of the Cathedral's eastern arm, and a boss in the choir vault featuring St Etheldreda probably marks the spot (Colour pl. 17*b*). Its appearance is imperfectly known, for like all other shrines, it was despoiled and broken up after the Dissolution. Certainly the coffin, traditionally of white marble, was raised on a stone, columned base. The superstructure and the decoration changed over the years, but they were always costly.[43] St Etheldreda was translated into the newly built presbytery in

---

[41] This section is added by Peter Meadows. For the furniture, organisation and finances of the cult of St Etheldreda, see especially Ben Nilson, *Cathedral Shrines of Medieval England* (Woodbridge, 1998), *passim.*

[42] Nilson, *Shrines*, p. 155. The sacrist's roll for 1372, for example, contains the item 'to the shrine of St Etheldreda by tally against brother Simon of Banham' (EDC 1/F/10/18). Banham was feretrar in 1371 (Greatrex, *BRECP*, p. 389).

[43] In 1144 Bishop Nigel requested 200 marks from the Priory in order to pay a royal fine, and this was provided

1252, and the dedication of the Cathedral was changed in her honour in that year.[44] Ben Nilson gives a description of the decoration in the second quarter of the twelfth century:

> The surface of the shrine . . . was of silver plate with figures in high relief, some gilded and some not, and set with beryls, onyxes, alemandines, pearls, amethysts, carnelians, sardines, emeralds, and one topaz. By far the most common stone . . . was 'crystal' (presumably quartz). On the east side were two crystal lions and other images, and the two sides supported sixteen figures each. On the western face were two images, including a majesty and a cross that was probably fixed to the apex of the lid.[45]

Over this was a wooden cover. In 1455 a new cover cost £12 7s. 6d. for carpentry, painting, gilt, nails, and a lining of linen cloth.[46] The accounts of John of Soham, feretrar in that year, list payments to the painter Robert Pygot in connection with this canopy. Included in the total payment seems to have been a new reredos for the shrine altar which backed on to the high altar. Painted panels that are probably from this reredos, illustrating scenes from Etheldreda's life, were discovered by James Bentham in the 1780s, forming cupboard doors in a cottage in Ely. Bentham presented them to the Society of Antiquaries of London, where they remain[47] (Colour pl. 20).

In addition to the legalised pillaging of the shrine for taxation purposes, and despite the fact that it was in the midst of a guarded cathedral in a monastic precinct, the shrine was nevertheless sometimes the object of attack by robbers. In 1324 they stole a large golden cross, traditionally the gift to the Cathedral of King Edgar; but the feretrar followed the thieves to London and retrieved the cross.[48] Another theft was recorded in 1385.[49]

Around the shrine were arranged the tombs of Etheldreda's saintly family; and objects of lesser devotion, such as the shackles, hung on the pillars of the presbytery.[50] On the east, north and south sides the shrine-area was enclosed by iron screens and tombs (the eastern arm of the Cathedral was the burial place of bishops and priors[51]), and on the west by the high altar reredos.[52]

---

largely by stripping silver from St Etheldreda's shrine (*LE*, iii. 89: p. 335; Nilson, *Shrines*, p. 140). In return Nigel endowed the shrine with the manor of Hadstock.

[44] BL, MS Harl. 3721, fo. 37 (*Chronicon Ecclesiae Eliensis*).

[45] Nilson, *Shrines*, pp. 37, 39, summarised from *LE*. For a translation of the *LE* inventory, see Simon Keynes, above, pp. 54–5. The variety of semi-precious stones was probably the result of offerings of jewellery at the shrine.

[46] Stewart, *Ely*, p. 131; Nilson, *Shrines*, p. 41.

[47] J. Fletcher, 'Four Scenes from the Life of St Etheldreda', *Antiquaries Journal*, liv (1974), pp. 287–9.

[48] Chapman, *Sacrist Rolls*, II, p. 31: 'Item to Brother Robert de Rickling for going to London to look for the silver and gold stolen from the feretrum'.

[49] CUL, EDR G1/2, fo. 54 (Register of Bishop Arundel). The thieves removed the wooden cover, broke the locks and stole rings and other jewels. The Bishop excommunicated them *in absentia*.

[50] The fetters hung up by a prisoner, Bricstan of Chatteris, who in 1116 was miraculously set free by St Etheldreda's and St Benedict's intervention: *LE*, iii. 33: pp. 266–9.

[51] For the monuments in the presbytery see N. Pevsner, *The Buildings of England: Cambridgeshire*, 2nd edn (Harmondsworth, 1970), pp. 364–9 and E. Esdaile, *The Monuments in Ely Cathedral* (Ely, 1973). Nigel (Bishop, 1133–69) was buried in the nave, next to the altar of the Holy Cross, at the east end; a Tournai marble slab, depicting a winged figure of the Archangel Michael holding the soul of the deceased Bishop, the lower part broken away and lost, which is thought to have been Nigel's, was found upturned in the floor of St Mary's church, Ely, in 1829, and now lies in the north choir aisle (Plate 12a); see S. Inskip Ladds, 'The Tournai Slab at Ely', *Trans., Cambs. & Hunts. Archaeol. Soc.*, V (1937), pp. 177–80. Hugh of Northwold (Bishop, 1229–54) and his successor William of Kilkenny (Bishop, 1154–6) were commemorated with similar monuments of Purbeck marble, recumbent effigies under canopies. Northwold's figure is flanked by a trio of cusped niches, each with a

Except at Mass times, pilgrims were admitted to the Cathedral to visit and venerate the shrine. Access to the shrine area was supervised by the feretrar and his clerk and deputies, who acted as guides. The almonry schoolboys were frequently employed to announce the opening of the shrine-area.[53] The feretrar's chamber seems to have been on the north side of the presbytery, perhaps near the 'processional way', which was the pilgrims' route to the Lady Chapel.[54] A 'watcher' was supposed to be on duty at the shrine 'all night and day', but this, evidently, was not enough to prevent the occasional burglary.[55]

It is thought that pilgrims entered the Cathedral by the door in the north transept[56] and proceeded past the stone wall backing the choir stalls, where there were mural paintings depicting the seven Saxon benefactors whose bones were preserved in niches there (Plate 9b). Entering the north choir aisle, they would pass under the raised passage which took the monks from their choir to the Lady Chapel, and would then enter the shrine area. Having made their devotion, inspected the rest of the presbytery, and perhaps visited the Lady Chapel, the pilgrims must have retraced their steps and exited by the same north transept door. Departure by the south was impossible, for the living quarters of the monks were located there.

Pilgrims were expected to leave an offering at Etheldreda's shrine, light a candle and perhaps obtain a keepsake of their visit. The offering might be money, or possibly a jewel. A candle of fragrant beeswax could usually be obtained in the Cathedral. Ely offered them at 4d. per pound; other cathedrals charged 6d. or 7d.[57] It is not clear whether the souvenir unique to Ely, 'St Audrey's chains', a brightly coloured silk necklace, was sold in the Cathedral as well as at the twice-yearly fair outside the precinct, although sales of silk are certainly shown in the feretrar's rolls.[58] There is no evidence of the common pilgrims' badges being sold at Ely.[59]

The feretrar's rolls of William Tylney (shrine-keeper, 1464–77) reveal, for the late

---

saint, and below his feet, a sculpture of the martyrdom of St Edmund (Plate 12b); see M. Roberts, 'The Effigy of Bishop Hugh de Northwold in Ely Cathedral', *Burlington Magazine*, cxxx (1988), pp. 77–84; Kilkenny's is similar but plainer: over his vestment he wears a Rationale, alluding to Aaron's breastplate, and his figure is flanked by censing angels (Plate 12c). Of quite a different order is the monument to William de Luda, on the south side of the presbytery: the tomb-chest is surmounted by a tripartite pillared canopy, crowned with gables and pinnacles (Plate 12d). This is so similar to the monument of Edmund Crouchback, Earl of Lancaster (d.1296), in Westminster Abbey that the same masons must have been responsible. See Phillip Lindley, 'The Tomb of Bishop William de Luda: An Architectural Model at Ely Cathedral', *PCAS*, lxxii (1984), pp. 75–87.

[52] VCH, *Cambs.*, IV, p. 70; Nilson, *Shrines*, p. 98. The sacrist's roll for 1349–50 mentions a door in the iron screen: 'Item for one pair of hinges for the wicket across from the shrine'.

[53] *E.g.* EDC 1/F/12/4, 1425–6, 'for four scholars helping in the time of the fair, for calling pilgrims and minding wax – 2s.'

[54] An undated fabric roll for the feretrar's buildings (EDC 1/F/12/6) locates his chamber on the north side 'opposite the doors of the shrine of St Etheldreda'; Nilson, *Shrines*, p. 98.

[55] *LE*, iii. 58: p. 306, *'totaque nocte et die'*.

[56] Atkinson, *Ely Monastery*, p. 28.

[57] EDC 1/F/12/1. The feretrars recorded receipt of offerings and sales of candles in their account rolls. Nilson, *Shrines*, p. 105.

[58] 'St Audrey's chain' is supposed to be the origin of the word 'tawdry'. Stewart, *Ely*, p. 190: 'Our women of England are accustomed to bear on the neck a certain necklace, bound and subtly made of silk, which they call the necklace of Etheldreda' – translated from the Latin of Nicholas Harpsfield, *Historia Anglicana Ecclesiastica*, ed. E. Campion (London, 1622), p. 86.

[59] B.W. Spencer, 'Medieval Pilgrim Badges', *Rotterdam Papers*, 1 (Rotterdam, 1968), pp. 137–53.

fifteenth century at least, something of the fluctuating numbers of visitors to the shrine through the year, for he divided his account of the offerings received into five seasonal sections.[60] Not surprisingly, the peak times for visits seem to have been around the time of the two fairs, in June and October; and pilgrimages in winter, when the Isle of Ely was usually impassable, were few and far between[61] (Colour pl. 2a).

Nilson's account of the Ely shrine reveals that, as a source of Priory income, the fortunes of the shrine fluctuated more or less in accordance with the fortunes of shrines elsewhere. 'For most times in most places the shrine offerings were a noticeable if not crucial element of church revenue.'[62] Over the medieval period, shrine income at Ely averaged about £50 *per annum*, or about four *per cent* of total Priory income. It rose gradually in the late fourteenth century to a high point of £94 9s. 10d in 1408–9, and then declined inexorably during the fifteenth century, though less dramatically, it seems, than in other cathedrals and monasteries.[63]

Monastery and town[64]

The monastic enclosure was bounded on the west by the Gallery, on the north by Steeple Row and Fore Hill, on the east by Castle or Broad Lane, and on the south by Back Hill (Plate 21a). At first there seem to have been two gates: one in Broad Lane, emerging into the monastic vineyard, and another (Almonry Gate) on the summit of the Fore Hill, where the market seems to have been held, and through which the dependents of the almonry had access to the daily distribution of alms.[65] Later, two further gates were formed on the north side. Steeple Gate, where there was a tower of St Peter, recorded as having been struck by a thunderbolt in 1111,[66] was the entrance for parishioners of Holy Cross church, and, later of Holy Trinity, when it was established in the Lady Chapel in 1566. Steeple Gate housed the parish bell. Sacrist's Yard Gate was for the use of the sacrist and his workmen.

There were two manors: the Bishop's manor of Ely Barton, and the Prior and convent's manor, which became known as Ely Porta when the great south-west gatehouse was built in the fourteenth century, and the manorial courts began to be held in its upper chamber (Colour pl. 6a). Broadly speaking, Ely Barton lay to the west and south of the monastic precinct, Ely Porta to the north and east; but in practice both manors had tenements, closes, hithes and rights scattered through the town.

Most of the traffic into and out of the town, and all the goods brought in for sale, came by water to the hithes east of Broad Lane, where the cut in the Ouse had brought

---

[60] Michaelmas to Fair (mid-October); Fair to Christmas; Christmas to Easter; Easter to 24 June; 25 June to time of indulgence (forty days granted by Pope Innocent IV to cover the feast of the dedication – see Evans, *Ordinances*, p. 39 n.)

[61] Nilson, *Shrines*, p. 115.

[62] *Ibid.*, p. 182.

[63] *Ibid.*, pp. 170–1. The feretrar's accounts are not a continuous sequence, so individual high or low years might have occurred to distort this pattern. See the tables of receipts recorded in the sacrist's and feretrar's rolls, *ibid.*, pp. 216–7.

[64] This section is an abridged and rearranged version of part of D.M. Owen, *The Medieval Development of the Town of Ely* (Ely, 1993).

[65] And where a meeting of the hundred of Ely was once held: VCH, *Cambs.*, IV, p. 5, quoting from *LE*, ii. 12: p. 91.

[66] *LE*, iii. 28: p. 264.

the river close to the foot of Ely's hill. Here was a network of narrow lanes leading to the warehouses and hithes. It seems likely that the area available as strand was increased by tipping and embanking, as was certainly done at Lynn: a late twelfth-century grant of eighteen roods of land on the hithe conveys to the grantee 'all the increase he can gain as far as his neighbours do'.[67] Here too was the important bridge leading across the river to the causeway over the fen, which ran on to Soham and thence to the higher ground to the east. After the turmoil of King Stephen's reign (1135–54), this commercial quarter grew rapidly. On the west side of Broad Lane, as early as 1163 × 77, Prior Solomon had conveyed sites for two dwellings beyond the vineyard,[68] and before the end of the century a plot on the same side was bequeathed by John the Chapman. At various points along the west side were pits or ponds used by tanners and also a horse mill which was granted by Walter de Snayleswell to the almoner in the early thirteenth century.[69]

The survival of original Priory charters or cartulary copies of grants has been irregular, and by no means all the growth in the town and its population can be documented. One significant hint is Bishop Hugh of Balsham's order (c.1258 × 86) forbidding the sacrist to continue to give a candle at Candlemas to each inhabitant because the increasing multitude of citizens would require 700 pounds of wax.[70] However, the best clues to the numbers of inhabitants and the spread of the town are to be found in surveys of the episcopal manor of Ely Barton made in 1222 and 1251. There was also a complete enumeration of houses in 1417, when the division of properties in the town between Bishop and monastic officials was finally settled, and a survey of Priory holdings was made in 1522–3. With the help of these full descriptions and other indications from obedientiary accounts it is possible to see how the town and its inhabitants waxed and waned.

The 1222 episcopal survey[71] opens with a list of the unbuilt areas of episcopal demesne, and a series of ten fisheries. This is followed by the names of dwellings belonging to the five knight's fees of Simon de Insula, Warin de Saham, Henry Pelrin, Stephen de Marisco and William Muschet. 144 free tenants held 161 dwellings 'across the water'. 13 tenants held between them 16 butchers' stalls. There were also customary tenants whose names are not given: 31 holders of full lands, 18 holders of half lands, 97 cottagers, including a number of widows, and 2 millers and 2 weavers.

The 1251 survey of episcopal properties[72] has little to add to that of 1222 except the names of a series of marshes, two windmills, and the four chaplains celebrating for the King and the Bishop (the Chantry on the Green, founded 1250). Many of the episcopal properties were already held or occupied by one or other obedientiary, and especially by the cellarer, the almoner and the keeper of the Lady Chapel. At the outset there seems to have been uncertainty about the lines of division originally drawn up at the creation of the bishopric, and by the early fifteenth century it was unclear what belonged to the Bishop and what to the Priory. There were evidently disputes, and an attempt to resolve them was made in 1417 by a renewal of the respective rentals made by Richard

[67] EDC 1/A/2, almoner's cartulary, fo. 1.
[68] BL, MS Egerton 3047, fo. 108[v].
[69] EDC 1/A/2, fo. 69.
[70] EDR G3/28, fo. 203.
[71] BL, MS Cotton Tiberius B. ii, fos. 86–231.
[72] EDR G3/27, 'The Old Coucher'.

Hildersham, clerk of the King's privy seal. This was followed by an inquest conducted by Robert Wetheringsete, Archdeacon of Ely, and Peter, monk of Ely, who were commissaries for three arbiters agreed by the Bishop and the Prior: Henry Ware, keeper of the King's privy seal, William Hankeford, chief justice of the King's Bench, and Roger Horton, justice of the same Bench.[73] Copies of the inquest were attached to an indenture of agreement signed by all parties. The inquest provided detailed lists of all the properties in the town, identified by 'P' (for *Prioratus*) or 'Ep' (for *Episcopatus*), and arranged systematically under the names of the roads, so that we have a complete directory of the town for this year.

The final listing of Ely properties is a rental of Priory properties made in the year 1522–3;[74] this throws some light on the fabric of the various structures. A tenement of the almoner on Broad Hithe is said to stand on a stone step, and on the east side of Broad Lane, the treasurer had Le Bordidhows, which suggests an elaborate timber building. Several inns are named: Le Spure and Le Cron in Broad Lane, Le Shipe at Broad Hithe, Le Angel at Croyes Lane leading down to Castle Hithe, and Le Swan in Walpole Lane. Other landmarks include Le Scolhous in Walpole Lane,[75] the well of St Etheldreda (first mentioned in 1251), in Potter Lane, a horsemill belonging to the almoner on Back Hill, and the Common Pinfold, which was situated at the corner of Cattes Lane and Akreman Street. Two monastic storeyards stood in Broad Lane. The barns of the almoner and sacrist are mentioned, and the general impression given is of a more exclusively agricultural community than that of the thirteenth century.

The area around and to the west of the episcopal palace was largely the sacrist's responsibility, through his oversight of the two parishes of Ely. By a charter of *c*.1109[76] Bishop Hervey granted to the sacrist in perpetuity the church of St Mary and the tithe of the Barton which belonged to it. There was already a nave altar at the Cross (*ad crucem*) with its officiating priest in the Priory church, and this served the lay population of the Priory, so that St Mary's, to the west of the monastic enclosure, was plainly intended for the bishop's tenants. Certainly by 1280, and probably well before, the sacrist had, close to St Mary's, his barn from which the farming operations of the monastic rectory were directed and into which the produce of tithes was collected. This, the 'Sextry (Sacristy) barn', an imposing erection which until the mid-sixteenth century was roofed with lead and afterwards thatched with reeds, stood on the site of the present-day Parson's almshouses[77] (Plate 21*b*). Its connection with the sacrist's headquarters in Steeple Row would have been via the green before the palace, until *c*.1400 Prior Walpole built the southern gate, the Porta, and so gave direct access to the inner barn, brewhouse, bakehouse and mill which were maintained in that part of the precinct by the chamberlain and granator. This sacrist's property was matched by the establishment in the thirteenth century of an almonry grange ('Aumbry Barns') at the north-west corner of High Row (High Street) from which the scattered town properties of the almonry were administered.

[73] BL, MS Cotton Vespasian A. xix, fos. 61–102.

[74] EDC 1/C/7, rental of priory properties, 1522–3.

[75] This was the town grammar school from which pupils emerged to make a riot with some of the young monks in 1527. PRO, STAC 2/17/223, petition of Thomas Dale of Semer, 12 September 1527, transcribed in Owen and Thurley, *King's School*, pp. 26–7.

[76] EDC 1/B/51.

[77] R. Willis, *A Description of the Sextry Barn at Ely, lately Demolished*, CAS, Quarto Publications, 7 (1843).

It seems likely (though it cannot be proved) that a weekly market was held outside the monastery's north gate continuously from at least the re-establishment of 970. In the early nineteenth century, when the market day was said to have been recently changed from Saturday to Thursday, the market itself was said to be held not by a charter but by prescriptive right.[78] Development of the area leading into the market place (Steeple Row and High Row) began in the early years of the See, and certainly by the time of Henry II's reign (1154–89). The enterprise was undoubtedly the Bishop's and took the form of the erection of booths, shops or stalls: first of all two on each side of St Peter's tower and later at least six on the opposite side of the road. These erections on the south side backed on to the northern wall of the lay cemetery; on the north side they formed the first stages of an infilled commercial area between the two streets leading east to the market-place, where subsequently the butchers' shambles were sited.

The Bishop's manor of Ely Barton was probably already in existence in Bishop Hervey's time, as soon as the division of the church lands had been made, and it lay on the south, west and north of the Priory. Everything to the west of the Gallery was in episcopal hands. We know, for example, that for fear of fire Bishop Nigel removed houses which stood too close to the west front of the cathedral, and that when Bishop Eustace built the *porticus* by which he went from his palace to the Priory, the bishopric still held land between the monks' refectory and the *porticus,* on which he allowed the convent to construct a cellar for ale.[79]

An early episcopal move to exploit the Barton estate began with the establishment of a fair. Henry I was induced to grant to the church of Ely and to Hervey the Bishop a seven-day fair, on St Etheldreda's feast and for three days before and after.[80] The importance of such an opportunity for regular trade was immense. It was intended in part, no doubt, to serve the needs of the Bishop himself for food, articles of luxury and building materials, and even more to provide for the Priory's omnivorous appetite for wood, stone, lead and glass to complete the new building of the church. In fact the clue is probably given by another charter of Henry I, this time to the Prior and convent, quitting them of all customs and tolls on timber, lead, iron and stone for the new building.[81] Those attending the fair seem to have set up their stalls or booths wherever there was spare ground. The lay cemetery seems to have been much used for the purpose, and the Broad Hithe was lined with them: the sacrist regularly accounted for rent of stalls on the Broad Hithe at fair time.[82] The precentor's accounts for early in Edward III's reign record receipts from booths in St Mary's parish, presumably built in front of dwellings belonging to the precentor. The cellarer in 1339 was putting up new booths near the monks' vineyard, and the almoner had in 1339 seven shops projecting from his walls into the market-place which seem to have been let at fair time. The seven-day October mart, another granted to the Prior and convent in 1312 for fifteen days at St Lambert (17 September) and a third, accorded to the Bishop in 1318, for twenty-two days beginning at the vigil of the Ascension,[83] provided ample opportunity for traders

---

[78] D. and S. Lysons, *Magna Britannia*, vol. II part 1 (London, 1808), p. 189.
[79] EDC 1/B/59. Eustace was Bishop, 1198–1215.
[80] Bentham, *Ely*, App.18* no. XIII (from EDR G3/28, p. 84).
[81] *Ibid.*, nos. XI (from EDR G3/28, p. 80) and XII (from *LE* iii. 21: p. 259).
[82] Chapman, *Sacrist's Rolls*, I, p. 124.
[83] VCH, *Cambs.*, IV, p. 50.

coming downstream from Cambridge, across the fen from Norfolk and Suffolk via the lodes, and upstream from Lynn and the Midlands.

The last years of Ely Priory[84]

The final decades of the Priory's existence are not well documented. Robert Wells or Steward was elected Prior in 1522 and guided the Priory and then the refounded Cathedral through the changes and chances of the Reformation and the Marian reaction until his death in 1557. It is a pity that we do not know more about this adroit character.

In 1515, during the vacancy-in-see following the death of Bishop James Stanley, William Fayrhaer, Vicar-General of Archbishop William Warham, conducted the final visitation of the Priory for which details survive.[85] No great misdemeanours were uncovered. The Prior was accused of spending over-much money on the estates, including Shippea Manor, where he could reside at less expense than in the Priory. The almoner was accused of feeding his workmen better than his secular priests; the granator was accused of supplying ale not fit for pigs to his servants, many of whom had left, and of withdrawing after-supper drinks from the monks, forcing them to send out into the town for it.[86]

Not long before Bishop Goodrich's visitation in 1534 ten young monks were admitted.[87] As Joan Greatrex has observed, 'an influx of young men drawn to the monastic life at Ely and professed within a space of only a few years speaks well for its internal regime and its external influence in the surrounding community.'[88] The monastic services were probably carried on satisfactorily. Indeed, the list of pensions awarded in 1539 specifically refers to four former monks as good choir men.[89] From 1533 change was in the air, and in 1535 Bishop Goodrich ordered the expunging of all references to the Pope from books in the Priory and diocese.[90] Ely escaped the dissolution of the smaller religious houses in 1536; it would be reasonable to assume that Prior Steward's visits to London in 1535–6[91] were in connexion with negotiations about the orderly surrender of the Priory when the time came, and for the award of favourable terms for the monks. In 1534 there were thirty-three monks; by 1539 the number had dwindled to twenty-four.

Of the twenty-three monks who (with the Prior) signed the deed of surrender,[92]

---

[84] This section is added by Peter Meadows.

[85] LPL, Register of Abp Warham, II, fo. 277. There was a further visitation by Bishop Goodrich in 1534 (EDR G1/7, Register of Bp Goodrich, fo. 3ᵛ).

[86] Evans, *Ordinances*, pp. 65–7.

[87] EDR G1/7, Reg. Goodrich, fo. 3ᵛ. The last ten names on the visitation list lack the title *dominus*, probably because they were not yet ordained priest. Five of these ten did not sign the surrender document in 1539 (John Hadenham, William Braunche, Gilbert Croxton, John Braffeld, and Lancelot Ely), presumably because they had died or gone elsewhere. There is no indication that they became beneficed clergymen (J. Foster, *Index Ecclesiasticus*, CUL, MS Add. 6750).

[88] Greatrex, *BRECP*, p. 383.

[89] *LP Henry VIII*, XIV, pt 2, p. 542. William Sewall, John Skelsyn and John Bury became minor canons; Robert Derham was not kept on, and his career is untraced.

[90] EDR G1/7, fo. 25. It was perhaps at this point that the name of the Pope was scored out of *Liber Eliensis*, together with that of St Thomas Becket.

[91] See p. 400, n. 37.

[92] Stevenson, *Supplement*, pp. 55–6, n. The original deed of surrender was examined and copied by James

fourteen became Canons, minor canons (or vicars choral), gospeller and epistoler in the New Foundation. All the monks received pensions. Of the nine monks not found posts in the Cathedral, two, Thomas Soham and Robert Sutton, were described in the list of pensions as 'an old man and weak' and 'aged and very sick' respectively.[93] Six probably became beneficed clergymen.[94] The careers of three, Thomas Agarston, Robert Derham and Thomas Soham or Nex, have not been fully traced. The first two were probably young;[95] but Thomas Soham had been made deacon in 1494, and had been subprior as recently as 1534.[96] Probably he died soon after the Dissolution.[97]

So ended eight hundred years of Ely monasticism; and those former monks ordered to remain watched and waited for the King's decision as to the future of his 'House' at Ely.

Bentham on 16 November 1744, when it was owned by Charles Parkin (1690–1765), Rector of Oxburgh, Norfolk 1717–65 (CUL, MS Add. 2957, fos. 166ᵛ–168). It was shown to Bentham by Samuel Knight (*q.v.* below, p. 273 and n. 79). On 8 July 1772 a copy was shown to Bentham by Thomas Watkins, precentor and registrar, when Bentham noted (fo. 166ᵛ) that Parkin was 'said to have left his curious writings to Pembroke Hall in Cambridge; where probably it may be deposited'. There are several monastic deeds of surrender at Pembroke College today, but there is no trace of the Ely document. Sir Ellis Minns listed the Parkin MSS in the 1890s, and the Ely surrender was not noted then. Possibly Samuel Knight never returned it to Parkin. I am grateful to Jayne Ringrose for information about the Parkin MSS.

[93] Thomas Soham has been confused with John Soham, ordained subdeacon in 1476 (EDR G1/5, fo. 216ᵛ); but John Soham had died before 1515, since he was not on Archbishop Warham's visitation list (LPL, Reg. Warham, II, fo. 277). Robert Sutton seems to have recovered, however, since the accounts show that he continued to receive his pension until 1552.

[94] William Hand became Rector of Brandon, Suffolk, and was deprived in 1554. William Wisbech or Salabanke was Rector of Whitton, Suffolk, was married and so was deprived in 1554, restored in 1559, and resigned in 1561; he was Rector of Creeting St Mary, 1560–75 (G. Baskerville, 'Married Clergy and Pensioned Religious in Norwich Diocese, 1555', *Eng. Hist. Rev.*, 48 (1933), pp. 60, 63, 218). Thomas Wilburton or Outlaw was for a few years 'divinity student' in the Cathedral until that post was abolished; he was (unmarried) Rector of Claxby, Lincs., 1551–75 (G.A.J. Hodgett, *The State of the Ex-religious and Former Chantry Priests in the Diocese of Lincoln 1547–1574* (Lincoln Record Society, 53, 1959). Details of these three are *ex inf.* Peter Cunich. Richard Denys was possibly Vicar of Hagnaby, Lincs., 1548–55; Thomas Over was possibly Rector of Kincote, Leicestershire, 1544–84; and John Whitby was probably Rector of Earl Stonham, 1548–56. J. Foster, *Index Ecclesiasticus*, CUL, MS Add. 6750.

[95] Agarston's pension was paid until Michaelmas 1546, so he probably died soon after this date. Robert Derham's pension was paid until 1553 at least.

[96] EDR G1/7, fo. 90ᵛ.

[97] PRO, LR 6/55/8, receiver's account, 1539–40, indicates that none of his pension was ever paid to him.

Benedictine Observance at Ely:
The Intellectual, Liturgical
and Spiritual Evidence Considered

JOAN GREATREX

At the time of the transition from Abbey to Cathedral Priory, a monastic community at Ely had been in existence for over four centuries. With the arrival of a Bishop as head of a newly created diocese, the monastic church became his Cathedral while he was the titular Abbot of the monastic chapter. From 1109, therefore, Ely was numbered with the other seven cathedral priories in England which had been instituted in the eleventh century by Lanfranc, the Norman abbot whom William the Conqueror had appointed as Archbishop of Canterbury.[1] Prior to this date the Abbey at Ely had claimed exemption from episcopal jurisdiction; it now had its own episcopal overseer who was often in close proximity to it and whose authority over its monks was a constant and ever present reality in chapter affairs.[2] The adjustments that must have been made by the seventy or so monks who experienced these traumatic changes are hidden from us, but the community under Prior Vincent (d. *c.*1128) and his successors was to continue to live the monastic life until 1539. From this period the names of 540 monks have been found in the surviving records, together with biographical details of some of their activities.[3] If we take the average span of monastic life to be twenty years and the average number of monks in the community at any one time after the Black Death to be forty, we may estimate that this figure of 540 named monks represents about 70 *per cent* of the total community; the remainder may continue to elude us because a large proportion of the medieval muniments and manuscripts of Ely Cathedral has been lost.[4] Almost 25 *per cent* of those named, however, are known to have survived as monks for twenty-five years or more, and there are unquestionably others who should be included in this category;

---

[1] The other cathedrals whose chapters consisted of Benedictine monks were Bath, Canterbury, Durham, Norwich, Rochester, Winchester and Worcester.
[2] The choice of prior and the appointment of monks to some of the obedientiary offices in the monastery, for example, were considered by the early bishops as part of their prerogative.
[3] The details are in Greatrex, *BRECP*, pp. 387–465.
[4] For a summary of the surviving muniments see D.M. Owen, 'The Muniments of Ely Cathedral Priory', in C.N.L. Brooke, D. Luscombe, G.H. Martin and D.M. Owen (eds.), *Church and Government in the Middle Ages* (Cambridge, 1976), pp. 157–76.

but the large number of missing dates of admission and of death deprives us of the desired information.

The local, or at least East Anglian, origins of most of the monks are indicated by their toponyms, or surnames, which generally denoted the towns or villages from which they came. On this assumption we know, for example, that there were at least twenty-four whose family connections were in Ely itself, while some thirteen came from Swaffham and nine from Wells.[5] Ramsey, Sutton, Wisbech and Walsingham each provided seven monks, while Lakenheath, Ixworth, Soham, Cambridge and Thetford were close behind with six each. It would seem that the inhabitants of the Isle of Ely were more closely attached to their cathedral priory than were the townsmen in more populated centres to theirs: the monastic community at Norwich, for example, included only twelve monks whose name was Norwich, just half the number of those at Ely who were named Ely.[6] Baptismal names of Ely monks also demonstrate regional peculiarities: apart from the universally popular John, Richard, Robert, William and several others, there were seven Ely monks by the name of Alan and five whose name was Laurence. Norwich Cathedral had only three Alans and one Laurence while Winchester had only one Alan (surnamed Bungey, a name that suggests an East Anglian origin) and one Laurence.[7]

It is these 540 named monks, whom we have thus ascertained to be for the most part of East Anglian parentage, who are the subject of this chapter. Three facets of monastic life at Ely have here been singled out for examination in order to elucidate the daily rhythm of activities shared by the members of the community in the later Middle Ages. The three aspects to be considered are: the monastic study programme in the cloister and the university; the monastic liturgy; and the individual monk's personal prayer and devotion.

Monastic studies in cloister and university

In common with all Benedictine monasteries, the monks of Ely were bound together in obedience to the Rule of their founder St Benedict (d. *c*.550); the reading of a passage from the Rule at the daily chapter meeting must have served as a constant reminder of the goal set before them. Yet this Rule is more appropriately described, in the words of St Benedict himself, as a guide for beginners; it was composed not only as a code of regulations but also as a series of practical exhortations directed toward the pursuit of, and perseverance in, the way of holiness through humility and mutual love.[8]

Immediately after his admission to the Cathedral Priory the aspiring monk commenced his studies. During the year of probation before he made his monastic profession he was expected to learn by heart the seventy-three chapters of the Rule, the one hundred and fifty psalms comprising the Psalter, and other portions of the

---

[5] Probably Swaffham Prior, but Wells presents a problem as there could be more than one place involved.

[6] These and other statistics provided here have been compiled from the data in Greatrex, *BRECP*.

[7] Even the nine Alans and nine Laurences at Christ Church, Canterbury, leave the Ely record unchallenged, the former having been a community twice the size of the latter. It might prove fruitful to compare Ely baptismal names with those found among the monks of Bury St Edmunds, Ramsey and Thorney when the requisite lists have been extracted from the records.

[8] The most recent edition of the Rule with lengthy notes and commentary is that by the American monk, Timothy Fry, *RB1980, The Rule of St Benedict* (Collegeville, 1981) (henceforth Fry, *RB1980*).

monastic office. Also part of the initial study programme were the novice's knowledge and understanding of the Rule, of subsequently promulgated monastic constitutions that applied to the English Benedictine houses, and of the customs in use at Ely.[9] For example, John Chelmsforth and his two brother novices, whose professions were made before Prior John de Bukton on the authorisation of the Bishop in February 1389, would have been examined beforehand on these and other learning requirements by a board of senior monks.[10] When the period of study and training had been completed, the novices petitioned for profession.[11] The actual words pronounced by every monk at his profession incorporate a threefold promise of stability, obedience and conversion of manners: this implied a lifelong commitment to remain in the Cathedral Priory, to obey the Prior unreservedly and to persevere in the daily struggle to purify the inner man.[12]

At Ely, ordination as acolyte usually followed within a few months of profession; in Chelmsforth's case it was four months after profession, but for another group of monks, Henry Madyngle and his fellow novices in 1404, it was only one month. The three major orders of subdeacon, deacon and priest were normally conferred in conformity with the minimum age requirements that were laid down for each in the canon law: seventeen, nineteen and twenty-four years respectively.[13]

If we discount possible dispensations – which allowed occasional slight, temporary adjustments, by lowering the age in a time of a shortage of priests – knowledge of these regulations enables us to estimate the ages of some of the Ely monk ordinands. Thomas Orewell, for example, who was one of the six professed with Henry Madyngle in November 1404, proceeded through the three major orders to become a priest within six months, while Madyngle remained a deacon for three years.[14] This delay is almost certainly explained by the fact that Madyngle must have been three years younger than Orewell. A scrutiny of the admittedly small number of Ely monks for whom there are records of the dates of profession and ordination encourages the suggestion that young men who applied for admission to Ely Cathedral Priory may often have been between twenty and twenty-three years of age and thus slightly older than those of Worcester and Canterbury priories, where many entered in their late teens. If some of the Ely monks received their early education in the Priory almonry school, there is no evidence for this, and it seems to have been a rare occurrence at other cathedral priories as

---

[9] One of Bishop William Gray's injunctions after his 1466 visitation concerned the instruction of novices and stated that the explanations of the texts being studied could be given in English in order to facilitate comprehension: Evans, *Ordinances*, pp. 58–9.

[10] See W.A. Pantin, *Canterbury College Oxford*, vol. iv, Oxford Historical Society, new series, xxx (1985), pp. 53–4 which describes the procedure at Christ Church, Canterbury. For Chelmsforth and Bukton see Greatrex, *BRECP*, pp. 397 and 393–4.

[11] A mid-to-late-14th-century 'exhortation' by the Prior or novice master to three novices who had so petitioned survives in the archives (EDC 1/G/1). The novices were reminded of the three requirements for the religious life laid down in canon law – obedience to superiors, renunciation of possessions and chastity of life – and were provided with references drawn from commentaries such as St Bernard's *De dispensatione et precepto*, Gregory the Great's *Moralia in Job*, Hugh of St Victor's *De institutione noviciorum*, and Hugh de Folieto's *De claustro anime*. In addition to its extreme rarity as an *ad hoc* admonition to aspiring monks, the exhortation provides evidence for books not otherwise known to have been in the Ely library.

[12] For further details concerning profession, its meaning and implications, see Fry, *RB1980*, pp. 449–66.

[13] A. Friedberg (ed.), *Corpus Iuris Canonici*, 2 vols. (Leipzig, 1879–81), II, Clementinarum, I.6.3. References to the timing of profession and ordination at Ely are to be found in Bishop Walpole's statutes of 1300 and in the chapter ordinances of 1314: Evans, *Ordinances*, pp. 15, 43.

[14] Greatrex, *BRECP*, pp. 423 (Madyngle) and 426 (Orewell).

well.[15] In the single instance of Robert Colville, however, his possible presence in the almonry school in the 1460s would serve as a plausible explanation for the ten years that elapsed between his first tonsure, when he was not yet a monk, and his ordination as priest.[16]

It seems clear that the years preceding final ordination were chiefly occupied in further study; for a few, like Colville, this included a period at Cambridge, but most of those who were selected for university study were probably sent after priestly ordination.[17]

Claustral studies in a young monk's early years were supervised by both senior monks and secular masters. Of the former, who were referred to as *instructores* or *informatores*, only two are known by name. In the 1360s Robert Sutton II received small sums for exercising this office from both the sacrist and the keeper of the Lady Chapel, who recorded small gifts of money on their accounts. Although Sutton does not seem to have been sent up to the university, his competence as a preacher must have been recognised by his brethren because he was selected to give the sermon in the Cathedral before Archbishop Wittlesey in 1373 on the occasion of his *sede vacante* visitation.[18] The other recorded monk *instructor*, Roger de Norwich I, combined his theological studies at Cambridge with his teaching assignments in the monastery. Since he obtained his doctorate in 1384–5, probably after some fifteen years of intermittent university study, the junior monks in the cloister would have shared in the benefits of his learning while he advanced through his own curriculum of study.[19] The only hired secular master known by name is John Dounham junior, described as *capellanus*, who in 1448 was appointed to teach grammar not only to the boys in the almonry school but also to the junior brethren in the cloister. A room within the monastery was to be assigned for the lessons, which were to take place between three and six o'clock in the afternoon and to last for one and a half hours.[20] The purpose of these classes was to instruct the monks in Latin grammar, for which a wide variety of texts was available in the fifteenth century, including frequent recourse to late classical grammarians like Donatus and Priscian as well as their later commentators. It must be remembered that the term 'grammar' had a wider application than it does today. It was understood to include, for example, the correct method of writing, etymology, syntax, prosody and *dictamen* (the art of letter writing), and many of the texts were interspersed with illustrative quotations from biblical sources. The theory of grammar, which was only introduced after a thorough grounding had been acquired, involved a more speculative approach in which 'logical analysis and philosophical concepts of grammar'[21] were considered.

---

[15] At Canterbury, four are named in 1468: *The Chronicle of John Stone, Monk of Christ Church, 1415–1471*, ed. W. Searle, CAS, Octavo Publications, no. 34 (1902), p. 106. Both at Rochester and at Winchester only one is known by name: John de Bradefeld and Nicholas de Bysshopestone: Greatrex, *BRECP*, pp. 593, 679–80.

[16] The details are in Greatrex, *BRECP*, pp. 398–9.

[17] Some monks of Christ Church, Canterbury and of Worcester began their university studies prior to priestly ordination.

[18] Greatrex, *BRECP*, p. 446.

[19] *Ibid.*, p. 427.

[20] CUL, EDR G2/3, item no. 46, which has been transcribed in Dorothy Owen and Dorothea Thurley (eds.), *The King's School, Ely* (Cambridge, 1982), pp. 25–6; see also Evans, *Ordinances*, p. 58.

[21] J.N. Miner, *The Grammar Schools of Medieval England: A.F. Leach in Historical Perspective* (Montreal, 1990), p. 144.

Several of these works of grammar were to be found in the novices' book cupboard in the Durham Cathedral cloister in 1395, and they were no doubt in common use among novices at many Benedictine houses since they are known to have been available on their library shelves. Thus it is safe to assume that Ely also possessed a number of grammatical texts in its monastic library, some of which may have been set aside for the novices. The prescribed reading material for Durham novices also included Hugh of St Victor's treatise entitled *De informacione noviciorum*, the Rule of St Benedict, several biblical works of reference and a number of devotional tracts.[22] The frequent occurrence of works such as these, and others like them, in many Benedictine libraries suggests that, although few Ely volumes and no medieval library catalogues survive, the nucleus of the monastic collection of books would have been similar to those at monasteries like Ramsey, Bury and Norwich.

Thirty-seven Ely monks are known to have been selected for advanced studies at the University of Cambridge between the 1330s and the 1530s, about half of whom returned with a degree.[23] For these monks, at least, the monastic library would have been a place of frequent resort, and the supply of texts must have been adequate for their preliminary studies in preparation for the halls of higher learning. In supporting their most promising monks in this way, at considerable cost to the community, the Prior and chapter were implementing the papal legislation of the 1330s which required 'the setting up of a common house of studies within the university to which one monk in twenty was henceforth to be sent'.[24] The presence of monk scholars at university was regularly entered on the annual account rolls of the monastic officers or obedientiaries who made contributions toward the maintenance costs. It is unfortunate that relatively few of the obedientiary accounts of Ely survive, and of those that remain many are fragmentary and illegible.[25] However, although the names and the number of monk students are often omitted from the details of payments on the accounts, it is possible to estimate that there were relatively few years when there was not an Ely monk at Cambridge. As far as can be ascertained there were generally two monk students, the prescribed number for a community of forty; but at times three and even four are recorded. It was Prior Crauden's initiative that lay behind the practical arrangements for the first Ely monks to be accommodated in Cambridge. They were lodged first in a hostel known as Crauden's Hostel (on the site of Trinity Hall); they next occupied Borden's Hostel on Trinity Street; and in the early fifteenth century they joined Benedictines from other monasteries in a common house of study called 'Monkis Place'. By 1483 the name of this last was Buckingham College; it was similar to the much earlier foundation of Gloucester Hall or College at Oxford.[26]

---

[22] [B. Botfield (ed.)], *Catalogi Veteres Librorum Ecclesiae Cathedralis Dunelm.* Surtees Society, 7 (1838), pp. 81–2. For other monastic libraries see my article, 'The Scope of Learning within the Cloisters of the English Cathedral Priories in the Later Middle Ages', in G. Ferzoco and C. Muessig (eds.), *Medieval Monastic Education* (London, 2000), pp. 41–55.

[23] Only one Ely monk is known to have attended university prior to the 1330s: John de Swaffham (II), who obtained a doctorate in theology, probably from Oxford, in 1289–90: Greatrex, *BRECP*, p. 446.

[24] J. Greatrex, 'Rabbits and Eels at High Table: Monks of Ely at the University of Cambridge, *c.*1337–1539', in B. Thompson (ed.), *Monasteries and Society in Medieval Britain, Proceedings of the 1994 Harlaxton Symposium* (Stamford, 1999), pp. 312–28, at p. 314.

[25] There are fewer than 400 account rolls in all, a large number of which are in the form of eighteenth-century transcripts. In contrast there are about fourteen hundred at both Durham and Norwich cathedral priories.

[26] This is a summary of Greatrex, 'Rabbits and Eels at High Table' (cit. in n. 24), pp. 313–14.

At Ely the policy was to send monks to Cambridge a year or two before, or shortly after, their ordination to the priesthood. John de Sautre and Walter de Walsoken were among the earliest residents in Crauden's Hostel in the late 1330s, the former commencing in 1339–40, about a year after receiving priest's orders, and the latter in 1337–8, about a year before being made priest.[27] In many cases neither the length of an individual monk's stay in Cambridge nor his course of study have been preserved in the records. Sautre was a student for at least eight years, possibly more, with no mention of his course of study, while Walsoken studied canon law for six years or more; neither of them, however, appears to have obtained a degree. The fact that canon law was considered an acceptable field of study for a cloistered monk requires comment. When the general chapter of the black monks first set up a house of study at Oxford in the 1290s, its stated purpose was a practical one: to produce competent and well informed teachers and preachers who would not be overshadowed by the friars, who had recently risen to prominence on account of their learning and their skill as preachers.[28] This is the context in which Richard Swaffham's progress in homiletics was put to the test when, as a student in Cambridge, he was assigned to preach in Ely Cathedral on Palm Sunday, 1479. Several other monk students were also given the opportunity to practise and improve their skill, by being licensed to preach in Cambridge.[29] While canon law studies were not strictly forbidden, theology was considered more appropriate for a monk. At Ely, however, almost half the monk graduates had degrees in canon law; at Norwich the number was less than a quarter, while at Worcester all the monks sent to university seem to have studied theology.[30] There is no obvious reason why policy differed so much from house to house. Of the Ely monks trained as canonists, only Thomas Dounham I in 1383 and Walter de Walsoken in 1349 were appointed by the bishop as penitentiaries in the diocese, at least as far as we know.[31] Since monks with theological degrees or with no known university connection were also called upon to perform this duty, no specialised legal training appears to have been deemed necessary. It has been suggested that the canon law curriculum was less intensive than its theological counterpart and for this reason would have proved a more feasible choice when part-time studies were undertaken. Some evidence exists for Ely to support this possibility, for example in the case of John Yaxham who studied canon law between c.1396–7 and 1415; in 1411–12, in the midst of his studies, he held the office of almoner.[32] The cases of John Cottenham and John Soham I may be similar, but the details are too sparse for certainty; and monk theologians like Roger de Norwich I (mentioned above) were also journeying back and forth between Ely and Cambridge in order to fulfil their dual obligations.[33]

On completing their studies the university-trained monks would have returned the books they had borrowed from the monastic library, checked their library holdings for

---

[27] Greatrex, *BRECP*, pp. 437, 455.

[28] W. Pantin (ed.), *Documents Illustrating the Activities of the General and Provincial Chapters of the English Black Monks, 1215–1540*, Camden Society, 3rd series, 45 (i), 47 (ii), 54 (iii) (1931–7) (henceforth, Pantin, *Black Monk Chapters*), ii, p. 75.

[29] Greatrex, *BRECP*, p. 447 (Swaffham), and pp. 423–4, where Henry Madyngle and three other student monks were licensed in 1415 to preach in any church in Cambridge appropriated to the Cathedral Priory.

[30] Greatrex, 'Rabbits and Eels at High Table', pp. 322–3.

[31] Greatrex, *BRECP*, pp. 405, 455.

[32] *Ibid.*, p. 465.

[33] *Ibid.*, pp. 400–1 (Cottenham); p. 439 (Soham); p. 427 (Norwich).

other books they had found most useful at Cambridge, and probably brought back some which they had been able to purchase. Lists and inventories from other cathedral monasteries furnish this kind of information; at Ely only a few references shed light on the contents of the library.[34] The copy of the Decretals, for example, that had been purchased for 3s. by Alexander de Ely, precentor in 1300/1, may have been among the volumes conveyed to Cambridge in the 1330s, as the existence of a library in the monk hostels in the early days would have been unlikely.[35] In 1410 John de Bukton II, who was probably the Priory treasurer at that time, came to the aid of Ely monks who like Yaxham were studying canon law at Cambridge by giving them a two-volume copy of the *Lectura super Decretales Hostiensis.*[36]

It may at first appear surprising that the precentor bought few books and provides in his accounts few details of the work assigned to the scribes in copying and repairing manuscripts. Most of the scribes can be identified as hired professionals by the fact that their wages are regularly entered on these accounts. Any monks employed would rarely have been mentioned because no payment would have been necessary; nevertheless, it is possible and even probable that some of the junior monks were assigned to assist the precentor, perhaps to update the library catalogue or the community chronicle.[37] Only a few surviving volumes bear personal ownership inscriptions. One of these is a collection of Martin Luther's works printed at Wittenberg in 1519; it was bought by John Skelsyn, trying to keep abreast of contemporary theological writings while he was a student at Cambridge in the early 1530s. Five others, all manuscripts dating from the eleventh to the early sixteenth century, bear the name and armorial insignia of the last Prior and first Dean, Robert Wells, alias Steward; most, probably all, of these had been in the monastic library before Wells inscribed them.[38]

However, monks like John Bukton I and John Skelsyn were probably responsible for a number of acquisitions to the library – to the mutual benefit of the community among whom there must have been a nucleus of studious monks, including both those whose education had been confined to the cloister and those who had been sent on to university.

Our familiarity with many of the details of the monks' daily activities relating to the organization of their domestic affairs and the administration of their properties, should not cause us to forget that their primary responsibility as Benedictines was a spiritual one which carried with it the obligation to study and meditate on the scriptures. This *lectio divina,* or prayed reading, nourished by the perusal of patristic writings and biblical commentaries, is an aspect of the daily monastic regimen which by its very nature remains largely hidden from our eyes.[39]

---

[34] R. Sharpe, J.P. Carley, R.M. Thomson and A.G. Watson (eds.), *English Benedictine Libraries. The Shorter Catalogues* (Corpus of British Medieval Library Catalogues 4) (London, 1996), pp. 127–31. Also EDC 1/G/1: see n. 11.

[35] CUL, MS Add. 2957 (Bentham transcripts), fo. 40.

[36] Greatrex, *BRECP*, p. 394.

[37] There is evidence of young Norwich monks working on a book catalogue and of an annual edition of a chronicle at Worcester; see Greatrex, 'Monk Students from Norwich Cathedral Priory at Oxford and Cambridge, c.1300 to 1530', *Eng. Hist. Rev.*, cvi (1991), pp. 555–83, at p. 575, and Greatrex, *BRECP*, p. 844, under Prior John Malverne.

[38] Greatrex, *BRECP*, p. 438 (Skelsyn); pp. 457–8 (Wells).

[39] For a discussion of what is implied by *lectio divina* in the Rule of St Benedict, see the many references in Fry, *RB1980*.

The monastic liturgy, said and sung

Monastic liturgy is to be understood as the prayer of the community assembled in choir for the daily conventual mass and the eight offices of psalms, lessons and hymns which were scheduled at fixed hours during the day.[40] These were public ceremonies, as distinct from the individual monk's private meditation and prayer, and as such were sometimes attended by resident corrodians, visiting guests, priory personnel and employees, and other members of the laity who lived near by or who came to offer gifts at the shrines of Etheldreda and her sister saints.[41] Their presence in small numbers in the Cathedral church is for the most part unrecorded but may safely be assumed; larger numbers, however, would have thronged the nave on greater festivals such as the Palm Sunday high mass. Until the 1360s the nave was also in regular use on Sundays throughout the year as the parish church of St Peter. Secular clergy officiated at the nave altar of the Holy Cross which adjoined the west side of the pulpitum or screen separating the monastic choir from the nave.[42] This arrangement, which also pertained at Rochester Cathedral, proved equally unsatisfactory in both cases.[43] Mutual complaints at Ely on the part of the monks and of the parishioners were voiced during Archbishop Reynolds's visitation in 1315, with the resultant injunction that a separate parish church be built in a suitable location.[44] The stone pulpitum had proved an ineffective barrier in blocking out the sound when services were in progress simultaneously on both sides, and both parties were being distracted in the performance of their rites and devotions. The monks, who at this time were preparing to launch an ambitious building programme that was carried out under priors John Crauden and Alan Walsingham, were slow in implementing this injunction to build the new church; in fact, it was not completed until the 1360s. Dedicated by Bishop Simon Langham as the church of St Cross, it was described in 1566 as little more than a lean-to on the north side of the nave towards its western end.[45] The new site was sufficiently remote not to interfere with the monastic community at prayer, but the parishioners' views are not recorded; it is possible that their church was originally more impressive.[46]

Among other problems that afflicted the monks were the freezing temperatures they endured in the winter months during divine office as they sat and knelt for long periods in the high vaulted choir. In *c.*1258 Prior Hugh de Balsham and the convent requested and received permission from Pope Alexander IV to wear caps (*pillei*) on the grounds that their church had been constructed *in frigido loco*.[47] Though not himself a monk,

---

[40] An example of the monastic horarium is given by David Knowles in his volume, *The Monastic Order in England*, 2nd edn (Cambridge, 1966), pp. 448–53.

[41] Corrodians were often retired lay personnel who had been in the service of the priory; they were provided with food and lodging for life, within the precinct or close by, usually in return for a specified single payment.

[42] T.D. Atkinson, 'Architectural Description of Cathedral and Precincts', in VCH, *Cambs.*, IV, pp. 82–3.

[43] The parishioners at Rochester Cathedral worshipped at the nave altar of St Nicholas until 1423: A. Oakley, 'Rochester Priory, 1185–1540', in N. Yates (ed.), *Faith and Fabric: A History of Rochester Cathedral 604–1994* (Woodbridge, 1996), pp. 29–55, at pp. 35–6.

[44] The Archbishop's *decretum* to this effect has been transcribed by Chapman, *Sacrist Rolls*, I, pp. 101–2, footnote.

[45] *Ibid.*, pp. 103–4; in 1566 the Lady Chapel became the parish church of the Holy Trinity.

[46] *Ibid.*, p. 103.

[47] W.H. Bliss, C. Johnson, J.A. Twemlow (eds.), *Calendar of Entries in the Papal Registers relating to Great Britain and Ireland. Papal Letters* (London, 1894–), i, p. 360.

Bishop Ralph de Walpole displayed a sensitivity to the needs of the weaker members of the community for whom St Benedict had shown special concern: he issued an injunction in 1300 ordering books and lighting to be provided at the night office for the juniors who were still engaged in striving to commit all the psalms and antiphons to memory and for the elderly whose memories were beginning to fail.[48] Walpole also decreed that as soon as a junior monk had received major orders he was to take on the responsibility for some role in the performance of the daily office as determined by the precentor.[49]

A clock had been installed in the cloister before 1300 so as to ensure the punctual operation of the monastic horarium.[50] However, there was a perennial problem of absence from some of the choir offices; this was a common failing within Benedictine houses, since many monks were burdened with administrative responsibilities. Bishop Walpole tackled the problem by ordering that no one was to be excused from the evening collation and compline which immediately followed.[51] A few years later, in 1314, Prior John de Fresingfeld and the Chapter agreed on ordinances requiring the Prior to set a good example by more frequent attendance at the divine office and the subprior and obedientiaries to do similarly and to take care to arrive on time and stay until the end of the service.[52] Both Archbishop Thomas Arundel in 1403 and Bishop William Gray in 1466 issued post-visitation injunctions in an attempt to control this abuse by allowing no exemptions from attendance unless there was an 'evident necessity' and licence had been previously obtained from the Prior.[53] It is uncertain how vicars deputising for absent obedientiaries were regarded, since they too were monks of the house to whom the same rules applied. Ely was just one of many Benedictine monasteries where *vicarii in choro* are recorded, although at Ely they occur only on some accounts of the sacrist and cellarer in the fourteenth and fifteenth centuries, when they were allocated up to 10*s.* per annum for their services.[54] William Burdelays is the only one known by name; he occurs on the sacrist's account for 1341–2, when he must have been a junior monk.[55] The sacrist, Nicholas de Copmanford, had heavy responsibilities that year, both as subprior at the time of Prior Crauden's death in September 1341, and as sacrist appointed by Bishop Montacute two months later; absent from the house on Priory business on frequent occasions, he must have been grateful to have his stall in choir occupied.[56]

An injunction of the monk-Bishop Robert de Orford draws attention to the important role of the precentor and the necessity of his unfailing attendance in

---

[48] Evans, *Ordinances*, p. 7.

[49] *Ibid.*, p. 15.

[50] Chapman, *Sacrist Rolls*, II, p. 6 (the account for 1291–2); see also Evans, *Ordinances*, p. 18.

[51] Evans, *Ordinances*, p. 17; collation (*collatio*) was the term assigned to the evening [period of] reading that preceded the office of compline.

[52] *Ibid.*, p. 36.

[53] *Ibid.*, pp. 52, 57. At an episcopal visitation in 1500 there were complaints concerning the absence from divine office of the precentor, Henry Iselham: Greatrex, *BRECP*, p. 418.

[54] *E.g.* EDC 1/F/2/8 (1340–2) (cellarer); Chapman, *Sacrist Rolls*, II, p. 30 (1322–3); EDC 1/F/10/36 (1478–9) (sacrist).

[55] Greatrex, *BRECP*, p. 394.

[56] *Ibid.*, pp. 399–400, for Copmanford's activities. I know of no evidence that the vicar sat in the stall of the monk for whom he was deputising, but it is at least a plausible suggestion.

choir to lead the chant.[57] His duties also included the repair of psalters, breviaries, antiphonals, bibles, missals and other service books as well as the supervision of scribes writing out new books to replace the old ones worn out through daily use. Annual Easter tables had to be compiled to show the dates of the movable feasts and rotas had to be prepared for the monks officiating at the many services.[58] The expenses involved in these labours occupy a significant place on the surviving precentor's accounts: in 1302–3 a scribe employed to copy the missing sections of an antiphonal was paid 7s. 10d by Alexander de Ely, precentor; the rebinding of a missal for the high altar and of books for the so-called 'three altars' on the north side of the presbytery received attention in the 1340s from John de Wells I; one gradual was illuminated in 1373–4 and twenty quires of another were scored for the use of the cantors, under the direction of Thomas de Thetford II (alias Pike); in 1447–8, 2s. was spent on binding a small psalter used by the novices, four of whom were Thomas Depyng, William Makeroo, William Power and John Wace.[59] These are just scattered examples to illustrate some of the duties that devolved on the precentor in addition to his role as librarian.

Instruction of the monks in musical chant was part of the precentor's responsibility as monastic choirmaster; the monks required training to ensure that the sung portions of mass and office were competently and reverently performed. On major feasts, such as those of St Etheldreda, the precentor called in others to sing with the monks, some of whom appear to have been professional singers receiving annual stipends.[60] It is likely that the professionals also provided voice training for some of the monks and perhaps for others who augmented the choir on festal occasions. The additional singers were described as belonging to several categories – clerks, friends and *diversi extranei* – ; who were usually rewarded with small gifts in cash or kind; in 1442–3, for example, knives and gloves were distributed to them by William Wells III, the precentor then in office.[61] On several occasions during the fifteenth century singing boys, *pueri in choro*, were also

---

[57] Evans, *Ordinances*, p. 33 (1307).

[58] There is frequent reference to the Easter tables in the precentor's account: *e.g.*, *pro tabula Paschali scribend' et reparand'* in 1300–1, for which the scribe received 3s., and two years later *pro tabula Paschali factur' de novo et illuminand'*, 4s.: CUL, MS Add. 2957 (Bentham transcripts), fos. 40, 41. The rotas were probably written on wax tablets such as the one in the cloister that required renewing (*renovand'*) in 1442–3: EDC 1/F/9/[12].

[59] CUL, MS Add. 2957 (Bentham transcripts), fo. 41; *ibid.*, fos. 43, 44; *ibid.*, fo. 45; *ibid.*, fo. 48. For the monks named, see Greatrex, *BRECP*, p. 406 (Ely), pp. 456–7 (Wells), p. 449 (Thetford), p. 403 (Depyng), p. 424 (Makeroo), p. 430 (Power), p. 452 (Wace).

[60] Among the professionals known by name are William de la Launt, Richard Haryngton and William Reede, who all appear on the precentor's 1483–4 account, EDC 1/F/9/[12]. Haryngton was also employed by the Keeper of the Lady Chapel five years earlier with an annual stipend of 13s. 4d, EDC 1/F/4/13. A few fragments of plainsong and polyphony have turned up in manuscripts associated with Ely because, after being discarded, they were re-used as binding leaves. One consists of four folios used as flyleaves in TCC, MS O.2.1 (the 'E' MS of *LE, cf.* Simon Keynes, above, p. 8, n. 26), for which see further below, p. 88 and n. 71. Another bifolium is now the rear flyleaf and pastedown of MS 23 (B.1) of St John's College, Cambridge, previously a Priory manuscript, and is described in Andrew Wathey, *Manuscripts of Polyphonic Music*, Supplement to RISM BIV 1–2, *The British Isles, 1100–1400* (Munich, 1993), pp. 15–17. The rest are loose folios (15th-century) from the bindings of late 16th and early 17th-century visitation records that belonged to the Bishop or the Dean and Chapter of Ely. They are catalogued among the Ely Diocesan Records as EDR O19/2/1, 2; O19/3/1–4; and O/19/5. For a brief description see N.R. Ker, *Medieval Manuscripts in British Libraries*, II (Oxford, 1977), pp. 627–8. Other fragments are as yet uncatalogued in the EDC archives (Colour pl. 18b).

[61] EDC 1/F/9/[12]; for William Wells III, see Greatrex, *BRECP*, p. 459.

rewarded by the precentor, who in 1408–9 paid Nicholas Chaunter 10s. for instructing the boys *in sua arte* for three quarters of the year.[62]

Cantors, monks and boys also sang at the Lady mass in the new Lady Chapel, a separate building on the north side of the presbytery, after its completion in 1349. Their presence there is recorded by the obedientiary who served as keeper of the Lady Chapel. John de Bukton II was in charge in 1383–4; he gave the boys 2s. for singing at the mass of St Mary and also rewarded some of his brethren for the same.[63] Monks, friends and clerks were given caps and knives for their services in 1426, while the boys received gloves and knives in 1446–7.[64] It is probable that similar entries appeared regularly on the accounts of the keeper of the Lady Chapel, but we shall never know because many of them, like those of the precentor, have been destroyed. On the latest surviving account of the keeper, that of 1514–15, monks as well as outsiders were recorded as singing in the Lady Chapel on various occasions during the year; they were rewarded with 'victualibus' which cost the keeper 8s. 1d.[65]

In one year, 1465–6, the precentor recorded a detail that is of more interest to us than it would have been to the monastic auditors: namely, that he brought in *extraneii* several times during the year to sing with organ accompaniment.[66] This was also the year in which the precentor, Gilbert Lakyngheth, arranged for Robert Colville, one of the youngest members of the community, to have organ lessons. Shortly afterwards Colville was sent to Cambridge to study, but after what seems to have been a brief sojourn there he returned to the monastery and continued his organ studies, for which the monk treasurer, Thomas Denver, paid 26s. 8d in 1473–4.[67] There were probably other monk organists, some of whom may have been taught by Colville and thus no expenses would have had to be entered on the account of the precentor or the keeper of the Lady Chapel. Professional organists like William Kyng, whose stipend was 13s. 4d for the year 1452–3, were also paid by the precentor.[68]

The precentor appears to have been in charge of all organ maintenance and repair in the Cathedral church. References to the location of the organs occur only when it was necessary to distinguish one organ from another, and these suggest that there were two:

[62] CUL, MS Add. 2957 (Bentham transcripts), fo. 47. In 1483–4 the *pueri in choro* shared 8d, given by the precentor for singing on a number of occasions (*per vices*), no doubt the feasts of St Etheldreda: EDC 1/F/9/9.

[63] CUL, MS Add. 2957 (Bentham transcripts), fo. 58.

[64] *Ibid.*, fos. 59, 60.

[65] *Ibid.*, fo. 64. Were the boys who on occasion sang for the precentor in the monks' choir the same boys who sang for the keeper of the Lady Chapel at the Lady mass in the Lady Chapel? And were the singing boys chosen from among those who were receiving an elementary education in the almonry school? There is no clear evidence to support either an affirmative or a negative answer to these questions. However, from a study of the almonry schools of other cathedral priories such as Norwich, I would suggest that Ely almonry school may have included both groups of boys; both would have been given instruction in grammar but only some would have been chosen to sing. See J. Greatrex, 'The Almonry School of Norwich Cathedral Priory in the Thirteenth and Fourteenth Centuries', in *Studies in Church History*, xxxi (1994), pp. 169–81, at pp. 178–9. Dr Roger Bowers sees the choristers as a 'sub-group of boys' within the almonry schools. He also suggests that, in the major monastic churches from the late 14th century, almonry schoolboys were trained to sing daily at the Lady mass in the Lady Chapel. See his 'The Almonry Schools of the English Monasteries c.1265–1540', in *Monasteries and Society in Medieval Britain* (cit. in n. 24), pp. 177–222, at pp. 208–10.

[66] CUL, MS Add. 2957 (Bentham transcripts), fo. 49; he paid them the impressive sum of 10s. 4d.

[67] Colville also received priest's orders in 1473–4. Other biographical details of this monk, who served as precentor and was later elected Prior, are in Greatrex, *BRECP*, pp. 398–9.

[68] CUL, MS Add. 2957 (Bentham transcripts), fo. 48.

the great organ, in the monastic choir (probably on the southern side), and another, smaller one, in the Lady Chapel.[69] There were major expenditures in 1396–7 on both organs, costing over £7, and again in 1406–7, when the monks decided in chapter to forego their pocket money for the year in order to make a collective contribution to the organ fund.[70]

The dearth of liturgical manuscripts that survive from Ely and the few extant fragments of what may have been part of an Ely customary severely restrict our knowledge of the actual performance or celebration of the daily mass and office. Only four folios from a volume of motets have been identified as having belonged to the Cathedral Priory; they have been preserved as flyleaves in a copy of the *Liber Eliensis* which is now MS 0.2.1 (1105) in the library of Trinity College, Cambridge. They are late thirteenth century polyphony for three or four voices intended to be sung during the Lady mass or at the high mass on Marian festivals.[71] Monks in priest's orders were required to say mass at least once every three days, and there would have been a rota of celebrants in operation for the daily high mass at the high altar, as for the Lady mass in the Lady Chapel and for the masses at other altars in the Cathedral church.[72] Some of these last would have been regular chantry or anniversary masses for the souls of deceased monks, friends and benefactors; secular priest chaplains as well as monks were on hand to fulfil these duties.

The survival of a monastic breviary and several psalters of Ely provenance allows us to gain some impression of the monks' performance of the daily office in choir. It should be pointed out, however, that nothing remains from any medieval English Benedictine house to explain 'how the many texts that varied from day to day were woven together to make up that mosaic of largely biblical texts that formed the Office'; nor do we know the details of when or where the additional devotions, including suffrages and litanies, were 'fitted in to the daily cursus'.[73] In chapters 8 to 18 of his Rule, St Benedict laid down the general scheme to be followed for each office or hour of the day and prescribed the order in which the psalms were to be distributed among them so that all one hundred and fifty psalms would be said during the course of a week.[74]

As accretions to the Benedictine office gradually multiplied, the accompanying rubrics grew correspondingly in length and complexity while at the same time there came to be an increasing divergence from the prescriptions of the Rule. A series of meetings of members of the English provincial chapter of black monks between 1277 and 1279 resulted in the issue of new statutes that aimed to reduce the number of

[69] *Ibid.*, fo. 46. At an episcopal visitation in 1500, Thomas Drayton and Simon Quaveney complained that the keeper of the Lady Chapel had not returned the organ to the Lady Chapel; presumably he had removed it for repair: Greatrex, *BRECP*, pp. 405, 432. An inventory taken at the time of the dissolution records the presence of three: 'Two paer of Organs' in the choir and 'A paer of Organs' in the Lady Chapel; see Bentham, *Ely*, p. 224.

[70] CUL, MS Add. 2957 (Bentham transcripts), fos. 46, 47; at Ely, the term used for pocket money was *gracie*. Several of the obedientiaries made regular contributions to this annual allowance which averaged about 4*s.* for each monk; it was to be spent '*pro suis necessitatibus*', Evans, *Ordinances*, p. 9.

[71] See the report by R. Bowers in I. Fenlon (ed.), *Cambridge Music Manuscripts, 900–1700* (Cambridge, 1982), no.13, pp. 44–7.

[72] Evans, *Ordinances*, pp. 7–8, 37.

[73] *The Monastic Breviary of Hyde Abbey, Winchester*, ed. J.B.L. Tolhurst, 6 vols., Henry Bradshaw Society (1932–42) (henceforth, Tolhurst, *Monastic Breviary*), VI, p. 143.

[74] *Ibid.*, VI, pp. 11–13. The word 'hour' may be used as an alternative to 'office'.

extraneous devotions and introduce more uniformity of observance.[75] Although a number of reforming measures were agreed, the monks soon encountered the opposition of Archbishop Pecham, who condemned the truncated office and ordered the bishops to ensure that its original, lengthier form be retained in the Benedictine monasteries within their dioceses. Pecham's letter written to the monk-Bishop of Ely, Hugh de Balsham, in November 1280 contained a stern rebuke directed at the Prior, John de Hemmingestone, whose support for the new measures had been sufficiently enthusiastic to lead him to contravene the Archbishop's order; it seems that he had been urging their adoption by the very monasteries which had been expressly forbidden to do so by the Archbishop himself during recent visitations.[76]

How universally these and later statutes concerning the divine office were implemented remains uncertain because of the inadequacies of surviving manuscripts. The thirteenth-century Ely breviary is among those examined by J.B.L. Tolhurst some sixty years ago; he identified many of the variations that continued to be followed by individual houses, but research in this area is far from complete.[77]

As the Ely manuscript demonstrates, the monastic breviary contained the variable texts for the feasts and *ferias* of the liturgical year. Hymns, collects and lessons might be given in full but were often, as always in the case of the psalms, indicated only by a cue consisting of the first few words. The psalter was a separate volume which would probably have been within the monk's reach for use with the chant. The late thirteenth-century Ely psalter now in the British Library is a volume in which the four gospels and the psalms have been bound together, with a kalendar of saints' days celebrated at Ely occupying the first few folios. Rubrics in the margins of the gospels indicated the sections that were appointed to be read on Sundays, and the final folios included the Te Deum and those Old Testament canticles that were in frequent use.[78] The Ely psalter in the Bodleian Library, Oxford, also thirteenth-century, has as its distinctive feature musical notation both in the margins and on several folios at the end.[79]

The ecclesiastical vestments were in the care of the sacrist, whose accounts record frequent expenses for the making and washing of albs and amices and the repair of chasubles and copes. Among the bequests from bishops noted in the continuation of the *Historia Eliensis* there is a chasuble from Bishop Hervey which was known as *pascha*

[75] See Pantin, *Black Monk Chapters*, I, pp. 60–101, where the 1277 statutes have been transcribed and *ibid.*, I, pp. 102–5 for a note and transcription of an existing fragment of those of 1279.

[76] *Registrum Epistolarum Fratris Johannis Peckham, Archiepiscopi Cantuariensis*, ed. C.T. Martin, 3 vols. (Rolls Ser., 1882–5), I, no. 126, pp. 150–1.

[77] Tolhurst, *Monastic Breviary*, vol. VI, *passim*; examples of Ely practice occur on pp. 61, 73, 85, 167, 176, 187, *etc.* Tolhurst attributed a 13th, rather than a 15th, century date to the Ely breviary (now CUL, MS Ii.4.20); this must be borne in mind while reading his commentary. N.R. Ker's attribution of a 15th-century date is now reckoned to have been a misprint.

[78] BL, MS Harl. 547; the calendar, highlighting the galaxy of women saints venerated at Ely, identifies its provenance. In addition to Etheldreda these include Sexburga and Wihtburga, her sisters, Ermenilda the daughter of Sexburga, and Werburga.

[79] Oxford, Bodleian, MS Laud Latin 95; it may be assumed that the major portions of the office were normally sung, despite the paucity of the references. Wharton's version of the *Historia Eliensis* supplies two: (1) on 2 March 1310, Robert de Swaffham, precentor, announced the election of John de Ketene, almoner, as Bishop, after which the monks took their places in choir to sing compline; (2) on 3 February 1310 the monastic community sang matins in the chapel of St Catherine: Wharton, *Anglia Sacra*, I, pp. 642–3. (A third late 12th-century psalter is in the Biblioteca Nazionale Braidense, Milan (MS A.F.xi); this I have not yet seen.)

floridum, i.e. Palm Sunday, and a cope from Bishop Nigel denoted as *gloria mundi*. The actual making of vestments such as these was sometimes undertaken by the monks themselves, among whom Guthmund and Ralph II, two twelfth-century Ely sacrists, were remembered for their achievements.[80] The inventory taken at the dissolution of the Cathedral Priory provides a partial list of the contents of the sacristy and includes a number of copes and chasubles distinguished only by their colour, but a few are described in slightly more detail as having embroidered designs of birds, beasts and flowers[81] (Colour pl. 19*a*). There is no mention of Queen Philippa's 'robe of purple-red velvet powdered with golden squirrels' which she is reputed to have given to Prior Crauden.[82]

The monk's personal prayer and devotion

Among his instruments of good works, St Benedict reaffirmed the precept of St Paul in urging his disciples to resort frequently to prayer[83] (Colour pl. 20*b*). In this command Benedict was alluding to the individual monk's private prayer as distinct from the daily liturgical prayer of mass and office performed by the community. The inner life of the medieval monk, like that of any practising Christian, remains hidden unless he or she chooses to reveal it or records thoughts and prayers in writings which later become public. Observations on the part of fellow monks may occasionally shed a ray of light in this quarter, as in the case of Ely's Prior Crauden; the account of his life and achievements extends beyond the ambitious building programme to describe his fervent spirituality: he 'was to be found frequently at prayer and in meditation in his chapel during the night watches'.[84]

The contemplative side of Benedictine life at Ely is exemplified by two monks who, having led active lives of service in administration in their early years, were allowed in later life to retire from office in order to devote themselves to prayer. One of these was Thomas de Elyngham II, who, in 1438 when in his mid-sixties and a professed monk for forty-six years, was released from the office of sacrist which he had held for nearly a quarter of a century. The other was John Grove, who served as assistant or *socius* to both the sacrist and precentor between 1396 and 1407, and probably longer because his request to transfer to the newly founded enclosed community of Bridgettines at Syon is dated ten years later, in 1417. Prior William Powcher wrote a warm recommendation on his behalf to the prior of Syon and so we may presume that he went to try his vocation there. However, within three years he had returned to Ely, probably because he had

---

[80]   Wharton, *Anglia Sacra*, I, pp. 618, 630. Guthmund and Ralph II are included in Greatrex, *BRECP*, pp. 414, 432; at Canterbury, Thomas Selvyston was described as an expert embroiderer of vestments, *ibid.*, p. 285.

[81]   Bentham, *Ely*, unpaginated following Volume II title-page; this inventory was probably taken after some of the items in the sacristy had been removed, possibly by individual monks for 'safe keeping'. There is an instance of the removal of a relic by a monk of St Swithun's, Winchester, for similar reasons: Greatrex, *BRECP*, p. 694, under Thomas Fygge. A cope of green velvet, embroidered with gold waterflower ornament, and the orphrey embroidered with figures of saints, of *c.*1470–1500, survives (Colour pl. 19*a*).

[82]   Wharton, *Anglia Sacra*, I, p. 650.

[83]   Fry, *RB1980*, Chap. 4, 56 (p. 185): *Orationi frequenter incumbere*; St Paul, I Thess. 5, 17: *Sine intermissione orate.*

[84]   Greatrex, *BRECP*, p. 401 (from LPL, MS 448, fos. 59–59ᵛ). His chapel, much restored, is part of the 8th Canonry house.

found the life too rigorous. By 1420 he was described as an elderly monk, an anchorite, living in reclusion and dispensed to eat meat. His cell was within the precinct and possibly in the presbytery of the Cathedral church.[85]

Only three surviving Ely manuscripts have any direct bearing on an individual monk's spiritual life and these can do no more than suggest what may have been common practice. Peter de Norwich II, for example, acquired a volume containing Latin treatises on the contemplative life by the mystical writer Richard Rolle, hermit priest of Hampole. Rolle had died in 1349, only a few years before Norwich entered the Cathedral Priory. The latter was sent to Cambridge where he obtained a doctorate in theology in 1364–5, but very little else is known about him during his remaining 40 years in the monastery. He must have acquired this volume towards the end of his monastic life, judging by the clear, neat hand in which the text is written. It contains a full-page illustration in colour of the Crucifixion and several decorated borders and initials.[86] In Norwich we may have a third monk who was drawn to the life of contemplative prayer which Rolle had described with great fervour.

The Ely breviary cum missal calls for further attention in this section because it may have been used as a *vade mecum* for a monk priest while he was obliged to be absent from the monastery.[87] Comparatively small for a handwritten volume – it measures six inches by eight, and three inches in thickness – it could be conveniently carried, and its contents would have enabled him to fulfil his liturgical duties *vis à vis* the daily monastic office and the mass.[88] Evidence of its personal and private use lies in the additional prayers and collects which have been inserted on blank folios together with the form of absolution used by the priest following the confession of a penitent.[89]

The third manuscript, now in the British Library, contains a miscellaneous collection of treatises and other material dating from the thirteenth to the fifteenth centuries. It has all the marks of being a personal collection, possibly passed down from one monk to another. Among the contents as they now exist are: treatises, prayers and meditations of St Anselm; a treatise on the passion of Christ by St Bernard; a litany of devotion to the blessed Virgin; extracts from the breviary; prayers to be said privately by the priest celebrant before, during and after mass; prayers and meditations calling on our Lady, St Benedict, St Etheldreda, St Bridget and other saints; and prayers for the welfare of family, friends and enemies. It is to be noted that many of the prayers and devotions are

---

[85] Greatrex, *BRECP*, p. 410 (Elyngham), pp. 413–14 (Grove). Atkinson suggests that the doorway to Grove's cell is still visible on the north wall of the north presbytery aisle close to the entrance of what is now Bishop Alcock's chapel, VCH, *Cambs.*, IV, p. 74. Anchorites were provided for in the Benedictine Rule, see Fry, *RB1980*, 169 and other references.

[86] The book is now Cambridge, St John's College, MS 23; it is one of those containing musical fragments described above in footnote 60. The hand must be late 14th or early 15th-century; Ker, *Medieval Libraries*, p. 78, described it as 15th. Could it have been a copy made by Norwich himself? His name occurs on fo. 1 above the list of contents.

[87] CUL, MS Ii.4.20; probably it was used by a succession of monk priests sent out to supervise the Priory estates or to act on behalf of the Prior and chapter in ecclesiastical and other affairs at home and abroad.

[88] If his memorisation of the psalms was inadequate he would also have needed a psalter. The suggestion concerning the way in which the breviary was used was made by Tolhurst, *Monastic Breviary*, vol. VI, p. 2. It is to be noted that most of the folios are well worn and darkened from extensive use.

[89] Examples of the prayers and collects are in the margins of fos. 69, 83, 171, 172ᵛ, 207, 241ᵛ; the absolution is inserted on fo. 319ᵛ. There is also, on fo. 207ᵛ, a rough method of calculating the date of Easter which might have proved useful on lengthy travels abroad.

written in the first person singular, and at some stage in the compilation a detailed index was added for ready reference. Several full-page illustrations in colour, like the one of Christ rising from the tomb bloody but victorious (Colour pl. 19*b*), would have served as aids to devotion, as would the set of praises addressed to the three Persons of the Trinity and our Lady, and the 'glorious invocation of our Saviour Jesu'; the last two are later additions in a cursive hand of the fifteenth century and the invocation is in English.[90] Though a unique survival from Ely, collections such as this were probably compiled by many monks to sustain and deepen the life of the spirit within by means of a frequent recourse to personal prayer.

Finally, while we can only imagine the splendours of the interior embellishment of Ely Cathedral in the later Middle Ages, with its stained glass windows, wall paintings and panels and the galaxy of images especially those adorning the Lady Chapel – all in vivid colour – we must also take them into account. There can be no doubt that for those who lived in their midst they served as powerful visual aids to devotion in bringing the spoken and written word to life.[91]

Conclusion

While there were a number of Ely monks who were highly regarded for their attainments, none has left a mark as a writer of distinction in the fields of theology, history or literature. Hugh de Balsham, Robert de Orford and John de Ketene, for example, all of whom were elected by their fellow monks to the see of Ely, appear to have been educated men; and university studies were generously supported by the Prior and chapter.[92] Nevertheless, only a few monks are known to us to have left any writings, virtually all of which are historical. A remarkable number of these, many no more than fragments, are in the form of chronicles that are centred on the Abbey and Cathedral Priory, the lives of the bishops and major events in Ely and the surrounding region. The authors and compilers for the most part remain anonymous, although the names of three twelfth-century monks, Gregory, Richard and Thomas, are attached to some of them.[93]

Surviving versions of the *Liber Eliensis*, or history of Ely, from the foundation of the Abbey to the later twelfth century were collated and edited by E.O. Blake in 1962 and some sections of the later continuations were printed in 1691 by Henry Wharton.[94] Other fragmentary chronicles remain in manuscript, waiting for an intrepid scholar to tackle and resolve the complex relationship between the different accounts. There can be no doubt that interest in the history of their monastery was alive and flourishing within the community until the dissolution, although in the early sixteenth century the evidence is little more than an unimpressive collection of historical data untidily copied from

---

[90] BL, Add. MS 33381; the prayers and meditations comprise most of the text, the Resurrection illustration is on fo. 78ᵛ, the praises of the Trinity and our Lady on fos. 185ᵛ and 186, and the glorious invocation on fo. 181ᵛ.

[91] Some of these visual aids to devotion are described elsewhere in this volume.

[92] Balsham founded Peterhouse, Cambridge; Orford was judged by Pope Boniface VIII to be a man of sound learning, Wharton, *Anglia Sacra*, I, p. 641; Ketene is one of the few Ely bishops whose donation to the monastery library has been recorded and preserved, *ibid.*, I, p. 642.

[93] These three monks are in Greatrex, *BRECP*, pp. 413, 434 (Richard I), 450.

[94] Dr Blake's edition of *Liber Eliensis* was published by the Royal Historical Society in the Camden Third Series, vol. xcii (London, 1962); some of the later continuations are in Wharton, *Anglia Sacra*, I, pp. 593–688.

various sources.[95] In addition, a small octavo volume recently identified contains the description of a pilgrimage to the Holy Land made by Ralph de Ickelyngton, or Iklingham, who became a monk at Ely around 1350; it is possible that he did not make the journey himself, but the work appears to be his own composition.[96]

The only literary figure of note, Alexander Barclay or Barkley, can hardly be claimed by Ely since he joined the community as a mature secular priest and left a few years later to become a Franciscan. During his stay, which covers an unknown period on either side of 1515–16, he wrote the *Mirrour of good manners*, the *Eclogues* and possibly a life of St Etheldreda; he also translated a life of St George which he dedicated to Bishop Nicholas West.[97]

Finally, it should be emphasised that all these facts, although of interest and significance in themselves, are much less important than the monks' continuing fidelity to study and prayer: activities of mind and spirit which are not subject to human assessment.

---

[95] BL, MS Harl. 3721 includes twenty folios of historical miscellanea mostly pertaining to or relevant to Ely Priory, probably compiled by an Ely monk copying from various sources what was of interest to him; one of these sources may be in LPL, MS 448. The extent of Prior Robert Wells's interest in history may have been limited to his own family origins (see his brief continuation and his genealogy in Wharton, *Anglia Sacra*, I, pp. 675–7, 686, under his family name, Steward). He certainly had a penchant for adding his name and armorial bearings to a number of Ely manuscripts, possibly those he removed from the library at the dissolution (Colour pl. 21*b*).

[96] This is now Oxford, Bodl., MS Rawl. C.958, pt 2, and the pilgrimage is on fos. 1–15; on fo. 15ᵛ the *explicit* is followed by *secundum Radulphum de Iklingham*, which implies that he was at least the author if not the actual pilgrim traveller.

[97] Greatrex, *BRECP*, p. 390; see also the *DNB* where details of his literary career are given.

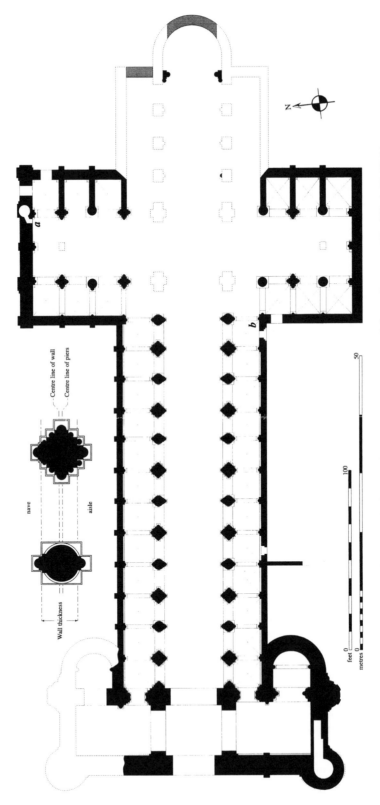

Figure 5. Ground plan of Simeon's Abbey church, late 11th century, reconstructed from Stewart, *Ely* (Chris Kellish)

nave

aisle

Wall thickness

Centre line of wall

Centre line of piers

a

b

N

feet 0   100

metres 0   50

The Architecture and Sculpture
of Ely Cathedral in the Norman Period

ERIC FERNIE

Norman rule in England brought with it a massive increase in the construction of buildings of all kinds, to the extent that, in the late eleventh and early twelfth centuries, most cities, towns, villages and manors would have resembled nothing so much as building sites. The Normans totally rebuilt almost every Anglo-Saxon cathedral and major abbey church, beginning in the 1070s with the cathedrals of Canterbury, Lincoln and Winchester, and the abbeys of St Augustine's, Canterbury, and St Albans. Winchester, begun in 1079 by Bishop Walkelin, was on a much larger scale than the earlier buildings, and was to be the model for Ely.

Shortly after his appointment as abbot in 1081 or 1082, Simeon, prior of Winchester and brother of Walkelin began in the Norman fashion to build a completely new church to replace the old Anglo-Saxon one (Figure 5). Following Simeon's death in 1093 there was an interregnum under William II until the appointment in 1100 of Abbot Richard in 1100, who continued the work until the eastern arm was ready for the translation of the body of St Etheldreda in 1106. Bishop Ridel (1173–89) 'completed the new work towards the west with the tower, even to the top'.[1]

Simeon's building, as one of the great churches of Norman England, provided a fitting setting for the shrine of Etheldreda. It belongs to a group of the nine or ten

---

I would like to express my gratitude to Jill Franklin, Stephen Heywood, Jane Kennedy, John Maddison, Peter Meadows, Richard Plant, Malcolm Thurlby and Jeff West for their invaluable help in the preparation of this paper, to Chris Kennish for digitising the drawings, and to the Research Committee of the Courtauld Institute of Art for a grant towards the cost of illustrations.

[1] For Simeon and Richard see *Liber Eliensis*, written between 1131 and 1174 (ed. Blake, p. xlvii); Bk. ii, ch. 118 (ed. Blake, p. 200): '*Translato autem Godefrido ad abbatiam Malmesberie Willelmi regis precepto venerabilis prior Wintoniensis ecclesie Simeon, frater Walchelini eiusdem ecclesie pontificis, Elyensi ecclesie abbas delegatur*'; *LE*, Appx D: p. 413: the *Winchester Annals* give Simeon's accession under the year 1082; *LE*, pp. xxvi–xxvii: the Ely *Chronicon* gives him thirteen years in office to his death in 1093, and *LE*, ii.137: p. 221 gives fourteen years. Richard: *LE*, Appx D: p. 414: Abbot from 1100 to his death in 1107, with a brief interruption. For the translation: *LE*, ii.144–5: pp. 228–31: '*Translata est . . . Aeðeldreða . . . post autenticum altare parato thalamo collocata.*' Ch. 145: '*Decenter itaque collocata, tanquam primiceria, Aeðeldreða virgine contra maius altare . . ., omnium sanctarum ibidem quiescentium . . . ossa . . . ad orientem versus pedes sancte Aeðeldreðe sollenniter reposuerunt.*' For Ridel see Wharton, *Anglia Sacra*, I, p. 631: '*Novum opus versus occidentem, cum turre usque ad cumulum fere perfecit.*' Stewart, *Ely*, p. 47, quoting from the 17th-century collection of transcripts in BL, MS Harl. 258, notes that in some sources *fere* ('almost') is omitted.

largest buildings of the eleventh century that are known to have been constructed in western Europe, which also rival the great churches of Early Christian Rome. Ely has – or had – an eastern arm of four bays, main transepts of four bays each, with aisles round three sides, an aisled nave, some of the most complex pier designs and the richest sculpture of the period, west transepts with a chapel off each arm, a large tower over each of the two crossings, and a cloister with monastic ranges. The apse contained the high altar and the shrines of Etheldreda and her female relatives, and the choir stalls ran under the crossing to the choir screen in the second bay of the nave. The elevation consisted of a main arcade, a spacious tribune gallery and a clerestory with a wall passage; and in the western transepts there were chapels at both ground and gallery levels and a multiplicity of passages riddling the walls and leading to the upper parts.

In the time of Eustace (Bishop, 1197–1215) a Galilee porch was added to the façade, and Hugh of Northwold (Bishop, 1234–52) extended the east arm. The crossing tower collapsed in 1322, leading to the building of the Octagon and the rebuilding of the Norman bays of the east arm. The north-west transept collapsed around 1500 and the north-west corner of the north transept in 1699[2] (Colour pl. 4a).

The following analysis of the surviving fabric, working from east to west, sets out the evidence for this description and provides the basis for a discussion of the function and sources of the building.

Eastern arm

Excavations have indicated that the eastern arm ended in an apse lying under bay five from the present east end[3] (Plate 3b). The west side of bay six is marked by a pair of large shafts on pilasters of Norman type which survive in the later fabric (Figure 5, p. 94). Their survival is unlikely to be accidental, both because the thirteenth-century extension took them as its point of departure and because they could easily have been removed at the time of the fourteenth-century rebuilding of the bays to the west. Their retention therefore suggests that they marked a liturgically significant feature (Colour pl. 11b). That this is likely to have been the entrance to the bay containing the high altar is indicated by a reference in the sixteenth century to the altar having stood between the tombs of Bishops Redman and Louth – that is, according to Browne Willis's plan of 1730, in the sixth bay from the present east end[4] (Frontispiece). Further, according to the *Liber Eliensis*, when Etheldreda was translated into the new east arm in 1106, she was placed near the high altar (*contra maius altare*). Since the vault of the sixth bay has a central boss with a representation of the saint (Colour pl. 17b), the shrine was probably located in this bay in the 1240s building, a position which, in the Norman building, would place it appropriately behind the high altar, in the apse. The *Liber* also says that

---

[2] '*Ipse* [Bishop Eustace] *construxit novam galileam a fundamentis versus occidentem*': BL, MS Harl. 3721, fo. 35ᵛ. Tracery on the buttress built to shore up the western crossing after the collapse of the north-west transept is comparable with that on the tomb chest of Bishop Redman (1501–5): Bentham, *Ely*, pl. 22, facing p. 184. For the 1699 collapse and repair see T. Cocke, 'The Architectural History of Ely Cathedral from 1540 to 1840', in *Medieval Art and Architecture at Ely Cathedral*, BAACT, 2 (London, 1979), p. 72.

[3] Robert Willis's excavations are reported in Stewart, *Ely*, pp. 24–9. The apse was squared off; in Willis's opinion, during construction.

[4] B. Willis, *A Survey of the Cathedrals of Lincoln, Ely, Oxford, and Peterborough* (London, 1730). See Stewart, *Ely*, pp. 128–9, for the 16th-century texts on the position of the high altar.

Etheldreda's two sisters, Sexburga and Wihtburga, and her niece, Ermenilda, were buried at her feet, that is, to the east of her. With the high altar in bay 5, the space available for the four shrines would have been no more than 14ft (4.3m) long at its deepest point. The apse was at some stage squared off, possibly to allow more room for the shrines.

The elevation of the eastern arm probably consisted of a main arcade, a tribune gallery, and a clerestory with a wall passage, as these are the elements of the surviving Norman elevation in the transepts and of the thirteenth-century extension, which would have been linked by the bays of the Norman eastern arm. The masonry joints of the shaft above the first pier from the crossing on the south side do not course with those of the wall of the adjacent fourteenth-century bay to one side, or the pier of the Octagon to the other. This suggests that the shaft is Norman.[5] If there was a shaft on this support, it is almost inevitable that there would have been a shaft on every support in the arm. This follows if all the supports were uniform, and equally if they alternated, as the evidence lies on a support which would have been a minor element, which implies a shaft of at least equal size on the major supports.

Main transepts

The transepts differed in two chief respects from their present form (Colour pl. 12*b–c*). In the original building they were four bays long, before one bay of each was lost to the Octagon in the fourteenth century. Secondly, each transept had aisles on all three sides. The end aisle differs from those of the normal kind along the sides of the arm in lying inside the transept wall rather than outside it. It supported a platform linking the galleries to east and west – hence the absence, in the arches leading to the galleries, of the subdividing column present in the other bays. Each of these end aisles was at some stage removed, and replaced with a narrower walkway, but their existence is established by four observations. The large triple respond in the centre of each end wall belongs with a pair of aisle bays but conflicts with the arcades of the extant walkways; the spandrels above the first supports in from the end walls have very uneven surfaces, especially evident in the south transept, suggesting that they have been altered; unevenness in the half-shafts where they rise above the springing point of the main arcade in the north transept suggests the same; and a large fragment of a groin vault is embedded in the later walkway of the south arm.[6] The bays of the east aisles are separated by transverse walls which appear at points to course with the arcade supports and hence to be original, making the bays into separate chapels and unusable for processions.

There is a major building break across the middle of the transept. It runs from the north-east corner of the main space of the north transept to the east end of the south aisle of the nave (points a and b in Figure 5, p. 94). Both ends are marked by breaks in

---

[5] The shaft has been examined from scaffolding by Philip Dixon and John Maddison (personal communication from John Maddison). See also M. Thurlby, 'The Romanesque Apse Vault at Peterborough Cathedral', in D. Buckton and T.A. Heslop (eds.), *Studies in Medieval Art and Architecture Presented to Peter Lasko* (Stroud, 1994), p. 178. Christopher Wilson appears to have been the first to recognise the possibly Norman date of this shaft.

[6] On the main transepts see also J.P. McAleer, 'A Note about the Transept Cross Aisles of Ely Cathedral', *PCAS*, 81 (1992), pp. 51–70, who illustrates the fragment of groin vault at plate 2.

the jointing of the masonry. The positions of the break indicate that the work of phase 1 lies to the east and south. This work can be identified by its rectangular arch orders, volute capitals and crude tooling. In the south transept these characteristics occur in the main arcades and aisles of the east and west sides and in the end wall, and in the north transept on the main arcade and aisle of the east wall. The work of phase 2 is characterised by arch mouldings and cushion capitals and includes all the parts of both transepts above and to the north and west of phase 1. The fact that the break does not coincide with any of the the main elements of the building suggests that it was due to an unplanned interruption in building works, probably associated with the abbatial interregnum of 1093 to 1100.[7] To have begun the south transept before the north would have followed the common practice of starting with the transept adjoining the east range of the claustral buildings.[8] Since half shafts do not occur in the south transept but are present in the east arm and the north transept, it is possible that the south transept also preceded the east arm. The exterior faces of the eastern walls of the transepts both have a similar narrow course near the top of the wall. This suggests that the whole of phase 1, including the parts of the east arm constructed before the break, was built in a single organised campaign, with courses of specific sizes running from one end of the build to the other.[9]

In addition to the differences in architectural form which help to define the break between phases 1 and 2, there are three other changes which occur within phase 1, concerning the windows, the shafts on the piers, and the alternation of supports. All the windows in the east walls of both transepts have been altered, but the window at the end of the east aisle of the south transept has a single undecorated rectangular order, while its equivalent in the north transept has nook shafts and billet mouldings. Secondly, in the south transept the piers (the second supports from the crossing on both the east and west sides) have no attached shafts on their main faces, while in the north transept the sole equivalent pier (the first support from the crossing on the east side) does.

The changes between the transepts in their windows and shafts can, then, be

---

[7] S. Ferguson, 'The Romanesque Cathedral of Ely: an Archaeological Evaluation of its Construction', PhD thesis (Columbia University, 1986), is the most complete and thorough study of the Cathedral, including detailed analyses of the masonry, the building phases, the internal development of forms, and their place in the context of Romanesque architecture. The only major point on which I disagree with her findings concerns the dating of phase 2. Ferguson places this in the 1090s rather than after 1100, on the following grounds. (1) There is documentary evidence that Ranulf Flambard continued the administration of the Abbey over the interregnum (pp. 98–9, 125–6). (2) There would have been insufficient time for Abbot Richard to have completed the building up to the third bay of the nave by the translation in 1106 (pp. 115–17). (3) There are forms of the type of phase 2 in buildings datable to the 1090s (pp. 140–53). (4) There is no break in the masonry between phases 1 and 2. To these points it may be responded: (1) This is a good point but it is not by itself conclusive. (2) It is only necessary for Richard to have completed the eastern arm for the translation. (3) The dating of architectural details is not susceptible to such fine distinctions as that between 1093 and 1100. (4) What matters most is that there is a break between the two phases, at the end of the north transept and at the junction between the south transept and the nave aisle. This overrides all the other points, not only because it exists but because of its unplanned position. The breaks in the masonry and the striking changes in the decorative elements are clear suggestions of a gap in years. The evidence does not indicate how long it was or when it started, but the interregnum of 1093 to 1100 is better than any other set of years.

[8] As for example at Norwich Cathedral; see E. Fernie, *An Architectural History of Norwich Cathedral* (Oxford, 1993), pp. 50–3.

[9] As for example at Selby; see E. Fernie, 'The Romanesque Church of Selby Abbey', in L.R. Hoey (ed.), *Yorkshire Monasticism: Archaeology, Art and Architecture from the 7th to the 16th Centuries*, BAACT, 16 (1995), pp. 40–9.

attributed to a simple desire for more decoration. The third change, however, in the alternation of the supports, must reflect differences of opinion about design principles. Counting south from the position of the lost south-east crossing pier, the south transept has a column, a pier and a column, and then the south wall. In the north transept the sequence, again counting out from the crossing, is a pier, a column, another pier and then the end wall (Colour pl. 12*b–c*). The difference can be explained in the following way. The third supports from the crossing would originally have carried the corner between the side walls and the arcade of the aisle across the end of the transept. For this purpose a column, being visually and actually less massive than a pier of the same width, could be thought to offer inadequate support. Having tried the column in the south transept, for the north the architect used a pier. The same problem produced the same response in the designing of the courtyards of Renaissance palaces. In the Palazzo Medici in Florence of the 1440s all the supports are columns – including those at the corners, which consequently form points of visual and possibly structural weakness. This, at any rate, appears to have been the view of later architects designing similar courtyards, such as Luciano Laurana at the Palazzo Ducale in Urbino, of the 1460s, where the corners are supported on piers.[10] A similar point is made by Vitruvius, who directs that columns at the corners of buildings 'must be made thicker by the fiftieth part of their diameter, because they are cut into by the air and appear more slender to the spectators'.[11] The solution in the north transept does, on the other hand, produce what many might feel to be the equal infelicity of having a pier in an alternating system next to what must have been the pier of the crossing.[12]

After the break, the transepts were completed, including the main arcades of the north and west walls of the north transept, and the upper storeys of both arms. The disruption of the northernmost spandrel in the west wall of the north transept indicates that this completion included the aisle across the end wall. The replacement walkways are, however, unlikely to have been built very much later as they have the same arch mouldings as used in phase 2.[13] It is not clear why the aisles were removed. There could have been a change of function, such as a discontinuation of processions at gallery level, but it is difficult to see why that would require removal. The change is therefore more likely to have been due to an assessment that the transepts would be improved in appearance without the encumbrance of the end aisles, but a means of passing from one gallery to another was still needed, hence the walkways. There are two other changes. At some point in phase 2 (or in the first half of the twelfth century) to judge by the capitals and mouldings of the blind arcading, the west aisle of the south transept was closed off by a wall some 10ft (3m) high, and secondly the doorway in the west wall of the west aisle of the south transept was refurbished and, at an unspecified date, was blocked up.

---

[10] For illustrations of these courtyards see P. Murray, *The Architecture of the Italian Renaissance*, 3rd edn (London, 1986), illustrations 36 and 49.

[11] Vitruvius, *De Architectura*, III, iii, 11 (ed. F. Granger, 2 vols. (London, 1931–4), I, pp. 178–9): '*Etiamque angulares columnae crassiores faciendae sunt ex suo diametro quinquagesima parte, quod eae ab aere circumciduntur et graciliores videntur esse aspicientibus.*'

[12] S. Inskip Ladds, *The Monastery of Ely* (Ely, 1930), p. 3, argues that the north transept must be earlier, because it has the right arrangement of supports, and the south later, because it lacked Simeon's guiding hand.

[13] Ferguson, 'Romanesque Cathedral of Ely' (cit. in n. 7), pp. 191ff, dates the replacement walkways to 1106–9.

Nave

The nave continues the elevation of the transept, with a main arcade, tribune gallery and clerestory (Colour pl. 8). The clerestory is built using the technique of oversailing, which is also present in the transepts. This occurs when a gallery wall is thicker than the wall of the main arcade below, in order to allow room for a wide passage within the wall at clerestory level without having to make the wall and the supports of the main arcade below correspondingly thick (Figure 6). Thus the external width of the nave at ground level is 44ft (13.41m) while at the wall-head, where it includes the wall-passages, it is 46ft (14.02m).

The construction of the nave appears to have proceeded swiftly, as details at its west end are comparable with those in the eastern arm of Peterborough Cathedral, which is datable to between 1118 and 1125, while the profiles of the Ely bases have suggested a date for the start of the nave of about 1115. These stylistic dates have been corroborated by a dendrochronological date in the 1120s provided by timbers re-used in the roof.[14] The nave is more unified than the transepts, with all the supports – both columns and piers – having an attached shaft on a backing pilaster. Minor changes indicate the following order of building (Figure 7).

The earliest work, continuing that of the north transept, is indicated by the rectangular pilasters on all the piers of the north main arcade and the second one on the south (and presumably in the first, lost, piers on both sides) (Figure 7, section A). West of pier 2 in the south arcade, the two corners of each pilaster are replaced with thin shafts, forming a bundle of three shafts with the main one (section B). The arches of the easternmost five bays, in both the north and south arcades, have (or, in the case of bay 1, presumably had) three orders, the first and third with angle rolls and the middle one a rectangular profile. The middle order changes to an angle-roll in bay 6 and after, again on both north and south sides (section C), while in the arches of the tribune gallery, on the face towards the gallery, bays 2, 3 and 4 have a rectangular middle order and bay 5 an angle roll, again on both the north and the south (section D). This means that all of the piers in the north main arcade must have been built first, followed by two with the same rectangular profile at the east end of the south arcade (A), then piers with the new profile of a triple shaft at least to pier 5 in the south arcade (B), and next, five main arcade arches and four gallery arches were built on both sides (C, D).

The change from rectangular to cylindrical pilasters in the piers therefore occurs at a random point in the building programme, nor is the change consistent, as the cylindrical forms on the pier faces begin on pier 3 of the south arcade while the rectangular arch orders continue to bay 5. The changes in the arches, however, are not random, as they occur in the same places on both sides of the nave. Most large Norman churches have a building break in the eastern bays of the nave. At Ely the frequency, the symmetry and

---

[14] For the parallels with Peterborough see Ferguson, 'Romanesque Cathedral of Ely', pp. 212–16, and for the bases, S. Rigold, 'Romanesque Bases in and South-east of the Limestone Belt', in M.R. Apted, R. Gilyard-Beer and A.D. Saunders (eds.) *Ancient Monuments and their Interpretation: Essays presented to A J Taylor* (London and Chichester, 1977), pp. 99–138, at 122, 123 and 135 n. 183. See W.G. Simpson, 'Archaeological Survey of Ely Cathedral', 7th Report for the Dean and Chapter (University of Nottingham, 1988), p. 1, for a felling date for the timber between 1105 and 1140; this bracket is derived from timber re-used in the later roof which could have come from anywhere in the length of the previous roof.

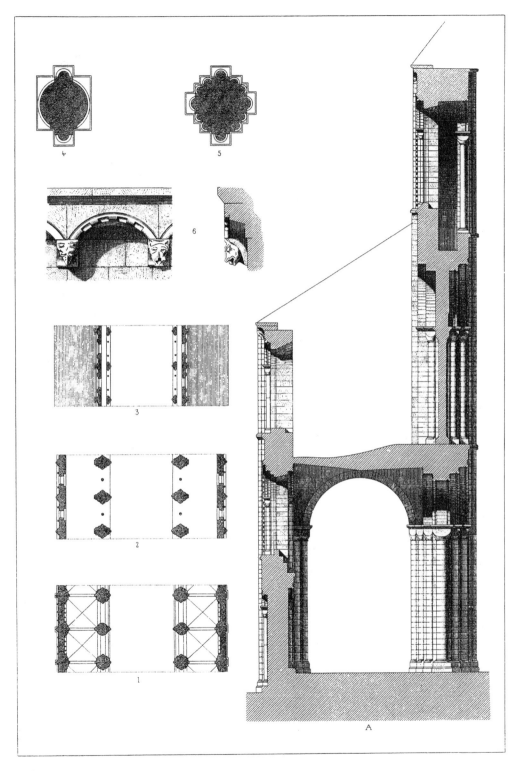

Figure 6. Cross section of nave and aisle walls (V. Rupprich-Robert, *L'architecture Normande* (1884–9), II, pl. LXIA)

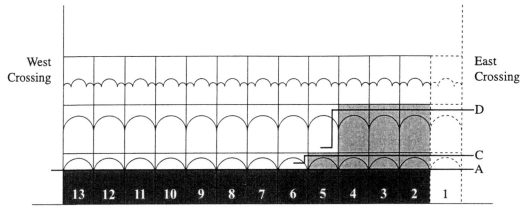

Nave: north elevation

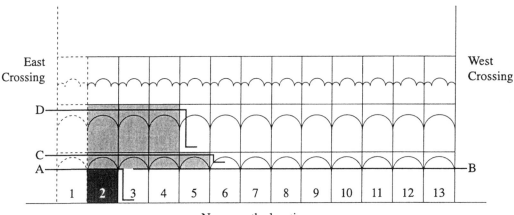

Nave: south elevation

Figure 7. Phases in the north and south walls of the nave (Chris Kellish)

the stepping back of storeys to the east all suggest that these were planned, possibly to recoup the finances of the project, at a point which would both provide a roof for the part of the church housing the monastic services and afford sufficient buttressing against the westward thrust of the north and south arches of the crossing. Such planned breaks contrast with the unplanned character of the break across the main transepts.

A break also seems to have occurred at the same place in the north aisle wall, as there are changes in the rectangular orders at the ends of the blind arcading from bay 6 westwards and in the abaci of the capitals from bay 7. In the south aisle, because the aisle wall was built to the west end of the cloister, similar changes only occur in bay 10. The change from plain transverse arches to those with angle rolls does however occur in the same place in both aisles – where one would expect, at the sixth bay.

The choir screen is located between the second piers of the nave in Browne Willis's plan of c.1730, before the removal of the furniture (Frontispiece). Its form is recorded in sketches of the 1760s by James Essex (Plate 3c) which formed the basis of a reconstruction by William St John Hope[15] (Plate 3c). The screen had three open arches, the central one providing an entrance and the flanking ones set on a plinth and hence like windows, the trio forming an arrangement similar to the entrance to a chapter house, such as that at Durham. The flanking openings had unusual segmental arches with joggled voussoirs set inside them. The scalloped capitals and chevron provide decoration similar to that in the upper parts of the south-west transept, which, together with the quatrefoils in the frieze across the top, might suggest a date in the second half of the century.

Western transepts

These consisted of a full-scale crossing and two arms. The surviving south transept has three different elevations on the interior faces of its three sides. The east wall has a ground storey with a chapel, a gallery level also with a chapel, and a clerestory with a passage, equivalent to the three storeys of the nave. The south wall has five levels of blind or open arcading plus a clerestory passage on the same level as that of the east wall, while the west wall also has five levels and a clerestory, but with the third and fourth levels different from those on the south wall (Plate 5a). On the exterior the sequence is the same on all three sides of the transept (Plate 5b). There is a plain dado, then rows of arches, the second of which was originally open to the wall passage behind it.[16] Remains of blind arcading above the level of the Galilee vault indicate that the western wall of the transept originally continued across the western face of the crossing. What survives of the north transept follows the same pattern as the south, with some differences in decoration such as the use of the Greek key instead of chevron.

This part of the building provides another indication, like parts of the main transepts and the nave, of the way in which the amount and complexity of decoration increased as the church was built. On the interior, by contrast with the single layers which decorate the aisles of the nave, the blind arcading is two and sometimes three layers thick, and the interlaced arcading of a remarkably impressionistic rather than geometrical character. On the exterior the plainness of the dado cannot be attributed to its being of an earlier date, as it is likely to be of the same date as the highly ornate interior face at this level. It must rather indicate the architect's wish to provide a strong plain element at the base of the wall. By contrast, the increase in the amount and sophistication of each successive band in the storeys above is due to changes of style over time. The sophistication is, however, restricted to the design, as much of the masonry is of very poor quality. The south arm uses similar motifs to the west end of the nave, so that there is no reason to date its commencement later than the 1120s. From the blind arcading below the clerestory upwards, however, elements such as keeling and crockets suggest a break and a date in the second half of the century.[17] The roof lines on the north and south

---

[15] W.H. St John Hope, 'Quire Screens in English Churches', *Archaeologia*, 68 (1917), pp. 43–110, and *idem*, 'The Twelfth-century Pulpitum or Roodloft formerly in the Cathedral Church of Ely; with some Notes on similar Screens in English Cathedral and Monastic Churches', *CAS Communications*, xxi (1919), pp. 19–73; G. Zarnecki, J. Holt and T. Holland (eds.), *English Romanesque Art 1066–1200* (London, 1984), item 518. Maddison, *Ely Cathedral*, pp. 35–7, dates the screen after the burial of Bishop Nigel in 1169.

[16] R. Plant, 'English Romanesque Architecture and the Holy Roman Empire', PhD thesis (Courtauld Institute of Art, University of London, 1998), p. 227.

[17] Ferguson, 'Romanesque Cathedral of Ely' (cit. in n. 7), pp. 226, 247–50, 259, dates the lower parts of the west transept to 1120s because of the use of similar decorative details to those in the nave. As with her re-dating of

faces of the tower indicate roofs with an angle at the ridge of approximately 70° – steeper, as befits their later date, than the approximately 90° angle of the nave roof indicated on the east face of the tower.[18]

Stairs

There are the remains of six staircases to the upper parts of the building, namely fragments of one behind the north respond in the east arm, at clerestory level but probably beginning at least at gallery level, that in the eastern turret of the north transept façade from ground level, one in the east turret of the south transept façade from gallery level, one in the west turret of the south transept façade, from clerestory level, one in the south-west corner of the south-west transept, also from ground level, and the sixth in the east tower of the south-west transept, from gallery level. It is possible that there were matching stairs on the south side of the eastern arm and in the north-west transept, but the absence of one in the south main transept indicates that symmetry was not a rule.[19] The turret at the south-west corner is noteworthy both for being ten-sided and in having a pronounced lean. The foundations must have started to sink during building, as the lean begins to be corrected at the fifth row of blind arcading above the dado, in the same way as that on the nearly contemporary campanile at Pisa.[20]

Sculpture and painting

Carving occurs on capitals, portals and corbels, as well as, in the very latest phases of the building, on blind arcades.[21] In phase 1, between 1083 and 1093, it is characterised by two-dimensional, flat figures and foliage on plain surfaces especially of the volute capitals, and by chip carving. There are capitals with this type of carving on the columns of the main arcades and on the responds of the south transept (Plate 4d), and on the respond to the east of the cloister doorway in bay 2 of the south aisle of the nave. There is also the portal to the cloister in the west aisle of the south transept, in the bay next to the corner with the nave, of which only the bevelled and chip-carved hood-mould survives (Plate 4b).

---

the nave, this date has also been corroborated, firstly by the dendrochronological evidence published by Simpson, 'Archaeological Survey of Ely Cathedral' (cit. in n. 14), p. 1; secondly by the masons' marks, which show that the western transepts were a continuation of the build of the nave (K. Fearn, 'Ely Cathedral Masons' Marks in the South-West Transept', MA thesis (University of Nottingham, 1993)); and thirdly by the coursing of the masonry from the nave into the transept (K. Fearn, P. Marshall and W.G. Simpson, 'The South-West Transept of Ely Cathedral: Archaeological Interpretation' (University of Nottingham, n.d. [post-1995]), p. 25). As cited in n. 1, above (Wharton, *Anglia Sacra*, I, p. 631), the completion of the western transepts and tower can be attributed to Bishop Ridel, who died in 1189.

[18] Fearn, Marshall, and Simpson, 'South-West Transept', p. 55, roof sections.

[19] For the stair in the eastern arm see J.P. McAleer, 'Some Observations about the Romanesque Choir of Ely Cathedral, *Jnl., Society of Architectural Historians*, 53 (1994), pp. 89–92.

[20] In E. Fernie, 'Observations on the Norman Plan', in *Medieval Art and Architecture at Ely Cathedral* (cit. in n. 2), figure 1 and p. 6, I discussed the possibility that the Galilee formed part of the plan of the original Cathedral even if it was not built with it. The walls are immensely thick for a porch of c.1200 and more in keeping with the walls of the western transepts, but only excavation of the foundations would reveal whether they are of old build with the façade itself.

[21] G. Zarnecki, *The Early Sculpture of Ely Cathedral* (London, 1958).

Work in phase 2, between 1100 and some time in the 1120s when the west end of the nave was reached, is three-dimensional and deeply undercut. There is decoration of this kind on isolated cushion capitals on the east galleries of the north and south transepts (Plate 4*d*). The greater part of it, however, occurs on three doorways. An arch was inserted into the doorway of phase 1 in the west aisle of the south transept, consisting of nook shafts and a roll moulding with spiral thongs and foliage, and a human head in the round at the keystone. Immediately to the west of this, in bay 2 of the south nave aisle, is the portal known as the Monks' Doorway. This is composed of similar elements and cut in the same way as the transept portal, but is more complex, with four orders that become richer toward the centre, a trefoil arch with representations of monks in the spandrels, dragons on the orders, and heads on the abaci and at the keystone. The doorway is bonded into the aisle wall, with a shallow course for the abaci, and a deep one for the capitals, extending west some 3ft (1m) after which the masonry is a patchwork.[22]

The portal in bay 9, known as the Prior's Doorway, has a tympanum with Christ in majesty supported by angels, and three orders, the outer of which had lions for bases and capitals (Plate 4*a*). The absence of a tympanum would have permitted the use of crosses in processions entering the Monks' Doorway (Plate 4*b*), while the tympanum in the Prior's Doorway suggests that it was the guests' entrance – like the public portal on a facade, the commonest place for such sculptural display. The corbels on the exterior of the south transept and the nave have a mixture of human, animal and grotesque heads, the human ones being closely comparable to those on the portals. The Prior's Doorway is not bonded into the aisle wall to either side of it, but since the Monks' Door, with sculpture identical in character to that of the Prior's Doorway, is contemporary with the aisle, it follows that the Prior's Doorway is also, however it was put in place.

Though only a few fragments of polychromy now remain, there is no reason to doubt that all of the masonry on the interior would originally have been painted. The most extensive survival is the foliate decoration in bay 3 of the south aisle of the nave. This is comparable with the carved foliage on the adjacent portals, suggesting that the painting was carried out shortly after the completion of the aisle in the late 1120s or 1130s. The exterior was probably intended to be painted as well, though no evidence for this survives at Ely.

Monastic buildings

The design for Simeon's church would have included a cloister and claustral ranges (Figure 5, p. 94). While nothing earlier than the middle of the twelfth century remains standing, the presence of the cloister is indicated by the sills of the windows in the south aisle of the nave, which are higher in bays 4 to 9 than in bays 10 to 13 in order to accommodate what must have been the lean-to roof of the north walk. The arcading is lower in bay 3 presumably because the builders had not yet taken account of the need to

---

[22] The knobs on the cusps of the trefoils are missing in Bentham's engraving (Bentham, *Ely*, plate VI, opp. p. 35), but their restoration may be acceptable given the tiny fragment of bevel surviving on one cusp and their use on the fourth doorway surviving from phase 2, that inserted into a doorway of the first phase in the north wall of the north transept, just to the east of the break, and one on the door from the main wall passage of the south-west transept to the upper chapel.

accommodate the cloister roof.[23] The eastern or Monks' Doorway would appropriately have led into the bay of the nave behind the choir screen.

There is no indication of the east range apart from the rough masonry below gallery level in the western half of the central section of the end wall of the transept, where a slype or similar building may have abutted. Further south on the site, two walls of the kitchen survive to full height with architectural details which suggest a date in the second or third quarter of the twelfth century (Colour pl. 5b). The building was recorded by Essex apparently in a more complete state (Plate 3a). The space between the nave and the kitchen would accommodate a square cloister and a south range for the refectory, probably placing the kitchen near the middle of the length of the range, rather than at the more usual west end. The Prior's Doorway in bay 9 and changes in details in the aisle wall to the west indicate that the west wall of the original cloister would have abutted between bays 9 and 10, one bay further east than the later cloister. It is unclear if a west range was intended or built. There would have been room for it in line with bays 10 and 11, between the cloister and the chapel of the western transept, but there is evidence for a window in bay 10, which would conflict with any abutment.

Separate from the claustral square and hence from any connection with Simeon's original plan, the infirmary lies to the east and can be dated to c.1160–80 on stylistic grounds (Colour pl. 5a). It consists of a hall of nine bays with aisles and a clerestory, the arcades supported on alternating cylindrical and polygonal columns, and at the east end an aisled chapel with a rib-vaulted sanctuary. The capitals are a study in variations on the theme of the scalloped form. Those in the nave include the straightforward, the triangular, the positive alternating with the negative, those with volutes and those enveloped in waterleaf scrolls. Those in the chancel are fittingly more complex, being composed of two tiers with, for example, waterleaf forms above cylindrical-shaped scallops.[24]

Geometry

The unit used in the designing of the plan seems to have been 5ft 6in. (1.68m) long, or one third of a perch of 16ft 6in. (5.03m). The nave is 33ft (10.06m) or two perches wide, each aisle 16ft 6in. (5.03m) or one perch wide, and the arcade walls 5ft 6in. (1.68m) thick, giving a total of 77ft (23.48m) (Figure 8), or 14 units in width. The nave, from the interior face of the west wall of the main transepts to the interior face of the west end of the nave, is 220ft (c.67m) or 40 units long, the western arm to the interior of the façade is 264ft (c.80.5m) or 48 units, and the remaining eastern parts of the building, from the interior face of the west wall of the transepts to the chancel arch, 110ft (c.33.5m) or 20 units. The cloister side was 132ft (c.40.2m) or 24 units, as were the western transepts internally, if the north transept mirrored the south. The 48-unit length of the western

[23] The same error is evident in the windows of the west wall of the transept abutting the cloister at Norwich; see Fernie, *Norwich Cathedral* (cit. in n. 8), p. 57.

[24] Bentham, *Ely*, plate L. Anne Holton-Krayenbuhl, 'The Infirmary Complex at Ely', *AJ*, 154 (1997), pp. 118–72. Essex and Bentham thought that the kitchen was a chapel and the infirmary a Saxon church. These misidentifications are nonetheless understandable, as each structure is clearly related in form to an ecclesiastical building type. On the relatively meagre remains of other buildings of the 12th century in the College, see Holton-Krayenbuhl, pp. 123, 135–41, figs. 13–16, and 'The Prior's Lodgings at Ely', *AJ*, 156 (1999), pp. 300–6 and 331.

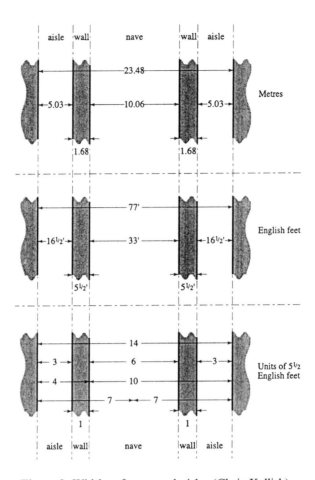

Figure 8. Widths of nave and aisles (Chris Kellish)

section taken as the side of a square produces a diagonal of 68 units, or 20 units extra, which is the length of the eastern section. The proportion between the side of a square and its diagonal is a near standard formula in large Norman churches in England.

Neither the perch nor the proportion is used in the elevation. This is made up of piers of between 17ft 7in. and 18ft 4in. (5.38 and 5.57m), an arcade storey of between 27ft 3in. and 27ft 8in. (8.31 and 8.44m), arcade and gallery of between 52ft 5in. and 53ft 5in. (15.98 and 16.28m) and a full elevation of approximately 73ft 7in. (22.44m). While the disjunction between plan and elevation may seem odd, it also occurs at Winchester and at St-Étienne in Caen. It is also a striking coincidence that almost the only piece of documentary evidence we have for an elevation in relation to a ground plan (or at least for how one architect measured them) draws the same distinction. That is, Antonio da Vicenza's late fourteenth-century sketches of Milan Cathedral give the dimensions of the plan in feet and those of the elevation in braccia.[25]

---

[25] For the dimensions, tolerances and proportions of the plan see Fernie, 'Observations on the Norman Plan' (cit. in n. 20), pp. 1–7. On related examples see Fernie, *Norwich Cathedral* (cit. in n. 8), pp. 94–100. Ferguson,

Functions and sources

The brief for Simeon's building would have required a setting for a high altar and four shrines, space for choir stalls and a choir screen, aisles for processions, and an imposing size. The church built from the 1080s to the late twelfth century contains many changes in otherwise uniform sequences of forms, but they are mostly matters of detail such as the profiles of orders, abaci and mouldings. On the face of it there is no reason to question the assumption that the building as completed, apart from its decorative elements, was as Simeon's architect designed it. The change in status and function from abbey church to monastic cathedral in 1109 does not appear to have led to any remodelling of those parts already constructed nor to any alterations in the design, other than in masonry details, of those parts still to be built.[26]

The design of Ely is clearly based on that of Winchester, and as Winchester had been under construction for only a few years when Ely was begun, the new building must have been modelled on plans rather than a standing structure. Ely shares with Winchester all of its major features, including its scale, an east arm and transepts of four bays, aisles on all three sides of each transept, with that at the end forming a platform inside the building, an aisled nave with two doorways to the cloister, some alternation of supports, a western massif, and an elevation consisting of a main arcade, a tribune gallery and a clerestory with a wall passage. Ely lacks the crypt, the ambulatory and the towers on the corners of the main transepts of Winchester, and has different forms of piers and alternation as well as chapels off the east face of the western massif.

Winchester and Ely have overall dimensions comparable with those of the imperial cathedrals of Speyer and Mainz in the Rhineland, and, at least in length, with those of churches such as Old St Peter's or St Paul's-outside-the-Walls in Rome. These contrast sharply with almost all other churches of the eleventh century in western Europe, including buildings in Normandy such as St-Étienne in Caen, despite its having had Duke William himself as patron. Old St Peter's had a total interior length of *c*.436ft (*c*.133m), St Paul's over 420ft (*c*.128m), Speyer Cathedral *c*.416ft (*c*.127m), Winchester *c*.515ft (*c*.157m), and Ely over 400ft (122m), against St-Étienne at *c*.276ft (*c*.84m). The contrast between St-Étienne and Ely can be illustrated by overlaying the plans of each on to that of an Early Christian model such as St Paul's[27] (Figure 9).

'Romanesque Cathedral of Ely' (cit. in n. 7), p. 63, n. 12, notes that she has not found the English foot in the smaller parts of the building. This is a good basis for accepting a third of a perch (1.68m) as the unit used, which need have no relationship to the English foot. Only the length of the main transepts, at a little under 180ft (54.86m), is not made up of 5ft 6in. (1.68m) units. The explanation for the length may lie in a parallel between the 2–3–2 relationship of the width of the nave and the flanking sections of the aisle and arcade wall and the width of the nave and aisles in the centre and the length of each transept beyond (51ft 4in. – 77ft – 51ft 4in. (15.66m – 23.46m – 15.66m), and 22ft – 33ft – 22ft (6.7m – 10.06m – 6.7m)). The figures for the elevation are much less trustworthy than those for the plan, as floor levels and wall heads are frequently changed and all levels are subject to subsidence. The measurements were taken in the west bay of the south wall of the south transept and in the even numbered bays of the south wall of the nave, except for the clerestory, which was only measured in bay 8. For the Milan figures see J. Ackerman, 'Ars sine scientia nihil est', *Art Bulletin*, 31 (1949), p. 88 and n. 14.

[26] *LE*, iii. Prol: p. 237: '*Textus autem libri huius de duorum constat episcoporum tempore, Hervehi scilicet ipsius loci, sicut novimus, episcopi primi, sed aliunde sacrati, et Nigelli secundi, sed primi illic consecrati.*'

[27] Fernie, 'Observations on the Norman Plan' (cit. in n. 20), p. 4.

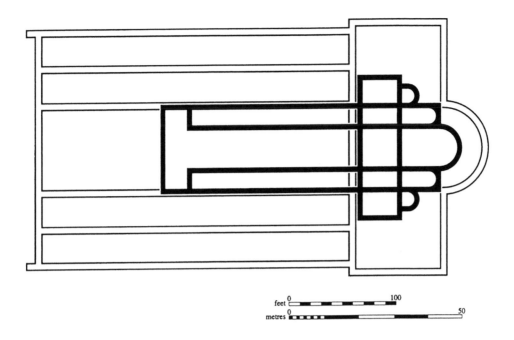

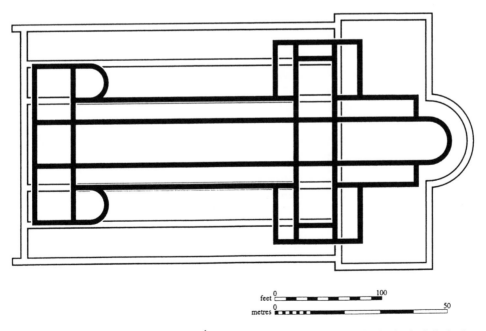

Figure 9. Comparative plans of St-Étienne in Caen (*above*) and Ely Cathedral (*below*), laid over a plan of St Paul's Rome (Chris Kellish)

The platforms at the ends of the main transepts are not to be confused with the aisles on the transept ends at, for instance, the cathedral of Santiago de Compostela in north-west Spain, which are proper aisles lying outside the end wall of the transept. They are taken directly from Winchester, which in turn derived them from a source in Normandy such as St-Etienne in Caen. It has been suggested that such platforms were intended to meet the requirements of Anglo-Saxon liturgical practice, but the source in Normandy renders the explanation unnecessary.[28] The change from platforms to walkways at the ends of the main transepts cannot be explained by the change in status from abbey to cathedral, because Winchester, the source of the platforms, was designed as a monastic cathedral from the start.

The constructional formula known as oversailing, of which the example at Ely is the earliest surviving in England, can be traced back to St-Étienne, where it was developed out of the deep blind arcading on the transept walls of earlier buildings such as the abbey churches of Bernay and Jumièges.

The best source for the west transepts as a concept is the most obvious one, namely Winchester, though the form is not that of a great rectangular block, but rather of a standard Norman main transept with chapels, such as that at St Augustine's in Canterbury. The predilection for grand western massifs on churches in the Empire is doubtless relevant in that a general reference was almost certainly intended, even if no specific influence is evident.[29]

Turning to the decorative elements, the sculpture of phase 1 can be associated by its stone type with the production of the quarry at Barnack, nearby in eastern North-amptonshire, and by its style and motifs with the Bayeux Tapestry and related manuscripts of the eleventh century.[30] The changes introduced in phase 2 to the sculpture, the pier forms and the arch mouldings are part of a revolution in architectural decoration which takes place in the late 1080s and 1090s and which forms the basis of Norman decoration thereafter. The sculpture of phase 2 belongs to the same group as that in the crypt at Canterbury Cathedral, in the transepts at Worcester Cathedral, and in the east arm of the abbey church at Romsey, that is, work of between the 1080s and the 1120s. These parallels support the likelihood that the Monks' and Prior's Doorways, like the corbels, were built in the 1120s with the nave bays which they adorn.[31]

---

[28] A. Klukas, '*Altaria superiora*: The Function and Significance of the Tribune in Anglo-Norman Romanesque', PhD thesis (University of Pittsburgh, 1978), p. 312.

[29] Examples include the cathedral of Nevers in eastern France (*c.*1030), the abbey of St Trond in Belgium (1055–82, without a central tower), the cathedral of Trier in the Eifel (*c.*1050), and S. Antonino at Piacenza in North Italy (11th century), a distribution which suggests a common source in the Empire. On this see Plant, 'English Romanesque and the Empire' (cit. in n. 16), pp. 204–6. See also J.P. McAleer, 'Le problème du transept occidental en Grande Bretagne', *Cahiers de civilisation médiévale*, 34 (1991), pp. 349–56. Sir Alfred Clapham, *English Romanesque Architecture before the Conquest* (Oxford, 1930), pp. 90 and 94, suggested that the western transept at Ely was derived from the Anglo-Saxon church there, on the basis of the entry in the Anglo-Saxon Chronicle for 1036 to the effect that the burial of the Aetheling Alfred was 'low in the sacred earth, to the steeple full nigh in the south aisle [*portice*], to lie of the transept west'. This is however unconvincing, not only because the form in the Norman building has a straightforward ancestry in a Norman context, but also because the description of a *porticus* next to the steeple calls to mind an arrangement like that in the Anglo-Saxon church of All Saints at Brixworth, which has nothing in common with a transept.

[30] Zarnecki, *Sculpture at Ely* (cit. in n. 21), pp. 11–12.

[31] Zarnecki, *Sculpture at Ely*, pp. 19–37, and Zarnecki, 'The Romanesque Capitals in the South Transept of Worcester Cathedral', in *Medieval Art and Architecture at Worcester Cathedral*, BAACT, 1 (Leeds, 1978), p. 41. The sculpture of the Monks' and Prior's Doorways used to be dated as late as the 1170s. Zarnecki was the first

Influences

Despite the fact that it was part of the east Midlands diocese of Lincoln, Ely stands at the head of the school of Norman church building associated with the diocese of East Anglia, with experimentation in pier forms a characteristic of the group. Its chief monuments are the abbey of Bury St Edmunds (which may be contemporary with Ely), the cathedral at Norwich, and the abbeys or priories at Castle Acre, Binham, Wymondham and Thetford, and, in the Fenland closer to Ely, at Peterborough, King's Lynn, Crowland and Thorney.[32] Ely, Bury, Norwich and Peterborough constitute an unrivalled concentration of very large buildings in one region, whereas other large buildings such as the cathedrals of Winchester, London and Durham do not appear to have been dependent on their hinterlands or other buildings in the vicinity. This may be a consequence of the wealth of the area in this period.

Finally, though the influence is probably not direct, Ely forms part of the overall relevance of Norman Romanesque, in both Normandy and England, to the origins of Gothic in northern France. This is particularly so with the experimentation with wall passages and their attendant oversailing, as in the cathedrals of Noyon, Laon and Chartres. The resulting openness of the architecture is most evident at Ely in the thinness of the columns in both the gallery and the clerestory. In their lightness and thinness these features are the very antithesis of the weight and mass normally associated with the Norman style of building.

---

to clarify the sculptural history of Ely and in particular to put the arguments for the dating of phase 2 on a rational basis in the first half of the century. J.A. Franklin, 'The Romanesque Cloister Sculpture of Norwich Cathedral', MA thesis (University of East Anglia, 1980), presented the case for a date in the first quarter of the century in advance of the dendrochronological evidence. G. Zarnecki, 'Some Observations concerning the Romanesque Doorways of Ely Cathedral', in C. Harper-Bill, C.J. Holdsworth and J.L. Nelson (eds.), *Studies in Medieval History presented to R. Allen Brown* (Woodbridge, 1989), p. 351, acknowledges the case for this even earlier date. T.A. Heslop, *Norwich Castle Keep: Romanesque Architecture and Social Context* (Norwich, 1994), p. 33, dates the Ely portal sculpture about ten years after the portal of Norwich Castle, and therefore in the 1120s. Ferguson, 'Romanesque Cathedral of Ely', pp. 153–66, identifies a number of Anglo-Saxon sources.

[32] On the pier forms see B. Cherry, 'Romanesque Architecture in Eastern England', *JBAA*, 131 (1978), pp. 1–29, and L. Hoey, 'Pier Form and Vertical Wall Articulation in English Romanesque Architecture', *Jnl., Soc. Architectural Historians*, 43 (1984), pp. 258–83, and on the architectural context E. Fernie, *The Architecture of Norman England* (Oxford, 2000). On Thorney see J.C.E. Ayton, 'Thorney Abbey, an Architectural Analysis of a Romanesque Fen Abbey-Church', MA thesis (Courtauld Institute of Art, University of London, 1998), and on the East Anglian buildings in particular, see *e.g.* Fernie, *Norwich Cathedral* (cit. in n. 8), pp. 145–55.

The Gothic Cathedral:
New Building in a Historic Context

JOHN MADDISON

For its richness, sophistication and originality the Gothic work at Ely has achieved a prominent place in English architectural history. Early writers have served the building unusually well, and more recently stylistic problems, questions of iconographic significance, and issues of restoration and authenticity have been given detailed consideration.[1]

---

[1] The earliest useful account of the building is in Browne Willis, *A Survey of the Cathedrals of Lincoln, Ely, Oxford and Peterborough* (London, 1730), pp. 331–401, 549–51. Bentham, *Ely* (1771; 2nd edn. 1812) is an exceptionally full and reliable history in which the discussion of the architecture reflects Bentham's pioneer status in this field and includes the ideas of James Essex. Several of the engravings are unusually objective records of the building. George Millers, *A Description of the Cathedral Church of Ely* (Ely, 1807, 3rd edn 1834), makes some advances in its treatment of the architecture. These works were superseded by Stewart, *Ely* (1868), in which the new standards of Victorian archaeological writing, close observation of the fabric and patient examination of the fabric rolls and other accounts inform a scholarly account that includes an important contribution by Robert Willis. Charles W. Stubbs, *Handbook to the Cathedral Church of Ely*, 20th edn (London, 1898) is comprehensive and has some fresh observations. Chapman, *Sacrist Rolls* (1907) tabulates the late 13th and 14th-century fabric rolls and includes a discussion in which they are related to the standing architecture and probable liturgical arrangements of the church. S. Inskip Ladds, *The Monastery of Ely* (Ely, 1930) and Atkinson, *Ely Monastery* (1933), though primarily concerned with the conventual buildings, also discuss the Cathedral and its liturgical layout, and set it in the context of its monastic buildings. Atkinson's account of the Cathedral in VCH, *Cambs.*, IV, pp. 50–82, contributes new material and interpretations. N. Coldstream and P. Draper (eds.), *Medieval Art and Architecture at Ely Cathedral*, BAACT, 2 (London, 1979), has two important articles on the Gothic campaigns: P. Draper, 'Bishop Northwold and the Cult of St Etheldreda', pp. 8–27, and N. Coldstream, 'Ely Cathedral: the Fourteenth-Century Work', pp. 27–46, as well as J. Fletcher, 'Medieval Timberwork at Ely', pp. 58–71. Important observations on the 14th-century work are made by Christopher Wilson in 'The Origins of the Perpendicular Style and its Development to circa 1360', PhD thesis, University of London, 1979, pp. 185 ff; some of them were published in his *The Gothic Cathedral* (London, 1990), pp. 197–9. Phillip Lindley, 'The Monastic Cathedral at Ely, circa 1320 to circa 1350', PhD thesis, University of Cambridge, 1985, was the first extended treatment of the 14th-century work and led to a series of articles including: 'The Fourteenth Century Architectural Programme at Ely Cathedral', in W.M. Ormrod (ed.), *England in the Fourteenth Century: Proceedings of the 1985 Harlaxton Symposium* (Stamford, 1986), pp. 119–29; 'The Imagery of the Octagon at Ely', *JBAA*, 139 (1986), pp. 75–99; and '"Carpenter's Gothic" and Gothic Carpentry: Contrasting Attitudes to the Restoration of the Octagon and the Removals of the Choir at Ely Cathedral', *Architectural History*, 30 (1987), pp. 83–112. N. Coldstream, 'The Lady Chapel at Ely: Its Place in the English Decorated Style', in Malcolm Barber, Patricia McNulty and Peter Noble (eds.), *East Anglian and Other Studies Presented to Barbara Dodwell*, Reading Medieval Studies, 11 (Reading, 1985), pp. 1–30, is a substantial treatment of the building which initiated the 14th-century campaigns on the Cathedral. Maddison, *Ely Cathedral* (2000) is a history of the architecture of the Cathedral aimed at the general reader in which design is discussed in relation to its purpose, historical context and probable intended meanings.

Among the matters which remain to be more fully considered is the degree to which the Gothic additions and alterations were affected by earlier work at Ely. The structural failings of the standing fabric were a major spur to new building at the Cathedral after 1200 and often determined its form. But it can also be argued that some of what is original and idiosyncratic in the design and detail of these new elements arose from close study of the Cathedral itself.

The completion of the west front and tower

Ely's western block was the last great work of the Norman Cathedral, begun in the first half of the twelfth century but left incomplete in about 1140 (Colour pl. 3a). Before the stoppage the now ruinous north-west transept had been built up to the fourth storey of the exterior – a dwarf gallery of rounded arches that was originally open to the weather – whereas the south side had halted at tribune level.[2] The completion of the western transepts and the building of the west tower were funded by Geoffrey Ridel (Bishop, 1174–89).[3] Problems of settlement, which have dogged the west end throughout its history, had already manifested themselves in the twelfth century. Ridel's superstructure reinstated vertical alignments, but by adding massively to the pressure bearing down on the inadequate foundations, stored up trouble for the future. The interest of his work, as a document of the English transition to Gothic, lies in the meshing of new French ideas with the pre-existing Anglo-Norman framework.

The new mason completed the eastern tribune gallery of the south-west transept following the Norman design of the north-west transept but with novel details. He introduced early Gothic volute capitals and elegant classical bases. Disdaining the Norman key pattern of the north side, he executed the tribune arches with plain keel mouldings.[4] On the south and west elevations of the interior, the precedent of the north arm required a blind triforium, which now became a trefoil arcade, resembling the choir triforium at Noyon (c.1175–85) (Plate 5a). A more complex trefoil arcade was used on the exterior, where it corresponds with that on the north arm but was enclosed from the start (Plate 5b).

In the clerestory Ridel's mason accepted the Ely formula of a central window flanked by narrower blind panels, but made all the arches pointed. Inside he achieved a clean Gothic effect with blank lancet arcading at the corners, but on the exterior he felt obliged to sustain the decorative intensity of the Norman front with surface ornament. The incompetent masonry pattern of the Romanesque tribune offered a precedent upon which he could be expected to improve. Three new repeat ornaments were essayed in the

---

[2] See K. Fearn, P. Marshall and W.G. Simpson, 'The South-west Transept of Ely Cathedral', unpublished University of Nottingham report (1995) for the Dean and Chapter (EDC 4/10B/3), in which an analysis of mortar, masonry and masons' marks produces a building sequence which is plotted onto the survey drawings of J. Atherton Bowen.

[3] 'Novum opus versus occidentem, cum turre usque ad cumulum fere perfecit': BL, MS Harl. 3721, fo. 34. Some copies omit 'fere' ('almost'), e.g. BL, MS Harl. 258, as quoted in Stewart, Ely, p. 47. For dendrochronological dates of timbers in the tower ranging from after c.1040 to after 1180 see 'List 65. Nottingham University Tree-Ring Dating Laboratory Results: General List (R.E. Howard et al.)', Vernacular Architecture, 27 (1996), pp. 78–80.

[4] They are similar to those of Noyon choir, begun c.1148, and the early Gothic work at Canterbury that followed the fire of 1174.

lowest course of the south-west clerestory, and a design of deeply incised right-angled triangles was chosen, doubtless for its boldness. In the event, however, conspicuous failures of vertical registration led to its abandonment above the clerestory arches. That the remains of the north-west transept clerestory show no sign of this treatment implies its construction after the shortcomings of the southern clerestory had emerged. Economy was also a factor: for the internal bases of the clerestory – invisible from the ground – cheap hollow chamfers like those in the nave of St Mary's, Ely, were preferred to the solitary and much more expensive classical base proposed in the south-west corner.[5]

The clerestories formed part of a common building campaign with the middle section of the west front and tower, where cusped oculi, repeated all over the transept and tower, are used to flank the western crossing arch.[6] The west face of the tower was not designed for a high roofed structure into which this arch could have opened; and the possibility, canvassed by Bentham and Essex, of a large-scale forerunner to the present Galilee is not supported by recent archaeological examination. In its original state the west crossing arch must therefore have framed a subdivided window, all trace of which has since been lost.[7]

The structure of the tower is typically Anglo-Norman with multiple storeys and layers of mural passages. But whereas wall passages and access doorways tend to be round-headed, all prominent or decorative arches are either trefoiled or pointed. These self-consciously modern details are moreover combined in an external elevation whose orderly uniformity contrasts with the more varied and ornate Norman towers at Norwich and Bury St Edmunds. This reaction against the ornamental variety of later Romanesque can be related to early Gothic work in France, notably the internal south transept elevation of Noyon. But the effect is heavier here. In the lower level of the three-storey internal elevation of the tower, the thick inner wall is carried on a forest of slender, double columns. These mask the difference between the windowed western wall and the other sides which at this level were abutted by roofs (Colour pl. 8c). The doubled shafts run across the western windows, and this counterpoint is used boldly in the rising shafts and niches of the south-west transept turret (Colour pl. 3c). This large ten-sided turret was a companion for the west tower, and Ridel's mason clearly wanted to establish a relationship by means of similarly proportioned Gothic niches. This was very difficult to combine with the double shaft rising in the centre of each facet of the earlier work. The solution was to reduce it to a single shaft which in the first two added storeys would divide pairs of narrow niches. In the stage above it ran straight through the centre of the single arch. This striking prototype of Early English Gothic syncopation plainly arises from the conflicting demands of new and old work.[8]

[5] St Mary's church was rebuilt and reconsecrated in the episcopate of Eustace (1197–1215): Bentham, *Ely*, p. 145, n. 4.
[6] These oculi resemble the rose windows in the south transept of Notre-Dame-en-Vaux at Châlons-sur-Marne of *c.*1140–57.
[7] These issues are discussed in J. Maddison and H. Richmond, 'Ely Cathedral: The Galilee Porch', an unpublished archaeological report (2001) for the Dean and Chapter (EDC 4/10B/9).
[8] The southern tower of Chartres is dated before 1145. Its second-storey windows are set in tall bays whose paired decorative arches have a common central shaft which rises from a corbel at the apex of each window, a partial precedent for the unusual design of the Ely turret.

The external detail of the main tower is graduated according to height (Plate 5c). Above the early Gothic capitals and mouldings of the first storey is a reversion to simpler Romanesque details, and shaft rings introduced in the third main stage are given up in the fourth. The intended form of the tower top is uncertain, but twelfth-century squinches below the later octagon clearly imply an octagonal top which would have related to the form of the western transept turrets (Plate 4c). There are numerous precedents in France for square towers that turn octagonal at the top, including the early Gothic towers of Chartres and La Trinité at Vendôme. A group of comparable local tower summits, including the roughly contemporary St Mary's, Swaffham Prior and the early thirteenth-century octagons at Barnack and Elm, may be related in different ways to the Ely work.

The completion of the west front was accompanied by extensive and closely comparable building activity in the monastery.[9] It would have been surprising therefore if there had been no contemporary modifications elsewhere in the Cathedral, especially as Ridel's interest in the eastern part of the church is known to have included the repair of the principal shrine with quantities of silver and a scheme of painted decoration encompassing the episcopal throne and parts of the choir.[10] Some of the existing thirteenth-century painted decoration in the nave and transepts may have its origins in Ridel's scheme, but there is no documentary suggestion that the fragmentary archaeological evidence of a late twelfth-century remodelling of the south choir aisle is to be connected with him. The Norman aisles, which extended four bays east of the central crossing, have all but disappeared; but two features embedded in the fourteenth-century south choir aisle could be contemporary with Ridel. One, a mass of masonry in the tribune,[11] seems to have belonged to an early pointed vault and the other is a line of late twelfth-century chevron ornament on the wall bench in the aisle below.[12] The vault fragment could imply an early remodelling of the Norman south aisle. It suggests that the tribune level in the three western bays of the eastern arm – about 3 feet (1m) higher than that of the nave and transepts – predates not only Hotham's fourteenth-century remodelling but also the building of Bishop Northwold's presbytery in the thirteenth century.

[9] Any discussion of Ridel's work and its significance for the development of early Gothic needs to take into consideration the architecture of Ely's infirmary. This highly sophisticated but essentially Romanesque building uses closely allied ornament – shaft rings, keel mouldings, outward-pointing chevron ornament and other features. The former hall in the west range (running along the Gallery) is another close relative of Ridel's west front work. See Dixon's chapter on the monastic buildings, pp. 147 and 149 below.

[10] '*Duo latera feretri Sce. Etheldrede et partem cumuli de argento perpulcre reparavit . . . cathedram magni altaris et medietatem chori depixit*': BL, MS Harl. 3721, fo. 34.

[11] This came to light when an old tank was removed from bay 9 (numbering from the east) as part of recent repairs in the south choir. The vault fragment rises through the present tribune floor and projects from the wall that divides the south tribune from the adjacent triangular compartment of the Octagon. It is roughly pointed in shape and includes at least one re-used diagonally tooled Norman stone with a chamfer of the same size as that on the early Norman wall bench in the north transept. The painted decoration of the nave and transept arcades is regarded as 13th-century but the painted imbrication of the drum pier next to St Edmund's Chapel in the north transept resembles the tympanum of the infirmary north door.

[12] Whether the chevron moulding is *in situ* is open to debate. It is neatly laid, lies above a bench riser of diagonally tooled stones and has a smooth top implying a bench or sill rather than a built-in string. The base courses of the Norman choir wall are detectable externally in the three western bays of the eastern arm and the clearest evidence is in the organ blower chamber on the north side where the Norman chamfered offset is plainly visible.

The Galilee porch

It is recorded that Eustace (Bishop, 1197–1215) built a new Galilee.[13] The apparent mismatch between Eustace's episcopate and the style of the porch has produced various explanations. Robert Willis and David Stewart both thought it later than Eustace;[14] but Sir Gilbert Scott insisted, by a comparison with St Hugh's choir at Lincoln (begun in 1192) and the western porches of St Albans (begun in the abbacy of John de Cella, 1195–1214), that Eustace could have built the Galilee.[15] Stewart later recanted,[16] but some authors have returned to the possibility of the porch embodying different phases and others attempt to divorce the interior from the outer side walls.[17] Eustace's later life was not conducive to building. Having pronounced the Pope's Interdict in 1208, he fled to France and was unable to regain his see and temporalities until after 1213. If this pushes the building of the Galilee back to 1197–1208, that would make the assured design and ornate Gothic detail remarkable. It could not however have been built entirely between 1213 and 1215, so T.D. Atkinson's suggestion that the work was funded posthumously by Eustace has a certain plausibility.[18] The question of how long it was delayed is more difficult. Whatever its liturgical function,[19] it is clear that the side walls of the porch, which reproduce the massive thickness of the Norman westwork, were abutments for the overburdened piers of Ridel's tower.

This thickness meant that lateral buttresses for the porch vault were unnecessary, so the side walls could be decorated with continuous arcades related to those of the western transepts (Plate 6*a*). Two equal wall arcades on the Galilee correspond to the lower three zones of the Romanesque work, and the two upper storeys tie in exactly. Even the chevron string of the transepts is carried round the top of the porch with a row of visually rhyming half-dogtooth. The unusual moulded corner piers have a local precedent in the twelfth-century west tower of St Peter's, Northampton, and a thirteenth-century parallel in the west front of Peterborough.[20] On the west elevation

---

[13] '*Ipse construxit novam galileam a fundamentis versus occidentem*', BL, MS Harl. 3721, fo. 35ᵛ.

[14] Stewart, *Ely*, p. 53.

[15] Scott's lecture at Ely, in which these views were expressed, was published in Charles Merivale, *St Etheldreda's Festival. Summary of Proceedings . . . at the Bisexcentenary Festival . . . at Ely* (Ely, *c*.1874). The early date for the Galilee was reiterated in the third of Scott's posthumously published *Lectures on the Rise and Development of Medieval Architecture delivered at the Royal Academy* (London, 1878–9), I, p. 127. In a note added by Scott in 1878, shortly before his death, he wrote 'It is fair to say that Professor Willis doubted the date given to this Galilee.' The account given of the building of the west front of St Albans in the *Gesta Abbatum*, ed. H.T. Riley (Rolls Series, 28), vol. I, p. 219, quoted in VCH, *Herts.*, II (1908), p. 485, implies that the work done by John de Cella was abandoned before half of it had reached the *tabulatus domitialis*. It was ruined by frosts in the winter of 1197–8 and seems to have made very little progress over the next thirty years. Stuart Harrison in 'The Thirteenth-Century Front of St Albans' in M. Henig and P. Lindley (eds.), *Alban and St Albans*, BAACT, 24 (London, 2001), p. 176, suggests how the document might be related to the standing work, and Lawrence Hoey in 'The Gothic Reconstruction of the Nave and Presbytery of St Albans', *ibid.*, p. 187, regards the present porches as the work of de Cella albeit altered by Lord Grimthorpe.

[16] D.J. Stewart, 'Ely Cathedral', *The Builder*, 2 April 1892, pp. 266–8, at p. 267.

[17] *E.g.* P. Brieger, *English Art 1216–1307* (Oxford, 1968), p. 187, and N. Pevsner, *The Buildings of England: Cambridgeshire*, 2nd edn (Harmondsworth, 1970), p. 346.

[18] Atkinson, *Ely Monastery*, p. 5.

[19] For a discussion of the meaning and use of Galilee buildings see R. Halsey, 'The Galilee Chapel', in N. Coldstream and P. Draper (eds.), *Medieval Art and Architecture at Durham Cathedral*, BAACT, 3 (London, 1980), p. 59.

[20] Corner piers of this kind are also a common feature in major French churches, such as those of Charente and

the arcades become niches for sculpture with scooped backs, their ornate arches varying subtly in different storeys. Slender shafts frame both the triple window and below it the portal whose dimensions relate only to the levels of the vaulted interior. Here the wall thickness allows an impressive display of deep arcades in two stages (Figure 12, p. 126). The complex lower stage has a tall arcade of trefoiled arches on slim marble shafts. These are linked by miniature vaulting to colonettes rising from a deep shelf and appearing between the main shafts. It is this arrangement and some of the moulded detail that are comparable with the western porches of St Albans, as Scott observed. Similar ideas are also found in buildings of the 1220s, including the cloisters of Mont-Saint-Michel in Normandy, completed in 1228, and the triforia of Worcester and Beverley.

The upper chamber is stark with rubble side walls. Its triple lancets are devoid of internal mouldings and nothing distinguishes this interior from other rough-and-ready tribune spaces in the Cathedral (Plate 6b). The original access arrangements were too tortuous to imply anything more than the occasional liturgical use for which the internal singing galleries at the west ends of Wells, Salisbury and Lichfield cathedrals are thought to have been built.[21] The upper room was approached from one of the western transept corner turrets, via the western tribune passage which once penetrated the tower corners and opened into tall passages in the upper walls of the porch.

There are some perplexing inconsistencies of detail in the Galilee, especially in the external arcading of the side walls, but the relative unity of the moulding profiles suggests that these are not especially significant in terms of chronology. The subtle building break between the inner doorway and the rest of the Galilee implies that the remodelling of the door was delayed until the porch could provide shelter.[22] The sophisticated ornaments of the door arch were interpreted by Pevsner and others as Scott's restoration. But close examination during recent repairs revealed that whereas Scott was responsible for the central pier, detached marble shafts as well as the vesica and its associated foliage, much of the arch ornament is authentic.[23] It and the comparable details of the outer portal arch argue for a date after c.1220 and invite

---

Vienne. The angle of the Romanesque north transept of Christchurch Priory is expressed in this fashion. Keel mouldings are a feature of early Gothic architecture, seen in Ridel's work at Ely and, for example, the late 12th-century parts of the nave of Selby and in Roche Abbey; but they are found later at Beverley in the 1220s and in the slender central column of the Morning Chapel at Lincoln, the roof of which has been dated by dendrochronology to c.1230. Locally, keels are found in mid-13th-century architecture (e.g. above the chancel arch in the nave of West Walton church where in one south aisle window, bar tracery is combined with sophisticated foliage ornaments like those of the two Galilee portals).

[21] It is evident from an engraving in Bentham that the upper chamber was roofed, and there are faint traces of the roof profile cutting across the decorative masonry of Ridel's front. The singing galleries of Wells, Salisbury and Lichfield are compared in John Atherton Bowen's drawing in T. Ayers (ed.), *Salisbury Cathedral: the West Front. A History and Study in Conservation* (Chichester, 2000), figure 44, p. 74. They are discussed in J. Sampson, *Wells Cathedral West Front: Construction, Sculpture and Conservation* (Stroud, 1998), pp. 168–73, and J. McAleer, 'Particularly English? Screen Facades of the Type of Salisbury and Wells', *JBAA*, cxli (1988), pp. 147–9.

[22] Re-used pieces of decorative Norman masonry in the walls of the upper chamber may come from the former west door.

[23] *Buildings of England: Cambridgeshire* (cit. in n. 17), p. 346. John Maddison and Hugh Richmond, 'Ely Cathedral: The Galilee Porch', unpublished report for the Dean & Chapter, 2001 (EDC 4/10B/9), p. 12. The work of Bernasconi and Scott is compared in two illustrations of the west door in Gerald Cobb, *English Cathedrals: The Forgotten Centuries* (London, 1980), pls. 131 and 132.

comparison with the rosette-studded mouldings of the Dean's Eye at Lincoln and the inner arch of the south transept door at Westminster Abbey (*c.*1246–59). Graffiti of bar tracery and of a cinquefoiled arch – similar to those on the tomb of Bishop Northwold (before 1254) – show that the porch was serving as a temporary tracing-house in the mid-thirteenth century (Figure 10). The high position of some of the drawings implies scaffolding and perhaps that the porch was then in the course of completion.

Such features appear to move the Galilee towards the episcopate of Hugh de Northwold (1229–54), whose documented works at Ely include the construction of a timber spire on top of Ridel's tower. This structure, which may be represented in Northwold's counter-seal of *c.*1229, was described by Matthew Paris as 'that most excellent steeple'.[24] The settlement of the tower, plainly evident in the distortion of the western nave bay and in the clerestory of the south-west transept, is also detectable in the inward movement of the Norman west door jambs prior to their remodelling in the thirteenth century. So the building of the porch, projected in the time of Eustace, could have been delayed until the decision to add a spire made additional abutment more urgent.

The presbytery of Bishop Northwold

In Northwold's time (1229–54) there is physical evidence of extensive reconstruction at the Cathedral, but the only elements which contemporary documents ascribe to him are the western spire and the new six-bay presbytery at the east end.[25] His recorded expenditure on the presbytery, some £5,040, may have amounted to three quarters of the total building fund. Constructed between 1234 and 1252, the presbytery is the most refined and richly detailed English building of its period. It represented a sensational departure in the development of the Cathedral, altering the whole balance of the building and placing massive emphasis on the presence of St Etheldreda. The cults of the Virgin Mary, whose chapel was in the south aisle, and of Ely's principal virgin saint were now united in surroundings of unprecedented splendour and powerful symbolic meaning. Etheldreda's sprouting staff, that first miracle of her hagiography – the sign of her virginity and elect status – is probably alluded to in the exceptionally luxuriant foliage decoration of the building.[26]

---

[24] Mention of the spire ('*turrim excellentissimam*') is found in the *Chronica Majora* of Matthew Paris published by H. Luard, Rolls Series, 57 (1872–83), vol. V, p. 322. Wharton, *Anglia Sacra*, I, p. 636, also mentions and locates the spire: '*Ipse etiam construxit de novo turrim lygneam versus Galileam ab opere cementario usque ad summitatem. . .*' (BL, MS Harl. 3721, fo. 37). For an illustration of Northwold's counter-seal see Maddison, *Ely Cathedral*, p. 44. Northwold's predecessor Bishop de Burgh received grants of oaks from the royal forests in 1226 and 1229 for rebuilding the *turris* of his church. This could have been for a free-standing bell-tower or for the central tower. The King granted oaks for the western steeple in 1234–5. See W.G. Simpson and C.D. Litton, 'Dendrochronology in Cathedrals', in Tim Tatton-Brown and Julian Munby (eds.), *The Archaeology of Cathedrals* (Oxford University Committee for Archaeology Monograph 42, 1996), p. 194.

[25] The building accounts for the presbytery are in BL, MS Cotton Tiberius B ii, fos. 246–8, and are printed in Draper, 'Bishop Northwold and the cult of St Etheldreda' (cit. in n. 1), p. 27. They commence in 1239–40, which is described as '*anno vij ab inceptione nove fabrice ecclesie de Ely*' and end in 1250. The dedication of the presbytery and a summary of Northwold's work at Ely are found in the *Chronica Majora* of Matthew Paris (cit. in n. 24).

[26] The idea that the foliate decoration of the presbytery celebrates the virginity of Etheldreda is discussed in Maddison, *Ely Cathedral*, p. 50, where it is proposed that the six sprouting vault-shaft brackets round the site

Figure 10. Drawings of *c.*1250 scratched on the inner
walls of the Galilee (Maddison, *Ely Cathedral*, p. 56)

The Early English version of Gothic in which marble shafts play so prominent a part – used at Canterbury after the fire of 1174, and then developed at Lincoln from the 1190s to the 1240s – is used at Ely with great assurance (Plate 7a). But the vertical proportions, bay and aisle dimensions appear to have been determined entirely by the Norman work.[27] Whether Northwold's arcade and unfashionably tall tribune gallery exactly replicated the earlier levels has been open to dispute.[28] The surviving early vault fragment in the south tribune of bay 9 however suggests that the level of the present east arm tribune was a feature of the earlier choir bays and not an innovation by Northwold. The need to follow the early external elevation also meant a low outer tribune wall. This survives only in two bays on the south side; and its corbel table, carried on foliage knots and heads, is probably a reference to the lost corbel table of the Norman choir[29] (Colour pl. 4d).

Putlog holes for scaffolding show that work proceeded in even stages right across the presbytery; but there is evidence of details being tried out and modified in the light of their visual impact, indicating where one part of the work was temporarily ahead of the rest.[30] For example, limestone cores, found exclusively in the two eastern responds, were rejected in favour of drums of Purbeck marble when it came to the piers. But some of the most interesting modifications occur in the tribune, where the piers and arches were built first and were then, as a separate operation, filled with a central column and richly decorated tympanum. The filling design appears to have been evolved in the north-east bay, where the details are different from all the others. It must have been noticed that

---

of the shrine and high altar are deliberately contrasted with the tightly furled brackets further east, in a re-enactment of the miracle of the flowering staff. The rich brackets can also be compared with those in the nave and chapter house at Lincoln where they are uniform throughout the work.

[27] Here there is a comparison with the internal elevation of the early Gothic choir of St Étienne at Caen. The levels at Caen were evidently closely modelled on those of the 11th-century work there which resemble Norman Ely (see Fernie, above, p. 107). Although Caen is earlier and plainer, the distribution of decorative detail also corresponds in a very general way with the Ely presbytery. Caen's late 12th-century date and dependence on the early Gothic work at Canterbury have been convincingly argued by Lindy Grant, 'The Choir of St Etienne at Caen', in E. Fernie and P. Crossley (eds.), *Medieval Architecture in its Intellectual Context. Studies in Honour of Peter Kidson* (London, 1990), pp. 113–25. There is unlikely to be a direct relationship between the Gothic work at Ely and Caen. It appears rather that their closely related contexts produced independent designs of a similar character.

[28] Draper in 'Bishop Northwold and the Cult of St Etheldreda' (cit. in n. 1), p. 9, suggests that only the clerestory corresponds with the Norman level and that the gallery sill was raised to bring the proportions of the elevation closer to contemporary fashion, whereas the conventional interpretation was offered by Robert Willis in Stewart, *Ely*, p. 78: 'Hugh de Northwold ... built his own work so as to place its architectural members within and without at the same levels as the corresponding parts of the Norman work'. A reconstruction of the choir of Winchester (from which Norman Ely is partly derived) indicates an even more pronounced difference between the choir tribune there and those in the rest of the building. See J. Crook, 'The Romanesque East Arm and Crypt of Winchester Cathedral', *JBAA*, cxlii (1989), pp. 1–36.

[29] The north transept east wall preserves the Norman external tribune elevation.

[30] Aspects of the archaeology of Northwold's work and of the eastern arm as a whole are considered in J. Maddison, 'The Choir of Ely Cathedral: an Archaeological Report on the Eastern Arm of the Cathedral', unpublished report (2001) for the Dean and Chapter (EDC 4/10B/10). Alterations to the aisle windows and the remodelling of most of the outer tribune walls inhibit a full understanding of the building order. At the lower level, the coursing of the regular buttresses and dado wall is absolutely consistent up to the fourth course above the present plinth moulding. Above this a disturbance on the north-east buttress of the north aisle suggests that the south aisle and east wall were temporarily ahead of it. The thick buttresses which formed the junction with the Norman eastern arm do not course with the rest of the aisle masonry and were evidently added after the completion of the lower aisle walls.

the low bases of the completed foliate tribune piers could not be seen from the ground. The central column of the north-east bay was therefore raised up on a high base. That this was subsequently considered to be too high is shown by the fact that the bases of the other central columns are all slightly lower.[31] In this bay alone, moreover, the central oculus of the tympanum was first intended to be open.[32] It was subsequently blocked, and all the other central oculi were built blind. Finally, the foliage knots on either side of the oculus are smaller than those in the other tribune tympana, which confirms that this experimental first bay prompted the refinement of the design. When it came to the clerestory the bases were raised up on a stone sleeper so that they could be seen from the floor. On the other hand, the variation in the foliage brackets which support the main vault shafts can be interpreted as an iconographic device, indicating the position of the shrine and alluding directly to the miracle of Etheldreda's sprouting staff[33] (Plate 7c).

The moulded roof-line on the external east face of the Octagon suggests that Northwold's roof, replaced in Essex's rebuilding after 1757, may have extended over the Norman choir bays to the former crossing tower.[34] The vault of the presbytery, whose construction would have followed the building of the roof, is a relative of the somewhat earlier tierceron vault of Lincoln nave, supported externally by flying buttresses and finished at the west end with a richly moulded arch. This arch is now partially concealed by the adjacent vault of Hotham's bays, but once marked the division between presbytery vault and the open timber roof of the choir bays.

In the design of the east wall, Northwold's mason partially evaded the historical constraints which had determined the cross-section of his presbytery (Colour pl. 4b). It is a typical Early English lancet composition with niched and arcaded buttresses, and is slightly at odds with the levels of the building behind. The east windows of the aisles were replaced in the fifteenth and sixteenth centuries and the rebuilding of the tribunes in the fourteenth century destroyed their original gable profile. But the end fenestration of the tribune survives on the north side. Here, significantly, the archaic corbel table of the south elevation has been abandoned in favour of strictly contemporary details.

---

[31] There are further small differences in the bases on the south side. I am grateful to Peter Draper for this observation and for the suggestion that the supply of adequate lengths of Purbeck marble might also have affected the decision on the base height.

[32] The difference between the upper and lower stones of this oculus imply that the decision to build it blind may have been taken halfway through its formation. There are interesting variations in the rear masonry of the other tribune tympana on the north side. Some tympana have lumps of ashlar amongst the rubble fill. On the south side a coat of limewash makes examination difficult but the tympana appear to be all rubble.

[33] See n. 25. There are other alterations in the detail. Two tribune spandrel oculi above the north-east pier have redundant water run-offs at the base, of the kind associated with external detail, and were probably a mistake by the executant mason. Other inconsistencies may indicate changes of mind by the designer. The north aisle wall bench has a hollow chamfer like that of the Galilee Porch, in contrast to the plain chamfer of the south side. The north aisle vault shaft capitals have minute, almost invisible ornaments that are omitted on the south aisle capitals. In the clerestory, large through-stones forming a powerful cantilever at the base of the tas-de-charge are of two patterns, chamfered and plain, with the majority of chamfers found on the south side. Two external clerestory arches on the north side (bays 3 and 4) have an order of dogtooth which the others lack, perhaps implying an economy drive in the closing years of the project. But contradicting this apparent parsimony are the impressive carved head stops, all but hidden within the clerestory passages and also found on the northern clerestory exterior.

[34] Essex's drawing of the choir roof records a scissor-truss design like that of the nave: BL, Add. MS 6772, fos. 220–1, illustrated in Thomas Cocke, The Ingenious Mr Essex, Architect (Cambridge, 1984), p. 53.

Internally, the former contrast between ornate Gothic and the austere early Norman bays appears to have been mitigated by new stalls which would have run westward through the crossing to the pulpitum in the first bay of the nave.[35] The housing for the bones of the Saxon benefactors which lay under the stalls on the north side was recorded in an eighteenth-century drawing by Michael Tyson, and this shows at the lower level a cinquefoiled arcade with a dogtooth surround, interpreted by T.D. Atkinson as a thirteenth-century feature[36] (Colour pl. 22c). This interpretation has since been disputed in favour of a fourteenth-century date consistent with the tower collapse of 1322.[37]. But a comparison between the details shown by Tyson and the most ornate parts of the Galilee would suggest that the benefactors' tombs pre-dated the collapse. The Galilee's plainer upper external wall arcades also provide a comparison with some recently rediscovered timber arches of the thirteenth-century stalls[38] (Plate 8a). The choir fittings would doubtless have related to other furnishings further east, probably including the setting of the choir altar, the high altar and the altar and shrine of Etheldreda.[39] The shrine pedestal of Etheldreda, reconstructed graphically from a series of Purbeck marble fragments by Atkinson (Figure 4, p. 67), had a syncopated arcade, like that of the Galilee interior, with foliage-decorated bases similar to those of the west door. Above this were richly moulded two-stage nodding arches with gables. Reliefs of censer-bearing angels that have recently come to light may also have formed part of this ensemble.[40]

The completion of the presbytery and the general rededication of the whole building in 1252 initiated a period of tranquillity. Of the other thirteenth-century features in the Cathedral, the arched recess in the north cloister walk, the conical tops of the main transept turrets and the nave roof would all have been completed by the dedication.[41] But the three bar-tracery windows of the south transept chapels probably date from the third quarter of the century. They, like some of the graffiti of the Galilee walls, register the impact of Henry III's rebuilding of Westminster Abbey, which had established bar-tracery as the fashion to follow after 1246. At the very end of the century, the tripartite canopy of the tomb of William de Luda (Bishop, 1290–8) indicates, in its close

---

[35] In the Norman Cathedral this would have been the second bay of the nave.

[36] VCH, *Cambs.*, IV, p. 64.

[37] Lindley, 'The Imagery of the Octagon' (cit. in n. 1), provides a full and convincing discussion of the tombs of the benefactors and their related paintings. His interpretation of the dogtooth ornament drawn by Tyson as the artist's attempt to render 14th-century fleurons would be more plausible were it not for other details of the lower level arcading – the capitals, cusps and pierced spandrels – which look 13th-century.

[38] Kate Fearn, 'Medieval and Later Woodwork from the Choir of Ely Cathedral', *JBAA*, cl (1997), pp. 59–75, at p. 60. These 13th-century arches are survivors of some twenty-nine such units recorded in John Bacon's late 19th-century inventory of woodwork then in store at Ely (EDC 4/6/7). A felling date of *c.*1220 has been determined by dendrochronology.

[39] Draper, 'Bishop Northwold and the Cult of St Etheldreda' (cit. in. n. 1) has the best discussion of these liturgical arrangements.

[40] Atkinson's reconstruction is illustrated in VCH, *Cambs.*, IV, p. 71. The form of the shrine base is discussed in N. Coldstream, 'English Decorated Shrine Bases', *JBAA*, cxxix (1976), pp. 15–34, at p. 17. Purbeck marble fragments which may be associated with the shrine are now housed both in the north aisle of the presbytery and in the newly established stone store at Ely (catalogue numbers 427, 441, 467–8, 911 and 1101).

[41] For the nave roof see W.G. Simpson, 'Ely Cathedral – The Nave Roof', unpublished University of Nottingham report (1996) for the Dean and Chapter (EDC 4/10B/5). Some of its findings were published: W.G. Simpson and C.D. Litton, 'Dendrochronology in Cathedrals' (cit. in n. 24), pp. 183–210. Dendrochronology suggests that the nave roof was rebuilt with a good deal of re-used Norman timber *c.*1240.

resemblance to that of Edmund Crouchback (*c.*1297) at Westminster Abbey, the continuing dominance of the king's masons[42] (Plate 12*d*).

The Lady Chapel

The commencement of a new Lady Chapel to the north of the eastern arm on Lady Day 1321 ushered in another forty years of architectural upheaval.[43] It was linked by a spacious passage to the north aisle of the Norman choir and by a separate high level route leading to its sanctuary from the choir enclosure of the monks. This segregation of access may have arisen from comment in Bishop Walpole's visitation injunctions of 1300 about the mingling of the monks and the female laity in the existing Lady Chapel in the south presbytery aisle.[44]

However, the fall of the crossing tower in February 1322 changed everything. Now the triumvirate of John Hotham (Bishop, 1316–37), Prior John of Crauden and the sacrist, Alan of Walsingham, was engaged in three separate building campaigns at the Cathedral: the Lady Chapel, the new octagonal choir with its lantern and belfry, and the rebuilding of the Norman choir bays. Close correspondences of architectural detail suggest that one master mason began these works and also undertook the remodelling of the Prior's house. After 1322 what had begun as a discrete if lavish building in which to honour the Virgin and invoke her intercession became a campaign for the salvation of the Cathedral. The obligation to restore the coherence of the building as a whole was now paramount.

Of the progress of the Lady Chapel after the catastrophe of 1322 and during the previous building season very little can be said.[45] Some of the earliest parts are likely to be those that were involved with the linking passage on the southern side. The upper walls can hardly be earlier than the mid-1330s, and the building was not dedicated until 1352–3.[46] A list of sources for the design would include the earlier Lady Chapel at Peterborough (1272–90) – now lost but built in an analogous position and on a similar scale – and St Stephen's Chapel, Westminster, which had been gradually rising since 1292, as well as Bishop Kirkby's chapel of St Etheldreda at his Holborn palace.[47] If the double planes and subtle vertical linkages of the Ely walls were anticipated by St Stephen's wall arcades, the Ely mason went much further in the modelling of his design, scooping the wall surface into a series of swinging curves to provide seats at dado level and niches for sculpture above. These distinctive curves are also found in the window jambs of Prior Crauden's

[42] Phillip Lindley, 'The Tomb of Bishop William de Luda: An Architectural Model at Ely Cathedral', *PCAS*, lxxii (1984), pp. 75–87.

[43] Wharton, *Anglia Sacra*, I, p. 651. See Coldstream, 'The Lady Chapel at Ely' (cit. in n. 1).

[44] For Walpole's injunctions see Evans, *Ordinances*, pp. 6–23. For the original access to the new Lady Chapel, see P. Dixon and J. Heward, 'A Report on the Lady Chapel Bridge, Ely', unpublished archaeological report (1999) for the Dean and Chapter (EDC 4/10B/12).

[45] Demolition work to allow for the building of the Chapel is however recorded in the sacrist's roll for 1322–3: Chapman, *Sacrist Rolls*, II, p. 28.

[46] The side window tracery is similar in pattern to the earliest tribune gallery tracery of Hotham's choir bays, *i.e. c.*1330. The proto-Perpendicular character of the east and west windows and the blind tracery gablets high on the east wall suggest the mid-to-late 1330s.

[47] Nicola Coldstream also suggests the northern Lady Chapel of Bury St Edmunds, whose foundation stone was laid in 1275: 'Ely Cathedral: the Fourteenth-Century Work' (cit. in n. 1), p. 35. The importance of the work at St Stephen's Chapel for the Octagon at Ely is explained in Wilson, *The Gothic Cathedral* (cit. in n. 1), pp. 197–8.

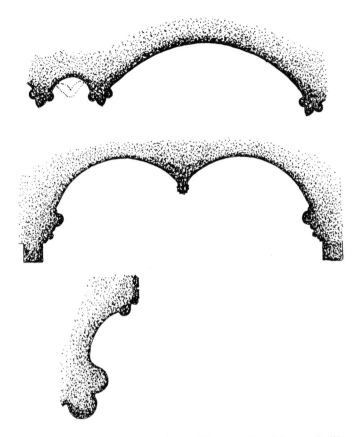

Figure 11. Curved 'casement' mouldings at Ely. Upper: Galilee
west wall niche; middle: Lady Chapel wall arcade; lower: window
jamb in Prior Crauden's Chapel

Chapel in 1324–5 where, as John Harvey pointed out,[48] they constitute the earliest
English instance of the 'casement' moulding that was to become a *leitmotif* of the
Perpendicular style. These important features show every sign of being derived – at Ely –
from the swept backs of the Galilee's west wall arcades (Figure 11). The subdivisions of
the Lady Chapel dado, as D.J. Stewart observed, can likewise be seen to derive from the
syncopated internal arcades of the porch[49] (Figure 12, p. 126). It may be significant
therefore that the search by other writers for prototypes of the Lady Chapel relief
sculpture has also led back to the mid-thirteenth century, and notably to Salisbury.
Comparisons are to be found there in the tomb of Giles de Bridport (d.1262) and the
narrative cycle in the chapter house, which offer a similar combination of arcades and
spandrel sculpture.[50] Geographically, these are remote comparisons, so it is important

[48] John Harvey, *The Perpendicular Style* (London, 1978), p. 34 and figure 1. The casement moulding was
developed at Ely in the tribune window jambs of Bishop Hotham's choir bays, in the contemporary rere-arches
of the Lady Chapel window heads and somewhat in the remodelled tribunes of Northwold's presbytery.

[49] Stewart, *Ely*, p. 142.

[50] Phillip Lindley considers these 13th-century prototypes in his thesis 'The Monastic Cathedral at Ely' (cit. in
n. 1), p. 189, and also mentions the choir dado arcades at Worcester.

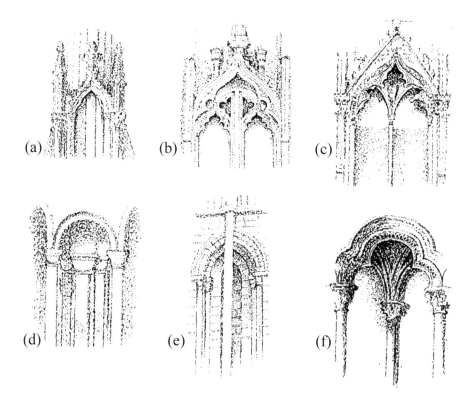

Figure 12. 14th-century details with earlier relatives at the Cathedral: (a) Octagon niche; (b) Lady Chapel tabernacle; (c) Lady Chapel wall arcade; (d) redundant respond and wall-walk arch, north transept (late 11th and early 12th centuries); (e) south-west transept turret detail (1180s); (f) internal arcade of Galilee Porch (13th century)

not to overlook the putative fragments of Etheldreda's shrine base. This, as we have seen, appears to have combined relief sculpture with nodding arches above syncopated arcades. A relationship between the shrine base and the Lady Chapel would have been entirely appropriate, given the important association between the Virgin and Ely's virgin saint.[51]

The oculi which ventilate the vault are similar to those in the east gable of Exeter Lady Chapel (completed *c.*1280), but also invite comparison with the work of Bishop Ridel in the west tower, which in spite of its age may have been of interest to the fourteenth-century mason (Colour pl. *7c–d*). In the main turret of the south-west transept he may well have found the inspiration for the interpenetrating shafts and arches of his uniquely complex wall piers, in particular for the motif of the arch divided at its apex by a central shaft rising through the storeys (Figure 12). This is not to discount comparable features in more recent buildings, but to acknowledge the role of the old fabric in moving the imagination of the mason in a particular direction.[52] A clear interest in old work can also be detected in

[51] Etheldreda enthroned and the Coronation of the Virgin are the two principal bosses of the presbytery vault. The principal shrine base at St Albans which was constructed before 1308 also has spandrel figures including censing angels. See Coldstream, 'English Decorated Shrine Bases' (cit. in n. 40), p. 18.

[52] It has been suggested that the Lady Chapel oculi are insertions (see n. 55), but their rather incoherent masonry

at least one contemporary Cambridgeshire parish church and in both the Octagon and Bishop Hotham's choir bays.[53] In their different ways, moreover, the Octagon and Bishop Hotham's choir bays display similar tendencies. The delayed completion of the Lady Chapel accounts for a number of inconsistencies in the detail of its ornate interior above the level of the wall arcades. The stone lierne vault, whose span of 46 feet is exceptional, does not relate well to the wall piers, and this has led to speculation that it may be considerably later.[54] Alternatively the somewhat botched detailing is explicable in terms of a project begun in 1321 and finished by other hands in the 1340s.

The Octagon

The Octagon stonework, carried out between 1322 and 1328,[55] is more consistent than either the Lady Chapel or the Decorated western bays of the eastern arm, which indicates the priority given to its construction. Its unusual plan and elevations arose from both practical and programmatic considerations, and the credit for its design has to be shared between the sacrist, Alan of Walsingham, the mason, John, and the royal carpenter William Hurley.[56]

One practical reason for the octagonal plan is implied by the *Chronicon*: the search for firm ground may have inspired the sacrist to take a step back from the failed Norman crossing foundations.[57] Another consideration, at least so far as the culminating Lantern is concerned, may have been the original octagonal top of the west tower. But the suggestion that the centralised form carries traditional connotations of a mausoleum – referring both to the burial of the Saxon benefactors on its northern side and in a more general way to the shrine of Etheldreda – is also very plausible.[58] If, as has been suggested here, the housing of the benefactors' bones survived the collapse, this was another factor that had to be put into the brief for the new work, for it defined

---

surrounds are arguably all of a piece with the generally poor masonry of the spandrels. The Octagon windows have oculi in the corresponding position and such openings are used in the late 13th-century Lady Chapel at Exeter. The tendency to bifurcate arches and foiled forms with rising shafts is present in French late 13th-century architecture (St Urbain at Troyes, begun 1262; the choir of Sées, begun *c.*1270). Related 13th-century English experiments include the nave of Lichfield (1260s) and the chapter house vestibule at York (1290s). In the early 14th century, the vertical division of tracery forms is seen above the bell openings in the tower of Grantham.

[53] The lavish 14th-century aisles of the church at Over (Cambs.) exhibit striking revivals of 13th-century detail including shaft rings and water-holding bases on the bay wall arcades and, on the porch, corner piers like those of the Ely Galilee and the Peterborough west front.

[54] F. Woodman, 'The Vault of Ely Lady Chapel: Fourteenth or Fifteenth Century?', *Gesta*, 23 (1984), pp. 137–41.

[55] W.G. Simpson, J. Heward and P. Dixon, 'An Archaeological Report on the Octagon', unpublished report (2001) for the Dean and Chapter (EDC 4/10B/11), contains the most recent work on the Octagon, including a discussion of the documentary evidence, an analysis of the structure, and record drawings of some of the masonry.

[56] A biography of William Hurley is given in John Harvey, *English Mediaeval Architects*, revised edn (Gloucester, 1984), pp. 154–5. Harvey has suggested that Master John may be synonymous with John de Ramsey, an architect much involved with early 14th-century work at Norwich. See Harvey, p. 163 (John the Mason VII) and p. 240 (John de Ramsey I). Also Arthur Whittingham, 'The Ramsey Family of Norwich', *AJ* 137 (1981), pp. 285–9.

[57] Wharton, *Anglia Sacra*, I, p. 644.

[58] The *martyrium* function of the Octagon was first proposed by Jean Bony in *The English Decorated Style: Gothic Architecture Transformed, 1250–1350* (Oxford, 1979), p. 40, and was connected with the special significance of the benefactors' tombs by Lindley, 'The Imagery of the Octagon' (cit. in n. 1), p. 91.

part of the route for pilgrims approaching the shrines in the presbytery[59] from the north transept entrance. It also formed the back of the northern choir stalls. Although the new crossing was to be octagonal, there were thus compelling reasons for an entirely traditional approach to the planning of the stalls, which would form a rectangular box running through the centre of the Octagon.

For the internal elevation of the Octagon, one possibility would have been to continue the three-storey design of the Norman Cathedral in some fourteenth-century guise. But with the difference in tribune heights between the eastern arm and the rest of the building, this option was problematic. The difficulties of reconciling conflicting levels in this new central feature would have argued forcefully for the more autonomous design that was built. At ground level the angled aisle arches and the triangular vaulting compartments thus created were determined by the eastern arm arcade height. The internal transition to the lower pitches of the transept and nave aisles is concealed in shadow. From the start, however, the mason would have known that these four new aisle arches would be largely hidden from the monastic choir by the stall backs and could not easily be perceived as the base of his design. The junction of the stall ends and their masonry backing walls with the angles of the piers would moreover encroach upon the sort of boldly projecting shafts that were necessary for the visual support of the vault and Lantern that were to be added between 1328 and 1340. The shafts therefore commence as compact triplets fitting into the octagon's angles, and the stone decorative tabernacles – whose supporting brackets are decorated with reliefs of the life and miracles of St Etheldreda (Plate 10c–d) – are the means by which their projection is considerably increased[60] (Plate 9a). But there was more to this arrangement than its practical effect. If we reinstate the stalls in a photomontage, it becomes clear that from the monks' viewpoint these tabernacles formed the visual base of an upper-level architectural composition that was both coherent and complete (Plate 8c). This careful integration of architecture and furnishing is surprisingly uncommon in greater medieval churches, where the accommodation of stallwork was more usually acknowledged in the summary curtailment of inconvenient projections in an elevation that was otherwise uniform with the rest of the building. The stalls themselves, built between 1338 and 1348, are more sober than the exuberant detail of the Octagon, reflecting rather the architecture of Hotham's choir bays[61] (Plates 8b, and 15b for misericord details).

---

[59] An inscription on the wall of the north choir aisle in bay 8 invites prayers for benefactors to the Church: '*pro animis benefactorum ecclesie Eliensis et omnium fidelium defunctorum*'. The original layout of the stalls is illustrated in the plan in Willis, *Survey of Ely* (Frontispiece).

[60] In Maddison, *Ely Cathedral*, p. 67, I have suggested that the relief on the north-west bracket (adjacent to the nave) represents *The Death of Tondberht* rather than the traditional identification as *The First Translation of Etheldreda*, and that the sequence of large head stops on the Octagon aisle arches illustrates precepts in the 1st Epistle of Peter which are appropriate to the conduct of a monastic community.

[61] The Gothic remodelling of St Rémi at Rheims is one of many examples of an elevation in which vaulting shafts, which in other bays rise from floor to springing, are begun on corbels to allow the backs of the choir stalls to pass beneath. These historiated corbels are a precedent for the Ely reliefs of the life and miracles of Etheldreda. The stalls are discussed in detail in Fearn, 'Medieval and Later Woodwork' (cit. in n. 38). I am grateful to Edward Maddison for the photomontage. Tracery possibly from the desks of the 14th-century stalls is incorporated in two 19th-century desks currently used in the Lady Chapel. Of similar date is the much restored screen fragment now enclosing the Chapel of St Edmund in the north transept, the tracery of which is copied from Hotham's clerestory. This is suggested (Maddison, *Ely Cathedral*, p. 82) to have been the screen of the chapel of the Holy Cross, west of the pulpitum in the nave (Plate 13d).

Having abandoned the levels of the surrounding work, it was possible to build very large windows whose sill-passages are linked to the adjacent clerestories by stairs. The window heads correspond to the new crossing arches whose keystones come just below the timbers of the thirteenth-century nave and east arm roofs. The increased height of the crossing required new roofs for the transepts, whose Norman tie beams would have cut across the arches.[62] The solution here was a type of mansard roof whose silhouette survives in the north and south external Octagon elevations and in the oddly-shaped gable of the north transept (Colour pl. 4a). The low ridge of these novel roofs was devised to come below the gallery of windows lighting the Octagon roof space, a feature compromised to the east and west by the steep pitch of the thirteenth-century nave and choir roofs. A similar window gallery is a feature of the recently completed chapter house at Wells, and there is a close comparison between William Hurley's great timber tierceron vault at Ely and that of the chapter house, if one mentally removes its column and central cone of ribs.[63] In 1315 the archiepiscopal visitation of the monastery at Ely had been made by a commissary, John de Bruton, a canon of Wells,[64] and small talk on this tense occasion would surely have turned to the new chapter house at his own Cathedral. These discussions would perhaps have been remembered by the Ely sacrist when in 1322 the idea of an octagonal structure gradually evolved.

The exalted crossing arches represented an interesting problem for any proposed vault over the rebuilt choir bays (7–9), which would have to match the height of Northwold's presbytery ridge rib. When such a vault was eventually built, probably before 1337, its moulded western arch was almost a storey below the Octagon's eastern opening. Reference in the sacrist's roll of 1345–6 to carpentry work carried out 'above the new *supercilium* [literally 'eyebrow'] it is an editorial insertion against the three altars' probably refers to the closing of this gap with a timber tracery tympanum.[65]

In the Octagon the mason dealt roughly with the Norman work in certain areas (taking down a bay from each arm, slicing through the sculpted capitals of the transept tribunes and building an ugly if necessary buttress across one jamb of the ornate Monks' Door), but there are places where the detail acknowledges the design of the Romanesque fabric. The principal shafts of the new crossing piers correspond exactly with the diameter of the Norman masts[66] in the nave, while the brackets supporting the corner tabernacles have a crenellated rim which is clearly intended to resemble and even imply the continuation of the distinctive Norman billet string under the tribune of the nave and transepts. Whether the tabernacles were built to accommodate sculptures has been debated, but in their present state they form a niche housing a bundle of three shafts which rises behind the nodding arch to support the springing of the Octagon vault (Plate 9a). This configuration can be related to the dado arcade of St Stephen's

[62] See below. Jean Bony points to the requirement for transept roofs without tie beams in *The English Decorated Style* (cit. in n. 58), p. 40.

[63] This comparison is made in Maddison, *Ely Cathedral*, p. 68 and pls. 54, 56 and 57.

[64] For the visitation of 1315 see Chapman, *Sacrist Rolls*, I, pp. 101–2. John de Bruton (d.1342) was Prebendary of Haselbere in Wells Cathedral, 1312–39 (Le Neve, *Fasti, 1300–1541*, VIII, p. 48).

[65] Chapman, *Sacrist Rolls*, II, p. 137. See 'The remodelling of the presbytery tribunes', below, and notes 94, 96 and 97 for the argument behind the relocation of '*tria altaria*'. In this interpretation of the new vault, the 'old *supercilium*' would have been the western transverse arch of Northwold's vault.

[66] The shafts which rise from floor to roof.

Chapel, Westminster, but it also has a Romanesque precedent at Ely in the north transept where the central arch of the twelfth-century wall walk frames three shafts of a redundant eleventh-century respond, above which a single shaft rises to the clerestory[67] (Figure 12, p. 126). One further detail that has been shown to derive from the existing fabric at Ely source is the design of the trefoil sculpture brackets (now occupied by Redfern's seated Apostles) (Plate 10*b*). These were copied from the central gable of de Luda's tomb,[68] an observation that attests to the mason's searching examination of his surroundings at Ely.

Close co-operation between mason and carpenter was critical and there is plenty of evidence, in the stone fabric, of preparation for the remarkable timber vault and lantern (Figure 13). Repairs by Essex and others have removed some elements of the medieval carpentry and more research is required before the whole of the original structure and the method of its assembly are properly understood[69] (Plate 11). Timber vaults, intended to give the impression of stone, had their heyday in the late thirteenth and early fourteenth-century England when simulation, visual complexity and interchange between the crafts could produce work of unparalleled richness and ingenuity. They were used by the King at his chapels at Windsor and Westminster, and also in the great octagonal chapter house at York, so it is doubtful if the Octagon mason ever considered the possibility of a stone vault over so great a span.[70] Early photographs record the original decoration of the vault webs which were painted to resemble window tracery[71] (Plate 10*e*). The repetition of foiled shapes was linked to repeated forms in the openwork tracery that partly covers the Octagon window heads. This further twist in the illusion helped blur the distinction between wood and stone, contributing to a glorious cobweb of different tracery patterns rising from the windows through the vault

---

[67] T.D. Atkinson argued (in VCH, *Cambs.*, IV, p. 63) that the niches were too shallow to accommodate statues, but this has been challenged by Lindley in 'The Imagery of the Octagon' (cit. in n. 1), p. 82, in which he points out that the niche bases are deep enough to accommodate figure sculpture. He suggests that masonry fragments of two figures holding scrolls came from these niches. Since the establishment of the stone store and cataloguing of the collection more than 20 further fragments have come to light. The first of the pieces mentioned by Lindley is now 875 in the stone store catalogue and the smaller piece is 826. Of the other pieces the most relevant is 535 which is a portion of a draped figure with a scroll with fragmentary blackletter. Other pieces include 339, 349, 358, 494, 517, 518, 524, 526, 531, 535, 585, 586, 658, 672, 713, 716, 720, 721, 724 and 821. The significance of St Stephen's Chapel for the elevation of the Octagon is put forward by Christopher Wilson in *The Gothic Cathedral* (cit. in n. 1), pp. 196–8.

[68] An observation made by Wilson in 'The Origins of the Perpendicular Style' (cit. in n. 1), p. 187.

[69] A reconstruction of the Octagon timberwork was published by Cecil Hewett in *English Historic Carpentry* (London, 1980), pp. 161–4, and with further detail and analysis in *English Cathedral and Monastic Carpentry* (Chichester, 1985), p. 122. The most recent research is by Simpson, Heward and Dixon (cit. in n. 55). For an analysis of the engineering, see J. Heyman and E.C. Wade, 'The Timber Octagon of Ely Cathedral', *Proc., Institution of Civil Engineers*, 78 (1985), part 1, pp. 1421–36.

[70] The new royal chapel at Windsor, in completion in the autumn of 1243 was, according to the King's instruction, 'to have a high wooden roof made after the manner of the new work at Lichfield, so that it may appear as stonework', R. Allen Brown, H.M. Colvin and A.J. Taylor, *The History of the King's Works*, II (London, 1963), p. 868. Timbers were prepared for the wooden vault of St Stephen's Chapel, Westminster, by William Hurley in 1325 and stored until it became possible to assemble them in 1345: *ibid.*, I, pp. 514 and 517.

[71] Some painting appears to have been carried out in 1334: Chapman, *Sacrist Rolls*, II, p. 73. The other reference to vault painting is in 1337, and is usually associated with the masonry vault of Hotham's bays (*cf.* n. 75), but given the protracted construction of the Octagon and Lantern it is possible that this was the completion of the Octagon painting. Tracery patterns were also painted on the Lady Chapel vault webs, and are visible in the east bay. The date is uncertain.

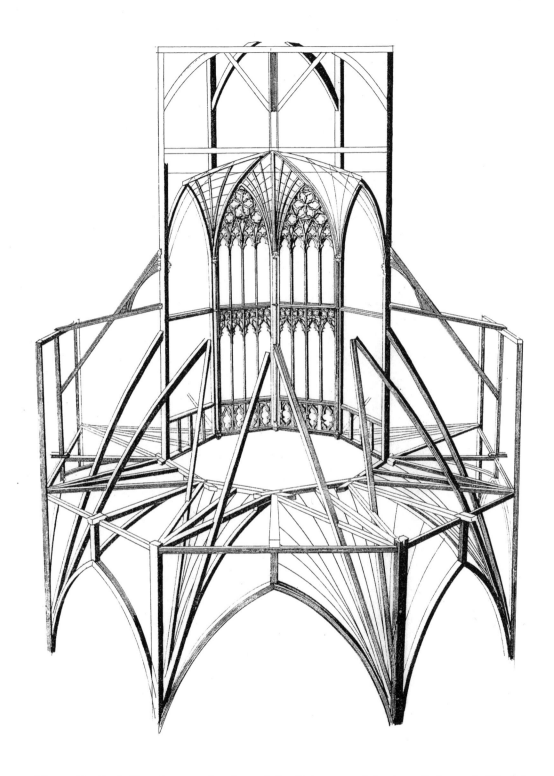

Figure 13. Cecil Hewett, reconstruction of the Octagon and Lantern timberwork (*English Cathedral Carpentry* (London, 1974), fig. 76, p. 87)

and into the lantern. With the exception of the present decorative painting and the Lantern window tracery, the Victorian restoration has been shown to correspond very closely with the medieval form both inside and out.[72]

Hotham's bays

The remodelling of the three bays east of the crossing by John Hotham (Bishop, 1316–37) represents an object lesson in how build in harmony with earlier work (Plate 7b). In its subtle evocation of Northwold's presbytery, moreover, it avoids the overt revivalism that characterises the self-effacing fourteenth-century naves at Beverley and Westminster Abbey. Local regard for the thirteenth-century presbytery is expressed in the fourteenth-century *Chronicon*, which describes it as the 'great and beautiful fabric rising above the tombs of the Holy Virgins' and attributes its survival in the disaster of 1322 to the protection of God and the merits of Etheldreda.[73]

Hotham's accounts are lost, but the costs of Bishop's and sacrist's masons sharpening their chisels are noted separately in the roll of 1323–4. After this there is silence until 1337, when Hotham had died and the sacrist was obliged to deal with unfinished aspects including the painting of the vault and the provision of fittings.[74] The building sequence suggests three phases.[75] The first phase made a start in the aisles. The second built the south internal elevation and raised the outer tribune walls; and the third built the north internal elevation, the north aisle vault, the high vault and the upper buttresses and flyers. Associated with this final phase are alterations to the south main elevation of the second phase.

The idea that the three earlier bays were crushed by the fall of the tower is not wholly consistent with the surviving Norman choir masonry at tribune and clerestory level on the south side next to the Octagon.[76] Work appears to have begun with the remodelling of the aisle walls, and on both sides the central bay (8) has a window whose tracery and mouldings can be directly related to forms in the Octagon and could therefore have been

---

[72] This is established by Lindley in '"Carpenter's Gothic" and Gothic Carpentry' (cit. in n. 1). See also Meadows, below, pp. 320–1.

[73] '*Illa tamen pulcra et magna fabrica eminens supra Sanctarum Virginum sepulcra*' (BL, MS Harl. 3721, fo. 42). For Hotham's responsibility for the work and its cost (£2034 12s. 8¾d), see Wharton, *Anglia Sacra*, I, p. 647.

[74] Chapman, *Sacrist Rolls*, II, pp. 47–8, 83 and 117.

[75] The phases are discussed in detail in Maddison, 'The Choir of Ely Cathedral' (cit in n. 30), pp. 5–31. The account given here revises that in Maddison, *Ely Cathedral*. The recent repairs to the Purbeck marble are described in Jane Kennedy, 'The Repair of Purbeck Marble in the Choir of Ely Cathedral', *Transactions, Association for Studies in the Conservation of Historic Buildings*, 20 (1995), pp. 30–2.

[76] The mast at the north end of bay 9 was re-used as a vault shaft by the 14th-century masons. From scaffolding it was possible to see that it is Norman throughout its height except where the capital and springing of the 14th-century vault interrupt it. The mast on the opposite side of Hotham's bays is however a 14th-century replica. Richard Gem suggested that the Norman choir elevation at Ely had an alternating system in which 'the minor piers had attached shafts (for which evidence survives) on their face to the presbytery', in 'The Romanesque Cathedral of Winchester: Patron and Design in the Eleventh Century', in T.A. Heslop and V.A. Sekules (eds.), *Medieval Art and Architecture at Winchester Cathedral*, BAACT, 6 (London, 1983), p. 11, n. 25. This was challenged by Philip McAleer in 'Some Observations on the Romanesque Choir of Ely Cathedral', *Jnl., Society of Architectural Historians*, 53 (1994), pp. 80–94. He suggested that the mast in bay 9 (south) was 14th-century. The matter seems to be settled by the survival at the wall head of the Norman mast complete with its pilaster backing. Fixed into the angle of the mast at about 10 feet from the ground, and now behind the choir stalls, is a large iron staple which indicates a significant medieval fixture.

built between 1322 and 1328. The adjacent windows to east and west begin with a similar moulding, but this changes in the head where the tracery is also of a different sort.[77] These departures mark the beginning of the second phase, in which the main internal elevation of the south side was rebuilt up to the wall head, excluding the tracery of the central clerestory window and the open-work tracery filling of the two south-eastern tribune bays (7–8). This work and the major phase which followed probably post-date the completion of the bulk of the octagon masonry in 1328.[78]

The first idea for the elevation is represented in the south-west bay. The levels mainly agree with those of the presbytery. The piers, set on tall plinths to compensate for the lower floor level, answer Northwold's multiple shafts in courses of sumptuous stratified Purbeck, and in the arches, spreading Decorated mouldings and fleurons balance the sculptural riches to the east. The crenellated strings and arcade profiles relate to the Octagon, and in place of the solid tympana of the presbytery the southern tribune of bay 9 has a lively pattern of flowing tracery with minute – effectively invisible – trails of ballflower. The four main cusps are tipped with animals. Other fantastic and obscene creatures, too small to register beyond a few feet, decorate the solitary tabernacle which projects at clerestory string level on the division with bay 8. This attention to the smallest details contrasts with the main spandrels, in which knots of Decorated foliage or heraldic shields set against rather mean fields of diaper look like components of an unfinished scheme.

The second phase of building on the south side incorporated one important structural change. An early scheme for buttress arches below the tribune roof is represented by a stump projecting from the inner wall between bays 8 and 9. This implies a lower buttress arch of more or less the same pitch as those in Northwold's presbytery. It would appear to have been part of a scheme in which Hotham's bays would continue the low outer wall of Northwold's tribune. The decision to have the much higher outer wall that we see today was connected with a new plan to build buttressing arches of a much steeper pitch than those of Northwold. These rise through the tribune roof and push against the lower wall of Hotham's southern clerestory where they overlap the already completed foliage ornament of the window jambs. This change in the buttressing is of considerable significance in the subsequent history of the eastern arm. It shows that Hotham's masons had become aware of developing structural problems in Northwold's work – problems which would soon require the replacement of nearly all his buttresses – and had determined to avoid similar difficulties in the new bays. The latter possibility might explain why the clerestory wall was not originally built to take flying buttresses and could also account for the isolated tabernacle whose thick, flat marble top would have made a good impost for timber. Tracery and mouldings show that the second phase also

[77] Stewart, *Ely*, p. 122, first pointed out the change in the mouldings of the window heads in these bays. There are comparable changes in the arcade, pier 8/9 having different mouldings from the rest.

[78] Stewart, *Ely*, p. 101, noted the more unified character of this northern elevation and concluded correctly that it was later than the south. Wilson in 'The Origins of the Perpendicular Style' (cit. in n. 1), p. 195, argued convincingly that the mason of this new work was William Ramsey, who was made chief surveyor of the King's works in the Tower of London and other castles south of the Trent in June 1336. He had been appointed to build the new chapter house and cloister at Old St Paul's in July 1332 and in May 1337 was appointed to advise on the completion of the presbytery at Lichfield. See Harvey, *English Mediaeval Architects* (cit. in n. 56), pp. 242–5. The profiles and other details of his work at Lichfield can be closely compared with the work of the third phase in Hotham's bays. See also Whittingham, 'Ramsey Family' (cit. in n. 56), pp. 285–9.

completed the aisle and tribune walls on the north side and initiated work on the main internal north elevation. But apart from some isolated Purbeck features at the extremities, the bulk of the northern elevation is clearly the work of another designer, who must have taken over in the mid-1330s and completed the project.[79]

By studying this masterly north elevation and examining the masonry of the bays opposite, it is possible to see that there are physical alterations to the standing work on the south. The slender fourteenth-century counterparts of Northwold's foliate brackets which rise between the spandrels of the southern arcade appear to have been inserted later than the main build[80] (Plate 7d–e). The spandrels of the arcade and tribune may likewise have been modified to allow the introduction of cusped, blind trefoils as a contemporary reference to the pierced spandrels of Northwold's work[81] These may be alterations by the mason of the third phase, and it was clearly in this phase that the two empty southern tribune arches were given their very delicate open tracery and the central window of the clerestory built to match those on the north. The pierced quatrefoil parapets were also an addition, and in the tribune they are roughly hacked into the bases of the second phase.[82] In these ways the deficiencies of the earlier design were corrected through a careful reappraisal of Northwold's work.

On the new north elevation it was possible to change details that could not easily be altered on the south. The two central piers and arches of the main arcade have some different profiles, and, significantly, the new vault shafts of the main elevation now project powerfully like those of Northwold and incorporate at their bases moulded stumps for the pierced parapets.[83] The boldness of the vault shafts, contrasting so strikingly with those opposite, indicates that the new mason was thinking about the impressive stone lierne vault which he now had to build. It is a close relative of his vault in the north aisle which is notably richer than the plainer vault of the south aisle.[84] This elaboration of the aisle, appropriate to the pilgrims' route to the Lady Chapel and the shrines, is a fitting prelude to the sumptuous, somewhat earlier, portal to the Lady Chapel passage. Built along with the high vault were the flyers and buttress towers whose pinnacles have an elegance that is displayed in all the work of the third phase.

---

[79] These Purbeck features might represent the using up of stored materials from the second phase.

[80] Their tops do not connect properly with the tribune string above, whose lower moulding has been cut away to accommodate them.

[81] The insertion of the spandrel tracery can be deduced from its ugly clash with the masonry surround of the tabernacle above the tribune at 8/9. The profiles resemble those of the inserted tracery in the tribune bays 7 and 8.

[82] These little parapets are now entirely 19th-century restorations. John Bacon, 'A Record of the Restorations and Repairs Etc done in and about Ely Cathedral since 1818', 1871 (EDC 4/6/2), fo. 98, notes 'The peculiar Tracery filling on each side the three bays of the Triforium of Bishop Hotham's exquisite Specimens of the Middle Pointed style, and of an unusual degree of beauty were carefully repaired, and the ancient cresting of the Triforium and Clerestory were entirely replaced; the corbels richly coloured and gilt, the shields in the spandrills [sic] illuminated, and the sunk trefoils painted, a dark blue, relieved with small stars in gold'; Bacon does not give a date, but the repair of the eastern arm interior was initiated by Dean Peacock with the assistance of Robert Willis in 1844. See Meadows, below, pp. 308–10.

[83] The realisation that the new parapets on the south side hid the moulded bases of his and his predecessor's central tribune pillars must have prompted the unusually tall bases of the north tribune, a revisiting of the problems encountered in Northwold's tribune.

[84] There are also differences in the handling of the vault springers in the two aisles.

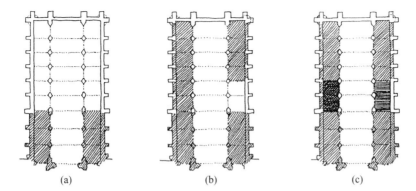

(a)   (b)   (c)

Figure 14. The remodelling of the presbytery tribunes: (a) stage 1: Bishop Northwold's 13th-century presbytery (bays 1–6) with Bishop Hotham's 14th-century bays (7–9); (b) stage 2: the 14th-century work is extended to encompass Northwold's tribune (bays 1–6 north and 1–4 south); (c) stage 3: light wells are created by the removal of the roofs in bays 5 and 6

The remodelling of the presbytery tribunes

The completion of Hotham's bays was followed by an extensive campaign of remodelling in the tribunes of Northwold's presbytery (Figure 14).[85] The date of this remodelling has been open to question but its purpose is clear. It provided improved abutment and was built in response to the outward rotation of the thirteenth-century buttress towers. This had compromised the upper flying arches and threatened the stability of Northwold's high vault whose spread is indicated in the outward curve of the clerestory walls. The remodelled tribunes resemble one another closely but are actually two distinct campaigns, with subtle variations in the mouldings and different buttress designs (Figures 14 and 15). The north side has a version of Hotham's buttresses which rejects his slender pinnacle in favour of a heavy one. The heavy pinnacles also appear on the south tribune, but the section is markedly different, omitting the wall-like upper mass and pierced walkway in favour of a steep upper arch and more separated pinnacle tower. On the north, the masonry of the lower buttress arches shows that they were tackled cautiously in alternating pairs, whereas on the south the uniform masonry suggests greater confidence. The outer tribune walls, built to correspond with the higher level established by Hotham, have uniform windows and, at the aisle ends, matching spires on Northwold's corner turrets.[86]

This extensive remodelling was not however the only fourteenth-century alteration that was made to Northwold's tribunes. At some time two southern bays (5 and 6) were unroofed to create a light well for windows which were inserted in the inner tribune

---

[85] This remodelling affected bays 1–6 on the north and 1–4 on the south.

[86] Whereas the southern campaign hacked away the base of the clerestory pilaster buttresses completely to join its lower arches to the wall plane, the north side retained much of this masonry. The northern arches are therefore steeper. The dimensions of the two turret vices are different. Details of the tribunes and the various phases of the remodelling are in Maddison, 'The Choir of Ely Cathedral' (cit. in n. 30), pp. 41–7.

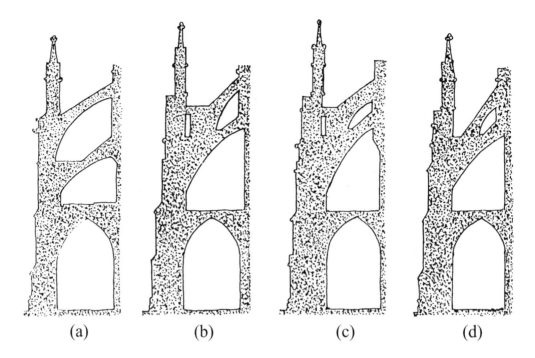

(a)   (b)   (c)   (d)

Figure 15. The developing design of buttresses in the eastern arm: (a) Bishop Northwold's 13th-century buttress section (with mid-14th-century pinnacle); (b) rebuilt buttress of bays 1–6 north; (c) buttress of Bishop Hotham's bays; (d) rebuilt buttress of bays 1–4 south

openings, presumably to light St Etheldreda's shrine and the high altar. The tracery follows the pattern of Hotham's tribune.[87] A similar but not exactly contemporary alteration in the equivalent position on the north side required the unroofing of the two western bays of the major fourteenth-century north tribune remodelling just discussed (Colour pl. 4c–d).

The sequence of these four different alterations to Northwold's presbytery tribunes has not been convincingly explained by earlier writers, and its chronological relationship to the alterations in the presbytery aisles has been unclear. Robert Willis was the first to address the problem and illustrated his argument with a sectional drawing.[88] He confined his analysis to the south side, however, and concluded that the first alteration of all was the unroofing of the southern tribune bays 5 and 6. He associated this work and its new internal tribune windows with John Barnet (Bishop, 1366–73) – perhaps mistakenly – and deduced that the remodelling of the southern tribune bays 1–4 must have followed it 'after a very considerable time'. He therefore described the windows of tribune bays 1–4 as 'late Decorated or Perpendicular', implying the closing years of the

---

[87] Two buttresses on the south side – 5/6 and 6/7 – were underpinned in 1866 and their upper arches rebuilt. The medieval tribune closure at 5/6 which had been built over an arch was taken down and a new closure formed on an iron girder. This is described in Bacon, 'Record of Restorations' (cit. in n. 82), fo. 158.

[88] Willis's argument is outlined in Stewart, *Ely*, pp. 76–81, and was first put forward in a paper at the RIBA in 1848.

fourteenth century. This account failed to acknowledge two important issues: firstly, the differences between the fourteenth-century buttresses in bays 1–6 (north) and 1–4 (south), and secondly the fact that in bays 5 and 6 (north) the tribune had been remodelled twice. His explanation has never been seriously challenged, and although Atkinson in 1953 asserted that the major remodelling of the tribunes was undertaken in the mid-fourteenth century, no evidence was put forward in support of this view.[89] More recent scholarship has therefore swung back to the interpretation advanced by Willis.[90]

The sacrist's roll of 1357–8 describes payments for a pair of windows on the north side of a place called 'three altars' (*tria altaria*).[91] This reference has for many years been taken to describe two windows in the north aisle (bays 4 and 5) but these can be shown to date from the 1370s and are too large and complex to be composed of the 67 pieces of stone specified in the roll.[92] More likely candidates are the two light well windows inserted in Northwold's northern inner tribune openings in bays 5 and 6. All the stone appears to be original, as the windows are sheltered from the weather by their recessed position. The moulded pieces – mullions, tracery and sills – amount to the total of 67 accounted for in the sacrist's roll. According to this roll, the glass for these windows was (unusually) provided to the glazier by the sacrist.[93] It was probably the relatively new glazing removed from the fourteenth-century outer tribune windows, now made redundant by the removal of the roof. The place called '*tria altaria*' cannot, therefore, have been the north aisle as is commonly supposed, and is probably the name given by the monks to the central part of Hotham and Northwold's work which contained the choir altar, high altar and the shrine altar.[94] The evidence of the roll implies that the major remodelling of Northwold's tribunes precedes this alteration of 1357–8.

New aisle windows in the presbytery

The new levels of light admitted by the numerous new windows of the mid-fourteenth-century tribune rebuilding would have made the thirteenth-century aisles, with their narrow lancets, appear gloomy. It appears now that this disparity was first addressed on the initiative of John Barnet (Bishop, 1366–73). Certain windows 'in the Lady Chapel next to the high altar' – meaning the old Lady Chapel in the south presbytery aisle – were, according to the sacrist's roll of 1374–5, built in the previous year. The funds had been recouped from Barnet's estate.[95] The three uniform windows (bays 4, 5 and 6)

---

[89] VCH, *Cambs.*, IV, p. 59.

[90] Draper, 'Bishop Northwold and the Cult of St Etheldreda' (cit. in n. 1), p. 22, n. 5.

[91] Chapman, *Sacrist Rolls*, II, p. 180. In the roll of Robert of Sutton for the year from Michaelmas 1357 to Michaelmas 1358, under the heading '*Custos novi operis*' the first entry is: '*In lxvij petris empt. pro ij fenestris ad tria altaria versus boream faciendis £3 3s 4d.*'

[92] Stewart, *Ely*, p. 121, first made this erroneous connection and has been followed by subsequent authors. Evidence for the identification of the aisle windows with the 1370s and with Bishop Barnet is advanced below.

[93] '*Solut. Willielmo Gerry pro ij fenestris vitriis de novo faciendis de materia D[omi]ni ad tria altaria versus boream £4 15s.*': Chapman, *Sacrist Rolls*, II, p. 180.

[94] In the north presbytery aisle, it has been suggested, there were chapels to St John, St Martin and St Benedict. If *tria altaria* was in the middle of the north aisle, as has been suggested, the sacrist would not have troubled to write more than once '*versus boream*' as all windows in this part of the north aisle were towards the north.

[95] Stewart, *Ely*, p. 139, quotes the reference from the roll for 25 January 1374 to 24 January 1375: '*De receptis de executoribus domini Johannis Barnet nuper episcopi Eliensis ad facturam cujusdam fenestrae in capella beatae Mariae juxta magnum altare factae in anno precedente xx li.*' He assumed however that it referred to

which light Barnet's place of burial are identical in every respect to the two windows in the north aisle (bays 5 and 6). This uniform group tallies with the five ascribed to Bishop Barnet by the *Chronicon:* 'The same indeed caused to be made three windows in the presbytery in the south part of the church and two in the north part.'[96]

The use of flowing tracery in Barnet's work, based on one window-pattern of Hotham's aisles, demonstrates that the remodelling of the outer tribunes and their buttresses, undertaken out of structural necessity, had initiated a switch in the design policy at Ely. Hotham's bays had deferred to the work of Bishop Northwold, but once structural problems had forced the remodelling of the thirteenth-century tribune it became the policy to remodel Northwold's aisles to conform with Hotham's, even though by the 1370s flowing tracery was passing swiftly out of fashion. This new discipline moreover, enforced for more than a century, ensured that the remaining presbytery aisle bays were slowly converted – in the heyday of Perpendicular – by two groups of late fifteenth-century aisle windows with outmoded Decorated tracery scarcely distinguishable from that of Bishop Barnet.

Four windows in the north aisle have distinctive carved shields in the jambs. In bays 2–4 they bear the arms of William Gray (Bishop, 1454–78) but are blank in bay 1. Gray's austere Purbeck monument once stood nearby between the piers of bay 2 and is now known through an engraving in Bentham and some fragments in the stone store.[97] Its rigid Perpendicular character contrasts with the archaic flowing tracery of Grey's aisle windows. The second group of fifteenth-century aisle windows includes the east window of the north aisle and the windows of bays 1–3 in the south aisle.[98] As to their date, it is clear that the east window of the north aisle was overbuilt by the masonry of Alcock's chantry and would therefore pre-date its foundation in 1488.[99] The window which was made in 1483–4 by the resident master mason Thomas Peyntour, 'opposite the tomb of St Alban', would also have been in this area but cannot be identified with certainty.[100]

The two lavish chantry chapels which occupy the eastern aisle bays present both similarities and remarkable contrasts. The chapel of John Alcock (Bishop, 1486–1500), on the north side, was only fitted into its space with the greatest difficulty (Plate 13*a*). The aisle wall was cut away to accommodate it and whereas its lower zones present a reasonably orderly assembly of panelling and shafting, there are some strange asymmetries. More extraordinary is the chaos above, where the jostling together of the canopies hid some of the sculptures so effectively that even the sixteenth-century

---

the 14th-century Lady Chapel east window. Lindley, in 'The Monastic Cathedral of Ely' (cit. in n. 1), p. 115, was the first to suggest that it might also be interpreted as a reference to the old Lady Chapel in the south aisle next to the high altar.

[96] '*Ipse fecit fieri tres fenestras in presbiterio ex parte australi ecclesie et duas ex parte aquilonai*': BL, MS Harl. 3721, fo. 59.

[97] See Stewart, *Ely*, p. 130 and Bentham, *Ely*, plate XX (dated 1764). The principal fragments from Gray's tomb are nos. 994–8 in the stone collection.

[98] Within this group 2 and 3 (south) are distinguished by distinctive floral cusp terminations.

[99] The date of Alcock's chapel is recorded on a foundation stone now preserved in the chapel.

[100] Harvey, *English Mediaeval Architects* (cit. in n. 56), p. 231. The position of the tomb of St Alban is implied in the description of Bishop Gray's place of burial: '*Sepelitur inter duas columpnas marmoreas per feretra Sti Albani et Ste Ermenilde*' (BL, MS Harl. 3721, fo. 63ᵛ). Stewart, *Ely*, p. 129, adds '*ad corneram capellae Johannis Alcock*' from an untraced source.

iconoclasts could not find them. The only properly integrated element is the fan vault, a separate structure sprung from Northwold's walls and piers. The anomalies might be explained if the chapel had been planned originally for a larger space such as the more ample bays of Worcester Cathedral, Alcock's previous see.[101]

The chantry of Nicholas West (Bishop, 1515–33) on the south side of the presbytery was planned to fit its site with considerable care, incorporating and altering the pre-existing tomb of Louis de Luxembourg (Bishop, 1437–43) (Plate 13b). The date 1534 occurs in an inscription on its west wall, and it is known that the sculptor Edmund More was at work on its imagery between 1523 and 1533.[102] The design followed the layout of Alcock's chapel, with a central entrance and a tomb recess on the outer wall of the aisle, but there the similarity ends. In the new chapel the most advanced late Gothic forms are arranged in an entirely orderly fashion, now effortlessly incorporating French Renaissance ornament (Colour pl. 13c). The fifteenth-century southern aisle window is concealed by screenwork and the east wall breaks through Northwold's aisle end to form a new termination with a Perpendicular window. This singularly assertive departure from a code of practice which had hitherto protected the unity of the presbytery fenestration signalled that the monastic community no longer had the authority to control the architectural contributions of the bishops. Its disorder had been the cause of West's visitation of 1515.[103]

The alteration of the west tower and fifteenth-century work in the nave and transepts

The structural instability of the west tower was a cause of recurrent anxiety in the later Middle Ages. The crowning octagon was probably introduced shortly after Bishop Barnet's alterations in the presbytery aisles. This much can is suggested by the design of its four windows, which resemble those built at Witchford (Cambs.) before the reconsecration of the church in 1376.[104] As with so much of the Gothic work at Ely, this octagonal structure was not a new thought; it was the projection of Bishop Ridel's late twelfth-century octagonal base. The fate of Northwold's spire is not known, but as the engravings in Bentham and Browne Willis show, the new western octagon also had a spire, albeit a small and slender one. If a date in the late 1370s can be accepted, it appears that this work preceded the very substantial reinforcement of the western

---

[101] Ironwork identical in character to the gates of Alcock's chantry is found in the south door to the cloister and uprights forming the Victorian entrance gates to gardens in the College. The south door gate seems to be intact and its measurements and design could suggest that it came from the entrance to the Galilee porch, altered in the late medieval period by the introduction of two four-centred arches. This alteration, probably prompted by the failure of the slender trumeau, was removed by Bernasconi in 1802. My suggestion (Maddison, *Ely Cathedral*, p. 97) that Alcock's contribution of two gates to the Cathedral was documented arose from a mistranslation of the Latin (Wharton, *Anglia Sacra*, I, p. 675) and should be discounted. Alcock's responsibility for this work is however likely, given the design.

[102] Harvey, *English Mediaeval Architects*, p. 207.

[103] Maddison, *Ely Cathedral*, p. 98; VCH, *Cambs.*, IV, p. 73. [There was a third chantry chapel, that of Richard Redman (Bishop, 1501–5), which was probably formed in the north choir aisle by screening off one or more bays, and possibly entered from the presbytery where his monument is sited. A deed relating to the chantry's endowment survives (EDC 1/B, Box 29). The vestments and altar frontals of this chapel were listed in the inventory of 1539 (CCCC, MS 120, p. 341; Bentham, *Ely*, Vol. II, unpaginated, following title page) – Peter Meadows].

[104] VCH, *Cambs.*, VI, p. 177.

crossing undertaken around the period 1405–7, when the mason John Mepsale (Meppershall) is recorded to have built the northern arch.[105] This was one of four identical arches that reinforced the four axes of the western crossing and originally completely concealed Ridel's ornate arches. That the northern side was in greater trouble than the south is indicated by the bracing of the north-west bay of the nave. All this was a substantial undertaking and may have inhibited other major architectural projects for some time. It is clear however that the rebuilding of the north transept gable with two large Perpendicular windows is earlier than the hammer beam roof which rides across them. The roof is identical to that in the south transept, the likely completion of which in c.1430 has been established by dendrochronology[106] (Colour pl. 12a) This expensive re-roofing operation may imply the structural failure of the fourteenth-century mansards. But if the new roofs were characteristic of their period, the painting of the rafters with repeated quatrefoils (now much overpainted) was probably intended to tie in with the earlier decoration of the Octagon's vault webs.

There are later references to donations by Thomas Bourchier (Bishop, 1443–54) and William Gray (Bishop, 1454–78) towards the repair of the tower, and in 1476 Master Thomas Peyntour was paid for further strengthening work.[107] The fall of the north-west transept probably occurred somewhat later and must have immediately preceded the construction of the large sloping mass of masonry standing in place of its original western wall. The blind tracery of its plinth suggests the end of the fifteenth century, and as with West's chantry there is no obvious sign of an attempt to replicate or respond to earlier architectural forms. The details indicate moreover that only a reduced, single-bay replacement of the original transept was contemplated.

As in so many monastic churches, the nave received less attention than the choir and presbytery. Apart from one window in the south aisle (bay 2) which has tracery similar to Hotham's second phase, there are very few signs of fourteenth-century work. This is partly because the parish of Holy Cross, which might have been expected to contribute to improvements, had been moved into a purpose-built church against the north aisle of the nave, begun in 1359 and dedicated by Simon Langham (Bishop, 1362–6).[108] Only the seventeenth-century cladding of the six western nave bays and the previous scarring indicated in Daniel King's engraving of 1655 reveal its former existence.[109]

The remodelling of the nave and transept tribunes was well underway by 1487–8 when battlements were built on the south side of the nave by Thomas Peyntour.[110] This probably dates the rebuilding of the tribune and its windows as well as the tracery of six matching windows formerly in the south aisle.[111] There seems to have been general agreement between the various campaigns that a common window tracery form was desirable but the north nave tribune is distinguished from the others in reincorporating

---

[105] Harvey, *English Mediaeval Architects*, p. 203. In 1405–6, a mason of the county of Huntingdon was paid 6s. 8d for surveying defects in the west tower and 1s. was paid to the groom who was sent to find him (*ibid.*, p. 154). This may also have been Mepsale, who is documented periodically at Ely between 1389 and 1418.

[106] Simpson and Litton (cit. in n. 24), pp. 185–9.

[107] Wharton, *Anglia Sacra*, I, pp. 672–3.

[108] Chapman, *Sacrist Rolls*, I, p. 101, II, p. 193; Wharton, *Anglia Sacra*, I, p. 662.

[109] This alteration is dated 1662 by a stone and involved alterations and rebuilding up to the corbel table of the tribune where there are some classical replacement corbels.

[110] Harvey, *English Mediaeval Architects*, p. 231.

[111] They are recorded in Bentham, *Ely*, Vol. II, pl. I.

the Norman corbel table at the new eaves level. The reinstatement of this feature may have been motivated by economy but it helps to relate the new wall to the Norman clerestory.[112] This conservative approach to an alteration at the end of the medieval period at Ely is a modest late expression of the important transaction between past and present that is a unifying theme in many of the building campaigns by which the Norman Cathedral was gradually dressed in Gothic forms.

[112] At Walsoken (Norfolk) the north aisle was rebuilt in the early 16th century, reinstating the late 12th-century corbel table.

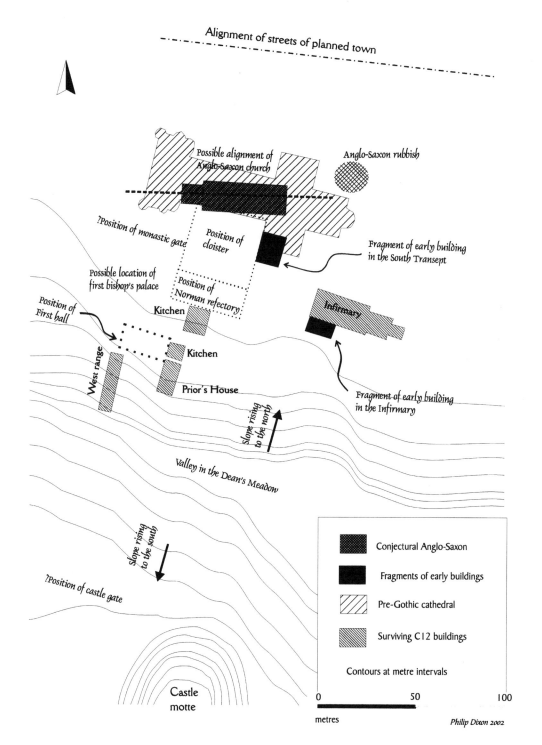

Alignment of streets of planned town

Possible alignment of Anglo-Saxon church

Anglo-Saxon rubbish

?Position of monastic gate

Position of cloister

Fragment of early building in the South Transept

Possible location of first bishop's palace

Position of Norman refectory

Position of First hall

Kitchen

Infirmary

West range

Kitchen

Prior's House

Slope rising to the north

Fragment of early building in the Infirmary

Valley in the Dean's Meadow

Slope rising to the south

?Position of castle gate

Castle motte

▨	Conjectural Anglo-Saxon
■	Fragments of early buildings
▨	Pre-Gothic cathedral
▨	Surviving C12 buildings
	Contours at metre intervals

0   50   100

metres

Philip Dixon 2002

Figure 16. Plan of the monastic site and buildings to *c.*1300 (Philip Dixon, based on T.D. Atkinson's survey)

The Monastic Buildings at Ely

Philip Dixon

Introduction

Ely is remarkable for the extent and quality of its surviving monastic buildings, which include structures which at other former cathedral priories have been lost, such as the guesthouses, prior's houses, and infirmary and almoner's ranges. It is remarkable, too, that the surviving buildings are almost all still in use, and that most preserve some or all of their pre-Reformation timberwork in floors and roofs. This unusual quality of preservation, however, is very partial: for reasons which are discussed at the end of this section, the central buildings of the complex have almost all gone. Nothing above ground now remains of the chapter house, dormitory or rere-dorter or of the buildings to the north-east of the Cathedral, and only the merest vestiges stand of the cloister, dormitory undercroft and the refectory. Thus though the overall pattern of the monastic precinct is sufficiently well established by the detailed studies of Atkinson and others,[1] some of the detail of even quite significant elements of the layout is still doubtful, and we can understand it only by analogy with better preserved structures elsewhere. This is particularly unfortunate for our understanding of the developing plan at Ely, in that the surviving structures show a fascinating sequence of alteration and rebuilding, especially during the fourteenth and fifteenth centuries; but it is now not possible to be certain how far these changes affected the buildings around the cloister.

The Anglo-Saxon monastery

The obscurity of certain parts of the medieval monastery is compounded in the pre-Conquest period. Indeed, the very location of the earliest monastery is much in doubt. The settlement of Cratendune may perhaps be represented by the site on the slope to the west of the present city of Ely.[2] This is stated to have lain at a distance of a mile from Etheldreda's new monastery,[3] which corresponds reasonably well with the distance of

---

[1] The most complete and accurate account is provided by Atkinson, *Ely Monastery*; for recent studies of parts of the complex see Anne Holton-Krayenbuhl, 'The Infirmary Complex at Ely', *AJ*, 154 (1997), pp. 118–72, and *ead.*, 'The Prior's Lodgings at Ely', *ibid.*, 156 (1999), pp. 294–341.

[2] In Fen Road, on the western slope of Ely island, excavated in 1999. See also Simon Keynes, above, p. 12 and n. 48.

[3] *Liber Eliensis* (ed. Blake), Intro., p. 4.

the recent excavations from the site of the present Cathedral precinct. To the west of the Cathedral, graves have been found under the grass of Palace Green, and further remains and some occupation debris were revealed a little to the west, behind the frontages of St Mary's Street, but none of these tells us more than that the site was occupied before the end of the Anglo-Saxon period. Of perhaps greater significance for the understanding the location of the monastery itself is a substantial foundation, a small part of which was observed immediately to the west of the Cathedral at the corner between the Galilee porch and the south-west transept, when the surrounding pavement was relaid.[4] The alignment of this fragment differed from that of the present Cathedral, and corresponded with that of the parish church of St Mary, to the west. Excavations between the Cathedral choir and the Lady Chapel, carried out in 2000, showed quite considerable quantities of occupation debris of the middle and later Saxon periods, indicating the presence nearby of rubbish dumps, such as might be expected towards the periphery of a settlement.[5] A comparison with other early monastic sites, such as St Augustine's, Canterbury, Jarrow, or Whitby, suggests that one might have expected to find a series of small churches arranged along a single axis; in these early monasteries the location of dormitories, refectories and other ancilliary buildings is not regular and their layouts are quite various.[6] In the absence of better information, it may be suggested that the buildings of the early monastery lay in the general area of the present nave, on an alignment about 10 degrees further to the north than the present line, and that the domestic quarters (which are not likely at this period to have been in the form of a cloister) extended no further to the east than the transepts of the present Cathedral. Etheldreda's abbey was damaged by Viking raiding, and seems to have been abandoned.[7]

The late Anglo-Saxon monastery

During the great reformation of monastic life towards the end of the tenth century, the old church and monastery were rebuilt by Bishop Æthelwold and Byrhtnoth, formerly Prior of Winchester, but their work is described only in vague terms in the *Liber Eliensis*.[8] This was the complex which survived to the later eleventh and early twelfth centuries. It presumably consisted of the church (about which most is said) and several ranges of monastic buildings. It seems likely enough that these latter included a cloister, in the then new fashion of late Carolingian architecture,[9] and that it had the whole

---

[4] A. Taylor, T. Malim, and C. Evans, 'Field-work in Cambridgeshire: October 1993 – September 1994', *PCAS*, 83 (1994), pp. 167–76, at p. 173.

[5] Excavations were carried out by Cambridge Archaeological Unit. I am grateful to Alison Dickens of CAU for discussing the results of the work with me before publication. The attribution of the pottery is given by spot dating, without further analysis. The use of the area for rubbish during the Saxon period is in strong contrast to the rarity of material from the post-Conquest period, when the adjacent choir and chapel were constructed and in use.

[6] H.M. and J. Taylor, *Anglo-Saxon Architecture* (Cambridge, 1965), pp. 136–42, 250–4, 338–42, 654–5; the status of the excavated remains at Whitby as an ecclesiastical site has recently been questioned ('Anglo-Saxon "planned town" revealed this month in Whitby', *British Archaeology*, 64 (April 2002), p. 4).

[7] See Simon Keynes, above, pp. 14–15 and nn. 60–1.

[8] *LE*, ii. 1: pp. 72–3.

[9] Walter Horn and Ernest Born, *The Plan of St Gall. A Study of the Architecture and Economy of, and Life in a Paradigmatic Carolingian Monastery* (Berkeley, 1979), I, pp. 241–310. See also E. Fernie, *The Architecture of the Anglo-Saxons* (London, 1985), and M.W. Thompson, *Cloister, Abbot and Precinct in Medieval Monasteries* (Stroud, 2001).

range of conventual buildings about it. A part of this work may have left what seems to be the ghost of an earlier structure in the masonry of the southern wall of the south transept; certainly, the existence here of some of the domestic buildings of the late Saxon monastery would explain the order of construction of the new Norman church, whose south transept and its adjacent walls, butting up against these earlier buildings, were built a little before the northern and western sides of the north transept. Fragments of other buildings which may have formed part of the early monastery survive beside the twelfth-century works of the infirmary, and may have survived from the earlier monastery. Finally, at the southern end of the present precinct, a mound, generally known as Cherry Hill, has long been taken to be the remains of a motte-and-bailey castle. For this there is some plausibility, and the contours of the land to the south of it suggest the former existence of a platform which could represent one or two fortified courtyards attached to the motte.[10] The position of this earthwork indicates that it was once a castle built to confront the monastery from the southern side of the steep valley which once extended eastwards across the Gallery into the Dean's Meadow (Figure 16, p. 142).[11] Implications of this are that the castle was constructed in the immediate aftermath of the post-Conquest Ely uprising, and before the reformation of the 1080s and 1090s, and also that this southern area (which has been part of the monastery since at least the fourteenth century) lay outside the Anglo-Saxon precinct, which may therefore have been contained within the space marked out by the Green, the southern valley, the eastern arm of the present Cathedral, and the High Street.

The layout of the monastery

At least by the twelfth century, the general layout of the monastery had been established (Figure 16, p. 142). The buildings within the precinct fell into six or seven distinct groups. The first, the core area immediately to the south of the Cathedral nave, beside the south transept, was the cloister and its surrounding buildings, principally the dormitory, refectory and chapter house. Here the monks ate, slept, and met at regular chapter meetings, and it was from here they passed through the day and night doors to their church in the crossing and eastern arm of the Cathedral. To the south and west of this central area lay the house of the Prior and probably that of the Bishop, with a range of associated lodgings that was added as a guest hall at the end of the twelfth century. To the east of the cloister lay the monks' cemetery, perhaps with a chapel. Here, at least by the later twelfth century, stood the infirmary and a cluster of buildings for officials such as the cellarer, the chamberlain and the pittancer. These three clusters of buildings lay to the south of the Cathedral, and constituted the main monastic complex.

Immediately to the east of the Cathedral, and located so close to its east end that it seems likely that the arrangement belongs to a period before Northwold's extension of the presbytery after 1230, lay the outer or forinsec hostelry, probably a timber-framed

---

[10] No excavations seem to have taken place here, and the mound was heavily scraped and heightened by Bentham in the late 18th century: EDC 4/6/3, pp. 34–5. The ground occupied by the baileys was stripped in the 20th century to produce a football field.

[11] Excavations in 1999 on the site of the King's School theatre have shown a considerable depth of alluvial deposits in this valley: the present land surface is largely horizontal as far as the southern side of Prior Crauden's Chapel, but even in the later Middle Ages the valley seems to have been about 16ft (5m) deeper.

and thatched guest house with its kitchen and service buildings inside a walled close. This was entered from the town by its own gate in Steeple Row (now the High Street). To the north-east of this complex lay the almoner's offices, with accommodation for a school; to the west, north of the Cathedral, lay an old hall and other buildings which may already have been part of the sacrist's establishment, where works on the buildings were planned and carried out, and where the funds were reckoned up, and goldwork for the altars and liturgical objects were put together. This department probably always had a separate entrance on to the High Street, for the convenience of unloading building materials. The present-day entrance (Sacrist's Gate) belongs to a fourteenth-century rebuilding, and the earlier approach may have been a little to the west of this point, where excavations have revealed a pathway[12] (Plate 14*b*). The sacrist's department stood beside the lay cemetery on the northern side of the Cathedral, which had its own entrance from the main road through the Steeple Gate, where the charnel house stood.[13] A final area lay at the extreme south of the site, where the great gate and adjacent storehouse stood beside the earthwork of the old castle, and represent the agricultural area of the precinct.[14]

It is not easy even to estimate how much of this complex was already standing by the time of the Conquest. The scar of an early building on the south wall of the south transept marks the position of a range running north and south. This may well have been the dormitory at the eastern side of an early cloister, since the location of the two cloister doors in the southern wall of the nave (the Monks' and the Prior's doors) shows that a full-sized cloister aligned with the present Cathedral was already in place or planned by no later than the second quarter of the twelfth century, and a now-blocked opening in the western wall of the south transept suggests that at least this end of the cloister was standing by the last quarter of the eleventh century.[15] How far any reconstruction had by then extended to the rest of the monastic complex is unknown. It seems unlikely that the Abbot, Prior or monks would have found it acceptable for long to occupy the old buildings of the Saxon monastery without any rebuilding. However, the turbulent years of the monastery between the Conquest and the start of the rebuilding of the Abbey church under Simeon (Abbot, 1082–93), and the subsequent troubled years of Rufus, seem unpropitious periods in which to have reconstructed the monastic complex. It may thus have been the case that parts of the old monastery survived long into the Norman occupation.

Even if late eleventh- or early twelfth-century domestic buildings were erected, however (perhaps in the central area of the cloister, where the heart of the monastery lay), the earliest dated sections now to be seen outside the Cathedral itself are on the edge of the monastery. These are: on the southern side of the infirmary complex, where

---

[12] A. Holton-Krayenbuhl, T. Cocke and T. Malim, 'Ely Cathedral Precincts: the North Range', *PCAS,* 78 (1990), pp. 47–69.

[13] Atkinson, *Ely Monastery,* pp. 148–9.

[14] The sacrist's department was supplied with a great barn beside the church of St Mary, to hold the produce which made up a significant part of the works income. This was destroyed in 1842: R. Willis, *A Description of the Sextry Barn at Ely, lately Demolished,* CAS, Quarto Publications 7 (1843). Willis's drawings made at the time show an aisled structure with scissor braces and secondary rafters, which suggest a date around the middle of the 13th century.

[15] I am grateful to Dr Geoffrey West for discussion about this point.

walls predating the work of *c.*1180–90 survive among the canonry houses;[16] in the ruined building (presumably a kitchen) next to the great hall, the trumpet capitals and keel-moulded shafts of which suggest a date in the later twelfth century; and in the vaulted basement of the Prior's house, which belongs to the second and third quarters of the twelfth century.[17] What happened to the monastic buildings during the three generations between the Conquest and the building of the middle and later twelfth century therefore remains very doubtful, but the considerable extent of this late Romanesque rebuilding suggests that some of the late Saxon structures, at least of the outer buildings, may still have been standing long after the start of the great rebuilding of the monks' church.

The Norman monastery

The buildings around and connected with the Prior's house provide us with our first tolerably complete picture in detail of the monastic buildings at Ely. Excavations below the undercroft of the later Queen's Hall revealed a substantial wall running from north to south, approximately parallel to the long axis of the Prior's house.[18] It seems likely that this was the gable end of a large building, against which the Prior's house was built, and which at its western end, next to the Prior's house, had kitchens, of which some traces still survive. Against the southern end of this supposed large building there was constructed during the last quarter of the twelfth century a long thin range, which still survives among the buildings of the School next to the Gallery. Its purpose was to provide a tall ground-floor hall beside a small two-storeyed extension southwards.[19] These structures produced a U-shaped complex, which perhaps consisted of the ground-floor hall and a kitchen flanked by the two-storeyed Prior's house to the east, and perhaps by a guest hall and two-storeyed chambers to the west; such a layout would be comparable, for example, with the early eleventh-century hall and chambers arranged in the Bishop's suite at Norham, or the first layout of Durham Castle.[20] It has been assumed since the time of Bentham that these buildings formed from the first the lodging of the Prior, who had been given a new and increased status in the monastery, because the Abbot was after 1109 the Bishop and was in consequence a more remote figure.[21] This is by no means certain, however, and the silence of documents on this matter makes it difficult to distinguish in particular the initial lodgings of Prior and Bishop. The multiplication of halls in this complex (three 'great' halls, the northern one perhaps a replacement for an earlier hall,

---

[16] Holton-Krayenbuhl, 'Infirmary Complex' (cit. in n. 1), pp. 136–9.

[17] Holton-Krayenbuhl, 'Prior's Lodgings' (cit. in n. 1), p. 301. In the text, the structures are referred to as the Prior's house, despite uncertainty about its proper original designation. Tree ring dates giving a bracket *c.*1165 × 85 have been obtained for the roof of the stone wing: Dendrochronological Laboratory, Department of Archaeology, University of Nottingham. My thanks to Dr R.R. Laxton.

[18] The excavations are referred to by Holton-Krayenbuhl, 'Prior's Lodgings', p. 305: I am grateful to her for information on this point.

[19] Probably in 1187 or a year or two later: dates from the original roof timbers have been supplied to me by the Nottingham Dendrochronological Laboratory (cit. in n. 17). My thanks to Dr R.R. Laxton.

[20] P. Dixon and P. Marshall, 'The Great Tower in the Twelfth Century: the Case of Norham Castle', *AJ*, 138 (1993), pp. 410–32. For Durham see M. Leyland, 'The Origins and Development of Durham Castle', in D. Rollason, M. Harvey and M. Prestwich (eds.), *Anglo-Norman Durham, 1093–1193* (Woodbridge, 1994), pp. 404–24.

[21] Thompson, *Cloister, Abbot and Precinct* (cit. in n. 9), p. 89; Holton-Krayenbuhl, 'Prior's Lodgings' (cit. in n. 1), pp. 333–5.

and one two-storeyed private hall) seems an excessive provision. The placing of the medieval Bishop's palace is still wholly uncertain, and it may be that the large two-storeyed northern hall represents a thirteenth-century rebuilding of part of this establishment (which would then extend northwards towards the south-west transept of the Cathedral), and not that of the Prior.[22] In any case it is worth noting that a detached complex for the Prior, wholly removed from the cloister, is a development more frequently associated with the later Middle Ages.[23]

To the north and east of these buildings stands the ruin of what was probably a square structure with tall vaulted round arches and high round-headed windows. This was mistakenly considered by Bentham to have been the Chapter House,[24] and has very tentatively been identified as a private chapel comparable with the Bishop's Chapel at Hereford. Almost certainly, however, it was the monastic kitchen, sited beside the refectory on the southern side of the cloister, and kept separate from the Prior's apartments at this time by a small open courtyard[25] (Colour pl. 5b). The building presumably contained a central chimney shaft, with fires and set-pots in the middle of the room, surrounded by a vaulted ambulatory or aisle.[26] The Norman refectory presumably stood between the kitchen and the southern walkway of the cloister: the existing fragments here belong to the late thirteenth-century rebuilding. To the east of the cloister, the Chapter House was partially investigated in 1892, and found to be rectangular,[27] and a passage, the inner parlour, and perhaps a warming house are to be expected on the ground floor below the dormitory. All this would be conventional planning, and there are references in the archives to the dormitory, privy dormitory and other rooms, but we have no direct evidence for their location.

Of the rest of the monastic buildings within the precinct we know little at this period. Towards the end of the twelfth century, when the guest halls at the western side of the site were being completed, the present infirmary hall was constructed[28] (Colour pl. 5a).

---

[22] For the uncertain location of the Bishop's palace see Atkinson, *Ely Monastery*, p. 161, and Holton-Krayenbuhl, 'Prior's Lodgings', pp. 297, 333–5. Both, however, regard this two-storeyed hall as an adjunct of the Prior's house rather than that of the Bishop. The significance of the door of the hall at first floor level running northwards may be that it communicated with the Bishop's apartments to its north. Bishop Northwold is recorded as having constructed a hall, which might accord with the first phase of this great hall: Wharton, *Anglia Sacra*, I, p. 636; Atkinson, *Ely Monastery*, p. 161. This may, however, have stood near or under the towers later built by Bishop Alcock at the end of the 15th century: C. Hussey, 'Ely Palace, Cambridgeshire', *Country Life*, 9 June 1928, p. 850.

[23] Thompson, *Cloister, Abbot and Precinct*, pp. 76–8.

[24] Bentham, *Ely*, Addendum, p. 7.

[25] Atkinson, *Ely Monastery*, pp. 60–1, draws attention to descriptions in the 1649 survey of 'the monks' kitchen built with stones arched over and covered with lead' and of the dimensions 33ft square, which corresponds with the surviving remains. Fernie draws attention to the large size of the windows and suggests the parallel with Hereford (*The Architecture of Norman England*, pp. 205–6), but concedes that the designation as kitchen is most likely. George Millers had believed that the structure was the Chapter House: *A Description of the Cathedral Church of Ely*, 3rd edn (Ely, 1834), p. 109.

[26] Parallels for this arrangement are not obvious, but the extreme rarity of 12th-century kitchens (that at Ely being the only English example to stand higher than its foundations) makes realistic comparison impossible.

[27] Its size (76 by 33ft) is almost exactly equal to that, for example, at Durham: *CAS Communications*, viii (1895), pp. 242–3. Atkinson, *Ely Monastery*, p. 55, points out that the worked stone found in the excavations suggests at least that there had been a rebuilding in the 13th century.

[28] The architectural detail suggests a date in the third quarter of the 12th century. The first reference to an infirmary lies in the period 1159 × 69, and therefore may refer to this building: Holton-Krayenbuhl, 'Infirmary Complex' (cit. in n. 1), p. 167.

It is clear that it was built immediately to the north of an existing building, and it is striking that its alignment does not accord with that of the Cathedral, nor with that of the various adjacent monastic buildings around the cloister, which share the main axis of the church. The infirmary alignment corresponds instead with that of the simple vaulted building to its south, and so it is possible that it preserves the arrangement of earlier buildings, which had survived the twelfth-century rebuilding of the monastery.[29] The infirmary was constructed as a three-aisled hall with a chapel at its eastern end, similar to those at Peterborough, Canterbury Cathedral Priory, or (complete, but rather later) in the hospital at Chichester. Its western end was set square with the end of the pre-existing building, and the infirmary contained nine bays, their arches supported on alternating pairs of piers with trumpet capitals. At the eastern end of the hall a single round-headed door led into an aisled chapel of five bays, with a simple two-cell vaulted sanctuary beyond; and a door, still extant, gave access from the western bay of the chapel to the adjacent monks' cemetery.[30] By no later than the 1230s, another door perhaps led from the north aisle of the hall to a passageway which crossed the cemetery and passed through the aisle wall of the choir, to give a covered access to the church.[31] Immediately after the completion of the hall, a rectangular wing was constructed over the pre-infirmary building, set at right angles to its west end; this was probably to provide storage and accommodation for the cellarer, and is now part of Canory House.[32]

The Gothic monastery

By the beginning of the thirteenth century the monastery had arrived at the arrangement of buildings which it was to preserve until the end of the Middle Ages (Figure 17, p. 151). During the next two generations two major developments took place, in the cloister and in the Prior's ranges. In the first place, fragments of surviving ashlar show that the main buildings of the cloister were rebuilt: the Chapter House seems to have been the first to be reconstructed, in the middle of the century, and the refectory followed during the second half of the century, perhaps c.1270.[33] This certainly suggests that these significant elements of the monastery were by then regarded as obsolete, and perhaps too small; it is also further evidence that they therefore had been built no later than the eleventh century, since they were so soon to be replaced, and their rebuilding was a substantial project, which perhaps began after the completion of Northwold's

---

[29] The discrepancy in alignment may have led to Bentham's supposition that the infirmary was a relic of the Saxon church, a not unreasonable conjecture at the time: Bentham, *Ely,* pl. 4, and Stevenson, *Supplement, Addenda,* pp. 9–10 and pl. 58. Holton-Krayenbuhl, 'Infirmary Complex', p. 137, suggests that the early building was a chapel, associated with the monastic graveyard to its north.

[30] For a full description see Holton-Krayenbuhl, 'Infirmary Complex'.

[31] The doorway in the aisle wall of the choir of the Cathedral, which is now blocked, is still clearly visible, together with its roof crease. The door in the infirmary was in the lower storey of Powcher's Hall, but has now been rebuilt.

[32] Atkinson, *Ely Monastery,* p. 107; so too, more cautiously, Holton-Krayenbuhl, 'Infirmary Complex', p. 164.

[33] For the dates see Atkinson, *Ely Monastery,* p. 59, quoting documents in Bentham, *Ely,* p. 218. The bases of the attached shafts in the refectory resemble those of Vale Royal Abbey, which are later than 1277. I am grateful to John Maddison for this observation. A number of ashlars from broad-chamfered pointed openings of similar date have been preserved in the Cathedral stone store, and perhaps come from the refectory, as do fragments of bar tracery.

presbytery in 1252. In the second place, significant additions were made to the building complex to the south-west of the precinct: a new two-storeyed hall (which forms the core of the existing Great Hall) was built beside the older ground floor hall next to the Prior's house. This may have been intended to replace the old hall, and probably re-used its kitchen.[34] A new range was extended southwards along the street now called the Gallery, from the southern end of the old west range to the edge of the watercourse into Dean's Meadow, thus increasing the accommodation of the twelfth-century guest hall.[35]

Further construction works clearly took place elsewhere in the precinct, but their details are now obscure: the undercroft of the dormitory was linked to the infirmary by an elaborate walkway which was to become known as the 'Dark Cloister', and which contained a song school at first floor level,[36] and the infirmary itself was perhaps increased in size by the building of a second wing, the 'Black Hostelry', extending from the south side of the aisle opposite the third and fourth bays: this was intended to provide accommodation for visiting Benedictine monks, and is the first clear sign of that segregation of apartments which is a feature of the fourteenth century. It is clear that two periods of construction are represented here, these being taken to be of the earlier thirteenth century and the financial year 1291–2, when stone and timber were bought for a new house next to the infirmary.[37] This is not however certain, since the date of the roof, which seems to belong to the second phase of construction, is later than expected.[38] The first phase remains without clear date.

The prospect of the construction of the Lady Chapel, begun in March 1321, seems to have led to a reorganisation of the works yard under the control of the sacrist. This involved the rebuilding of the precinct wall fronting the High Street between the Goldsmith's Tower and the new Sacrist's Gate, and the construction of a series of sheds, workshops and storage buildings[39] (Plate 14*b*). The collapse of the central tower of the Cathedral in February 1322, when work on the new Lady Chapel had just begun, greatly compounded the problems of the builders, but seems not to have caused much remission in the pace of the work: the scale of the projects undertaken is shown by the way in which all the surviving fragments of the monastic buildings at Ely display rebuildings or additions belonging to the second and third quarters of the fourteenth century. In addition to the rebuilding of the sacrist's offices, where work continued until about 1334,[40] substantial additions were made to the infirmary ranges, and to the Prior's apartments.

[34] This is the structure which is generally identified as the Prior's guest hall, but which might have been the southern element in the Bishop's palace complex. See above, n. 21.

[35] The sequence is discussed in Holton-Krayenbuhl, 'Prior's Lodgings' (cit. in n. 1), pp. 302–11. Atkinson saw the two phases of building in the two-storeyed Great Hall, but draws attention to the difficulty of distinguishing them: *Ely Monastery*, pp. 80–1.

[36] A wall of this, and of the dormitory undercroft, remains, and is illustrated in Maddison, *Ely Cathedral,* p. 86.

[37] Atkinson, *Ely Monastery*, p. 110; Holton-Krayenbuhl, 'Infirmary Complex', p. 164.

[38] The roof of this Hostelry is of crown-post construction with octagonal capitals and rather long posts. While this might suggest a date of *c.*1300 (comparable with the hall at Fressingfield (Suffolk): *cf.* Eric Mercer, *English Vernacular Houses. A Study of Traditional Farmhouses and Cottages* (London, 1975, pl. 55), the tree-rings point to a late 14th-century or later date, in the range 1390–1410 (for this my thanks to Dr R.R. Laxton).

[39] Atkinson, *Ely Monastery*, pp. 142–7; excavations within the 19th-century range to the west of Sacrist's Gate have revealed an earlier pathway running south from the street, and the foundations of buildings which may include the shops bought from the Bishop *c.*1322 by Alan of Walsingham to increase the size of his department: for a report see Holton-Krayenbuhl *et al.,* 'Ely Cathedral Precincts: the North Range' (cit. in n. 12), pp. 47–69.

[40] Atkinson, *Ely Monastery*, p. 143.

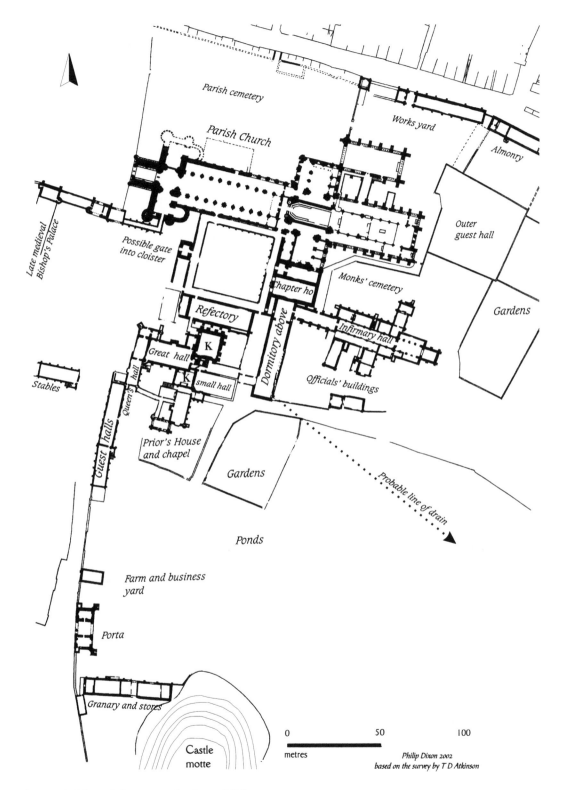

Parish cemetery

Parish Church

Works yard

Almonry

Late medieval
Bishop's Palace

Possible gate
into cloister

Outer
guest hall

Chapter ho

Monks' cemetery

Gardens

Refectory

Dormitory above

Infirmary hall

K

Great hall

K small hall

Officials' buildings

Stables

Queen's hall

Guest halls

Prior's House
and chapel

Gardens

Probable line of drain

Ponds

Farm and business
yard

Porta

Granary and stores

Castle
motte

0   50   100

metres

Philip Dixon 2002
based on the survey by T D Atkinson

Figure 17. Plan of the monastic site, c.1500

In the infirmary a new range was built projecting from the north aisle of the hall, facing the Black Hostelry, after 1334.[41] This is now known as Walsingham House, and contained a hall and chamber above a vaulted basement, probably with their own garderobe, providing accommodation that in the last resort would have been suitable for female relatives of the monks.[42] To the west, Powcher's Hall represents a complete rebuilding of the northern aisle of the infirmary, to produce a pair of first-floor rooms above basements. These developments (which continued into the fifteenth century in the range beside the Black Hostelry and in a grand rebuilding of the upper storey of Powcher's Hall in the early sixteenth century) (Plate 14a), demonstrate a significant change in the infirmary complex: between 1200 and the early fourteenth century the emphasis moved from the communal treatment of the sick in what was presumably an open hall (as at Chichester and elsewhere, with screened cubicles in the aisles), to the construction of separate apartment blocks, for specific functions within the infirmary, and also for the accommodation of monastic officials away from the cloister. We hear of chambers for the cellarer, sub-prior, chamberlain and pittancer, as well as for the infirmarian himself, who may have had a room above the Dark Cloister.[43] By the early sixteenth century the infirmary was wholly enclosed by two-storeyed ranges, and it seems that at this stage or earlier the roof of the central nave of the building was removed, to produce a long thin internal courtyard, from which these adjacent buildings could borrow light[44] (Colour pl. 5a).

While these works were in hand, the Prior's complex was substantially rebuilt. Additional guest rooms were provided by extending the west range southwards to the edge of the valley.[45] The private hall, above its twelfth-century vault, was rebuilt in 1324–5 for Prior John de Crauden, and was beautified by an elegant chapel and a timber-framed chamber used as a study, both at first-floor level[46] (Colour pl. 5c). The Great Hall was substantially rebuilt, and linked across the screens at first floor level with a flying gallery over the kitchen to the Prior's private hall. At the upper end of the Great Hall, a door from the dais led through a crooked passage to a tall and exquisite first floor chamber, of c.1330, now in the Headmaster's House; this was probably intended for guests of the highest rank. The name 'Queen's Chamber' is found in the records,[47] and the traditional association with Queen Philippa is chronologically possible but not supported by any definite documentation. From the south-eastern corner of the Queen's Hall a flying bridge extended across the courtyard to reach a platform beside Prior Crauden's study, from which another bridge ran to the first floor doorway of his private

[41] Holton-Krayenbuhl, 'Infirmary Complex', p. 149; tree-ring dates for rafters and boards suggest a felling date of 1332–3 (Nottingham Dendrochronological Laboratory), which accords with the reference to a new chamber in 1334–5: D.J. Stewart, 'Distribution of the Buildings of the Dissolved Monastery at Ely', *AJ*, 54 (1897), pp. 174–85, at p. 182.

[42] Holton-Krayenbuhl, 'Infirmary Complex', p. 169.

[43] *Ibid.*, pp. 168–9.

[44] The chapel at its eastern end, however, remained in use, and was still roofed: Holton-Krayenbuhl, 'Infirmary Complex', pp. 169–70.

[45] Probably in the period 1302 × 22: date from alterations to the roof of the 12th-century range. My thanks to Nottingham Dendrochronological Laboratory.

[46] Priory House contains boards (on the stair turret) of c.1294 × 1320, and studs of 1327–8, in both cases re-used much later, but probably originally belonging to these alterations.

[47] A brewhouse was located '*inter cameram regine*' and the monks' bakehouse, in 1258: Atkinson, *Ely Monastery*, p. 87. But this certainly predates the present building.

chapel. The result of all these works was to provide a continuous walkway around the whole of the Prior's and guest apartments, so that all who used these spaces could avoid returning to ground level.[48] The works here were completed after the middle of the century, when the rebuilding of the Great Hall was completed by the erection of a vast timber roof in 1352.[49] This is of the grandest scale, but utilises large but short timbers, so that many of the rafters and braces are end-scarfed out of two or three pieces – perhaps a sign of the shrinking of resources after more than thirty years of continuous building. It was nevertheless followed by the construction of a new church of Holy Cross for the parish, on the north side of the Cathedral nave; this was begun in 1359 and was finished by c.1364.[50]

All the works so far described were located to the north of the valley which runs into Dean's Meadow. There is no information about the extent and nature of the buildings in and around the old castle mound, until towards the end of the fourteenth century, when a large storehouse and a new grand gatehouse were built. This latter, the Ely Porta, has ever since served to provide the principal access to the precinct (Colour pl. 6a). Some such gate as this on the western side of the precinct was of course essential, since the gates which opened from Steeple Row (High Street) all gave access to distinct areas and yards, and not directly to the monastic buildings themselves, and one may suspect that the Porta replaced a service gate to the farmyards, which may even have superseded the old castle gate. If this was the only western gate, however, its position is odd, since the Porta was far from the cloister, and led directly to the farmyard and offices, and then to the houses of the Prior and the Bishop, and the guest houses, and not at all to the cloister. To get into the core monastic buildings one would have expected to find a gateway facing towards the western walk of the cloister, perhaps leading towards an outer parlour, but there is little evidence for this, and some against it.[51] Above the gatekeeper's lodge and other office rooms – including, at least by 1541, a gaol[52] – the Porta contained a great chamber, used for the monastery's administration and manorial courts, and it was set beside a large agricultural building, part granary and part business accommodation, which had recently been completed.[53] This was appropriately enough treated as the farming end of the precinct, and may well have contained other buildings, now replaced by those of the School. The building of the Porta after

---

[48] This treatment of linking what are essentially separate buildings by bridges is not new: it formed part of Henry III's modification at Westminster in the middle of the 13th century (R. Allen Brown, H.M. Colvin and A.J. Taylor, *The History of the King's Works*, I (London, 1963), pp. 121, 494–504, and *ibid.*, II, pp. 912–13). Its use at Ely is unusually thorough, however, and may be prefigured in the high-level flying gallery which led to the Lady Chapel, as this latter was designed no later than 1322–3: P. Dixon, 'Gateways to Heaven: The Approaches to the Lady Chapel, Ely', *PCAS*, 91 (2002), pp. 63–72.

[49] Nottingham Dendrochronological Laboratory dates: 1352, with an alteration to the louver truss in 1367.

[50] Maddison, *Ely Cathedral*, p. 79.

[51] The gate of the Bishop's Parlour is mentioned in 1300, and may have been this entrance: Atkinson, *Ely Monastery*, p. 65. The extensive lands of the Bishop in this area clearly made direct access difficult. A grant by Eustace at the beginning of the 13th century refers to problems in bringing beer to the refectory, and land for a cellar was accordingly given between the latter and a *porticus* (which may mean passageway) from the palace to the church: Atkinson, *Ely Monastery*, p. 63. The 16th- and 17th-century surveys give no sign of a gate, though the rearrangement of the Bishop's accommodation in this area after the building of the Porta c.1400 and before the Dissolution may have confused the picture.

[52] Atkinson, *Ely Monastery*, p. 183.

[53] Nottingham Dendrochronological Laboratory's date for its roof timbers: 1386–7.

1397, and of the granary beside it, brought to an end the great period of building which had continued for most of the fourteenth century.

During the following decades, when much was done to embellish the Cathedral, with the addition of chantry chapels, and the major intervention on the western tower, very little is known to have been constructed in the precinct. The southern part of the western guest houses was re-roofed in 1478,[54] and the western walk of the cloister may have been replaced at about this time or a little before,[55] but it was not until the next century that works began again. The rest of the cloister was rebuilt c.1509–10, when the works are mentioned in the sacrist's rolls.[56] We do not know whether any other claustral buildings were restored at this period, but the rebuilding of the cloister presumably disturbed the library, which at this period seems to have lain within the cloister walk.[57] The roof of the Norman hall of the Prior's house was replaced in 1524–5, as part of a modernising of this area.[58]

The piecemeal expansion of the precinct was brought to an abrupt end by the dissolution of the monastery in 1539. The new College which replaced it expanded the establishment considerably, to a total of no fewer than 76 people, nine of whom were to have their own houses.[59] Prior Steward, now appointed the first Dean, continued to occupy his apartments, which remained the Deanery until the twentieth century. The increasing segregation of the monastic buildings during the fourteenth and fifteenth centuries had provided suitable locations for the required separate residences. Five of the eight new Canons were allocated sections of the infirmary complex, which by this period consisted of a series of independent dwellings grouped around a narrow courtyard.[60] Others were accommodated in the almonry and the sacristy, and in the new hall which was part of the rebuilt Priory House.[61]

The cloister and its buildings, however, were not immediately abandoned. Despite the segregation of the canons' residences, a refectory and dormitory were still required, since the minor canons, schoolmasters and others were to live in common, and the 'gret hall' and the adjacent monastic kitchen were allocated to their use in 1541.[62] It is possible that the small dormitory over the Dark Cloister (west of the infirmary) was retained, while the great dormitory and its rere-dorter were demolished. Perhaps because it lay below this dormitory, the Chapter House, which was retained for use by the new foundation, required alterations.[63] A new library was constructed in c.1550

[54] Nottingham Dendrochronological Laboratory; my thanks to Dr R.R. Laxton.
[55] Atkinson, *Ely Monastery*, p. 49.
[56] *Ibid.*, pp. 40–50.
[57] *Ibid.*, pp. 50–1.
[58] *Vernacular Architecture*, 24 (1993), p. 40.
[59] Atkinson, *Ely Monastery*, p. 14.
[60] Holton-Krayenbuhl, 'Infirmary Complex' (cit. in n. 1), p. 160 and illustration 29.
[61] So Stewart, 'Distribution of the Buildings' (cit. in n. 43), pp. 178, 183; Holton-Krayenbuhl, 'Prior's Lodgings' (cit. in n. 1), pp. 336–7.
[62] CCCC, MS 120, p. 320, transcribed in Stewart, 'Distribution of the Buildings', pp. 175ff, and by Atkinson, *Ely Monastery*, pp. 180–5. Both identify this 'grete hall' as the building which is now the Bishop's House. Holton-Krayenbuhl, 'Prior's Lodgings', p. 336, however, suggests that the reference is to the old refectory; this is difficult, since the same document refers to 'vaults under the same [grete hall]' while the refectory was pretty certainly single-storeyed; additionally, the 'frayter', presumably meaning the monks' refectory, was in this document listed for demolition.
[63] Bentham, *Ely*, pp. 226–7; Atkinson, *Ely Monastery*, p. 56.

above the western walk of the cloister, presumably to replace a less convenient reading area which one would expect to have been in the northern walk; this last was probably now dismantled.[64]

Decay and demolition continued during the next century. The chapter house, repaired in c.1541, had vanished by 1649, and the old monks' kitchen was at that time listed for dismantling, effectively removing the core of the monastery.[65] The west range of the cloister, with its library, still stood in 1649, but was removed perhaps in the later seventeenth century, when the modernising of the surviving prebendal houses began.[66] The effect of the demolition or alteration of these buildings was to remove the cloister and the linking corridors and structures which had been formed to unite the complex, and to divide the surviving elements of the monastery into four major blocks: the farmstead, the Prior's house, the infirmary and the High Street buildings, separated by gardens and pathways, in a form which, as late as the nineteenth century, preserved in its enclosures many of the property boundaries of the medieval precinct.[67]

---

[64] Atkinson, *Ely Monastery*, pp. 50–1: the evidence for the new library is a note in the Augmentation Office books relating to the selling of plate worth £265 to pay for it.

[65] The parliamentary survey of 1649 (EDC 8A/1/13) is printed and discussed by Atkinson, *Ely Monastery*, pp. 190–8, relying on the transcript by Stewart.

[66] These changes are glimpsed in the tree-ring dates for some of the buildings: the roof of Canonry House, 1617–8; eastern roof of Powcher's Hall, early 17th century; roof of Queen's Hall, early 17th century (dates from Nottingham Dendrochronological Laboratory).

[67] The removal of the fishponds and other ancient elements is recorded by John Bacon (EDC 4/6/3, fos. 39–48); for discussion see Atkinson, *Ely Monastery*, pp. 158–9.

The Library and Archives 1109–1541

NIGEL RAMSAY

The creation of the see of Ely, with the Bishop's *cathedra* or formal seat in the church of what had been Ely Abbey, cannot have been a wholly welcome development for the Ely monks. They gained a measure of greater dignity, including (in time) the notional right to elect successive bishops; but they lost a considerable proportion of their estates and income. It is unclear how far they had to surrender to the Bishop their archives for these lost estates; they undoubtedly will have had to hand over a large quantity of records, so that tenants' names and obligations were known.

No English bishop in the Middle Ages appears to have thought seriously of setting up a library for his successors' convenience – only at the beginning of the seventeenth century was Lambeth Palace Library established – and it is likely that the monks were left in possession of their books. After the death of Abbot Simeon (which was in 1093), these totalled 287; 79 were service-books of one kind or another, which means that the library comprised 208 volumes.[1]

No doubt some books – perhaps even a few dozen – were new works that had been commissioned by Abbot Simeon as his Abbey's part in the early Norman drive to re-stock the country's more important monasteries; virtually nothing is known of any book production at Ely in this period, however. Most of the other books were presumably survivals from the Abbey's pre-Conquest collection, and would have been regarded with some disfavour – at least by those monks who were supportive of the Norman regime. Three books survive which may have formed part of the pre-Conquest collection – an eighth-century Gospel-book which had some abbatial estate records and other material added to its flyleaves;[2] an eleventh-century pontifical, which may have been housed at the Abbey when not needed by visiting bishops of Elmham;[3] and a mid eleventh-century volume containing the Dialogues of Gregory the Great and

I am grateful to Joan Greatrex, Michael Gullick, Nicholas Karn, Simon Keynes and Peter Meadows for commenting on a draft of this chapter: they have saved me from a number of errors.

[1] *Liber Eliensis*, ii. 139 (ed. Blake, pp. 223–4). The service-books comprised 19 missals, 8 lectionaries, 2 benedictionals, 22 psalters, 7 breviaries, 9 antiphoners and 12 graduals.

[2] The volume was dismembered in the 16th century and is now divided between CUL, MS Kk.1.24, BL, MS Sloane 1044, fo. 2 and BL, MS Cotton Tiberius B.v, fos. 74, 76; see N.R. Ker, *Catalogue of Manuscripts containing Anglo-Saxon* (Oxford, 1957), no. 22, and Simon Keynes, above, p. 5 and n. 14.

[3] CCCC, MS 44, which certainly was in the Priory library in the later Middle Ages; *cf.* Ker, *Cat. MSS Anglo-Saxon*, no. 33. Its presence at the Abbey cannot simply be assumed, however.

De compunctione cordis of Ephrem the Syrian, which seems likely to have been in the Abbey library.[4] Other books can only be guessed at. For instance, the *Historia Eliensis* asserts that Alfred turned into English the whole of the Old and New Testaments, and although this statement could simply be derived from some later writer, such as Ailred of Rievaulx, it is surely just as likely that there was actually a copy of an Alfredian or other vernacular version at Ely.[5]

Tantalisingly, the next Ely inventory of the Priory's goods, in 1143 or a little later, concludes with the observation that Bishop Nigel found in a cupboard (*in armario*) a good number of books 'which it would tire the reader if we stopped to list them'.[6] The likelihood, however, must be that the restocking of the library with patristic texts will have continued, since that was a major national programme for all the greater churches. If it had lacked them, Ely will now have received or made copies of such patristic texts as St Augustine's *City of God* and *Confessions* as well as his works on the Psalms and on St John's Gospel, and the *Letters* of St Jerome and the *Register* and *Moralia* of Gregory the Great.[7] It will also have acquired the texts of canon law and precept compiled by Archbishop Lanfranc and others.

By Lanfranc's *Constitutions*, which had been drawn up for Canterbury Cathedral Priory in the 1070s but were made applicable to other monastic cathedrals,

> on [the first] Monday [of Lent] . . . before the brethren go in to chapter, the librarian should have all the books save those that were given out for reading the previous year collected on a carpet in the chapter-house; last year's books should be carried in by those who have had them, and they are to be warned of this by the librarian in chapter the previous day . . . The librarian shall read out a list of the books which the brethren had the previous year. When each hears his name read out he shall return the book which was given to him to read the year before, and anyone who is conscious that he has not read in full the book which he received shall confess his fault, prostrate, and ask for pardon. Then the aforesaid librarian shall give to each of the brethren another book to read, and when the books have been distributed in order he shall at the same chapter write a list of the books and those who have received them.[8]

At Ely, as at other Benedictine houses, the librarian (*custos librorum*) was the Precentor, and the library remained his responsibility throughout the Priory's history, even after it had ceased to be particularly appropriate for one whose primary duty was to conduct the monks' services and their music. He was, of course, also responsible for the provision and upkeep of service-books, but the Constitutions are silent about this, since (with certain exceptions) the use of service-books in the choir was forbidden: the monks were required to learn their services – and their psalter – by heart during their novitiate.

The newly established Priory also followed a national pattern in preparing a fresh account of its early history and the lives of the saints who had founded and inspired it.

---

[4] LPL, MS 204; *cf.* Ker, *Cat. MSS Anglo-Saxon*, no. 277; and *cf.* below, p. 262.

[5] R.M. Wilson, *The Lost Literature of Medieval England*, 2nd edn (London, 1970), p. 67.

[6] *LE*, iii. 50: p. 294.

[7] *Cf.* N.R. Ker, *English Manuscripts in the Century after the Norman Conquest* (Oxford, 1960), pp. 7–8.

[8] *Monastic Constitutions of Lanfranc*, ed. and trans. D. Knowles, Nelson's Medieval Classics (London, 1951), p. 19; revised edn, by C.N.L. Brooke, Oxford Medieval Texts (Oxford, 2002), pp. 28–31.

At the instigation of Hervey, the first Bishop of Ely (1109–31), a Latin work was compiled, from tenth-century vernacular records, of the house's restoration in the tenth century and of the lands acquired for it by Æthelwold; this is the *Libellus quorundam insignium operum Beati Æthelwoldi*.[9] An account of the deeds of Hereward (*Gesta Herwardi*), by an unnamed monk of the Cathedral Priory, perhaps dates from this time,[10] and so too does the monk Gregory's metrical version of the Life of Etheldreda.[11] Under Norman rule, the monks were positively being encouraged to celebrate and regularise their history, and it is striking that – up to a point – they were even allowed to record the doings of Hereward, anti-Norman rebel that he was. The new Priory was able to nurture its sense of tradition.

Hervey's policy was continued by his successor Nigel (Bishop, 1133–69), who gave two churches – St Andrew's, in Whittlesey, and Impington (Cambs.) – to the Priory, to provide for the making and repairing of the Church's books.[12] It was also in Nigel's time, and almost certainly with his encouragement or even at his bidding, that the monks set about producing a cartulary in which their Church's privileges (since the time of King Edgar) and other grants to the house were transcribed in full: the earliest version of this which is now extant is Trinity College, Cambridge, MS 0.2.41, pp. 81– 159. The first 64 of these pages are perhaps datable to between April 1139 and the end of 1140.[13] They include four royal charters, charters and writs concerned with the creation of the bishopric of Ely and the consequent separation of lands between bishop and monks, and conclude with three letters of Pope Innocent II, 1139, relating to Bishop Nigel's attempt to recover alienated lands by sending a delegation to Rome with the originals of some of these documents. The cartulary then continues with further papal letters, coming down to 1152. The whole cartulary was copied, with additions, as British Library, MS Cotton Tiberius A.vi, fos. 99–120,[14] while another collection of these and other royal and papal privileges and writs, down to Geoffrey Ridel's election to the bishopric (1173), was compiled late in the twelfth century or early in the thirteenth: British Library, MS Cotton Titus A.i, fos. 24–55ᵛ.[15] The first two of these compilations are in volumes that also contain other archival materials: the Priory was evidently being careful to make copies of miscellaneous texts, such as the late eleventh-century *Inquisitio Eliensis*.[16]

There is only ambiguous evidence for the Priory taking any particular interest in its title deeds – the grants and confirmations of its lands, which it had retained in 1109. Few of its surviving original charters from this period have endorsements from the twelfth century, and certainly none that gives any indication about their arrangement; nor is

---

[9] See *LE*, p. xxxiv; Blake dates one of the manuscripts of this to 1139 × 40. See also Simon Keynes, above, p. 7.

[10] *LE*, pp. xxxiv–vi.

[11] Datable to 1116 × 31; see Pauline A. Thompson and Elizabeth Stevens, 'Gregory of Ely's Verse Life and Miracles of St Æthelthryth', *Analecta Bollandiana*, cvi (1988), pp. 333–90.

[12] Grant by Bishop Nigel and confirmation by Prior William, to be printed in Nicholas Karn (ed.), *English Episcopal Acta: Ely 1109–97* (British Academy, forthcoming), nos. 32 and 44.

[13] *LE*, pp. xxxiv, xl. See also Simon Keynes, *Anglo-Saxon Manuscripts and other items of related interest in the Library of Trinity College, Cambridge*, Old English Newsletter, *Subsidia*, vol. 18 (1992), pp. 41–3, for a description of this MS.

[14] *LE*, pp. xxxix–xl.

[15] *Ibid.*, pp. xxv, xli.

[16] For the *Inquisitio Eliensis*, see Simon Keynes, above, pp. 7, 50.

there any reason to think that a cartulary of these non-royal land grants was made.[17] On the other hand, it is clear that the monks in this period were looking very closely at some of their charters, for they decided to forge at least one more: this is nothing less than the charter of Bishop Hervey's, in which he specifies and separates from the lands of the bishopric the lands which he has granted to the Cathedral Priory for the use of the monks.[18] The immediate or direct explanation of this forgery is that it enhanced very considerably the extent of the episcopal grants to the monks. However, the context for its making is that the separation of the estates was an extremely long-drawn-out process that was not completed until the late 1150s or early 1160s: that is to say, the Priory and the bishopric had – to some extent – to run their estates in tandem for a good half-century. It is accordingly possible that there was no clear separation of title-deed charters either; this would explain the failure to produce a cartulary proper, for either bishopric or Priory, until the next century.

In both 1222 and 1251 (or 1249–50?), surveys were made of the episcopal estates,[19] and the making of the later survey has plausibly been linked to the making of the first episcopal cartulary, British Library, MS Cotton Claudius C.xi.[20] To the making of the cartulary might also be linked the drawing up of a later thirteenth-century inventory of royal and other charters, most of which undoubtedly relate to the bishopric (British Library, MS Cotton Nero C.iii, fos. 202–207[r]): these charters are stated to be in *punctis* (or small containers) lettered [A], B, C and D, and it is striking that a similar arrangement was in use for the Priory charters in *c*.1300.[21] Did the bishopric and Priory charters share the same arrangement because they were in fact still kept together? It is suggestive, too, that the first Priory cartulary also dates from near the end of the thirteenth century (Liber M; EDR, G3/28)[22] (Plate 16*a*); the hand that wrote most of

---

[17] One charter with an endorsement from this period is King Edgar's grant to Ælfhelm of the West Wratting estate that subsequently came to the Abbey and was retained by it in 1109: this 10th-century charter (S 794; *cf.* Simon Keynes, above, p. 5) is now the oldest document in the Cathedral's possession (Plate 1*b*). It was not copied into any of the Priory's medieval cartularies. It is not clear, however, why Dorothy Owen has suggested that it only came to Ely after the confused re-sorting of cathedral muniments in the 1660s: D.M. Owen, 'The Muniments of Ely Cathedral Priory', in C.N.L. Brooke *et al.* (eds.), *Church and Government in the Middle Ages. Essays Presented to C.R. Cheney* (Cambridge, 1976), pp. 157–76, at p. 159.

[18] The forgery (now BL, Harl. Ch. 43 H.4) is printed in *Sir Christopher Hatton's Book of Seals*, ed. L.C. Loyd and D.M. Stenton (Oxford, 1950), no. 420; *cf. LE*, pp. l–li. Bishop Hervey's authentic charter for separating the estates is still in the Cathedral archive (EDC 1/B/49); it is printed by Miller, *Abbey & Bishopric*, pp. 282–3, appx. iv, and discussed at pp. 75–6 and 200. For the forgery of pre-Conquest charters (*e.g.* Edgar's confirmatory grant of AD 970, S. 779), see Simon Keynes, above, p. 21; Hervey's charter will be in Karn (ed.), *Ely 1109–97* (cit. in n. 12). I am grateful to Dr Karn for discussing it with me.

[19] Miller, *Abbey & Bishopric*, pp. 5–6; VCH, *Cambs.*, IV, pp. 35–7. In each copy of the later survey, it is dated to the 21st year of Bishop Hugh (Northwold), *i.e.* 1249–50. The book *'de inquisicionibus maneriorum Episcopatus'*, made in 32 Henry III [1247–8], and which in 1584 (a time when the See of Ely was vacant) was in the custody of the Queen's Remembrancer in the Exchequer, was presumably another copy of the later survey; it is cited in Bodl., MS Ashmole 799, f. 100[v].

[20] Owen, 'Muniments of Ely Cathedral Priory' (cit. in n. 17), p. 161. She refers to the Great Coucher, EDR G3/27; but the copy of the mid 13th-century survey in this cartulary is of much later date than that in Claudius C.xi.

[21] *Ibid.* At the Priory, A.I, *etc.*, was used for royal charters, B.I, *etc.*, for episcopal charters. The heading is now missing from the inventory in Nero C.iii, which was originally in roll form and made no earlier than 1272; it has (sub-) headings for *punctis* B, C and D. *Punctum* A was for royal charters, and B for royal, episcopal and some other charters.

[22] *Cf. LE*, pp. xli–ii, dating it to the 'last years of the thirteenth century' and comparing its 'handwriting and general appearance' to Bodl., MS Laud. Misc. 647, which he dates (p. xxv) to 1290 × 8; G.R.C. Davis, *Medieval*

this volume has been thought by D.M. Owen to resemble the hand that endorsed the Priory's royal and episcopal charters of between 1066 and 1300.[23] In the 1270s the Priory also began to maintain a register in which copies were entered of miscellaneous documents concerning it (chiefly, presentations to Priory benefices, grants of pensions and corrodies, appointments of proctors or proxies to Parliament and Convocation, confirmations of episcopal instruments, and Priory Chapter ordinances): this substantial volume (now British Library, Add. MS 41612[24]) did service as a register until about 1370, and was then used as a formulary for another century and a half – as is shown by the headings and marginal notes in a variety of late medieval hands. It is still bound in its medieval boards (although they are now without any leather or tawed skin covering).

English monastic libraries in the twelfth and thirteenth centuries were not housed in rooms of their own: they were normally kept in the cloister, either on the side nearest to the church[25] (which would have been one of the warmer parts of the convent, where the cloister was on the south side of the church) or in the east walk. In the twelfth century, books were generally kept in chests, not wall-cupboards; this can be seen to have been the case at Ely, since one twelfth-century manuscript (Bodl., MS Bodley 582 [*S.C.* 2204][26]) still has its medieval binding with tawed skin tabs protruding at each end of its spine, to protect it in the chest where it would have rested on its fore-edge (long outer side) (Colour pl. 18*b*).

In the thirteenth century an elaborate cupboard-recess was constructed (out of a doorway) in the north walk of the cloister, near the cloister's east door – the classic place for a book-cupboard at this date – and it can safely be assumed that the Priory's books were now transferred from their chests into this. It was presumably divided into two, since the earliest Priory press-mark occurs in two forms: a square-shaped (or Greek) cross resting on either one or two uprights.[27] (Plate 16*c*) These marks appear to date from the fourteenth century, however, and they do not occur in as many as might be expected of the (disappointingly few) manuscripts that survive from this period.

Less ambiguous, but not much more substantial, are the clues afforded by the precentor's account rolls. His duty of providing scribes (*i.e.*, if necessary paying

---

Cartularies of Great Britain (London, 1958), no. 369, dating it to '*c*.1290–1300'; and Owen, 'Muniments of Ely Cathedral Priory', pp. 161–2, suggesting a date of about the 1320s.

[23] Owen, 'Muniments of Ely Cathedral Priory', p. 161. More than one hand was responsible for the endorsements, however: compare *e.g.* BL, Harl. Ch. 43. H. 4 and 5.

[24] Davis, *Medieval Cartularies*, no. 375; formerly known as the Leconfield or Petworth cartulary. It was very inaccurately calendared by Horwood for HMC, 6th *Report*, appx., pp. 289–300, but is well described in British Museum, *Catalogue of Additions to the Manuscripts, 1926–30* (London, 1959), pp. 83–4.

[25] *Cf.* F. Wormald, 'The Monastic Library', in F. Wormald and C.E. Wright (eds.), *The English Library before 1700* (London, 1958), pp. 15–31; reprinted in Ursula E. McCracken *et al.* (eds.), *Gatherings in Honor of Dorothy E. Miner* (Baltimore, Md., [1974]), pp. 93–109.

[26] Bodley 582 stayed at Ely long enough to receive the cross-on-one-bar press-mark, but was later at Windsor; it has a late medieval press-mark M. 23, which is not an Ely press-mark.

[27] The mark of a cross resting on a single support occurs in *e.g.* BL, MS Harl. 1031 (illustrated hence by C.E. Wright, *Fontes Harleiani* (London, 1972), pl. ix (e)); Cambridge, Pembroke College, MS 308; Cambridge, Trinity College, MS O.2.1; and Bodl., MS Bodley 582; a cross resting on a double support occurs in CCCC, MSS 44 and 416; CUL, MSS Gg.1.21 and Ii.2.15; and Bodl., MS Rawl. Q.f.8. A little disconcertingly, it appears also to have been written in CCCC MS 335, although mostly now torn out: this is an early 15th-century collection of texts about Mahomet *etc.*, and must be supposed to have been a substitute (with replica press-mark) for an earlier occupant of its place in the cupboard. It is not certain, also, that this door-recess *was* a cupboard in the 13th or 14th centuries: John Maddison questions this general assumption.

professional scribes from outside the Priory) for the writing of books, and especially of antiphoners, was specifically reiterated in Bishop Ketton's ordinances of 1314.[28] Just thirteen of his rolls survive today, ranging in date from 1329–30 to 1534–5;[29] twenty-seven were extant in the eighteenth century, when James Bentham made his transcripts.[30] They show him to have been spending a few shillings each year on maintenance of service books and other books – principally their binding or rebinding – as well as on the purchase of materials: parchment (and its preparation), ink, threads, paper (first mentioned in 1360–1), clasps and boards. More years than not, he also paid for a scribe (for a particular term of days or to write a specific book). In 1299–1300 he paid 3s. for a book of (canon law) Decretals and 6d. for writing a *Summula* (subject not stated); in 1320–1 he bought a *Speculum Gregorii* (i.e., Adalbert of Metz's collection of extracts from St Gregory's *Moralia*) for 2s.; in 1373–4 he paid £1 2s. 9d. for the illumination of a customary and a gradual; and in 1396–7 he paid 1s. to a clerk for bringing from Lynn a book called *Clement* (presumably the canon law collection known as the Clementines). In this last year there is also mention of John Dallyng as the 'present scribe', retained at an annual rate of £3. In 1341(?), there may have been as many as eight scribes engaged in correcting or amending books ('*in emend[acione] libr[orum]*').[31]

In the fourteenth century Ely had its own *lector* to instruct the brethren, and successive bishops of Ely gave books to the community: Ralph Walpole (d.1302) gave books of papal decretals, Robert Orford (d.1310) a precious 'portifory' (i.e., breviary), and John Ketton (d.1316) 'a good book, called the Confessors' *Summa*', and Simon Montacute (d.1345) commissioned a missal and a benedictional.[32] The Priory had enough books that it could lend ten volumes to Roger of Huntingfield, for his life; they were duly received back from his executors in 1329.[33] It is only slightly contradictory to this picture of bookishness that Bishop Orford, who had been Prior of Ely, had his election by his brethren to the bishopric quashed by Archbishop Robert Winchelsey (a distinguished theologian) on the grounds of his 'insufficient learning'; such allegations might be politically motivated, and Orford sufficiently impressed the

---

[28] Evans, *Ordinances*, p. 40.

[29] EDC, 1/F/9/1–13.

[30] Excerpts by both Bentham (in CUL, MS Add. 2957) and Gullick relating to books have been printed: Michael Gullick (ed.), *Extracts from the Precentors' Accounts concerning Books and Bookmaking of Ely Cathedral Priory* (Hitchin, 1985). Two of the 13 survivors were transferred in the later 20th century from Rochester, where they had evidently been sent by error in the 1660s.

[31] Joan Greatrex, 'The English Cathedral Priories and the Pursuit of Learning in the Later Middle Ages', *Jnl. of Ecclesiastical History*, xlv (1994), pp. 396–411, at p. 405.

[32] Wharton, *Anglia Sacra*, I, pp. 640 (Walpole '*contulit ad inspectionem Claustralium librum perpulchrum Decretorum*' and '*librum similiter Decretalium cum glossa ordinaria et Innocentii*'), 641 (Orford: '*Portiforium preciosum quod modo est in Capella Prioris*'), 642 (Ketton: '*unus bonus liber, vocatus Summa Confessorum*') and 649 (Montacute: '*scribere fecit unum pulcrum Missale et unum Benedictionale, que in capella remanent Prioris*').

[33] The books are listed in a copy of the receipt given to his executors, printed in Richard Sharpe *et al.* (eds.), *English Benedictine Libraries: The Shorter Catalogues*, Corpus of British Medieval Library Catalogues, 4 (London, 1996), pp. 129–30. Similarly, three books – '*bibliotecam et ystoriam et librum platearii*' – had been lent for life to John de Watford, Rector of the Priory living of Sudbourne (Suff.), in 1277: BL, Add. MS 41612, fo. 3. Watford was granted a 22-year lease of the manor of Wisbech a fortnight later, and in 1278 he was retained by contract to be the Priory's physician (*ibid.*, fos. 10–11[r], 11[r]); the 'book of Platearius' was the book of medical samples of the Salernitan physician Matthaeus Platearius (d.1161). The '*biblioteca*' will have been a bible, and the '*ystoria*' was doubtless the *Historia scholastica* of Petrus Comestor.

1(a) Ely Cathedral from the river, by J.B. Pyne, 1850, in the Deanery

1(b) Ely from the south-east, distant view, *c.*1850; private collection

2 (a) Ely Cathedral from the fens

2(b) Aerial view

3(a) West tower, *c.*1820, by R.H. Essex

3(b) West tower and St Catherine's Chapel, from the Bishop's garden

3(c) West tower and south-west transept from The Gallery

4(a) North transept and Lady Chapel from north-west

4(b) East end and Lady Chapel (John Buckler in 'extra-illustrated Bentham', EDC 14/24)

4(c) Thomas Girtin, Ely Cathedral from the south-east, 1793–4 (Ashmolean Museum, Oxford)

5(a) Firmary Lane (John Carter, BL, Add. MS 29927, fo. 152)

5(b) Monastic kitchen: Bishop's House, exterior

5(c) J.M.W. Turner, Ely Cathedral from the south-east (private collection)

6(a) Ely Porta (John Buckler, in 'extra-illustrated Bentham', EDC 14/24)

6(b) Prior Crauden's Chapel (John Buckler, in 'extra-illustrated Bentham', EDC 14/24)

7(a) North tribune from Lady Chapel

7(b) South tribune, earlier work

7(c–d) West tower and Lady Chapel oculi

8(a) View into Cathedral through Galilee Porch (John Buckler, in 'extra-illustrated Bentham', EDC 14/24)

8(b) Nave looking east

8(c) West tower interior, looking upwards

8(d) View into the south-west transept, *c.*1850

9 J.M.W. Turner, view of Octagon (Aberdeen Art Gallery & Museums Collections)

10(a) C.E. Kempe, design for colouring Octagon (EDC 4/5/83)

10(b) Octagon and Lantern, upward view

10(c) Central boss of Lantern

10(d) Lantern interior

11(a) Choir looking east, by R.H. Essex, *c.*1830
(Victoria & Albert Museum)

11(b) Choir looking east

11(c) Sir Gilbert Scott's reredos

12(a) Angel roof, south transept

12(b) North transept, view

12(c) South transept, view

13(a) James Essex's screen, surmounted by the organ; Charles Jenyns, *c.*1840

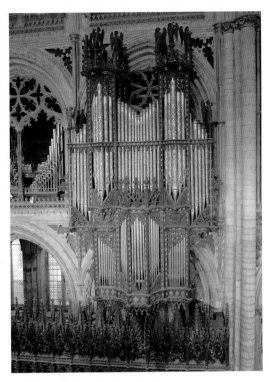

13(b) Organ case, designed by Sir Gilbert Scott

13(c) Bishop West's Chapel, by R.H. Essex, 1824

13(d) Prior Crauden's Chapel, interior

14(a) Medieval stained glass, Lady Chapel

14(b) 16th-century glass, nave west window

14(c) 18th-century glass, St Peter, by Pearson

14(d) 19th-century glass, in traditional style: the Baptism of Christ, by Wilmshurst

14(e) Wilmshurst's design for a baptistry window, 1850

15(a) Noah window, nave south aisle, by Alfred Gérente, 1850

15(b) History of St John the Evangelist, south choir aisle, by Clayton & Bell, 1871

15(c) Christ the healer, south choir aisle, by Henry Holiday, made by Powell's of Whitefriars, 1891

15(d) Glass in Bishop West's Chapel, by Sir Ninian Comper, *c.*1939–45

16(a) Monument to Dean Henry Caesar (d.1636)

16(b) Monument to Humphry Smith (d.1743), by John Sanderson

16(c) Monument to Bishop Allen (d.1845), by James Legrew

17(a) St Etheldreda, in Benedictional of St Ethelwold, late 10th century (BL, Add. MS 49598, fo. 90v)

17(b) St Etheldreda, roof boss in presbytery

17(c) St Etheldreda, stained glass roundel, in Chapel of St Edmund & St Dunstan

17(d) St Etheldreda, stained glass by James Pearson (d.1805), in the Bishop's House

18(a) List of Ely monks, in the *Liber Vitae* of the New Minster, Winchester, 1031 (BL, MS Stowe 944, fo. 27)

18(b) Leaf from a 15th-century Ely gradual, for Trinity Sunday (EDC 1/G/7)

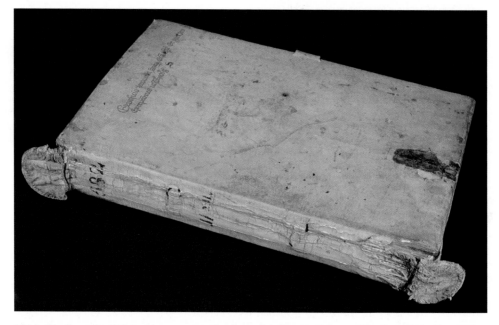

18(c) Binding of a 12th-century manuscript from the Chapter Library (Bodl., MS Bodley 582)

19(a) Ely cope

19(b) Christ rising, in a volume from the priory library (BL, Add. MS 33381, fo. 78v)

19(c) Mortuary roll of Bishop Hotham (d.1337) (Canterbury Cathedral, Charta Antiqua E 191)

20(a) Life of St Etheldreda, panels from shrine reredos (Society of Antiquaries of London)

20(b) Monk praying, in a 15th-century Priory breviary (CUL, MS Ii.4.20)

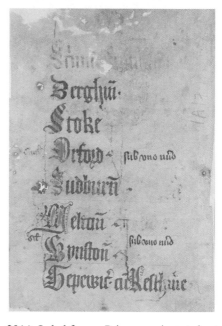

20(c) Label from a Priory muniment chest

21(a) Foundation charter, 10 sept, 1541, initial (EDC 2/1/1)

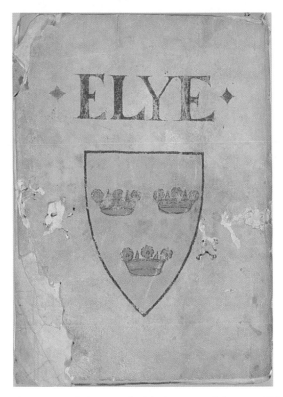

21(b–c) MS decorated with the arms of the see of Ely and of Steward, by Dean Robert Steward in the 1540s
(EDC 1/C/3)

22(a) Ely tabula: the forty knights quartered on the Abbey (Roy Hallett)

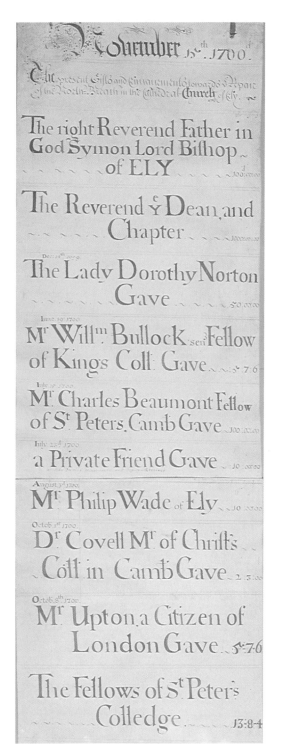

22(b) Roll of benefactors, 1699–1700 (EDC 4/5/15)

22(c) Michael Tyson, drawing of Wulfstan, Archbishop of York, one of the 'Ely benefactors', 1769 (Bodl., Gough Maps 225, fo. 35ᵛ)

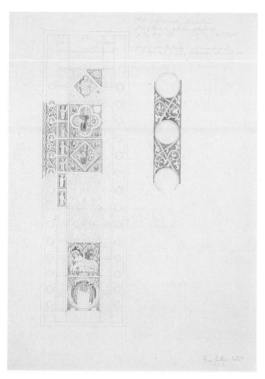

23(a) Robert Willis, drawing of the Hildesheim
ceiling (Victoria & Albert Museum)

23(b) Nave ceiling

23(c) Nave ceiling, bay

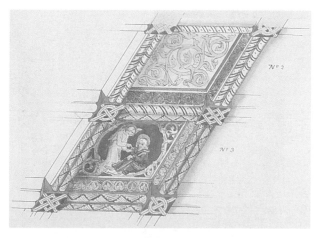

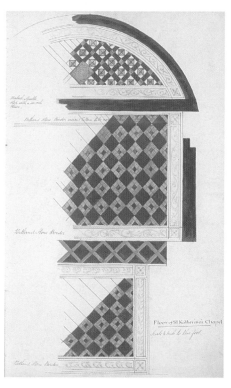

24(a) David Stewart, ceiling designs for south-west transept, *c.*1845 (EDC 4/5/167)

24(b) John Bacon, design of the floor in St Catherine's Chapel, by Sir Gilbert Scott (EDC 4/6/2, fo. 35)

24(c) Anonymous watercolour, 1858, of the slab over Bishop Allen's vault in the retrochoir (EDC 4/5/370)

25(a) Andrew Perne (Dean, 1557–89) (Peterhouse, Cambridge)

25(b) Henry Caesar (Dean, 1614–36)

25(c) Bishop Matthew Wren (Pembroke College, Cambridge)

26(a) Bishop Cox's funeral procession, 1581, shown in reverse

26(b) 'Long procession' in the Cathedral ('extra-illustrated Bentham', EDC 14/24)

27(a) Bishop Cox's funeral procession, 1581, shown in reverse

27(b) Watercolour of the Octagon, *c.*1850

28(a) Bishop James Yorke, by D. Monier, in the Old Palace

28(b) Bishop Bowyer Sparke, by Sir William Beechey, in the Old Palace

28(c) Bishop Sparke as donor of the east window, by Wailes

28(d) Dean Peacock as Isaiah, nave ceiling

28(e) Henry Styleman Le Strange, ceiling portrait by T. Gambier Parry

29(a) Bishop Peter Walker at the service to launch the Appeal, 1986

29(b) The Cathedral Choir on Liverpool Street Station, 1986

30(a) Royal Maundy, 1987. HM the Queen and Bishop Peter Walker

30(b) Queen Elizabeth the Queen Mother and Dean William Patterson, 1988

30(c) Sir Jocelyn Stevens and Dean Higgins, on the occasion of the granting of English Heritage funds for the restoration, 1992

31(a) Four bishops of Ely at the enthronement of Anthony Russell, 2000. Left to right: Stephen Sykes (Bishop, 1990–9), Peter Walker (Bishop, 1977–90), Anthony Russell, Edward Roberts (Bishop, 1964–77)

31(b) New Chapter, 2000. Back row, left to right: Canon Peter Sills, Canon John Inge, Canon Brian Watchorn. Front row: Susan Pope (Chapter Canon, 2002), Dean Michael Higgins, Lady (Rosemary) Hughes (Chapter Canon, 2002)

32(a–b) Processional Way, exterior and interior

Pope, in a personal examination at Rome, that he had his election confirmed and was consecrated forthwith.[34] Of Prior Crauden's abilities, a generation later, there could never be any doubt. Just to the north of his chapel, he built a chamber where he held conference with his brethren about matters of canon law and the Priory's business; and here he also had his study, with books, for such time as could be spared.[35]

The Priory's archives must also have been growing rapidly, from about the mid thirteenth century onwards. At some point between 1241 and 1254, it was decided that two monks should be placed in charge of the Priory's financial administration, and they were to render an annual account of receipts and expenses;[36] from 1261 these two monks were replaced by (monk) treasurers, who were empowered to control the expenditure of all monks with departmental duties (or obediences). In 1300 Bishop Walpole ordered all the obedientiaries to present bi-annual accounts before a committee of six or seven monks.[37] Today, only about three hundred of the obedientiaries' account rolls survive, but even after the ravages of neglect and wear over several centuries, it is noticeable that several of the sequences commence in the late thirteenth or early fourteenth centuries: the treasurers' rolls are extant from 1281–2 onwards, the sacrist's from 1291–2, the precentor's from 1329–30 (though in the eighteenth century the sequence began with a roll of 1299–1300), the granator's from 1307–8, the pittancer's from 1308–9, and the cellarer's from 1313–14 (from [1280] in the eighteenth century).[38]

In 1304 the Prior and Chapter imposed the obligation of presenting accounts upon their manorial officials; the accounts were to be audited by three monks.[39] This system, which required the bailiffs and reeves to go each year to Ely, was ultimately replaced by a system of auditing on each manor, and with professional auditors instead of monks,[40] but it should still have produced a stream of about twenty manorial accounts into the archives for each year.[41]

The Priory's archives also gained in complexity as the different obedientiaries began to build up their own, separate sets of records. The pittancer, for instance, may have kept some of the Priory's land grants,[42] and he certainly had them transcribed into his own register or cartulary (compiled in the late thirteenth or early fourteenth century; now lost[43]). The sacrist, who had considerable estates under his own control, recorded

[34] W.A. Pantin, *The English Church in the Fourteenth Century* (Cambridge, 1955), p. 19.

[35] Wharton, *Anglia Sacra*, I, p. 649.

[36] Evans, *Ordinances*, p. 1. For some discussion of Ely accounting practices, see R.A.L. Smith, 'The *Regimen Scaccarii* in English Monasteries', *Trans., Royal Historical Soc.*, 4th ser., xxiv (1942), pp. 73–94, at pp. 80–3; reprinted in Smith's *Collected Papers* (London, 1947), pp. 54–73, at pp. 61–3.

[37] Evans, *Ordinances*, p. 21.

[38] I owe statistics and dates of the (approximately) 299 surviving rolls to the kindness of Joan Greatrex and Peter Meadows; for the precentor's account of 1299–1300 see Gullick, *Extracts from the Precentors' Accounts* (cit. in n. 30), p. 7.

[39] Evans, *Ordinances*, p. 28.

[40] *Ibid.*, p. xvi, n. 2.

[41] Infinitely fewer survive – perhaps a total of around 150 in the Dean and Chapter Archives, for the manors of Kingston, Melton, Lakenheath and Winston (Suff.) and Swaffham Prior, Wentworth, Whittlesey rectory and Witcham rectory (Cambs.), as well as some more among the records formerly held by the Church Commissioners and the Evanses (who acted as registrars for both the Dean and Chapter and the Church Commissioners). I am grateful to Peter Meadows for details of these.

[42] See the endorsements on BL, Lord Frederick Campbell Charters ii.3 and xxvii.27.

[43] This book belonged in 1730 to James West, and was perhaps destroyed in the fire when almost all of his collection of MSS perished, in 1737; an excerpt from the book was transcribed by Thomas Hearne and is

copies of documents relating to his office, and had his own customary.[44] The almoner twice had deeds copied into registers of his own, in the fourteenth century; and the precentor also had a store of muniments relating to his endowments.[45] Finally, like most cathedrals and major houses, the Priory will have owned or housed elements (or more) of the archives of other institutions. For instance, in 1446, when it acquired Mullicourt Priory, it gained that house's entire archive.[46]

In 1299 the Priory had secured from the Crown, at a cost of £666 13s. 4d, the concession that in future vacancies of the see, the Priory would not be taken into the Crown's hands (as it had been in 1286, 1290 and 1298). Custody of the bishopric itself, during episcopal vacancies, was an even costlier prize, which was secured in 1329, by a perpetual concession to the Priory of the right to have the custody during each vacancy, for an annualised rent of £2000.[47] It was consequently very much in the Priory's interests for it to keep its own records of the episcopal estates; this was made much easier by the fact that many of the lay officials of the bishopric also held comparable offices under the Prior and Chapter. The Priory seems also to have been asked to confirm most episcopal grants shortly after they were made.

There were also occasionally losses of archival materials, which prompted the making of fresh records. The rebels in June 1381 destroyed various rolls and documents in Ely; they attacked both the Priory and the episcopal buildings (mounting the Cathedral pulpit and assaulting the episcopal prison), and it is not certain if the destroyed documents had belonged to the monks or the Bishop.[48] In 1401 there was a fire of Ely muniments, and again it is unclear whose these had been.[49] It could have been because of this fire or simply as a result of a more general confusion as to the ownership of estates by the Priory and bishopric that a major new composition had to be drawn up between the two. All their estates in Ely were surveyed in 1416–17, under the eye of the Archdeacon of Ely and one of the monks, and in December 1417 a formal agreement (or *laudum*) was reached between Prior Powcher and Bishop Fordham as to the demarcation of their respective estates.[50]

---

printed in H.E. Salter (ed.), *Remarks and Collections of Thomas Hearne*, XI (Oxford Historical Soc., o.s. lxvii, 1915), pp. 334–6.

[44] Owen, 'Muniments of Ely Cathedral Priory' (cit. in n. 17), pp. 162–3.

[45] *Ibid.*, p. 163. The almoner's cartularies are BL, Cotton MS Vesp. A.vi, fos. 90–133 (Davis, *Medieval Cartularies*, no. 373; its index was completed in the 15th century, seemingly by a hand which occurs frequently in BL, MS Egerton 3047) and EDC 1/A/2 and 2A (Davis, *Medieval Cartularies*, no. 374. 2A, a single detached leaf, is to be rebound into the volume).

[46] The actual royal licence to incorporate Mullicourt is now BL, Lord Frederick Campbell Charter xxvii.29.

[47] *Cal. Fine Rolls, 1327–37*, pp. 120–1; see also Rose Graham, 'The Administration of the Diocese of Ely during the Vacancies of the See, 1298–9 and 1302–3', *Trans., Royal Historical Soc.*, 4th ser., xii (1929), pp. 49–74, at 53, 60. There is a copy of the grant in BL, MS Royal 12 D.xi, fos. 19ᵛ–20ᵛ. For some of the complications involved in the Priory's administration of the bishopric, see *e.g.* PRO, E135/22/25 and 24, for proceedings in the Exchequer and a draft writ from the vacancy of 1298–9.

[48] *Cf.* VCH, *Cambs.*, IV, p. 34 n. 86.

[49] In CUL, MS Mm.1.53, fo. 158, Thomas Baker noted that a composition was made between the Bishop and the Archdeacon on 13 Nov. 1401, '*intra paucos menses post combusta Registrorum Eliensium munimenta*'; Baker derived his knowledge '*e libro quodam chartaceo in Fol:, qui olim erat Liber Freckley, nunc Tabor habet*', as excerpted by Matthew Wren, Bishop of Ely 1638–67. John Tabor was Wren's Registrar, 1638–45.

[50] Printed in Bentham, *Ely*, Appx., pp. *27–34, and calendared in *CPR, 1416–22*, pp. 183–95; discussed in VCH, *Cambs.*, IV, pp. 38–9, Dorothy Owen, *The Medieval Development of the Town of Ely* (Ely, 1993), pp. 20–6, and Dorothy Owen, above, pp. 71–2.

Just a few years before this, the Priory had commenced a register in which copies of miscellaneous documents – grants, leases, presentations, licences, confirmations, manumissions and so forth – were entered over the next hundred and more years.[51] It is comparable to the register that was maintained in the thirteenth and fourteenth centuries (BL, Add. MS 41612), except that an effort was made to render it more user-friendly, by entering the copies on a roughly alphabetical basis (*bulla* under b; *commissio, confirmatio, concessio*, but also *carta*, under c): it was thus easier to use it as a formulary.

At some point close to the middle of the fifteenth century (not before 1446, and probably in the 1460s), a far more significant archival project was undertaken: the writing of a new cartulary. Most of this massive compilation survives, although it was divided into two parts before the end of the seventeenth century, and its larger section is now in the British Library[52] and the shorter in the Bodleian Library.[53] The latter, which once formed the last six quires and was foliated 278–349, has additions (from fo. 92[v] onwards) in fresh hands, copying documents of *e.g.* 1461, and this might suggest that the previous part was begun at an earlier date. The cartulary is arranged on a systematic basis, and contains copies of a fair proportion of the title-deeds of the Priory. Each copy is given a title, and a reference to the chest (number), letter and number where the original might be found. The British Library section begins imperfectly, at [chest i,] A.1.25, and the Bodleian at *cista* (or chest) iiii, N.11. From the references to the documents' numbers, it is clear that there was an almost simultaneous numbering of the documents, and – thanks partly to the survival of three medieval archive-chests with their labels – it is apparent that there was also a complete overhaul of how and where the documents were stored (Plate 16*b*). The royal and episcopal charters retained their letters and numbers (A.1, B.1) and were placed in *cista* i; this and other chests were subdivided into separately lettered compartments or *scrinia*, and, a little later, arabic numbers were added to the individual documents or bundles of documents within each *scrinium*. *Cista* ii contained *scrinia* C to E, which comprised documents relating to Ely itself and parishes in the southern half of the Isle of Ely; *cista* iii, in *scrinia* F to M, had the charters of estates in Cambridgeshire, Norfolk, the northern part of the Isle of Ely, and Suffolk; *cista* iv, in *scrinia* N to T, had the charters of the cellarer's and hosteller's augmentations and of the Priory's London estates; *cista* v had two *cophini* (boxes) containing the pittancer's muniments, mortmain licences, distraints and copies of leases; and *cista* vi had two *cophini* labelled 1Y and 2Y which contained further Ely deeds.

---

[51] EDR, G2/3 (Davis, *Medieval Cartularies*, no. 377); it was known as Liber B in the diocesan registry for much of the 18th century, and was later called the Almack MS, from its having belonged to Richard Almack, FSA, and his son H.H. Almack, before its purchase for the see of Ely by Lord Alwyne Compton, Bishop of Ely, in 1889. Its contents (481 documents) are analysed in detail by J.H. Crosby in CUL, MS Add. 6394, pp. 89–140.

[52] BL, MS Egerton 3047 (Davis, *Medieval Cartularies*, no. 371); in the 18th century it was Liber L in the diocesan registry. See discussion by A.J. Collins in *British Museum Quarterly*, v (1930–1), pp. 113–14; British Museum, *Catalogue of Additions to the Manuscripts, 1926–30*, pp. 228–30; and Owen, 'Muniments of Ely Cathedral Priory' (cit. in n. 17), pp. 164–5. The latest dated entry in it that I have noticed is of Aug. 1469 (fo. 243[v]).

[53] Bodl., MS Ashmole 801, fos. 74–143 (Davis, *Medieval Cartularies*, no. 372). Note that early additions (*e.g.* on fo. 89[v]) had only the final number supplied; additions on *e.g.* fos. 92[v]–95[r] had no *cista* reference supplied. Two documents might have the same final number (*i.e.*, form part of the same small bundle or packet): *cf.* the sequences for *cista* v. X on fos. 302–303[r] and 303[v]–307[r], which have final numbers 1, 4, 5, 8, 10, 12, 14, 16, 18, 19, and 1, 3, 4, 5, 6, 9, 10, 11, 12, 13, 18, 19, 23, 24, 26, 28, 28, 29, 28, 29, 30.

Cista iv and *cista* v also each had some overflow of royal and episcopal charters.[54] The making of the cartulary and the overhaul of the archives were separate exercises, and the latter may have continued as late as the 1460s, and the former into the 1470s; but they were made to operate in tandem, and thus be far more effective as a system of records management, thanks to each document having its number endorsed on it as well as entered in the cartulary: one could therefore easily cross-refer from the one to the other. And as an additional aid to the searcher, alphabetical indexes were compiled and added to this and to other Priory cartularies (such as Liber M, EDR G3/28) at about the same time.

By the fifteenth century, a similar overhaul is likely to have been needed by the Priory's book-collection. The cupboard in the cloister wall-recess must long since have proved too small: the majority of the books press-marked with the square-shaped cross, which it has been suggested were housed in it, were of eleventh- or twelfth-century date. Later acquisitions must have been housed elsewhere. Approximately forty books survive from the medieval library, and between one-third and a half of these date from the thirteenth to sixteenth centuries.[55] Their subject matter differs rather from that of the earlier books: instead of pontificals, calendars, gospel-books and other books for liturgical or related use, and patristic works (as by Saints Jerome, Gregory and Ambrose, and the ninth-century Amalarius of Metz), there are works of theology by more recent authors, such as the Dominicans Thomas Aquinas, Roger Dymock (against Lollard heresies) and William Peraldus, a book of provincial constitutions (*i.e.*, ecclesiastical governance; no canon law books are known to survive), the spiritual writings of Richard Rolle, and several volumes of Ely chronicles and histories. A few of these books, which in no cases have the square cross press-mark, have a two-part arabic number (such as 6.32) written at the top of a leaf at the front; a further four or five manuscripts which are not otherwise known to have been at the Priory, have similar two-part numbers. In full sequence, these numbers are 6.21, 6.32, 6.41, 6.60, 7.3, 8.17, 10.45, 12.20 and 19.20[56]; only numbers beginning with 6, 8 and 10 are on books definitely from Ely. Their significance is an almost total mystery. Should one assume that – if they *are* press-marks – there were presses numbered 6, 8 and 10, each with up to 60 books (a total of 180 books), or that there were presses numbered 6, 7, 8, 10, 12 and 19, each with up to 60 books (a total of 360 books), or even that there were twenty presses, each with up to 60 books (giving a total of 1200 books)? By comparison with other major religious houses, Ely might well have had a few hundred volumes in its library; but it is most unlikely that it had as many as a thousand. The early fourteenth-

---

[54] These details of the chests are partly taken from Owen, 'Muniments of Ely Cathedral Priory', p. 164. Chests i–iii are now in the Ely Museum; chest iii is illustrated here, as Plate 16*b*, and, both open and closed, in Dorothy Owen, *The Library and Muniments of Ely Cathedral* (Ely: Dean and Chapter of Ely, 1973), plate 1, and a label from chest iii is *ibid.*, plate 2 (Colour pl. 20*c*). Note that since Egerton 3047 contains in its principal hand and in its main sequence items that were in the overflow in *cista* v, it must postdate the placing of these documents in that chest.

[55] Almost all are detailed in N.R. Ker (ed.), *Medieval Libraries of Great Britain: A List of Surviving Books*, 2nd edn (London: Royal Historical Soc., 1964), pp. 77–8, and its *Supplement*, ed. Andrew G. Watson (London: Royal Historical Soc., 1987), p. 35.

[56] The MSS with these numbers are: CCCC, MS 131 (= 6.21); Bodl., MS Bodley 762, ff. 149–272 (= 6.32); CUL, MS Ii.4.22 (= 6.41); EDC 1 (= 6.60); National Library of Wales, MS 735C (= 7.3); Oxford, Balliol College, MS 49 (= 8.17); Bodl., MS Laud. misc. 647 (= 10.45); CCCC MS 397 (= 12.20); Oxford, Magdalen College, MS lat. 17 + Westminster Abbey, MS 34/3 (= 19.20).

century Franciscan union-catalogue of English libraries, the *Registrum Anglie de Libris Doctorum et Auctorum Veterum*, makes no mention of Ely.[57] The precentor's accounts give no hint of the library being vast, and show expenditure on book-maintenance to have been concentrated on service-books; suggestively, too, they include one entry, in 1301–2, for the making of a new cupboard for book storage.[58] That sounds more like the scale of things at Ely, and also accords with the fact that no room is known that might have held three, six or twenty large book-presses; and yet there must be some explanation for the two-part numbers.

Far more helpful to modern historians was another operation that was effected upon the library's contents, in about the 1470s or a little later. This was to inscribe at the foot of the first and last page of each book the words *'Iste liber pertinet ecclesie Eliensi'* ('This book belongs to the Church of Ely') (Plate 16d). Hitherto the Priory's books seem to have had no statement of their ownership. Where he judged it necessary, the same scribe also wrote a summary list of a book's contents at its front, on, say, a flyleaf. The library was certainly now in as good order as the archives.

The last couple of generations before the dissolution of the Priory are a time about which surprisingly little can be said. There is only one precentor's account from the sixteenth century.[59] It would be surprising if printed books were not being acquired for the library, but only one has so far been identified.[60] A little historical writing is known to so far have taken place, but it was more a matter of existing chronicles being continued or updated than of fresh material being composed. So far as record-management was concerned, the employment of lay professionals as registrars (such as Ely's Robert Bredon, BCL, in the 1460s and 1470s)[61] was now seen by the Crown as good practice for all monasteries, and was accordingly imposed by Henry VIII in his injunctions of 1535;[62] but there was doubtless already a successor to Bredon in place at Ely.

Other interest that was taken in the Cathedral Priory was of a more historical nature. At some point in the mid to late 1530s John Leland, the self-appointed investigator of English libraries' medieval authors, came to Ely. He found relatively little to interest him: fewer than a dozen works, including Bede upon Genesis, Aldhelm's *De laudibus virginitatis* and *Carmen de virginitate*, the *Itinerarium* of Antoninus, the *Variae* of

---

[57] *Registrum Anglie de Libris Doctorum et Auctorum Veterum*, ed. R.H. Rouse and Mary A. Rouse, Corpus of British Medieval Library Catalogues, 2 (London, 1991).

[58] Gullick (ed.), *Extracts from the Precentors' Accounts* (cit. in n. 30), p. 7.

[59] EDC 1/F/9/10 (for 1523–4).

[60] The name of John Skelsyn (documented 1532–9) is in a copy of Martin Luther's *Collected Writings and Sermons* (Wittenberg, 1519): Greatrex, *BRECP*, pp. 438–9.

[61] Bredon is referred to as *'registrarium nostrum'* in 1473 in the Priory register formerly Liber B (EDR G2/3), fo. 120: W.A. Pantin, 'English Monastic Letter-Books', in J.G. Edwards, V.H. Galbraith and E.F. Jacob (eds.), *Historical Essays in Honour of James Tait* (Manchester, 1933), pp. 201–22, at p. 207; *cf.* also Emden, *Register*, p. 90, for employment of Bredon, a notary public, as the Prior's secretary in 1469–70, 1474–5. A possible predecessor to Bredon at Ely was John Dounham, who was Priory grammar-master (see EDR G2/3, fos. 35–6 (1465, 1459)), corrodian (*ibid.*, fos. 88–9 (1466)) and a chaplain at the Chantry on the Green at Ely (*East Anglian Notes & Queries*, n.s. vi (1895–6), p. 278 n. (before 1478)); his name is scribbled at the front of the Priory register, BL, Add. MS 41612. *Cf.* also Emden, *Register*, p. 198.

[62] BL, Cotton MS Cleopatra E. iv, fo. 21; printed by G. Burnet, *History of the Reformation of the Church of England*, ed. N. Pocock, 7 vols. (Oxford, 1865), IV, pp. 217–22, at p. 221. *Cf. L & P Hen. VIII*, VIII, pp. 24–5, no. 76 (3).

Cassiodorus, several biblical commentaries, and a work by Vitruvius – no doubt his *De architectura*.[63] Far smaller houses could yield more to interest Leland.

Finally, in 1535, even as Henry VIII's commissioners were starting to visit the monasteries for the purpose of taking their surrender, one of these men, Sir John Prise (or ap Rhys or Rheseus), came to Ely. He took a historical interest in monastic foundation charters, and for some reason he lit upon the royal licence to the Cathedral Priory to incorporate Mullicourt Priory, 1446 (now British Library, Lord Frederick Campbell Charter xxvii.29). This very unremarkable document he presumably bore away; it is endorsed *'Refertur in regio Regesto ad verbum. J. Rheseus, Regestor.'*[64] This slight loss was a foretoken of what was to come.

---

[63] Leland's list is printed in Sharpe (ed.), *English Benedictine Libraries: The Shorter Catalogues* (cit. in n. 33), pp. 130–1. It is conceivable that the Vitruvius is to be identified with the 12th-century copy that in the late 16th century received a scribble *'Andreas Pearne est meus summus amicus'* ('Andrew Pearne is my greatest friend'; Pearne (or Perne) was Dean of Ely from 1557 to 1589) and that in 1887 was described as no. 38521 in cat. 375 of the bookseller B. Quaritch, and is now in the Berlin Staatsbibliothek (where it has the shelfmark Cod. lat. fol. 601; *cf.* C.H. Krinsky, 'Seventy-Eight Vitruvius Manuscripts', *Jnl. of the Warburg and Courtauld Institutes*, xxx (1967), pp. 36–70, at p. 48). The Berlin MS containing this and other texts will be discussed by H. Gneuss in a supplement to his *Handlist of Anglo-Saxon Manuscripts* in *Anglo-Saxon England*, 33 (forthcoming, 2004?).

[64] Prise's collection of 'transcripts (or possibly originals)' of the foundation charters of monastic houses is discussed by N.R. Ker, 'Sir John Prise', *The Library*, 5th ser., x (1955), pp. 1–24, at pp. 2–3; reprinted with addenda in Ker, *Books, Collectors and Libraries. Studies in the Medieval Heritage*, ed. A.G. Watson (London and Ronceverte, W. Va., 1985), pp. 471–95, at 472–3. See also a brief note in S.E. Kelly (ed.), *Charters of St Augustine's Abbey, Canterbury, and Minster-in-Thanet*, Anglo-Saxon Charters, iv (Oxford, 1995), pp. lix–lx. On two pre-Conquest charters at Bury St Edmunds Abbey, for instance, Prise wrote endorsements similar to that on the Ely licence: see C.W. Goodwin, 'On Two Ancient Charters, in the Possession of the Corporation of King's Lynn', *Norfolk Archaeology*, iv (1855), pp. 93–117, at p. 93.

The Dean and Chapter,
Reformation to Restoration: 1541–1660

The period from the Reformation to the Restoration was the most momentous and most turbulent in all the thirteen centuries since St Etheldreda founded her church at Ely. Events between the 1530s and 1650s had a greater impact and a longer-lasting significance than the destruction of the Abbey by the Danes in 870, the foundation of the bishopric of Ely in 1109, or the mid nineteenth-century reforms carried out by the Ecclesiastical Commission. Twice Ely was dissolved. For twenty-two months between November 1539 and September 1541, and again for eleven years from April 1649 until the summer of 1660, the institution that was Ely Cathedral ceased to exist. Moreover, this was the century when the purpose of Ely and all other cathedrals was most deeply questioned. Medieval cathedrals had a clear purpose, the *opus Dei*: the worship of God in the ceaseless round of services in the church; human endeavour had no higher earthly end. A Protestant cathedral, however, seemed to many an oxymoron, for to most Protestants God was not to be worshipped with pomp and organs in the repetition of the hours of the divine office, but with intellectual assent to his Word. It was not clear how, if at all, cathedrals fitted into this new understanding of the divine order.[1]

Suppression and refoundation

Early in 1538 the gossip in East Anglia was that Ely Priory was about to be dissolved; to suppress the chatter the government put the rumour-mongers in the stocks and ordered the Prior and Convent not to sell or alienate any of their property.[2] The story was premature, but with the lesser monasteries already swept away and a variety of schemes under discussion for the remodelling of English cathedrals, few could have expected Ely

I am grateful to John Maddison, Peter Meadows, Jane Tillier and my colleagues in the History Department of Keele University for their comments and assistance in the preparation of this chapter.

[1] See especially D. Marcombe and C.S. Knighton (eds.), *Close Encounters: Cathedrals and English Society since 1540* (Nottingham, 1991) and P. Collinson, 'The Protestant Cathedral, 1541–1660', in P. Collinson, N. Ramsay and M. Sparks (eds.), *A History of Canterbury Cathedral* (Oxford, 1995), pp. 154–203.

[2] *LP Henry VIII*, XIII, pt 1, no. 102. Norwich Cathedral Priory was the first to be 'transposed' in May 1538: I. Atherton *et al.* (eds.), *Norwich Cathedral: Church, City and Diocese, 1096–1996* (London and Rio Grande, 1996), p. 507.

to survive unchanged.[3] It was hardly unexpected, then, when on 18 November 1539 Prior Robert Steward and the twenty-three monks solemnly surrendered their monastery and all its possessions to royal commissioners, so dissolving the Priory. The King's intention was to refound Ely as a cathedral governed by secular priests, but in the interim Steward and thirteen of the monks were instructed to tarry at Ely and continue celebrating services, while the remaining eleven, described as aged, sick or the worst monks, were dismissed.[4]

For the next twenty-two months the church at Ely was neither a priory nor properly a cathedral, but 'the kynges howsse'. The fourteen ex-monks presumably continued a pattern of services similar to the one which they had previously celebrated, but the affairs of the Church were in the hands of the Crown, which began to lease out its lands and properties.[5] Bereft of a resident governing body, the Church fell prey to the greed not only of the Crown, which stripped it of around three hundredweight of precious metal, but also of its Bishop, Thomas Goodrich, who had some of the lead from its roof.[6] This liminal period ended on 10 September 1541, with the sealing of the royal charter reconstituting the Cathedral[7] (Plate 17a and Colour pl. 21a). Robert Steward was re-appointed to head the community, as the first Dean. Eight prebendaries were appointed: three former senior Ely Priory monks[8] and five senior clerics connected with the King, Bishop, or Cambridge University. These nine formed the Dean and Chapter, the governing body of the Cathedral. Two of the first prebendaries, the noted reformers Richard Cox and Matthew Parker, probably oversaw the implementation of the rest of the foundation according to the general pattern applied to other former monastic cathedrals. The Crown's stated reasons for refoundation were threefold: that true religion and worship of God should be propagated; that boys should be liberally educated in letters; and that Christ's poor should be succoured.[9] In pursuance of the first aim there were also eight minor canons or vicars choral, all of them former Ely monks (three of whom had been identified as 'good choir man' two years earlier, and one of them as 'discreet'); a gospeller (to chant the gospel) and an epistoler (to read the epistle), also former Ely monks; eight lay clerks or singing men; eight choir boys; and a master of the choristers. To fulfil the Cathedral's educational role there was a grammar school of 24 scholars and two masters. In partial fulfilment of the Cathedral's charitable function there were six almsmen (or bedesmen). And there was a domestic staff,

---

[3] H. Cole (ed.), *King Henry the Eighth's Scheme of Bishopricks* (London, 1838). The declining number of monks at Ely, down from 32 in 1536 to 24 in 1539, perhaps suggests a realisation that the monastic life would not survive long: Evans, *Ordinances*, p. x.

[4] *LP Henry VIII*, XIV, pt 2, nos. 542, 584; XV, no. 1032. See also Owen, above, pp. 74–5. Between 1538 and 1542 Henry refounded 8 former monastic cathedrals (Ely, Canterbury, Carlisle, Durham, Norwich, Rochester, Winchester and Worcester) and created 6 new cathedrals (Bristol, Chester, Gloucester, Osney [shortly afterwards transferred to Oxford] and Peterborough, as well as Westminster, dissolved in 1550).

[5] PRO, E314/13/1, m. 1; *LP Henry VIII*, XVI, nos. 503(50), 1500, pp. 722, 727.

[6] *LP Henry VIII*, XIV, pt 2, no. 777. Goodrich later made restitution in his will: PRO, PROB 11/37, fo. 76ᵛ.

[7] *LP Henry VIII*, XVI, no. 1226(11).

[8] Robert Hammond, formerly sub-prior, John Ward, formerly sacrist, and John Custans, formerly steward of the lands. For the prebendaries see: *LP Henry VIII*, XIV, pt 2, no. 542; *DNB*; Bentham, *Ely*, II, pp. 243, 247, 249–50, 253, 257, 260, 265; Le Neve, *Fasti*, VII: *Ely, Norwich, Westminster and Worcester Dioceses*, ed. J. M. Horn (London, 1992), pp. 15, 17, 19, 21–2, 24, 26–7.

[9] G.W. Kitchin and F.T. Madge (eds.), *Documents relating to the Foundation of the Chapter of Winchester AD 1541–1547* (London, 1889), p. 44.

particularly to maintain a common table: two sextons, two porters, a butler, two cooks and a caterer.[10]

The refoundation of the Cathedral was codified in statutes issued in June 1544.[11] Drawn up by three royal commissioners, the conservative bishops Nicholas Heath of Worcester and George Day of Chichester, and the reformer Richard Cox, one of Ely's own prebendaries, they were a variation of the standard statutes devised by these commissioners for most of England's new foundation cathedrals.[12] It is not clear to what extent these statutes were fully enforced. None of the new cathedrals' statutes was properly authenticated under the royal Great Seal; some of the provisions were probably redundant from the start. The establishment of the common table must have been weakened by the provision that married members could opt out. Indeed it may never have been established, except for the choristers and grammar school boys. The marriage of clergy dealt a severe blow to a system which envisaged a quasi-monastic rule of life, with the members dining and worshipping together daily. Elizabeth later famously tried to banish wives from all colleges and cathedrals, but Bishop Cox of Ely rebuked her and the Queen's wishes went unheeded.[13] Other parts of the statutes were quickly made redundant by the speed of religious change after the publication of the first Book of Common Prayer, 1549. The prayers set out in the statutes were abolished that year, and the posts of gospeller and epistoler became superfluous. Nevertheless, although the former office quickly disappeared, an epistoler continued to be appointed until the early nineteenth century.[14] Finally, parts of the statutes were simply ignored by local custom and practice. By 1551, for example, the number of minor canons had dropped from eight to six, while the number of lay clerks varied, with the Chapter sometimes paying for temporary supernumeraries.[15]

Early in Elizabeth's reign, an attempt was made to remove some of the anomalies and revised statutes were issued.[16] These too were legally ambiguous, for the first article of the metropolitical visitation of the Cathedral in 1608 asked whether each member swore on admission 'to observe such Statutes as have beene hitherto used as

---

[10] Owen and Thurley, *King's School*, pp. 30–3; *LP Henry VIII*, XIV, pt 2, no. 542. The Chapter was also charged with maintaining four divinity students at the universities, but the obligation to find these was dispensed with by the King in 1545, who took back the Suffolk manor of Barnham in recompense: *LP Henry VIII*, XX, pt 1, no. 777, p. 389; *CPR, 1550–3*, pp. 173–4; C.S. Knighton, 'The Provision of Education in the New Cathedral Foundations of Henry VIII', in *Close Encounters* (cit. in n. 1), pp. 18–42, at pp. 26–34.

[11] CCCC, MS 120, p. 284; EDC 2/1/4 (c), a copy made in the 1580s.

[12] S.E. Lehmberg, *The Reformation of Cathedrals: Cathedrals in English Society, 1485–1603* (Princeton, 1988), pp. 91–2; A.H. Thompson (ed.), *The Statutes of the Cathedral Church of Durham* (Surtees Society, 143, 1929), pp. xxxviii–lii. Cox was additionally Archdeacon of Ely.

[13] I. Payne, *The Provision and Practice of Sacred Music at Cambridge Colleges and Selected Cathedrals c.1547–c.1646* (London, 1993), p. 192; J. Bruce and T.T. Perowne (eds.), *Correspondence of Matthew Parker* (Parker Society, Cambridge, 1853), p. 151.

[14] Payne, *Provision and Practice*, pp. 193–8.

[15] *Ibid.*

[16] CCCC, MS 120, pp. 205–40. These, and the other surviving copies (EDC 2/1/4 (b) and Bodl., MS Gough Camb. 27, pp. 163–82) are undated, and although they state that they have been passed under the Great Seal, no entry on the patent rolls has been found and the original copy had been lost by 1666: *The Statutes of the Collegiate Church of Ely* (London, 1817), pp. 138–43. These statutes must be later than the 1559 act empowering the Queen to amend cathedral statutes (1 Eliz. I c. 22) but are probably earlier than the institution of a theology lecturer at the Cathedral by 1562–3 (EDC 3/3/4, fo. 7) who is not mentioned in the statutes. For the confusion surrounding cathedral statutes under Elizabeth see also J. Saunders, 'The Limitations of Statutes: Elizabethan Schemes to Reform New Foundation Cathedral Statutes', *JEH*, 48 (1997), pp. 445–67.

statutes'.[17] They made some minor changes, notably in the Protestantisation of the liturgy, but the Cathedral and its governance were little changed. The Cathedral envisaged in these statutes was still a corporate body living together and devoting its principal resources to the daily round of corporate prayer. This was, by Elizabeth's reign, a profoundly conservative view of the reformed church, and it begs the question of how far religious change affected Ely.

Religious change

The early Reformation had come forcefully to Ely, through Bishop Goodrich, who, though he accommodated himself to Queen Mary at the end of his life, was an energetic, evangelical reformer close to Archbishop Cranmer[18] (Plate 19*a*). The Cathedral still bears witness to Goodrich's reforming zeal and the thoroughness with which it was enacted. In June 1535 Goodrich ordered that the hated names of the Pope and St Thomas Becket be erased from all books. In the Dean and Chapter's copy of the *Liber Eliensis* every reference to either person has been scored through.[19] The shrine of St Etheldreda, at the heart of the medieval Cathedral, was swept away. When it was dismantled, probably in 1539, the discovery that it was made of 'common stone' and not, as had been thought, of fine white marble was trumpeted by the reformers as evidence that the Roman church had blinded and corrupted the laity:

> Thus was her tomb degraded and debased one degree, which makes the truth of all the rest to be suspected. And if all Popish miracles were brought to the test, they would be found to shrink from marble to common stone, nay from stone to untempered dirt and mortar.[20]

The purging of the Cathedral's cultic associations was symbolised by the change of dedication at the Cathedral's refoundation, from St Peter and St Etheldreda to the Holy and Undivided Trinity.[21] The Cathedral was also purged of its images: every one of the 147 statues of Mary and other saints in the Lady Chapel was systematically beheaded, and the statues in Bishop West's chantry chapel were similarly mutilated to render them innocuous. Although it is not known when the iconoclasm was carried out, it was

---

[17] EDR, F5/41, fo. 118.

[18] D. MacCulloch, *Thomas Cranmer: A Life* (New Haven and London, 1996); M. Aston, *England's Iconoclasts*, vol. I: *Laws against Images* (Oxford, 1988), p. 238, n. 51; F. Heal, 'The Bishops of Ely and their Diocese during the Reformation Period, ca. 1515–1600' (PhD thesis, University of Cambridge, 1972), pp. 16–23, but underestimating Goodrich's reforming zeal in the 1530s and 1540s.

[19] HMC, *12th Report, Appx, pt ix, Manuscripts of the Duke of Beaufort, K.G., the Earl of Donoughmore, and Others* (London, 1891), pp. 393–4; compare the copy of the *Liber Eliensis* in Trinity College, Cambridge (MS O.2.1), which contains no such erasures.

[20] *LP Henry VIII*, XIII, pt 1, no. 192; Maddison, *Ely Cathedral*, pp. 102–3.

[21] *LP Henry VIII*, XVI, no. 1226 (11). The reformed dedication was illustrated in the iconography of the new seal matrix (Plate 17*b*), which showed an image of the Trinity on one side, with God the Father enthroned, supporting Christ on the Cross and the Holy Spirit as a dove, and Henry VIII enthroned on the other side, almost as an earthly reflection of the Heavenly Lord: Maddison, *Ely Cathedral*, p. 103. The Cathedral's dedication changed several times in the Middle Ages. In the 10th century Dunstan dedicated the rebuilt Abbey to St Peter and the Blessed Virgin Mary, but on the completion of the new presbytery in 1252 Bishop Northwold rededicated the church to St Mary, St Peter and St Etheldreda. Mary had dropped out of the Cathedral's dedication by the Reformation, probably as a consequence of the construction of the Lady Chapel in the 14th century.

probably in response to Goodrich's injunctions given at Ely on 21 October 1541 for the suppression of all images[22] (Plate 18*a–b*).

The worship in the newly refounded Cathedral was, however, otherwise little changed under Henry VIII – a situation epitomised in 1546–7 when the Dean and Chapter acquired new hymnals and processionals and marked the King's death (January 1547) with a requiem mass at a cost of £3 13*s.* 2*d.*[23] The surviving evidence will not allow a clear judgement on the enthusiasm with which either the liturgical and theological changes under Edward, or their reversal under Mary, were carried out at the Cathedral.[24] The Edwardian Chapter did contain a conclave of committed Protestants, particularly Cox, Parker, Edward Leeds and William May.[25] Their impact on life at Ely, however, was probably muted since most of them were busy elsewhere, as the Bishop's vicars general, as heads of Cambridge colleges or, in the case of Cox, as Chancellor of Oxford University.[26] Throughout the Edwardian Reformation the Chapter was headed by a natural trimmer, Robert Steward, a man gifted in the art of self-preservation, who was successively Prior and Dean from 1522 until his death in 1557.[27] Nevertheless, most of the Cathedral's plate and vestments were sold in the early 1550s and some of the proceeds were spent in building and equipping a new library, which might suggest an attempt to turn the Cathedral from a house of intercessory prayer to a hub of reformed, evangelical learning.[28] Shortly thereafter, the Marian reaction virtually wiped the prebendal stalls clean, with seven vacancies in the first sixteen months of the Queen's reign: five by deprivation, one by resignation and one by death.[29] The new appointments were not, however, particularly zealous proponents of a reinvigorated Roman Catholicism, and Mary's principal legacy to Ely was the transfer in 1556 of the presentation to the eight prebendal stalls from the Crown to the Bishop of Ely.[30] Only three

---

[22] VCH, *Cambs.*, IV, p. 61; Aston, *England's Iconoclasts*, I, p. 269n.; W.H. Frere and W.P.M. Kennedy (eds.), *Visitation Articles and Injunctions of the Period of the Reformation*, 3 vols (Alcuin Club Collections, 14–16, 1910), III, pp. 68–9. Previous historians have suggested other dates for the iconoclasm: Lehmberg, *Reformation of Cathedrals* (cit. in n. 12), p. 104, suggests *c.*1547, while Atkinson, *Ely Monastery*, p. 16, suggests that the damage was done during the Commonwealth. West's chantry, however, suffered before 1635 when its statues were described as having been 'disarm'd, dislegg'd and beheaded': L.G.W. Legg (ed.), 'Relation of a Short Survey of the Westerne Counties . . . 1635', *Camden Miscellany XVI*, Camden 3rd Series, 52 (1936), p. 92.

[23] EDC 3/3/2, fos. 3d, 5. Henry died on 28 January 1547; his funeral rites at Windsor took from 3 to 16 February, while churches throughout the land held a solemn dirge and requiem mass on 8–9 February: J. Loach, 'The Function of Ceremonial in the Reign of Henry VIII', *Past and Present*, no. 142 (February 1994), pp. 43–68, at pp. 56, 59; J.J. Scarisbrick, *Henry VIII* (London, 1968), p. 496.

[24] The loss of almost all of the Chapter's financial records before the 1560s makes it difficult to assess the implementation of reform and reaction at the Cathedral.

[25] For these see Bentham, *Ely*, and *DNB*.

[26] See CCCC, MS 120, p. 322, for Cox's excuse that 'a iust impediment by commaundment' kept him away from Ely and 'my numbre of affayres' meant that 'I me selfe shall have lytyll leysure' to fulfil the office of receiver.

[27] W. Dugdale, *Monasticon Anglicanum*, ed. J. Caley, H. Ellis, and B. Bandinel, 6 vols in 8 (London, 1817–30), I, p. 468; *DNB*; Bentham, *Ely*, II, p. 227; see also Appendix 2, below.

[28] *The East Anglian*, 3rd ser., 8 (1899–1900), p. 377. A series of articles on Cambridgeshire inventories, from transcripts by J.J. Muskett, was published in *The East Anglian; or, Notes and Queries on Subjects connected with . . . Suffolk, Cambridge, Essex and Norfolk*, ed. C.H. Evelyn-White, 3rd ser., 6 (1895–6) to 10 (1903–4), and in collected form was printed as *Cambridgeshire Church Goods. Inventories for the County and the Isle of Ely, for various Years, 1538–1586*, transcribed J.J. Muskett, ed. C.H. Evelyn-White (not published, [*c.*1908]).

[29] Cox, Parker, May, Richard Wilks and Robert Hammond were deprived, Leeds resigned, and Anthony Otway died.

[30] *CPR, 1555–7*, p. 523; the deanery remained in the gift of the Crown.

prebendaries were deprived on Elizabeth's accession: John Yonge, who died in prison *c.*1580; John Bykerdyk; and Thomas Peacock.[31] The rest of the Chapter conformed in 1558–9 and were more representative of the Cathedral body under Mary – none more so than Steward's successor as Dean, Andrew Perne (Colour pl. 25*a*).

Perne was an enigmatic and controversial figure. Of a minor Norfolk gentry family, he had initially attracted the attention of the evangelicals Matthew Parker and Bishop Goodrich. Through them he secured a Cambridge fellowship and, by 1551, appointment as a royal chaplain to King Edward. Under Mary, however, he quickly adopted a more conservative stance and was soon rewarded with the mastership of Peterhouse and, in November 1557, the deanery of Ely. While he turned against the reformers with whom he had once consorted and suppressed Protestantism, his investigations into heresy as Vice-Chancellor of Cambridge saw no burnings and he even sheltered from the Marian storm John Whitgift, a convinced Protestant and at that time one of Peterhouse's junior fellows. At Elizabeth's accession Perne conformed again and kept all his preferments, but he was never able to shake off a reputation for covert popery, which his latest biographer thinks is 'very possibly' justified. Gabriel Harvey, his bitterest enemy and a man who dipped his pen in more gall than did most academics, fulminated 'What an Ambidexterity, or rather Omnidexterity had the man, that at one and the same meeting, had a pleasing Tongue for a Protestant, a flattering Eye for a Papist, and a familiar nod for a good fellow'.[32]

Perne not only symbolised the ambiguous nature of the Marian reaction in Ely: he also muted the impact of religious change at the Cathedral under Elizabeth.[33] Some of the obvious trappings of popery were disposed of. A crozier, a mitre and some of the bells had been sold by 1563, and two chalices after 1564; instead, the Cathedral was provided with what was necessary under the 1559 Prayer Book: one communion cup, two patens and a great silver flagon.[34] Otherwise the winds which blew so strongly from Geneva and buffeted the Elizabethan church were no more than gentle breezes by the time they reached Ely. Richard Cox, appointed Bishop in 1559, filled those prebends not already occupied by trimmers with worthy parish clergy such as Thomas Willet (who had been his chaplain in the days of Edward VI)[35] or Cambridge academics, some of them decidedly conservative in outlook like Henry Hervey, Master of Trinity Hall, who retained his preferments under Henry, Edward, Mary and Elizabeth and who in 1570 was accused of lukewarmness in religion.[36] Of Cox's early appointments, only Matthew Hutton and John Whitgift were unquestionably outstanding; both left Ely to have greatness (and an archbishopric) thrust upon them elsewhere, Hutton at York and Whitgift at Canterbury.[37] Pressure to move the Cathedral in a more Protestant direction

[31] Le Neve, *Fasti, 1541–1857*, VII, *Ely* (cit. in n. 8), pp. 17, 21, 26.

[32] P. Collinson, 'Andrew Perne and his Times', in D. McKitterick (ed.), *Andrew Perne: Quatercentenary Studies* (Cambridge Bibliographical Society, monograph no. 11, 1991), pp. 1–34; *DNB*; Bentham, *Ely*, II, pp. 228–9.

[33] C. Marsh, 'Piety and Persuasion in Elizabethan England: The Church of England meets the Family of Love', in N. Tyacke (ed.), *England's Long Reformation 1500–1800* (London, 1998), p. 152.

[34] Frere and Kennedy (ed.), *Visitation Articles* (cit. in n. 22), III, pp. 143–4; EDR B2/4, p. 54; EDC 2/2A/1, fo. 1 (reversed). There were also in 1593 eight silver spoons.

[35] Bentham, *Ely*, II, p. 253; A. Willet, *Synopsis Papismi* (London, 1634), sigs. a^v, a2^r.

[36] Bentham, *Ely*, II, p. 250; *DNB*.

[37] *DNB*; P. Lake, 'Matthew Hutton – a Puritan Bishop', *History*, 64 (1979), pp. 182–204; J. Raine (ed.), *The Correspondence of Dr. Matthew Hutton* (Surtees Society, 17, 1843); P.M. Dawley, *John Whitgift and the Reformation* (London, 1955); J. Strype, *The Life and Acts of John Whitgift*, 3 vols. (Oxford, 1822).

was only gentle. By 1563 the Chapter had created a new post, theology lecturer, to lecture weekly for a stipend of £20 a year. The first known holder was Prebendary Thomas Steward, younger brother of the late Dean, who had spent Mary's reign in exile sitting at the feet of the Scottish reformer John Knox.[38] Subsequently the lectureship was sometimes used to augment the stipend of a favoured minor canon,[39] but some of the lecturers were noted preachers – none more so than Andrew Willet, who held the post for three years, probably in the early 1580s before his father Thomas resigned his prebend in his favour[40] (Plate 19c).

There is some evidence that the musical establishment was run down from the 1560s, partly because of Protestant doubts about the role of music and singing in worship. In 1576 Bishop Cox expressed his hope to Archbishop Grindal that 'the Cathedrall churches would be brought to some better frame touchinge exercise of learninge, whose exercyse now is onely in singinge and very little in aedifyinge'.[41] No concrete initiative seems to have arisen in response to Cox's criticisms, and the worship at the Cathedral remained only half reformed, as a painting of his funeral service in 1581 suggests (Colour pl. 26–7). In this, a wooden communion table stands, rail-less and covered with a white cloth over a green table carpet, at the east end of the choir, while the minister, wearing a white surplice over a black cassock, stands on its north side. A large square catafalque with a pyramidal canopy stands in the middle of the choir. The stalls on the north side of the choir are occupied by 38 seated figures, five of whom (presumably the choir men) are dressed like the minister at the communion table. In front of the stalls are 29 laymen seated on benches, while further laity stand around the hearse and in a gallery around the Octagon. From a high pulpit in the middle of the north stalls, a bishop, in a black cap, and a black chimere over a white rochet, delivers the sermon.[42]

The fabric of the Cathedral and College bore the marks of religious change to a far greater extent than the worship. The departure of the monks left much of the precincts potentially unused. In October 1541 the King had ordered his commissioners to allot to the Dean, prebendaries and other staff 'convenyent dwelling howses and placeis to be devided sorted and assigned to them'. The former monastic buildings were carved up: the cellarer's lodgings to the first stall, the almonry to the seventh stall, the great hall and the knights' chamber to the minor canons, and so on; surplus buildings were demolished.[43] After 1559, most of the Cathedral church, apart from the choir where the liturgy was celebrated, was redundant and empty. With the prebendaries usually

[38] EDC 3/3/4, fo. 7; C.H. Garrett, *The Marian Exiles: A Study in the Origins of Elizabethan Puritanism* (Cambridge, 1938), p. 299.

[39] EDC 3/3/10, fo. 10; EDC 3/1/3B, fos. 13^v, 62, 88–91.

[40] Willet, *Synopsis Papismi*, sigs. [a3^v], b^v. Daniel Wigmore, at first schoolmaster at Ely and then prebendary and archdeacon, was another good preacher who held the post of lecturer for many years under James I and Charles I: EDC 3/1/3B, fos. 61, 76^v; EDR B2/31, fos. 1, 106, 109, 161; Le Neve, *Fasti, 1541–1857*, VII, *Ely* (cit. in n. 8) pp. 13, 15, 17; Owen and Thurley, *King's School*, p. 15.

[41] LPL, MS 2003, fo. 7.

[42] Atkinson, *Ely Monastery*, pp. 187–90; P. Blakeman, *The Book of Ely* (Buckingham, 1990), p. 19. I am grateful to John Maddison for help in interpreting this painting.

[43] CCCC, MS 120, pp. 319–20, as excerpted, paraphrased and discussed by D.J. Stewart, 'Distribution of the Buildings of the Dissolved Monastery at Ely', *AJ*, 54 (1897), pp. 174–85; Atkinson, *Ely Monastery*, pp. 180–5; Owen and Thurley, *King's School*, pp. 33–5.

absent,[44] Cox has left an enduring image in his description of the Cathedral in 1561 as 'vast', with 'rooms plenty and several', and where, save for one resident prebendary, 'doves and owls may dwell there for any continual housekeeping'.[45] Parts of the Cathedral were turned to other uses. The stone *mensa* of the former high altar was re-used as a gravestone in the south aisle.[46] The south-west transept, formerly the bishop's chamber, became a store room.[47] The passageway between the Cathedral and the Lady Chapel became chambers for the almsmen.[48] By the early seventeenth century (and probably earlier) the nave was used as the principal preaching space, as in other cathedrals.[49] The Chapter House was used for the diocesan consistory court.[50] Other parts of the building were used only on exceptional occasions. Episcopal visitations were sometimes conducted in front of the former high altar (although the Chapter House was a more common venue).[51] As in some other churches, the eastern arm was used as a site for burials, suggesting that it retained some of its former sanctified aura.[52] In particular, the area immediately before the old high altar was used for the burial of bishops and deans who clearly wished to be associated with the pre-Reformation bishops who had been buried there.[53] The brasses to Bishop Goodrich (in full vestments) and Dean Tyndall (in full academic dress) were both placed here (Plate 19a–b), as was the floor slab to Dean Bell and the elaborate monument to Dean Caesar (Colour pl. 16a). Bishop Cox's floor slab was also placed here but its Latin inscription was defaced within twenty years of his death, showing that not all iconoclasm at Ely happened in the middle of the sixteenth century.[54] The south aisle of the eastern arm, meanwhile, was slowly being turned into a mausoleum to the Steward family. Dean Steward's floor slab was placed here as were the monuments to his relatives Robert Steward (d.1570) and Sir Mark Steward (d.1603), the latter proudly sporting an entirely

[44] EDC 2/1/4 (b), fos. 15–16.

[45] Bentham, *Ely*, II, pp. 250, 257, 260; J. Bruce and T.T. Perowne (ed.), *Correspondence of Matthew Parker* (Parker Society, Cambridge, 1853), p. 151. Cox feared that the Queen's edict ejecting priests' wives from cathedrals would mean that no prebendary would reside at Ely.

[46] VCH, *Cambs.*, IV, p. 69.

[47] Atkinson, *Ely Monastery*, sheet II; Stevenson, *Supplement to Bentham*, plate facing p. 73; R. Holmes, *Cromwell's Ely* (Ely, 1975), p. 53.

[48] VCH, *Cambs.*, IV, p. 62; EDC 8A/1/13, fo. 11ᵛ. The almsmen had initially been assigned the new dorter: Atkinson, *Ely Monastery*, pp. 182–3.

[49] EDR, B2/31, fo. 108. There was also a 'lytle pulpyt' on the north side of the choir: EDR B2/23, fo. 38; EDC 3/1/2, fo. 29; it is illustrated in Bishop Cox's funeral painting. The nave may also have been used for baptisms: when a new font was erected in 1693 it was placed in the nave, possibly on the site of the former font: G. Cobb, *English Cathedrals: The Forgotten Centuries* (London, 1980), pp. 85, 91.

[50] EDR B2/31, fo. 160ᵛ.

[51] W. M. Palmer, 'The Archdeaconry of Cambridge and Ely, 1599', *Trans., Cambs. & Hunts. Archaeol. Soc.*, 6 (1938–47), pp. 6, 13, 15; EDR B2/4, p. 3; B2/6, p. 3.

[52] In King's College chapel in Cambridge, for example, the east end, beyond the choir, was reserved for burials: T. Cooper (ed.) *The Journal of William Dowsing: Iconoclasm in East Anglia during the English Civil War* (Ecclesiological Society, Woodbridge, 2001), plate 23.

[53] The plan of the Cathedral reproduced above as the Frontispiece, from B. Willis, *A Survey of the Cathedrals of Lincoln, Ely* (London, 1730), shows the location of monuments; several, including those of Goodrich, Tyndall and Caesar, were subsequently moved. Few prebendaries were buried in the Cathedral.

[54] C.H. Cooper and T. Cooper, *Athenae Cantabrigienses*, 3 vols (Cambridge, 1858–1913), I, p. 442. The Cathedral lost almost all of its medieval glass, but when this was done is not known. It should be noted that there is no evidence that William Dowsing, who wreaked his iconoclastic ire on so many East Anglian churches in 1643–4, visited either the Cathedral or any other churches in the Isle of Ely: Cooper, *Journal of Dowsing*, pp. 19, 46, 402.

fictitious but politically expedient claim to descent from the royal house of Stuart. Bishop Heton's monument was placed here a few years later (Plate 20*b*) and after the Restoration the south aisle of the eastern arm became instead the preferred place of burial for Ely's bishops.

The Lady Chapel was left a large, barren space,[55] until in September 1566, the Dean and Chapter agreed that Holy Trinity parish should have it for their parish church. The former Holy Trinity church (built between 1359 and *c.*1362) was a lean-to against the the north nave aisle. Apart from being too small, it was described as 'very uncomelye, and noysome and dangerous', and it can never have been satisfactory, blocking up some windows and making the Cathedral 'darkened' and 'very unholesome for want of thorrowe ayre'; it was therefore demolished. The parishioners were also granted the Goldsmith's Tower in the north range of the College as a belfry, and with an eye to a quick profit, the Dean and Chapter sold them the Cathedral's smallest bells.[56]

The most notable example of the recycling of buildings was the bishop's palace, which, during the long vacancy of the see after Bishop Cox's death, 1581–1600, was frequently used as a prison for recusants.[57] The emptiness of the palace also proved attractive to the Master and Fellows of Trinity College who, in 1593, petitioned to move their college there during an outbreak of plague in Cambridge.[58] Despite such examples of radical interpretation of the geography of Cathedral and College, Ely did not, at least until the 1650s, see the wide-scale demolition of superfluous parts of the fabric that occurred at other cathedrals such as Norwich.[59]

The Genevan breeze, so gentle in the 1560s and 1570s, blew more forcefully in the 1580s and 1590s. While the see was vacant, patronage of the prebends passed to the Crown. The Queen preferred conservatives, but she faced pressures from courtiers of a more forward bent.[60] This, and the pervading Calvinism of the Church and university establishment in the 1580s and 1590s, meant that the Chapter became moderately Calvinist, especially after the death of Dean Perne in 1589. Humphrey Tyndall (Dean, 1591–1614) was a leading 'moderate Puritan',[61] and several of the active prebendaries shared his theological outlook, particularly Andrew Willet, Edmund Barwell and Hugh Booth.[62] The donation

---

[55] It was used for the examination of ordination candidates by the Archdeacon of Ely: Owen and Thurley, *King's School*, p. 48.

[56] EDC 8A/1/26, a copy made in 1649; A. Holton-Krayenbuhl, T. Cocke, and T. Malim, 'Ely Cathedral Precincts: The North Range', *PCAS*, 78 (1989), pp. 47–69, at p. 65; W.H. Frere (ed.), *Registrum Matthei Parker*, 3 vols. (Canterbury and York Society, 1928–33), II, pp. 456–8. Holy Trinity had apparently had its bells seized by royal commissioners in July 1552: *The East Anglian*, new ser., 9 (1901–2), pp. 7–8. The parishioners of Holy Trinity continued to use the Lady Chapel until 1938: VCH, *Cambs.*, IV, p. 83.

[57] *Acts of the Privy Council, 1588*, pp. 167–8; HMC, *5th Report* (London, 1876), pp. 406–7; HMC, *Marquess of Salisbury*, XIV (London, 1923), pp. 29–30; HMC, *Report on Manuscripts in Various Collections*, III (London, 1904), pp. xi, xiv–xv; LPL, MS 2008, fos. 1, 12, 19, 25, 33, 41, 43, 44, 46.

[58] BL, MS Lansdowne 75, fo. 18.

[59] Atherton *et al.* (eds.), *Norwich Cathedral* (cit. in n. 2), pp. 502–3, 529, 638. For destruction during the Interregnum see below, pp. 191–2.

[60] P. Collinson, in Collinson, Ramsay and Sparks (eds.), *Canterbury Cathedral* (cit. in n. 1), p. 168.

[61] P. Lake, *Moderate Puritans and the Elizabethan Church* (Cambridge, 1982), pp. 228, 242, 328.

[62] For these men see: Le Neve, *Fasti, 1841–57*, VII, *Ely* (cit. in n. 8); N. Tyacke, *Anti-Calvinists: The Rise of English Arminianism c.1590–1640* (Oxford, 1987), p. 12; Lake, *Moderate Puritans*, pp. 193, 237, 242, 328; V. Morgan, 'Country, Court and Cambridge University, 1558–1640: A Study in the Evolution of a Political Culture', PhD thesis, University of East Anglia, 1983, III, p. 539; H.C. Porter, *Reformation and Reaction in Tudor Cambridge* (Cambridge, 1958), p. 208.

by the Chapter of £5 to the city of Geneva in 1590 symbolised its theological allegiance in the closing years of Elizabeth's reign.[63]

That position was, however, not fixed. From the 1590s cathedrals and the universities were the seed-beds of the avant-garde conformism or Arminianism which leached out into the wider church and, eventually and controversially, in the 1630s, captured the ecclesiastical hierarchy. It was a more sacramentally and ceremonially focussed piety, with a greater role for music and an emphasis on the physical fabric of the church building.[64] At Ely the loss of the treasurer's accounts before 1604–5 renders certainty elusive, but an enhanced role for the music within the liturgy may have begun through the influence of Thomas Neville (2nd stall, 1587–1615): as Master of Trinity College, Cambridge (1593–1615), and Dean of Canterbury (1597–1615), he oversaw increased expenditure on the musical establishment of both those institutions.[65] There are certainly signs of renewed emphasis on the conduct of services at Ely from the early years of James's reign, with significant expenditure on the music and monthly communion.[66] The real turning point, however, probably came with the episcopate of Lancelot Andrewes (Bishop, 1609–19), an Arminian noted for his concern with the celebration of the liturgy. His friend Isaac Casaubon described a service at the Cathedral attended by Andrewes on 5 August 1611, Gowrie day. The choir sang psalms as the Bishop solemnly processed in, there was a service of Mattins, Andrewes preached, and then the eucharist was celebrated.[67]

Clear leadership was provided by the coincidence of a succession of Arminian bishops – Andrewes, John Buckeridge (1628–31), Francis White (1631–38) and Matthew Wren (1638–67) – and two deans – Henry Caesar (1614–36) and William Fuller (1636–46) – who were all noted for their support for cathedral music and ceremonial worship.[68] The new direction can be detected in Bishop Andrewes's instructions of 1616 that the minor canons 'forsake and leave that loiteringe kynde of lyfe whiche many of them too longe have used and followed', and in Wren's visitation articles for the Cathedral of 1638, which stressed the orderly conduct of the services and the upkeep of the fabric and asked whether the minor canons attended the service diligently and properly vested, 'without private reading of their owne, or talking with others', and whether the church

[63] EDC 3/1/1, fo. 14.

[64] Tyacke, *Anti-Calvinists*; P. Lake, 'Lancelot Andrewes, John Buckeridge and Avant-Garde Conformity at the Court of James I', in L.L. Peck (ed.), *The Mental World of the Jacobean Court* (Cambridge, 1991), pp. 113–33; P. Lake, 'The Laudian Style: Order, Uniformity and the Pursuit of the Beauty of Holiness in the 1630s', in K. Fincham (ed.), *The Early Stuart Church, 1603–42* (Basingstoke, 1993), pp. 161–85; N. Tyacke, 'Lancelot Andrewes and the Myth of Anglicanism', in P. Lake and M. Questier (eds.), *Conformity and Orthodoxy in the English Church, c. 1560–1660* (Woodbridge, 2000), pp. 5–33.

[65] R.D. Bowers, 'The Liturgy of the Cathedral and its Music, c.1075–1642', in Collinson, Ramsay and Sparks (eds.), *Canterbury Cathedral* (cit. in n. 1), pp. 439–40.

[66] EDC 3/1/2, fo. 29; Ian Payne, below, p. 233.

[67] P.A. Welsby, *Lancelot Andrewes, 1555–1626* (London, 1958), pp. 103–4. The so-called 'Gowrie Plot' of 1600 was an apparent attempt to kill James VI of Scotland by John, 3rd Earl of Gowrie and his brother, Alexander, the Master of Ruthven; the King ordered that the anniversary of his deliverance, 5 August, should thereafter be made a day of solemn thanksgiving: D.H. Willson, *King James VI and I* (London, 1956), pp. 126–30.

[68] For these, see: *DNB*; Tyacke, *Anti-Calvinists* (cit. in n. 62), pp. 171–80, 222–3, 266–7; *The Petition and Articles exhibited in Parliament against Dr Fuller, Deane of Ely, and Vicar of S. Giles Cripple-gate* (London, 1641). Nicholas Felton (Bishop, 1619–26) was an exception to the series, as an evangelical Calvinist, but he made little impression on the diocese, preferring life at court: K. Fincham, *Prelate as Pastor: The Episcopate of James I* (Oxford, 1990), pp. 33, 268, 292, 296, 311.

was kept free from defilement by dogs, hogs, doves and daws.[69] It can also be seen in expenditure on the choir. In 1617–19, over £48 was spent on choir furnishings, including 11½ yards of cloth and 3¾ yards of velvet for the communion table, 13½ yards of crimson grain taffeta and 7½ yards of purple grain cloth, along with lace, embroidery and repainting.[70] Further sums were spent on carving for the King's visit in the autumn of 1636.[71] By the late 1630s, in accordance with Arminian ideas, the communion table was railed, candles stood upon it, and it was called an altar.[72]

The Chapter, however, remained theologically diverse under the first two Stuarts. There were convinced Arminians such as Jerome Beale (3rd stall, 1616–31), and convinced Calvinists such as Ralph Brownrigg (5th stall, 1621–59), who had unsuccessfully opposed Beale's candidature as Master of Pembroke College, Cambridge, in 1619.[73] Until his death in 1621 Andrew Willet remained an advocate of further reformation within the church of England and a critic of the worship of cathedral churches, increasingly at odds with the theological drift of the church establishment.[74] Other prebendaries were noted more for their eccentricities than their theological standpoint, including John Bois (1st stall, 1615–44). He was such a hypochondriac that he was forced to abandon the study of medicine because 'whatsoever disease he read of, he was troubled with the same himself'. Thereafter he adhered to a strict but unconventional rule of life, following a system of fasting of his own devising, being particularly attentive to the rubbing and picking of his teeth after every meal, standing far from a window whenever he studied (frequently from 4 am to 8 pm without a break), and never going to bed with cold feet. Despite the rigours of this routine, he lived to the ripe age of 83.[75] English cathedrals and universities have always attracted a goodly number of eccentrics.

The Dean and Chapter's estates

In 1541 Henry VIII endowed the Dean and Chapter with lands said to be worth £995 a year, all formerly possessions of the Prior and Convent. The new Cathedral did not, however, receive back all those lands that had been surrendered in 1539. A collection of manors and other properties, worth approximately £266 a year, was retained by the Crown.[76] Ely's income, compared with other former monastic cathedrals, made it considerably less wealthy than Canterbury, Durham or Winchester, but better off than Norwich, Rochester or Carlisle; it was also wealthier than any of Henry's new cathedrals.[77] More than half of the income was assigned to fixed outgoings, principally

---

[69] EDR B2/31, fo. 160; EDR F5/41, fos. 77–8.

[70] EDC 3/1/2, fos. 85, 97.

[71] EDC 3/1/1, fos. 159, 164; EDC 3/1/2, fos. 212ᵛ, 223ᵛ.

[72] EDC 3/1/2, fo. 232; R.H. Gibbon, 'Account Book of the Dean and Chapter of Ely, 1604–1677', *Church Quarterly Review*, 115 (1932–3), p. 223.

[73] Tyacke, *Anti-Calvinists* (cit. in n. 62), pp. 45–6, 48–50, 222, 240.

[74] Anthony Milton, *Catholic and Reformed: The Roman and Catholic Churches in English Protestant Thought, 1600–1640* (Cambridge, 1995), especially pp. 18–22, 25.

[75] A. Walker, 'The Life of that Famous Grecian Mr. John Bois', in W. Allen, *Translating for King James* (London, 1970), pp. 134, 147–8, 152.

[76] *LP Henry VIII*, XIV, no. 1226(11); Stevenson, *Supplement*, pp. *2–*15; PRO, SP5/4, fo. 57.

[77] Lehmberg, *Reformation of Cathedrals* (cit. in n. 12) pp. 88–9; Atherton *et al.* (eds.), *Norwich Cathedral*, p. 666. Ely was also less wealthy than the short-lived Westminster Cathedral.

the wages, stipends and diet of the members of the foundation, and £125 was payable to the Crown for tenths and first fruits.[78]

The estates were spread across East Anglia, with a central core of manors, rectorial and other lands, and advowsons in Cambridgeshire and the Isle of Ely. Here were the Cathedral's most valuable properties, such as those in and around Ely itself, and the manors of Melbourn cum Meldreth in Cambridgeshire, and Sutton in the Isle, so prosperous in the sixteenth century that it was nicknamed 'Golden' Sutton. There was also a valuable group of properties in west Suffolk and west Norfolk, including Lakenheath manor. Further afield was an even more diverse and scattered assortment of lands and rights, including a couple of small manors in Suffolk, tenements in London, tithes in Essex, and the profits of jurisdiction of the five and a half hundreds of Wicklaw in east Suffolk (the Liberty of St Etheldreda).[79] These properties were let to tenants according to the system of beneficial leases prevalent among cathedrals. In return for a fixed, and usually small rent, the lessee received a long lease of the property;[80] the profit to the lessee from an improved estate could be as much as double the annual rent.[81] There were two mechanisms by which the income of the Dean and Chapter was partially safeguarded. First, the lessee would pay a lump sum or fine at the sealing of the lease.[82] Second, the profits of the manor court were usually reserved to the Dean and Chapter, although they were granted away for a fixed sum in a few leases. Such profits, although fluctuating, could be considerable, averaging over £150 a year in the late 1630s.[83]

Every October at the annual audit the accounts were cast and the stipends paid by the prebendary appointed Treasurer for the year.[84] The Dean received £120 7s. 6d. a year and each prebendary £20. In addition each received a dividend of any rents paid in kind, with the Dean always receiving a double share: in 1635 these extra emoluments brought the money received by the Dean to £177 12s. 6d. and by each prebendary to £38 13s. 10d. There were also the profits of any fines, for which no accounts have survived.[85] Although all the estates were held in common, by 1551 a system of prebends appears to have existed, under which properties were assigned to individual members just as each obedientiary had held part of the Priory's estates before the Reformation. The dean or prebendary had the nomination to benefices attached to his prebend; in return, each might have to bear the cost of any arrears in the revenues of his properties, or pay the cost of calling a Chapter if he wanted any lease within his block to be sealed in a hurry.[86]

[78] EDC 2/1/4 (c); Bentham, *Ely*, pp. *40–*42.

[79] The valuations are those made by the commissioners of the Court of Augmentations: Stevenson, *Supplement*, pp. *2–*15; VCH, *Cambs.*, IV, p. 160; Miller, *Abbey & Bishopric*, p. 30; PRO, E134/44 & 45 Eliz I/Mich 39.

[80] A clause in a lease of Melbourn manor in 1565 directing the lessee to keep 200 of the Dean and Chapter's sheep on his land may have been erroneously copied from a much earlier lease: EDC 2/4/1, fos. 49–51.

[81] VCH, *Cambs.*, IV, p. 177.

[82] Fines were not accounted for in the audit book (EDC 3/1/1) nor were they entered in the treasurer's or the receiver's accounts (EDC 3/1/2, EDC 3/3), and so they are known only from incidental references: EDC 2/1/4 (b), fo. 15; Katherine Fuller, EDC 6/1B/1660/4, letter to the Dean and Chapter, 11 October 1660.

[83] EDC 2/4/1, fos. 57ᵛ–8ᵛ, 64–5ᵛ, 85, 106ᵛ–7; EDC 6/2/3, fos. 2ᵛ–3, 4; EDC 6/2/2.

[84] In 1589 the Dean and Chapter agreed that the audit should begin on 17 October and end on 27 October; in 1610 this was shortened to a maximum of 6 days beginning on 18 October: EDC 2/2A/1, p. 2; EDC 3/1/2, p. [iii].

[85] EDC 3/1/3B, fos. 48–50; EDC 2/1/4, fo. 16.

[86] CCCC, MS 120, pp. 288–9; EDC 3/1/2, pp. [i, iii]. It is not clear how long the system lasted, but it was

Initially, as before 1539, many properties were let on long leases – some for as many as 90 years – and the practice continued, despite attempts to end it, until leases longer than 21 years were outlawed by Act of Parliament in 1571.[87] Thereafter, however, the Chapter found it hard to resist pressure from tenants wanting long leases, and there was a corresponding rise in leases granted for three lives, a custom which the Chapter tried repeatedly but vainly to stop.[88]

Like any landowner, the Dean and Chapter sometimes had problems asserting their rights, especially over the more far-flung properties, such as their share of the salt-rents collected in Terrington on the edge of the Wash,[89] or their ownership of the manor of Charles in West Wratting, in south-west Cambridgeshire, which was contested for a century.[90] Their difficulties, however, were compounded by aspects of their own practice. Properties often remained in the same families for generations. The lease of the manor of Melbourn was held by the same family from the 1560s until the 1720s, while the lease of the rectories of Holy Trinity and St Mary's in Ely, granted in the mid sixteenth century to the Steward family, relatives of the Dean, passed by marriage in the 1630s to the person whom history has recorded as the Chapter's most famous tenant, Oliver Cromwell.[91] The boundaries of the Chapter's and lessee's properties could become confounded. As the Chapter tended to rely on tenants to produce surveys, an obligation they sometimes resisted, the confusion easily increased.[92] In 1576 the Chapter obtained the Queen's grant of a commission to survey their lands, but they employed Nicholas Massey, son of one of their tenants, as their surveyor; he used his position to steal deeds from the chapter house which he sold to others who then used them to defraud the Dean and Chapter of certain rents and properties.[93]

The Dean and Chapter sometimes had problems with their own tenants, although their tendency to let estates to themselves, their families or other members of the foundation considerably reduced the likelihood of such friction.[94] However, the Chapter's lack of control over lessees could sometimes sour relations between those lessees and the sub-tenants of those estates. Stuntney manor, for example, was let by the Chapter to Simon Steward, brother of the first Dean; he barred rights of way on the manor, allowed his sheep to trespass on neighbouring properties, and denied rights of common to others to force the copyholders to sell their lands to him.[95] The two greatest problems, however, were not of the Chapter's own making: the difficulties associated with fen drainage, and the ever-present possibility that Ely, in common with other cathedrals, would lose all its estates to the Crown and greedy courtiers.

---

apparently still in operation in 1610: EDC 3/1/2, p. [iii]. For the monastic obedientiaries see S.J.A. Evans, *The Medieval Estate of the Cathedral Priory of Ely: A Preliminary Survey* (Ely, 1973), pp. 8–9.

[87] EDC 2/4/1, fos. 3–22, 49–51, 44–5; EDC 6/2/1, p. 108; Frere and Kennedy (eds.), *Visitation Articles* (cit. in n. 22), III, pp. 143; statute 13 Eliz. I c. 10.

[88] BL, MS Lansdowne 58, fo. 8; EDC 6/2/1, pp. 109–10; EDC 2/2A/1, pp. 1, 57–8; J. Strype, *Annals of the Reformation*, 7 parts in 4 vols. (Oxford, 1824), III, pt 2, p. 72.

[89] PRO, E134/37 Eliz/Hil 6; E134 8 Jas I/Hil 16; E134/17 Chas I/East 9.

[90] VCH, *Cambs.*, VI, pp. 192, 196; PRO, C3/58/8, C3/202/47.

[91] VCH, *Cambs.*, VIII, p. 69; W.C. Abbott (ed.), *The Writings and Speeches of Oliver Cromwell*, 4 vols. (Cambridge, Mass., 1937–47), I, pp. 12, 82–101.

[92] EDC 2/2A/1, p. 143; Katherine Fuller, letter to the Dean and Chapter, 11 October 1660, EDC 6/1B/1660/4.

[93] *CPR, 1575–8*, p. 86; PRO, C21/E13/15.

[94] EDC 8A/1/8, fo. 1; VCH, *Cambs.*, VIII, pp. 169, 196.

[95] VCH, *Cambs.*, IV, pp. 41–2.

The joint issues of fen drainage and enclosure caused the greatest friction between Chapter, lessees and peasantry. In the sixteenth century, drainage schemes were usually conducted by commissions of sewers composed of local gentry and including the Dean and some prebendaries, which gave the Chapter a key role in the process and ensured a level of consensus between the Chapter, its tenants, and the inhabitants of the lands to be drained. In the early seventeenth century, however, grander schemes were proposed, using improved Dutch drainage technology, and encompassing the drainage of vast acreages of the fens, including some of Ely's own lands. The drainage undertakers effectively sidelined the commissions of sewers and the Ely Chapter. These ambitious schemes tended to be very unpopular with the inhabitants of the fens, who saw them as a means of enriching the undertakers at their own expense.[96] The Dean and Chapter were caught between the two sides of the disputes. The Chapter's relations with the undertakers were difficult, especially with Sir Miles Sandys and his son, Sir Miles Sandys the younger, who were lessees of their manors of Mepal and Sutton. The Sandyses were deeply unpopular with their own undertenants and they were already in dispute with the Dean and Chapter over rights of common in Mepal when, in 1622, they proposed the drainage of around 4,000 acres in Sutton. The scheme did not progress smoothly. The undertakers received less land in the enclosure award than they had expected, and blamed the Dean and Chapter. The poorer inhabitants of Sutton believed that the Chapter had conspired with the undertakers in robbing them of their commons, and in 1649 they petitioned Parliament for restitution.[97] In 1637 Chapter, the Bishop, some Cambridge colleges and several JPs petitioned the King, claiming that the process of allotting recently drained and enclosed land had been unfair. Although Charles agreed to investigate the matter, he upbraided all the petitioners as inciters of discontent.[98] These cases typify the largely unhappy experience of the Cathedral (and fenland society in general) with drainage schemes in the 1620s and 1630s.

Such vexations, however, paled alongside the greatest challenge to face the Cathedral before 1640, not only in its estate management, but to its very existence: the attempts to divest it of all its lands. The wealth of Ely and other cathedrals, coupled with their ambiguous position within a Protestant church, left them vulnerable to proposals to strip them of their assets. Sir Francis Walsingham, one of Elizabeth's secretaries of state, had the estates of Ely Cathedral valued as if he was considering divesting it of some or all of its lands – a procedure previously visited upon the estates of several sees, and one which would be used again on the See of Ely.[99] In the 1580s and 1590s claims were raised that a legal flaw in Henry VIII's refoundation of cathedral chapters meant

---

[96] Heal, 'Bishops of Ely', pp. 309–11; K. Lindley, *Fenland Riots and the English Revolution* (London, 1982); *Acts of the Privy Council, 1575–7*, p. 134; BL, Add. MS 33467, especially fos. 36, 48, 119, 131; PRO, C181/5, fos. 9ᵛ–11ᵛ, 20, 103, 175ᵛ–78. The Dean and prebendaries were appointed commissioners of sewers, but their wider powers were circumscribed by their inclusion on commissions for gaol delivery and oyer and terminer for the Isle of Ely only, and not for Cambridgeshire or other counties.

[97] PRO, C2/Jas I/E7/39; C2/Chas I/G34/8; C5/550/98; C21/E3/15; C21/E7/11; VCH, *Cambs.*, IV, pp. 149, 159; HMC, *7th Report* (London, 1879), p. 75; Lindley, *Fenland Riots*, pp. 38, 40.

[98] PRO, PC2/48, pp. 128–9; Lindley, *Fenland Riots*, pp. 93–4.

[99] P. Collinson, in Collinson, Ramsay and Sparks (eds.), *Canterbury Cathedral* (cit. in n. 1), p. 156; Northamptonshire Record Office, Finch-Hatton MS 105, fos. 1–3; Inner Temple Library, Petyt MS 538, fos. 122–4; F. Heal, 'The Tudors and Church Lands: Economic Problems of the Bishopric of Ely during the Sixteenth Century', *Economic History Review*, 2nd series, 26 (1973), pp. 198–217, at pp. 202–4.

that their lands still belonged to the Crown. Although Norwich was the first to be challenged, the uncertainty spread to others, including Ely. Some of Ely's tenants in Norfolk, probably influenced by the contest over Norwich's lands, stopped paying their rent to the Chapter on the grounds that the estate properly belonged to the Queen.[100] Ely's response was twofold. First, in 1587 and 1591 the Chapter procured new letters patent from the Crown, regranting them all the lands with which they had been previously endowed. Secondly, and in consort with other cathedral chapters, they obtained an Act of Parliament in 1593 confirming the validity of Henry's refoundation of cathedrals. Neither the new grants, nor the confirmatory statute, came cheap: the Chapter claimed that they had utterly wasted the stock of the church. To replenish it, the Chapter decreed that an extra half-year's rent would be levied on all their tenants in 1594 to replenish the church's reserves, and that any tenants who refused would not have their leases renewed in future.[101]

If some of the estate management – the fixed rents, the long leases, the lack of proper estate surveys – smacks of improvidence, the Chapter should not be accused of incompetence. Most Ely deans and prebendaries were, as Cambridge heads and fellows, already skilled in managing a corporation, its properties and revenues. Much of their policy was designed to produce an immediate return, with little thought for the future. No doubt it suited the Chapter members to swell their own incomes, if necessary at the expense of their successors, but their greed might also make the Cathedral look less of a prize to those who eyed its wealth and contemplated its disendowment. Matthew Parker and William May, two of the first prebendaries, had, as Master of Corpus and President of Queens' respectively, helped to save Cambridge colleges from the threat of dissolution under Henry VIII partly by adroitly manoeuvring college accounts to convince the King that they were insolvent bodies not worth suppressing.[102] The management of Ely's estates was conducted on not dissimilar lines. Furthermore, the century between the refoundation and the outbreak of the Civil War saw the Chapter's annual income rise from around £1,000 to about £1,300, while expenditure, though it too rose, was kept under control and the level of rent arrears did not grow out of hand. These were not insignificant achievements in a century when the survival of cathedrals was repeatedly challenged.[103]

The Cathedral and the wider world

If cathedrals were no more than 'dens of loitering lubbers' to their opponents, excrescences on the body of a church not yet fully reformed,[104] to their proponents

[100] Atherton *et al.* (eds.), *Norwich Cathedral* (cit. in n. 2), pp. 528–9, 670–1; PRO, E134/37 Eliz I/Hil 6, SP12/157, fo. 72.

[101] PRO, C66/1303, mm. 1–6, C66/1377, mm. 15–17; statute 35 Elizabeth c. 3; EDC 2/2A/1, p. 52; EDC 3/1/1, fo. 23.

[102] C.N.L. Brooke, *A History of Gonville and Caius College* (Woodbridge, 1985), p. 47. For Perne's care of university government and his possible roles in securing the 1570 statutes of Cambridge University and the 1576 corn rent act see: Collinson, 'Andrew Perne' (cit. in n. 32), p. 11; J. McConica (ed.), *The Collegiate University*, The History of the University of Oxford, III (Oxford, 1986), p. 542.

[103] EDC 3/3/69, 3/1/2.

[104] C. Cross, '"Dens of Loitering Lubbers": Protestant Protest against Cathedral Foundations, 1540–1640', in D. Baker (ed.), *Schism, Heresy and Religious Protest*, Studies in Church History, 9 (1972), pp. 231–7.

they had a vital role in the world beyond the cathedral and precinct: a chapter was the council of the bishop and guardian of the see during vacancies; a cathedral should dispense charity and promote education to assist the poor; and a cathedral was the mother church of the diocese, ensuring that the light of true religion spread through all its daughter churches.

The Chapter took its role as protector of the diocese seriously, refusing in 1569, for example, to confirm a reversionary lease on the Bishop's estate on the grounds that it would ruin the poor of that and neighbouring properties.[105] During the nineteen-year vacancy of the see until the consecration of Martin Heton in February 1600, while the Queen was happy to see the episcopal revenues diverted into her coffers, the Dean and Chapter's role as guardians of the temporalities of the see was even more carefully discharged. They produced lengthy objections to an arrangement by which Heton gave up many of the see's best properties to the Crown, before reluctantly confirming the transaction.[106] The long vacancy in fact made little difference to the life of the Chapter, beyond the temporary reversion to the Crown of the patronage of the prebends and the absence of episcopal visitations of the Cathedral.[107]

The Henrician statutes charged the Chapter with various charitable obligations, repeated in the Elizabethan revision. The Chapter was to maintain six almsmen and a grammar school of 24 boys under two masters, it was to distribute £20 to the poor every year and spend a similar sum on maintaining bridges and roads, and the duty of hospitality was laid upon the dean and prebendaries. These obligations represented a major work of welfare in a small town where the maintenance of communications across the fens was vital work.

Intended to be 'poor men pressed down by want and afflicted with poverty, wounded and maimed in war, or worn down with age, or otherwise weakened and reduced to poverty and wretchedness' the almsmen included maimed soldiers, at least one man who had been robbed of his possessions, and a smattering of former servants of the church.[108] Their stipend being small (£6 3s. 4d a year), in the 1560s at least the Chapter allowed them 'to go abroad for their better living'. As might be expected of such a mixed bunch, some absented themselves from the Cathedral completely, preferring life in London while still receiving their stipend.[109] The Chapter took more care over its other charitable obligations. Andrew Willet persuaded the Chapter to augment the stipends of three vicars of parishes whose impropriate tithes the Chapter held.[110] Various schemes were devised for distributing the £20 a year to the poor, with some of the money given to the indigent on the

---

[105] HMC, *Report on the Pepys Manuscripts* (London, 1911), pp. 157–8.

[106] BL, MS Lansdowne 54, fo. 74; HMC, *Marquess of Salisbury*, XIV, pp. 114–15; EDC 2/2A/1, p. 62. For the details of the vacancy and the exchange of 1599–1600, see Heal, 'Bishops of Ely', pp. 284–96.

[107] For a different verdict, claiming that, but for the long vacancy, Ely might have become 'the most distinguished and successful' of the new foundation cathedrals, see D.M. Owen, 'From Monastic House to Cathedral Chapter: The Experiences at Ely, Norwich, and Peterborough', in Marcombe and Knighton (eds.), *Close Encounters* (cit. in n. 1), p. 15.

[108] EDC 2/1/4 (c), fo. 8ᵛ, cap. 27; 2/12/8, fo. 34; 2/4/1, fos. 66, 112ᵛ; *LP Henry VIII*, XVI, p. 477, no. 985; *Cal. of State Papers, Domestic, 1595–7*, pp. 149–50, 399; *Cal. of State Papers, Domestic, 1598–1601*, p. 198; *Cal. of State Papers, Domestic, 1661–2*, p. 9.

[109] EDC 8A/1/13, fo. 11ᵛ; EDR B2/4, pp. 54, 56; EDC 3/5/2, acquittance of Richard Dudley, 1641–42. Compare EDR F5/41, fo. 176.

[110] Willet, *Synopsis Papismi* (cit. in n. 35), sig. [b4].

Chapter's estates but most going to the poor in Ely itself. Whatever means were used to distribute the money, it was generally accounted for, with any underspend in one year being carried forward to the next. There were also smaller sums for extraordinary occasions, such as the wedding of a daughter of a Cathedral servant.[111] The money for bridges and roads was similarly carefully shepherded.[112] The Dean and Chapter were responsible for maintaining the high bridge over the Ouse on the Ely-to-Stuntney road and five other bridges and causeways in the fens.[113] In addition the Dean appointed a bridgekeeper with a stipend of £2 13s. 4d a year; his job was to chain the high bridge at night, allow boats to pass and collect their tolls, beacon the causeway during floods and keep it repaired.[114] Although their management of bridges and causeways was sometimes criticised, the Dean and Chapter did take their responsibilities seriously and discharged them better than other local landowners discharged their similar obligations.[115]

Of all the Cathedral's charitable endeavours, the grammar school, founded in 1541 (replacing the Priory's almonry school) and given statutory basis in 1544, had the greatest local impact.[116] There were 24 foundation boys, maintained by the Chapter. The statutes decreed that they should be poor and friendless, but the Dean and Chapter, who in 1551 decided that the Dean should appoint to eight of the places and each prebendary to two, tended to appoint their own relatives or the sons of Cathedral officers and servants.[117] Other pupils were accepted on a fee-paying basis. The school witnessed a golden age under the mastership of James Speight (1562–96). In the 1570s Andrew Willet (the future prebendary) was sent to the school by his father, Prebendary Thomas Willet, and he later recalled that there were then over 300 pupils attending the school, while Dean Tyndall claimed that the school was then 'renowned for excellent teachinge and orderinge of yougth amongste the best free schooles of England'.[118] After Speight, however, the school went into a steep decline, reaching a nadir under William Pamplyn (1605–9). He was accused of a long catalogue of abuses: incompetence, extortion, absenteeism and failing to attend services in the Cathedral; there were allegations that his cross-dressing daughter encouraged the boys to wear her clothes; and claims that at night the townsfolk resorted to the school for dancing. Rapidly falling numbers and the complaints of parents led to Pamplyn's dismissal by the Dean.[119] Thereafter the fortunes of the school recovered as the schoolmasters were given additional responsibilities (minor canon, sacrist and the like) to augment their meagre stipend. The school was the only part of the Cathedral foundation to continue after 1649, and it appears to have functioned right through the 1650s.[120]

---

[111] CCCC, MS 120, pp. 339–40; EDC 3/1/1, fos. 1, 15, 24, 27, 30, 33, 106ᵛ, 114ᵛ, 132, 142ᵛ.

[112] EDC 3/1/1, fos. 22ᵛ, 25ᵛ, 28ᵛ, 31, 34ᵛ, 37, 43ᵛ, 45ᵛ, 48ᵛ, 98ᵛ; EDC 3/3/4, fo. 4d; EDC 3/3/10, fo. 14; EDC 3/3/13, fo. 11.

[113] EDC 8A/1/48.

[114] EDC 3/1/1, fos. 4ᵛ, 48ᵛ, 109, 112ᵛ, 146; EDC 8A/1/1, p. 126.

[115] PRO, E134/18 Chas I/Mich 4; *Calendar of State Papers, Domestic, 1638–9*, pp. 202–3.

[116] Owen and Thurley, *King's School*, pp. 1–3, 35–43. That the school existed from the refoundation of the Cathedral is suggested by the list of pupils in PRO, E314/13/1, mm. 3–4.

[117] Owen and Thurley, *King's School*, pp. 36, 43–4.

[118] *Ibid.*, pp. 4, 55; Bentham, *Ely*, II, p. 254; A. Willet, *An Harmonie upon the Second Booke of Samuel* (Cambridge, 1614), dedication.

[119] Owen and Thurley, *King's School*, pp. 55–7.

[120] *Ibid.*, pp. 5–6, 64–5; EDC 8A/1/48.

If, through its charitable and educational work, the Cathedral had a significant local impact, especially on Ely itself, in the field of religion the Cathedral stood apart from local and diocesan life. The monastic chapter at Ely had had little perceptible impact on the diocese,[121] and the refounded Dean and Chapter continued in a similar vein. The Cathedral was not used as a venue for the regular clerical synods which the bishops of Ely held until the 1580s.[122] Neither the Reformation nor its reverse under Mary was led from the Cathedral. When Bishop Goodrich wanted the gospel to be spread to his parishioners, he relied on the appointment of noted Protestants to parochial livings, rather than to the Cathedral, to awaken his people.[123] There was one attempt to place the Cathedral at the heart of the Marian reaction in the diocese: two Wisbech men were convicted for heresy before four judges, including Prebendary John Fuller (also Chancellor of the diocese) and Dean Steward, and were burned at Ely on 9 October 1555, but otherwise the Chapter gave no clear lead to the diocese.[124] The story was much the same after 1559. The Cathedral played little role in the reimposition of Protestantism in the 1560s and 1570s, or in the emerging disputes over the nature of the Elizabethan settlement such as Archbishop Whitgift's suppression of Puritan nonconformity in the diocese in 1583–4.[125] Even under James I and Charles I, when cathedrals all over England developed as the home for Arminian sacramentalism, it was not Ely Cathedral which provided liturgical and theological leadership within the diocese. Contemporaries looked for inspiration to the episcopal chapel of both Andrewes and John Buckeridge in Ely House, London, or to the college chapels in Cambridge, but not to the Cathedral.[126]

More surprisingly still, the Cathedral failed to provide a lead in the suppression of heresy under Elizabeth. In the second half of the sixteenth century, Cambridgeshire and the fens were one of the centres of activity of the Family of Love, a shadowy heretical group which claimed that scripture should be interpreted allegorically, humans could achieve perfection by spiritual 'illumination', only Familists could be saved, and that the true godly could lie and dissemble to avoid persecution. Though there were probably never more than a few hundred Familists at any one time, their radical creed found converts in and around Ely. Although some Elizabethan clergy attacked the Family of Love with the vigour and persistence of convinced heresy hunters, Familists met a more ambiguous response from Ely Cathedral. There were probably more Familists in the village of Balsham in Cambridgeshire (where the Rector was none other than Andrew Perne, Dean of Ely) than anywhere else in the world. When, in 1574, their existence was

[121] Owen, 'From Monastic House to Cathedral Chapter' (cit. in n. 107), p. 4.

[122] D.M. Owen, 'Synods in the Diocese of Ely in the latter Middle Ages and the Sixteenth Century', in G.J. Cuming (ed.), *Studies in Church History*, 3 (Leiden, 1966), pp. 217–22.

[123] F. Heal, 'The Parish Clergy and the Reformation in the Diocese of Ely', *Proc. CAS*, 66 (1977), pp. 141–63, at p. 151. Dorothy Owen has shown how the machinery of synod and visitation, in which the Cathedral played only a very minor role, was used to bring the Reformation to the diocese: D.M. Owen, 'The Enforcement of the Reformation in the Diocese of Ely', *Miscellanea Historiae Ecclesiasticae*, 3 (1970), pp. 167–74.

[124] J. Foxe, *Acts and Monuments*, ed. G. Townsend and S.R. Cattley, 8 vols. (London, 1837–41), VII, pp. 402–6. The preacher at the burning was Thomas Peacock, who in the following year was appointed a prebendary of Ely.

[125] P. Collinson, *The Elizabethan Puritan Movement* (London, 1967), pp. 243–72.

[126] PRO, C115/N9/8848–9; Welsby, *Lancelot Andrewes* (cit. in n. 67), pp. 129–30; Tyacke, *Anti-Calvinists* (cit. in n. 62), pp. xviii, p. 71, and figure 1; Tyacke, 'Andrewes and the Myth of Anglicanism' (cit. in n. 64), p. 25.

brought to his attention, Perne launched an investigation but quickly satisfied himself with their outward show of conformity and left them undisturbed. The suppression and persecution of the Family of Love was left to others. There were Familists in Ely city too, likewise little bothered by the ecclesiastical authorities. One of them may have been Robert Hinde, under-master at the Cathedral grammar school, curate of Stuntney and minor canon of the Cathedral.[127] The relationship between the Family of Love and Ely Cathedral is unclear, and may always remain so, but it was somewhat different from the model of a cathedral as the promoter of 'true religion' and a beacon of orthodoxy shining its pure gospel light into the dark corners of the diocese that many expected.[128]

One of the principal reasons why Ely Cathedral figured so little in diocesan life was that it remained overshadowed by Cambridge University. Since most of the Chapter were Cambridge fellows, and many of them heads of Cambridge colleges, they played out their politicking and theological disputes at the university. In 1564, for example, a set disputation was held before the Queen on the relative authority of scripture and the Church. One side of the debate was led by Matthew Hutton, prebendary of Ely, the other by Andrew Perne, Dean of Ely, and the contest was chaired by Richard Cox, Bishop of Ely. It quickly turned into an unedifying contest and Perne came close to denouncing Hutton as a heretic.[129] Though the main actors were three Ely Cathedral men, the disputation was held in Cambridge University and not at the Cathedral. Between the 1540s and the 1640s it was Ely, and not Cambridge, which was the ivory tower insulated from the outside world.

Great scholars tended not to do their greatest work at Ely. John Bois, having helped translate the Bible and edit St John Chrysostom's works, retired in 1628 to Ely where he busied himself with Cathedral administration, not academic work. Andrew Willet, 'the wonder of the world' in Joseph Hall's judgement, spent eight hours a day in his study and produced a new learned tome every six months, but it was at his rectory of Barley, Hertfordshire, not his prebend at Ely, that he undertook his work[130] (Plate 19c). From Elizabeth's reign onwards, prebendaries came to Ely – if they came at all – for a break, for rest and relaxation from the rigours of university life, and not to work for the inspiration and enlightenment of the fens or the defence of the national church.

If the Cathedral did not dominate the diocese, it did command the city of Ely. In such a small place, more than a tenth of the 400 householders said to reside there in 1563 would have held a Cathedral office; if those with other connections to the Cathedral – the workmen and domestic servants – are included along with the household and staff of the bishop, then the control of the church over the city is clear. Furthermore, there was no counterweight to the Cathedral or Bishop. Ely was not an incorporated town and municipal authority lay in the hands of the Dean and Chapter's manor court of Ely Porta, the Bishop's manor court of Ely Barton, and the feoffees of Thomas Parsons's

---

[127] C. Marsh, 'Piety and Persuasion in Elizabethan England: The Church of England meets the Family of Love', in N. Tyacke (ed.), *England's Long Reformation 1500–1800* (London, 1998), pp. 141–65; C. Marsh, *The Family of Love in English Society, 1550–1630* (Cambridge, 1994), pp. 171, 193–4, 213–17, 265–87. I am grateful to Dr Marsh for discussions about the Family of Love, Perne and Hinde.

[128] W.T. Mellows (ed.), *The Foundation of Peterborough Cathedral A.D. 1541* (Northamptonshire Record Society, 13, 1941), p. 104.

[129] Collinson, 'Andrew Perne' (cit. in n. 32), pp. 7–9.

[130] *DNB*.

charity: the Bishop, Dean and Archdeacon, and nine others.[131] The Dean and Chapter were patrons of the only two livings in Ely (Holy Trinity and St Mary's) to which they usually presented their own minor canons, and they ensured that there were no sermons in those churches; instead, all the parishioners were to troop into the Cathedral nave after Sunday morning service in their own churches for a sermon. The Dean and Chapter thereby ensured attendance at the Cathedral, and paid an officer to enforce 'good order in sermon time'.[132]

Ely thus escaped the jurisdictional disputes between chapter and corporation which racked so many other cathedral cities,[133] but there was some opposition to the Cathedral and its policies within the town. On New Year's Day 1638, a great crowd gathered on the green in front of the Cathedral at the time of the service, and made 'a great noyse and disturbance . . . by the Roasting of a catt tied to a spitt . . . and there a Fier made about it one the Greene'. This was noted as 'a great prophanation . . . both of day and the place', and was taken at the time as an intended criticism of the ceremonialism of the Cathedral.[134] There were also criticisms about the way the prebendaries let their houses in the College, with complaints not only that some of their lessees were usurers or of evil fame, but also that the residents of the College claimed exemption from the duties incumbent upon other townsfolk.[135] That most of the complaints about the conduct of sermons in the Cathedral, the ways in which the Dean and Chapter restricted and regulated other religious expression, including parochial life, in Ely, and the running of Parsons's charity, only surfaced in petitions to Parliament in 1641 as the hierarchy of the Church of England began to totter, bears witness to the controlling hand of the Cathedral in Ely, where economic, political and religious power were firmly under ecclesiastical control.[136]

1640–49: the lingering death of Ely Cathedral

From the opening of the Long Parliament in November 1640, Ely, in common with all other English and Welsh cathedrals, suffered a slow, lingering death. Although the Act abolishing cathedrals was not passed until 1649, the writing had been on the wall for deans and chapters since 1640. Attempts by the Church to return itself to the days of King James, such as the reforms proposed by a committee including Prebendary Ralph Brownrigg, failed,[137] and Ely, together with all other cathedrals, was battered and assaulted both in London and locally. Bishop Wren was under parliamentary investiga-

---

[131] VCH, Cambs., IV, pp. 42–3; Holmes, Cromwell's Ely (cit. in n. 47), p. 14; HMC, 4th Report (London, 1874), p. 84. The total population of Ely was probably around 1,800 people.

[132] EDR, B2/31, fo. 108; EDC 3/1/2, fo. 53; Holmes, Cromwell's Ely, pp. 24–5. The nave may also have been used for baptisms: when a new font was erected in 1693 it was placed in the nave, possibly on the site of the former font: G. Cobb, English Cathedrals: The Forgotten Centuries (London, 1980), pp. 85, 91.

[133] C.F. Patterson, 'Corporations, Cathedrals and the Crown: Local Dispute and Royal Interest in Early Stuart England', History, 85 (2000), pp. 546–71.

[134] EDR D2/51, fo. 15.

[135] EDR B2/31, fo. 160; Holmes, Cromwell's Ely, p. 24.

[136] Holmes, Cromwell's Ely, pp. 24–5; HMC, 4th Report, pp. 70, 84.

[137] A Copy of the Proceedings of some Worthy and Learned Divines, appointed by the Lords to Meet at the Bishop of Lincolns in Westminster, touching Innovations in the Doctrine and Discipline of the Church of England (London, 1641).

tion from December 1640: he was voted by Parliament unfit to hold office in July 1641 and was sent to the Tower the following December.[138] The Cathedral, too, came under attack,[139] and in 1641 spent £8 8s. 8d defending itself,[140] partly from the general attack on cathedrals, and partly from the criticisms of about a hundred townsfolk that it was a parasite on the religious and civic life of Ely. In August 1641 the House of Lords, having heard the petitioners and their witnesses (who included Oliver Cromwell), warned that it intended 'to take a course for a generall reformacion of the manner of service' in the Cathedral and also to order 'a fitting enlargment of allowances to Curates'.[141] Further problems soon followed for Dean Fuller, who was briefly imprisoned in the autumn of 1641 on the information of his London parishioners that he was a 'popish innovator', and again in July 1642 for reading a royal declaration from his London pulpit.[142] In 1642, though, there was not the attempt to purify the Cathedral of the trumpery of popery that some cathedrals endured.[143] The column of the Parliament's troops which entered Ely on 30 August 1642 came not to purge the Cathedral of its altar rails or organ, but to seize the Bishop (only recently released from the Tower), and the arms that he had allegedly been stockpiling.[144]

Until the autumn of 1643 the Cathedral functioned normally under increasingly difficult circumstances. Although the organ was repaired on 2 February 1643, on 25 March the Dean and Chapter expended 18d 'taking downe the Orgaines and Quier Cloathes'. This action may have been a gesture towards Puritan concerns about the worship, but services continued otherwise little changed for the remainder of the year. Monthly communions certainly continued until at least October 1643, and boys continued to be made choristers as places fell vacant until Christmas 1643.[145] The second half of 1643, however, saw Parliament's army tighten its grip on the Isle of Ely: following a royalist uprising in the Isle in May, a permanent garrison was established at Ely, with Cromwell as governor of the Isle.[146] Religious reformation followed in the train of the troops. It was in 1643, according to an entry in the Wilburton parish register, that the Book of Common Prayer 'was cut out and torn in pieces in all our churches in the Isle of Ely'. At the same time it was alleged that Cromwell had promised

---

[138] *DNB*. Antipathy to Wren in Ely, however, was muted compared to that from Cambridge and Norwich: *Articles of Impeachment of the Commons assembled in Parliament . . . against Matthew Wren* ([London], 1641); BL, MS Egerton 1048.

[139] The story in *The Arminian Haltered* ([London], 1641) that John Hobson, prebendary of Ely, 'one of the greatest Arminians in this Kingdome' had hanged himself in despair in July 1641 was false: there was no such person at Ely. But when mud was thrown, some of it was likely to stick.

[140] EDC 3/1/1, fo. 185ᵛ.

[141] HMC, *4th Report*, p. 70; Holmes, *Cromwell's Ely*, pp. 24–36. The details of the Lords' judgement are unknown.

[142] *DNB*; *Petition and Articles exhibited in Parliament against Dr Fuller* (cit. in n. 68).

[143] S.E. Lehmberg, *Cathedrals under Siege: Cathedrals in English Society, 1600–1700* (Exeter, 1996), pp. 26–7; Atherton *et al.* (eds.), *Norwich Cathedral* (cit. in n. 2), pp. 552–4.

[144] C. Holmes, *The Eastern Association in the English Civil War* (Cambridge, 1974), p. 55; *Joyfull Newes from the Isle of Ely* ([London], 1642). It has been alleged that the Chapter took steps to defend the Cathedral (Gibbon, 'Account Book' (cit. in n. 72), p. 223), but the expenditure adduced, of ironwork added to doors and fencing in the College, was probably merely routine maintenance.

[145] EDC 3/5/2 (1642–3); EDC 3/8/1. The same quantity of wine (three pints) was purchased for each eucharist as before.

[146] Holmes, *Eastern Association*, p. 73; HMC, *7th Report*, p. 550; B. Coward, *Oliver Cromwell* (Harlow, 1991), p. 26.

to purge the Isle of 'all the wretches and ungodly men' to make it 'a place for God to dwell in', and that consequently the Isle became a haven of sectaries and 'a meere Amsterdam'.[147]

The years between the autumn of 1643 and the spring of 1649 saw the gradual disintegration of the Cathedral. The audit in October 1643 was not held, probably because estates had been recently sequestered, and only vestigial accounts were kept thereafter.[148] Reformation of the services soon followed. On 10 January 1644 Cromwell wrote to William Hitch, the vicar choral and precentor (who oversaw the daily conduct of services) commanding him on the pretext of avoiding violence to amend the worship in the Cathedral:

> Mr Hitch, least the Souldiers should in any tumultuarie or disorderly way attempt the Reformation of your Cathedrall Church; I requier you to forbeare altogether your Quier seruice soe vnedifyinge, and offensiue, and this as you will answere it, if any disorder should arise thereupon. I advise you to Cattechise and reade, and expound the scriptures to the people not doubting but the Parliament with the advise of the Assemblie of Divines will in due tyme direct you farther. I desier the sermons may be where usually they have beene, but more frequent.

The letter and its warnings were ignored:

> Mr Hitch, notwithstanding this letter, continuing to Officiate in the church of Ely as before, Oliver Cromwell (with about forty soldiers or more armed with swords and guns, and a numerous rabble of disaffected people) came into the Quire with his hat on his head, and said thus to Mr Hitch as he was reading prayers viz. I am a man under authority, and am commanded to dismiss this assembly: upon which words Mr Hitch gave over reading. But then Oliver and his company, walking towards the Communion table, Mr Hitch proceeded in the prayers: And then Oliver in a rage coming down againe and laying his hand upon his sword, spake thus to Mr Hitch, viz leave off your fooling, and come down, and then drove him and all the assembly out of the church.

The story as we have it was told in 1707 by Thomas Bullis, an elderly lay clerk, who had been a fifteen-year-old chorister and an eye witness in 1644. It shows every sign of having been reworked and influenced by later accounts of Cromwell's dismissal of the Rump Parliament in 1653; Bullis had, no doubt, often dined out on the story in Restoration Ely.[149] There is, nevertheless, no reason to dismiss the story.

A reformed service, with the emphasis on the Word, continued at the Cathedral.[150]

---

[147] VCH, *Cambs.*, II, p. 181; J. Bruce and D. Musson (eds.), *The Quarrell between the Earl of Manchester and Oliver Cromwell*, Camden Society, 2nd ser., 12 (1875), pp. 73–4.

[148] EDC 3/1/3, p. 30; EDC 3/5/2; A.G. Matthews, *Walker Revised* (Oxford, 1948), p. 6.

[149] Bodl., MS J. Walker c. 3, fos. 368–9; EDC 3/8/1. Several versions of Cromwell's letter survive, each slightly different. I have preferred that copied in 1707 by Francis Fern from the original (now apparently lost) then said to be in the keeping of William Clark of Ely, for Fern added 'I have endeavoured to imitate Cromwell's spelling, and the dashes of his pen'. See also BL, MS Stowe 154, fo. 12; *Gentleman's Magazine*, lviii, pt 1 (1788), pp. 225, 318–19; J. Walker, *An Attempt towards recovering an Account of the Numbers and Sufferings of the Clergy* (2 parts, London, 1714), II, p. 23; *Writings and Speeches of Oliver Cromwell*, ed. Abbott, I, pp. 270–1.

[150] The story found in several histories that in January 1644 Cromwell locked the doors, pocketing the key, and that the Cathedral remained closed until the Restoration, is wrong: B.E. Dorman, *The Story of Ely and its Cathedral* (Ely, 1945), p. 47; Lehmberg, *Cathedrals under Siege* (cit. in n. 143), p. 39.

The Lady Chapel continued as the parish church of Holy Trinity throughout the 1640s and 1650s, with Hitch as minister until his death in 1658.[151] The radical divine William Sedgwick was appointed lecturer at the Cathedral in 1644, whence he got the name 'the apostle of the Isle'; from 1647 he was also known as 'Doomsday Sedgwick' after Christ appeared to him in his house in the College to proclaim the imminent end of the world.[152]

The other members of the Cathedral were already living in end times. The last recorded Chapter meeting was held on 2 January 1644, with only two prebendaries present, one of whom (John Bois) died twelve days later.[153] Although Wren presented John Montfort to the vacant stall, it is unlikely that he ever came to Ely.[154] From Lady Day 1644 the prebendaries' houses in the College began to fall to others.[155] Dean Fuller vacated the deanery on his presentation by the King (itself ineffective) to that of Durham in March 1646; the King then presented William Beale to the deanery, but he was never installed. Charles I was merely rearranging the deck chairs on the *Titanic*.[156] An ever-decreasing band of the Cathedral's minor officers soldiered on at Ely, largely because they had nowhere else to go, with nothing to do but draw their payments from Dean Caesar's benefaction and pray for the payment of their stipends out of the sequestered estates of the Cathedral.[157] By the time that deans, chapters and cathedrals were abolished by Parliament on 29 May 1649, Ely Cathedral had faded away like the Cheshire cat.

Ely's estates were then surveyed by the government and sold. The grander houses in the College were taken over by others: Cromwell had the deanery, his brother-in-law John Disbrowe one of the prebendal houses; by 1660 two of the prebendal houses had been partially converted into shops.[158] The cloister was demolished, and its timber and lead, valued at £89 14s. 4d. in April 1652, sold.[159] The Cathedral church did not, however, suffer as much as others. In March 1648 Parliament had described the Cathedral as being in a 'ruinous condition' and had ordered that an ordinance be drafted for its demolition and the sale of the materials 'for the relief of sick and maimed soldiers, widows and orphans'.[160] Nothing came of the order, and although the survival of the building is often ascribed to Cromwell's protection, it was more likely a combination of uncertainty, apathy, and the continued use of parts of its buildings by Holy Trinity and the free school.[161] Although the ornaments, furnishings and

---

[151] Matthews, *Walker Revised*, p. 82. Hitch's stipend was augmented by Parliament in 1647.

[152] *DNB*; C.H. Firth (ed.), *The Clarke Papers*, volume I (Camden Society, 2nd series, 49, 1891), p. 4; A.G. Matthews, *Calamy Revised* (Oxford, 1934), p. 432; Atkinson, *Ely Monastery*, p. 196.

[153] EDC 2/2A/1, p. 147; Le Neve, *Fasti, 1541–1857*, VII, *Ely* (cit. in n. 8), pp. 15–16.

[154] EDR F/5/41, fos. 124–5. Wren, imprisoned in the Tower and in defiance of reality, continued presenting to vacant prebends throughout the later 1640s and 1650s: Le Neve, *Fasti, 1541–1857*, VII, *Ely*, pp. 16, 19, 26, 28.

[155] EDC 8A/1/13, fos. 5, 9.

[156] *DNB*; Le Neve, *Fasti, 1541–1857*, VII, *Ely*, p. 11. Beale was formerly Master of St John's College, Cambridge; he had been deprived by Parliament in 1642 and was only recently released from three years' imprisonment for attempting to send college plate to the King.

[157] EDC 3/8/1; Matthews, *Walker Revised*, p. 6. Dean Caesar's benefaction was last paid at Michaelmas 1647.

[158] EDC 8A/1/7, pp. 18–19, 22–3; EDC 6/1B/1660/1, list of tenants 'that dwell about the Minster of Ely', 1660.

[159] EDC 6/2/37.

[160] *Journals of the House of Commons, 1547–1761*, 28 vols. (London, 1742–61), V, p. 478. For the damage done at other cathedrals see Lehmberg, *Cathedrals under Siege* (cit. in. n. 143), pp. 26–51.

[161] Gibbon, 'Account Book' (cit. in n. 72), 225. Despite various proposals, no English cathedral was, in fact, demolished during the Interregnum.

communion plate were either sold or stolen, neglect, not deliberate destruction, was the main enemy of the Cathedral church. With no maintenance work being carried on, the lime house, formerly used for storing building materials, was converted into a house.[162] In the late 1650s the Cathedral was described as being in a 'falling condition',[163] while John Gauden, only months before the Restoration, thought it 'horridly desolate and ruined' and fitting of Christ's last words on the Cross, 'Eli, Eli, lama sabachthani'.[164]

For Thomas Fuller, writing in the late 1650s, Ely Cathedral, often seen as the 'great ship of the fens', represented the ship of the Christian soul, buffeted and tossed about in the storms of the world, but journeying to its final destination in the hope of ultimate safety:

> in the lanthorn when the bells ring, the woodwork thereof shaketh, and gapeth and exactly chocketh into the joynts again; the lively emblem of the sincere Christian, who hath fear and trembling, yet stands firmly fixt on the basis of a true faith.[165]

The irony is that when Fuller visited Ely, the bells in the Lantern no longer rang and the fabric, then an empty shell, shook and gaped more than ever. The sight of the derelict and abandoned building was a more powerful image, a more spiritual experience, and more redolent of meaning than the inhabited church had been for a century. In the mid-sixteenth century Ely Cathedral had been an institution in want of a purpose. In the mid seventeenth century the building had, in its death, finally found a function.

---

[162] Holmes, *Cromwell's Ely* (cit. in n. 47), p. 54; EDC 6/1B/1660/1, list of tenants, 1660. Some lead from the Cathedral was, however, stolen in 1650: *Journals of the House of Commons*, VI, p. 493; EDC 8A/1/13, fo. 2.

[163] T. Fuller, *The Worthies of England*, ed. J. Freeman (London, 1952), pp. 46, 49. Thomas Fuller (1608–61) was a royalist and cleric who in the 1640s was ejected from some of his livings, including his prebend at Salisbury Cathedral: *DNB*; Matthews, *Walker Revised*, pp. 47–8.

[164] J. Gauden, *A Sermon preached in the Temple-Chapel, at the Funeral of . . . Dr. Brounrig* (London, (1660), pp. 157–8; the epistle dedicatory is dated 1 January 1659 [*i.e.* 1660]. Matthew 27:46, 'My God, my God, why hast thou forsaken me?' Half a century before, Sir Thomas Tresham had also been unable to resist the pun on Ely: HMC, *Various Collections*, III, p. xlii.

[165] Fuller, *Worthies*, p. 49.

Dean and Chapter Restored 1660–1836

PETER MEADOWS

Of the pre-Civil War Chapter there was not a single survivor. Only Bishop Matthew Wren remained, released from the Tower of London, where he had been confined since 1644 (Colour pl. 25c). He had not been inactive there, and into the 1650s he had continued to make appointments to the Chapter (notionally, of course, since the Cathedral establishment had been dissolved in 1644). The three prebendaries who had thus been pre-selected were Stephen Hall (1st stall, 1660–1), Vicar of Fordham and Fellow of Jesus College; Richard Ball (8th stall, 1660–65, 7th stall, 1665–84), Fellow of Pembroke College and Rector of Wilby and Westerfield, Suffolk, both appointed in 1652; and William Holder (3rd stall, 1660–98), Rector of Bletchingdon, Oxfordshire and a former Fellow of Pembroke.[1] Two of the minor canons and three of the eight lay clerks survived the Commonwealth, and were reinstated in 1660.[2]

Bishop Wren made some significant Chapter appointments in 1660. Henry Brunsell (4th stall, 1660–79), of Magdalen College, Oxford, had trained as a physician and changed to divinity in 1660. John Pearson (5th stall, 1660–1, 1st stall, 1661–73), whom Wren also made Master of Jesus College, was, in Bentham's words, 'sufficiently known in the learned world, by his excellent Exposition of the Creed'.[3] Wren's second son Thomas Wren (5th stall, 1661–79) had, like Brunsell, trained as a physician, and been ordained in 1660: he was also Rector of Willingham (1662) and Archdeacon of Ely (1663). Laurence Womack (6th stall, 1660–86) was Rector of Horninger and Boxford, Suffolk, and Archdeacon of Suffolk; in 1683 he became Bishop of St. David's, retaining his prebend. Joseph Beaumont (7th stall, 1660–5, 8th stall 1665–99) was a Fellow of Peterhouse who had been ejected in 1644: in 1662 Wren made him Master of Jesus College, and in 1663, after an irregular election, Master of Peterhouse.

---

[1] Bishop Wren's register was in existence at least until the late 18th century, but is now lost. Several transcripts were made from it, the most complete being that by James Bentham (CUL, MS Add. 2953).

[2] Reginald Gibbon, 'Small Beer of History', *Church Quarterly Review*, cxvii (1933–4), pp. 100–116, at p. 101.

[3] John Pearson (1613–86), Prebendary of Salisbury Cathedral and Rector of Thorington, Suffolk, was a supporter of Charles I and lost his preferments in the King's cause. He lived a life of study in London until the Restoration, and from 1654 to 1660 was (unpaid) lecturer at St Clement's, Eastcheap, where he preached a series of discourses which were published in 1659 as *An Exposition of the Creed*. It ran through many editions; Pearson last made alterations to the 3rd edition, 1669. In 1660 he was made a Canon of Ely, Archdeacon of Surrey, and Master of Jesus College, Cambridge. He was a leading figure in the Savoy Conference, 1661, in that year became Lady Margaret Professor of Divinity at Cambridge, and in 1662 was appointed Master of Trinity College. He became Bishop of Chester in 1673, and was buried in his cathedral in 1686.

This Chapter provided a period of stability in the 1660s and 1670s, and Holder and Beaumont lived until 1698 and 1699 respectively. They reflected very much Matthew Wren's High Church, Laudian convictions, and also his long and close connexion with Cambridge, where he had been President of Pembroke College and then Master of Peterhouse in the 1620s. The canons also provided examples of the typical means of obtaining a prebend which persisted until the mid-nineteenth-century reforms. Most canons were either relations of the bishop, or of the bishop's patron, or had been the bishop's chaplain. Many were fellows or masters of Cambridge colleges – especially Jesus, Peterhouse and St John's, where the bishop had rights of appointment or was visitor.

Although none of the canons was a pre-1644 survivor, almost until the end of the seventeenth century men appointed to the Chapter had begun their careers before the Civil War, and so can be said to have been partly conditioned by their experiences before and during that period of upheaval for the Church of England.

The deanery was a different matter. The appointment lay with the Crown. The first three Deans after the Restoration died in rapid succession: Richard Love, Master of Corpus[4] (Dean, September 1660 – January 1661); Henry Ferne, Master of Trinity[5] (Dean, February 1661 – March 1662); and Edward Martin, President of Queens'[6] (Dean, April 1662). No record of Chapter meetings between December 1660 and June 1662 has survived, so we cannot tell from that source how decisive these Deans' impact was on the Cathedral. Francis Wilford, Master of Corpus (Dean, 1662–7), was an assiduous attender, apparently never missing a Chapter meeting.[7] Amongst other things he pressed forward the work of Cathedral repair. The east end was restored, and the north aisle was refaced in 1662. The west tower was found to be dangerous and was

---

[4] Richard Love (1596–1661), son of an apothecary, was born in the parish of Great St Mary's, Cambridge. About 1628 he was made a chaplain to King Charles I, who recommended him for the mastership of Corpus Christi College, Cambridge, in 1632. Love managed to keep his mastership and preferments during the Common-wealth, and at the Restoration he recommended himself to Charles II by publishing two Latin congratulatory addresses, in which he excused his acquiescence during the Interregnum. He died at Corpus and was buried there.

[5] Henry Ferne (1602–62) was a Fellow of Trinity College, Cambridge, and in 1641 became Archdeacon of Leicester. At Leicester in 1642 he preached so impressively before the King that Charles made him a royal chaplain, and Ferne published his *Case of Conscience Touching Rebellion* (Cambridge, 1642). Attending the King at Oxford, he issued several pamphlets defending his first publication. Charles gave him a patent for the mastership of Trinity when it should next become vacant. Ferne was the last chaplain to preach before the King, at Carisbrooke Castle. He lived quietly during the Commonwealth, and published a series of pamphlets chiefly in defence of the reformed Church against the Roman Catholic. In 1660 Charles II made him Master of Trinity. In February 1662 he was consecrated Bishop of Chester, but died on 16 March 1662, and was buried in Westminster Abbey.

[6] Edward Martin (c.1588–1662), was a Fellow of Queens' College, Cambridge, 1617, and in 1627 a chaplain to Archbishop Laud. In 1632 he was elected President of Queens'. In 1642, at the start of the Civil War, he was active in the King's cause, and collected silver from the Cambridge colleges for the King. For this he was arrested, imprisoned, and deprived of his preferments. He suffered great poverty and hardship (John Walker, *Sufferings of the Clergy* (London, 1714), part II, pp. 154–6), and about 1652 fled to France, and later lived in Utrecht. In 1660 his preferments were restored. In 1661 he was one of the managers of the Savoy Conference to settle the contents of the Prayer Book. He became Dean in 1662 but died three days afterwards, on 28 April, and was buried in Queens' Chapel. He was the author of several books and pamphlets.

[7] Francis Wilford (c.1614–67), a Fellow of Trinity College, Cambridge from 1633, was appointed a chaplain to King Charles II in 1660; through the influence of Gilbert Sheldon, Bishop of London, he was recommended for the mastership of Corpus Christi College, Cambridge, and in 1661 was made Archdeacon of Bedford. He died in 1667 and was buried in Corpus Chapel. See Gibbon, 'Small Beer of History' (cit. in n. 2), p. 101.

restored at great cost. Perhaps Dean Wilford's hot temper (Bentham described him as 'arbitrary'[8]) pushed the work forward.[9]

Robert Mapletoft (Dean, 1667–77), once a chaplain to Bishop Wren, and Master of Pembroke College (1664), succeeded Wilford. Mapletoft lived hospitably at Ely as Dean, and was renowned for his acts of charity. He also continued work on the west tower; and to this work Bishop Benjamin Laney, Mapletoft's contemporary at Pembroke, gave £100, though faced with heavy expense in restoring the episcopal Palace at Ely. On his death in 1677 Mapletoft left 400 acres of wash-land[10] at Coveney to increase the lay clerks' stipends, and bequeathed to the Cathedral his library with £100 to fit up a room.[11] This was the beginning of the Cathedral library enjoined on the Dean and Chapter by the 1666 statutes. It was housed in the partitioned eastern aisle of the south transept, where it remained, augmented over the years, until 1970.[12]

Since 1541, the deanery had usually been held with the mastership of a Cambridge college, and this practice continued after 1660. Only two deans – Lambe and Allix – were not also heads of house in the period 1660–1836.

In common with other cathedrals, the restored Chapter in 1660 was faced with three main tasks: the restoration of Cathedral services and music; the repair of the Cathedral and College fabric; and the recovery of lands, rights and revenues. The first two tasks are covered in other chapters of this book. The third was perhaps the most crucial, since it was the revenue produced by the manors, rectories and other estates which enabled repairs and restoration to go on. It is perhaps slightly surprising, therefore, that the new order book, begun in 1660, makes no mention of the upheavals of the past twenty years, nor offers pious thanks to God for the Chapter's restoration. The first item of business was the granting of a minor place, and then most of the decisions were to do with property and the granting of leases, with the attendant fines which produced a large income for division amongst the Dean and Chapter.[13]

The extent of the dispersal of Chapter property had been such that the houses of the College itself had been occupied by interlopers, and two unauthorised tenants – Bell and Gotobed – had to be evicted. The Chapter Bailiff was ordered to survey 'the tenements by the churchyard' and report 'how many there bee of them, who nowe are tenants in them, and upon what termes'.[14]

---

[8] Bentham, *Ely*, p. 235.

[9] The bill of Robert Minchin, contractor for the tower and other works, was for £1066 7*s.* (EDC 3/1/2, memorandum of expenses, 1669).

[10] Grazing land which was liable to flood in winter.

[11] Robert Mapletoft (1609–77) was elected a Fellow of Pembroke College, Cambridge, in 1631, and was ejected in 1644 as a royalist and malignant. He lived quietly during the Commonwealth. In 1660 he was made Subdean of Lincoln Cathedral and in 1664 Master of Pembroke. He died in 1667 and was buried in Pembroke Chapel near Bishop Wren, his friend and patron.

[12] Thomas Hitch (1622–86), precentor, sacrist and from 1676 curate of Holy Trinity, was first librarian, and was 'to see the Library swept out and the Books rub'd or clean'd over, as often as he shall judge it necessary', and was allowed to borrow: EDC 2/2A/2, p. 144.

[13] EDC 2/2A/2. It was not until 1662 that Chapter meetings were properly recorded in the book, and the lack of record of the first two years after the Restoration is puzzling, since many important decisions must have been made then.

[14] EDC 2/2A/2, p. 8. The result of the survey is probably 'A note of the Tenants names that dwell about the Minister of Ely 1660' (EDC 6/1B/1660/1), which includes 'In the Mr of the Vialls chamber Goodman Gotobed. In the Lecturor Lodging Robert Bell'.

In the event, the recovery of the Chapter estates went quite smoothly. The King's letter of 22 June 1660 requiring all cathedral chapters to reduce leases from three lives to 21 years was duly received at Ely,[15] and the guidelines set down by King and Parliament in late summer 1660, that pre-1644 tenants and purchasers should be favoured where possible, and that interlopers who were ejected should receive compensation, seem to have been adhered to, with only a few recourses to the Royal Commission that was set up in October 1660 to arbitrate and adjudicate.[16]

It was thus vitally important that the Chapter knew what their rights were, and since the archives had been taken to London, along with those of other cathedrals, when their estates were ordered by Parliament to be sold in 1649, part of the task was to recover those records. Dorothy Owen has told the story of the bringing home of the records in 1660, not without loss, or dispersal to the wrong cathedrals.[17] And when they were returned, they were supplemented by surveys of most properties, which Parliament had ordered to be made in 1649, prior to their sale. This was valuable additional evidence in the process of reclaiming what were often scattered parcels of land.[18]

Before the Chapter could recover their property, they had to prove title to it. Hence the importance of the records. During his short tenure of the deanery, Dean Love was busy in summer 1660 in making his own search in London, in company with John Pegg, who had been deeply involved in making the Parliamentary surveys. Among the records recovered were 'surveys of the Vinyards in Holborn, the bell in Newgate, and for 2 tenements in Grace Church street, and . . . a Copy of a contract, of the baylywicke, and liberty of Saint Etheldred's in Suffolke, all belonging to the Deanery of Ely'.[19] Katherine Fuller, widow of Dean Fuller, returned several Chapter documents 'which my husband carefully preserved, that they might not be lost as many records of other churches have been in thes times'.[20] Dean Ferne continued the process, with some success, and a letter from William Ayloffe early in 1661 lists further records to be sent back to Ely, including (evidently) the medieval muniment chests.[21] In 1662 bailiffs were

---

[15] EDC 6/1A/1660/1.

[16] Ronald Hutton, *The Restoration: A Political and Religious History of England and Wales, 1658–1667* (Oxford, 1985), pp. 139–42. Eight cases are recorded in the archives (EDC 8A/6/1–18): at Mepal, Melbourn, Newton, Witchford, Ely and Quaveney. The most interesting case was that of Elizabeth Lilburne at Newton. She was the widow of the political agitator John Lilburne (c.1614–57), with 'foure small orphans', and claimed her purchase money with interest in compensation for loss of revenue at Newton and a lease for 21 years. She had also lost her Durham Chapter lands at Billingham (Co. Durham), as a result of 'forcible entries' made by the old tenants (EDC 8A/6/8).

[17] D.M. Owen, 'Bringing Home the Records: The Recovery of the Ely Chapter Muniments at the Restoration', *Archives*, viii (1968), pp. 123–9. Account rolls were received at various times from Norwich and Worcester. Two documents were received from York in 1999.

[18] The Parliamentary surveys are EDC 8A/1/1–77.

[19] EDC 6/1B/1661/1: receipt of Thomas Ayloffe to John Pegg, 12 January 1661.

[20] EDC 6/1A/1660/4, Katherine Fuller to the Dean and Chapter, 11 October 1660. In return she asked for a small lease or allowance, arguing that from leases which had fallen in during the Commonwealth her husband would have 'had his share in the profitts, if the power of the sword had not kept him and other loyall subjects from ther right, which fever by gods goodnesse being now removed, and he taken away immediately before this change when he should have reaped the fruits of his sufferings'.

[21] EDC 6/1A/1661/3, 13 March 1661. Ayloffe sent 'three longe Boxes of very ancient records sorted under the severall heades you will finde fixed upon the inside of their covers' and gave two others to Dr Pearson : 'I hope you will receive some satisfaction by these in what you desire . . .'

asked to bring to audit any court rolls which they had[22]; similarly, tenants of manors were to bring in their court rolls. In 1663 a special inducement was offered, 'that the party discovering to Dr Ball the two hundred acres of land belonging to the Church shall . . . have a Lease of the said Land'.[23] Similar requests for 'evidences' were made for several years.

As late as 1664, prebendaries who happened to be in London continued to search the records, removed in 1662 to Lambeth Palace, on one occasion at least, being assisted by the antiquary William Dugdale. Not everything was recoverable, but some records had been copied or noted by the indefatigable antiquary Bishop Matthew Wren, in a volume which he had filled at Ely before the Civil War, and in which he noted, on 15 October 1664, 'Now I find that the largest part of these records, from which I transcribed those things, have either perished utterly or have been removed or stolen in the wickedness of those times which lasted from early 1643 until 1660.'[24] The exercise was sufficiently successful for most, if not all, of the Chapter properties to be recovered speedily and without undue difficulty.[25] Documents continued to be returned, however, until at least 1683.

Chapter expenditure, rarely more than £900 annually before 1640, was £1682 in 1662, £1933 in 1664, and reached its highest point in 1669, of £2928.[26] Much money had to be borrowed from individual canons and from other sources. The 1669 expenses were swollen by £96 spent on entertaining Charles II when he came over from Newmarket 'to take a sight of the Cathedrall'.[27]

In the summer of 1662 the new Book of Common Prayer was received at Ely, complete with the Great Seal; and Richard Ball, canon in residence, was directed to read Morning and Evening Prayer from it and declare Chapter assent to it.[28] In 1666 new statutes were issued for the Cathedral, and were ordered to be 'laid up in the Chest with the common seale of the Church'.[29] They did not differ markedly from the Elizabethan statutes, and they formed the constitution of the Cathedral (except where changed by parliamentary legislation, especially in the mid nineteenth century) until 1936.

The sacrist was responsible for the Cathedral's plate. Thomas Hitch, appointed in 1667, had an inventory of plate and altar furniture appended to his patent.[30] The plate, presumably newly purchased in 1660–1 to replace the old items lost during the

---

[22] EDC 2/2A/2, p. 6. Also 'theire severall Greivances upon the dreyneing of the Fenns'; these grievances do not seem to have been preserved.

[23] EDC 2/2A/2, p. 15. The outcome of this has not been traced.

[24] EDR G2/1, column 360. *'Quia nunc reperio partem maximam eorum scriptorum, e quibus ista conscripsi, vel periisse funditus vel saltem ablatem subductamque esse per scelus temporum illorum que ab initio anni 1643 ad annum 1660 interlapsa sunt.'*

[25] In November 1677 the Chapter ordered 'That for the more easy and speedy finding of any Church-writings or Record the Present Registrar take an Assistant . . . to review all the said Records, to put them into good order and to make as perfect an index of them as can well be': EDC 2/2A/2, p. 128. A volume 'An Alphabetical Index to the Boxes in the Chapter House' (EDC 13/8/1) is probably the result of this review.

[26] These figures are as given by Gibbon, 'Small Beer of History' (cit. in n. 2), p. 104.

[27] Details of the entertainment were not preserved.

[28] EDC 2/2A/2, p. 3.

[29] EDC 2/2A/2, p. 53. The original volume, signed by Charles II and with the Great Seal attached, is EDC 2/1/6. See also Harvey Goodwin (ed.), *Statuta Ecclesiae Cathedralis Eliensis. Recognita per . . . Regem Carolum Secundum* (Cambridge, 1867).

[30] EDC 2/4/3, pp. 188–9.

Commonwealth, was all silver gilt, and consisted of a basin, two large candlesticks, two large flagons, two chalices with covers, and two patens.[31] The appearance of the altar has not been recorded in prints or drawings, and the description in Hitch's patent is of interest.[32] To left and right of the altar were curtains of blue serge. Over the altar were purple damask hangings, scarlet edged, with a gold and silk fringe. There were two altar cloths ('carpets'), one purple, and the other of purple and scarlet damask edged with a purple and gold fringe, with cushions to match. Hanging cloths and cushions were provided in the same materials for the bishop's and dean's stalls and the pulpit, and for the (prebendaries') stalls also there were provided 'Twelve turkey worke cushions'.[33]

John Spencer succeeded Mapletoft as Dean in 1677 (Plate 25a). Soon after his arrival he had to reprimand Henry Brunsell (4th stall, 1660–79) for bad behaviour, in taking away one of the three keys to the seal-chests, which should have been kept by the dean, subdean and treasurer, and refusing to give it up when required. Brunsell persisted in obstinate refusal, so that the Chapter had to break open the chest and have new keys made.[34] Dean Spencer was Master of Corpus Christi College and Archdeacon of Sudbury, and was reputed one of the greatest scholars of his age. He was an excellent administrator.[35] In his time the library was established. In 1679 John Moore, one of the great bibliophiles of the period, joined the Chapter (1st stall, 1679–91; Bishop of Ely, 1707–14) (Plate 25b).

During Spencer's time Peter Gunning (Bishop, 1675–84) first expressed the wish to move the choir stalls to the east end of the Cathedral. This would improve the vistas immeasurably. The Dean and Chapter would not countenance it, however, and the choir remained in the Octagon for another eighty years. Eventually, a legacy of £400 from Gunning was used to repave the choir in black and white marble. Dean Spencer made his own benefaction to the Cathedral: a white marble font, 'lavishly encrusted with cherubs'[36] and crowned with an elaborate wooden canopy (Plate 24b–c). Spencer died in 1693, and left a legacy of £100 for it, and further legacies to the minor canons, lay clerks, vergers, choristers and the poor of Ely.[37]

He was succeeded by John Lambe (Dean, 1693–1708), who was chaplain to William III and Mary II. Not only had he no Cambridge connection, but he lacked the degrees

---

[31] Of this plate, only the two candlesticks, still on the high altar, remain. There was a robbery in 1796, the details of which are not known. Wakelin was paid for repairing the plate and 'replacing what was stolen' (EDC 3/1/8).

[32] For liturgical practice in this period, including the burning of incense, see Thistlethwaite, below, p. 256.

[33] R.H. Gibbon, 'John Lambe, Dean of Ely, 1693–1708', *Church Quarterly Review*, cxix (1934–5), pp. 226–56, at p. 229.

[34] EDC 6/1B/1678/3, a memorandum of the reprimand. Henry Brunsell (1618–79), of Magdalen College, Oxford, trained as a physician but was ordained in 1660, and was appointed to a canonry the same year. He was made Rector of Stretham, near Ely, in 1662, and so was close at hand when business needed to be transacted. He died in 1679 and was buried in Stretham chancel.

[35] John Spencer (1630–93) was appointed a Fellow of Corpus Christi College in 1655, and kept his office by quiescence in the religious climate then prevailing. In 1667 he was elected Master of Corpus and appointed Archdeacon of Sudbury, and governed his college well. He succeeded John Pearson in his Ely canonry in 1672, and was appointed Dean in 1677. He was a great scholar, and his book *De Legibus Hebraeorum* (Cambridge, 1685), on the laws, rituals and beliefs of the Jews, was a pioneering work in comparative religion, though Spencer's religious orthodoxy was questioned as a result of it. He was buried in Corpus Christi Chapel.

[36] Gibbon, 'Small Beer of History' (cit. in n. 2), p. 113.

[37] £50 and the Deanery furniture to the minor canons and lay clerks; legacies to the vergers and choristers; and £20 to the poor of Ely. Bentham, *Ely*, p. 237.

of BD, DD or LLD laid down in the statutes. (This was remedied by royal mandate).[38] If he was not a great scholar, he was, however, capable, hard-working and diligent, and he resided mostly at Ely. In 1691 Sir Richard Onslow paid a huge fine for the renewal of a lease of property in Holborn,[39] and £900 of this was set aside for the Cathedral and its ministers. A new case and new pipes were acquired for the organ, for £380. The aisles and porch were paved at a cost of £40. £79 was spent on beautifying the east end of the choir.[40]

When the north-west corner of the north transept collapsed, in 1699, the Chapter turned quickly to schemes of repair, and agreed that for the next four years the treasurer would keep back £250 a year out of their dividends.[41] Robert Grumbold, a Cambridge builder, estimated for the repair work. Dean Lambe wanted a second opinion and consulted Sir Christopher Wren and Archbishop Tenison in London. Wren's opinion was that Grumbold's plan was a partial nonsense and his estimates for materials and labour were too high, and he advised obtaining a brief[42] for repairs, which, if circulated nationwide, might raise £1500. Lambe did so, but only £500 was received.[43] The full cost of repairs was eventually met, and the work was finished in 1702. Rolls of honour recording donations to the Cathedral's first organised appeal were made and ordered to be hung up in the Cathedral.[44]

The bishops of this period did not make much impact on the Cathedral. Francis Turner (Bishop, 1684–90) was deprived as a non-juror,[45] but not before appointing his brother Thomas Turner (7th stall, 1686–1714) to a canonry. After the Bishop's deprivation Thomas Turner never again attended a Chapter meeting or, apparently, kept a term of residence. About 1700 he wrote from Oxford seeking to be formally excused from keeping residence because he was over 60 and in poor health, and his College allowed him only three months' absence a year. Perhaps he was too comfortably settled at Corpus Christi College. The Chapter decided that they could not excuse him but would 'connive' at his absence by filling his term of residence – partly because he had contributed £100 to the north transept appeal and had given generously to relieve the smallpox in Ely.[46]

---

[38] John Lambe (1648–1708) died at Ely, and was buried at Wheathampstead (Herts.). Statutes, 1666, chapter 2, 'Of the qualifications, appointment and installation of the Dean'.

[39] The actual amount does not seem to have been recorded, but in 1725 Lord Onslow paid a fine of £6,000 for Holborn Vineyards (EDC 2/2A/2 , p. 378).

[40] Gibbon, 'John Lambe' (cit. in. n. 33), p. 232.

[41] EDC 2/2A/2, p. 223.

[42] That is, a royal letter soliciting donations.

[43] EDC 4/5/164. Further correspondence about the rebuilding is in EDC 4/5/42–51. In 1679 the Chapter, responding to the Bishop of Ely's request for contributions towards the cost of the new St. Paul's Cathedral, gave £150 to that project (EDC 2/2A/2, p. 151).

[44] EDC 4/5/15.

[45] A clergyman who would not swear the oath of allegiance to William III and Mary II because the former King, James II, was still alive.

[46] EDC 6/1B/1704/1, 'An account of our conniving at Dr Turners absence'. Turner renewed his application to be excused in 1704, offering as an inducement a substantial bequest to the Cathedral (EDC 6/1A/1704/1). When this came to the notice of Bishop Simon Patrick, he threatened Dean Lambe with a visitation of the Cathedral if Turner was not made to keep residence. All efforts to persuade Turner seem to have been in vain, however, and the Bishop finally left it to Turner's conscience whether he should sometimes reside for a short period at a pleasant time of the year. There is no evidence that this ever happened (Bodl., MS Rawl. lett. 92, fos. 19, 224, 228, 232, 249). Thomas Turner (1645–1714) was a Fellow of Corpus Christi College, Oxford, from 1672 and

Dean Lambe died in 1708, and his successor Charles Roderick (1st stall, 1691–1708) survived him by only four years.[47] The next Dean, Robert Moss (Dean, 1713–29) was a Fellow of Corpus and one of the university's best scholars and preachers, but suffered greatly from gout, which in later life almost incapacitated him. He had a house in Ormond Street, London, and came to Ely, infamous for its agues and damp-related illnesses, only in the summer.[48] Moss was fortunate in that his great friend Charles Ashton (4th stall, 1701–52), chaplain to Simon Patrick (Bishop, 1691–1707), had been made a canon. Ashton, who was also Master of Jesus College, was extremely business-like and efficient, and frequently deputised for Moss[49] (Plate 25d).

Letters between Ashton and Moss have survived.[50] They show Ashton in a favourable light, as straightforward, efficient in prosecuting Cathedral business, and modest about his own abilities. Before Moss's appointment, in Dean Lambe's time, Ashton cut through the confusion and the possibility of fraud in the Cathedral works, by drawing up regulations for the clerk of works and control of the workmen. The Treasurer's hold over expenditure on building and repair was strengthened, and the clerk of works was to act honestly and firmly 'at the peril of his place'.[51]

This was prudent, since there were major projects of repair to be undertaken after the collapse in the north transept had been made good. In 1706 the great south gate, Ely Porta, was repaired and reroofed; in 1707 the Lantern was ordered to be repaired; and in 1709 the south transept was repaired.[52] Ashton's vigilance was perhaps justified, since in a letter of 16 May 1709[53] he castigated two of his brethren, Francis Ferne (6th stall, 1690–1714) and James Smith (8th stall, 1702–15) as 'these two Supines', and doubted whether the audit could be properly performed when either of them was Treasurer. He suspected that on account of his efficiency he would be chosen Treasurer for the following year, though other canons had not taken a turn since he did it last; but 'for the sake of the Church I will not decline it'.

Early in 1716 a serious robbery took place in the Cathedral. A thief or thieves got into the Treasury in the south transept, forced open the Cathedral chest, and stole about

President from 1688. Among his charitable bequests were £6000 to Corpus, £1000 to Ely to augment the lay clerks' stipends (an estate at Stuntney was purchased in 1721 – see Thistlethwaite, below, p. 249), and £20,000 to the Corporation of the Sons of the Clergy (Bentham, *Ely*, p. 263, n. 3). He never married, but left £4000 to relations and friends.

47 Charles Roderick (1650–1712) was Head Master of Eton, 1682, Provost of King's 1689, and a Canon of Ely in 1691. He was buried in King's College Chapel.

48 Robert Moss (1666–1729) was made a Fellow of Corpus Christi College, Cambridge, in 1687, and from c.1700 was a chaplain successively to William III, Anne and George I. He was buried in the Cathedral's north choir aisle. His collected sermons were published in 8 volumes in 1736–8, with a preface by Zachary Grey and Moss's portrait engraved by Vertue.

49 Charles Ashton (1665–1752) lived at Jesus College except for his annual residence and Chapter meetings. He had no benefice. His great knowledge of classics, literature, *etc.*, resulted in no publications, but he assisted others with theirs; after his death his edition of Justin Martyr's *Apologies* was worked up from his MS by Frederick Keller and published in 1768. He was buried in Jesus College Chapel.

50 BL, Add. MSS 5831, fos. 106, 128, 130.b, 136; 6396, fo. 23. A typescript edition by Reginald Gibbon, using William Cole's notes on the letters and adding his own explanations, is at EDC 14/44/7. See also R.H. Gibbon, 'Ely Cathedral 1600–1720. Some Footnotes to Bentham's History', *Church Quarterly Review*, cxxx (1940), pp. 28–46.

51 EDC 2/2A/2, pp. 251–3: 25 November 1704.

52 EDC 2/2A/2, p. 261 (Ely Porta), pp. 271–2 (Lantern), p. 279 (south transept).

53 Probably to Dean Roderick.

£230 in coin. This sum included £112 belonging to the Bishop and £95 of Stephen Weston's,[54] as well as about £40 of Church money. Ashton was in the forefront of investigations into the robbery, which had come at a difficult time, when funds were low and the Chapter had 'a present Prospect of a vast Expense coming upon us'. Entry into the Treasury was not easy, and Ashton's feeling was that it was an 'inside job'. Suspicion fell at first on Henry Turner, an organ builder from Cambridge, who was known to have run up debts, and had recently departed from Ely. Soon Turner was thought not to have been the culprit, and Ashton and Samuel Hutton, Deputy Receiver, obtained a warrant to search the houses of the vergers and craftsmen. Ashton seems to have suspected a verger, Thomas Poole; but nothing was found. The mystery was never solved, and the loss to the Cathedral and the Bishop was made up out of revenue; but Dr Weston had to bear his own loss, having declined to take payment of his dividend by banker's order, and having left the sum at Ely for ready money to be used at his next residence.

All this was reported to Dean Moss in Ashton's letters; and such assiduity on Ashton's part could only have increased his usefulness in Moss's estimation. Moss was already appointing Ashton as his proxy for Chapter meetings, but when the other canons found that Moss expected Ashton to preside, superseding the Subdean, they became resentful, and in November 1715, at the Chapter, Thomas Tanner, who was Subdean, objected, and was supported by John Davies (5th stall, 1711–32) and Samuel Knight (7th stall, 1714–46). Ashton, who, as before, seems to have acted only 'for the sake of the Church', was acutely aware of the delicacy of the situation and advised Moss not to appoint him proxy in future (but give it to the Subdean). Moss however would have none of it and upheld his right to nominate Ashton to act for him.

Thomas Tanner, antiquary, a Fellow of All Souls College, Oxford, and a son-in-law of Bishop Moore (who while Bishop of Norwich made him Chancellor of that diocese and Archdeacon of Norfolk) held the 2nd stall, 1713–24 (when he resigned it for a canonry of Christ Church, Oxford)[55] (Plate 25c). Some of his letters show the tedium often experienced by canons during their periods of residence at Ely. Writing to Arthur Charlett, Master of University College, Oxford, during his first residence in December 1713, Tanner explained that the Dean and Canons who had gathered for the November Chapter had now left Ely.

> On the 26 of November they all left me to pass this dark time of the year here alone; where I have nothing to do but to mind my prayers and studies, a state of living very acceptable to one that is hurried all the rest of the year in a great town and a busy imployment. The situation of the place, buildings, solitude &c are very Monastick; and among other work I have out during my stay here, I intend to review the *Notitia Monastica . . .*[56]

---

[54] Stephen Weston (1664–1742) was a Fellow of Eton College and Vicar of Mapledurham, Oxfordshire, and in 1724 became Bishop of Exeter. He was a Canon of Ely from 1715 to 1717; whether his loss in the burglary precipitated the resignation of his stall is not known.

[55] Thomas Tanner (1674–1735) was Bishop of St Asaph, 1732–5.

[56] Bodl., MS Ballard 4, fo. 111, 1 December 1713. *Notitia Monastica or a Short History of the Religious Houses in England and Wales* was published at Oxford in 1695; by 1709 Tanner had a second edition ready, but this letter shows that he was still contemplating further revisions after 1709. Tanner was not the only prebendary interested in the history of the Cathedral. Samuel Knight (1675–1746) (7th stall, 1714–46) contemplated

The plain fact was that there was not enough for a Dean and eight prebendaries to do. They were required to assemble twice a year, in June and November, at the statutable Chapters. Otherwise each Canon had a month-and-a-half's residence each year, and at other times took himself off to his chief living or Cambridge college. The Cathedral was maintained by the minor canons, the organist and choir, and the registrar or chapter clerk. Unless the Canons chose to mix with the other officials there was scarcely any society in so small a town as Ely. Often, indeed, it was not wise to venture too far from the Cathedral, for the City was prone to outbreaks of disease. Ely had to be relieved from the distress of smallpox at least three times in the eighteenth century, in 1722, 1732 and 1750.[57]

John Frankland was Dean for five months only, in 1729–30.[58] During his time Thomas Kempton was appointed organist to succeed James Hawkins; and Browne Willis came to Ely to make plans of the Cathedral for his two-volume work on English cathedrals. For his care in making the plans the Chapter awarded him ten guineas[59] (frontispiece; Plate 26).

Frankland's successor was Peter Allix (Dean, 1730–58), a member of a French Huguenot family forced by the revocation of the Edict of Nantes in 1685 to take up residence in England[60] (Plate 29a). Allix's father conformed to the Church of England but was very Low Church in character. Peter Allix inherited what might be called his father's Puritanism. As R.H. Gibbon observed: 'He could not enter into full appreciation of a cathedral and of a system which placed worship first and edification second. On the whole, with much to recommend him, Dean Allix was not the ideal head for a cathedral establishment.'[61] William Cole the antiquary called him 'a weazel-faced and black swarthy complexioned Frenchman'.[62] Allix was Dean for 27 years. During this time both Ralph Perkins (6th stall, 1715–51) and Charles Ashton obtained leave of

producing a Cathedral history, as is evidenced by a letter to him from 'JW' [John Warburton?] (CUL, MS Add. 41, fos. 99–100), undated but perhaps c. 1720, in which Warburton encouraged Knight in his intention and offered him materials and further assistance. In the event, nothing was published by Knight, perhaps because he was more devoted to writing biography than to Cathedral history.

[57] EDC 2/2A/2, p. 353, 25 November 1722, on 'the extraordinary occasion of the calamity in Town by reason of the smallpox'.

[58] John Frankland (1674–1730) was appointed Dean of Gloucester, 1723, and Master of Sidney Sussex College, 1729. He died at Bristol.

[59] Browne Willis, A Survey of the Cathedrals of Lincoln, Ely, Oxford and Peterborough (London, 1730).

[60] Peter Allix (1679–1758) was made a Fellow of Jesus College by Bishop Simon Patrick in 1705. A later Canon of Huguenot descent was Thomas Duquesne (d.1793), the son of Gabriel, Marquis Du Quesne, of Dieppe, Normandy, who came to England after the revocation of the Edict of Nantes. Thomas Duquesne was Chancellor of St Davids and Rector of Honingham and East Tuddenham, Norfolk. He was presented to an Ely canonry in 1783 by Archbishop Cornwallis, as his option. He lived at East Tuddenham for more than 40 years, and 'visited the sick, comforted the afflicted, and relieved the necessitous' (Bentham). He left a legacy to the choir of Ely.

[61] Reginald Gibbon, 'The Order Book of the Dean and Chapter of Ely, 1729–1769', Church Quarterly Review, cxxiv (1937), pp. 250–65, at p. 252.

[62] William Cole (1714–82), antiquary, was Rector of Bletchley, Bucks. (presented by his friend Browne Willis) 1753–67, and retired to Waterbeach and (1770) to Milton, both close to Ely and Cambridge. He remained at Milton until his death, although he was also Vicar of Burnham, Bucks., 1774–82. He made large MS collections towards a 'History of Cambridgeshire', and counted among his friends and correspondents many antiquaries, including Horace Walpole, Thomas Gray and Richard Gough. 'Although he published no separate work of his own, he rendered substantial assistance to many authors by supplying them either with entire dissertations or with minute communications or corrections' (DNB).

absence from residence on account of their 'great age', and John Nicols (2nd stall, 1748–74) never attended a Chapter while Allix was alive (but was an assiduous attender after Allix's death).[63] At Allix's first Chapter the decision was taken that the Cathedral service, except for psalms, anthems and hymns, should be said 'with a distinct and audible voice', not sung, thus relieving the minor canons of any need for musical proficiency for a century to come.[64]

There was no open hostility during Allix's tenure, and most of his Chapters were uneventful and concerned with the management of the Chapter estates. A particularly long and vexatious dispute arose in 1736 with Sir Simeon Stuart of Lakenheath, over his complaint that the Dean and Chapter's gamekeeper was setting snares on his land. The case was sucked into the quagmire of Chancery and dragged on until 1760.[65]

Ely shared in the shock of the 1745 Jacobite rising and the Young Pretender's march into England. The November Chapter met while he was marching south. The Dean and four canons were absent, but the four present adopted an address of loyalty to King George II, with only Thomas Jones (1st stall, 1722–59), described by Gibbon as 'pugnacious, indomitable, and not very lovable', expressing dissent. His residual Jacobitism seems to have been forgotten, and he suffered no penalties for his disloyalty.[66]

The June 1748 Chapter decided to remove the wooden spire from the west tower of the cathedral. But when the citizens of Ely protested against the loss of a familiar landmark the decision was reversed, and the spire survived for another fifty years.[67] In 1749 a gallery was ordered to be built for the lay clerks, choristers and King's Scholars at sermon time, then held in the nave; it is not clear whether this gallery was attached to the west side of the screen, or occupied an archway in one of the aisles.[68]

Samuel Bentham, Chapter registrar,[69] had two sons who came to prominence at Ely in the second half of the 18th century (a third son was University Printer at Cambridge). Jeffrey Bentham was chorister, minor canon, precentor and master in the Grammar School for nearly fifty years.[70] James Bentham (1708–94) was appointed a minor canon in 1736; in 1779, partly in appreciation of the scholarship he had displayed in writing *A History of Ely* (1771), he was made a Canon (2nd stall, 1779–96)[71] (Plate 29c). Bentham

[63] EDC 2/2A/3, p. 16, 25 November 1732 (Perkins), p. 35, 14 June 1736 (Ashton). Ralph Perkins (c.1658–1751) was chaplain to Bishop Patrick, who appointed him Rector of Stretham in 1696. He resigned his fellowship at Queens' in 1699, but continued to reside there. He was appointed a canon in 1715 and resigned Stretham in 1727. He obtained leave of absence from Ely in 1736, aged about 78, divided his collection of books between the Cathedral library and Queens', and retired to London. He was a benefactor to the Corporation of the Sons of the Clergy and other charities. Ashton, of course, had laboured at Chapter business for more than thirty years.

[64] EDC 2/2A/3, p. 8, 25 November 1730.

[65] EDC 2/2A/3, p. 222, 25 November 1760.

[66] EDC 2/2A/3, p. 111, 25 November 1745, the Chapter 'beg leave to express our just indignation and resentment at the unnatural rebellion now carrying on, in favour of a Popish Pretender'; Reginald Gibbon, 'The Order Book' (cit. in n. 55), p. 258.

[67] EDC 2/2A/3, pp. 134, 136, 14 June and 15 August 1748.

[68] EDC 2/2A/3, p. 141, 14 June 1749.

[69] Samuel Bentham (1681–1723), was Vicar of Witchford, 1705–23, and became registrar after the resignation of his father Samuel Bentham in 1713.

[70] Jeffrey Bentham (1720–92) was also Vicar of Meldreth (1744), curate of Chettisham (1751) and curate of Holy Trinity, Ely (1776).

[71] Another man rewarded for his scholarship was Thomas Knowles (1727–1802), only son of John Knowles,

loved Ely and its Cathedral. In the town he was active in encouraging street improvements, and he was a leading promoter of the scheme for a carriage road between Ely and Cambridge. In the Cathedral Bentham was instrumental in bringing in James Essex[72] (Plate 30*a*) to save the Lantern, but was also a strong promoter of what Gibbon called 'the mad desire' to remove the choir to the east end[73] (Plate 29*c*). The start of the Lantern's restoration was almost the last act of Dean Allix's deanship, for Essex was appointed in June 1757 and Allix died the next year. The task of guiding the restoration fell to Allix's successor, Hugh Thomas (Dean, 1758–80), who was also, amongst other appointments, Master of Christ's College, Cambridge. [74] Bentham was soon busy lobbying for the choir's removal: by late 1759 he had had a plate printed and was sending it to potential benefactors (Plate 31*c*). Dr Nicols in London received 100 copies.[75]

Essex and Bentham pushed the scheme to remove the choir from the Octagon, a considerable achievement for Bentham, who was only a minor canon (he was also clerk of works for the project). While the Lantern was under repair, and the choir was being relocated, the Cathedral was out of action for thirteen years, and services were held in the Lady Chapel, where there was no organ and the only music was a metrical psalm pitched by one of the lay clerks.

The remodelling of the Cathedral raised the interest of antiquaries such as William Cole (Plate 29*d*) and Horace Walpole. In 1762 Cole sent Walpole a sketch of a stained glass panel, 'a full-length picture of St Etheldreda', which Bishop Mawson (Plate 29*b*) had removed for safety from Ely House, Holborn, to Ely Palace.[76] This panel was mentioned again in 1769 when Cole, in writing to Walpole, reported that 'a more ancient picture in glass of St Etheldreda . . . in more gaudy colours' had been found 'in a window of one of the prebendal houses' and was sent to Michael Tyson in Cambridge 'for him to take a drawing of it'.[77] Tyson gave the drawing to Cole, since Bishop

---

Chapter registrar. Thomas Knowles was Rector of Ickworth and Chevington (Suffolk), and domestic chaplain to Lady Hervey. He was a distinguished metaphysician, and for his literary merit he received the degree of DD from Archbishop Secker, and his canonry from Bishop Keene in 1779. He was later Vicar of Winston (Suffolk), and Lecturer at St Mary's, Bury St Edmunds, where 'as a public Preacher, he was much admired and esteemed, his person and mode of delivery being dignified, solemn and impressive.' (Bentham, *Supplement*, p. 21).

[72] James Essex (1722–84), Cambridge architect, worked extensively at King's College, Cambridge, Lincoln and Winchester Cathedrals, and for Horace Walpole at Strawberry Hill, Middlesex.

[73] Reginald Gibbon, 'The Order Book' (cit. in n. 55), p. 260.

[74] Hugh Thomas (1707–80) was a very successful pluralist. Bentham recorded an obituary notice in the *Middlesex Journal*, 20 July 1780: 'A Reverend Gentleman, lately deceased, is a melancholy proof of the great inequality of Church Livings; he was at once a Dean, a Master of a College, an Archdeacon of one Diocese, a Chancellor of another, and a Treasurer of a third; had four Prebendal Stalls in different Churches, two Rectories in Yorkshire, and a *Sinecure* in Wales. As this man had no less than twelve Livings; it is no wonder that eleven poor Clergymen should go without any.' (EDC 14/29).

[75] In the letter sending them (CUL, MS Add. 2960, fos. 54v–55, Bentham to Nicols, 5 February 1760), Bentham spoke of the difficulty of starting the subscription, especially among the gentlemen of Ely, most of whom were holding back until one of them should pledge an amount and thus indicate the appropriate level of donation. Bentham did not mention any opposition to his plan, but of course it would not have been in his interest to do so.

[76] *Horace Walpole's Correspondence with the Rev. William Cole*, ed. W.S. Lewis and A. Dayle Wallace, The Yale Edition of Horace Walpole's Correspondence, I (London, 1937), p. 31, Cole to Walpole, 3 November 1762. The glass was later 'placed in the middle of the three lowest lancet windows at the east end of the Cathedral' (Bentham, *Ely*, p. 290n.). An engraving of the figure is reproduced *ibid.*, opp. p. 45. The panel, which is small, is now set in the window of the chapel of SS Æthelwold and Dunstan, in the south transept.

[77] *Walpole's Correspondence with Cole*, ed. Lewis, I, p. 185. Michael Tyson (1740–80), Fellow of Corpus Christi

Mawson, on comparing the figure with the previous panel, by this time in a window at the Palace, preferred the previous one to be set into the East window of the Cathedral.[78]

Cole was on hand in 1769 when the medieval choir stalls were being dismantled, and he reported to Walpole:

> We made a curious discovery . . . about three weeks ago. An old wall being to be taken down behind the choir, on which were painted seven figures of six Saxon bishops and a Duke . . . of Northumberland, one Brythnoth: which painting I take to be as ancient as any we had in England; therefore I was very desirous to have a copy of it taken before it was destroyed.

Cole persuaded a Canon, probably his friend John Gooch, to order a stay of demolition until Tyson had made a copy of the wall paintings.

> I guessed by seven arches in the wall below the figures that the bones of these seven benefactors to the old Saxon conventual church were reposited in the wall under them, and accordingly we found seven separate holes, all of them full of the remains of the said persons . . .[79]

Tyson made a series of drawings (Colour pl. 22c), which Bentham hoped to have engraved for his *History*, but a benefactor could not be found for that plate.[80]

The architectural changes once again proved a severe strain on Chapter finances, and various recourses were employed – from an appeal, to borrowing on bonds, loans from individual prebendaries, and a generous donation of £1000 from Bishop Matthias Mawson.

Bentham is said to have derived his antiquarian interests from Thomas Tanner who was a prebendary while Bentham was growing up. During his time as a minor canon Bentham had ample opportunity to explore the mass of documentary evidence kept in the muniment room in the south transept. In 1756 Bentham printed and circulated a list of abbots, priors and deans of Ely, in order to obtain further biographical details.[81] He was gradually accumulating materials, and in 1761 he sent out proposals for publishing his *History of Ely*.[82] In 1764 printing was begun by his brother Joseph at Cambridge; but, as William Cole reported to Horace Walpole in 1768, the work was by no means complete by then. Cole wrote:

College, Cambridge, 1767, Vicar of St Bene't's, Cambridge 1773–6, and of Sawston, Cambs., 1772–6, and Rector of Lambourne, Essex, 1779–80, was an antiquary, friend of Cole and Richard Gough, and a skilful artist and engraver.

[78] There is no mention at this time of medieval stained glass in the Octagon angle windows. Two panels were sketched by William Stukeley some years previously (CCCC, MS 556, unpaginated) (Plate 10a): King Egfrid in the north-east window, and St Wilfrid in the south-east window. A plan on the following page of MS 556 makes the positions clear. Unfortunately, Stukeley does not say whether this was the only surviving stained glass. See P. Lindley, 'The Imagery of the Octagon at Ely', *JBAA*, 3rd ser., 139 (1986), pp. 75–99, at p. 91.

[79] *Walpole's Correspondence with Cole*, ed. Lewis, I, p. 160. The relics were installed in Bishop West's Chapel. See also Appx 3, below.

[80] Tyson gave the drawing to Cole in 1778, and Cole gave it to Richard Gough, who engraved it for his *Sepulchral Monuments* (London, 1786–99), I, pt 1, opp. p. clvi. Stevenson copied the plate for the *Supplement* to Bentham's *Ely* (Norwich, 1817), opp. p. 69. Tyson's drawings are in Bodl., Gough Maps 225, fos. 35–41.

[81] *A Catalogue of the Principal Members of the Conventual and Cathedral Church of Ely, viz. Abbesses, Abbots, Bishops, Priors, Deans, Prebendaries and Archdeacons; From the Foundation of the Church, A.D. 673 to the Present Year 1756* (Cambridge, 1756).

[82] EDC 14/24, 'extra-illustrated Bentham' (see n. 87, below), vol. 3, opp. p. 10.

I am desired by an old acquaintance who undertook twenty years ago to write an *History of the Cathedral of Ely* to help him forward this long-expected work into the world; and if I do not, I am much afraid it will never be done at all.

Bentham wanted Cole to write the biographies of the Bishops of Ely from Louis de Luxembourg onwards. 'All before this have been printed off; so that I have been very busy, having nothing else to do, in composing some of these lives'. Cole foresaw that if he did not write up the deans and prebendaries also, 'the book will never come out, which would be a great pity, for there are already very neatly engraved about fifty plates . . .'[83]

Bentham acknowledged Cole's contributions in his *History*,[84] but not, it seems, well enough for Cole, whose caustic comments in his own copy of the *History* were copied and printed by William Davis in 1814.[85] When Cole had read the *History* to the end, he could, it seems, contain himself no longer, for he wrote in condemnation of Bentham's very intellect: 'It needed only to look in the face of James Bentham, and be struck with wonder that so good a book could come from such Ideot appearance; to hear and see him open his mouth and talk to you, to be convinced that it was impossible for him to compose it.' Cole went so far as to claim that Bentham's brother, Professor Edward Bentham, 'whose custom it was every year, to spend a few months at Ely', was the real author.[86]

Cole's aspersions on Bentham's literary abilities and intellectual faculties need not, perhaps, be taken too seriously. Bentham's volumes of transcripts from Ely documents testify to his skill and assiduity as historian and antiquary.[87] The *History*, which was published in 1771, was a *tour de force*, especially in its reliance on original documents, and in its many detailed plates.Through the *History*, and his devotion to the Cathedral and its services, Bentham towered over the other mid-eighteenth century personnel at Ely. Yet his biographer stressed his modesty, diffidence and charity towards others.[88]

The Chapter, even before Bentham joined it in 1779, was quite hard-working: at the two statutable chapters there were never fewer than four Canons, usually five or six; but in 1774 Dean Thomas devised a cycle of attendance to provide five Canons at each

---

[83] *Walpole's Correspondence with Cole*, ed. Lewis, I, pp. 135–6, Cole to Walpole, 14 May 1768. A notebook of Bentham's, 'Prebendaries of Ely', an incomplete catalogue of prebendaries, with some biographical details, probably Bentham's preparation for the History, is at EDC 14/29.

[84] Bentham, *Ely*, Preface, p. iv, and in footnotes, *passim*.

[85] William Davis, *An Olio of Bibliographical and Literary Anecdotes and Memoranda Original and Selected* (London, 1814), pp. 109–26. Cole, for example, had a great regard for Bishop Mawson, who, Cole claimed, encouraged Bentham 'in every way in his power' in writing the *History*, and gave Bentham 'a good living in Norfolk', which, 'not quite suiting him', Bentham exchanged for Feltwell. Bentham prepared a lavish dedication to Mawson ('or his Brother for him') for the History; but Mawson died, the dedication was cancelled, and a new one was drawn up to Bishop Keene 'who might have been flattered with a Dedication to the 2nd part'. To Cole this smacked of ingratitude and self-seeking.

[86] *Ibid.*, p. 125. The Benthams, Cole continued (p. 126), were 'all worthy people . . . but . . . not like other people . . . they are as unlike in all their actions to the rest of mankind as it is possible to conceive, though without guile, and quite unoffensive.' Edward Bentham (1707–76) was a Canon of Christ Church, Oxford 1754–76, and Regius Professor of Divinity 1763–76.

[87] CUL, MSS Add. 2944–2962.

[88] William Stevenson, 'Memoirs of the Life of the Reverend James Bentham', in Bentham, *Ely*, pp. 1–20 (foreword), at p. 19. Stevenson, publisher of Bentham's work, owned an extra-illustrated copy of the *History of Ely*, which is now EDC 14/24.

Chapter (three being excused in rotation). The cycle was notable more for its ingenuity than its effectiveness, with little sign that it made the slightest difference to attendance; in June 1778 and June 1784 full attendance of all nine dignitaries was recorded.[89]

Before his death in 1770, Bishop Mawson gave money for new stained glass for the east window of the Cathedral. The glass painter James Pearson was commissioned, and a contract drawn up;[90] but nothing happened, and in 1776 John Warren (7th stall, 1768–79) was asked to investigate the progress of the project, or the lack of it, and if necessary to seek a legal opinion. In the event only one light (St Peter, removed to the nave north gallery about 1850) and a few coats of arms of canons, were made, and not put up until 1790[91] (Colour pl. 14c).

In 1775 the Chapter subscribed ten guineas towards the cost of a fire engine for the City. This would not have been effective in extinguishing blazes in the Cathedral roofs.[92]

In 1792 the south transept was considered as the site for the Sunday sermon (the benches which were brought out on Sundays were stored there) and Thomas Winter was asked to measure the transept and provide a plan.[93]

Throughout the eighteenth century most bishops managed to provide a canonry for a son, son-in-law, brother or nephew. William Powell (8th stall, 1717–41) was a nephew of Bishop William Fleetwood, and Charles Fleetwood (3rd stall, 1718–37) was the Bishop's son; Thomas Greene (3rd stall, 1737–80) was a son of Bishop Thomas Greene; Eyton Butts (7th stall, 1746–54) was a son of Bishop Robert Butts; John Gooch (4th stall, 1753–1804) was a son of Bishop Sir Thomas Gooch; Benjamin Underwood (3rd stall, 1780–1815) was the nephew of Bishop Edmund Keene; Thomas Waddington (5th stall, 1793–1815) was a son-in-law of Bishop James Yorke, and Philip Yorke (6th stall, 1795–1817) was the Bishop's son. Such men tended to be appointed young, and were usually well-provided with rich livings and lucrative offices, so that they tended to be amongst the most regular attenders at Chapter and provided an element of continuity (and often conservatism) in Cathedral affairs. More rarely, canons came up from the ranks, such as Caesar Morgan (4th stall, 1804–12), author of philosophical works.[94]

Bishops continued to be buried in the Cathedral in the period 1660–1836.[95] From the death of Benjamin Laney in 1677 to that of Matthias Mawson in 1770, each bishop's burial was commemorated by a monument. Peter Gunning's was exceptional in that it

[89] EDC 2/2A/4, pp. 31–33, Dean Thomas's cycle of attendance.
[90] Agreement (copy), EDR D9/9/2, in which Pearson is mistakenly called Preston.
[91] EDC 2/2A/4, p. 151, June 1790, order for the window to be put up; EDC 4/5/221, 8 August 1790, estimate by Robert Painter for erecting it.
[92] In 1802, for example, the Lantern was saved from destruction by a workman who hacked away timbers which caught fire after the Lantern was lined with candles to burn in celebration of the Peace of Amiens (John Bacon's book, EDC 4/6/2, fo. 78).
[93] EDC 2/2A/4, p. 167, June 1792.
[94] Caesar Morgan (1750–1812) was first promoted by his fellow Welshman, Hugh Thomas, Dean of Ely and Master of Christ's College, Cambridge (Morgan's college), who made him a minor canon and Master of the Grammar School. He became chaplain to Bishop Yorke in 1783, and Yorke provided him with a string of livings of increasing value, including Littleport (1791) and Stretham (1802), and in 1804 he was appointed a Canon.
[95] Except for Matthew Wren, buried in the crypt of the chapel of Pembroke College, Cambridge; Francis Turner (deprived as a non-juror) who was buried in Therfield church (Herts.); Sir Thomas Gooch, buried in the chapel of Gonville and Caius College, Cambridge; James Yorke, buried in Forthampton church (Gloucs.); and Thomas Dampier, buried in Eton College Chapel.

featured a semi-reclining effigy of the Bishop, his mitred head propped up by his hand[96] (Plate 24a). The monument of Benjamin Laney, and those of the bishops from Simon Patrick to Thomas Greene, were variations on the type of wall-monuments with inscriptions in panels, charged with each bishop's mitred coat of arms. Simon Patrick's is flanked by two flaming obelisks in pink marble;[97] John Moore's, by an unknown sculptor, is very elegant, the inscription following the folds of a suspended drapery, flanked by columns and grieving putti[98] (Plate 27a) William Fleetwood's monument has a tablet framed by columns and urns, with an open, scrolly pediment above[99] (Plate 27b); Thomas Greene's featured an urn flanked by columns and an inscription on drapery below.[100] Matthias Mawson's monument, by an unknown sculptor, is distinguished by its use of delicately coloured marbles; Edmund Keene (d.1781) was buried in Bishop West's chapel, with only an inscribed grave slab over his burial.

Robert Butts's monument[101] formed a break in the Ely pattern, for it featured a tablet charged with a bust of the Bishop, set against an obelisk backing, which carried Butts's mitred coat of arms, and many rococo scrolls and festoons (Plate 27c). When it was moved to the back of the choir stalls on the south side in the 1850s, it lost the obelisk, and the disjointed elements of the design now seem to hover somewhat unconvincingly (Plate 27d). Another monument of the obelisk type, to Humphrey Smith (d.1743), was formerly in the Lady Chapel, but was placed in the south cloister porch when Holy Trinity parish gave up use of the Chapel in 1938.[102] A bust of Smith in a circular cartouche is flanked on one side by palms and on the other by a lolling putto. Smith was active in fen drainage, and this is symbolised by an upturned urn spouting forth water (Colour pl. 16b).

In 1780 William Cooke[103] succeeded Hugh Thomas as Dean, and he was succeeded in 1797 by William Pearce.[104] In 1781 James Yorke was appointed Bishop of Ely.[105] Bishop

---

[96] Edmund Esdaile, *The Monuments of Ely Cathedral* (Ely, 1973), p. 10, tentatively, and without any evidence, attributes the monument to the workshop of Grinling Gibbons. A high, plain backing, crowned with a segmental pediment, was removed in the 1850s to display the stained glass behind it: see the plate in Bentham, *Ely*, opp. p. 203.

[97] By Edward Stanton (1681–1734); see the plate in Bentham, *Ely*, opp. p. 206.

[98] Originally on the north side of the presbytery; Essex moved it to the north choir aisle, and finally in the 1850s it was moved to the south choir aisle, backing the choir stalls.

[99] By Edward Stanton and Christopher Horsnaile. Since the 1850s Bishop Fleetwood's monument has stood beside that of his son, Charles Fleetwood (3rd stall, 1718–37), by Peter Scheemakers (1691–1781), in the north choir aisle, backing the choir stalls. The Bishop's monument was originally in the presbytery; Essex moved it to the south choir aisle, near to where Canon Fleetwood's originally stood.

[100] This was moved in the 1850s from the eastern south choir aisle to a position close to Bishop Moore's. See the plate in Bentham, *Ely*, opp. p. 210. Esdaile suggested that Horsdaile might have been the sculptor.

[101] By Sir Henry Cheere (1703–81). Esdaile, *op. cit.*, p. 13, cites two drawings by Cheere in the Victoria & Albert Museum, and illustrates one of them.

[102] It was designed by Smith's friend, the architect John Sanderson, and sculpted probably by Charles Stanley (1703–61).

[103] William Cooke (1711–97) was Head Master of Eton from 1743, but found the post too onerous and in 1748 exchanged it for a fellowship of Eton and the nearby rectory of Denham. In 1768 he became Rector of Stoke Newington, and in 1772 was made Provost of King's College, Cambridge. He had a large family, of twelve children; in later life he became mentally deranged.

[104] William Pearce (1744–1820) was a Fellow of St John's College, Cambridge, 1768–88. Bishop Yorke appointed him Master of Jesus College in 1789. He was Master of the Temple from 1787 until 1797, when he resigned it on being appointed Dean of Ely. He was also Rector of Houghton Conquest, (Beds.), 1786–1820, and Rector of Wentworth (Cambs.), 1799–1820.

[105] James Yorke (1730–1808). Some details of Yorke's life and episcopate were provided by E.A.B. Barnard, 'A Georgian Prelate: James Yorke, Bishop of Ely, 1781–1808', *Notes and Queries*, cxciv (1949), pp. 178–82, 204–8.

Yorke's benefactions to the Cathedral were frequent. Scarcely a year went by without his paying for some improvement or embellishment. In 1789 he asked for an inspection of the west tower.[106] In 1790 he gave £50 towards putting up the east window.[107] In 1794 he offered funding for work at the west end (the Galilee porch and west tower), to be carried out by James Wyatt.[108] In 1799 when further work was needed on the tower, Yorke commissioned a report from William Wilkins.[109] In 1800 he gave an altarpiece for Essex's reredos at the east end of the Cathedral, a painting of the angel releasing Peter from prison, attributed to Ribera.[110] In 1801 Yorke funded further repairs to the Galilee porch, according to plans by John Groves executed by Bernasconi, who made remarkably accomplished and durable tracery of Roman cement in the western arch.[111] Wyatt's work had unroofed the upper chamber of the Galilee porch, leaving an arch into the Cathedral. In 1806 Yorke paid for a new window to be inserted,[112] and in 1808 he bought sixteenth-century French stained glass to fill several of the openings[113] (Colour pl. 14b).

Bishop Yorke was succeeded by Thomas Dampier, translated from Rochester, who died in 1812. Dampier's successor was Bowyer Edward Sparke, Bishop of Chester, a protégé of the Duke of Rutland since he had been Rutland's tutor.[114] Sparke's twenty-four-year episcopate at Ely closes this chapter. He is chiefly remembered now for appointing two sons and a son-in-law to the Chapter, for being the Bishop who hanged or transported the Littleport rioters, and for being the last Bishop of Ely with secular jurisdiction in the Isle, abolished on his death, when he was buried with his sword of state.

Probably the most extraordinary appointment to a canonry in Sparke's time was that of Sir Henry Bate Dudley in 1815 (Plate 34a). This was almost certainly political, forced on Sparke by the Duke of Rutland, and, through Rutland, the Prince Regent. The sensational career of Bate Dudley (1745–1824), clergyman, journalist, controversialist and partisan of the Prince of Wales is too long to tell here: amongst the offences with which he was charged at various times were libel and simony.[115] His pugnacious nature (he once challenged an opponent to a duel) led to his nickname the 'fighting parson'. For ten years he lived in virtual banishment in Ireland before Sparke rescued him, first as Rector of Willingham (1812), and then in 1815 by means of the canonry. In 1812 Bate Dudley obtained a baronetcy from the Regent in repayment of a long-standing 'obligation'.

As chance would have it, the 'fighting parson' was in residence at Ely when riots

[106] EDC 2/2A/4, p. 144.

[107] *Ibid.*, p. 154.

[108] *Ibid.*, p. 188.

[109] *Ibid.*, p. 227.

[110] *Ibid.*, p. 233. The painting now hangs in the south transept.

[111] EDC 2/2A/5, p. 21. The Dean & Chapter paid £150 towards the cost.

[112] EDC 2/2A/5, p. 32.

[113] Peter Moore, *The Stained Glass of Ely Cathedral* (Ely, 1973), pp. 3–4. Yorke purchased this glass, which was probably from the church of St John the Evangelist, Rouen, at auction in London.

[114] Bowyer Edward Sparke (1759–1836), was Vicar of Scalford (Leics.), 1800–5, Vicar of St Augustine-the-Less, Bristol, 1803–10, Dean of Bristol 1803–9, and Bishop of Chester, 1809–12.

[115] For Bate Dudley see the *DNB, s.v.* Dudley, and the references cited there; also Arthur Aspinall, *The Letters of King George IV 1812–1830* (Cambridge, 1938), *idem, Politics and the Press, c.1780–1850* (London, 1949), and A. Aspinall (ed.), *The Correspondence of George, Prince of Wales, 1770–1812* (London, 1963–71).

broke out at Littleport in 1816 and swept on to Ely.[116] Bate Dudley immediately summoned the militia from Bury St Edmunds (all the canons were magistrates in the Isle of Ely) and rode at their head into Ely. The ringleaders were swiftly arrested, some at Littleport, and order was restored. Bishop Sparke held a special Assizes at Ely to deal with the rioters and summoned two London judges to sit with Edward Christian, the Chief Justice of the Isle. At the service before the trial, in the Cathedral, Bate Dudley preached the sermon.[117] Several of the rioters were condemned to death, others were transported to Australia for life, and more were imprisoned for a year in Ely jail.[118]

Bate Dudley was ambitious and avaricious: in 1820 and 1822 he lobbied secretly for the deaneries first of Ely, then Peterborough, but was twice unsuccessful. He secured a government pension in 1823 but lived only a few months to enjoy it.

John Henry Sparke (1794–1870), Bishop Sparke's elder son, was destined for preferment from an early age (Plate 34c). In 1817, while still an undergraduate, he and his brother Edward were appointed joint Registrars of the Diocese (Edward being aged only 12!).[119] Henry was next made a Fellow of Jesus College, in the Bishop's gift. When a canonry fell vacant in 1816 Henry was still under the age for 'priesting', so in the meantime his father appointed to the canonry John Henry Browne, Archdeacon of Ely (a notorious absentee), doubtless with a 'bond of resignation', a promise to resign when asked to do so. The moment came in 1818. On 16 August Henry was ordained priest; on the following day he was appointed Vicar of Stretham and sinecure Rector of Littlebury, Essex, Browne resigned his canonry and Henry was appointed to it.[120] The appearance of this twenty-four-year-old in a Chapter of sexagenarians must have been an interesting spectacle.

In 1819 Henry Fardell, a young clergyman who had the good fortune to marry Sparke's daughter Eliza, was provided with a canonry and a prosperous living.[121] The Bishop's younger son, Edward Bowyer Sparke (1805–79), followed a similar path through Cambridge, and was elected a Fellow of St John's (where James Wood (Dean, 1820–39) was Master) in 1826. A canonry fell vacant in 1826 and Sparke appointed his Pembroke College contemporary Benjamin Parke, a Norfolk clergyman.[122] When Edward Sparke passed his twenty-fourth birthday, in 1829, his father ordained him priest, Parke resigned his canonry, and Edward Sparke received the canonry and a collection of livings (Plate 35c).

---

[116] C. Johnson, *An Account of the Ely and Littleport Riots, in 1816* (Ely, 1893).

[117] Sir Henry Bate Dudley, *A Sermon Delivered at the Cathedral of Ely on . . . the 17th of June, 1816 . . . on the Opening of their Special Commisssion for the Trial of the Rioters* (Cambridge, 1816). His text was 1 Timothy 1, v. 9, 'The law is not made for the righteous man, but for the lawless, and disobedient'. He did not refer to the rioters directly, except to urge primary obedience to the laws of God 'under whose protecting providence we are enabled to assemble this day, to offer up our thanksgiving for deliverance from the terrors of devastation, amidst which, even this venerable temple was profanely marked to fall!'

[118] It cannot have been unconnected with the shock of the riots that in November 1816 the Chapter gave £100 for the employment of the poor at Ely, the money to be used at the magistrates' discretion (EDC 2/2A/5, p. 136).

[119] EDC 2/2A/5, p. 140.

[120] EDR G1/16, p. 14.

[121] Henry Fardell (1795–1854) was a son of John Fardell, deputy registrar to the Bishop of Lincoln. While engaged to be married to Eliza Sparke, he was made a Canon of Ely in 1819. He was Vicar of Waterbeach, 1821–54, Rector of Feltwell, 1823–31, and Vicar of Wisbech, 1831–54. He died at Ely, and his grave was the last to be dug at the east end of the Cathedral.

[122] Benjamin Parke (1759–1835) was Vicar of Tilney (Norfolk), 1805–35. He was a Canon of Ely 1826–9 and 1831–5.

Not even Bishop Sparke could entirely pack a Chapter of eight with his family and connexions. Two canons lived right through his episcopate (Cambridge and Jenyns).[123] Some of Sparke's other appointments were interesting. Bate Dudley no doubt was forced on him; but in 1822 he gave the third stall to George Gaskin, who had been Secretary of the SPCK since 1786.[124] The tutor to Sparke's children, William French, was appointed in 1831 (Plate 34d); the brilliant young Cambridge scholar William Selwyn in 1833 (Plate 35d), and the long-serving royal chaplain John Maddy in 1835.[125]

Apart from the scare of the Ely and Littleport riots, little seemed to trouble the steady course of the Bishop and the Dean and Chapter until about 1830. Sparke carried the Bible at the Coronation of King George IV in 1821 (the most opulent ceremony ever); and he paid for a thick coat of ochre paint to cover the Cathedral's interior in 1822. Henry Sparke became Chancellor of the Diocese in 1824, and Edward Sparke then became sole Registrar. Both offices were, of course, exercised through deputies.

The story that Bishop Sparke was so pleased by the appointment of his second son to a canonry that he threw a lavish ball at the Palace has not been confirmed by any contemporary reference, but it would seem plausible, and is a poignant symbol of the old order so soon to be swept away in Church reform. John Wade's *Extraordinary Black Book* first appeared in 1831 and showed the Bishop and his family in a thoroughly unfavourable light, as rapacious and exploitative. Wade put the Bishop's income at £27,742; J.H. Sparke's offices were listed (except his Norfolk livings of Gunthorpe and Bale) and calculated to yield £1803. Henry Fardell's offices (before he exchanged Feltwell for Wisbech) were shown to yield £2100 a year. E.B. Sparke was too newly installed to gain a mention. Wade observed with heavy irony 'For anything we know, his son and son-in-law may be amply qualified for these numerous endowments; indeed, they must be young men of extraordinary capabilities, to be able to discharge the duties of so many and important offices'.[126]

At about the same time a letter highly critical of the Sparkes appeared in *The*

---

[123] George Owen Cambridge (1756–1841) was a Canon of Ely and Rector of Elm cum Emneth, 1795–1841; he was also Archdeacon of Middlesex and a Prebendary of St Paul's, 1812–41. He edited the works of his father, Richard Owen Cambridge. George Leonard Jenyns (1763–1848) was Vicar of Swaffham Prior, 1787–1848, and Canon of Ely 1802–48. He inherited Bottisham Hall (Cambs.), in 1787. He had a great knowledge of farming, and was Chairman of the Board of Agriculture in London, and also Chairman of the Bedford Level Corporation in 1830. In the period 1810–20 he acted as unofficial surveyor and clerk of works at Ely. From 1840 he was excused attendance at Chapter on account of a debilitating illness. He was buried at Bottisham (Plate 34b).

[124] George Gaskin (1751–1829) was curate (1778–97) and then Rector (1797–1829) of Stoke Newington, and Rector of St Bennet's, Gracechurch Street, 1786–1823. He was Secretary of the Society for Promoting Christian Knowledge 1786–1823, and was involved in the Society's mission to the Scilly Isles, in promoting legislation for the relief of Scottish Episcopalian ministers, and in the fostering of Church institutions in the western United States. He edited the writings of Richard Southgate, who had left Gaskin his manuscripts.

[125] William French (1786–1849) was Master of Jesus College, 1820–49 (appointed by Bishop Sparke), and Rector of Monkton Moor (Yorks.), 1820–49. He was a mathematician, classicist and oriental linguist, and a skilful administrator. He began the restoration of Jesus College in the 1840s. He died at Jesus College and is buried at Brockdish (Norfolk). William Selwyn (1806–75) was Rector of Branstone (Leics.) 1831–46, and Vicar of Melbourn 1846–53. He was a Canon of Ely 1833–75, and Lady Margaret Professor of Divinity in Cambridge University, 1855–75. An amateur scientist, he had photographs taken at Ely of the Sun, 1863–73. He was the author of *Horae Hebraicae*. He was buried in the Chapter plot in Ely Cemetery. John Maddy (1766–1853) was Rector of Somerton, Suffolk, 1799–1853, and was a royal chaplain, 1806–53. He was buried at Bury St Edmunds.

[126] [John Wade], *The Extraordinary Black Book* (London, 1831), pp. 22–3.

Times.[127] Sent from Ely by 'Your constant reader, a Radical Reformer of every abuse',[128] it argued forcefully against the Archbishop of Canterbury's assertion that Sparke had been 'so moderate in bestowing preferment on members of his own family', and detailed the careers of the Sparke brothers and Henry Fardell since 1815.[129] In the writer's opinion, his research was 'almost of itself sufficient to convince any honest mind of the necessity of an immediate, full and effectual reform.'[130]

Nowhere was the view of the Bishop, or his sons, of the reforms in train or in prospect, ever expressed. When it came to the point, life tenure counted for much, and it was their successors who would bear the brunt. In the shake-up caused by the appointment of Bishop Allen as Sparke's successor in 1836 – by a Whig government – the Sparke brothers and the other diocesan officials prepared to defend themselves and refused to surrender their patent offices. The story of the momentous changes of the later nineteenth century belongs to another chapter; but in the early 1830s the momentum for change was seen to be building up, with the inquiry into cathedral revenues by the 1832 Royal Commission. The old order which had given Ely such continuity since 1660 was about to be shaken.

---

[127] *The Times*, 9 April 1831. This letter had been provoked by unwelcome comments on Sparke in Parliament, after the resignation by Henry Fardell of Feltwell so that he could be presented to Wisbech. Sparke wanted Feltwell for his younger son, but the presentation was alternate with the Lord Chancellor, and Sparke had to ask the Lord Chancellor to cede his turn. Sparke wrote two letters, the second not in his hand, but signed by him, and the Lord Chancellor in referring to the letters seemed to cast doubt on the soundness of Sparke's mind. On 31 March 1831 the Archbishop of Canterbury made a statement to the Lords in defence of Sparke, 'who, though he might be in an infirm state of body, was beyond all question, in a sound state of mind.' The Archbishop had had letters from Dr Clark, Sparke's physician, and another 'in reply to a note from one of the bishop's sons', testifying to Sparke's ability to transact business 'since his attack in May last' (1830). The Archbishop defended Sparke against the charge of nepotism 'but we are sorry to say that his observations were almost inaudible below the bar [of the House]'.

[128] The writer has not been identified.

[129] His estimate of their income was in excess of Wade's: J.H. Sparke, £4,500 *p.a.*; H. Fardell, £3,700; E.B. Sparke, £4,000.

[130] Adding, for good measure, the reminder that 'The Bishop of Ely . . . owes his appointment to one of our greatest boroughmongers and anti-reformers', namely, the 5th Duke of Rutland.

The History of the Fabric from 1541 to 1836

THOMAS COCKE

It is frustrating that we know so little of what was done to the fabric of Ely Cathedral during most of the seventeenth century. It is probable that works were in progress in 1632–3 when a wide variety of building materials was inventorised.[1] Even before Matthew Wren arrived as Bishop shortly before the Civil War, it is likely that the choir was refurbished, including perhaps some of the monuments. That of Bishop Hotham, as recorded in the mid-eighteenth century, seems to have been reworked at this stage, with a prominent Jacobean-style finial at one corner.[2]

Firm evidence is equally lacking for what was done in the following decades to destroy rather than renew the building and its contents. With the dissolution of the Cathedral establishment in 1644,[3] there would have been a cessation of regular maintenance; but how much outright destruction was there during the Civil War and the Interregnum? Oliver Cromwell, with his considerable personal links with Ely, is alleged to have ordered traditional worship in the Cathedral to cease, but the Cromwell connexion might, by analogy with that of Fairfax with York Minster, argue for greater protection of the Cathedral building.[4] The systematic iconoclasm practised against the Lady Chapel sculptures in the 1540s can be set against the immunity of the St Etheldreda capitals around the Octagon. The Parliamentary survey of 1649 offers firmer evidence for the fate of the Chapter buildings than for the Cathedral itself.[5] Greed for roofing-lead evidently resulted in the stripping of buildings such as Prior Crauden's Chapel and the chapter house, ultimately leading to the destruction of the latter.[6]

In 1660 the restored Dean and Chapter evidently faced a major backlog of repairs to the Cathedral and soon found that the cost of the work exceeded their financial resources. The relatively scarce evidence indicates that most of the urgent repairs were necessary in obvious places. The windows of the choir needed renewing and

---

[1] EDC 4/5/13, inventory of Chapter goods dated 26 November 1632, listing scaffolding, a glazier's vice and other building materials.
[2] Bentham, *Ely*, plate XVIII.
[3] See Ian Atherton, above, p. 191.
[4] Maddison, *Ely Cathedral*, pp. 109–10.
[5] EDC 8A/1/13; see also the edition by Atkinson, *Ely Monastery*, pp. 190–8.
[6] In 1647–8 there was a scheme to demolish the Cathedral and sell its materials for the benefit of 'sick and maimed soldiers, widows and orphans' (BL, Add. MS 5868, fo. 34ᵛ).

extensive repairs were necessary on the Octagon, the west tower and the north aisle. The elaborate tracery in the choir windows, not to mention the glass itself, would obviously have suffered during the twenty years of civil war and Commonwealth. Repairs were in progress at the east end in March 1663.[7] Attention must also have been given to restoring some 'beauty of holiness' to the choir. In June 1663 the Chapter resolved to ask the Bishop for leave to make a throne for him, presumably to ease him out of the place of honour on the south side of the choir occupied in other cathedrals by the dean but in Ely by the Bishop as successor to the Abbot.[8] The Octagon and west tower, exposed as they are to the full force of the winds across the Fens, would also have suffered from the lack of maintenance. Thomas Fuller described as a wonder of nature the way the ringing of the bells in the Octagon made the timbers of the Lantern open and shut, but a more realistic view of the phenomenon led to the disposal in 1662–3 of two of the bells and the transfer of the others to the west tower.[9] The west tower was repaired six years later with the help of £100 given by Bishop Laney.[10] The Chapter thanked the Bishop in an elaborate Latin letter which made eloquent references to the physical ruin to which the Cathedral had been reduced 'by the madness of those most barbarous times'[11] and the consequent financial ruin for the Chapter after nine years of repairs.[12]

The reason for the work on the north aisle is less obvious. Back in the fourteenth century the lay congregation of the Cathedral had been moved out of the nave into a separate parish church, dedicated to the Holy Cross, attached to and presumably parallel to the north aisle. Virtually nothing is known of its architectural character or even its precise dimensions. After the Dissolution, the parishioners must have been persuaded that the Cathedral's Lady Chapel offered better accommodation and the parish of Holy Trinity established itself there in 1566. The former church of the Holy Cross was left to moulder away and its ruins are schematically depicted in the *Monasticon* engraving of 1655[13] (Plate 23a). The date stone of 1662, still visible on the north face of the north aisle, shows that the opportunity was taken after the Restoration to tidy away what remained and to re-face the aisle.

It is typical of the financial problems which beset cathedrals in this period that even these works were enough to plunge the Chapter into debt, especially to its own members. By the end of 1662 the Chapter had to advance £160 from the canons' own dividends and two years later it had to borrow another £400.[14] The ready money necessary to pay the tradesmen was always scarce and so the temptation was always to borrow it from the dean or individual canons, against the security of future revenues. This practice could cause particular problems after the death of one of these dignitaries,

---

[7] EDC 2/2A/2, p. 13.

[8] *Ibid.*, p. 15. 'To make a motion to the Bishop about the erecting a Throne for him in the Quire; and for leave to use the other stalls, as is usuall in Cathedralls.' If there was such an attempt, it failed.

[9] EDC 4/5/7.

[10] EDC 2/2A/2, p. 82.

[11] '*Saeverrimorum temporum rabie*'.

[12] *Ibid.*, p. 83.

[13] William Dugdale, *Monasticon Anglicanum*, I (London, 1655), pl. facing p. 88; see also J. Alexander and P. Binski (eds.), *Age of Chivalry: Art in Plantagenet England, 1200–1400* (London: Royal Academy of Arts, 1987), p. 369, cat. nos. 384–5.

[14] EDC 2/2A/2, pp. 20, 45.

when his heirs sought to retrieve the capital.[15] In 1678 the Chapter formally acknow-ledged that they were 'sensible how much the Church suffers in the Credit and Interest thereof by their frequent wants of money to supply their present occasions'.[16]

Perhaps for these reasons, there appears to have been a lull in major works during the 1670s. Activity revived after the death of Bishop Gunning in 1682. Traditionally it was he who first formulated the idea of moving the choir out of its inconvenient site, blocking the crossing, into the east end, liturgically redundant since the abolition of the cult of St Etheldreda; and serious interest in the idea is confirmed by the appointment of a committee of two prebendaries to investigate the feasibility of accomplishing the 'late Bishop's designe of removeing and beautyfieing the Quire'.[17] Presumably they recom-mended against it since the next recorded decision was to resume the scheme of re-paving the existing choir – an improvement typical of the period – and to use £300 bequeathed by Gunning for this purpose.[18] Any unspent balance was to go to 'the use and advantage of the Church'.[19] The mason Robert Grumbold duly installed a pavement of black and white marble in 1685.[20] It demonstrates the long memory of the Cathedral community at Ely that the idea of moving the choir did not altogether vanish but sank underground, to emerge almost a century later in the scheme proposed by James Bentham and James Essex in 1759 and finally executed in 1771. An equally contemporary and more striking improvement to the furnishings was the provision of a white marble font in 1693, for which Dean Spencer left money in his will.[21] It survives, although exiled to the nineteenth-century church at Prickwillow, where it stands, in Pevsner's words, as 'a gilt goblet on a poor man's bare boards'[22] (Plate 24c). Unfortunately the elaborate carved cover supporting figures of Christ being baptized by St John has been lost. It must have rivalled any of the contemporary equivalents in the City of London churches (Plate 24b).

The next major event to affect the Cathedral fabric was due to an act of God rather than to any act of Chapter. On 29 March 1699 the north-west angle of the north transept collapsed, allegedly the delayed effect of an 'earthquake' some years earlier. It is tempting to suspect that an earth tremor was a convenient disaster with which to excuse previous neglect of a superfluous part of the Cathedral. However, whatever the omissions of their predecessors, the Dean and Chapter in 1699 reacted to the disaster with vigour. There is, besides, the testimony of John Dowsing, the Chapter Clerk, perhaps prompted by accusations of neglect, that 'to the Honour of this Society all first appearances of decay in this noble edifice have been always timely obviated by the extraordinary care and zeal of the Reverend Doctors and Canons; of this I have been a witness for two and twenty years'.[23]

---

[15] *Ibid.*, pp. 41–2.

[16] *Ibid.*, pp. 143–4.

[17] *Ibid.*, p. 179.

[18] Bentham, *Ely*, p. 204.

[19] *Ibid.*, p. 179.

[20] EDC 4/5/9, articles of agreement between Dean Spencer and Grumbold for repaving the choir 'after the manner of the Chappell belonging to the . . . Colledge commonly called Peterhouse.'

[21] Bentham, *Ely*, p. 236.

[22] N. Pevsner, *The Buildings of England: Cambridgeshire*, 2nd edn (Harmondsworth, 1970), p. 450.

[23] EDC 4/5/57. The Chapter had certainly not been idle in the preceding years, spending £100 in 1696 on 'beautifying the outside' (EDC 2/2A/2, p. 213).

It can be argued that the restoration of Ely's north transept in 1699–1702 was the first event in the architectural history of the Cathedral to be of international significance since the construction of the Octagon and Lantern four centuries before. And while the aesthetic results may not be as inspiring as Alan of Walsingham's work, the decision to rebuild the early Romanesque fabric as it had stood before the collapse is a landmark in the history of restoration in Europe.

As was standard with extraordinary projects affecting a cathedral fabric, the accounts for the restoration were kept separately from the standard chapter accounts, which covered the regular expenditure on the fabric. Fortunately the documents relating to these extraordinary expenses survive at Ely, and include not only the accounts and a list of benefactors but three letters sent by Dean Lambe when he visited London in August 1699 to gain expert advice on how best to further the project.[24] He was disarmingly honest about his own mixed motives, on the one hand wanting the best solution for the building and on the other fearful of the effect the repairs would have on his own pocket – 'such is the effect of clergy marriages'. In his brief visit he discussed the rebuilding with Archbishop Tenison and the Dean of Westminster on the ecclesiastical side,[25] as well as with Sir Christopher Wren and Samuel Foulkes, overseer of the masons at St Paul's Cathedral. We do not know what discussions may have preceded the crucial decision in June 1700 to rebuild 'exactly in the same manner and on the same foundations it stood before'.[26] This part of the building was of little use for a reformed Anglican cathedral, either for liturgy – since there were no processions and no side chapels – or for everyday maintenance. It was the south transept which housed the ancillary spaces, such as the Library, Chapter Room and vestries. The chief function of the north transept was to act as an entrance for the townspeople living to the north as opposed to that for the Canons from the south. This was of course especially important for the parishioners of Holy Trinity whose church was the former Lady Chapel.

It would not have been surprising if the repair had proved a minimal affair, perhaps reducing the transept by a bay or chipping away the architectural detailing.[27] Instead the transept was rebuilt according to its original design and to its original height (Colour pl. 4a). A Romanesque turret, complete with grotesque heads, was constructed at the north-west angle to match that surviving on the north-east. The latter was repaired and repointed in 1703.[28] Samuel Foulkes had stressed to the Dean that the 'cap or spire' was 'not an ornament only but a mighty strength, even as good as a buttress by reason of its weight'.[29] The only place where the original detailing was altered was in the western bay of the north front, where the round-headed gallery window was treated like those on the west front of the Wren Library at Cambridge, with slender double mullions and a transom, and the doorway below like the north doorway of St Mary le Bow in

[24] EDC 4/5/42–3, 164.

[25] Thomas Spratt (1635–1713), also Bishop of Rochester 1684–1713.

[26] EDC 2/2A/2, p. 229.

[27] Such devices were common during the restoration of French monastic churches damaged in the Wars of Religion and repaired in the 17th century. See T.H. Cocke, 'Gothique Moderne: The Use of Gothic in Seventeenth-Century France', in E. Fernie and P. Crossley (eds.), *Medieval Architecture and its Intellectual Context. Studies in Honour of Peter Kidson* (London, 1990), pp. 249–57, at pp. 254–5.

[28] EDC 2/2A/2, p. 247.

[29] EDC 4/5/42.

London, a design of receding voussoirs derived from Parisian 'hotels'. It seems unlikely that these contemporary features respond to elements in the original design. More probably, they were inspired by a desire to update the building, while respecting its overall architectural character.

Who was responsible for this energetic but subtle design? The obvious candidate is the man appointed to take on the rebuilding, Robert Grumbold, the leading mason in Cambridge and the regular choice of the Chapter when faced with any significant task. Grumbold had worked on the Wren Library himself and could easily have studied the St Mary le Bow doorway both by personal inspection – he knew both Wren and Foulkes personally – and through drawings. Grumbold however had little experience in replacing major elements of a major medieval building, let alone one in the Romanesque rather than the Gothic style. It may not be fanciful to suggest that there had been informal discussions between Grumbold and Sir Christopher Wren as to the best way forward, before Dean Lambe embarked on his own consultation with the Surveyor-General. By 1700 Wren had acquired through his official duties and other consultations a broad knowledge of both the stylistic character and the practical repair of the greatest medieval buildings of the country, ranging from the early Romanesque of Old St Paul's nave to the complex Perpendicular of the Divinity Schools at Oxford.

The way the rebuilding was funded is also of interest. In the event the costs were largely covered by individual donations. Of the final bill of £2637, £1100 came from the Chapter and the Bishop but nearly all the rest from individuals, ranging from various Cambridge Heads of Houses and Fellows and local gentry to 'Mr. Upton, citizen of London'.[30] The least productive source, though the most troublesome to organise, had proved to be the country-wide 'brief', which only yielded £500 net after the considerable expenses had been deducted. The Ely authorities suspected fraud or incompetence on the part of the collectors but it may be that Ely's plight meant little outside the diocese.[31]

By 1704 the Chapter felt 'loaded and surprized' by what they saw as 'vast and unnecessary charges' in the building works, so it is not surprising that the first half of the eighteenth century saw little work of consequence to the Cathedral.[32] That caution meant not blindness to the needs of the fabric but the greatest restraint in responding to them. For instance, a survey of the Lantern in 1707 revealed that many of the timbers were decayed and the leadwork thin and cracked, but only £40 was allowed to cover the worst defects.[33] In the event over £100 was spent. Even during this uneventful period it was, however, unusual for less than £100 to be spent on repairs in any one year, even if details of the expenditure are scarce.

For the modern student, perhaps the most intriguing intervention is one that did not happen. When the west tower was raised to its present height, in c.1400, it was capped by a wood and lead spire, similar to the 'Hertfordshire spike' found, for instance, not far

---

[30] EDC 4/5/52. The names of the donors were recorded not only in the accounts but also on a scroll designed for public display (EDC 4/5/15) (Colour pl. 22b); see G. Zarnecki et al. (eds.), *English Romanesque Art 1066–1200* (London: Arts Council of Great Britain, 1984), p. 370, no. 506. A similar scroll of benefactors had been prepared in 1695 to record all those who had contributed since 1660 (EDC 2/2A/2, p. 209).

[31] The Chapter recorded that 'these our hopes [of larger receipts from the brief] are not without some fears and suspicions attending them' (EDC 4/5/53).

[32] EDC 2/2A/2, p. 251.

[33] *Ibid.*, p. 271.

away at Baldock. In 1748 the Chapter resolved to remove the spire, presumably to save the expense of repair, but perhaps also for the aesthetic reason which 25 years before had nearly condemned the similar spires on the Lincoln west towers, which were considered to look 'ill', like 'so many Extinguishers set upon great candles'.[34] However, only two months later, the decision was rescinded upon 'the application of some of the principal Gentlemen of this Town', and a revised order was given to re-lead and repair the spire.[35] It was finally removed in 1802. As at Lincoln, where the attempt to remove the spires in 1725 had provoked a serious riot, there may have been a political dimension to the agitation, with a disaffected town suspicious of anything a Whig-dominated Cathedral establishment might do to diminish traditional features, especially following the descent by the Young Pretender into England only three years earlier.[36]

This seemingly quiet period saw the gradual emergence into prominence of the talented Bentham family, especially James who became the great historian of the Cathedral (Plate 29c). As noted elsewhere in this volume, the eventual fame of the latter meant that details are recorded of his career and those of his family, most of them lesser members of the Cathedral establishment, whereas usually the sources only deal with the most eminent – the Bishop, the Dean and well-connected Canons. The Bentham evidence indicates that, though it would be tempting to interpret the relative inactivity at Ely in terms of building during the first half of the eighteenth century as typical of Hanoverian lethargy and indifference to the inheritance of the past, during this period there was a growing concern to investigate the history of the building and to improve the liturgy celebrated there. The presence at Ely of the distinguished antiquary Thomas Tanner (Plate 25c) as a prebendary from 1713 to 1724, stimulated first Samuel Bentham and then his son, James, into years of research into the successive generations of the Cathedral establishment and also of the development of the architecture through the Middle Ages.

These years of 'underground' study help to explain the sudden change in the 1750s from relative quiet to major projects of repair and improvement. This was assisted by the energy and generosity of Bishop Mawson, translated to Ely in 1754 from Chichester where he had already instigated extensive work on that Cathedral (Plate 29b). A third stimulus towards a more vigorous approach was the involvement of a surveyor and architect who possessed a deep understanding of medieval buildings. James Essex of Cambridge, son of the joiner of the same name, was emerging by the 1750s both as Sir James Burrough's heir, as the leading source of architectural expertise in the region, and as successor to Robert Grumbold as chief contractor for any major building project (Plate 30a).

Essex's precocious interest in medieval antiquities will have led him to study Ely early in his career, but such was the close-knit world of Cambridge and Ely, that it would be hard to say whether it was James Bentham, still a minor canon, who persuaded the Chapter to commission Essex to make a survey of the whole Cathedral in 1757. It surely cannot be mere coincidence that just at this time Essex surveyed and prepared the

[34] PRO, State Papers Domestic (George I) 35, vol. 63, no. 51(2) and (3).

[35] EDC 2/2A/3, pp. 134, 136.

[36] T.H. Cocke, 'The Architectural History of Lincoln from the Dissolution to the Twentieth Century', in T.A. Heslop and V.A. Sekules (eds.), *Medieval Art and Architecture at Lincoln Cathedral*, BAACT, 8 (1986), pp. 148–57, at p. 150.

impressive series of measured drawings showing plans, elevations and sections of the Cathedral that were eventually published as illustrations to James Bentham's book.[37]

The comprehensive surveys which James Essex made of Ely (though his financial reward was only twelve guineas) and a few years later of Lincoln Cathedral, stand in succession to Sir Christopher Wren's famous analyses of the cathedrals of Salisbury, Old St Paul's and Westminster Abbey, published in *Parentalia* in 1750.[38] Essex's observations do not simply list the areas of structural concern, for instance in the roofing, where he expressed himself pungently as to the deficiencies of previous repairs; throughout, his account is informed by his understanding of the whole 'mechanism' of a great medieval building – in other words how each part depended upon another.[39] It was surely Essex who insisted that the first parts of the building to be repaired properly were the decayed Octagon and Lantern over the crossing, even if that meant leaving the potential danger of the outward-leaning roof over the eastern arm for another ten years. As Essex pointed out, the Lantern 'being a work of the greatest Importance, the neglect of it may be attended with the destruction of the Church . . . As nothing but a general substantial Repair of this Lantern can prevent it's Ruin, it would be the greatest Imprudence and Extravagance, to enter upon a partial one'.[40] This prudent prioritising of the structural safety of the Cathedral was accompanied by his championing of a major re-ordering, dictated by aesthetic and liturgical rather than architectural considerations. The plea in the 1680s to move the choir eastwards had not been forgotten in Ely and it was taken up enthusiastically by all those most concerned in the mid-century restoration: the Dean and Chapter, the Bishop and, not least, James Bentham and James Essex. The practical advantages of the move were that sound and warmth, instead of being dissipated upwards in the crossing, would be reflected back by a vault. In terms of aesthetics, the move would reveal the beauties of the crossing and also permit grand vistas along the nave and transept (Plate 31a). The avowed model for such a treatment of the centre of a cathedral was a building that was only just rising from the ground in the 1680s but by 1760 was an Anglican ideal – St Paul's Cathedral in London. The analogy was not inappropriate since one of the sources for Wren's octagonal plan for the crossing could have been Ely.

In the event, the removal of the choir was delayed until 1770–1 to enable the major repairs to be undertaken first (Plate 31b). Work began on the Octagon and the Lantern in 1757. Essex claimed that most of the great timbers in the Octagon had become rotten and needed replacement; but investigations in the mid nineteenth century and again in the mid twentieth showed that Essex retained a high proportion of them.[41] More conspicuous and more controversial was his reconstruction of the Lantern. We do not know how much of the medieval detailing had survived to Essex's day. The exposed

---

[37] Bentham, *Ely*, plates XLII–XLIV.

[38] Stephen Wren (ed.), *Parentalia, or Memoirs of the Family of the Wrens* (London, 1750).

[39] The only contemporary figure with expertise similar to that of James Essex was Francis Price, a carpenter by trade, but surveyor to Salisbury Cathedral from 1737 to his death in 1753 and author of *A Series of Particular and Useful Observations . . . upon . . . the Cathedral-Church of Salisbury* (London, 1753), of which plate 6 depicts 'A Section of the Church . . . shewing the Critical Mechanism of the whole Structure'.

[40] EDC 4/5/17, pp. 5–6.

[41] P. Lindley, '"Carpenter's Gothic" and Gothic Carpentry. Contrasting Attitudes to the Restoration of the Octagon and Removals of the Choir at Ely Cathedral', *Architectural History*, 30 (1987), pp. 84–112.

position makes it likely that the original pinnacles and tracery would have become unsafe and would have been simplified or removed during the 400 years or more since their construction. Their representation in Dugdale's *Monasticon* gives little help; that illustrating Browne Willis's survey of the Cathedral in 1730 offers rather more guidance, especially as to the leadwork[42] (Plate 11*a*). Essex kept the detailing simple, using Y-tracery for the windows, slender pinnacles and no buttresses. He would have been encouraged in this approach by two factors: firstly, the need for economy and secondly, his perception, typical for his age, that Gothic suffered from an excess of ornament, and its virtues would only be enhanced by paring off unnecessary detailing (Plate 11*b*).

The other major repair, ten years later, was perhaps even more remarkable. The thirteenth-century roof over the choir was essentially of the coupled rafter type and thus lacked any longitudinal stiffening through a ridge or purlins. The result, as in many other great medieval buildings – for instance the thirteenth-century roofs of Westminster Abbey and Salisbury Cathedral – was the 'racking' of the choir roof, with the tall trusses falling away eastwards from the crossing and gradually pushing the east gable so that it 'hung out of the perpendicular, near two Feet'.[43] It is not clear how Essex tackled the latter problem. One later source claimed that he screwed it back to the vertical, presumably using the kind of wooden 'cradle' devised by William Thornton in 1717 to solve a similar problem in the north transept in Beverley Minster.[44] Unlike Beverley, there is no print or any other record of such an apparatus, so perhaps Essex preferred a careful rebuilding. If so, it is a rebuilding which cannot be detected archaeologically.

The choir roof itself presents no such points of uncertainty. Many of the timbers are marked with the date 1768. Essex revised the design of the roof to avoid the structural weaknesses of the original but he retained its proportions, in particular the height. This contrasts sharply with the practice of James Wyatt at Lichfield and Hereford only a decade or so later when he deliberately lowered the pitch of the high roofs to save on timber and on lead, since the flatter pitch allowed the use of slates as covering.

Once both crossing and east end were secure, it was possible to embark on moving the choir. While the Chapter's decision is understandable since the traditional position created an awkward box at the heart of the Cathedral, the lack of care in the dismantling of the choir and in the treatment of the existing features at the east end are less easy to justify. The evidence suggests that Bentham was more to blame than Essex, since Essex complained of the way that the Ely Chapter, with Bentham as their clerk of works, did not heed his professional advice but took their own decisions[45] (Plate 31*c*).

The first design that Essex made, and the one that he himself favoured for the new choir was to place the organ over the altar, hard up against the east window (Plate 30*b*). Not surprisingly there was resistance to this unusual idea and in the event the organ was placed in the conventional position over the western screen[46] (Colour pl. 13*a*). The walls

[42] T.H. Cocke, 'The Architectural History of Ely Cathedral from 1540–1840', in N. Coldstream and P. Draper (eds.), *Medieval Art and Architecture at Ely Cathedral*, BAACT, 2 (London, 1979), pp. 71–7, at p. 74.

[43] Bentham, *Ely*, p. 284.

[44] George Millers, *A Description of the Cathedral Church of Ely* (London, 1807), p. 74.

[45] T.H. Cocke, 'James Essex', in R. Brown (ed.), *The Architectural Outsiders* (London, 1985), pp. 98–113, at p. 107.

[46] A set of 5 designs for the new choir survives at the Fitzwilliam Museum, Cambridge (*The Ingenious Mr. Essex, Architect. A Bicentenary Exhibition. Fitzwilliam Museum, Cambridge*, selected and catalogued by Thomas Cocke (Cambridge, 1984), p. 32) (Plate 30*b,d*). The west face of the screen is shown in the *Interior of Ely*

flanking the altar were bowed into an apse-like form, partly to accommodate the monument of Cardinal Luxembourg, one of the few monuments not dislodged by the new scheme. Essex was however careful to retain and restore the fourteenth-century stalls, when he moved them eastwards (Colour pl. 11a).

The aesthetic focus of the choir was altered by the generosity of Bishop Mawson, who offered to pay for the insertion of stained glass in the east window. While the Bishop took advice from Horace Walpole, he was not perhaps much helped by Walpole's verdict that the east window was 'the most untractable of all Saxon uncouthnesses' and, prudently, so it seemed, he went to the professional, James Pearson.[47] It is significant that Essex was one of the witnesses signing the contract with Pearson.[48] The window was to be a major piece of work, of a scale and quality to equal the earlier eighteenth-century windows at Westminster Abbey and Exeter Cathedral. It was to include both sacred subjects with the Nativity attended by angels in 'attitudes of joy' in the lower compartments and individual figures of the four Evangelists, St Etheldreda, St Peter and St Paul, and heraldic display with the arms of the King, the Bishop and other dignitaries. Unfortunately, the slow pace of the stained glass artist and the death of the Bishop in November 1770 prevented the completion of the project. The quality of the few fragments that were achieved, notably the head of St Etheldreda, shows the opportunity lost[49] (Colour pl. 17d).

Unfortunately there appears to have been virtually no recognition of the archae-ological importance of the enclosing walls of the choir, notably the western screen, which evidently was a rare survival of a major Romanesque screen. Again, Essex did at least record its detailing sufficiently for its design to be reconstructed, whereas Bentham makes no mention of it.[50] Much more attention was given to the dismantling of the tombs of seven Saxon 'worthies' encased in the choir wall, which were re-housed in Bishop West's chantry chapel[51] (Plate 13c).

The last major campaign of work on the Cathedral during this period focussed on the west end of the building, which had been examined in James Essex's survey but which in the event had received little attention. Again, much of the initiative came from the Bishop, James Yorke, a man of taste and aristocratic connections who was concerned to exploit the aesthetic possibilities of the building as well as to repair the fabric. It is no surprise that in 1794 he summoned the assistance of James Wyatt, just as Bishop Shute Barrington did at Salisbury and then at Durham Cathedrals in the same period. Wyatt's proposals for Ely were much less radical than for the other cathedrals, recommending the raising of the roof within the west tower so as to reveal 'a very beautiful part of the Saxon tower rich in columns and Arches clearly intended to be seen'.[52]

Cathedral by J.M.W. Turner in Aberdeen Art Gallery (Colour pl. 9), and in a painting by Charles Jenyns (Colour pl. 13a).

[47] W.S. Lewis (ed.), *Horace Walpole's Correspondence with . . . Cole*, 2 vols. (London and New Haven, 1937), I, p. 163.

[48] EDC 4/5/19.

[49] The figure of St Peter is preserved in the north nave gallery of the Cathedral (Colour pl. 14c) and the head of St Etheldreda in the Bishop's House.

[50] Essex's brief description of the screen was published in Bentham, *Ely*, Appendix, p. 3. A reconstruction using some drawings by Essex was published by W. St J. Hope in *Archaeologia*, lxviii (1917), pp. 43–110, at pl. ix, facing p. 43 (Plate 3c).

[51] See Appendix 3, pp. 401–4 below.

James Wyatt was, again as at Salisbury and Durham, the consultant architect, giving his advice from afar and then leaving the execution to other hands of whatever resulted. In the case of Ely it was John Groves, a colleague of Wyatt at the Office of Works, who was put in charge both of the repairs and improvements to the west tower and of similar work on the Galilee porch. The work on the latter has particular interest from the involvement of Francis Bernasconi, the stuccador who was extensively employed in church restorations of the early nineteenth century to reproduce fine Gothic mouldings in his patent plaster. The use of cement was criticised by John Carter in the *Gentleman's Magazine* as 'in all likelihood perishable and unfit for any length of time to withstand the vicissitudes of an English climate', although the article admitted that the models chosen for the mouldings and ornaments were 'for the most part, uncommonly sharp and correct'.[53] In the event the composition has worn better over the last 200 years than much of the more recent stonework.

The Chapter evidently sought advice on the west tower from other sources, in particular from William Wilkins senior, who had a considerable, though not uncontroversial reputation as a surveyor of historic buildings in Norfolk, not least at Norwich Cathedral. His involvement at Ely is confirmed by the brilliant paper delivered to the Society of Antiquaries in 1801 by his son the younger William Wilkins, which analysed and reconstructed the original appearance of the fourteenth-century Prior Crauden's chapel, long since converted into lodgings.[54]

The reports by Wilkins 'and many others' agreed that the west tower was 'in a very dangerous and dilapidated state' and a Chapter committee was formed in June 1799, empowered to take emergency measures as necessary.[55] Whoever directed the repairs of the upper parts, it was the proposals by Wyatt and Groves for the west porch which were agreed. Since Bishop Yorke was offering to pay, it may have been his influence which ensured that Wyatt and Groves (whom he had earlier employed on the Palace) would be the chosen team. Groves in turn delegated much of the supervision to his pupil, Charles Bacon, who petitioned for the title of 'Architect to the Dean and Chapter' in 1816 – the first time apparently that the title had been accorded – but he died prematurely in 1818.[56]

As at the east end, the climax of Bishop Yorke's generosity was to pay for the installation of stained glass in the west window in 1807. In this case, perhaps fortunately, the stained glass was made up of imported pieces from abroad, rather than depending on the energy of a glazier (Colour pl. 14*b*). (They were supplemented by two further panels given by Thomas Waddington in 1810). The roof of the Galilee was lowered so that sufficient light would illuminate the newly installed glass. This created a Romantic effect at the west end to balance that produced by clearing the Octagon 30 years earlier – not dissimilar to the vistas carefully orchestrated by Wyatt at Salisbury Cathedral.[57] A watercolour by J.M.W. Turner, now in the City of Aberdeen Art

[52] EDC 4/5/291–2.
[53] *Gentleman's Magazine*, lxxv (1805), pt 1, pp. 122–3.
[54] William Wilkins, 'An Account of the Prior's Chapel at Ely', *Archaeologia*, xiv (1803), pp. 105–12.
[55] EDC 2/2A/4, p. 227.
[56] EDC 2/2A/5, p. 135. He was not related to John Bacon and his son, also John Bacon, who were respectively clerk of works in the Cathedral in 1822–45 and 1845–88.

Gallery, shows the Cathedral clergy and even Essex's choir screen dwarfed by the architecture and the soaring shafts of light (Colour pl. 9).

More prosaically, Groves designed a new pulpit in a precocious neo-Romanesque style (Plates 41a and 48c). The provision of a pulpit was presumably connected with the re-arrangement in 1796 of the space in the crossing and transept cleared by the removal of the choir eastwards into a 'sermon place' where the Cathedral congregation could join with those of the town parishes without inconvenient to-ing and fro-ing.[58]

The final episcopal benefaction occurred just 30 years later when Bishop Sparke offered to fulfil his predecessor's intention and insert new stained glass in the east window. It is interesting to note that the letter of thanks from the Dean and Chapter to the Bishop expressly referred to this being 'the only requisite for the completion of the interior'. The Bishop would be putting 'the finishing hand to that fabric, which owes so much to your Lordship's predecessors'.[59] Less than ten years later the new Dean Peacock and his Cambridge friends William Whewell and Robert Willis would be looking at the Cathedral with very different eyes.

---

[57] T. Cocke and P. Kidson, *Salisbury Cathedral: Perspectives on the Architectural History* (London, 1993), p. 28.
[58] EDC 4/5/33.

Music and Liturgy to 1644

IAN PAYNE

Ely Cathedral was fortunate among English provincial cathedrals in that it boasted for the period 1541–1643 a number of very talented musicians. As early as 1614, Prebendary Andrew Willet was able to reflect proudly on Ely's distinguished musicians ('*insignos Musicos*'), singing the praises of Tye, White, Farrant, Fox, Barcroft, Jordan and Amner.[1] Most of these men were composers whose music has come down to us, and some also held posts at other institutions. Others – William Fox, George Barcroft and John Amner – spent their entire working lives at Ely, and therefore probably composed all of their surviving liturgical music for performance by the Cathedral choir. The Dean and Chapter archives shed considerable light on the careers of these men and on the musical establishment of which they were part, especially from the beginning of the seventeenth century. There are, of course, the usual *lacunae* in our knowledge, such as are caused by frequent gaps in the Receiver's accounts and the absence of a series of Treasurer's accounts for the Tudor musical establishment; and it must be stressed at the outset that ecclesiastical archives in general are seldom concerned with matters of musical detail,[2] and that Ely's are no exception. But these archival deficiencies are to some extent compensated for by the survival of exceptionally detailed post-1604 Treasurer's Accounts and a very full series of episcopal visitation staff–lists. Consequently, a tolerably clear picture of musical activity at Ely does emerge; and this is occasionally enhanced by the work of eighteenth-century Cathedral antiquaries such as Thomas Watkins (Precentor, 1736–76) and James Hawkins (Organist, 1682–1729).[3]

---

[1] Epistola Dedicatoria to his *An Harmonie upon the Second Book of Samuel* (Cambridge, 1614), quoted in EDC 14/9, p. 212. I owe my knowledge of this work to Dr R.D. Bowers.

[2] Numerous examples of this lack will be found in Payne, *Provision and Practice*, but not, unfortunately, from Ely.

[3] Watkins compiled, *c.*1764, a manuscript list of Cathedral officers from 1544 (EDC 2/9/3); and Hawkins copied much old music in score. (See Shaw, *Succession of Organists*, pp. 96, 101–2.) The work of such antiquaries, when applied to the earlier periods, must sometimes be treated with caution, as for example the absurd suggestion that the quite definitely post-Reformation anthem 'O almighty God' by George Barcroft (Organist, 1580–1610) is actually by Thomas Barcroft, who is stated in error to have been Organist of Ely in 1535. (The mistaken belief that the latter had been organist at Ely survived into the twentieth century: see A. Wilson, *Ely Cathedral: The Organs & Organists* (Ely, 1908), p. 14; the error is explained in Shaw, *Succession of Organists*, p. 99). The only Thomas Barcroft on the establishment when this anthem could have been composed was a lay clerk (d.1632: EDC 8A/1/1, p. 122).

The Reformation and the Elizabethan settlement 1541–1603

The New Foundation musical establishment

When, in August 1541, King Henry VIII's government refounded the Cathedral, it made essentially the same musical provision at Ely as at other cathedrals of the New Foundation.[4] Dated 20 June 1544, the new statutes provided for an adult choral force of eight minor canons and eight lay clerks.[5] The choir also included eight choristers with good, sonorous voices and suited to singing ('*vocibus sonoris et ad cantandum aptis*') and a Master of the Choristers, skilled in singing and in organ-playing ('*cantandi et organi pulsandi peritus*'), who was to teach the boys.[6] Although there is evidence at many New Foundation cathedrals (for example, Norwich and Peterborough) that the organist's duties, as they became more demanding towards the end of the sixteenth century, were shared by two or more individuals, there is no formal record that this was so at Ely before the Civil War, and all letters patent between 1559 and 1641 continue to assign both duties to one man.[7]

The earliest extant list of musical personnel, an undated document of *c.*1541, shows at least that the new musical establishment was fully staffed. Only the Master of the Choristers is named – one 'William Smith the elder' – of whom nothing else is known, although it is likely that he, at least, had served the former Benedictine monastery.[8] The remaining accounts for the 1540s, though incomplete, suggest that the choral establishment was up to strength; however between 1547 and November 1551 the number of minor canons had dropped from eight to six, which remained the norm up to the Interregnum; the number of full-time lay clerks was at its lowest in the 1560s, and between 1572 and 1640 it fluctuated between seven and nine, the shortfall being made

---

[4] EDC 2/1/4 (contains both Henrician and Elizabethan statutes). For a wider discussion of the musical implications of these statutes, and detailed lists of masters of the choristers, see Payne, *Provision and Practice*, pp. 191–2, 252; the musical ramifications of the statutes are considered in general terms by Shaw, *Succession of Organists*, pp. xviii–xxi. It should be observed that the salaries prescribed by the Henrician statutes were never paid; instead, the higher annual salaries stipulated in the Elizabethan statutes of 1565 (minor canons and master of the choristers £10 each; lay clerks £6 13*s.* 4*d*; choristers £3 6*s.* 8*d*: see EDC 2/1/4, c. 30, at fo. 11ᵛ) seem to have been anticipated since the 1540s. Although the Elizabethan statutes are in most respects virtually identical to the earlier ones, the subject of pre–1565 salaries is a typical example of statutory prescription lagging behind current practice.

[5] EDC 2/1/4, c. 20, at fo. 6ᵛ. The fact that both minor canons and newly–introduced laymen were required to be skilled in singing ('*cantando periti*') strongly suggests that all later contributed to the reduced, simplified textures of the post-Reformation polyphonic ensemble.

[6] EDC 2/1/4, c. 25, at fo. 7ᵛ. It is interesting to observe here that at Exeter Cathedral during the period covered by this chapter, the vicars choral equated such similar Latin phrases as '*vocis sonoritatem*' with 'sound or lowde voyces', and the stipulation that all singers should be '*in Cantus Scientia et Modulandi Voce sonora*' (according to a statute of 1544) with the possession of 'a laudable voyce, and skill in singinge agreeable' (Payne, *Provision and Practice*, p. 178).

[7] For Norwich and Peterborough, see Payne, *Provision and Practice*, pp. 261–2, 264–7; for letters patent, which seem to represent an Elizabethan attempt to make formal arrangements which had hitherto been informal, see below, pp. 228–30.

[8] CCCC, MS 120 'The boke of the erection of the King's newe College at Elye', p. 293. It was the government's intention, at the dissolution of the monasteries, that there should be 'as much continuity as possible with the former monastic personnel'. (See R.D. Bowers, 'The Liturgy of the Cathedral and its Music, *c.*1075–1642', in P. Collinson, N. Ramsay and M. Sparks (eds.), *A History of Canterbury Cathedral* (Oxford, 1995), pp. 408–50, at p. 426.)

up of singing-men who were paid for only part of the year. The choristers, in contrast, always numbered eight in the Dean and Chapter's accounts.[9]

A Period of Major Liturgical Upheaval, c.1547–c.1559

During the eight years which separated the birth of the New Foundation and the imposition of the first Book of Common Prayer in 1549, it is very doubtful whether the Cathedral's musicians could have been fully prepared for the sudden and seemingly cataclysmic change to their daily round of duties which this first vernacular liturgy would engender. Between the accession of Edward VI in 1547 and the enforcement of the Prayer Book two years later, the old familiar Catholic liturgy was tolerated by the new regime. But in June 1549 the use of the new English liturgy was enforced by statute, and the impact of this abrupt and unprecedented break with tradition had an immediate, deleterious and demoralizing effect on the staff of choral foundations everywhere: the familar Latin liturgy was discarded together with its rich heritage of elaborate polyphony, daily services were cut from ten to three, thereby reducing the numbers of staff required for their execution and leaving them with very little to do, and the 'members of former medieval choirs everywhere were changed at a stroke from actively participating in the liturgy to passively commentating on it'.[10] To make matters worse, the new liturgy made scarcely any provision for music and was hopelessly vague in its meagre musical directions. Then, three years later, when the plight of church music could hardly have seemed graver or more depressing, the first English liturgy was replaced by a newer and much more Protestant second Prayer Book, which was even less tolerant of polyphonic music than its predecessor. Such polyphony as was allowed under the new regime barely justifies that term: simple, predominantly syllabic, four-part music, more homophonic than contrapuntal, which pales into artistic insignificance beside the demanding Latin compositions of Henry VIII's reign, and which required a much lower degree of skill to compose and to perform it.

Ely was among the more fortunate foundations in one respect: at least its choir was not disbanded at the reformation of religion. Indeed, the 1540s saw the appointment of Ely's first distinguished Master of the Choristers, Christopher Tye; but it is typical of the paucity and lack of detail of New Foundation accounts for this early period that the Ely Cathedral archives contain not a shred of evidence for the copying or acquisition of polyphony or of service-books (most of which would have contained not one note of music) at this time of change. A supply of simple four-part settings of the Communion Service and the canticles would however have been required for the choir to participate fully in the new vernacular liturgy.

Hardly had the Ely musicians had time to adjust to the new liturgy, when they were forced to comprehend and wholly embrace an equally abrupt return to Henrician Catholicism: Mary Tudor acceded to the throne in July 1553 and the old Catholic liturgy was made compulsory by the end of that year. Because so much of the old Catholic polyphonic repertory had been lost or destroyed in the interim, and choral

---

[9] EDC 3/3/1–2; CCCC, MS 120, p. 289 (stray account dated 25 November 1551). For a summary of staff numbers based on accounting-records, see Payne, *Provision and Practice*, pp. 193–6.

[10] Payne, *Provision and Practice*, pp. 24–31, at pp. 24–5.

foundations were compelled quickly to acquire working repertories, the early years of Mary's reign saw a large increase in musical activity at some Old Foundation cathedrals and Cambridge musical foundations; but, once again, the Ely records, lacking Treasurer's accounts for this period, are completely silent.[11]

Fortunately, when the next (and final) reformation of religion occurred with the promulgation of the Elizabethan Prayer Book (1559), and the now-extinct repertory of Latin polyphony was discarded for the last time, Queen Elizabeth's personal wish was nevertheless to preserve 'the laudable science of music' in a liturgical context. Accordingly, the new Queen ensured the inclusion in the latest recension of the Prayer Book of a number of provisions which would preserve and safeguard the interests of 'such that delight in music': one much-quoted injunction, prepared by her commissioners during the summer of 1559, allowed 'a modest distinct song . . . that . . . may be as plainly understood as if it were read without singing': viewed against the recent background of florid Latin polyphony, the operative words 'modest' and 'distinct' would probably have had a sobering effect on highly-skilled singers of polyphony used to the richness and complexity of Latin polyphony; but that a 'song' (that is, an anthem or polyphonic canticle-setting) was allowed at all must, at the same time, have brought the choir considerable relief, following the period of musical attrition associated with the Book's two predecessors. The injunction further ruled that, at the beginning and end of Morning and Evening Prayer, 'there may be sung an Hymn, or such like song [*i.e.* anthem], . . . in the best sort of melody and music that may be conveniently devised, having respect that the sentence of the Hymn may be understood and perceived'.[12] This compromise greatly angered staunch Puritans, and may have seemed small recompense indeed for the extinction of the Marian Latin polyphonic repertory; but as a pro-musical measure it probably represented for those singers with longer memories a very definite and marked improvement upon the previous two Prayer Books, and especially on the short-lived second Book of 1552.

Music under the Elizabethan Organists: Tye, White, Fox and Barcroft

Although Christopher Tye's letters patent of appointment were dated 23 May 1559,[13] shortly before Elizabeth's commissioners issued the injunction quoted above, he was certainly in post during the years 1543–4 and 1546–7, and in November 1551, when he was included in the list of eight lay clerks.[14] He received half a year's salary at

---

[11] There are, for example, no references to polyphony at the New Foundation cathedrals of Norwich and Peterborough in this decade; compare this with the richly documented acquisitions at Old Foundations such as Exeter (see Payne, *Provision and Practice*, pp. 16–17): the difference, while striking, is more probably due to poorer documentation, than to any lack of musical ambition, at the New Foundations. For a detailed study of general Marian musical provisions, see *ibid.*, pp. 39–44.

[12] W.H. Frere and W.P.M. Kennedy (eds.), *Visitation Articles and Injunctions of the Period of the Reformation*, 3 vols (Alcuin Club Collections, 14–16; London, 1910), iii, p. 23 (quoted and discussed in P. le Huray, *Music and the Reformation in England 1549–1600* (London, 1967; 2nd edn, Cambridge, 1978), pp. 32–3; for further discussion of the Elizabethan Settlement see *ibid.*, pp. 31–5, and Payne, *Provision and Practice*, pp. 43–58).

[13] EDC 2/4/1, fo. 15^{r-v}.

[14] EDC 3/3/1–2, and CCCC, MS 120, p. 289. A useful summary of Tye's career is in A. Ashbee and D. Lasocki (eds.), *A Biographical Dictionary of English Court Musicians 1485–1714*, 2 vols (Aldershot, 1998), II, pp. 1107–9. The editors cite evidence newly discovered by David Mateer that Tye was a member of the Chapel Royal in October 1553, when he was allocated a livery for Queen Mary's coronation. Clearly, Tye's association with the

Michaelmas 1561;[15] and by Michaelmas the following year he had been replaced by another distinguished Cambridge musician, Robert White, who married Tye's daughter, Ellen. Prior to Michaelmas 1562, White had been a lay clerk at Trinity College, Cambridge, whose musical establishment (for which some of his superb large-scale Latin polyphony was probably composed, such as the Magnificat, and the antiphons *Regina coeli* and *Tota pulchra es*) had flourished under him; he presumably removed to Ely very soon after this date, for he was paid the full annual salary (£10) at Michaelmas 1563 and had probably served the Cathedral for the whole of that financial year. By Christmas 1566 White was installed in the organ-loft at Chester Cathedral, having left Ely shortly before.[16] It is indeed unfortunate that the archives provide no clue as to the state of music during the tenures of Tye and White, for both men were fine composers, and White's importance in particular has, until recently, been understated.[17]

White's immediate successor, at Michaelmas 1566, was John Farrant (the elder), a colourful and somewhat disreputable character, whose long, varied and chequered career probably began at Ely. Although there is some confusion between this man and another with the same name (who was probably his son),[18] it was certainly the elder man who served at Ely, where he was still in receipt of full salary at Michaelmas 1568.[19] He had left by Michaelmas 1572,[20] though a three-year gap in the accounts renders the precise date of his departure uncertain. Comments by the authorities of other institutions show that Farrant was a competent and able musician; and he had probably enjoyed a successful probationary period at Ely, because his letters patent of appointment, dated 10 December 1567, mention his diligent service.[21] But the Dean and Chapter of Ely had sailed uncomfortably close to the wind in appointing him, as is revealed by an episode which occurred at his next place of employment. Early in

---

Chapel makes it less certain that his music, and especially the large-scale Latin psalm-motets, was written for the Ely Cathedral choir. (For details of the Chapel Royal discovery, see D. Mateer, 'The "Gyffard" Partbooks: Composers, Owners, Date and Provenance', *Royal Musical Association Research Chronicle*, xxviii (1995), pp. 21–50, at pp. 25–6 and 44 n.74. It is likely that his fine six-part Mass *Euge Bone* (which may have been composed as a doctoral exercise in 1545 or 1548: see *The Mass Euge Bone*, ed. N. Davison (n.p., 1978), Preface) and his four-part Mass 'The Western Wind' (arguably the best of three related works with this title, the other two being by Sheppard and Taverner: see *The Western Wind Mass*, ed. N. Davison (London, 1970), Preface) date from his period at Ely, but there is no evidence that either was performed there.

[15] EDC 3/3/3.

[16] On White at Cambridge, see D. Mateer, 'Further Light on Preston and Whyte', *Musical Times*, cxv (1974), pp. 1074–7; Payne, *Provision and Practice*, pp. 35, 37, 218, 253, 277–8; and I. Payne, 'The Musical Establishment at Trinity College, Cambridge, 1546–1644', *PCAS*, lxxiv (1985), pp. 53–60. White's Ely tenure is documented in Payne, *Provision and Practice*, p. 253; and in Shaw, *Succession of Organists*, pp. 97–8, who also documents his tenure at Chester (p. 62).

[17] See H. Benham, *Latin Church Music in England c.1460–1575* (London, 1977), p. 212; much more instrumental in bringing this composer some of the recognition he deserves have been recent recordings, and accompanying liner-notes, such as *Robert White: Tudor Church Music*, by P. Phillips and the Tallis Scholars (Gimell 454 930–2; 1995), and articles such as P. Phillips, 'Sonorous Settings: the Music of Robert White', *Musical Times*, cxl (1999), pp. 31–6.

[18] A courageous attempt to sort out this confusion is in Shaw, *Succession of Organists*, pp. 34–6, though the present writer finds it hard to accept the suggestion that Farrant (the elder)'s career spanned the period 1566–1634 and that he 'was some 90 years old when he died'.

[19] EDC 3/3/8.

[20] EDC 3/3/9. At Michaelmas 1573 Farrant's successor, William Fox, received for the first time the increased full salary (£13 6s. 8d.) for the post of *informator choristarum*.

[21] EDC 2/4/1, fo. 84.

February 1592 Farrant, having been rebuked by the Dean of Salisbury Cathedral for abusing his (Farrant's) wife, threatened him with a knife, exclaiming 'Durst thou seek to take away my living . . . by God's wounds I will cut thy throat!' The Dean escaped with his life; but Farrant, whom Watkins Shaw has aptly described as 'almost certainly the only cathedral organist actually to have threatened to murder his dean', must have expected to be deprived of his office of organist, because he quitted his post two days later, before the day of reckoning.[22]

Following Farrant's hasty departure, the post of Organist and Master of the Choristers passed in succession to two Ely men who, as far as is known, spent the whole of their working lives in the service of the Dean and Chapter. First, on 30 October 1572 William Fox was granted letters patent of appointment, on exactly the same terms as Farrant, except that the annual salary had risen to £13 6s. 8d.[23] He is subsequently named in the annual accounts from 1572–3 to 1577–8,[24] and was buried on 10 September 1579.[25] If little is known about Fox, however, the same cannot be said of his successor, George Barcroft,[26] who was to live long enough to oversee a marked increase in the fortunes of the Cathedral's musical establishment. He must have succeeded Fox at Christmas 1579, for at Michaelmas 1580 he was paid for three quarters of the year.[27] Described as a BA in his letters patent of 10 January 1583,[28] Barcroft, who became a minor canon (or 'vicar', as such officers were known at Ely) in 1592–3,[29] gave continuous service until sickness overtook him, between Midsummer and August 1610. He was paid for the last time at Michaelmas of that year.[30]

If, as seems likely, Robert White managed successfully to steer the Cathedral music through the turbulent waters of sudden change from Marian Catholicism to Elizabethan Anglicanism after Queen Elizabeth I's accession in November 1558, his efforts have left no trace in the Cathedral archives. Whilst the financial records of some other cathedrals testify to the purchase of service-books, metrical psalms and some basic polyphonic repertory in the 1560s and 70s,[31] the Ely accounts tell us nothing at all about the state of its music at this period. These were difficult times for church musicians everywhere: virtually all provincial church musicians were struggling with woefully

---

[22] The Salisbury saga is fully told in Shaw, *Succession of Organists*, p. 259, from which the present brief account is extracted.

[23] EDC 2/4/1, fo. 102v.

[24] EDC 3/3/9, 3/3/12.

[25] Shaw, *Succession of Organists*, p. 99.

[26] *Ibid.*, p. 99, pointing out both that one man of this name was ordained priest in 1590 by the Bishop of Peterborough having become vicar of Dullingham, Cambs., in 1589 (presumably while still a deacon), and that another was a lay clerk of Durham Cathedral who died in 1639. (Perhaps the latter is identifiable as a second George Barcroft who occurs just twice in the Ely records, as a chorister under George senior, at the episcopal visitations on 27 September 1608 and 24 May 1610 (EDR B2/29, fo. 28; EDR B2/31, fo. 3). The chorister does not appear in the next list, dated 5 May 1613 (EDR B2/31, fo. 109). Given the Ely man's illness in 1610, it is most unlikely that he is identical with the Durham musician.) The Ely Barcroft is almost certainly identical with the sizar of this name who was a chorister at Trinity College, Cambridge, between 1575 and 1577, and proceeded BA in the following year: for references and discussion see Payne, *Provision and Practice*, pp. 254–5.

[27] EDC 3/3/13.

[28] EDC 2/4/1, fo. 138[v].

[29] EDC 3/3/21.

[30] At Midsummer 1610 one of the lay clerks (Thomas Barcroft) signed for his salary (EDC 3/1/2, fos. 39–40[v]); and in August the Treasurer bestowed a gift of 10s. 'uppon Mr Barcroft in his sicknes' (EDC 3/1/2, fo. 42).

[31] Payne, *Provision and Practice*, ch. 3.

inadequate stipends which had not risen to keep pace with inflation; many had Catholic sympathies, and even those who had not must have been very concerned for their future careers. And matters were scarcely more encouraging on the musical front. It is hard to believe that even simple polyphonic music with the 'reports and repeatings which may induce any obscureness to the hearers', which was the bane of hard-line reformers,[32] could have flourished at Ely during the long episcopacy (1559–81) of Richard Cox. Sometime tutor to Edward VI and a personal supporter of Christopher Tye,[33] Bishop Cox had earlier (1550) presided over a thorough reformation of the music at St George's Chapel, Windsor Castle.[34] He 'was very active in the Reformation of Religion' during the reign of his young pupil and, during Mary's 'reign of persecution, [being] a zealous defender, and constant in the use, of the English liturgy', had fled to Frankfurt.[35]

A glimpse of this simple, four-part Elizabethan repertory is provided by Ely's valuable collection of liturgical music manuscripts. Although their repertory is extensive, it is salutary to reflect that all of the pre-Civil War works that they contain are post- Restoration transcripts. These compositions, by Tudor, Jacobean and Caroline composers, which were presumably copied from the Cathedral's original part-books, comprise the usual mixture of Chapel Royal fare topped up with pieces by Ely and other provincial composers. For example, an organ-book, Music MS 4 (EDC 10/7/4), contains 27 pieces of service-music and responses on its recto side and 39 anthems on its verso. The impression left by the pre-Civil War repertory represented in this particular manuscript is that the service-music tends to be by earlier composers (for example, Thomas Tallis and Nicholas Strogers) and predominantly four-part, while the anthems, notwithstanding a considerable number of four-part pieces, are more ambitious, larger-scale works by later composers, such as Orlando Gibbons and Thomas Tomkins.[36] It is tempting to speculate that the original Ely exemplars of Tallis's and Tye's four-part services were very early acquisitions, followed closely by the music of Strogers, Farrant and Fox; but although music by predominantly Jacobean and Caroline composers may have originally entered the Cathedral repertory during one of the two pre-Civil War copying projects, any or all of these works could have been added after the Restoration. One of the most important features of these music manuscripts, though, is that they include works by three men who spent their entire working lives in its service. Of these, John Amner (Organist and Master of the Choristers from 1610 to 1641) emerges as the most important, in terms of both his musical ability and the amount of his music – some

---

[32] Le Huray, *Music and the Reformation* (cit. in n. 12), p. 25. (This oft-quoted phrase is from Archbishop Holgate's injunctions to the Dean and Chapter of York, issued in 1552.)

[33] *Biographical Dictionary of English Court Musicians* (cit. in n. 14), II, pp. 1108–9.

[34] Le Huray, *Music and the Reformation*, pp. 24–5. There is firm evidence that Cox's reforming zeal did not diminish on his translation to Ely. In 1603 Roger Goade, Provost of King's College, Cambridge, since March 1570, replied to the accusation that he had breached the College Statute requiring Organs in Divine Service', which were alleged now to be lacking. After denying that he had removed the organ personally, he had this to say: 'at his [that is, Goade's] first coming to be Provost [in 1570], the Commissioners appointed by authority from the Queen's Majesty, viz. the then Bishop of Ely [Richard Cox] . . . & others coming into the Coll[ege] Chapel did appoint & Command to have them taken away, & sold to the College['s] use, which was done' (King's College Archives, MS vol. entitled 'Visitations', p. 130).

[35] Bentham (1812), p. 193.

[36] See the inventory of contents in J. Bunker Clark, *Transposition in Seventeenth Century English Organ Accompaniments and the Transposing Organ*, Detroit Monographs in Musicology, 4 (Detroit, Mich., 1974), pp. 166–70.

of it four-part – that is transmitted by the manuscripts. But also represented are two Elizabethan organists, William Fox and George Barcroft. Fox's anthem *Teach me thy way, O Lord*[37] is very workaday indeed; Barcroft's music, which includes two four-part anthems (*O almighty God, mercifully hear* and *O Lord, we beseech thee*) and some morning and evening canticles,[38] is cast in the same mould, but shows a competent technique and reasonable mastery of the elements of word-setting and the *lingua franca* of English polyphony. To accompany this probable musical diet of monophonic (and perhaps metrical) psalms and simple, workaday homophonic, four-part anthems and service-music, the 1560s had witnessed a marked decrease in the number of minor canons and lay clerks who were paid a full annual stipend, and a corresponding increase in the number of those who received payment for only parts of a year. Thus, for example, in 1560–1 eight lay clerks' names appear in receipt of full salary; the next surviving account (1562–3) records only five such names, but no fewer than eight others who were paid for only part of the financial year. Both accounts show that only three minor canons were paid full salary in the two years concerned.[39] Not until 1598 would their number be set again at six;[40] and not until the 1620s would the complement of lay clerks be destined to reach or exceed the statutory number of eight,[41] though this body was always subject to wide fluctuations. This trend may signal a rise in the employment of part-time lay clerks, and may have represented a means of saving money, as well as usefully covering gaps in the recruitment of permanent singers. The engagement of part-timers was especially popular at Old Foundations such as York Minster and Hereford, where it achieved something approaching official sanction;[42] but there is no record of its formal implementation at Ely prior to the early 1630s, when it was conceded for the first time that 'half' places were being filled (see below, p. 237).

Although the late sixteenth-century archives shed very little light on musical activity at Ely Cathedral, it is not unreasonable to assume that the situation there in Elizabeth's reign was not so very different from that which is documented in institutions elsewhere. Generally speaking, musical activity in English cathedrals coasted along between the Reformation and about 1580 with purchases of service-books when necessary and the maintenance of a basic working repertory of four-part anthems and services. Not until the 1580s and 1590s is there widespread general evidence of a musical renaissance, when musical activity begins to quicken. At Ely, however, such a change in climate can only be inferred, because there are no Treasurer's accounts before 1604–5, and the Elizabethan Receiver's accounts – as has been stated above – do not record the acquisition of musical materials necessary for the execution of choral services. The major new musical development at this period in Ely – the allocation to one of the lay clerks of instrumental-teaching duties which previously had been the contractual obligation of the Organist and Master of the Choristers – is exceptionally well documented and will be discussed later, in a postscript to this chapter. But two other

---

[37] R.T. Daniel and P. le Huray (eds.), *Sources of English Church Music 1549–1660*, Early English Church Music, Supplementary Volume 1 (London, 1972), p. 103.

[38] *Ibid.*, pp. 76–7.

[39] EDC 3/3/3–4.

[40] EDC 3/3/26.

[41] EDC 3/1/2, fos. 99–102[v].

[42] Payne, *Provision and Practice*, pp. 224–7.

barometers of musical activity – the provision of polyphony and increased expenditure on the organs – will be considered here.

A period of musical expansion, c.1603–c.1639

An awakening of interest in the choral service, c.1603–c.1614

In his seminal study of music and the English Reformation, Peter le Huray noted a sea-change in the fortunes of cathedral music which he attributed, in part, to 'the emergence of a 'high-church' party within the Anglican church during the early years of the seventeenth century': this movement, he argued, was both 'a reaction against the spirit of Geneva' and 'a new and positive concern to justify the existence of an independent national church . . . which was seen more and more as the true continuation of all that was best in the European Catholic tradition'.[43] While the High Church movement cannot be said to have been either popular or widespread before the 1630s, 'wherever it flourished', continued Peter le Huray, 'especial attention was paid to the outward forms and observances of daily worship'.[44] A renewed interest in the cultivation of polyphonic church music is evident in provincial cathedrals from this time: 'after c.1603, the records of the statutory musical establishments show a unity of purpose in the attitudes of their authorities towards the provision and practice of church music which is truly impressive. Major programmes of organ-building and repair, and substantial music-copying projects, in particular, seem to be almost universal . . . and may suggest that polyphony was being used on a daily basis, rather than being reserved simply for holy days and important feast-days',[45] with perhaps the anthem and canticles at both Morning and Evening Prayer, and the Kyrie and Creed at the ante-Communion, being sung in polyphonic settings. A much-improved quality of archival coverage would seem to indicate that such expansion was real, rather than an illusion fuelled simply by the chance survival or greater detail of Jacobean documents.

At Ely, this change is documented in minute detail and with exemplary clarity by the sequence of Treasurer's accounts beginning in 1604–5.[46] The very first account shows the organist, George Barcroft, in receipt of a large sum of money (26s. 8d.) 'for pricking of churche songes',[47] presumably anthems, and a total of £2 13s. 8d. being expended on 'work aboute the organs'.[48] In 1606–7 a much larger sum, £13 6s. 8d., was found for 'repairing the Church Organs',[49] and a further 68s. for wainscot for the organs and for painting them;[50] and at Michaelmas of the following year the stairs to the organ-loft were mended and additional small repairs to the instrument carried

---

[43] Le Huray, *Music and the Reformation*, p. 46.

[44] *Ibid.*, p. 47.

[45] Payne, *Provision and Practice*, p. 78. (For a detailed breakdown of expenditure, and discussion, see the section headed 'Musical Expenditure at Ely, 1604/5–1642/3: a Case Study', in *ibid.* pp. 87–92.)

[46] EDC 3/1/2: this one volume of Treasurer's accounts records, for each financial year, both the quarterly payments of salary and the miscellaneous disbursements which are such a rich source of information about musical provision.

[47] EDC 3/1/2, fo. 7.

[48] *Ibid.*, fos. 7ᵛ and 8ᵛ.

[49] *Ibid.*, fo. 22.

[50] *Ibid.*, fo. 22ᵛ.

out.[51] In the latter year also, Barcroft received a fee of 20s. 'by Mr Deane & the chapters apoyntment':[52] extra payments made for music-copying are usually identified as such, and in the absence of such a qualification the inference here must be that Barcroft was increasingly busy in the organ-loft.

At this time a set of articles of inquiry was prepared for the Archbishop of Canterbury's metropolitical visitation of the Cathedral in July 1608. These articles show a concern with the conduct and quality of the choral service, testify to a growing High Church awareness and bear a quite striking resemblance to the Laudian visitation articles of the 1630s. They ask, for example, 'whether the number of those that serve the Quire . . . be kepte full and the Quire sufficientlye furnished with hable [*sic*] singers, and dayly service theire [*sic*] songe [*sic*]', and 'whether the Choristers be well ordered and the [statutory] number of them furnished'.[53] Unfortunately, as is usual in visitations of this period, no replies to these questions have survived. It is not impossible that some of the articles were framed in advance and aimed at known defects, though they seem often to be routine: at Ely, on this occasion, the choral force would seem to have been effectively at full strength; whether all of the singers were 'hable', however, is an open question.[54]

The Ely musicians were presumably very pleased by the translation to the see, on 22 September 1609, of Lancelot Andrewes.[55] A distinguished High Churchman, and an early patron and friend of the three leading High Church divines, William Laud, John Cosin and Matthew Wren,[56] Bishop Andrewes would surely have approved of the fresh musical endeavours which were rapidly gathering momentum at the Cathedral, for at Michaelmas that year, Barcroft and the lay clerks William Stonard, Thomas Roose and John Locar, were paid a total of £3 10s. 'for prickyng songuis in the newe bookes'.[57] The qualification 'newe' is significant here, in that it shows that this was a new project; whether these 'songuis' (or anthems) were newly composed, or merely transcribed from older and perhaps badly-worn part-books, is not clear; but it is very likely indeed that the project involved the pricking (that is, copying) of some new compositions.[58]

---

[51] EDC 3/1/2, fos. 28, 29.

[52] *Ibid.*, fo. 28.

[53] EDR B2/29, fo. 3[r-v] (from Articles 4 and 9).

[54] This paragraph follows closely the discussion in Payne, *Provision and Practice*, pp. 77–8. The subject of musical incompetence is never raised in the Ely archives; and even the more mundane matter of discipline is not as well documented in the New Foundations as in the Old, though it is an open question whether the reason for this is that singing men at the former were better behaved than their Old Foundation brethren, most of whom were organized in colleges of vicars choral, or that these colleges had a greater ability to cause the authorities trouble. Whatever the explanation, however, there is no evidence that the Dean and Chapter of Ely at any time during this period were faced with the problems of disputes between, or drunkenness or other unruliness among, members of their musical staff.

[55] Bentham (1812), p. 198.

[56] Le Huray, *Music and the Reformation*, p. 60.

[57] EDC 3/1/2, fo. 35[v]. It should be noted that this William Ston(n)ard is not identical with his namesake who, from Christmas 1608, was Organist and Master of the Choristers at Christ Church, Oxford (see Shaw, *Succession of Organists*, p. 210): the Oxford man was in his post until at least Michaelmas 1631, while the Ely Stonard was paid every year as a lay clerk until he was replaced at Christmas 1630 (EDC 3/1/2, fo. 169[v]). A William 'Stannard', doubtless a son or relative of the adult lay clerk, was however a chorister at the episcopal visitation on 21 October 1596 (EDR B/2/16, fo. 37), and he may be identical with the Oxford musician.

[58] The composer William Stonard, who wrote a number of verse anthems as well as evening canticles for full choir (see *Sources of English Church Music* (cit. in n. 37), p. 140), is usually assumed to be the Oxford man, though a five-part setting of the evening canticles by 'Mr Stonard' is found among the Ely manuscripts (*e.g.* EDC 10/7/4: see Bunker Clark, *Transposition* (cit. in n. 36), p. 167) and some music by Stonard is also transmitted in the

In 1610, amid continued use of the organ, as signified by the manufacture of 'a new parre of bellowes', the Cathedral's musical life was tinged with sadness: Barcroft became sick and, presumably, died.[59] He was replaced by John Amner, one of the greatest English provincial composers of the early seventeenth century and the man destined to oversee the late flowering of the pre-Civil War musical establishment.[60] Amner, who was baptised at Ely on 24 August 1579,[61] was listed as a chorister at the episcopal visitation of 22 October 1593.[62] For two or three years immediately following Amner's appointment the spirit of Barcroft lingered on: in 1610–11 the Chapter found £6 to pay off Barcroft's debts, and granted Amner £6 8s. 4d. 'for prickinge of songes' – presumably in the new books begun by his predecessor;[63] and in 1611–12 and 1613–14 small sums were expended on organ-repairs.[64] It was inevitable that a musician of Amner's ability would soon stamp his personality on the musical environment in which he worked:[65] in May 1613 he took the B.Mus. degree at Oxford;[66] and in 1615 his *Sacred Hymnes* was published in London[67] (Plate 22*b*). The size and generally high musical quality of this collection, comprising sacred anthems arranged like contemporary madrigal-prints in sections of pieces in from three to six parts, some with accompaniment for viols, shows that, just five years after his appointment, Amner was already a prolific and accomplished composer; and versions of music from his publication were sung both at Ely Cathedral and by cathedral and collegiate choirs elsewhere.[68]

Dean Henry Caesar and the musical establishment 1614–36

In October 1614, Henry Caesar succeeded Humphrey Tyndall as Dean.[69] Caesar, a man 'suspected of Popish leanings' in his youth, would prove to be the staunchest supporter of Cathedral music yet, and a great personal benefactor of the new Master of the Choristers (Colour pl. 25*b*). The first sign of a strong and productive working relationship between the two men is found among the Treasurer's accounts for 1618–19, which record the payment to Amner of 40s. 'by Mr Deane and Mr Archdeacon's appointment'.[70] The reason for this fee is not stated, but from 1624–5 Amner received the same

Peterhouse Caroline part-books (see *Sources of English Church Music*, p. 140). But the presence of music in Ely and Cambridge sources does not, of course, prove that they were composed by a local man.

[59] EDC 3/1/2, fo. 42.

[60] There is no record of a patent in his name, but he apparently replaced Barcroft as Master of the Choristers (and therefore as Organist also) at Midsummer 1610, since he received his first stipend the following Michaelmas (EDC 3/1/2, fo. 40).

[61] Shaw, *Succession of Organists*, p. 99.

[62] EDR B2/13, fo. 18.

[63] EDC 3/1/2, fo. 47.

[64] *Ibid.*, fos. 53, 67.

[65] To his Ely colleague, Andrew Willet, Amner the musician was already deemed worthy of praise as early as 1614, four years after his appointment (see above, n. 1).

[66] Shaw, *Succession of Organists*, p. 99.

[67] John Amner, *Sacred Hymnes: Of 3. 4. 5 and 6 Parts for Voyces and Vyols* (London, 1615); modern reprint, *The English Madrigalists*, 40 (London, 2000).

[68] Although Amner's music was popular in Ely and Cambridge, the surviving evidence suggests that very little of it travelled farther afield in the composer's lifetime: see below, p. 244 and n. 133.

[69] Bentham, *Ely*, p. 91.

[70] EDC 3/1/2, fo. 97ᵛ. Perhaps Dean Caesar's influence lay behind the expenditure, in 1616–17, of 28s. 10d. on 'repayring the instrument for the church and makinge a new stoppe in it' (EDC 3/1/2, fo. 85).

amount annually.[71] It is possible that the initial stimulus for these payments was Amner's composition of his Second Service, dedicated to Dean Caesar;[72] or perhaps it was triggered by Amner's sterling efforts in preparing the choir's part-books – almost certainly the 'newe bookes' begun in 1608–9 by Barcroft, Stonard and others – for binding in Cambridge: 'Item: [paid] to Mr Williams of Cambridge for bindeing the bookes in the Quier and for mending and stringing them, 12s. 6d.'[73] The careful wording of this extract strongly suggests that Barcroft's books had seen heavy service during the ten years of their existence, and it is even possible that Williams was being paid for rebinding them. But, whatever their condition, their content was certainly deemed adequate to fulfil the requirements of the choral service, since the accounts report no further copying of polyphony for almost two decades. A period of fifteen years period separated the century's initial flurry of musical activity, which had begun in 1605, and ended in 1619, with the binding of the choir's part-books, from the late but glorious flowering of music which would represent the high-water mark of musical achievement at pre-Civil War Ely (1636–43), and these years probably saw a consolidation of Barcroft's and Amner's earlier efforts under the protective and encouraging patronage of the extremely pro-musical Dean Caesar. No fresh purchases of paper or payments for the copying of polyphony are recorded at this time; but the organ continued to be used,[74] and even repaired,[75] in the interim; and the Treasurer's accounts had been peppered with references to the purchase of unspecified service-books for the choir since 1605.

In personal terms, the second decade of the century was good to Amner, whose career gained an added dimension when, in March 1617, he was ordained deacon by Bishop Lancelot Andrewes,[76] and combined the duties (and therefore also the salaries, respectively £3 6s. 8d. and £2 10s. per quarter) of the post of Organist and Master of the Choristers with that of a 'vicar choral', or minor canon, like Barcroft before him.[77] The extra income must have been most welcome, since the Organist and Master of the Choristers at Ely had always, by statute, been additional to the number of lay clerks and was therefore not entitled to receive a lay clerk's stipend in addition to his pay as organist. Nothing specific is known of Amner's duties prior to 1631–2, when he was awarded 40s. 'for playing one [i.e. on] [the] organs the last yeare 1631, at the beginning

---

[71] EDC 3/1/2, fo. 135.

[72] *Sources of English Church Music*, p. 76. The evening canticles are published as *Magnificat and Nunc Dimittis from the Second Service – Caesar's Service*, ed. A. Greening, Oxford Church Services, no. S578 (Oxford, 1967), and the *Te Deum*, ed. Greeening, Cathedral Music Ltd., CM 560 (Chichester, 1994): much of the writing for full choir is in four parts more usually associated with the 'short service' idiom, though the trebles (*medius decani* and *medius cantoris*) do sometimes divide to produce five-part polyphony (SSATB). Perhaps this writing for two trebles, rather than for the usual English choral disposition of SAATB, was intended to make the music more distinctive.

[73] EDC 3/1/2, fo. 97v.

[74] This is suggested by the regular payments for blowing the organs documented in the Treasurer's accounts.

[75] In 1620–1 40s. was found 'for mending the Organs and for stuffe for them', and in 1621–2 6s. 8d. was paid 'to the Joyner for mending the Organs' (EDC 3/1/2, fos 109ᵛ, 116). The next repair, in 1627–8, cost 2s. 2d. (EDC 3/1/2, fo. 155ᵛ).

[76] Shaw, *Succession of Organists*, p. 99.

[77] Amner appears to have joined the ranks of the minor canons at Christmas 1617, since his first recorded payment of the stipend was made in March 1618 (EDC 3/1/2, fo. 87ʳ⁻ᵛ). In the same year, in stark contrast to his musical duties, he received 2s. 6d. 'for powder and shot to kill dawes and other vermin in the Church' (EDC 3/1/1, fo. 96).

of sermons'.[78] The year 1630–1 seems, in fact, to have witnessed a great interest in the Cathedral organs, since listed among the extraordinary expenses (*expensa forinsica*) of this year is a mysterious reward of 2*s*. 6*d*. 'given to Mr Mudd by Mr Dean for playing on the Orgaines'. He is almost certainly identical with either John Mudd, Organist of Peterborough Cathedral (1583–1631), or Thomas Mudd, his son and, from 9 June 1631, his successor there;[79] no one with this surname is known to have been on the foundation at Ely.

The early 1630s also saw Caesar showing a close personal interest in the admission of selected lay clerks. On 15 December 1632, for example, he personally 'bestowed the singing man's place (lately voide by the deathe of Thomas Barcroft) upon Rob[er]t Claxton of Ely'.[80] (Claxton, who had been a chorister of the Cathedral,[81] would succeed Amner in the organistship and, as we shall see, apparently fully justified the Dean's confidence in him.) Two other explicitly personal appointments are recorded at this period, including the award of 'halfe a singing mans place' to Torell Adam, on 2 January 1633.[82]

But the Dean is best remembered for his generous bequest to the Cathedral's musicians, and it is perhaps in acknowledgement of this that his memorial in the Cathedral refers to his '*Charitate in hujus Ecclesiae Chorum et Musas Cantabrigienses ultimo Testamento Munifici*'[83] (Colour pl. 16*a*). This story is told most fully in one of the Dean and Chapter manuscripts, though Bentham gives a slightly different version of events. According to the former account, Caesar bequeathed £1000 towards the annual augmentation of the salaries of each minor canon and lay clerk (40*s*.) and chorister (33*s*. 4*d*.), and a further £1000 for the foundation of two fellowships and two scholarships at Cambridge. The total sum (£2000), however, was allegedly given by the Dean's nephew and executor, Sir Charles Caesar, to King Charles I at the time of his troubles, and was never subsequently recovered.[84] Supporting documents transmitted in the same manuscript, outlining the fate of this benefaction, suggest that in 1639, after Sir Charles Caesar had cleared his uncle's estate of this sum, Archbishop Laud persuaded him to lend the money to the King, on promise of repayment of the principal sum, with interest. In 1654, when the parliamentary commissioners summoned Dame Jane Caesar, Sir Charles's widow, to answer for the sum, she declared that neither she nor the Cathedral had ever received it, and that it had certainly been lent to the King.[85] Bentham reports the first part of this story, up to and including the royal loan, but states that Sir Charles did indeed pay the annuities both to the Cathedral and (in respect of the fellowships and scholarships) to Jesus College, Cambridge, and further, that after

---

[78] EDC 3/1/2, fo. 179ᵛ. Whilst it is possible that this activity was not new in 1631, and that his unspecified annual 40*s*. fee had been paid in respect of such organ-playing ever since 1619, there is no proof of this, and the possibility is weakened by the fact that the entry identifies the activity with the previous year only. However, Amner only ever receives one fee, and after this date it is always stated to be in payment for his organ-playing.

[79] EDC 3/1/1, fo. 141. (Further on the Mudds, see Payne, *Provision and Practice*, pp. 265–6.)

[80] EDC 6/2/1, p. 121.

[81] Claxton is listed as a chorister at the visitations of 2 June 1615 and 15 May 1616 (EDR B2/33, fo. 21; B2/31, fo. 161), and subsequently served as a lay clerk from 1624 (Payne, *Provision and Practice*, p. 256).

[82] EDC 8A/1/1, pp. 122, 121.

[83] Bentham, *Ely*, p. 230, n. 4.

[84] EDC 14/9, p. 153.

[85] *Ibid.*, p. 224.

his death his widow, and finally her eldest son, Sir Henry Caesar, continued to pay them 'for some years', although he concedes that in the times of the 'usurpation' the Cathedral did not receive these annuities.[86] Bentham's account would seem to be correct. A separate account book survives which records payments of the benefaction, by Sir Charles Caesar and his widow.[87] From 1639 until 1647 the recipients, including lay clerks, vicars and choristers, signed for their payments, which were still being made three and a half years after the cessation of the choral service.

Music and the Laudian revival, c.1636–9

When Dean Caesar died, in 1636, he was succeeded by William Fuller, who was, as Bentham put it, a man of 'great Royalist sympathies'.[88] Three years earlier, William Laud had become Archbishop of Canterbury and, together with some powerful and influential supporters, 'both in Court, our Universities, and else where', complained one of his most bitter Puritan opponents, they 'grew very great bold, [and] insolent, and their opinions spread themselves like a dangerous Leprosie, over the whole body of our Church'.[89] Staunch advocates of Arminianism, and passionate believers in the 'beauty of holiness' and the importance of ornament in ritual, Laud and his supporters strongly encouraged certain highly controversial innovations which, being found offensive in some quarters, were savagely caricatured by Puritan critics in the following terms: in one local Laudian showcase – Peterhouse, Cambridge – for example, they lamented that the chapel 'hath bene soe dressed up and ordered soe Ceremoniously that it hath become the gaze of the University', that in many college chapels there were 'diverse bowings and cringeings' to the altar, and the practice of kneeling and facing eastwards for the Litany and Doxology, and also that incense was burned.[90] In April 1638 Matthew Wren, who during his mastership of Peterhouse (1625–34) had introduced extremely High Church choral services there,[91] was translated to Ely. He was 'a zealous advocate for promoting order and discipline in the Church, which he endeavoured (in concert with Archbishop Laud) to raise to a higher pitch than the licentiousness of the times would permit',[92] and the Cathedral, and especially its music, was now in the firm grip of Laudianism.

Although music was a minor issue compared with the major differences in religious belief that separated Arminian and Puritan factions, there is no doubt that the performance of sacred polyphony, and even the mere presence in church of an organ, was seen by some to be popish.[93] However, by the mid-1630s many centres of church music were experiencing their greatest musical renaissance since the reign of Queen Mary, and Ely was no exception. The first sign of this activity in the Cathedral, in the

---

[86] Bentham, *Ely*, p. 231, n. 1.

[87] EDC 3/8/1.

[88] Bentham, *Ely*, p. 231.

[89] W. Prynne, *Canterburies Doome* (London, 1646), p. 159.

[90] London, British Library, MS Harl. 7019, beginning at fo. 52; quoted and discussed in Payne, *Provision and Practice*, pp. 159–60.

[91] Payne, *Provision and Practice*, p. 94; and see chapters 6 and 9 for a detailed account of Laudianism in Cambridge musical establishments.

[92] Bentham, *Ely*, p. 201.

[93] Payne, *Provision and Practice*, p. 80.

years 1635–9, is in repairs to the organ. On 24 May 1636 10*s.* was paid 'for taken out the Orgaine Pipes & scouring them, & for mending the keyes & doores of the Orgaines', 3*s.* 8*d.* worth of materials were provided for the same work, and Dean Caesar consented to pay Amner 5*s.* 'for his Paines in helping to retune the Orgaines'.[94] On 27 June the following year the larger sum of £1 7*s.* 2*d.* was 'laid out on mending the Orgaines, for workmanship and materialls'.[95] Although one stimulus for this work, which included cleaning and perfuming the church, and painting the pulpit, was an impending royal visit,[96] these entries testify not only to the greater use of the organ, owing possibly to the singing of polyphony – and verse music at that – on a daily basis, but also to the importance of the instrument's decent appearance.

An even more impressive indication of the sudden rise in importance of the role of choral participation in the daily round of services is the major programme for the refurbishment, replenishment and safekeeping of the Cathedral's polyphonic repertory which was personally supervised by John Amner. On 11 April 1637 he was paid £1 14*s.* 7*d.* 'for 35 quier of paper, at 16*d.* the Quier, & for the Carriage forom [*sic*] London to Ely', and a further £1 10*s.* 'for the binding of the Bookes of the Quier, and for his Joarnie to Cambridge about them'.[97] Between 5 and 8 November 1637 Amner was allowed £5 'for his paines in pricking the Newbookes of the Quier', and on 26 March 1638 a joiner received 6*s.* for constructing a cupboard in the choir for the music books'.[98] The project was finally completed sometime before 19 November 1639 with a payment to Amner of £3 2*s.* 'for his further paines in the Anthem Bookes for the Quier'[99] – the 'paines' referring most probably to his completion of the copying. This fresh paper was presumably for a set of 'Newbookes', which were to be bound before the music had been transcribed: whether Amner simply recopied the old repertory, or added new music, it is impossible to tell, although the latter explanation is perhaps the more likely of the two alternatives. But if the total amount spent on copying was £8 2*s.*, and if the almost universal rate for music-copying of 4*d.* per folio was applied,[100] then Amner would have copied no fewer than 486 folios of music, a considerable task that could easily have resulted in a set of ten part-books, or perhaps even a larger set: two of Amner's unpublished anthems, *O sing unto the Lord* and *Sing, O heavens*, which must have been composed for the Cathedral choir, are in seven parts (SSAATBB)[101] and it is quite possible that such lavish and luxurious settings could have found their way into part-books prepared at the height of Laudian influence.

[94] EDC 3/1/2, fo. 211ᵛ.

[95] *Ibid.*, fo. 222.

[96] *Ibid.*, fo. 212ᵛ.

[97] *Ibid.*, fos. 221, 224.

[98] *Ibid.*, fos. 230, 232.

[99] *Ibid.*, fo. 242.

[100] See Bowers, 'Liturgy of the Cathedral' (cit. in n. 8), p. 440 and n. 149, and the references there cited.

[101] See *Sources of English Church Music*, p. 75. Anthony Greening, in his liner-notes to the compact disc *Cathedral Music by John Amner*, performed by P. Trepte and Ely Cathedral Choir (Hyperion CDA66768; 1995), questions whether Amner 'felt unable to divide his tenor line' in these pieces. This is very probable, given that the tenor voice was apparently the least important in choirs of this period (there is firm documentary evidence for this fact at Exeter Cathedral in 1613 and at Norwich in 1620: see Payne, *Provision and Practice*, pp. 100–11); and relatively few verse solos were given to it. Greening also suggests that Amner may have performed such large-scale pieces in the 'resonant acoustics of the Lady Chapel', even though this building then served as the parish church of Holy Trinity.

The decline and eventual abolition of choral services *c.*1640–3

Sadly, the tremendous promise of these preparations was not destined to be realised, as fate dealt the Cathedral music a double blow. First, Amner died, and was buried on 28 July 1641;[102] he was replaced by the very able Robert Claxton, the lay clerk in whom Dean Caesar had earlier placed great trust, and who served in his new capacity certainly from Christmas, and very probably from Michaelmas, 1641. For the first time in the Cathedral's history the Organist was permitted to continue to receive his pay as a lay clerk.[103] The other problem was a looming national crisis quite outside the control of the Dean and Chapter.

The four remaining pre-Civil War Treasurer's accounts suggest that, although the Cathedral probably made full use of its new materials, there was no need for further major expenditure on musical provision. A few service books were acquired; and in 1641–2 some repairs were made to the organ, testifying to its continued use.[104] Despite such illusions of normality in the first two years of the decade, there was good reason to believe that an ill wind was blowing, and that a violent storm would follow. The account for 1642–3 lacks the customary list of salaries ('*pensiones*'); and in the quarter ending at Christmas 1642 the organ-blower is for the last time actually stated to have blown the organs, even though he continued to receive his stipend for the remainder of this year.[105] Such *lacunae* are sure signs of the running-down of choral services and perhaps of a little confusion. That some attempt was being made to maintain a choral presence as late as 10 January 1644 is, however, suggested by the fact that, on that very day, Oliver Cromwell wrote to the Precentor, ordering him 'to forbear altogether your quire service, soe unedifyeing and offensive', lest his troops 'should in any tumultary or disorderly way attempt the reformation of the cathedral church'.[106] Although there is no evidence that Cromwell personally approved of the vandalism that was so often meted out by parliamentarian soldiers to church fabric and property, it is quite clear that this letter contained a veiled threat: there is no specific record that the Ely organ, unlike some organs elsewhere, was broken up, but it is not impossible that some damage was done, since after 1660, £65 was expended on the purchase of a fresh instrument, rather than on repairs to the old one.[107] The optimistic assessment, however, is that perhaps the Cathedral did 'forbear' in good time its choral services, and manage to end with some dignity one hundred years of music and worship as a New Foundation cathedral.

---

[102] Shaw, *Succession of Organists*, p. 99.

[103] Amner naturally disappears from the accounts in the quarter ending Michaelmas that year (EDC 3/1/2, fo. 269ᵛ); his replacement is referred to simply as 'the Organist' and not named. But in the next quarter, ending Christmas 1641 – the first of the following financial year (1641–2) – Claxton is both named and styled Master of the Choristers (EDC 3/1/2, fo. 272ᵛ). In this light it is almost certain that Claxton took over for the whole quarter ending Michaelmas 1641, even though he is not identified.

[104] EDC 3/1/2, fo. 278.

[105] *Ibid.*, fos. 288ᵛ, 289ᵛ, 290ᵛ, 291ᵛ.

[106] P.A. Scholes, *The Puritans and Music* (Oxford, 1934), p. 223. The original apparently bore the date '1643' but this, of course, is Old Style (on the basis that the year began on 25 March). See also Payne, *Provision and Practice*, p. 167.

[107] EDC 3/1/2, fo. 305.

Postscript: The rise of instrumental music at Ely, *c.*1567–1643[108]

Although an obligation on the part of masters of the choristers to teach instrumental music to their young charges can in some institutions be detected long before the Edwardian Reformation,[109] the first positive evidence of the practice at Ely is in the letters patent of John Farrant (1567), which instruct him to teach the choristers both singing and instrumental music (*'ad docend' et instruend' choristas in arte musica, tam cantando quam instrumenta musicalia'*).[110] The letters patent of all subsequent pre-Civil War holders of this office at Ely required their recipients to teach instrumental music, though the precise nature of such teaching was not originally specified. For practical reasons, in ensuring a supply of 'sufficient deputies' to play the organ, keyboard instruments were widely taught in choral establishments;[111] but, at many cathedrals, including Ely, choristers were also taught to play the viols.[112] Although one early instance of the teaching of viol-playing to cathedral choristers is known,[113] the consensus of most cathedral archives is that the systematic teaching of viols began to be sponsored by capitular bodies, and pursued with vigour, only in the 1590s.[114] According to Thomas Watkins's manuscript 'Members or Officers of the Cathedral Church of Ely', there were three other instructors in music and the viols at Ely before the Civil War: (1) from 1580 to 1587, Edward Watson, lay clerk; (2) from 1605 to 1635, Thomas Wiborough, lay clerk; (3) from 1642, Robert Claxton, the Organist.[115] The first of these men, who had been a lay clerk since 1572–3,[116] certainly taught instrumental music from 11 December 1583, the date of his contract;[117] but it is very probable that he had begun these duties in 1579–80, because in that year he received a sudden increase in his annual salary, from the statutory £6 13*s.* 4*d.* to £8.[118] By his will (proved 8 July

---

[108] This section draws heavily on Payne, *Provision and Practice*, chapter 8, *passim* and pp. 256–8, where details are given about the three 'Instructors in Musick', Edward Watson, Thomas Wiborough and Robert Claxton, discussed below.

[109] As, for example, at Lincoln, where William Horwood, Master of the Choristers, was in 1477 contracted to teach them to play the organ, and the most apt the clavichord also (Payne, *Provision and Practice*, p. 135 n. 2).

[110] See above, n. 21.

[111] Payne, *Provision and Practice*, pp. 134–7, at p. 134.

[112] *Ibid.*, pp. 137–45.

[113] At Exeter Cathedral, in May 1550, the Dean and Chapter authorised the purchase of a set of viols and the appointment of an *informator choristarum* to teach them, clearly in compliance with the injunction of Edward VI's commissioners, in October 1547, that the choristers should be taught by him 'to play upon Instrumentes' (see Payne, *Provision and Practice*, pp. 231–2). At Canterbury Cathedral the purchase of a set of viols, for the domestic use of the choristers and their master, was agreed in 1574 (Bowers, 'Liturgy of the Cathedral' (cit. in n. 8), p. 438).

[114] The Ely material is discussed in I. Payne, 'The Provision of Teaching on the Viols at Some English Cathedral Churches, *c.*1594–*c.*1645: Archival Evidence', *Chelys*, xix (1990), pp. 3–15. A similar trend, exceptionally well-documented, began at Trinity College, Cambridge, in the mid-1590s: see I. Payne, 'Instrumental Music at Trinity College, Cambridge, *c.*1594–*c.*1615: Archival and Biographical Evidence', *Music & Letters*, lxviii (1987), pp. 128–40.

[115] EDC 2/9/3, p. 28, 'Informator Christar. Extraordinarius'.

[116] EDC 3/3/9.

[117] EDC 2/4/1, fo. 137. The two Latin verbs chosen for the description of his teaching duties (*'in instrumentis musicis pulsandis et inflandis'*) respectively suggest keyboard and wind instruments (possibly recorders), but not viols.

[118] EDC 3/3/13.

1587), he bequeathed to 'Thomas Jordan Chorister in Ely church al my books for the Cittern virginalls bandora or lute'.[119] But there is no evidence that he owned or offered teaching on viols.

Firm evidence for viol-teaching at Ely emerges abruptly with the earliest surviving of the Treasurer's account, in 1604–5, and suggests both that the Cathedral authorities attached great importance to the activity (which gained momentum in the first decades of the seventeenth century), and that it may have been practised for some years previously. In this year one of the lay clerks, Thomas Wiborough, received 6s. 8d. 'for teaching the schollers on the vialls' and a further 17s. 10d. 'for charges aboute the vialles';[120] and in the following year, in addition to his payment for teaching, his material costs (17s.) were itemised as 'strings for the violls, & mending of them, & for 2 new sticks [i.e. bows]'.[121] Wiborough continued to receive his allowance (which in 1606–7 was increased to 26s. 8d. and included the cost of 'a newe violl')[122] virtually every financial year until 1634–5, when the duties passed to another lay clerk, Robert Claxton.

Under Claxton, the teaching (and presumably therefore also the playing) of viols acquired a higher profile and much greater significance than ever before. In March 1637, he was accorded for the first time the new title of 'Master of the Violls', such was deemed to be the importance of his duties.[123] This title was supernumerary, not statutory, and is the closest that the Dean and Chapter came, before the Civil War, to a *de facto* division between more than one individual of duties that traditionally were discharged by one man, the Organist and Master of the Choristers. When, on 28 October 1641, after replacing John Amner in the latter office, Claxton received his letters patent of appointment, these still included the traditional obligation to teach instrumental music;[124] but he retained the title of 'Master of the Violls' in respect of these duties. Payments for viol-teaching and maintenance apparently ceased at Michaelmas 1643.[125] However, a final pre-Restoration reference to the instrument occurs at a strange time and place: the Parliamentary survey of 'The Singing Schoole', carried out between June and July 1649, reported that, 'at the staie[r]s hend over against the schoole dore [there is] another roome with a place taken out of it for a place to play upon the vyall in'.[126]

No survey of music and liturgy at Ely before 1643 would be complete without a brief

[119] EDC 2/8A/1, fo. 9^{r–v}. (In Payne, *Provision and Practice*, it is stated, in error, that Watson bequeathed 'instruments' to Jordan, whereas in fact he left only music-books.) Thomas Jordan was a chorister at the visitation of 30 March 1584 (EDR D2/14, fo. 28^v) and also served briefly (1596–1600: EDC 3/3/24, 3/3/28) as a lay clerk: he is probably to be identified with the Master of the Choristers of the same name who served King's College, Cambridge, 1605–6 (see Payne, *Provision and Practice*, p. 272). A lay clerk there 1606–25, and a conduct 1626–31 (died), his will mentions virginals, a lute and a 'bandore', but not viols (*ibid.*, p. 304).

[120] EDC 3/1/2, fos. 7 and 8, respectively. Further on the musical Wiborough family, see *Biographical Dictionary of English Court Musicians*, II, p. 1149.

[121] EDC 3/1/2, fo. 15^v.

[122] *Ibid.*, fo. 22. In the following year, the annual allowance for viol-strings was settled at 13s. 4d.

[123] *Ibid.*, fo. 220.

[124] EDC 8A/1/1, p. 120. According to his letters patent, Claxton seems to have warranted an increase in his salary (£15 6s. 8d), probably in respect of his important instrumental-teaching duties.

[125] EDC 3/1/2, fo. 29^v.

[126] EDC 8A/1/13, fo. 12. Payne, 'Provision of Teaching on the Viols', p. 7, reads 'head' for 'hend', *i.e.*, end, in error.) Shaw, *Succession of Organists*, p. 100, reads 'vyallin' for 'vyall in', almost certainly in error, since the two words are separated by a small space in the manuscript; furthermore, Claxton in 1638–9 purchased 'a newe violl for the Choristers Singing schoole' (EDC 3/1/2, fo. 243^v).

discussion of one of the most elusive questions that face music historians of this era, namely, whether the choristers used viols to accompany verse music (that is, music in which solo singers alternate with the full chorus) in a liturgical context, or whether they were confined to domestic and recreational use. That they were certainly used in the latter way is beyond question. Indeed, it was for private, domestic performance that Amner's own *Sacred Hymnes* (1615) was primarily intended, just as were the numerous earlier and contemporary English printings of madrigals whose title-pages proclaimed them to be apt for viols and/or voices.[127] Although stringed instruments may sometimes have been used liturgically,[128] there is no hard evidence that they were so employed, and the logistics of using them in formal five- or six-part consorts anywhere near choir-stalls, to say nothing of processional use, would have been formidable.[129] The consensus remains, therefore, much as Peter le Huray reported it more than thirty years ago:

> The Dean and Chapter of Ely . . . provided viol lessons for the choristers during the later years of the sixteenth century. There is nothing to show that viols were ever used in the cathedral, however; but in 1615 the cathedral organist, John Amner, published a set of Sacred Hymnes for voices and viols designed for the amateur. The organist of Lichfield Cathedral, Michael East, also published quite a few verse anthems for voices and viols: he had been for a short time under Amner at Ely. But again there is no evidence that viols were actually used in the cathedral [services].[130]

To illustrate the point, le Huray chose for discussion Amner's Christmas verse-anthem, *O ye little flock*, a magnificent, colourful and dramatic work for six voices and viols, from this very collection; and the negative evidence that viol consorts were not used in such pieces, either at Ely or anywhere else, is succinctly conveyed by le Huray's notes to his modern edition of this work. Many pieces which survive with viol accompaniment also exist in versions with accompaniment for organ only, and the two versions are sufficiently different to render them incompatible with each other. Amner's masterpiece is no exception: the organ-part preserved in Ely Music MS 1 transmits a text that is 'substantially different' from the printed 1615 consort version, the triple-time Alleluia section is missing altogether and the final chorus is shorter by roughly six bars. The conclusion, then, must be 'that either viols or organ were used in performance'.[131]

No more fitting end could be made to this chapter than this reference to one of the greatest works by John Amner, the quality of whose ideas and grasp of technique were, as John Morehen rightly observed, 'far above the standard of much music even by Chapel Royal composers', and much of whose sacred music he considered to be 'only slightly inferior to the best of [Orlando] Gibbons's music'.[132] Although Amner's sacred

---

[127] For discussion of this phrase, see E.H. Fellowes, *The English Madrigal Composers* (2nd edn., Oxford, 1948), pp. 77–8; C. Monson, *Voices and Viols in England, 1600–1650: The Sources and the Music* (Ann Arbor, Mich., 1982), pp. 285–6.

[128] Payne, *Provision and Practice*, pp. 150–3.

[129] Le Huray, *Music and the Reformation*, p. 129.

[130] *Ibid.*, pp. 128–9. Further on Michael East at Ely, where he served as a lay clerk in 1609 and 1610, see Payne, *Provision and Practice*, p. 74.

[131] John Amner, *O ye little flock*, ed. P. le Huray (Oxford, 1964), reprinted as Church Music Society Reprints, no. 47, 1982), editorial note.

[132] J. Morehen, 'Sources of English Cathedral Music, *c.*1617–*c.*1644', 3 vols., unpublished PhD thesis, Cambridge, 1969, I, p. 180.

music was more widely disseminated than that of his predecessors Fox and Barcroft,[133] his music did not travel widely beyond the Cambridge area until after the Restoration. It was popular at King's College and Peterhouse in the 1630s (the latter had autograph copies of twelve works by him included in its choral part-books),[134] but his work is poorly represented elsewhere: only Caesar's Service was sung at Durham Cathedral in this decade; and only a single anthem by him is listed among the texts of those sung in the Chapel Royal in the mid-1630s. Very shortly after the Restoration, however, with the translation of Dr John Cosin from the Mastership of Peterhouse to the see of Durham, no fewer than four anthems and a service were added to the polyphonic repertory of that cathedral between 1660 and 1665.[135] And yet, despite the uneventful contemporary reception-history of his music outside Ely and Cambridge, Amner has emerged not only as one of the greatest provincial composers of the period, but also as one of Ely's greatest organists. It was, after all, under his direction that the musical establishment, facilitated by the increasing awareness of music as an ornament of worship, first documented in the first decade of the seventeenth century and encouraged by such clerics as Dean Caesar, flourished until its tragic demise in 1644. As for Amner, and indeed Tye and White before him, their music remains their most eloquent memorial.

---

[133] According to *Sources for English Church Music*, pp. 103 and 77 respectively, Fox's single anthem survives only in a contemporary Ely source: and only one of Barcroft's two extant anthems found its way to Cambridge, where it was copied into an autograph organ-book by Henry Loosemore, Organist of King's College, in c.1627–31 (see Payne, *Provision and Practice*, pp. 73, 114–15). Such negative evidence is not, however, conclusive: both men may have composed music which did travel more widely but has vanished along with the sources which transmitted it.

[134] Morehen ('Sources of English Cathedral Music', I, p. 181) lists fifteen Peterhouse pieces copied in Amner's hand, twelve of his own composition together with William Byrd's *Prevent us, O Lord*, Thomas Morley's *Teach me thy way* and Thomas Tallis's *Discomfit them, O Lord*. (The fact that Amner took the trouble of copying these pieces surely implies that they were in the Ely repertory.) He suggests (p. 182) that 'Amner may well have visited Peterhouse on one of his visits to Cambridge, possibly in 1637' (see above, p. 239) and, further, that Amner probably knew the Master, Dr John Cosin, given the latter's close friendship with Bishop Andrewes. The Peterhouse 'Caroline' part-books 'were compiled as a fairly haphazard accumulation of any music that happened to be at hand' for use by its semi-professional choir (Payne, *Provision and Practice*, p. 99); the contents are varied, but include much music by local composers such as Robert Ramsey (Organist of Trinity College, c.1615–44) and Henry Loosemore, some of it apparently in holograph pre-copied parts.

[135] Morehen, 'Sources of English Cathedral Music', I, pp. 179–80.

Music and Liturgy 1660–1836

Nicholas Thistlethwaite

It was probably some time after the Restoration of Charles II to the throne before the Cathedral's musical foundation regained its full strength. The Treasurer's accounts resume with the Michaelmas quarter 1660 and are set out in their pre-war form, but some of the entries are blank. Robert Claxton was paid £10 13s. 4d. as *Informator*, Organist and lay clerk, and a further £1 'for teaching the Chiristers on the Violls as in former yeares', but the blank space in the accounts where payment to eight choristers should have been recorded suggests that they had yet to be recruited. Similarly, Claxton received a further allowance 'for 2 quarters for playing on the Orgaines before Sermon', but it is unlikely that an organ was in place as early as the summer of 1660.[1]

Two other lay clerks besides Robert Claxton survived from before the war: Miles Cadman had been admitted in 1635; and John Bradford as long ago as 1618. Both were paid £3 6s. 8d. for the Michaelmas quarter 1660.[2]

The first evidence for the re-appearance of choristers is found at Christmas 1660 when the Dean ordered them to be given a gratuity of four shillings.[3] In the following summer £65 was spent upon 'the Orgaine bought for the use of the Quier and for the bringing of it down to Ely', and payments (£2 a year) to an organ blower resume.[4] By October 1661 the singing men were once again at full strength: the accounts for the Michaelmas quarter record the names of four lay clerks (the three survivors, plus Thomas Bullis), four other full-timers (John Davies, Robert Bird, Anthony Brignal and Samuel East) and two 'demis' (John Johnson and John Adams).[5] By the following quarter (Lady Day 1662) the second group of four have been admitted as lay clerks, and later in the year stipends were raised to £10 a year for the men and £4 a year for each of the eight choristers.[6]

The first post-Restoration reference to music books occurs in March 1662 when Claxton was paid five shillings 'for pricking some Musik'.[7] It is unclear how much of the old music library survived. In June 1662 the Chapter agreed 'that it be left to Dr Holder,

---

[1] EDC 3/1/2, fos. 296ᵛ–8.

[2] *Ibid.*, fo. 297.

[3] *Ibid.*, fo. 304.

[4] *Ibid.*, fo. 305.

[5] *Ibid.*, fo. 306.

[6] *Ibid.*, fos. 306–7.

[7] *Ibid.*, fo. 309ᵛ.

to content Claxton and the rest for the Foureteene singing Bookes, and they to remaine to the Church'[8] and this (with the contents lists of three part-books in use in the mid-1660s)[9] suggests that choir members were compiling their own books in a haphazard way as need arose. Claxton was paid £5 'for 7 Singing bookes' and the other lay clerks received ten shillings each 'for theire Singing Bookes', which thereupon became Church property.[10]

At the same time the Dean and Chapter sought to regularise other matters pertaining to the Cathedral services. It was decreed that each prebendary should preach on three Sundays during his residence (the other Sundays being supplied by the Lecturer); the five minor canons were to officiate in turn at the first morning service (fixed at 5 a.m. in summer and 6 a.m. in winter).[11] The second morning service (which the choir attended) was to be at 10.30 with Evensong at 4.30 p.m. The Sunday morning service, consisting of Mattins, Litany, Communion (or Ante-Communion) and Sermon, began at 9 o'clock. The Chapter also issued regulations for the vicars choral and singing-men, imposing fines for unauthorised absences and instructing the Precentor to keep a record of defaulters.[12]

By 1663, therefore, the rhythm of the daily service had been re-established and the principal functionaries were restored to their places. Claxton, however, appears as Organist and *Informator Choristarum* for the last time in the Christmas quarter of 1662. He continued to be paid as a lay clerk and as master of the choristers, but it is unlikely that he was able to undertake any duties. In the accounts for 1663–4 he was described as being 'infirm, under an Apoplexie'[13] and he was buried on 2 March 1669.[14] In his place the Chapter appointed John Ferrabosco, who was paid a full quarter's stipend (£7 10s. as Organist, and £2 10s. as *Informator*) at Lady Day 1663. Ferrabosco (1626–82) was the descendant of a family of musicians from Bologna, some of whom had settled in England and found employment in the royal household. At Ely he was allowed £5 for his removal expenses[15] and a further £10 'to provide his chamber of necessaryes'.[16] The Chapter later paid for work on his lodging[17] and in 1671 made him a gift of £3 when he received the Cambridge degree of Bachelor of Music.[18] When he died in 1682, they laid out 17s. 10d. on his funeral.[19]

One of the most pressing tasks facing Ferrabosco when he arrived in Ely was the need to restore the music library. The earliest surviving manuscripts are two organ books largely in his hand.[20] One (MS 4) consists chiefly of pre-war repertoire – services and anthems by Tallis, Byrd, Gibbons, Amner, Barcroft, Henry Loosemore, Tye and

---

[8] EDC 2/2A/2, p. 8, 20 June 1662.

[9] EDC 10/1A/3–4.

[10] EDC 3/1/2, fo. 309ᵛ.

[11] EDC 2/2A/2, p. 6, 20 June 1662.

[12] *Ibid.*, pp. 14–16, 23 June 1663.

[13] EDC 3/1/2, fo. 334.

[14] *Ibid.*, fo. 375. Not 1668, as stated by Shaw, *Succession of Organists*, p. 100.

[15] *Ibid.*, fo. 325ᵛ.

[16] EDC 2/2A/2, p. 15, 23 June 1663.

[17] EDC 3/1/2, fo. 333.

[18] *Ibid.*, fo. 408ᵛ.

[19] EDC 3/1/5, 1681–2, *Soluciones forinsecae.*

[20] Described in J. Bunker Clark, *Transposition in Seventeenth Century English Organ Accompaniments and the Transposing Organ*, Detroit Monographs in Musicology, 4 (Detroit, Mich., 1974), pp. 64–5, 159–70.

Farrant, as well as a few more recent compositions by Child, Mudd and Ferrabosco himself.[21] The other (MS 1) includes a much greater proportion of new repertoire – anthems by Michael Wise, William Holder, Edward Lowe, George Loosemore, Benjamin Rogers, Ferrabosco and a good deal more Child.[22] The earlier book may well have been begun in the mid-1660s, and the glimpse it provides of the Ely repertoire at that time is largely borne out by the inventories of the three lost part-books.[23] This was a period of intense activity in the music library. In 1663–4, for example, Thomas Danks, bookseller, was paid £5 14s. 'for severall Singing Bookes & Organ bookes' and a Mr Delamain was paid £3 16s. for entering 94 services and 199 anthems in four singing men's part-books; £6 was paid to four lay clerks for 'pricking' a further seven books. Although much of this must have been 'old' repertoire, some was not. 'Mr Irish of Windsor' was paid £1 3s. 'for a Service & some Anthems of Dr Childes'. Four years later another nineteen shillings was spent on Windsor anthems, and John Adams, one of the lay clerks, was paid £2 for entering them and other pieces in the music books. Adams, indeed, seems to have been the principal scribe during these years, and payments to him reveal peaks of activity in 1667–9 and 1675–7.[24]

Despite the creditable progress made during Ferrabosco's tenure, the expansion of the music library accelerated remarkably under his successor. James Hawkins (Organist, 1682–1729) had been briefly Organist of St John's College, Cambridge.[25] He was a prolific composer, and the Ely books contain many anthems and settings by him.[26] His arrival led to so much activity that the Dean and Chapter took fright at the expense, and in 1693 ordered

> That the Organist shall not be allowed any bill for pricking books, setting any chorus or composing any Anthem . . . unless his designe shall be first allowed . . .[27]

Their concern is understandable: in eight years payments to Hawkins for 'pricking' had averaged £6 12s.; over the next ten years this figure fell to £2 19s. 7d.[28]

How many of Hawkins's own compositions were performed at Ely during his tenure is unclear. The largest collection is found in MS 7, a handsomely bound volume entitled 'Mr Hawkins' Church Musick', containing fifty-six anthems (of which all but eight are verse settings) and six services; it has the appearance of a fair copy perhaps prepared in hope of publication.[29] Probably more indicative of the working repertoire in Hawkins's day is MS 2 – an organ book largely in Hawkins's hand, which includes fifteen of his anthems; this volume, together with several others[30] from the same period, provides clear evidence that the music of earlier Ely composers (Tye, White, Farrant, Barcroft,

---

[21] EDC 10/7/4 (Music MS 4).

[22] EDC 10/7/1 (Music MS 1).

[23] EDC 10/1A/3–4.

[24] EDC 3/1/2 *passim*. Adams served the Dean and Chapter in various capacities, and sometimes received consolidated payments which included 'pricking' amongst other activities. These have been discounted. Delamain's voucher, with details of the music he entered is catalogued as EDC 10/1A/1.

[25] Shaw, *Succession of Organists*, pp. 101, 362.

[26] See I. Spink, *Restoration Church Music, 1660–1714* (Oxford, 1995), pp. 243–53, for a sympathetic discussion of Hawkins's compositions.

[27] EDC 2/2A/2, p. 204, 22 November 1693.

[28] EDC 3/1/5, 1685–1703, *passim*.

[29] EDC 10/7/7 (Music MS 7).

[30] EDC 10/7/2, 3, 5, 6, 18 (Music MSS 2, 3, 5, 6, 18).

Amner and Ferrabosco) continued in use alongside that of Hawkins's contemporaries (among them Wise, Purcell, Blow, Turner, Aldrich and Tudway). Nor should Hawkins's own 'invention' – the chanting service – be forgotten. This alternated passages of chant sung by the full choir with short polyphonic sections sung by a semi-chorus. Hawkins is known to have written two services in this style, and the idea spread to Norwich, Peterborough, Lincoln, Exeter and Bristol.[31]

As a footnote to this discussion of the music library in Hawkins's time the acquisition of the two volumes of Dr Croft's *Anthems* in 1726–7 should not be overlooked. Printed collections became increasingly important to the replenishment of music libraries as the century advanced, bringing about a standardisation of repertoire and encouraging the circulation of new music.

The Cathedral choir under Ferrabosco and Hawkins was of essentially the same size and composition as that of Amner's later years.[32] The 1666 Statutes reduced the number of minor canons (or vicars choral) to five, who also served as chaplains of Holy Trinity and St Mary's parishes, and curates of Stuntney and Chettisham; one senior minor canon usually served as Lecturer (*Praelector Theologicus*), another as Precentor with the statutory duties of selecting music for the services, maintaining discipline within the choir, and reporting absentees to the Chapter; a third was Sacrist and Epistoler.[33] Each vicar received £15 a year, plus small sums in respect of his other offices. The eight lay clerks were paid annual stipends of £10, and the eight choristers £4. These numbers were maintained until *c.*1850 (below, p. 340) although, as in the 1630s, the singing men were regularly augmented by the appointment of two 'demis' (effectively probationers on half pay) who succeeded by seniority to vacant places.

Little is known of the lay clerks, except their names.[34] Of the seven appointed in 1661, four retained their posts for upwards of forty years, including John Adams who died in office in 1715.[35] He and his colleague Thomas Bullis senior augmented their incomes by serving as bailiffs to the Dean and Chapter and by pricking music into the choir books; Anthony Brignal was a carpenter; in a later generation, Wenham Powers (lay clerk 1731–86) was Ely's Coroner.[36]

The Chapter was aware of the lay clerks' financial insecurity and made periodic attempts to relieve it. In 1668–9 they took legal opinion about recovering Dean Caesar's bequest to the choir but presumably were given no hope of success.[37] In 1677–8 they took steps against two prebendaries who had failed to pay the customary 'residence money' to the vicars and singing men by ordering the Receiver to deduct the disputed forty shillings from the prebendaries' stipends at Michaelmas each year.[38] Dean Mapletoft, who died in 1677, bequeathed one hundred acres of washland[39] at Coveney

---

[31] On the chanting service, see Spink, *Restoration Church Music*, pp. 245–7; Ruth M. Wilson, *Anglican Chant and Chanting in England, Scotland and America 1660–1820* (Oxford, 1996), pp. 103–14.

[32] Payne, *Provision and Practice*, pp. 195–6.

[33] For relevant extracts from the 1666 Statutes, see Spink, *Restoration Church Music*, pp. 429–33.

[34] The names were recorded in the audit books each year, and by the second quarter of the 18th century most of the appointments appear in the order books.

[35] EDC 2/2A/2, p. 317, 24 June 1715.

[36] C. Johnson, *Cathedral Lay Clerks* (Ely, 1897), p. 33.

[37] EDC 3/1/2, fo. 380ᵛ.

[38] EDC 2/2A/2, pp. 131, 137–8, 26 November 1677, 3 April 1678.

[39] Grazing land which was liable to flood in winter.

to increase the singing men's stipends on condition that they attended early prayers. The Chapter therefore required the lay clerks to act in turn as monitors of attendance at 'the 6 of Clock Prayers' and to make a fortnightly return to the Receiver who would adjust payments accordingly.[40] Later, they gave the singing men leave to let the ground for three years, 'to their best advantage'.[41]

Another substantial benefaction accrued to the lay clerks in 1714, when Prebendary Thomas Turner left £1000 to the Dean and Chapter for the augmentation of the singing men's stipends. After protracted negotiations, the Dean was authorised in 1721 to purchase 111 acres at Stuntney for £1121, which provided a yearly rental of at least £60. An annual payment of £4 12s. was to be made to the prebendary occupying Turner's former stall and the remainder was to go to the lay clerks. Appropriately, the estate became known as 'Singing-men's Farm'.[42]

It was the task of the *Informator Choristarum* to recruit and train boys for the choir. In practice, the post was combined with that of Organist except for a period during Ferrabosco's tenure, when John Blundeville (1669–74) and Robert Robinson (1674–82) received the *Informator's* stipend of £10.[43] Blundeville, whose father was a singing man and Master of the Choristers at Lincoln,[44] and Robinson were both lay clerks, as was Thomas Bullis, senior, who regularly received £10 a year between 1676–7 and 1681–2 'for teaching the Choristers'.[45] This may have been a continuation of the office of Master of the Viols (above, p. 245): the accounts for 1677–8 include the only post-1660 reference to 'Strings for Vialls' and the mending of a viol. On Hawkins's appointment in 1682 the post of *Informator* was again attached to the organistship, and the payments to Bullis cease (though the younger Bullis was given £5 'for his services during the vacancy of the Organist's place'[46]); Robinson, however, received his £10 as a gratuity, over and above his lay clerk's stipend, until he disappeared from the records in 1690.

The *Informator* was expected to ensure a steady supply of suitable boy singers by maintaining a 'Singing School' in which both choristers and potential choristers were taught to sing. The regulations drawn up following Hawkins's death for his successor probably describe the system which had been in place for many years. No boy was to be a candidate for a chorister's place 'unless he has been under the Instruction of our *Informator Choristarum*, more than half a year'. The *Informator* was to have five shillings a quarter 'of every One of our Scholars that learn of him to sing, before any such be chosen a Chorister; & 5s p[er] Q[uarte]r. the first year only after he is chosen a Chorister; & 1s at the Entrance of every One into his Singing School'.[47] It would seem

---

[40] EDC 2/2A/2, p. 136, 3 April 1678.

[41] *Ibid.*, p. 157, 14 June 1681.

[42] *Ibid.*, pp. 322, 324, 332, 347, 354, 25 November 1716, 14 June 1717, 25 November 1718, 25 November 1721, 25 November 1722. Also, Johnson, *Lay Clerks*, p. 13.

[43] EDC 3/1/3–4, 1669–82, *passim*. It is sometimes claimed (*e.g.* Shaw, *Succession of Organists*, p. 100) that John Jackson, later of Wells Cathedral, was briefly *Informator* during 1669. It is true that 'Mr Jackson' was allowed 6s. in 1668–9 but not at all clear that this has anything to do with the choir (EDC 3/1/2, fo. 385ᵛ).

[44] N. Thistlethwaite, 'Music and Worship, 1660–1980', in D.M. Owen (ed.), *A History of Lincoln Minster* (Cambridge, 1994), pp. 78, 83. The younger Blundeville had been a chorister at Lincoln and the Chapel Royal, and after his stint at Ely went on to Lichfield, Dublin, York and finally Durham where he died in 1721; see Spink, *Restoration Church Music*, p. 226.

[45] EDC 3/1/2, fo. 450ᵛ.

[46] EDC 2/2A/2, p. 162, 14 June 1683.

[47] EDC 2/2A/3, p. 4, 25 November 1729.

that until 1696 the Chapter provided Hawkins and his predecessors with a room for this purpose (possibly the old Singing School described in the 1649 Parliamentary Survey); there are references to payment of 'Chimney money . . . for a fire hearth in the Singing School' (1671–2) and to the existence there of an organ (1685–6).[48] However, from 1696 Hawkins was paid twenty shillings a year 'in consideracion of his finding a schoolroom in which he teaches the Quire to Sing'.[49] It would seem that the room provided by Hawkins was attached to his house (the location of which is unknown) because his probate inventory refers to a 'School Room' containing a pair of virginals.[50]

The frequency and nature of choir practices remain obscure. Throughout the period Organists were paid expenses for 'Musick meetings', 'meetings at the Singing Schoole', and 'trying Anthems',[51] at the rate of one shilling per meeting. There were between three and twelve meetings each year, and the purpose of the reimbursement may be indicated by the entry for 1669–70, when Ferrabosco was paid eleven shillings 'for treatm[en]ts at Singing meetings'[52] – 'treatments' possibly meaning refreshments. Whether they were exclusively private occasions is unclear – an entry for 1682–3 records two shillings 'Spent upon the Quire men and at a publicke Meeting'.[53] This is not the only entry to refer specifically to the participation of the singing men in the meetings: were they in the nature of a club at which music was tried and refreshment imbibed, rather like those musical clubs which gave rise, at about this time, to the Three Choirs Festival? On the other hand, the later references (after 1686) to 'trying Anthems' are more likely to be rehearsals of music intended for performance in the Cathedral.

These meetings continued throughout Hawkins's tenure, possibly with his encouragement; but other aspects of his work gave cause for concern. Soon after his arrival the Dean and Chapter allowed him

> To be absent at Bury, for the teaching of children there in Musick three days in a fortnight and no more. Provided that he take care for the Supply of his two Places of Organist and Informator, in his absence . . .[54]

Possibly as a result of this extra-curricular activity, standards at Ely slipped, and in 1698 the Chapter resolved

> That Mr Hawkins, our Organist, shall not be allowed to absent himself from the Service of the Church one day, or teach any persons to sing or play, in the County, unless he carefully teach the Choir at home three afternoons, at least, in every week; and unless the proficiency of the quire be very evident, and a Sensible progress be made, as well by those of the Lay-clerks, who are willing to learn, as by the Children, within the space of three Months next ensuing . . .[55]

---

[48] EDC 3/1/2, fo. 417; also, EDC 3/1/3, *Soluciones domesticae*, 1685–6.
[49] EDC 2/2A/2, p. 212, 14 June 1696.
[50] EDC 2/8B/42.
[51] EDC 3/1/2, fos. 344ᵛ, 370ᵛ; EDC 3/1/3, *Soluciones domesticae*, 1688–9.
[52] EDC 3/1/2, fo. 400ᵛ.
[53] EDC 3/1/5, *Soluciones domesticae*, 1682–3.
[54] EDC 2/2A/2, p. 178, 14 June 1684.
[55] *Ibid.*, p. 218, 14 June 1698.

Hawkins remained at Ely for a further thirty years, so presumably there was a substantial improvement in musical standards or else the zeal of the Dean and Chapter proved a temporary phenomenon.

Expenditure on the Cathedral organs was frequent in the late seventeenth century. The fate of the pre-war organ is unknown. Although no reference has been found to its destruction, the importation of an organ 'for the use of the Quier' in 1661 (above, p. 245) implies that any surviving instrument was derelict. There are payments in 1664 for carriage of organ parts, work on the organ loft (the pulpitum?) and twenty-eight days' attendance by the organ blower (while it was being voiced?) but whether this concerned the 1661 instrument or the renovation of a pre-war relic is not known.[56] This work had ceased to give satisfaction by 1682 when the Dean and Chapter recorded their thankful acceptance of Dr Holder's 'intended Gift to our Organ and our readiness to compleat the Great Organ according as he hath desired'.[57] Holder was a prebendary of Ely (and later of St Paul's) as well as being Sub-Dean of the Chapel Royal and brother-in-law of Sir Christopher Wren. He was also a composer whose anthems and services appear in the Ely books, and his interest and occasional presence must have been of benefit to the Cathedral's musicians. It seems that he proposed a scheme for the organ's reconstruction to be funded jointly by himself and the Chapter, and they had the good sense to accept. Thomas Thamer, a Cambridge organ-builder, undertook the work, which was more or less complete by 1685 when (inconveniently) Thamer died at Ely, putting the Chapter to the expense of 'watching the corps and removing it'.[58]

Thamer's efforts evidently left something to be desired, for in 1688–9 Gerard Smith reconstructed the chair organ at a cost of £120.[59] Despite mutterings about his workmanship and an adverse report from William Preston, another organ-builder, who said it was not worth more than £80,[60] Smith went on in 1691 to build a new Great Organ at a cost of £300. It was originally to have stood within the existing case on the pulpitum, but the Chapter decided to have a new one, for which Smith was paid £100 in 1693.[61]

Smith's work gave the Cathedral an instrument which, with only minor alterations, survived until 1830. It was cleaned and repaired occasionally, and in 1735–6 Henry Turner, a Cambridge organ-builder, added a trumpet.[62] When the Cathedral was re-ordered in 1769–70 the organ was re-erected on Essex's new screen (Colour pl. 13a); the accounts record the payment of £100 to an unnamed builder, which other sources say was the London firm of Byfield and Green; 'Mr Green' received ten guineas in 1781–2 'for gilding the Organ'.[63]

Ferrabosco and Hawkins were figures of some consequence: musicians and composers

[56] EDC 3/1/2, fo. 333ᵛ.

[57] EDC 2/2A/2, p. 159, 14 June 1682.

[58] EDC 3/1/5, *Soluciones domesticae*, 1684–5.

[59] *Ibid.*, *Soluciones domesticae*, 1689–90; but see EDC 4/5/218 (particulars of Smith's work), which gives the cost as £130.

[60] EDC 4/5/218.

[61] EDC 2/2A/2, p. 203, 14 June 1693. See also EDC 4/5/220, the fragment of an agreement with Smith for the Great organ case.

[62] EDC 3/1/5, *Expensae necessariae*, 1735–6.

[63] EDC 3/1/7, 1769–70; 1781–2. José Hopkins, 'Organs in Ely Cathedral before 1851', *Journal of the British Institute of Organ Studies*, 21 (1997), p. 7.

with reputations outside Ely. The same could not be said of their immediate successors. Thomas Kempton (Organist 1729–62) was born in Ely in 1702 and admitted as a chorister ten years later.[64] He was probably apprenticed to Hawkins. It seems that he was assiduous in his duties, keeping the music books in good order and composing a number of services and anthems (including a chanting service which was performed regularly at Ely until the 1950s) but he could claim neither Ferrabosco's musical pedigree nor Hawkins's technical accomplishments. When he died in 1762 the three of them had served the Cathedral successively for exactly one hundred years. For the next few years such stability was to prove elusive. John Elbonn succeeded Kempton but died six years later in 1768.[65] In his place, the Chapter appointed David Wood,[66] but he left in 1774 to be admitted as a gentleman of the Chapel Royal.[67] They thereupon took the novel step of placing an advertisement in the *Cambridge Journal* and the *St James's Chronicle* for a new Organist, 'well skilled in, and used to Church-Musick . . . [and able to] . . . produce a sufficient testimonial to his good life and conversation',[68] and duly appointed James Rodgers;[69] but he was enticed away to Peterborough Cathedral in 1777.[70] Next came Richard Langdon, Organist of Exeter Cathedral 1753–77. He was sworn in at Ely on 26 November 1777, but was appointed Organist of Bristol Cathedral seven days later, on 3 December.[71] After these comings and goings, the Cathedral was served for fifty-two years by Highmore Skeats, father (1778–1804) and son (1804–30). Skeats senior seems to have been appreciated by the Chapter: £10 *per annum* was added to his stipend in 1795, 'in consideration of his long services in our Cathedral', with an immediate gift of seven guineas.[72] Both he and his son composed anthems and settings, and the younger Skeats, especially, was active in maintaining and adding to the Cathedral's music books – during the 1810s and 20s he often received annual payments of between £15 and £23 for his work.[73] His father's removal to Canterbury Cathedral, and his own to St George's Chapel, Windsor, is probably evidence of a reasonable competence, even in those days of patronage.

Securing an adequate income must have been a preoccupation for Organists throughout this period. Following Hawkins's death (1729) the Chapter agreed that his successor should have £20 a year as Organist, £10 as 'a farther bounty from the Church', £10 as *Informator Choristarum*, £2 'for playing to the psalm before Sermon', and £1 for the Singing School. There were further payments (*cf.* above p. 249) for teaching choristers and copying music.[74] Organists usually also held one of the Cathedral's minor offices (Hawkins was cook; Skeats senior became bridgekeeper in

---

[64] EDC 2/2A/2, p. 288, 25 November 1712; Shaw, *Succession of Organists*, p. 102.

[65] EDC 2/2A/3, p. 232, 25 November 1762.

[66] *Ibid.*, p. 255, 14 June 1768.

[67] Shaw, *Succession of Organists*, p. 102.

[68] EDC 2/2A/4, p. 34, 14 June 1774.

[69] *Ibid.*, p. 36, 7 September 1774.

[70] Shaw, *Succession of Organists*, p. 222.

[71] *Ibid.*, pp. 39, 114, 404.

[72] EDC 2/2A/4, p. 197, 25 November 1795.

[73] EDC 3/1/8–9, 1810–30, *passim*.

[74] EDC 2/2A/3, p. 4, 25 November 1729. The troublesome payments for teaching choristers were eventually commuted into an annual payment of £4 made to the Organist by the Chapter: *ibid.*, p. 155, 25 November 1751.

1789), yet their total annual income can seldom have exceeded £60 before 1795 when Skeats got his extra £10. Like Hawkins before and Robert Janes after them, the Organists of the period 1730–1830 must have relied upon private music tuition to augment their incomes. Others were aware of the problem. Thomas Du Quesne, a Prebendary who died in 1793, left £100, the interest on which was to be paid to the Organist, 'as an encouragement towards having & keeping a good one',[75] and in 1816 the Chapter increased Skeats junior's stipend by £20, 'in Expectation that he will use his best endeavours for the improvement of our Choir'.[76] As a result, Skeats's income from the Cathedral in 1817–18 was £84 6s. 8d., plus £14 8s. 4d. for copying[77] – a modest enough sum for a professional man.

The financial position of the lay clerks was even less favourable. They each received the stipend of £10 provided by the statutes, together with a share of the residence money (above, pp. 248–9) and income from Singing-men's Farm. The latter rose steadily from approximately £85 in 1788 to £332 in 1830,[78] but even so, inflation meant that the eight lay clerks of 1830 were significantly worse off than those of 1730.

During this period most of the lay clerks whose origins can be traced had sung as boys in the Cathedral, and in due course many of them supplied sons to fill the ranks of choristers. (Nineteen of the forty choristers admitted between 1814 and 1837 appear to have been children of lay clerks.[79]) The same families cropped up in different generations – for example, three John Fortingtons served as lay clerk (1758–74, 1789–1805, 1810–37) and no fewer than ten of Thomas Kempton's descendants were choristers, the last at the beginning of the twentieth century.[80] Having their roots in Ely, the singing men of this period tended to remain there. Francis Winter, for instance, retired as a chorister in 1736 and was immediately admitted as a 'demi'. He had to wait until the 1740s for a full place, but was still serving in the early 1790s alongside John Pigot (1754–1810), Worth Marshall (1758–1812) and William Marshall (1758–96). Having the freehold, and limited means of support, the singing men of this period often continued in office well into their seventies (with what effect may be imagined) and organists could be faced with a choir of which several members were disabled by age or infirmity from fulfilling their duties. It was decided in 1795 not to levy fines on Winter for non-attendance 'on Account of his great Age and infirmity'[81] but he continued to receive a stipend until his death in 1799, when he must have been about eighty years old.

There were occasional attempts to tighten up the lay clerks' discipline. In 1754 it was decreed that any singing man absenting himself without leave from service more than twice in one week would be fined one shilling for each absence in excess of that number (perhaps implying that constant attendance was by no means the norm).[82] In 1767 a fine of 2s. 6d. was introduced for any singing man tempted to leave before the end of the

---

[75] EDC 10/2B/1.
[76] EDC 2/2A/5, p. 136, 25 November 1816.
[77] EDC 3/1/8, 1817–18.
[78] EDC 10/3A/1–2, lay clerks' estate, accounts, May and November 1788 and 1830.
[79] Based on a comparison of lists of choristers in the quarterage books (EDC 3/7/2–3) with lists of lay clerks from the order books.
[80] EDC 2/12/7.
[81] EDC 2/2A/4, p. 197, 25 November 1795.
[82] EDC 2/2A/3, p. 190, 25 November 1754.

Sunday sermon.[83] There were individual misdemeanours. Francis Winter was censured (1750) for 'going abroad' for several days after leave had been refused, William Cullen was fined (1786) 'for his disobedience and improper conduct to our Precentor', and Worth Marshall was temporarily suspended (1794) for fathering an illegitimate child, though he was reinstated when the Chapter was satisfied that he had provided for its maintenance.[84] A generation later, the Chapter were less inclined to be lenient, and Thomas Bennett and Arthur Bland were expelled in 1829 for 'general misconduct and neglect of duty'.[85]

The singing men's duties remained much the same as in Hawkins's day. The meetings for 'trying anthems' seem to have petered out within a few years of his death, and there is no further reference to a rehearsal until 1817 when the Chapter required lay clerks and choristers to attend a weekly 'full' rehearsal in the Cathedral lasting one hour.[86] In 1745 they were ordered to take turns at giving out the metrical psalm at the Sunday sermon, and in 1763 it was decreed that each newly-appointed vicar or singing man would be expected to compile his own collection of anthems and services in a ruled book supplied by the Cathedral and which would become the Cathedral's property on his departure.[87]

Little changed for the choristers, either. They attended the Singing School and were expected to be able to read the psalms 'distinctly' before being admitted to the choir.[88] Otherwise, the Cathedral authorities played no part in their education unless they qualified for a place at the King's School. In 1814, for instance, five choristers were also King's Scholars, though the proportion thereafter declined, in part as the fortunes of the school waned.[89] When they ceased to be choristers they received an apprenticeship premium of £20 or (occasionally) assistance with further education.[90] In 1816 the Chapter instituted a Christmas bonus of £8 for the boys, and in 1822 Skeats was ordered to present an annual report at the Audit on the choristers' conduct and proficiency.[91] Throughout the period, the boys were recruited from the city. Most were admitted between the ages of nine and eleven and (1814–37) served an average of 5½ years, although seven years was not uncommon, and Charles Ling (1813–22) managed 9¼ years.[92]

The choir continued to sing from manuscript part-books, some of which had been begun many years earlier. The singing men were expected to compile their own books, which explains both the absence of complete sets and the inconsistencies between books of apparently similar date.[93] Unfortunately, no treble books have survived from the eighteenth century.

---

[83] EDC 2/2A/3, p. 250, 14 June 1767.

[84] *Ibid.*, p. 151, 25 November 1750; EDC 2/2A/4, p. 123, 25 November 1786; p. 181, 14 June 1794; and p. 187, 25 November 1794.

[85] EDC 2/2A/5, p. 265, 14 June 1829.

[86] *Ibid.*, p. 146, 25 November 1817.

[87] EDC 2/2A/3, p. 110, 25 November 1745; p. 235, 14 June 1763.

[88] *Ibid.*, p. 91, 14 June 1742; p. 114, 14 June 1814.

[89] EDC 3/8/2, *passim.*

[90] These arrangements seem to have been formalised only in 1817 (EDC 2/2A/5, p. 146, 25 November 1817) but may have been in existence earlier (*cf.* EDC 2/2A/2, p. 121, 14 June 1677).

[91] EDC 2/2A/5, 25 November 1816, p. 136; 14 June 1822, p. 199.

[92] EDC 3/8/2, *passim.*

[93] EDC 2/2A/3, p. 235, 14 June 1763. Occasional attempts were made to bring order to the music library: *e.g.* EDC 2/2A/4, p. 187, 25 November 1794; EDC 2/2A/5, p. 115, 14 June 1814.

Only tentative conclusions can therefore be drawn about repertoire at this period. A volume of services in score, possibly in Kempton's hand and in existence by 1754, consists largely of seventeenth-century settings (Gibbons, Patrick, Ferrabosco, Child, Rogers, Aldrich and Portman among them) still apparently in regular use.[94] Similarly, when Thomas Watkins the Precentor had a book of anthems compiled for his use in 1764, this also reveals a preponderance of earlier material, including Purcell (7), Hawkins (8), Tudway (3), Aldrich (4), Humfrey (4), Rogers (3), Turner (2) and single entries for Byrd, Gibbons, Tallis, Loosemore, Batten, Bullis and Ferrabosco. The most 'modern' entries are four anthems by James Kent (1700–76) and three by William Boyce (1711–79).[95]

Firmer evidence survives from the early nineteenth century. A manuscript book entitled 'A list of the Services & Anthems that are used in the Cathedral Church of Ely', and with a footnote, 'for the Precentor', was compiled between 1815 and 1830[96] and lists ninety-four anthems and twenty-five services, all presumably in use during the 1820s.[97] Some earlier full services are included (Tallis, Byrd, Gibbons, Child, Creighton, Rogers) but the eleven verse services are all of the eighteenth century, including settings by Nares, Kent and Skeats. The anthems are grouped into three categories – full, verse, and full with verse (a popular style c.1800). The most represented composers are: Kent (11), Handel (7), Greene (5), Purcell, Haydn, Clarke, Smith, Stephens, Boyce (4), and Child (3); Byrd, Wise, Battishill, Croft and Bullis merit single entries, and the two Skeats contributed nine anthems between them. Much of the repertoire was drawn from printed collections of cathedral music to which the Chapter subscribed – among them, Greene's *Anthems* (1742), Boyce's *Cathedral Music* (1756) and collections by Bond (1790–1), Kent (1796–7), Clarke (1799–1800), Stephens (1804–5), Ebdon (1816–17), Whitfield (1823–4) and Camidge (1829–30).[98] These provided a vast resource upon which successive Organists drew freely for the music-books.

Broadly speaking, the pattern of services established in 1660–2 endured with only minor changes until the mid nineteenth century. The five vicars officiated in turn at the daily offices but found some difficulty on Sundays in juggling the demands of the Cathedral and those of their four chaplaincies. In 1695, for example, Bentham and Silvertop had to be reminded 'not [to] goe to Stuntney or Chetsham to officiate there till after first and second Service shall be ended in the Cathedral'.[99] Not all the vicars were, in any case, diligent in performing their Cathedral duties. An order of 1685 recorded that

> The Dean & Chapter are credibly inform'd that, notwithstanding the many Exhortacions & admonitions to a more diligent attendance upon Divine Service, it is (in their absence especially) very much neglected, to the great dishonour of God & the Scandall of the Church . . .

---

[94] EDC 10/7/13.

[95] EDC 10/7/8.

[96] EDC 10/1A/5. A subsequent hand made revisions and alterations during the 1830s.

[97] This assumption is supported by the surviving part-books of the period (*e.g.* EDC 10/7/40, 45, 58) and an organ book begun in 1823 (EDC 10/7/54).

[98] The dates are those upon which the Chapter resolved to purchase the collections or paid for them; information from the order books or audit books.

[99] EDC 2/2A/2, p. 208, 14 June 1695.

and instructed the Precentor to enforce the fines laid down in the Statutes.[100] The vicars would sometimes get others to undertake their duties, and an order of 1708 stipulated that the Litany should henceforth always be chanted by one of the minor canons, 'instead of lay clerks chanting of it by former custome'; a further order (1744) required that 'the Minor Canons do read the first Lesson at Prayers instead of the Singing men'.[101]

The Precentor appointed the canticle setting and anthem for each service. Unfortunately, combination papers (music lists) survive only from 1868 onwards, so it is hardly possible to know whether the choice of music reflected the changing liturgical seasons. The only slight evidence survives in one of the inventories of lost part-books from the mid-1660s. The contents of the Bass book include anthems designated for particular festivals: Christmas, Easter and Whitsunday, but also Epiphany, Ash Wednesday, Good Friday, St Peter's Day, All Saints' Day, and New Year's Day.[102] Clearly, some attempt was being made to distinguish holy days.

Another (less expected) way of marking holy days was the use of incense. William Cole records that it was the practice to burn incense at Ely at the great festivals until Thomas Greene (3rd stall, 1737–80) objected on the ground that it gave him a headache.[103] Eleven vouchers dating from between 1708 and 1747 survive as evidence that 'frankincense' was purchased at Christmas and (probably) Easter.[104] Probably it was burned in a fixed censer, continuing a practice that was fairly common in cathedrals and college chapels during the seventeenth century. There is also evidence for the seasonal decoration of the Choir with rosemary and bay at Christmas – again, a common usage.[105]

The frequency of Holy Communion varied. In 1668 the Chapter decreed that, in addition to the three principal festivals (Christmas, Easter, and Whitsunday), Communion should be celebrated on the first Sunday in Lent, the Sunday nearest to St Bartholomew's Day (24 August) and at the two general Chapters (June and November).[106] By 1682 it had been increased to include the first Sunday in every month as well as 'all the great festivalls', though this had never included the Ascension because a fair was held in Ely on that day.[107] It is not clear what the practice was in the first half of the eighteenth century, but in 1781 the Chapter agreed that Communion would be administered every Sunday 'during the Summer half Year', and on the third Sunday of each month during the winter, 'as has been lately customary'.[108]

Holy Communion (or Ante-Communion, when there was no celebration) concluded the Sunday morning service, comprising Mattins, Litany, Communion and sermon. Following the Nicene Creed, the congregation at the Choir service moved westwards to the 'Sermon-place', where they were joined by the congregations from Holy Trinity and

[100] EDC 2/2A/2, p. 180, 14 June 1685.
[101] *Ibid.*, p. 276, 25 November 1708; EDC 2/2A/3, p. 104, 14 June 1744.
[102] EDC 10/1A/2.
[103] Cole MSS, BL Add. MS 5873, fo. 326.
[104] EDC 14/18.
[105] EDC 3/1/5, *Soluciones domesticae*, 1679–80.
[106] EDC 2/2A/2, p. 80, 25 November 1668.
[107] EDC 2/11, responses to Bishop's visitation enquiry, 1682.
[108] EDC 2/2A/4, p. 99b, 25 November 1786.

St Mary's, and many others who had not attended service anywhere. An organ voluntary was played while people took their seats, and one of the lay clerks then led the singing of a metrical psalm from the organ loft, to which the choir had removed after the Creed. The sermon followed.[109] On Sacrament Sundays, those who wished to make their communion returned to the Choir after this, and the vergers were instructed to shut the Cathedral doors after the departing sermon congregation, 'that no-body may pass through the Church in Sacrament time'.[110]

It is not clear how much of Ante-Communion was sung. By the early nineteenth century it was probably the 'Kyrie' (actually, the responses to the Commandments), the Sanctus (sung after the Litany) and the Creed. This may have been the pattern since the 1660s, although the surviving part-books of that period contain at least one setting of the Gloria in Excelsis.[111]

Instructions for singing the morning and evening service survive from 1702–8, and indicate that the Apostles' Creed, Confession, Absolution and both Lord's Prayers were sung on a monotone[112] (Plate 22c). However, in 1730 the Chapter decreed that the service should 'be read for the Future with a distinct & audible Voice except the Psalms & Hymns & Anthems which are to be sung as usual'.[113] What abuse this was meant to correct is not known, but the practice continued until the 1840s.[114] By 'hymns' was meant canticles, and the music books contain many settings of the alternative canticles for evening prayer (Cantate Domino and Deus Misereatur) as well as the Magnificat and Nunc Dimittis.

The Cathedral statutes required that 'none of the canons or others who serve in the choir should enter the choir at the time of divine service without the dress appropriate to the choir'.[115] There is no convincing evidence for choir dress before the nineteenth century, but a Chapter order of 1756 decreed 'that neither Singing men nor Singing boys appear at Church on a Sunday without a Surplice'.[116] (Were surplices not required on week-days?) In 1817, however, the Chapter resolved to give newly-elected choristers a surplice (had parents been expected to provide them before this?), and later in the same year undertook to provide an additional surplice, 'that they may always appear clean and decent at divine Service in the Cathedral'.[117] So by this date the choristers (at least) always wore surplices when attending to their duties.

One of the other candidates for the organistship at Windsor when Highmore Skeats, junior was appointed was a young man of twenty-four named Robert Janes.[118] He was

---

[109] Before the re-ordering of 1770 the sermon-place was to the west of the pulpitum, where, in 1749, the Chapter ordered a gallery to be built for 'the Singing Men Choristers & as many of the Kings Scholars as it may contain' (EDC 2/2A/3, p. 141, 14 June 1749). John Bacon has left a colourful account of a Sunday morning sermon of the early nineteenth century (EDC 4/6/2, fos. 63–6), by which date the sermon place was in the first three bays of the (present) choir, to the west of Essex's screen.

[110] EDC 2/2A/3, p. 203, 25 November 1756.

[111] EDC 10/7/3. The setting is by Loosemore.

[112] EDC 10/1A/3. See Spink, *Restoration Church Music*, pp. 413–16.

[113] EDC 2/2A/3, p. 8, 25 November 1730.

[114] See W.E. Dickson, *Fifty Years of Church Music* (Ely, 1894), pp. 64–5; however EDC 10/7/23 (Music MS 23), which is probably late eighteenth century in date, contains Thomas Ebdon's responses from Durham.

[115] Spink, *Restoration Church Music*, p. 433.

[116] EDC 2/2A/3, p. 203, 25 November 1756.

[117] EDC 2/2A/5, pp. 140, 145, 14 June, 25 November 1817.

[118] Shaw, *Succession of Organists*, p. 348.

unsuccessful at Windsor, but was appointed to Skeats's post at Ely on 25 November 1830.[119] Janes's arrival coincided with the commencement of an era of reform which would gradually bring about far-reaching changes to a musical establishment that had changed little since the 1660s.

---

[119] EDC 2/2A/5, p. 292, 25 November 1830.

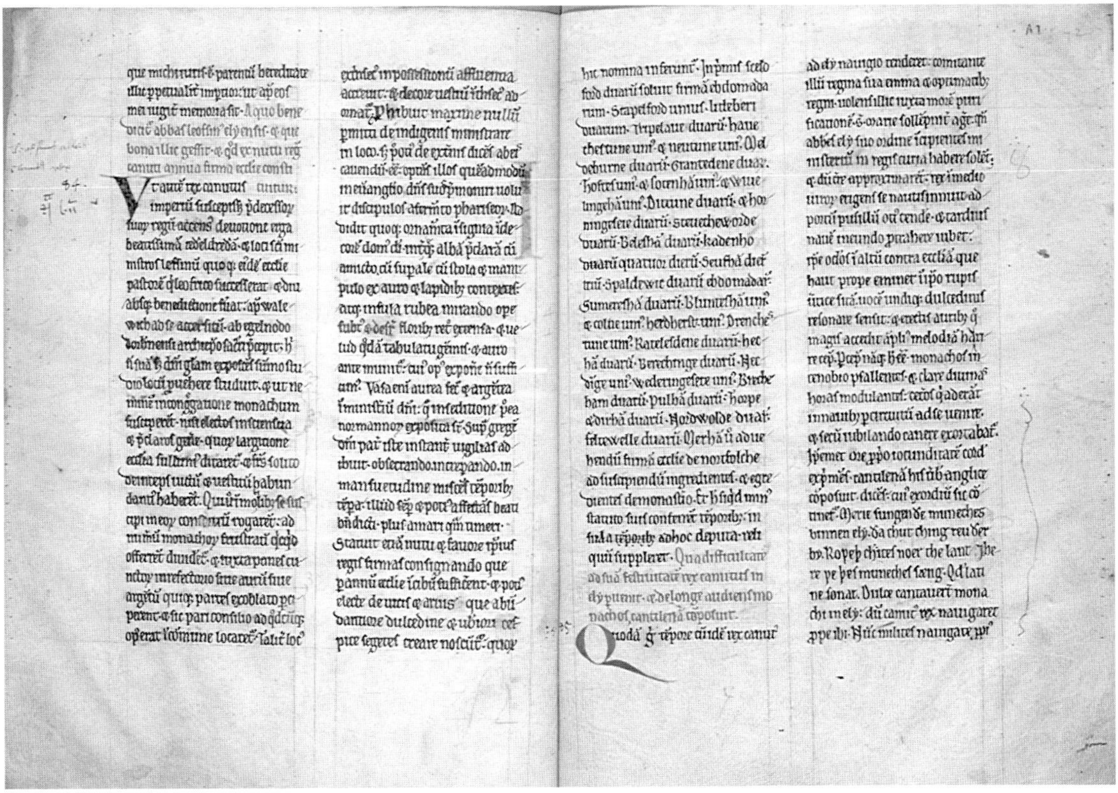

Plate 1(a) *Liber Eliensis* (EDC 1): Cnut's song, Book II, chapter 85, 'Merrily sung the monks of Ely' (indicated by arrow)

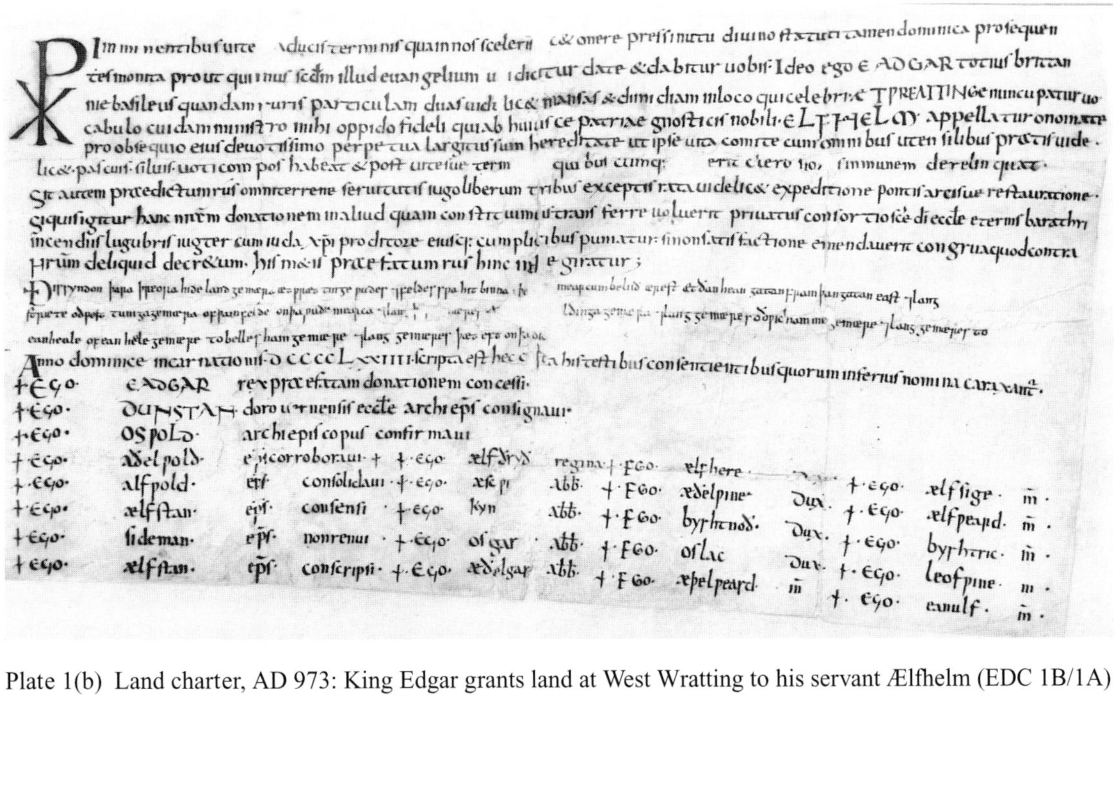

Plate 1(b) Land charter, AD 973: King Edgar grants land at West Wratting to his servant Ælfhelm (EDC 1B/1A)

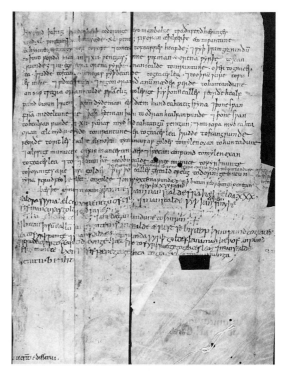

Plate 2(a) Regulations of the thegns' guild at Cambridge, in an 8th-century gospel-book from Ely (BL, MS Cott. Tib. B. v, vol. I, fo. 75)

Plate 2(b) Ely farming memoranda: lists of goods supplied to Thorney Abbey, pigs on Ely estates, details of fen rents, *etc.*, preserved as sewing guards in 17th-century bindings (BL, Add. MS 61735)

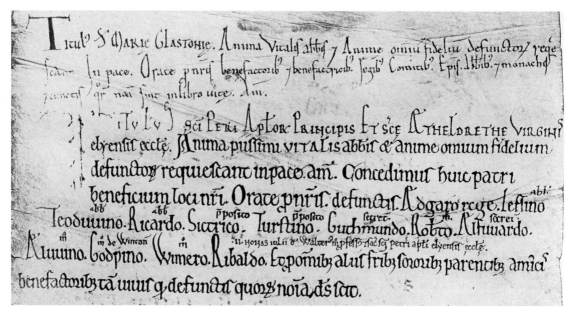

Plate 2(c) Ely titulus: commemoration of King Edgar and several abbots, priors and sacrists of Ely Abbey, in the mortuary roll of Abbot Vitalis of Savigny (d.1122) (L. Delisle, *Rouleau mortuaire* (Paris, 1909), pl. XLV)

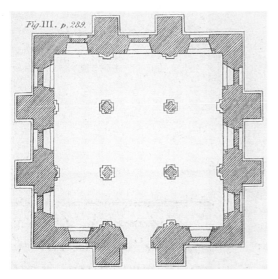

Plate 3(a) Plan of the 'chapter house' (monastic kitchen) (Stevenson, *Supplement*, pl. L, figure III)

Plate 3(b) Robert Willis, plan of the Cathedral's Norman apse and east end, sketched for D.J. Stewart's *Ely*, 1868 (EDC 14/36/1/49)

Plate 3(c) W.H. St John Hope, reconstruction of the elevation of the Norman nave pulpitum, destroyed in 1770 (*PCAS*, xxi (1919), pl. 1, facing p. 19)

Plate 4(b) The Monks' Door and the south transept door, both partly blocked by a buttress supporting the Octagon

Plate 4(a) The Prior's Door, opening into the former cloister on the south side of the nave

Plate 4(d) Norman capitals in the south transept

Plate 4(c) West tower interior, looking upward: angle squinches built to support a spire

Plate 5(a) South-west transept restored
(*Illustrated London News*, 27 Sept. 1845)

Plate 5(b) South-west transept, west front and lower part of turret

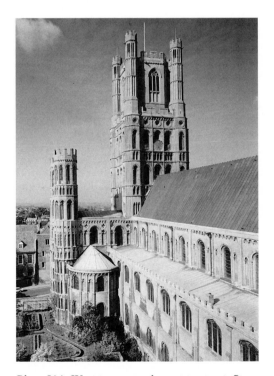

Plate 5(c) West tower, south-west transept; St Catherine's Chapel as restored by Robert Willis (Crown copyright. NMR)

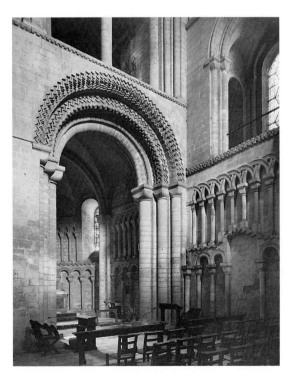

Plate 5(d) St Catherine's Chapel, interior

Plate 6(a) Galilee Porch, exterior

Plate 6(b) Galilee upper chamber, unroofed *c.*1800

Plate 6(c) Galilee Porch, interior and west portal

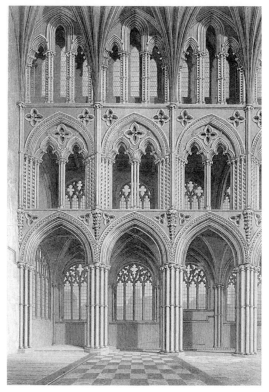

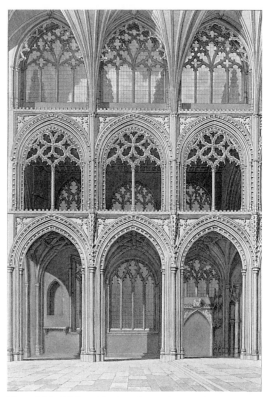

Plate 7(a) Bishop Northwold's presbytery, looking south, drawn by E. Mackenzie, engraved by F.J. Havell (George Millers, *Ely* (1834), pl. IX)

Plate 7(b) Bishop Hotham's presbytery bays, looking north (Millers, *Ely* (1834), pl. VIII)

Plate 7(c–e) Wall brackets in presbytery: (c) Bishop Northwold, east end; (d) Bishop Hotham, south side; (e) Bishop Hotham, north side

Plate 8(a) Remains of 13th-century choir stalls, in the cathedral wood store

Plate 8(b) 14th-century choir stalls, with 19th-century carved panels

Plate 8(c) Photomontage of the 14th-century stalls relocated in the Octagon space, showing the arrangements which lasted until 1770

Plate 9(a) Octagon tabernacle, 1320s

Plate 9(b) Painted tabernacle showing Wulfstan, Archbishop of York, over niches containing benefactors' bones, north backing wall of choir stalls (engraved after Michael Tyson's drawing (1769))

Plate 9(c) Tabernacle in the Lady Chapel 1330s or 1340s

Plate 9(d) Tabernacle in Prior Crauden's Chapel, c.1325

Plate 10(a) William Stukeley, sketch of medieval stained glass in the Octagon, showing St Wilfrid and King Ecgfrith (CCCC, MS 556)

Plate 10(b) View of Octagon niches, filled with James Redfern's seated Apostles (Crown copyright. NMR)

Plate 10(c) John Carter, drawing of Octagon capital: Etheldreda made Abbess (BL, Add. MS 29927, fo. 157)

Plate 10(d) The death and burial of Etheldreda, Octagon capital

Plate 10(e) Painted decoration of the Octagon vault, partially restored c.1850, later overpainted by Thomas Gambier Parry

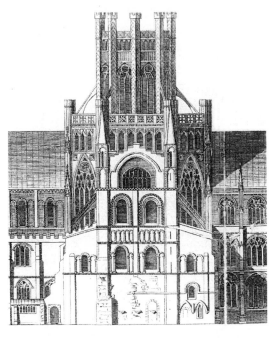

Plate 11(a) Lantern before 1760 (Bentham, *Ely*, pl. XLII, detail). Drawn by J. Heins, engraved by P.S. Lamborn

Plate 11(b) Lantern, after James Essex's restoration

Plate 11(c) Lantern as remodelled by Sir Gilbert Scott, from west tower

Plate 12(a) Slab of Tournai marble, believed to have been the monument to Bishop Nigel (d.1169); discovered in St Mary's church, Ely, in 1829

Plate 12(b) Monument to Bishop Hugh de Northwold (d.1254)

Plate 12(c) Monument to Bishop William de Kilkenny (d.1257)

Plate 12(d) Monument to Bishop William de Luda (d.1299)

Plate 13(a) Bishop Alcock's chapel

Plate 13(b) Bishop West's chapel

Plate 13(c) Tombs of Anglo-Saxon benefactors,
in Bishop West's chapel

Plate 13(d) 14th-century screen, now enclosing
St Edmund's chapel, thought to have been from
the altar of the Holy Cross in the nave

Plate 14(a) Former monastic buildings around Firmary Lane, viewed from the Cathedral's south transept

Plate 14(b) Sacrist's Gate and remains of bell-tower

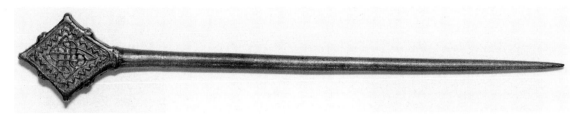

Plate 15(a) Gilded bronze pin found in the tomb of Archbishop Wulfstan of York (d.1023) when the remains of Anglo-Saxon benefactors were disturbed in 1769 (Society of Antiquaries of London)

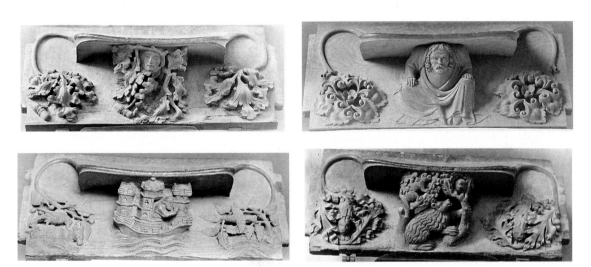

Plate 15(b) Misericords, from Octagon choir stalls (James Heber Taylor)

Plate 15(c) Stained glass figures in tracery lights, Lady Chapel (Crown copyright. NMR)

Plate 16(c) Ely ownership mark, in several 14th-century Priory manuscripts (CUL, MS Gg.1.21)

Plate 16(d) 'This book belongs to the Church of Ely' ('Iste liber pertinet acclesie Eliennis): ownership inscription, c.1470s (CUL, MS Ii.2.15)

Plate 16(a) Priory cartulary: a copy of King Edgar's foundation charter (EDR G3/28, p. 64, right hand column)

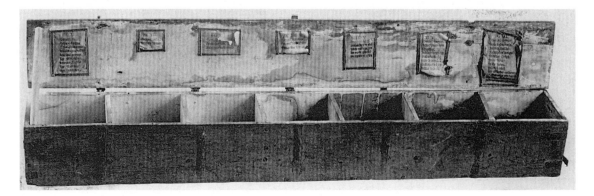

Plate 16(b) Late 15th-century muniment chest

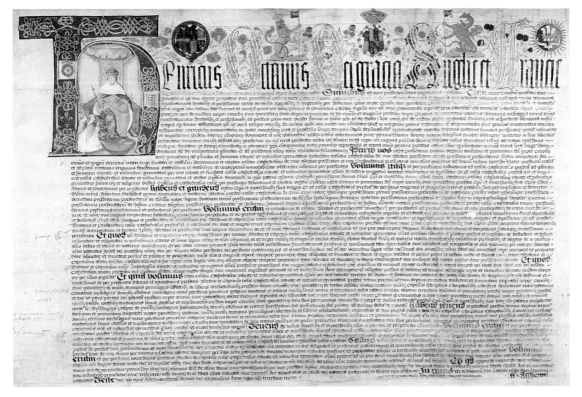

Plate 17(a) Charter of King Henry VIII, 10 Sept. 1541,
establishing the Dean and Chapter of Ely Cathedral (EDC 2/1/1)

Plate 17(b) Seal matrix of Henry VIII's new Foundation, showing the Holy Trinity and the King enthroned;
illustrated in reverse

Plate 18(a) Iconoclasm: figure sculptures hacked away, in Bishop West's chapel

Plate 18(b) Iconoclasm: heads of statues knocked off, in the Lady Chapel

Plate 19(a) Brass of Thomas Goodrich (Bishop, 1534–54)

Plate 19(b) Brass of Humphrey Tyndall (Dean, 1591–1614)

Plate 19(c) Andrew Willet (5th stall, 1587–1621), rubbing of his brass in Barley church, Herts.

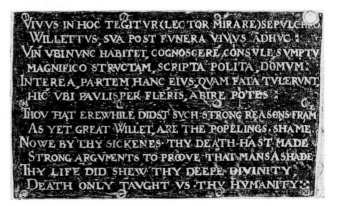

Plate 19(d) Andrew Willet, epitaph of his brass

Plate 20(a) Monument to Martin Heton (Bishop, 1600–9)

Plate 20(b) Monument to Sir Robert Steward (d.1570)

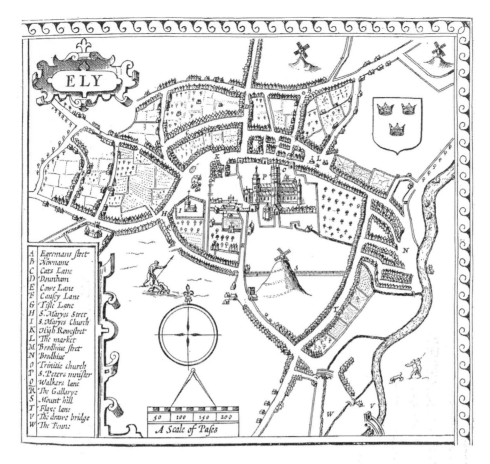

Plate 21(a) John Speed's map of Ely, *c.*1610

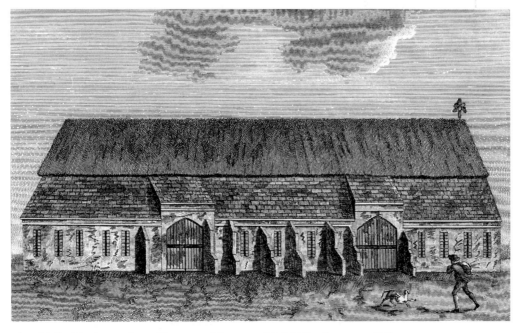

Plate 21(b) The Sextry barn (*European Magazine*, 34 (1798), pl. opp. p. 296)

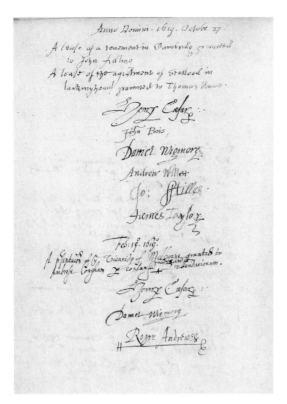

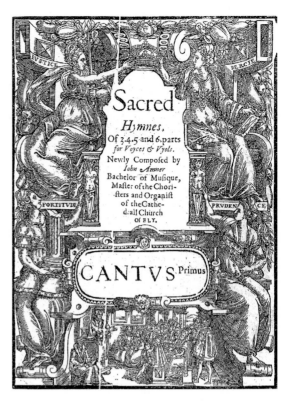

Plate 22(a) Chapter Order Book (EDC 2/2A/1), meetings of 27 October 1619 and 19 February 1620: with signatures of Dean Henry Caesar and Canons

Plate 22(b) Title page of John Amner's *Sacred Hymnes*, 1615

Plate 22(c) Directions for chanting the service in Ely Cathedral, *c.*1700 (EDC 10/1A/3)

Plate 23(a) Daniel King, preparatory drawing of Ely Cathedral from the north, for the engraving in Roger Dodsworth and William Dugdale, *Monasticon Anglicanum*, vol. I (1655), here shown in reverse, having been drawn to suit the engraver (Society of Antiquaries of London)

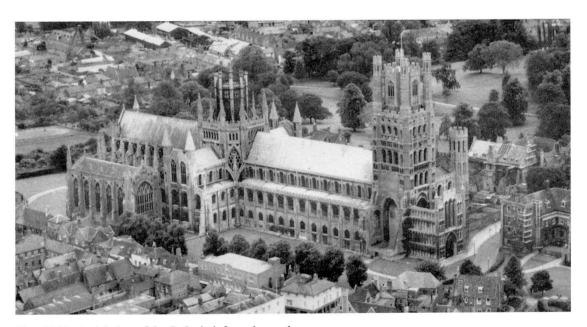

Plate 23(b) Aerial view of the Cathedral, from the north

Plate 24(a) Monument to Peter Gunning (Bishop, 1675–84), south choir aisle

Plate 24(b) Dean Spencer's font and cover, 1693, in Bentham, *Ely* (pl. XXXV): drawn by J. Heins, engraved by P.S. Lamborn

Plate 24(c) Dean Spencer's font, in Prickwillow church since 1865

JOANNES SPENCER S.T.P.
Decanus Eliensis, & Collegii Corporis Christi
Apud Cantabrigienses Custos.

Plate 25(a) John Spencer (Dean, 1677–93)

Reverendus admodum THOMAS TANNER Asaphensis Episcopus

Charles Ashton D.D.

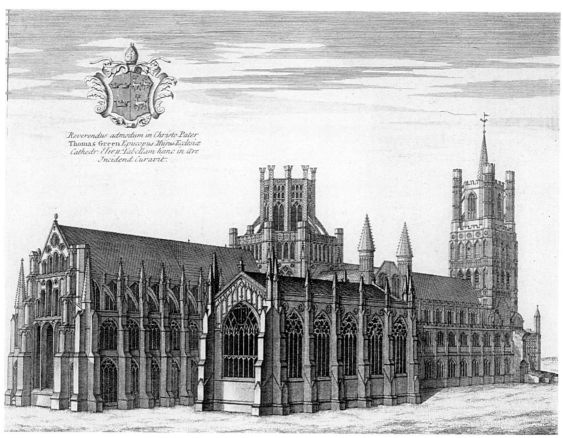

Plate 26(a) The Cathedral from the north-east,
drawn and engraved by J. Harris for Browne
Willis, *Survey* (1730)

Plate 26(b) J. Harris, west front, for Browne
Willis (1730)

Plate 27(a) Monument to John Moore (Bishop, 1707–14)

Plate 27(b) Monument to William Fleetwood (Bishop, 1714–23), by Edward Stanton and Christopher Horsnaile

Plate 27(c) Design for monument to Bishop Butts, by Sir Henry Cheere (Victoria & Albert Museum)

Plate 27(d) Monument to Robert Butts (Bishop, 1738–48)

Plate 28(a) Samuel Buck, view of Ely (1745), central section (CUL, Views.x.1, no. 145)

Plate 28(b) High Street, looking west: 18th-century watercolour (City of Ely Council)

Plate 29(a) Peter Allix (Dean, 1730–58)

Plate 29(b) Matthias Mawson (Bishop, 1754–70), possibly by Thomas Bardwell, in the Bishop's House

Plate 29(c) James Bentham (2nd stall, 1779–96), engraving, 1792, after a drawing by T. Kerrich

Plate 29(d) William Cole (1714–82), antiquary, engraving after a drawing by T. Kerrich

Plate 30(a) James Essex (1722–84), sketch portrait after a miniature by W.S. Lambourn (Downing College, Cambridge, MS Bowtell 63.5, fo. 1013)

Plate 30(b) East end with organ over altar screen, proposed by Essex in 1768

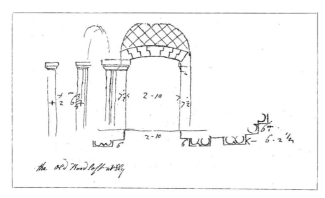

Plate 30(c) James Essex: sketch of the Norman pulpitum, 1760s. It was from this and other sketches that Hope made his reconstruction, reproduced as Plate 3(c) (BL, Add. MS 6768, p. 122)

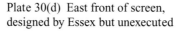

Plate 30(d) East front of screen, designed by Essex but unexecuted

Plate 31(a) View of the Octagon, as proposed to be cleared, 1763 (Bentham, *Ely*, pl. XLI). Drawn by J. Heins, engraved by P.S. Lamborn

Plate 31(b) View of the choir, looking west, by J. Newman, 1773 (Cambridgeshire Libraries)

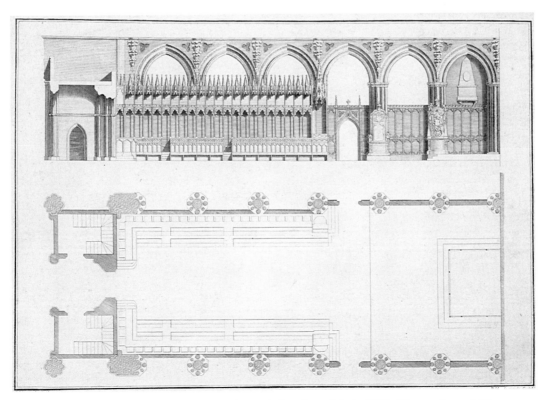

Plate 31(c) James Essex, prospectus plate, plan and elevation of choir (CUL, Views.x.1, no. 144)

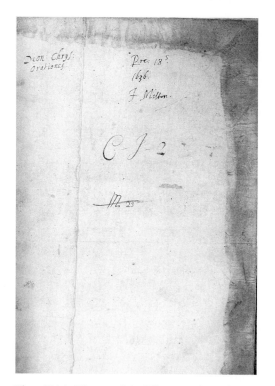
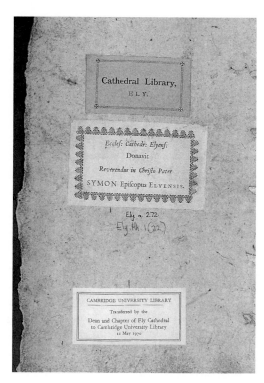

Plate 32(a) History of the Library: John Milton's signature, 1636, and later book-plates (CUL, Ely.a.272)

Plate 32(b) Charles Mason (1699–1771), owner of pre-Conquest charters of Ely: etching by J. Bretherton (Downing College Cambridge, MS Bowtell 48)

Plate 32(c) George Millers (1776–1852), Cathedral historian (EDC 14/37D/1)

Plate 33(a) William and Hilkiah Burgess, west front of the Cathedral with north-west transept notionally restored, 1810

Plate 33(b) William Anslow, south-east view of Ely Cathedral, 1813

Plate 34(a) Sir Henry Bate Dudley (5th stall, 1815–24), by Gainsborough

Plate 34(b) George Jenyns (8th stall, 1802–48)

Plate 34(c) John Henry Sparke (6th stall, 1818–24, 5th stall, 1824–70)

Plate 34(d) William French (3rd stall, 1831–49)

Plate 35(a) George Peacock (Dean, 1839–58)

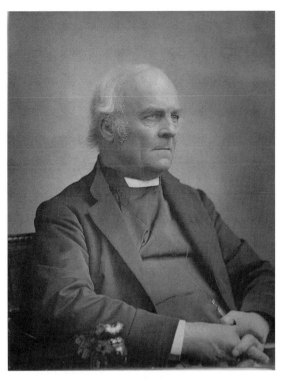

Plate 35(b) Harvey Goodwin (Dean, 1858–69)

Plate 35(c) Edward Bowyer Sparke (4th stall, 1829–31, 7th stall 1831–79)

Plate 35(d) William Selwyn (6th stall, 1833–75) (EDC 14/27)

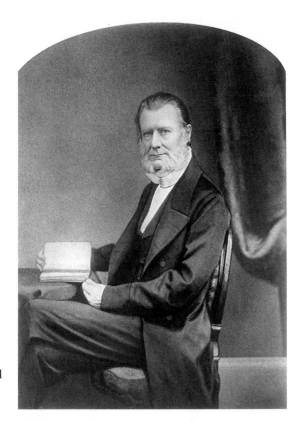

Plate 36(a) Robert Willis (1800–75, Jacksonian Professor of Natural and Experimental Philosophy and architectural historian (CUL, CAS E85)

Plate 36(b) Design for Ely altar chairs by Robert Willis (EDC 14/36/1/4)

Plate 36(c) Altar chair designed by Robert Willis, carved by Ollett

Plate 37(a) David Stewart (1814–98), minor canon and architectural historian (EDC 14/37D/2)

Plate 37(b) Stewart's sketch of the east end completed with turrets, one of which was executed by Edward Blore (EDC 14/36/2/25)

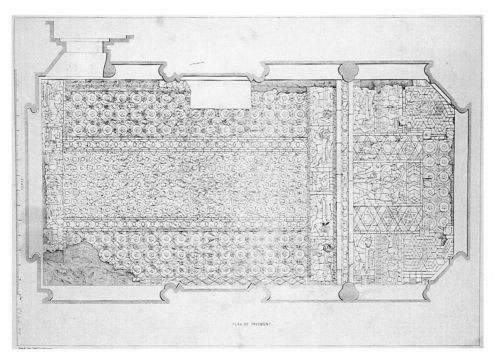

Plate 37(c) Prior Crauden's chapel monograph: plan of pavement (EDC 14/36/3/8). Lithograph by Day & Son from Stewart's drawing

Plate 38(a) Cathedral from the east, *c.*1855, showing James Essex's lantern (Victoria & Albert Museum)

Plate 38(b) Cathedral from the east, after 1879, showing Sir Gilbert Scott's Lantern and Octagon pinnacles

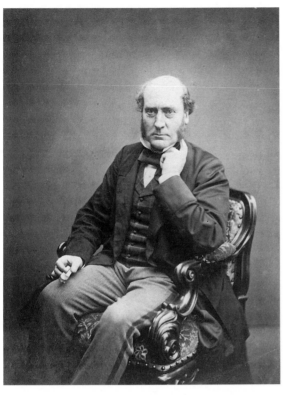

Plate 39(a) Sir Gilbert Scott (1811–78), architect (National Portrait Gallery)

Plate 39(b) The central 'Octagon' of Ely Cathedral, as proposed to be restored. Appeal engraving, 1859 (EDC 4/5/79)

Plate 39(d) Sir Gilbert Scott, design for the Lantern, 1862 (EDC 4/8/9)

Plate 39(c) Scott's sketch, from appeal engraving, with suggested spire (EDC 4/5/80)

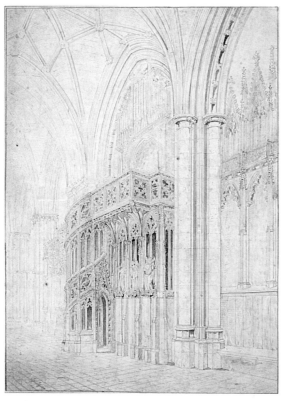

Plate 40(a) Sir Gilbert Scott, design for organ staircase, *c.*1849 (EDC 4/8/8)

Plate 40(b) Organ staircase, as executed

Plate 40(c–e) Michel Abeloos of Louvain, choir stall panels before staining: (c) Jacob's ladder; (d) Jonah and the whale; (e) Supper at Emmaus

Plate 41(a) Sir Gilbert Scott's screen, and John Grove's pulpit, *c.*1860
(B.E.C. Howarth-Loomes)

Plate 41(b) Scott's pulpit, in the Octagon

Plate 42(a) Thomas Gambier Parry, nave ceiling: portraits of Henry Davies, Alfred Clay and Henry Styleman Le Strange 'my friend' (Crown copyright. NMR)

Plate 42(b) Thomas Gambier Parry (1815–88)

Plate 42(c) Adoration of the Shepherds and Magi: sketch design by Gambier Parry

Plate 43(a) Charles Merivale (Dean, 1869–93)

Plate 43(b) Charles Stubbs (Dean, 1893–1906)

Plate 43(c) Benjamin Hall Kennedy (3rd stall, 1867–89)

Plate 44(a) Brass by J. and
L. Waller, 1850, covering
grave of George Basevi,
architect, in north choir aisle

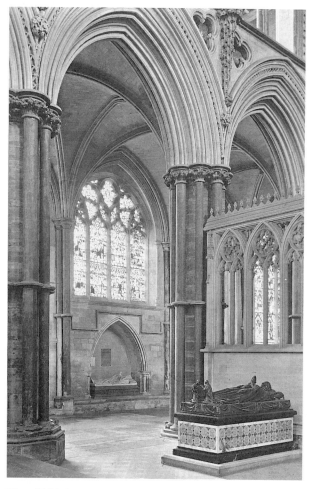

Plate 44(b) Monument to William Hodge Mill (8th stall,
1848–53), designed by Sir Gilbert Scott, in original setting
behind High Altar (Crown copyright. NMR)

Plate 44(c) Monument to James Russell
Woodford (Bishop, 1873–85), by G.F.
Bodley. Nave north aisle

Plate 45(a) Visitors to 1200th anniversary celebrations, 1873, including (left to right) Bishop E. Harold Browne, Bishop Harvey Goodwin, T.L. Claughton and Bishop James Russell Woodford (Cambridgeshire Libraries)

Plate 45(b) Cathedral bedesmen, late 19th century

Plate 46(a) William Emery and his wife in the study of the 5th Canonry house, now the Deanery

Plate 46(b) View of the study in the Deanery

Plate 46(c) Opening of the Church Congress at Ely, 1910

Plate 47(a) Edmund Chipp (Organist, 1867–86)
(*The Musical Times*, 1 March 1902, p. 160)

Plate 47(b) Basil Harwood (Organist, 1887–92)
(Royal College of Music)

Plate 47(c) Cathedral lay clerks, *c.*1895, with, in the centre, Thomas Tertius Noble (Organist, 1892–8),
and Precentor J.H. Crosby behind

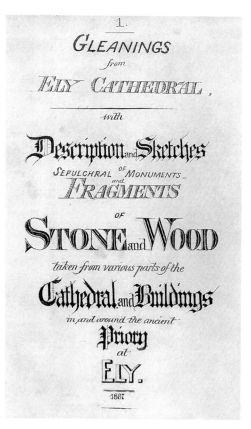

SCREEN — PROBABLY AT EAST END OF AISLE —
BEFORE 16ᵗʰ CENTURY

Plate 48(a) John Bacon's MS account, *Gleanings from Ely Cathedral*, 1887 (EDC 4/6/7)

Plate 48(b) Stone screen, probably from the south-east corner of the presbytery, now lost. Illustration in *Gleanings*

OAK · PULPIT

Plate 48(c) Oak pulpit, designed by John Groves, 1781, now lost. Illustration in *Gleanings*

WINGS OF ALTAR SCREEN · FORMERLY IN TRINITY PARISH CHURCH

Plate 48(d) Screen, late 17th century, perhaps for the high altar, later in Holy Trinity church, now in the east end chapel of St Etheldreda. Illustration in *Gleanings*

Plate 49(a) Frank Robert Chapman (Canon, 1879–1910), antiquary; detail of a photograph of the Dean and Chapter, 1901

Plate 49(b) Seiriol Evans (Precentor, 1923–9), Cathedral historian; Dean of Gloucester (1953–73) (Gloucester Cathedral)

Plate 49(c) Cathedral library, in the eastern aisle of the south transept: imperfect view

Plate 50(a) Dean and Chapter, 14 June 1901. Left to right: Frank Chapman (Canon, 1879–1910); William Emery (Canon, 1870–1910); Vincent Stanton (Ely Professor and Canon, 1889–1916); Charles Stubbs (Dean, 1893–1906), Alexander Kirkpatrick (Regius Professor of Hebrew, 1882–1903; Dean, 1906–36); Edward Lowe (Canon, 1873–1912), Bishop William Macrorie (Canon, 1892–1905)

Plate 50(b) Choir, c.1910 (in the centre, A.W. Wilson (Organist), Dean Kirkpatrick, Precentor J.H. Crosby)

Plate 51(a) Vincent Henry Stanton (first Ely Professor and Canon, 1889–1916)

Plate 51(b) John Martin Creed (Ely Professor and Canon, 1926–40)

Plate 51(c) Bishop Gordon Walsh (Canon, 1944–67)

Plate 51(d) Christopher Stead (last Ely Professor and Canon, 1971–80)

Plate 52(a) Visit of HRH the Duchess of Kent to the King's School, late 1930s

Plate 52(b) Lionel Blackburne (Dean, 1936–50), drawing by E.O. King, 1913

Plate 52(c) Visit of Queen Mary and Queen Elizabeth, 21 January 1938

Plate 53(a) Lady Chapel, looking west, while still in use as Holy Trinity Church (Crown copyright. NMR)

Plate 53(b) Lady Chapel looking east, after restoration

Plate 54(a) Bishop West's Chapel, view with Bishop Sparke's altar-monument

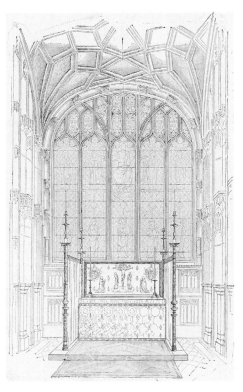

Plate 54(b) Sir Ninian Comper's design for new altar furnishings, 1938

Plate 54(c) Bishop West's Chapel, looking east

Plate 55 Aerial view of Ely, *c*.1975 (Cambridge University Collection of Air Photographs)

Plate 56(a) Appeal brochure, Ely in Peril, 1952

Plate 56(b) Gwen Raverat, woodcut used for Appeal poster

Plate 56(c) 'Death watch beetle' Appeal brochure, 1952

Plate 57(a) West tower under scaffolding, 1973

Plate 57(b) 1980s restoration: reconstruction of north aisle roof, 1987 (Crown copyright. NMR)

Plate 58(a) Dean Hankey and Chapter, 1968. Back row, left to right: Sir Will Spens (Steward), Robin Martineau (Bishop of Huntingdon and Canon, 1966–72); Peter Moore (Canon, 1967–74); Ben Mason (Chapter Clerk). Front row: Geoffrey Lampe (Ely Professor and Canon, 1960–71); Patrick Hankey (Dean, 1951–70); Bernard Pawley (Canon, 1959–70)

Plate 58(b) Dean Carey and Chapter, 1975. Back row, left to right: Derek Butler (assistant verger); Philip Brown (Chapter Clerk); Julian Thompson (Precentor); Alan Franklin (Head Verger). Front row: Eric Wall (Bishop of Huntingdon and Canon, 1972–80); George Youell (Canon, 1970–82); Michael Carey (Dean, 1970–82); Christopher Stead (Ely Professor and Canon, 1971–80); Anthony Morcom (Canon, 1974–84); Dean's dog, Piers

Plate 59(a) Octagon altar, designed by George Pace

Plate 59(b) Bishop's seat and stalls, by George Pace

Plate 60(a) Arthur Wills (Organist, 1958–90)

Plate 60(b) Dean Hankey, Arthur Wills and choir, mid-1960s

Plate 61(a) 1300th anniversary, 1973: recalling the arrival of King Cnut in the 10th century, the Bishop of Ely (Edward Roberts) and the Bishop of Huntingdon (Peter Wall) arrive at Ely by boat on 23 June 1973

Plate 61(b) The Archbishop of Canterbury, Michael Ramsey, after preaching the sermon on St Etheldreda's Day, 23 June 1973

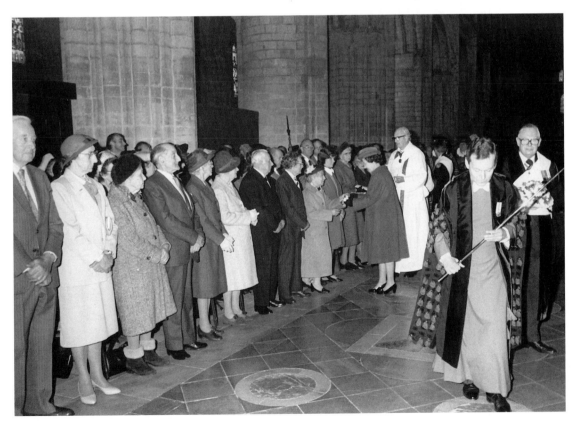

Plate 61(c) HM The Queen distributes the Royal Maundy, 1987

Plate 62(a) Dean Patterson and Chapter, *c.*1985. Left to right: Gordon Roe, Bishop of Huntingdon (Canon, 1980–8); Dennis Green (Canon, 1980–2000); William Patterson (Dean, 1983–9); Murray Macdonald (Canon, 1982–9)

Plate 62(b) Dean Patterson and Cathedral restoration: cleaning and refurbishment of nave ceiling (*Cambridge Evening News*)

Plate 62(c) Dean Patterson: cartoon by Garnett

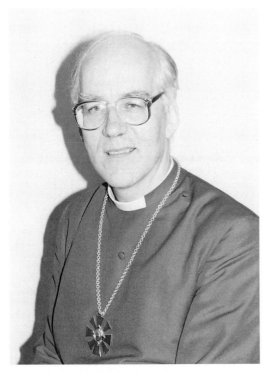

Plate 63(a) Stephen Sykes (Bishop, 1989–99)

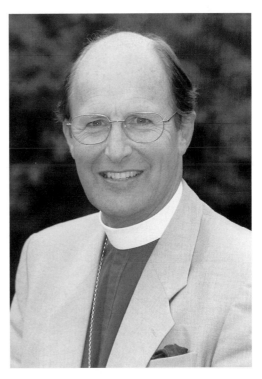

Plate 63(b) Anthony Russell (Bishop, 2000–)

Plate 63(c) Michael Higgins (Dean, 1991–2003)

Plate 64(a) Christ and Mary Magdalene, south transept, by David Wynne, 1967

Plate 64(b) Christus, west end, by Hans Feibusch, 1981

Plate 64(c) St Etheldreda, east end, by Philip Turner, 1960

Plate 64(d) Christ in Majesty over pulpit, by Peter Ball, 2000

The Library and Archives 1541–1836

NIGEL RAMSAY

The process of creating a new, secular Cathedral in the place of the monastic Cathedral Priory was protracted. The Priory of St Etheldreda and St Peter was reconstituted as the Cathedral Church of the Holy Trinity by royal letters patent dated 30 August 1541. It was endowed with the greater part of the Priory's estates on 10 Sept. 1541.[1] Statutes for its governance were issued only in 1544.[2] According to Gilbert Burnet, Archbishop Cranmer 'had projected, that in every cathedral there should be provision made for readers of divinity, and of Greek and Hebrew; and a great number of students, to be both exercised in the daily worship of God, and trained up in study and devotion, whom the bishop might transplant out of this nursery into all the parts of his diocese.'[3] In the event, however, this scheme came to nothing, and the New Foundation (or ex-monastic) cathedrals were set up without any indication that a scholarly or educational role was to be required of them. Rather, it was assumed that the cathedrals' governing body of canons (or prebendaries, in the word that soon came to be applied to the holders of the endowed [choir-]stalls) would be pluralists, with other posts in the Church or a university: accordingly, the members of each cathedral's governing Chapter were allowed and, in time, even expected to be absentees for most of the year, coming to their cathedral only to fulfil their statutory terms of residence and to attend an annual or twice-yearly General Chapter meeting where major items of business were transacted.

At this date, every cathedral in England already had a fair-sized library; some cathedrals, such as Canterbury and Durham, had formed collections that ranked among the largest in the land, far exceeding those of the collegiate and university libraries at Oxford and Cambridge. In their holdings of patristic texts, however, the cathedrals would have been deemed deficient, since they possessed these works in the form of manuscripts – frequently, twelfth- or thirteenth-century manuscripts – and not

I am grateful to Peter Meadows for commenting on a draft of this chapter and saving me from a number of errors.

[1] *L P Henry VIII*, XVI, pp. 575–6, no. 1226 (11) and (12).

[2] CCCC, MS 120, p. 247–84; EDC, 2/1/4 (c), a copy made in the 1580s. On the statutes, see Ian Atherton, above, p. 171.

[3] G. Burnet, *The History of the Reformation of the Church of England*, ed. N. Pocock, 7 vols. (Oxford, 1865), I, p. 477; see further D. MacCulloch, *Thomas Cranmer: A Life* (New Haven and London, 1996), pp. 264–5, for such a scheme at Canterbury Cathedral.

as printed books. In short, the cathedral libraries were seen as having old-fashioned book-stocks, and yet there was no canon of new editions, by approved modern scholars, with which to replace those stocks. In 1549 Edward VI issued injunctions that included the direction that every cathedral should set up a library and obtain within a year copies of the works of Saints Augustine, Basil, Gregory Nazianzen, Jerome, Ambrose, John Chrysostom, Cyprian and Theophylact, as well as Erasmus.[4] Nothing is said of specific editions, and it is striking that Erasmus is the only modern author. It is not clear, however, if any cathedral immediately complied, and it is certainly very doubtful that Ely did so.

The first mention of the formation of a new library at Ely comes from a memorandum made by the Cathedral in July 1552, in connexion with an inventory of its goods: it was asserted that although £265 10s. 6d. had been raised by the sale of plate (including two 'plates' or silver covers from 'the ghospell booke', weighing over twenty ounces), £105 10s. of this had been spent on necessary repairs, including the 'buyldynge of one newe Lybrarye and furniture of the same, with bookes and other necessaries'.[5] This sounds very promising; the library was built over the west walk of the cloister.[6] There is, however, an incidental bequest in the will of Thomas Goodrich, Bishop of Ely, in 1554: 'whereas my officers have receyved Lead of the College of Ely, to thuse of my Late buyldinge ther, I gyve unto the said College in recompence for the Leade so receyved the Residue of my bookes unbequeathed so that they will make up their Lybrarye and take order for the safe keeping and good ordering of the same. And yf the Deane and Chapter refuse my said bokes for recompens I will then that they be sold by myne Executors.'[7] The bequest proved acceptable, for there survives an acquittance from the Dean and Chapter to Goodrich's executors for 66 books, a mitre and a crozier.[8] But it is puzzling that the wording of Goodrich's bequest implies that he was proposing to initiate the library; had no books yet entered the newly constructed library room? Still, whatever his books' titles may have been, the library will now have got off to an early start, ahead of perhaps every other English cathedral.

In the early 1560s, a few years into Elizabeth I's reign, Archbishop Parker and other prominent ecclesiastics took concerted steps to check up on the book provision of the cathedrals. As Vice-Chancellor of the University of Oxford and Dean of Christ Church, Richard Cox has long been notorious for having led the destruction of Oxford's university library, in about 1549: there is even said to have been a bonfire of the books.[9] For Protestant publications, however, Cox was zealous, and as Bishop of Ely (1559–80) he included a question about the state of the library among the enquiries put to the Cathedral at his visitation in 1564. One of the replies was that

---

[4] W.H. Frere and W.M. Kennedy (eds.), *Visitation Articles and Injunctions of the Period of the Reformation*, 3 vols. (Alcuin Club Collections, 14–16, 1910), I, p. 135, and II, p. 136.

[5] *The East Anglian*, new ser., 8 (1899–1900), p. 377. See Atherton, p. 173, n. 28, above. The same words are quoted by Atkinson, *Ely Monastery*, p. 50, citing an inventory in PRO, Augmentation Office, Misc. Books, E315/495.

[6] Atkinson, *Ely Monastery*, pp. 50–1, citing a reference to the library in the Parliamentary Survey (1649).

[7] PRO, PROB 11/37, fos. 76ᵛ–77ʳ: will of Thomas Goodrich, 24 April 1554, proved 13 Oct. 1554. I am grateful to Ian Atherton for both drawing my attention to this bequest and giving me a transcript of it. Goodrich had received the lead for the gallery that he had built at his palace in Ely.

[8] D.M. Owen, *The Library and Muniments of Ely Cathedral* (Ely, 1973), p. 5.

[9] See Andrew Watson, 'The Post-Medieval Library', in *Unarmed Soldiery. Studies in the Early History of All Souls College* (Oxford: All Souls College, 1996), pp. 65–91, at p. 73.

'the liberary is not well furnisshed but theare is Bookes and divers also have ben carryd awaye'.[10]

At the end of his life, Cox followed Goodrich's example and bequeathed to the Cathedral 'toward the furnishing of the library there suche bookes of the olde Doctors Writing of Divinitye which my executors shall thincke most expedient.[11] He was a biblical scholar – he had translated Acts and Romans for the Bishops' Bible – and had also been a member of the commission responsible for the compilation of the first English communion service (1548), the first prayer book (1549), and, probably, the first ordinal (1550). An inventory of his possessions at the time of his death gives the titles of 175 works at his manor at Downham and a further 21 at Fenstanton; it is not known if there were also books in London for his executors to make their choice from.[12] The books at Downham, it has been observed, 'fall, for the most part, within the strikingly narrow range of the working library of an active reformer. Here are no *belles lettres*, no poetry, no rhetoric, none of the ancient historians, dramatists, or philosophers, certainly no natural philosophy, almost nothing . . . that suggests reading for pleasure or for curiosity's sake.'[13] But the Continental Protestant theologians were well represented: there were many books by Bullinger, Bucer, Calvin, Peter Martyr, Brentz and the like, as well as a few by such Englishmen as John Bale and John Jewel. The Ely Cathedral library will have benefited enormously.

The Cathedral Priory library was not forgotten meanwhile, even though it seemingly was ignored by the Dean and Chapter in their corporate capacity. Some of the medieval manuscripts were surprisingly quick in attracting the attention of antiquaries. It is true that it was only from late in Elizabeth's reign that the textual importance of England's medieval patristic manuscripts began to be appreciated, and that run-of-the-mill canon law texts were to be ill valued for centuries. But for manuscripts that related to the history of the English Church and, especially, to Ely there was a considerable demand – and the man who led this was in an extraordinarily strong position to take what he wished, for he was none other than the first Dean of the New Foundation, Robert Steward.

The first Dean was also the last Prior, and it is impossible to say when Robert Steward first began appropriating Cathedral Priory manuscripts for himself. Monks sometimes wrote their name inside a book, but that did not imply anything more than temporary custody of it: on the monk's death, if not sooner, it reverted to the community. Steward, however, went further than any other monk, by adding in a drawing of his own coat of arms (Colour pl. 21*b*). He claimed to be of the Scottish royal family of Stewart, and to be entitled to bear its arms with the augmentation of honour of *argent a lion rampant gules debruised by a ragged staff*, granted by Charles VI, king of France, after Andrew Stewart had slain the lion of Balliol with a ragged staff.

Modern scholarship, in the person of J.H. Round, the arch exposer of spurious

---

[10] EDR, B2/4, p. 53. John Christian (for whom see below, n. 27) also replied that the library was well furnished, as he believed, with books, 'but they [*i.e.*, the minor canons, *etc.*] have not free access unto yt'; *ibid.*, p. 56.

[11] E.S. Leedham-Green, 'Bishop Richard Cox', in R.J. Fehrenbach and E.S. Leedham-Green (eds.), *Private Libraries in Renaissance England. A Collection and Catalogue of Tudor and Early Stuart Book-Lists*, I, (Binghamton, New York, and Marlborough, Wilts., 1992), pp. 3–39, at pp. 4–5.

[12] See *ibid.*, pp. 10–39, for an edition of the two book-lists.

[13] *Ibid.*, pp. 6–7.

pedigrees, has revealed Steward's claim to be an imposture.[14] Still, the presence of the Steward arms in a medieval book is of use today as a pointer to its having probably come from Ely Cathedral: Steward owned at least half a dozen manuscripts, and it seems that they may all have come from the Priory, with the exception of the British Library's Cotton MS Julius A.i, which includes a cartulary of the nearby priory of Chatteris: this cartulary might have come – directly or indirectly – from Chatteris, but it is not impossible that it, too, was removed by Steward from the Ely library or archives, after the dissolution of Chatteris (1538), since Ely had some measure of oversight over Chatteris.[15]

Steward drew (or had drawn for him) a shield with his arms, dated 1513, in a late twelfth- or early thirteenth-century version of book II of the *Liber Eliensis* combined with a short cartulary of royal and papal privileges etc. for the Cathedral Priory (BL, MS Cotton Titus A.i, fos. 1–57[16]); twice, with the date 1522, in a thirteenth-century copy of Alexander Nequam's *Corrogationes Promethei* and other works (Bodleian Library, MS Laud Misc. 112; *S.C.* 1573); with the date 1531, in a twelfth-century collection of the lives of Ethelwold, Etheldreda, Wihtburga, Werburga and other saints (BL, MS Cotton Caligula A.viii, fos. 59–191[17]); *Philomena*, by the thirteenth-century poet, John of Howden (BL, MS Harl. 985, fos. 1–43[18]); undated, but while still Prior, the mystical writer, Richard Rolle's *Incendium amoris* and *Melos amoris* (Cambridge, St John's College, MS 23); and, also while still Prior, a pre-Conquest volume of the Dialogues of Gregory the Great and the *De compunctione cordis* of Ephrem the Syrian (Lambeth Palace Library, MS 204[19]). Some if not all of his collection passed to his relative Augustine Steward, of Norwich (d.1597), and although the latter is known to have owned manuscripts that came from elsewhere,[20] the ownership of an Ely book by Augustine Steward may reasonably be taken to indicate that it had previously belonged to Robert. On that basis, it is suggested that Robert also owned the twelfth-century Ely pontifical which is now Cambridge, Trinity College, MS B.11.10.[21] He also both owned

---

[14] For Steward's ancestry, see W. Rye, 'Oliver Cromwell's Descent from the Steward Family', *Genealogist*, n.s. i (1884), pp. 150–7, W. Rye, 'The Steward Family and Cromwell's "Royal Descent"', *ibid.*, ii (1885), pp. 34–42, and – pinning on Robert responsibility for the claim to Scottish ancestry – J.H. Round, 'Oliver Cromwell and his "Stuart" Descent', *Genealogist*, n.s. x (1894), pp. 18–19, expanded by Round in his *Studies in Peerage and Family History* (London, 1901), pp. 135–41. An unconvincing attempt to rebut Rye and Round was made by Sir Henry Steward, 'Cromwell's Stuart Ancestry', *PCAS*, xxvii (1926, for 1924–5), pp. 86–122.

[15] Cotton Julius A.i contains Steward's arms on fo. 2ᵛ and the Chatteris cartulary at fos. 71–188, but they surely went together; the volume was made up, doubtless by Sir Robert Cotton, from a variety of sources (*e.g.* a Brut that is perhaps from Pipewell Abbey and a Pipewell cartulary). *Cf. The Cartulary of Chatteris Abbey*, ed. Claire Breay (Woodbridge, 1999), p. 107.

[16] Described in *Liber Eliensis* (ed. Blake), p. xxv; Steward became Prior only in 1522, and in 1513 was a junior monk, studying at Cambridge [Greatrex, *BRECP*, p. 457].

[17] Noticed in *LE*, pp. xxxiv n. 1, xxvii n. 3 and 52 n. 2; and see Wulfstan of Winchester, *The Life of St Æthelwold*, ed. M. Lapidge and M. Winterbottom (Oxford, 1991), pp. clxxi–clxxv.

[18] C.E. Wright, *Fontes Harleiani. . .* (London, 1972), p. 316, expressed doubts as to whether Robert Steward owned this, and suggested that the arms and inscription on fo. 43 'may be a fabrication' by Augustine Steward.

[19] See N.R. Ker, *Catalogue of Manuscripts containing Anglo-Saxon* (Oxford, 1957), no. 277.

[20] *E.g.*, Bodl., MS Bodley 130 (*S.C.* 27609), an 11th-century herbal, and Lincoln Cathedral, MS 243, *Dubia sacrae scripturae*, 15th century, both perhaps from Bury St Edmunds abbey.

[21] See J. Brückmann, 'Latin Manuscript Pontificals and Benedictionals in England and Wales', *Traditio*, xxix (1973), pp. 391–458, at pp. 411–12, with further references; R.W. Pfaff, 'M.R. James and the Liturgical Manuscripts of Cambridge', in Lynda Dennison (ed.), *The Legacy of M.R. James* (Donington, Lincs, 2001), pp. 174–93, at pp. 181–2.

and wrote historical notes in a fifteenth-century volume full of material relating to the Cathedral and bishops of Ely: Lambeth Palace Library, MS 448. His own additions include his own genealogy, stated to be compiled from the heralds' rolls in 1522 (his own arms being described as: *silver, a fess checky with azure and silver*, augmented by Charles VI of France with a red lion), a list of priors (fo. 96ᵛ) and a series of rather short accounts of the bishops of Ely, from John Alcock (1486–1500) to Thomas Goodrich (1534–54).[22] Finally, it is clear that he did not remove everything that his arms are drawn in, for the Ely Chapter archive still contains a copy of the detailed return to Henry VIII of the Priory's estates, 1540–1[23] (Colour pl. 21*b–c*).

What Steward removed might well otherwise have perished; equally possibly, it might have been removed by some other collector, who would doubtless have been less keen to leave clues for posterity as to where it came from. Matthew Parker, the future Archbishop of Canterbury, was one of the first set of prebendaries (2nd stall, 1541–54): did he pass by the opportunity that he then had to acquire medieval books from Ely? In both Corpus Christi College and the University Library at Cambridge there are Ely manuscripts that he gave or bequeathed to these institutions, but he did not usually either inscribe the date when he acquired a book or the provenance that he knew or believed it to have. Is it just coincidence that five Ely manuscripts which he gave to Corpus (MSS 44, 131, 335, 393, 397 and 416) and one in Cambridge University Library (MS Ii.1.33; its Ely provenance admittedly far from certain) all either have had their fifteenth-century Ely ex-libris scratched out or lack it altogether? It is only thanks to press-marks or other evidence that they can be identified as coming from the Cathedral Priory.

As Archbishop of Canterbury (1559–75), Parker helped to make medieval English history, and especially the history of the English Church, a respectable and wholly justifiable subject of study. The history of Ely Cathedral was soon to be regarded as a subject worth taking up by local and national antiquaries. As yet, these early students of Ely are shadowy figures, known today only from incidental mentions in miscellaneous sources. Little can be said, for instance, of Alexander Evesham, gentleman, save that he was of a Herefordshire family, 'traveled France, Norway, &c., and after lyved in Courte', and in 1591 owned Sutton Court, London.[24] That he was particularly interested in Ely is shown by a surviving translation that he prepared of Henry VIII's confirmatory charter of 1 June 1510, in which the celebrated charters of Kings Edgar and Edward the Confessor are recited in full (now Bodleian Library, MS Tanner 141,

---

[22] The genealogy and the accounts of bishops were printed hence by Wharton, *Anglia Sacra*, I, pp. 686–8 and 675–7.

[23] EDC 1/C/3; mentioned by Chapman, *Sacrist Rolls*, I, pp. v–vi, and illustrated opposite p. vi (fos. [iiᵛ–iiiʳ]) and before p. vii (fos. [iᵛ–iiʳ], with drawing of Steward's arms). His arms are also in EDC 1/C/8, a copy of the 1417 *laudum*. Steward may also have owned LPL, MS 92, a 13th-century Bracton; this certainly belonged to Nicholas Steward, of the Temple (probably identifiable as Robert's father) and to Augustine Steward. M.R. James thought that a drawing in it of the Steward arms 'looks like the work of Robert Stewarde': *Descriptive Catalogue of the Manuscripts in the Library of Lambeth Palace* (Cambridge, 1932), p. 152.

[24] *The Visitation of Herefordshire made by Robert Cooke, Clarencieux, in 1569*, ed. F.W. Weaver (Exeter, 1886), p. 28. He owned an Evesham Abbey charter of 3 Henry III [see *ibid.*], and, in 1591, BL, MS Harl. 615 (Robert Cooke's genealogies of the gentlemen of Herefordshire, Worcestershire, Gloucestershire and Shropshire); he supposedly copied a collection of arms of the nobility, now BL, MS Harl. 214 [Wright, *Fontes Harleiani* (cit. in n. 18), p. 147]. He died on 28 Dec. 1592 at Lady Stafford's house, Westminster [note in MS Harl. 615, f. 1].

fos. 7–22[r]). Tantalisingly, too, it was noted by an eighteenth-century prebendary that in 1590 Evesham had made and translated into English a whole folio-sized volume of collections about the bishops and abbots of Ely.[25] Where is it today? Where and how did he find his source materials?

As Archbishop of Canterbury, Parker also took an active interest in seeing that every English cathedral kept its records in good order. For Ely, as for the other New Foundation cathedrals, little thought seems at first to have been given to the value – financial and administrative, if not historical – of the Priory archive; it was as if the Foundation was to begin with a *tabula rasa*. It is true that the Cathedral's statutes of 1544 laid on the Dean the duty of safeguarding 'the charters, muniments, court rolls and writings without waste, saving their reasonable use', and it was also required that a double room be set aside as the 'common treasury': an outer room was to house the ordinary writings (account books, court rolls, bonds, rentals and inventories of goods and lands) and an inner room was reserved for the Chapter's seal, statutes, Henrician letters patent of foundation and endowment, and other muniments of title, all these being kept in a chest with three locks, of which the keys were held by the Dean, Vicedean and Treasurer.[26] However, the room that was to serve as the treasury for the next three centuries was the distinctly insecure vestry that is on the west side of the south transept (although it should be said that the vestry then had partition walls that extended up to the ceiling).

The custody of a record of Chapter decisions and, probably, of the book containing the Chapter's annual accounts was entrusted to the registrar (or Chapter clerk), but this was not a senior appointment. In 1562 the office of registrar was held by the usher of the Cathedral school, John Christian, who was aged twenty-three.[27] It was probably in the following year, 1563, that Archbishop Parker's commissioners issued injunctions for the Cathedral that are largely concerned with record-keeping. The Chapter was directed 'that your register book wherein you do record any things passed under your common seal or otherwise belonging to your said church be comely and decently bound in one volume', 'that you do not seal anything which is not first registered in your common register book and also proved as well before the company', and 'that you make a true, full and perfect inventory of your plate, ornaments, jewels and other moveable of the church, and the same do deliver indented . . . within xxxi[ty] days next following.'[28] It is not clear what prompted these injunctions, and although the register with transcripts was maintained,[29] neither indented copy of the inventory survives.

The Cathedral's medieval documents may simply have been generally left alone, possibly remaining in the fifteenth-century chests of which three survive (Plate 16*b*). A

---

[25] Note by Samuel Knight, prebendary, in CUL, MS Add. 49, fo. 93[v]; he refers to this volume as belonging to Peter le Neve, the herald and record-keeper.

[26] See above, n. 2, for copies of the Henrician statutes. These provisions were repeated in the re-issued statutes granted by Elizabeth I and Charles II.

[27] J.H. Crosby, 'Extracts from an Elizabethan Apposition and Ordination Book', *The Elean*, n.s. 35 (April 1918), pp. 5–7. Christian is first mentioned as a schoolmaster in 1560 and as registrar in 1561; he vacated the latter post by 1567; he was also a vicar choral (EDC 2/9/3, pp. 32, 67).

[28] The injunctions, which are undated, were printed by Stevenson, *Supplement*, p. 18 n. 4, and, better, by Frere and Kennedy, *Visitation Articles* (cit. in n. 4), III, pp. 143–4.

[29] Transcripts of indentures etc., as signed and sealed at each Chapter meeting, were entered in EDC 2/4/1 (the 'First Parchment Leiger', 1537–1616; succeeded by 'Leiger Book 2', EDC 2/4/2, for 1615–39).

fair proportion of the Priory's original charters is still extant, and in this the Cathedral compares very favourably with the bishopric, of which the original charters are almost all lost.[30] The half-century from the mid 1530s to the mid 1580s was a hazardous time for ancient documents of all kinds. Ely Cathedral certainly did not come through unscathed. Particularly at risk were miscellaneous medieval documents – for instance, those that related to members of the monastic community or that were of extreme antiquity and of no conceivable financial utility. The chance survival, as fragments used for bookbinding, of three pieces of an early eleventh-century set of farming memoranda of the Abbey suggests the sort of loss that was doubtless now taking place. The date of the book in which these fragments were incorporated, 1575, perhaps points to a period that was of particular peril – the archiepiscopate of Parker's successor, Edmund Grindal (1576–83).[31] Did some Cambridge bookbinder acquire a whole store of old Ely parchments to use in his work?

By the late sixteenth century, it was apparent that the prebendaries were not going to be resident at Ely except when it was required of them. Such pressure as there had been in the later 1540s and 1550s for the creation of a library of patristic theology must now have been largely dissipated. It was not until the late seventeenth century that Bishop Cox was to have a successor who concerned himself with the Cathedral's book provision. The long-lived Andrew Perne, who was Dean from 1557 until 1589, was bookish in the extreme, but hardly to the Cathedral's benefit.[32] He appears to have resided at Ely for a month each year, and to have gone there regularly for the annual audit in late October, and occasionally at Midsummer and Christmas; he also kept at Ely part of his enormous personal library, including some manuscripts.[33] His concerns, however, were for the libraries of Cambridge University and, above all, of Peterhouse, of which he was Master and to which he bequeathed most of his library. It was from Ely that came the eighth-century Northumbrian manuscript of the Gospels of Luke and John, which he bequeathed to Cambridge University Library.[34] When making his will in 1588, Perne displayed a generous concern for the further education of boys from the Ely grammar school; more by way of token, one feels, was his bequest of 'all my Centuriells that I have at Ely to the Colledge library of Ely, to be kept by a keper to be appoynted thereunto by the deane and Chapter there, by an Inventory Indented.'[35] The wording of

[30] At some point, in the 16th or 17th centuries, at least four of the Priory's cartularies (with transcripts of its charters) passed into the archives of the bishops of Ely; was this connected with some attempt to make good the bishopric's loss or was it the result of the two posts, of Chapter registrar and episcopal deputy registrar, being held by the same person?

[31] The two farming memoranda are today part of BL, MS Add. 61735; see further Simon Keynes, above, p. 6. For losses at Canterbury Cathedral in Grindal's time, see N.L. Ramsay, 'The Cathedral Archives and Library', in P. Collinson, N.L. Ramsay and M.J. Sparks (eds.), *A History of Canterbury Cathedral* (Oxford, *etc.*, 1995), pp. 341–407, at p. 377.

[32] Many aspects of Perne's life and interests are discussed by P. Collinson, D.J. McKitterick and Elisabeth Leedham-Green, *Andrew Perne: Quatercentenary Studies* (Cambridge Bibliographical Society, Monograph 11, 1991).

[33] *Ibid.*, pp. 16, 105.

[34] CUL, MS Kk.1.24; see further Simon Keynes, above, p. 5, noting the book's added Ely texts of the 10th century.

[35] *Perne: Quatercentenary Studies*, pp. 114–15. By 'Centuriells' (or 'Centauries', in the PCC text of his will) Perne meant perhaps an edition of Mathias Flacius, *Ecclesiastica historia*; this was commonly called the Magdeburg centuriators.

this bequest shows that the Cathedral's library still had no keeper, although it was less than ten years since it had received Bishop Cox's divinity books.

Perne's successors as Dean, like his Chapter contemporaries and successors, seem to have neglected the library that Goodrich and Cox had furnished. After the list of 66 books received from Goodrich's executors, there survives only one booklist before that made in 1796: this is of books returned to Ely in the early 1660s, following the Restoration.[36] It is of only 22 volumes, and comprises works by St Augustine, St Ambrose, St John Chrysostom and St Jerome as well as by Erasmus and the Reformers Sabellicus and Conrad Pellican. A second version of the list adds one volume, of the *Controversies* of Dr Willet, the former prebendary. Had the rest of the library been lost in the Civil War or its aftermath, or had it already been lost in earlier decades? None of the books, with the possible exception of nine volumes of the works of St Augustine, survived into the second half of the twentieth century. In 1948 J.B. Oldham, the historian of bookbindings, commented to the Cathedral's assistant librarian on how very odd he found it that he did not come across a single sixteenth-century Cambridge binding in the Library, despite the enormous number then produced in Cambridge.[37]

Even by the time of Archbishop Grindal, antiquaries were beginning to enlarge their interests to include archival material. In the late sixteenth and early seventeenth centuries, Ely's medieval charters suffered serious depredations. Mapping out the details of how or when such losses occurred is as treacherous as attempting to chart streams that run through quicksands. Take, for instance, the herald Sir Richard St George (d.1635), Norroy and then Clarenceux King of Arms. He owned at least one book that was doubtless from the Priory library – a copy of the *Liber Eliensis*[38] – and he probably had a substantial collection of medieval charters, since in c.1640 his son, Sir Henry St George, owned a great many.[39] Sir Richard certainly owned one document (in book format) from Ely, a copy of the composition between Bishop John de Fordham and the Prior and Chapter, 1417 (now British Library, MS Harl. 329).[40] At least ten of his medieval books were acquired by Sir Simonds D'Ewes (d.1650), generally at dates that are not now known.[41] D'Ewes acquired some of the most remarkable of all the charters that were ever in the Cathedral archive, including Henry I's foundation of the see of Ely, 1109 (BL, Harl. Ch. 43 C. 11), and the two twelfth-century charters purporting to be Bishop Hervey's and Bishop Nigel's separation from the bishopric of the lands which each by his charter has granted to the Priory for the use of the monks (BL, Harl. Ch. 43 H. 4 and 5).[42] How did D'Ewes get hold of such treasures? The

---

[36] See below, pp. 269–70, where it is noted that there are two versions of this list, one dated 1661 and the other 1663.

[37] Letter to the Revd Eric Yates, 30 Dec. 1948; EDC 13/5/1948/15.

[38] Bodl., MS Laud Misc. 698 (*S.C.* 1583). This had earlier belonged to Archbishop Parker and then to his son John: cf. list of 1575 × 90 printed by Sheila Strongman, 'John Parker's Manuscripts: An Edition of the Lists in Lambeth Palace Library MS 737', *Trans., Cambridge Bibliographical Soc.*, vii, pt 1 (1977), pp. 1–27, at p. 18, no. 50. The book was acquired by Archbishop Laud in or before 1633.

[39] Sir Henry St George owned the charters numbered 61–169 in L.C. Loyd and Doris Mary Stenton (eds.), *Sir Christopher Hatton's Book of Seals* (Oxford, 1950); none of these is from Ely.

[40] A.G. Watson, *The Library of Sir Simonds D'Ewes* (London, 1966), p. 304, List B, no. 228.

[41] A.G. Watson, 'Sir Simonds D'Ewes's Collection of Charters, and a Note on the Charters of Sir Robert Cotton', *Jnl., Soc. of Archivists*, ii (1960–4), pp. 247–54, at p. 252; cf. Watson, *Library of Sir Simonds D'Ewes*, p. 36.

[42] Printed in *Hatton's Book of Seals*, nos. 419, 415 and 420; see further *ibid.*, pp. xxxix–xl. Virtually all of D'Ewes's charters were acquired by Robert Harley, Earl of Oxford, in 1705, and passed with the Harleian manuscripts to the British Museum on its foundation in 1753.

suspicion must be that he did so directly from the Cathedral – he lived not far away, at Long Melford (Suff.) – but nothing is certain. They might have come from Sir Richard St George. All that can be stated is that these were years of peril for the Chapter's medieval archive, and yet that the years of Civil War and Protectorate that were to follow were a time of even greater losses for all cathedrals in England, as their archives and libraries were seized and removed to London. York Minster and Chester Cathedral were now to lose all of their medieval charters.[43] Ely was more fortunate, insofar as its archives were concerned; its library may have suffered badly, however. It is a period about which little can be written about either collection, so absolute is the chasm in the records until 1660.

The restoration of the monarchy in 1660 was rapidly followed by the return of the Church of England to its pre-1643 state. The sales of episcopal and cathedral estates that had taken place in the late 1640s and 1650s were rendered null and void. New leases of all the estates were granted, and lease-renewal fines were payable to bishops and chapters.[44] Even at the time, no one could do more than guess at what the total size of this compensatory windfall to the Church amounted to. Individual bishops and chapters must have had a fair idea, but they saw no reason to divulge this knowledge to anyone else. Gilbert Sheldon, Bishop of London, attempted to discover what he could by writing to various bishops and deans, but had little success. Dean Wilford wrote to assure him that none of the post-Restoration Deans of Ely – of whom there had been four – had received £1000 for fines, 'of which little or none came to Dr Martin's share or mine'.[45] From the mid sixteenth century until almost halfway through the nineteenth century, the sharing out of fines was treated by deans and canons as a private matter, to be arranged among themselves – like that almost equally important and certainly more contentious exercise of their office, the allocation of the ecclesiastical benefices that were within their patronage. At Ely, as at perhaps most other English cathedrals, no Chapter records were ever kept to indicate precisely what sums of money derived from fines were allocated to whom, or on what grounds benefices were awarded to whom.[46]

On the other hand, none of the new crop of fines could be paid if the Chapter did not know whom to ask for them. There was an archival dimension to the matter. The Chapter needed to be able to produce its title deeds and counterparts of leases, especially if litigation took place, and as a more practical matter, it needed to be able to consult its rentals, terriers, court-books and other administrative and legal records, in order to know whom to ask for what sums. What were its estates worth, and on what terms were they rented or leased out?

By parliamentary ordinance of 30 April 1649, the records of all the deans and

---

[43] K.M. Longley, 'Towards a History of Archive-Keeping in the Church of York. II. The Capitular Muniments', *Borthwick Institute Bull.*, i (1975–8), pp. 103–18, at 103–4; *Chartulary or Register of the Abbey of St Werburgh, Chester*, ed. James Tait, pt I (Chetham Soc., n.s. 79, 1920), pp. xxviii–xxxi.

[44] See discussion by I.M. Green, *The Re-Establishment of the Church of England, 1660–1663* (Oxford, 1978), pp. 61–79, and Ronald Hutton, *The Restoration: A Political and Religious History of England and Wales, 1658–1667* (Oxford, *etc.*, 1985), pp. 140–2, 172–3.

[45] Bodl., MS Tanner 141, fo. 45: Francis Wilford to Gilbert Sheldon, 8 Dec. 1662. Tanner 141 contains a variety of letters and calculations about the size of the Church's windfall.

[46] The dividend derived from fines can, however, be calculated with reasonable accuracy from the 1790s onwards; I am grateful to Peter Meadows for this information.

chapters had been brought to Gurney House in the Old Jewry, London.[47] In 1654 they were removed to the Excise Office in Broad Street. In each location it is clear that they were badly looked after, the different chapters' archives becoming confused with each other: by 1660, a major exercise in record-sorting was called for. The Dean and Chapter of Ely paid one William Ayloffe and his brother Thomas to do this, and in late 1660 and early 1661 they sent down some quantity of materials, including what must have been the three medieval chests with Priory documents: 'three longe Boxes of very ancient records sorted under the severall heades you will finde fixed uppon the inside of their covers'.[48] Identification was not always an easy matter, however: many of the cathedrals' records, especially of their estates, will not have given any clue as to which cathedral they belonged to. Some of the Ely prebendaries went up to London to join in the search: Dr John Pearson and Dr Richard Ball took part in the hunt, in 1661 and 1662. A letter from Pearson to Dean Ferne reveals a little more of the story:

> For my part I have not bin idle, though ill: I have sent downe all the records which can as yet be gained, and by the time that my servant brings you this Letter, I hope they will come to your hands. I send downe now 11 Letters from Mr Alexander Broome, which are to recover the improved Rents of the Vicaridges whose Leases were out y[e] last yeere, and therefore (not having bin sold) were payable to the State, and given by the Parliament to the King; the King hath given them to us againe for the repaire of our Church, and by these Letters they are recoverable.[49]

The whole matter of the dispersed and confused records gradually proved to be far more complicated than anticipated. In London, the distinguished antiquary Sir William Dugdale was ultimately brought in, in about 1663 and 1664: he had the range of historical knowledge which enabled a more-or-less accurate set of identifications to be made, though a further Ely prebendary, Dr Joseph Beaumont, was also involved in 1664.[50]

A few documents had never been taken by the Parliamentary agents. Some had been carefully concealed from them. Brian Walton, Bishop of Chester, wrote to Dean Ferne in 1661 to recommend the case of Dean Fuller's widow. Dr Fuller had died shortly before 1660, and had thus missed sharing in the profits from the lease-renewals. Walton thought that it might be some motive for Ferne's generosity that Fuller had 'preserved the charter of the Church confirmed by King James, with all the former charters, as also the booke of all the lands belonging to the Church in the severall Counties, with ther valews and reprisalls, which his widdow freely delivered up to the Deane and Chapter, and if they had fallen into some hands might have miscarried, and without which I beleeve they had been in the Darke as concerning the revenuew of the Church.'[51]

Some other documents were held locally, following normal practice. For instance,

[47] Offer or proposal of William Ryley, c.1660, in Bodl., MS Tanner 141, fo. 109[r-v]; printed by D.M. Owen, 'Bringing Home the Records: the Recovery of the Ely Chapter Muniments at the Restoration', *Archives*, viii (1967–8), pp. 123–9, at pp. 124–5.

[48] Owen, 'Bringing Home the Records', p. 127, from EDC 6/1A/1661/3, William Ayloffe to Henry Ferne, 13 Mar. 1661.

[49] Bodl., MS Tanner 49, fo. 54: John Pearson to Henry Ferne, 11 Mar. 1660/1; punctuation modernised.

[50] Owen, 'Bringing Home the Records', p. 128.

[51] Bodl., MS Tanner 49, fo. 51: Brian Walton to Henry Ferne, 7 Mar. 1660/1.

stewards of manorial courts and lessees of Chapter manors would often retain various manorial documents, since they needed these in order to hold the courts and maintain their own rentals. The Chapter order of 20 February 1664, that letters 'be sent to all those that have any of the Church writeings to demand the same',[52] may not have been the most effective way to approach matters. On the other hand, some people clearly held on to Chapter documents with no good cause: as late as 1677, the Chapter felt it necessary to threaten to bring a lawsuit against Captain Pegg and two others if they did not quietly deliver the Cathedral writings in their hands.[53] Pegg had been involved in the making of the Ely Parliamentary Surveys in 1649, and in 1660 had actually helped Dean Love in the identification of Chapter records at the Excise Office in London.[54]

Did the Chapter do all that it could to regain its records and estates? A generation later, the prebendary Thomas Tanner was to write, asserting the importance of good record-keeping: 'I am sure we at Ely have lost two good Houses in London since the Reformation.'[55] More immediately, one of the questions put by Bishop Gunning in his visitation of the Cathedral, September 1676, was: 'Have you a perfect Terrier of all your Lands, Mannors & Tenements, together with the Rights, Priviledges, Customes and Immunities belonging to every Mannor fairely written in Parchment and layed up and kept in the Archives of the Church?'[56] Over a year later, in November 1677, the Chapter finally took its record-keeping in hand. The Registrar was directed to take an assistant to review all the records, put them into good order and make as perfect an index of them all as could well be; the Chapter bailiffs were ordered to provide details of all the copyhold (i.e., manorial court) tenancies, to be fairly written out; a particular care was to be had to look for any evidence of the Cathedral's ecclesiastical jurisdiction, or of quit-rents or other estates that anciently belonged to the Cathedral but were now withheld or hidden from it; and the Treasurer's audit-accounts, or loose sheets of paper, were in future to be properly transcribed into a book.[57] An alphabetical index to the boxes in the Chapter House (at least 39 in number) was duly made;[58] it is a disappointment to any historian of the Cathedral Priory, since it provides negligible coverage of the medieval records, but it did service for half a century. A neatly written audit-book was also commenced.[59] No surviving record appears to be identifiable as the 'fairly written' terrier or account of all the copyhold tenancies, however; nor is it clear if any hidden estates were discovered.

Next to nothing is known about the fate of the pre-Civil War library of printed books. In principle, it was removed to London along with the muniments, and should also have been recoverable at the Restoration. A list survives of about 22 volumes of writings of the Fathers and certain of the sixteenth-century Reformers which are stated to have been returned to Ely on 15 August 1661; puzzlingly, however, the same books, with one

[52] Order Book, 1660–1728: EDC 2/2A/2, p. 19.
[53] Owen, 'Bringing Home the Records', p. 134.
[54] *Ibid.*, p. 126.
[55] BL, MS Stowe 749, fo. 138: Thomas Tanner to John Anstis, 15 Feb. 1720/1.
[56] CUL, MS Add. 41, fos. 287–291, Article 23.
[57] Order Book, 1660–1728: EDC 2/2A/2, pp. 128–30 (22 Nov. 1677). Samuel Bentham senior acted as chapter clerk or registrar from *c.*1677 (until 1713): EDC 2/9/3, p. 68.
[58] EDC 13/8/1.
[59] EDC 3/1/5; it opens with the year 1677–8.

additional volume of Dr Andrew Willet's *Controversies*, are elsewhere stated to have been sent to Ely two years later, on 4 December 1663.[60] Quite apart from being such a pathetically small total, these were a battered and depleted group: the sets of the works of St Augustine and St John Chrysostom were each wanting one or two volumes, there was only the fifth volume of St Jerome's works, and Dr Willet's book had lost its cover. For a post-Restoration cathedral that was under a moral obligation to put itself into full repair, this was plainly something that cried out to be remedied. Would the Dean and Chapter rise to the challenge? Ely being so close to Cambridge, its Chapter always included a number of learned divines who were members of the university – in the seventeenth and eighteenth centuries it was common for them to be heads or fellows of such colleges as Jesus, Peterhouse or St John's, with which the Bishop of Ely had close political and historic links – but by the same token these men tended to think of their own college or the university library when they came to consider making their will and disposing of their books. When coming to Ely for their statutory 50 days' annual residence, they had doubtless been in the habit of bringing with them some books of their own or from their college library. The nearness of Cambridge to Ely must have seemed to many to obviate the need for a library at the latter.

Robert Mapletoft, although Dean only since 1667, decided that positive action was called for, and in his will (dated July 1676; proved two days after his death in August 1677), he bequeathed to the Dean and Chapter 'my Library of Books (the small Reserves from the late plundering times) with what I have since added to it', and £100, of which two-thirds was to be spent on 'choice Books' while the rest was to go 'to prepare and fit up some convenient place in Church for a Library, for the common use in the times of the severall Residences. The Dean and every Prebendary to have his key, and to admit such of the Petty [*i.e.* minor] Canons, and Schoolmasters as they shall allow of, and no others, save such, as some one of the Canons or the Dean shall [re]spond for, to the free use of it. And I commend earnestly to [their] care and prudence to provide for the preservation of the said Books.'[61] Shrewdly, Mapletoft couched the whole legacy in the form of an offer which would only have effect if the Dean and Chapter undertook to carry out its terms within six months. This they duly did, although slightly over six months later.[62]

After the Restoration, the Dean and Chapter had set aside the southernmost bay of the western side of the south transept as their Archive Room and Chapter House. They now, in 1678, decided to make the facing bay (*i.e.* the southern bay of the east side of the same transept) into the library; it had hitherto been their vesting room. The Vice-Dean,

---

[60] EDC 3/2, 1660–1 and EDC 6/1B/1663/1; I owe these references to Peter Meadows. See also Owen, *Library and Muniments of Ely Cathedral* (cit. in n. 8), p. 5, for another version of this list, possibly derived from EDC 6/1B/1663/1.

[61] Transcript of Mapletoft's will by Thomas Baker, CUL MS Mm.1.37, pp. 239–45; there are accounts of Mapletoft by Baker, in MS Mm.1.49, pp. 191–2, and by H. Mapletoft (nephew), 1713, in BL, MS Harl. 7043, p. 233. Dean Mapletoft had been chaplain to Bishop Wren and remained Wren's protégé; he asked to be buried near Wren, in the chapel of Pembroke College, Cambridge. An excerpt of the part of the will that relates to the setting up of the Ely library is printed by Owen, *Library and Muniments*, pp. 5–6. He also bequeathed £100 to Cambridge University, towards buying the library of Jacobus Golius (d.1667; *cf.* J.C.T. Oates, *Cambridge University Library: A History. . .* (Cambridge, etc., 1986), pp. 430–4)) or some other use.

[62] Order Book, 1662–1728: EDC 2/2A/2, pp. 130 (preliminary consideration, 22 Nov. 1677), 133 (acceptance, 3 April 1678).

Dr Laurence Womack, was deputed to see to shelves being fitted, and the Dean was authorised to spend £20 or more in buying books. The room was ready, presumably, by the next Audit, in November 1678, when Thomas Hitch, sacrist, became the first of a long succession of minor canons to be appointed library keeper.[63] He was to take care to see that the room was swept, and the books rubbed or cleaned over, as often as he judged necessary; for his pains he was to be allowed to borrow any book for up to three weeks, to take to his chamber.

Over the next few years the stock of books in the library was built up. A few books were bought in response to Chapter orders, the first of these purchases being the *Bibliotheca Patrum* and the Councils [of the Church]: in June 1681 Dr John Moore was asked to buy these, in the best edition.[64] Moore, a prebendary since 1679, was one of a succession of members of Chapter who acted for it over the next few decades as (in effect) its bookbuying agents, buying books in London or elsewhere and arranging for them to be brought to Ely. In 1685 it was also he who arranged for the transport to Ely of Dr Richard Ball's books: Ball, who had been a prebendary since 1660, Rector of the Chapter living of Bluntisham (Hunts.) and Master of the Temple, had bequeathed his entire library to the Cathedral.[65] Ball's legacy was sufficiently large that a fresh catalogue of the library was made, in 1686–7, by Samuel Hutton – just four years after he had made a first one.[66] But the combined cost of these two catalogues – £4 3s. – was exceeded by the £5 7s. 6d paid to Hutton in 1699 for a third catalogue.[67]

Not one of these catalogues survives, and it is therefore their relative costs that are now the clearest measure of the scale of Bishop Simon Patrick's generosity that was shown in 1698, when he gave a large collection of books to the library. More subjectively, a generation later Patrick's biographer was to describe Patrick's gift as forming 'by much the best part' of the library, despite its already containing the whole libraries of Dean Mapletoft and Dr Ball.[68] Many of the books given by Patrick had previously belonged to his brother John, who was a bookman to his fingertips: 'there were few in his time who had so extensive a knowledge of Books'.[69] He had died in 1695, bequeathing to his brother Simon his entire library, 'which cost him above £1000, and [was] all that he was worth, except some legacies to some particular friends'.[70]

The influence of the bishops of Ely on their Cathedral in the seventeenth and eighteenth centuries cannot be over-stressed. Directly, they may appear to have had relatively little to do with the Cathedral, save in occasional gifts or even rarer

---

[63] *Ibid.*, p. 144 (25 Nov. 1678).

[64] *Ibid.*, p. 157 (14 June 1681).

[65] Audit Book, 1677–8 – 1720–1: EDC 3/1/5, *sub anno* 1684–5, *s.v. Solutiones Domesticae*; *cf.* the entry for Ball in EDC 2/9/2, *s.v.* Stall 7.

[66] Notes by Thomas Watkins in EDC 2/9/3, p. 18. Hutton was vicar choral from 1678 until his death, at the age of 68, in 1718: *ibid.*, p. 10.

[67] *Ibid.*

[68] Samuel Knight, Life of Symon Patrick: CUL, MS Add. 20, fo. 136.

[69] *Ibid.*, fo. 118. Dr John Patrick lived in London, being Preacher of the Charterhouse (see *DNB*); he also had prebends in Chichester and Peterborough Cathedrals. An account of him is given by Samuel Knight in his continuation to Simon Patrick's autobiography (CUL, MS Add. 36, pp. 227–85); naturally enough, this continuation is not included in Alexander Taylor's 9-volume edn of Patrick's *Works* (Oxford, 1858), but it is printed in *The Auto-Biography of Symon Patrick, Bishop of Ely* (Oxford, 1839), pp. 203–52, the account of John Patrick being at pp. 237–41.

[70] *Auto-Biography of Symon Patrick*, p. 174; and Patrick, *Works*, IX, pp. 541–2.

visitations. Indirectly, however, their role was of overwhelming importance, since they were free to appoint whom they wished to its eight prebendal stalls. A learned bishop could – if there were vacancies enough during his episcopate – create a learned Chapter. The bishopric's connexions with the university of Cambridge were so close that it was common enough throughout the seventeenth and eighteenth centuries for men of some scholarly distinction to be appointed to the see, and in the early eighteenth century there was a remarkable succession of scholarly holders of the see: Simon Patrick (1691–1707), John Moore (1707–14) (Plate 25b) and William Fleetwood (1714–23). Moore, in particular – who has already been mentioned as a bookloving prebendary (1679–91) – was responsible for a series of appointments to canonries that must have made of the Chapter a remarkably lively, scholarly group, when its members gathered together for, say, the annual late November audit.

Today, undoubtedly, the best-known of Moore's appointees is his son-in-law, Thomas Tanner (2nd stall, 1713–24), author of the *Notitia Monastica* and (published posthumously) the *Bibliotheca Britannico-Hibernica* (Plate 25c). Tanner's passionate interest in England's medieval monastic houses and medieval writers made him ideally qualified to investigate Ely's muniments; he must be the only canon ever to have read through the *Liber Eliensis* some years before he first joined the Cathedral body.[71] He was certainly also responsive to the specific charms of the College at Ely: in a letter which he sent to the antiquary Browne Willis in December 1713, during his first 50-day stint of residence, he referred to 'my self, who was never more Monastic than at present, being got here into the Stall and lodgings of the Subprior, Celarer or some such Officer – and hither I have brought the *Notitia Monastica*, in order to revise it for a new Edition.'[72] He spent a great deal of time during one of his residences in looking at the medieval obedientiary rolls, and drew up a set of chronologically arranged notes on Ely's medieval events and personnel, including the names of all the obedientiaries, from the eleventh century down to 1535.[73] A preliminary draught or working paper of his also survives – a list of those monks who were *Custos capelle BVM*. This has a particular value (and poignancy) today because it shows that Tanner was able to consult 23 rolls of the *Custos capelle*, whereas only 16 are now extant.[74]

Like his father-in-law, Tanner collected manuscripts of all sorts, as well as information, and it has sometimes been suggested that he was more than merely careless in his dealings with the Ely archives,[75] but the charge seems ill-founded. He often borrowed manuscript materials, to work on, and after his death his brother John wrote to Archdeacon Knight that 'on most, if not all the Books and Papers he had of other Peoples, he had pinned or pasted a piece of paper, and writ thereon whose they were,

---

[71] *Cf.* Tanner's notes for his *Bibliotheca* in BL, MS Add. 6261, fos. 15–16ᵛ, derived from Bodl., MS Laud Misc. 647.

[72] Bodl., MS Willis 44 (*S.C.* 16337), fo. 31: T. Tanner to B. Willis, College in Ely, 13 Dec. 1713.

[73] CUL, MS Add. 49, fos. 3–26ᵛ.

[74] CUL, MS Add. 41, fo. 257ʳ⁻ᵛ; one of the 16 extant rolls has only been in the archive since 1909, having been returned to Ely in that year from Worcester, to which it had presumably been allocated by mistake in the 1660s [*cf.* Chapter Minutes, EDC 2/2B/4, 28 Sept. 1909].

[75] *E.g.*, A. Jessopp, in HMC, 12th *Report*, Appx., pt 9, p. 392; and see the denial of these suggestions by M.J. Sommerlad, 'The Historical and Antiquarian Interests of Thomas Tanner', D.Phil. thesis, University of Oxford, 1962, p. 312. There are three possible exceptions: Bodl., MSS Cambs. Rolls 3 (Priory taxation details, 14th cent.), 4 (account of *Custos capelle BVM*, 45 Edward III) and 5 (Priory account as tax collectors, 1456).

and by this means I delivered several things (some belonging to the Chapter of Ely, to yourself) before they were enquired after'.[76] John Tanner was writing in connexion with the transcripts of mid-seventeenth-century state papers which had been made for Dr John Nalson (1684–6), and of which more than half were acquired by Thomas Tanner and thus passed with the rest of his collection into the Bodleian Library, Oxford.[77]

Tanner's heart was perhaps always in Oxford, where he later obtained a further canonry (causing him to resign that at Ely), and his historical interests were national rather than local in scope. But he clearly saw the potential scholarly value in the Ely muniments' content, and he was a friend and encourager of Dr Samuel Knight, to whom Bishop Moore had also given a canonry in Ely (7th stall, 1714–46). In the late 1720s, Knight wrote a Life of Bishop Simon Patrick, having already written Lives of Erasmus (1724) and Colet (1726).[78] Throughout the 1720s he toyed with the idea of writing a history of the Cathedral, once telling Bishop Gibson: 'Since I have been here upon my residence, I have taken some pains in looking over and transcribing several of our ancient charters belonging to this Church. I find more than I expected, or (as I think) have been taken notice of; which almost tempts me to set about the History and Antiquities of this Church.'[79] Knight never did complete such a history, however; it was as though he himself shared in the viewpoint that he attributed to John Colet: 'he could by no means admire that anxious and laborious Sort of Learning, that was to be gained by the running through all sorts of Books.'[80] Knight had served his time in the world of book-based work – once, he had even made a catalogue of all the printed books in Cambridge University Library[81] – and now he was free to write a more stylish or 'polite' form of history.

From the point of view of later generations, it is perhaps more important that the Ely Chapter archives and library were well maintained in this period than that they might have been used for the compilation of a substantial history of the sort that, for instance, Peterborough Cathedral had been given by Simon Gunton, supplemented by Simon Patrick (1686). The Chapter Order Book and Audit Book show continuing concern both for the library and for good record-keeping. In 1732 Dr Ralph Perkins, whom Bishop Fleetwood had made a Canon in 1715, gave half of his own library to the Cathedral (and the other half to Queen's College, Cambridge). The Chapter deputed

---

[76] Bodl., MS Ballard 4 (*S.C.* 10790), fo. 145: 'A Copy of a Letter to Mr Archdeacon Knight . . .'

[77] Peter Beal, *Index of English Literary Manuscripts*, vol. II, *1625–1708*, pt 2, *Lee-Wycherley* (London, 1993), p. 82; Nalson had acquired the papers of his relative, Bishop Williams, according to William Cole [BL, MS Add. 5822, fo. 96ᵛ; and *cf.* MS Add. 5841, fo. 4ᵛ, and *Catalogue of the Stowe Manuscripts in the British Museum*, 2 vols. (London, 1895), I, p. 682 (MS 1058)].

[78] He withheld the Life of Patrick from publication, possibly for political reasons: see Thomas Hearne, *Collections*, vol. X, ed. H.E. Salter (Oxford Historical Society, lxvii, 1915), p. 317; a manuscript of it is CUL, MS Add. 20.

[79] *Letters . . . to and from William Nicolson*, ed. J. Nichols, 2 vols. (London, 1809), I, pp. *340–1; see also J. Nichols, account of Knight, in *Literary Anecdotes of the Eighteenth Century*, 9 vols. (London, 1812–15), V, pp. 354–63. Knight's accounts of bishops, deans, canons and archdeacons of Ely are in CUL, MS Add. 49, fos. 29–43. He was a member of the Society of Antiquaries from its revival in 1718, and in 1720 wrote to it, to solicit other members' assistance with his intended 'History of the Church and Town of Ely': Society of Antiquaries, Minute Book I, *s.v.* 10 Feb. 1719/20.

[80] S. Knight, *Life of Dr John Colet, Dean of S. Paul's in the Reigns of K. Henry VII and Henry VIII* (London, 1724), pp. 76–7.

[81] Hearne, *Collections*, X (cit. in n. 78), p. 317; *cf.* D.J. McKitterick, *Cambridge University Library: A History. The Eighteenth and Nineteenth Centuries* (Cambridge, 1986), p. 45.

Knight to write and thank him and say that it readily allowed his great age and infirmities to be *legitimum impedimentum* to the last year's and any future residence.[82] The librarian, Thomas Ellis, was given five guineas for cataloguing the books and assisting Dr Charles Ashton in putting them into good order.[83] The presence in many of the library books of a label recording Perkins's gift is testimony to the size of the collection; its many surprises include a Sarum missal of 1555 and a Catechism of the Reformed Churches, in Greek (London, 1655).[84]

In 1737 the Chapter showed its corporate keenness for augmenting the library stock in the longer term, by recommending that in future all members of the Cathedral should – instead of giving a 'treat' – make a gift of money for the use of the library: £10 from a Dean, £5 from a prebendary and £1 from a minor canon.[85] For the next hundred years and more, this was duly done, although the donors often preferred to give actual books rather than sums of money. In June 1746 fresh library rules were drawn up, requiring a general recall of books by 1st June every year, so that the librarian could give an account at the next General Chapter of any that were missing.[86] A monthly recall of all books had been directed in 1721, but had presumably been found to be ineffectual.[87] Later in 1746 it was agreed that the library room could be enlarged, when needed, by taking in the vestry of the vicars choral.[88]

Some of the credit for the decisions about the library in 1746 should perhaps be given to the minor canon who was its keeper from 1744 until 1768: James Bentham.[89] For the better keeping and maintenance of the Chapter's records at about this time, credit is unquestionably owing to the Registrar, Thomas Watkins. This minor canon who was also curate of Holy Trinity, Ely, proved to be an exceptionally intelligent and diligent custodian of its muniments. It was of course the duty of the Registrar (or Chapter clerk) to maintain the Chapter's Order Books – until the mid twentieth century, the holder of the post remained the custodian of all the Order Books, whatever their date – but Watkins's labours far exceeded his duties.[90] He indexed each of the Order Books. In 1744 or 1745 he produced a List of members or officers of Ely Cathedral, 1544–1744 – a careful and intelligent compilation, with both references and comments on matters of interest, and even a list of sources used.[91] In 1752 it was doubtless Watkins who inspired the Chapter order that transcripts be made for the Steward's use of all the Cathedral's

---

[82] Order Book, 1729–69: EDC 2/2A/3, p. 16. In the event, Perkins lived until 1751, reportedly to the age of 96: *Gentleman's Magazine*, xxi (1751), p. 236.

[83] EDC 2/2A/3, p. 20. Ellis was a vicar choral from 1728; he was an MA of St John's College, Cambridge.

[84] The missal (London: John Kingston and Henry Sutton, 1555) is now CUL, Ely c. 260; the *Catechismus Ecclesiarum Reformatorum* is mentioned in EDC 13/2/4 (iii).

[85] EDC 2/2A/3, p. 50 (25 Nov. 1737). A list of references to such gifts is entered at the back of this volume. A book for recording library benefactions was ordered at the same date, but has not survived.

[86] *Ibid.*, p. 113 (14 June 1746).

[87] EDC 2/2A/2, pp. 344–5 (14 June 1721).

[88] EDC 2/2A/3, p. 114 (25 Nov. 1746).

[89] Appointed 8 May 1744: EDC 2/2A/3, p. 102, and *cf.* EDC 2/9/3, p. 18. Replaced 14 June 1768: EDC 2/2A/3. p. 255. For Bentham, see further P. Meadows, above, pp. 203–6, and see below, pp. 276–7.

[90] A generally appreciative account of Watkins is given by R.H. Gibbon, 'The Order Book of the Dean and Chapter of Ely, 1729–1769', *Church Quarterly Review*, cxxiv (April–Sept. 1937), pp. 250–65, at pp. 256–61. His association with the Chapter lasted for 52 years. For his unsuccessful application for the post of auditor (1750), see A. Gibbons, *Ely Episcopal Records . . .* (privately printed, Lincoln, 1891), pp. 58–60.

[91] EDC 2/9/3; for most posts it has not yet been superseded for the years covered.

manorial court rolls for the past eighty or ninety years, the older ones being 'laid up in the Chapter House with the other originals to be preserved as perfect as may be for our use.'[92] The manorial rolls tended to get battered and worn, being taken to each manorial court session. Also in 1752, Watkins was given five guineas for the indexes that he had made to various court rolls, and in 1754 he received a further ten guineas, for indexing twenty-nine volumes of court rolls.[93] And at the same time he produced an invaluable survey of what each Chapter estate ought to yield; typical of his approach, this provides the fruits of a careful sifting of historical evidence, including the Parliamentary Survey of Chapter properties (1649) and even documents as old as account rolls from the Cathedral Priory, to indicate what each manor or lesser estate had returned and ought to be producing at the present time.[94] Watkins was a born indexer, and even before he became Precentor (1764 (?)) he had turned to indexing the Cathedral's music manuscripts.[95]

Cambridge in the second and third quarters of the eighteenth century was positively brimming with antiquaries who would have pounced at any opportunity to remove historic documents from the ancient Cathedral located so conveniently nearby. Take, for instance, Charles Mason, Woodwardian Professor of Geology and Rector of Orwell (Cambs.); he was a Fellow of Trinity College from 1725 until 1762, when he resigned in order to marry[96] (Plate 32b). He is mentioned earlier in this volume as owner of two pre-Conquest royal charters for Ely Abbey,[97] and it might seem reasonable to suspect that these had only recently left the Ely Cathedral muniments. He appears to have been a friend of Samuel Knight,[98] but it would be quite unfair to blacken Knight's reputation on that score. In 1749 he must have earned the thanks of Thomas Watkins by lending for transcription into the first book of Chapter Acts the only known copy of the indenture of 10 June 1600 by which Elizabeth I received dozens of Ely episcopal manors in return for certain other lands and properties. For

---

[92] EDC 2/2A/3, p. 158 (14 June 1752). This had previously been called for in 1721: *ibid.*, p. 70.

[93] *Ibid.*, pp. 159 (14 June 1752), 187 (14 June 1754).

[94] EDC 14/8; briefly discussed (as MS 8, *alias* Liber G) by D.M. Owen, 'The Muniments of Ely Cathedral Priory', in *Church and Government in the Middle Ages. . .*, ed. C.N.L. Brooke *et al.* (Cambridge, etc., 1976), pp. 157–76, at 172. For its compilation in *c.* 1753, see p. 1, 67; for use of account rolls of St Etheldreda's Liberties in Suffolk of as early as 1 Henry VI, see p. 54; for medieval and later payment of Ely Farthings, see p. 65.

[95] See *Catalogue of Ancient Choral Services and Anthems, preserved . . . in the Cathedral Church of Ely*, ed. W.E. Dickson (Cambridge, 1861), and *cf.* E.F. Rimbault, 'Musical Manuscripts at Ely', *Notes & Queries*, 5th ser., iii (Jan.-June 1875), p. 484, for a 'Catalogue of the Church Musick at Ely, 1754' conjecturally by Watkins. Watkins had been in receipt of the precentor's stipend since before 1764: EDC 2/9/3, p. 14.

[96] For Mason's antiquarian interests, see J. Nichols, *Illustrations of the Literary History of the Eighteenth Century*, 6 vols. (London, 1817–31), III, pp. 545–6; contemporary criticisms of his uncouth ways and geological incompetence or bungling are reported in D.A. Winstanley, *Unreformed Cambridge. A Study of Certain Aspects of the University in the Eighteenth Century* (Cambridge, 1935), pp. 168–9, 259–60. A more favourable picture is given by William Cole, in BL, MS Add. 5834, fo. 8ᵛ: 'a very ingenious Man, an excellent Mechanic, a good Antiquary & no bad Geographer: witness a most accurate Map of Cambridgeshire, which he has made from a personal Visitation of almost every Spot in the County. . . He has also large Collections for an History of the same County, Part of Mr Layer's & Part of Mr Rutherford's Collections.' For Dr Jeremiah Milles (d.1784) he made a transcript of the *Liber Eliensis* (later in the Phillipps collection; sold as part of the library of W.A. Lindsay, Sotheby, 14–16 Feb. 1927, lot 390, when bought by the bookseller Halliday). Several volumes from his collection, on bellringing and other topics, were acquired by John Bowtell and are now at Downing College, Cambridge.

[97] Above, p. 5, n. 13; *cf.* Owen, 'Muniments of Ely Cathedral Priory' (cit. in n. 94), pp. 172–3.

[98] *Cf.* Bodl., MS Eng. Lett. d.43, fo. 77, letter of C. Mason to S. Pegge, 9 Mar. 1760.

some reason this had never been transcribed into the Dean and Chapter's book of Confirmations.[99]

However, the indenture of 1600 evidently came from the Ely episcopal archive, and it is in fact very possible that the Anglo-Saxon charters were from the same source.[100] The muniments of the see of Ely were kept mostly in Cambridge, and it is apparent that they were woefully ill-kept in the eighteenth century. In the mid 1720s the Bishop's principal registrar, William Balaam, lent the key of his office to the Nonjuring scholar Thomas Baker, letting him transcribe whatever he wanted; subsequently, Balaam even sent material to Baker's room at St John's College.[101] This was reasonable, given that Baker was punctilious in the extreme. But in about 1766 the deputy registrar, Thomas Higgins, shot himself, and a quantity of the muniments was subsequently sold as waste paper to a Cambridge grocer; several dozen volumes were bought from the latter by Samuel Peck, a fellow of Trinity College.[102] In 1776 the antiquary William Cole was lent some medieval deeds relating to Swavesey priory from the Chapter archives, by the prebendary John Warren: a note by Cole makes clear that this removal was simply for the purposes of a particular claim about tithes.[103] Given that context, this loan also seems reasonable enough, and it may fairly be contrasted with the state of affairs in the episcopal archives. In the following year, 1777, Cole remarked that neither Green, the episcopal registrar at Cambridge, nor Smith, his deputy, could read medieval writing.[104] And just a few years later, Cole noted that eight volumes of Ely diocesan wills from before the time of Henry VIII were lost, 'though known to be existing within these thirty years'.[105] Clearly the archives of the Chapter and those of the bishopric were very differently managed.[106]

James Bentham has always had a slight cloud over his scholarly reputation. It is as though his contemporaries – and later generations, too – could not credit a mere minor canon with the writing of such a careful and thorough major work of scholarship as his *History and Antiquities of the Conventual and Cathedral Church of Ely* (1771) unquestionably is.[107] Maliciously, William Cole suggested that Bentham's brother, Edward, had a major share in writing the book.[108] Others have wondered if it was

---

[99] The 1749 transcript is in EDC 2/2A/1, pp. 151–67; it was verified by Watkins and a lay clerk, Matthew Eburn.

[100] One of Mason's charters, the grant by Eadwig to Archbishop Oda, had belonged to Bishop John Moore: see White Kennett's note in BL, MS Lansd. 969, fo. 111[v]. Moore himself could be ruthless in his collecting methods, to judge from an anecdote recounted by John Bridges, *The History and Antiquities of Northamptonshire*, 2 vols. (Oxford, etc., 1791), II, p. 45. See also Simon Keynes, above, p. 17.

[101] F. Korsten, *A Catalogue of the Library of Thomas Baker* (Cambridge, etc., 1990), pp. xxi–ii. Baker was once able to transcribe a letter of Charles I and two Chapter Orders (1683 and 1684) directly from 'the Church Book. . .at Ely': CUL, MS Mm.1.43 (=Baker's vol. 32), p. 313; but that was surely exceptional.

[102] Gibbons, *Ely Episcopal Records* (cit. in n. 90), p. 79, supplemented by D.M. Owen, *Ely Records. A Handlist of the Records of the Bishop and Archdeacon of Ely* (Cambridge, [1971]), p. viii.

[103] W.M. Palmer and Catherine Parsons, 'Swavesey Priory', *Trans., Cambs. and Hunts. Archaeol. Soc.*, i (1904), pp. 29–48, at 32n.

[104] *Ibid.*

[105] BL, Add. MS 5822, fo. 208.

[106] In 1741 the Cathedral received from the antiquary Thomas Martin of Palgrave, apparently as a gift, a survey of episcopal lands, 1538–9: EDC 1/C/4; the prebendary Clement Tookie collected this from Martin.

[107] For an appreciative and defensive account of Bentham, see Nichols, *Literary Anecdotes* (cit. in n. 79), III, pp. 484–94.

[108] See Cole's notes in his copy of the *History*, as printed by William Davis, *An Olio of Bibliographical and Literary Anecdotes and Memoranda* (London, 1814), pp. 109–26, at p. 125. Did Cole feel aggrieved because he

not the poet Thomas Gray (d.1771) who first developed the theory of gothic architecture as originating in the intersecting of the blank arcading of round arches.[109] Exceptionally for an Ely minor canon, Bentham was later in his life given a prebend in the Cathedral, by Bishop Keene (1779). But that he had himself painstakingly gathered the materials for his book is shown beyond all doubt by the survival of nineteen volumes of transcripts and excerpts, neatly copied out in his own hand, and now in Cambridge University Library.[110] Furthermore, a letter that he sent in 1762 (when still a minor canon) to Dr A.C. Ducarel suggests that he was entirely dependent on the presence and goodwill of the Chapter registrar for access to the muniments: he offered to send what information he could find in the Chapter 'Registry' about endowments of vicarages in the diocese, and explained that 'At present it happens that the Registrar of the Church is at London; but, I hear, will return to Ely in about a fortnight's time; when I will not fail to get what informations I can, and let you know.'[111] Perhaps because the episcopal archives were so much easier to access, Bentham drew far more on them than on the records at Ely; Augustus Jessopp observed, perhaps unfairly, that he 'sometimes went far afield in search of information which lay ready to his hand very near home'.[112]

The closing years of the eighteenth century and the first two decades of the nineteenth were a high point in the history of the library, at least in terms of its financing and its general use. These were of course also years of increasing prosperity for the Dean and Chapter, who could readily afford to improve the library's funding. In 1784 James Bentham's younger brother Jeffery, minor canon and librarian, was given ten guineas for writing a new catalogue and putting the library into order:[113] it is possible that this catalogue is in part or in substance incorporated in that dated 1796, which is the earliest surviving catalogue of the post-Restoration library.[114] Gifts of all kinds came at this time: in 1798, for instance, the Chapter thanked the Bishop of Ely for his gift of *Athenian Letters* and Francis Maseres, Baron of the Exchequer, for a 'valuable gift' of unspecified books.[115] In 1785 another of James Bentham's brothers, the former University Printer, Joseph Bentham, gave 49 volumes, all printed at Cambridge since 1743. In 1802 the Revd Mr Ferraby was thanked for presenting a 'book of Old Grants' – presumably a stray from the muniments.[116] From 1790 to 1805, the Chapter subscribed three guineas a year to Dr Robert Holmes's work of collating

---

had himself prepared (and lent to Bentham) Lives of seven late medieval Bishops of Ely? Cole's work, now CUL, MS Add. 4153, is one of his few original compositions.

[109] N. Pevsner, *Some Architectural Historians of the Nineteenth Century* (Oxford, 1972), p. 5.

[110] MSS Add. 2944–62; Add. 2944–59 are the sixteen volumes of Bentham's 'Notitia Ecclesiae Eliensis'. The notebooks were all acquired from Jarrold & Sons of Norwich in 1889, and had once been used by Bentham's continuator, William Stevenson. Some of the medieval accounts excerpted in them have subsequently decayed and been lost, giving Bentham's work a particular value for modern scholars. Bentham was ready to let other scholars use his transcripts: for instance, his excerpts from the accounts of the sacrist and of the *custos capelle BVM* were drawn on by Thomas Pownall for his 'Observations on Ancient Painting in England', printed in *Archaeologia*, ix (1789), pp. 141–56.

[111] Nichols, *Literary Anecdotes* (cit. in n. 79), III, p. 489 n.

[112] HMC, 12th *Report*, Appx, pt ix, p. 389.

[113] Chapter Order Book, 1770–1804: EDC 2/2A/4, p. 107 (25 Nov. 1784).

[114] EDC 13/1/1; this has additions down to 1812.

[115] EDC 2/2A/4, pp. 215, 217 (10 June and 25 Nov. 1798).

[116] *Ibid.*, pp. 114–15 (1785), 245 (14 June 1802).

the Septuagint.[117] From about 1795, the Chapter also began subscribing two or three times that sum annually for newspapers.

In 1814 these developments came to a head, as a general overhaul of the library and its management was decided on. Recognition that the library was being used as a reading room (perhaps partly for the newspapers?) is reflected in the decision to spend £27 on a stove for it.[118] The librarian was given an assistant, whose duty it was to light the fire when wanted and to sweep out the room, for £2 a year.[119] A month later the major step was taken of giving all Chapter fees for the sealing of documents to the library, for the purchase of books.[120] The Ely library was henceforth to be as well funded as that of any other cathedral in the land. A month later still, the Chapter resolved to spend £100 (borrowed against future sealing fees) on filling gaps in the library, especially in its holdings of 'Dictionaries, Historical Works and other books of reference'.[121] Rearrangement of the books next followed, the London bookseller Robert Triphook being paid £31 10s. for this. A further £1 10s. 2d. was paid for 'Wire Work for the Library': this will have been for the enclosure that was later known as the Lattice, and which was a necessary security measure for housing the rarest or most valuable books, in a library which had never used chains to secure books to the shelves. Finally, still in 1815, Triphook was paid £29 6s. 10d. for making a new catalogue: *Catalogus Librorum qui in Bibliothecâ Cathedralis Eliensis adservantur*.[122] Fifty copies of this were printed.[123] No author's name appears on the title-page. Credit for its compilation has wrongly been given to the minor canon George Millers, who in 1803 had been appointed epistoler, sacrist, librarian and under schoolmaster, and who in 1816 was paid £10 'for the trouble he has had in arranging the library'[124] (Plate 32c). Millers was an astute individual, who has the distinction that in the first edition of his *Description of the Cathedral Church of Ely* (1805), he was apparently the first person to use the term 'Early English';[125] but the London bookseller seems to have been the victim of his own title-page's anonymity. Triphook's work is 138 pages long and has about 2500 entries. It is, in the then fashionable manner, a classed catalogue, arranged by subject; it is not in shelf order, although shelf-marks are given. There are principal headings, such as Theologia, Jurisprudentia, Politica, Artes et Scientiæ, and Literæ Humaniores; and within these are sub-headings, such as (under Theologia) Biblia Polyglotta, Hebraica et Græca, Biblia Latina, Bibliorum Sacrorum Interpretes, Liturgiæ, and Works of Eminent English Theologians. Overall, theology occupies about half the volume.

Just a few years later, in August 1820, a library borrowers' register was commenced,

---

[117] See the Audit Book, 1789–1818: EDC 3/1/9. See the entry on Robert Holmes in the *DNB* for a short account of his labours in collating manuscripts, 1788–1805 – an enormous undertaking, supported by numerous subscribers.

[118] EDC 3/1/9, *sub anno* 1814; the stove was purchased from Messrs. Downe and Saunders.

[119] Chapter Order Book, 1805–41: EDC 2/2A/5, p. 118 (25 Nov. 1814).

[120] *Ibid.*, p. 120 (23 Dec. 1814).

[121] *Ibid.*, p. 121 (23 Jan. 1815).

[122] EDC 3/1/9, *sub annis* 1815 and 1816.

[123] The print run is stated in a note in a copy in the Ely Cathedral Modern Muniment Room. An interleaved copy, with additions down to 1887, is EDC 13/1/2.

[124] EDC 2/2A/5, p. 136 (25 Nov. 1816).

[125] Pevsner, *Some Architectural Historians* (cit. in n. 109), p. 29 n. 2.

and this enables the use of the book stock to be assessed.[126] In the first full calendar year, 1821, there were fourteen borrowers, who took out a total of 67 works. The minor canons made the greatest use of the library, as might be expected of such full-time residents; William Metcalfe took out twelve works, George Millers ten and John Griffith nine. Of the prebendaries, George Jenyns was the most assiduous, with ten works, followed by Sir Henry Bate Dudley with six. A few volumes of sermons were taken out: Isaac Barrow's sermons by Jenyns, Dean Moss's by the prebendary, George King, Dr Pearce's by Millers and Bishop Horsley's *Charges and Tracts* by Dudley. John Henry Sparke borrowed volume I of Hampson's *Memoirs of Wesley*. Henry Fardell, prebendary, borrowed Burn's *Ecclesiastical Law*, and Jenyns took out both Blackstone's *Commentaries on the Laws of England* and Thomas Blount's *Law Dictionary* (1717). The history of Ely Cathedral was to prove a perennial favourite among library borrowings, and in this year Dean Wood signed for Millers's *Description of the Cathedral Church*, Metcalfe and John Henry Sparke borrowed the first volume of Dugdale's *Monasticon Anglicanum*, Dean Wood and Archdeacon Cambridge borrowed Bentham's *History* with its *Supplement*, and Bentham's *History* on its own was borrowed by both Dudley and Griffith. The fact that there is no date of borrowing of Bentham's *History* by Griffith (though he returned it on 20 November) suggests that he received it direct from Dudley (who took it out on 13 September and is stated to have returned it on 23 October); certainly, the coincidences that on the same day, 10 Nov., both Metcalfe and Dudley borrowed different volumes of G. Tomline's *Memoirs of the Life of Pitt* (1821), and that on the day that Metcalfe returned volume I, Archdeacon Cambridge signed it out, suggest that the residents of the College discussed their reading with each other. Indeed, when Cambridge returned volume I, it was shortly afterwards taken by the prebendary, George King.

Competition for popular historical or biographical works is, however, scarcely indicative of any attempt at scholarship. The most serious reading that can be pointed to is of Mabillon's *De Re Diplomatica* or *De Liturgia Gallicana* by Millers (3–29 December) and of *Reports on the Poor Population* (1811) and a volume on *Population Enumeration* by his fellow minor canon, Metcalfe (6–14 March and 29 May–12 June, respectively). That Metcalfe four years previously had been deemed by the local establishment – and, no doubt, Sir Henry Bate Dudley – to have acted too sympathetically towards the Littleport rioters, and been demoted from the magistrates' Bench, is in the light of this perhaps unsurprising. But was it any less surprising that within two decades the prebendaries' world would be transformed and that they would be reduced in both wealth and number? No longer would they have the leisure to pass their terms of residence in reading William Coxe's *History of the House of Austria* or Izaak Walton's *Lives* of John Donne, Sir Henry Wotton, Richard Hooker, George Herbert and Bishop Robert Sanderson.

---

[126] EDC 13/4/1.

Life at the Cathedral 1836–1980

FRANCES KNIGHT

Introduction

When George Augustus Selwyn published his provocatively-entitled pamphlet *Are Cathedral Institutions Useless?* in 1838, it was Ely that he had in mind.[1] All that Selwyn had had to hand when he began work were the statutes and charter of Ely Cathedral, and he positioned little extracts from them at the head of every chapter. He also had personal knowledge: his elder brother, William, had become a residentiary canon of Ely a few years earlier. G.A. Selwyn answered his question with a resounding negative: cathedral institutions were certainly not useless! Indeed, he believed that they contained the potential for renewing the whole Church. In eleven succinct chapters, Selwyn set out an entire manifesto for a remodelled cathedral. The residentiary canons would assume the form of an ancient council, advising the bishop and helping him run the diocese. They would receive sufficient income from their cathedral preferment to make unnecessary the holding of other livings, and they would all live constantly at the cathedral, offering hospitality and advising visiting clergy on everything from church finances to disputed points of theology. The residentiary canons would make preaching their special function, going about the diocese interpreting the bishop's charge, explaining changes in the law,[2] providing sermons in parishes where preaching was poorly performed and generally serving as models of homiletic excellence. The canons would be learned men, devoted to scholarship and to defending the Christian faith. They would use the resources of the cathedral for the education of grammar school boys, ordinands and missionaries, and Selwyn envisaged an elaborate system which would enable 'poor and friendless orphans' to proceed from parish national school to university, and thereafter to ordination and an incumbency. Once the canons had been worn out by scholarship, by preaching in large, crowded churches, and the frequent travelling to distant parts of the diocese, Selwyn envisaged them vacating their stalls and retiring to small, rural benefices.[3]

I am very grateful to Peter Meadows for his comments on an earlier draft of this chapter.

[1] G.A. Selwyn, *Are Cathedral Institutions Useless? A Practical Answer to this Question Addressed to W.E. Gladstone Esq., M.P.* (London, 1838).

[2] Selwyn was thinking of the Civil Registration Act, which was implemented in 1837 and was much resented among clergy who believed that the civil registration of births and marriages undermined the importance of baptism and holy matrimony.

[3] Selwyn, *Are Cathedral Institutions Useless?* pp. 7–9, 13, 23–5, 27–35, 58, 65–6, 73.

Over the next century and a half, Selwyn's vision of Ely was partially enacted, but he would hardly have approved of the much-reduced status of the mid-twentieth-century Cathedral. Selwyn put forward his proposals in the very different climate of the 1830s, and it is intriguing that he linked them explicitly to the template of Ely, without it apparently appearing either ridiculous or hypocritical. Ely Cathedral in the 1830s was rather far from Selwyn's vision. 1836 was a significant year. In April the Cathedral mourned the passing of its Bishop, Bowyer Edward Sparke. The death of Sparke marked the end of the legal jurisdiction of the bishops of Ely. Previously, bishops had been responsible for appointing all the law officers in the Isle of Ely (a sizeable area which included Wisbech and several other towns such as Chatteris, March and Whittlesey). Even the magistrates, although technically appointed by the Crown, were selected on the recommendation of the bishop. This explains a great deal about the unpopularity of the Church in the Isle and in the Fens during the unrest which had been such a prominent feature of the early nineteenth century.[4] The Bishop had also been responsible for meeting court expenses, and for maintaining his own prison; to do this he had the power to levy taxes. In 1836 at least five of the residentiary and minor canons were magistrates at the Quarter Sessions in the Isle of Ely.

In that year, Sparke's son-in-law, Henry Fardell, Vicar of Wisbech, a prominent magistrate and poor law guardian, occupied the first stall in the Cathedral. In the summer of 1836, Fardell was much occupied with trying to quell protests against the New Poor Law. The lock on the entrance gates of his house in Wisbech was hacked off in the middle of the night, and he believed that his property was about to be subject to an arson attack.[5] The second stall was occupied by the extremely elderly George Cambridge, Archdeacon of Middlesex. The third was in the possession of William French, Master of Jesus College, Cambridge (Plate 34d). John Maddy, a royal chaplain who also held a clutch of Suffolk livings and was newly installed at Ely, held the fourth. The fifth was held by Bishop Sparke's elder son, John Henry, who had had so much church preferment bestowed upon him by his father that, together with Canon Fardell, he had made an unwelcome appearance in John Wade's *Extraordinary Black Book* in 1831.[6] In 1836, in addition to his Ely canonry, J.H. Sparke was Chancellor of the diocese and the incumbent of four East Anglian parishes, and resided mainly at his recently-acquired estate of Gunthorpe in Norfolk. He was also a Justice of the Peace for Norfolk and for the Isle of Ely (Plate 34c). William Selwyn, the cleverest member of a very clever family, held the sixth stall.[7] Selwyn was thirty years old in 1836, and over the

---

[4] There had been riots in Littleport and Ely in 1816. The classic accounts are by an anonymous Member of the Inner Temple, *A Full and Correct Report of the Trials for Rioting at Ely and Littleport in May 1816* (London, 1816), and C. Johnson (who was a lay clerk at Ely Cathedral), *An Account of the Ely and Littleport Riots in 1816* (Ely, 1893). For a more recent, if somewhat tendentious account, see A.J. Peacock, *Bread and Blood: a Study of the Agrarian Riots in East Anglia in 1816* (London, 1965), pp. 59–64; also B.M.G. Smedley, *Holy Trinity, Ely: In Search of a Vanished Parish* (London, 1998), pp. 43–5.

[5] H. Fardell to Lord John Russell, 7 July 1836. PRO Microfilms HO52 (Public Order, Discontent and Protest 1820–1850), Reel 30, Box 28, fo. 70.

[6] John Wade, *The Extraordinary Black Book* (London, 1831), pp. 22, 528.

[7] His younger brothers were George Augustus Selwyn, Bishop of New Zealand, and Sir Charles Jasper Selwyn, MP and Lord Justice. A fourth brother, William Kynaston Selwyn, died at the age of 22 shortly after graduating from Trinity College, Cambridge, where he achieved various academic distinctions. See Laetitia Frances Selwyn, *Memorials of Four Brothers* (Richmond, 1885). For Selwyn see also the memoir by J.S. Wood,

next forty years was to make considerable contributions both to Ely and to Cambridge University. He had been at Eton with Bishop Sparke's younger son, Edward, and both men became fellows of St John's College, Cambridge, in the late 1820s. It may well have been Edward Sparke's prompting that brought Selwyn to Bishop Sparke's attention (Plate 35d). Edward Sparke occupied the seventh stall. He had been diocesan Registrar since 1824, and was Vicar of Littleport and Rector of Feltwell, both within fairly easy reach of Ely (Plate 35c). The eighth stall was held by George Jenyns. He was 73 in 1836, but still on the magistrates' bench. Jenyns owed his social position to having inherited the Bottisham estate in Cambridgeshire from a second cousin of his father in 1787.[8] He possessed a great knowledge of farming, and had served as chairman of both the Board of Agriculture and the Bedford Level Corporation (Plate 34b). Over this diverse collection of Bishop Sparke's friends and relations presided the Dean, James Wood. Three years later he would be succeeded by George Peacock, who would also become William Selwyn's brother-in-law.[9] In the 1830s 'the College', as the Cathedral precincts were known, had something of the air of a genteel family business.[10]

Ely and Cambridge

In 1836 the matter that most concerned the Dean and Chapter was the Ecclesiastical Commission's Second Report, with its proposal that the number of residentiary canonries be reduced to four, and its other recommendations which 'would, if carried into effect, materially impair the constitution of our Capitular body and also affect the comfort of the college residences . . .'[11] They sent a memorial to the Commissioners, the first salvo in what was to be an on-going hostility between the two bodies. In addition to protesting against any loss of patronage rights or appropriation of Dean and Chapter estates, they suggested that their proximity to Cambridge University would make the linking of canonries to inadequately endowed university offices a possibility.[12] Thus the Dean and Chapter themselves identified what was to be an important feature at Ely Cathedral for the whole of the period with which this chapter is concerned, the annexation of certain stalls to certain professorships.

In December 1836 they sent a longer, more indignant and defensive memorial, this time in response to the Ecclesiastical Commission's Fourth Report.[13] It reveals something of the way in which they saw themselves. They understood that the Cathedral revenues were theirs; why should they be expected to use their own money to supply the spiritual needs of commercial and manufacturing areas, as the Commissioners

---

President of St John's College, Cambridge, in W. Selwyn, *Pastoral Colloquies on the South Downs. Prophecy and Miracles* (Cambridge, 1876).

[8] Leonard Blomefield (formerly Jenyns), *Chapters in my Life* (Bath, 1887), pp. 4, 12.

[9] Frances Selwyn was married first to George Peacock and then after his death, to another member of the Chapter, William Hepworth Thompson, in 1866. Thompson gave up his canonry on appointment as Master of Trinity College, Cambridge in 1867.

[10] This continued for some decades. In 1841 Bishop Allen appointed his brother-in-law, John Ashley, to the second stall. In 1867 Solomon Smith, a minor canon, appointed his son as curate of St Mary's, Ely, and in 1880 E.H. Lowe, the son of a residentiary canon, was nominated to Holy Trinity, with the additional duty of chaplain to the Dean and Chapter.

[11] EDC 2/2A/5, p. 348, 3 June 1836.

[12] EDC 2/12/2, pp. 62–3, 23 June 1836.

[13] *Ibid.*, pp. 69–79, 20 December 1836.

demanded? Why should their patronage rights be transferred to the Bishop, when the rights of other patrons remained untouched? How could daily worship be maintained in the Cathedral, if the number of residentiary canons was halved? They claimed that under the present arrangement there was always a senior cleric available to preach on a Sunday, and that they did not have to call on outsiders for assistance. Their own vision of themselves was slightly different from that of G.A. Selwyn; rather than working with the Bishop to maintain good order in the diocese, they regarded it as their role to protect the parochial clergy from any undue exercise of episcopal authority. Apart from the 'highest matter' of maintaining cathedral worship, the Dean and Chapter saw their function as primarily academic. They were the clerical intelligentsia who must be given time to study so that they could respond to the needs of 'an highly educated and intelligent people'. They reiterated their call for two or three canonries to be annexed 'to certain important offices, connected with the advancement of sacred learning in the University of Cambridge'.

When the much-resented proposals of the Ecclesiastical Commissioners' Fourth Report became law as the Cathedral Act in 1840, it must have given the canons of Ely some consolation to see that their numbers were to be reduced to six, not four, and that two canonries were to be annexed to the Regius professorships of Hebrew and Greek.[14] Their claim to a special relationship with Cambridge University, fifteen miles distant, had been recognised. The 1840 Act resulted in the Regius Professor of Hebrew, William Hodge Mill, being collated to the eighth stall on the death of Canon Jenyns in 1848. Thereafter the eighth stall was occupied by Hebrew professors until 1932, after which it was reassigned to the Regius Professorship of Divinity until 1940, when it was suspended. The only Professor of Divinity to hold the stall was the progressive Charles Raven, who ruffled some feathers by declaring himself a pacifist in 1932, the year he went to Ely (Plate 51c).

The other canon-professorship lasted forty years longer. The first occupant was Canon Selwyn's old tutor, James Scholefield, the Regius Professor of Greek, who was collated to the third stall at Ely on the death of William French in 1849. Three years later, the heads of the Cambridge colleges, together with the Regius Professors of Divinity, Greek and Hebrew, were asked for their views on the recent annexation of the chairs of Greek and Hebrew, and were canvassed about the possibility of two more Ely canonries being attached to Cambridge divinity professorships, an idea which had emerged from the deliberations of the Commission of Inquiry into Cambridge University. Their replies reveal almost universal satisfaction with the existing arrangement, and general eagerness to see the poorly endowed Norrisian chair of Divinity similarly annexed to Ely, together with a newly created divinity professorship.[15] In the event, the annexation of two further Ely canonries to professorships never materialised. Greek professors held the third stall at Ely until 1889, when the chair was secularised.[16] The stall was then attached to the newly created Ely chair of Divinity, first held by Professor Vincent H. Stanton (Plate 51a). The Ely chair existed until the retirement of

---

[14] 3 & 4 Vict. c.113, paras. 12–13. Previously the professorships had been worth only £40 each.

[15] Their answers are preserved verbatim as an appendix to the *Report* of the Cathedral Commission, 1855.

[16] Notable among them was Benjamin Hall Kennedy (1804–89), previously Headmaster of Shrewsbury School, and author of the standard school textbook *Kennedy's Latin Primer*, first published in 1866 (Plate 43c).

Professor G.C. Stead in 1980, by which time Cambridge was clear that it was wrong to restrict a professorship to ordained Anglicans. The Cathedral's contribution to the professor's salary was also by then far too small to influence the University's decisions. Among the nine holders of the Ely chair were some distinguished names in twentieth-century British theology, including John Martin Creed (Plate 51*b*), E.C. Ratcliff and Geoffrey Lampe, men who very much maintained Selwyn's vision of a scholarly and resident clerical intelligentsia.

Traditionally, Cambridge undergraduates have bicycled to Ely on summer afternoons, and the nineteenth-century alumni of Cambridge were encouraged to look upon the Cathedral as one with which they had a special relationship. When stained glass began to be put in, one window was paid for by Cambridge-educated judges, another by the bachelors and undergraduates of the University.[17] Prince Albert appears in stained glass in the robes of the chancellor of the University.[18] By the mid-1850s, the Chapter which twenty years before had been dominated by magistrates and legal matters was dominated by Cambridge professors. In addition to the two Regius Professors, Thomas Jarrett and William Hepworth Thompson, William Selwyn was Lady Margaret Professor of Divinity, and the Dean, George Peacock, was Lowndean Professor of Astronomy. We may imagine university gossip, and perhaps theological discussion, as a feature of Chapter dinners. But Ely belonged to the Fens, not to the university world. It was not Christ Church, Oxford. Once he was appointed Dean, Peacock moved mentally as well as physically from Cambridge to Ely. In his Cambridge days he had breakfasted on Sundays with Herschel and Babbage, and he was a lifelong friend of Adam Sedgwick.[19] He had played an important role as a university reformer,[20] but after his move to Ely he seems to have neglected his professorship, and he is now remembered not as a scientist but as the Dean who commissioned Sir Gilbert Scott's restoration of Ely Cathedral.

Peacock was succeeded in 1858 by Harvey Goodwin, who later recorded that the vacancy had prompted much speculation in Cambridge. 'There was a kind of Cambridge tradition that the post should always be offered not merely to a Cambridge man, but to a man actually connected with the University of Cambridge, a Head, a Professor or some such person.'[21] Little had changed when Charles Merivale succeeded Goodwin in 1869. Merivale did not come directly from Cambridge, having turned down the Regius chair of Modern History on the grounds that the £300 salary was too small and the expense of taking a house in Cambridge too great. The deanery at Ely was however a much more attractive prospect. He told his sister-in-law 'I shall like nothing better than living in a solitude and stepping out in half an hour into the gaiety of Cambridge.'[22] To another correspondent he wrote 'The deanery of Ely cum Cambridge seems especially suitable to my tastes and habits. The dean and four

[17] EDC 2/2A/6, p. 231, 15 June 1857.
[18] The Queen and Prince Albert paid for their portraits in this window themselves. See EDC 2/12/2, p. 179.
[19] *Dictionary of National Biography*, vol. XV, p. 583.
[20] Peter Searby, *A History of the University of Cambridge*, vol. 3 (Cambridge, 1997), pp. 455–9.
[21] *Memoir of the Life of Harvey Goodwin DD, Bishop of Carlisle, Written by Himself* (printed for private circulation only, Cambridge, 1880), p. 138.
[22] Judith Anne Merivale (ed.), *The Autobiography and Letters of Charles Merivale, Dean of Ely* (Oxford, 1898), p. 384. Merivale to Mrs J.E. Frere, 12 November 1869.

canons will be Johnians, and I expect the wags will call us "St John's in the Wilderness . . ."'[23]

Despite the proliferation of professors from the late 1850s, there is no sense of the Ely Chapter being at the forefront of the intellectual debates on evolutionary theory or biblical criticism that were then raging. The interests of this generation seem almost antiquarian. Jarrett spent much of his time transliterating oriental languages into Roman characters according to a system of his own devising. Selwyn translated Tennyson into Latin. Benjamin Hall Kennedy is best remembered as the author of the *Latin Primer*.[24] The Cathedral library contained 10,000 volumes but had almost nothing by nineteenth-century authors. It did not acquire *Essays and Reviews* or *Origin of Species*.[25] In the mid and late 1850s the library was mainly used by Jarrett, Thompson and Selwyn, and by H.J. Carter, curate of the Ely parish of Holy Trinity. They continued to digest a solid diet of eighteenth-century High Church divinity, lightened by Walter Scott's novels, Voltaire's *Letters*, Blomefield's *Norfolk* and Gunning's *Reminiscences of the University, Town and County of Cambridge from the year 1780*.[26] They were the last generation of Ely clergy who continued to read the eighteenth-century divines; their late-nineteenth and early twentieth-century successors tended to use the library only for light reading, histories of Ely Cathedral and other works of East Anglian interest being the most popular. The last person to make any sustained academic use of the Cathedral library was the liturgical scholar and Ely Professor, E.C. Ratcliff. He borrowed eight of the nine books that were loaned in 1956, all theological works in Latin.[27] Easy transport links to Cambridge lessened the need for an academic library for Ely's academic residents, and in 1970 the Cathedral library was transferred to the University, after portions of it had already been sold off.[28]

Until the mid-twentieth century, Cambridge University and the Ely Chapter continued to have links that went beyond the annexation of stalls to chairs. Canon professors continued to become heads of colleges after a spell at Ely: Alan E. Brooke became Provost of King's, Charles Raven became Master of Christ's, J.S. Boys Smith went to St John's and Alexander Kirkpatrick and William Telfer both became Masters of Selwyn (a college founded in memory of G.A. Selwyn). While they were at Ely, they spent time writing – mainly biblical commentaries, and works on the early Church. In 1916 Chapter funds were used for the purchase of a lexicon of patristic Greek, an item clearly regarded as essential for the work of the Chapter to continue.[29] Some of them tried to make their learning accessible to the Cathedral congregation. It was remembered that the Hebraist Canon Kennett, in a sermon in the late 1920s, had urged his listeners to imagine themselves as pious young Jews at the time of Antiochus Epiphanes, 'the altar spluttering with guttering FA-AT!'[30] What they imagined is not

---

[23] Merivale (ed.), *The Autobiography and Letters of Charles Merivale*, p. 386. Merivale to the Revd Frederic Metcalfe, 27 November 1869.

[24] See n. 17, above.

[25] *Catalogue of the Books Contained in the Library belonging to the Dean and Chapter of the Cathedral Church of Ely* (Ely, 1884).

[26] EDC 13/4/1, Library borrowing register, 1820–85.

[27] EDC 13/4/2.

[28] See also N. Ramsay, p. 361, below.

[29] EDC 2/2A/9, p. 19, 31 July 1916.

[30] Various authors, *Tribute to Ely Theological College 1876–1964* (privately printed, n.d.), p. 29.

recorded, but the anecdote does reveal something of the mental world of the canon professors.

By the 1950s the University was beginning the process of removing the restrictions which limited the tenure of the three divinity professorships to priests of the Church of England. It was decided to secularise the Lady Margaret chair, and to make the Regius and Ely chairs open to men in priest's orders in any province of the Anglican Communion. The Chapter responded by pointing out that from whatever part of the Anglican Communion the Ely Professor might come, he would still be expected to take an oath of allegiance to the Queen.[31] If the Chapter had thought that change would stop there, they were mistaken. In less than twenty years, it became apparent that any continuing link between the University and the Cathedral was most unlikely to be sustained. In 1973, just two years after his appointment, the Ely Professor Christopher Stead indicated to the Chapter that he thought that he would not be replaced, and they began negotiations with the Chairman of the Divinity Faculty Board to retain the link between the two institutions in some other form.[32] In 1978 Professor Stead put forward a three-pronged proposal, whereby either a canonry would be permanently assigned to a university teaching officer (not necessarily from the Divinity Faculty), or a new post (analogous to that of High Bailiff) would be created for him, or the teaching officer would be given some other Cathedral post. This scheme did not make much headway, and may even have been killed off by other members of the Chapter, who appeared to favour a vacant canonry being assigned to a clergyman occupying a diocesan post.[33] After Stead's retirement in 1980, little evidence remained of the historic link between the Ely Dean and Chapter and the University of Cambridge.

The Cathedral Foundation

The period under discussion saw the reduction in the number of residentiary canons from eight to four,[34] and since 1980 the number has been reduced to two. But Ely Cathedral was always far more than the Dean and Chapter, powerful though they were. At the beginning of the period, the residentiary canons each resided for roughly two months every year, and lived elsewhere at other times. Until 1938 they continued with two-month periods of residence, but with the difference that by then they were living in Ely all year round, presumably attending the Cathedral on a regular basis, even when not 'in residence'. After 1940, when the number of canons was reduced from six to four, periods of residence became shorter and more frequent.

It was the minor canons who provided continuity and maintained the daily round of worship in the Cathedral. For part of the period they were also heavily involved in teaching, initially at the Cathedral grammar school (later known as the King's School) and then at the choristers' school. Until 1878 there were five minor canons, who also occupied the statutory offices of *praelector theologicus*, epistoler, sacrist, sub-sacrist, precentor, registrar, auditor and librarian. In addition to their duties at the Cathedral

[31] EDC 2/2A/10, p. 330, 30 January 1954.
[32] EDC 2/2A/12, p. 118, 1 December 1973, p. 126, 6 April 1974.
[33] *Ibid.*, p. 267, 4 March 1978.
[34] Two canonries were suppressed in 1853 and 1854, as a result of the Cathedral Act, 1840; one was suspended in 1938, and another was suppressed at the end of Professor Raven's tenure in 1940.

they took charge of the Dean and Chapter chapelries and parishes of Prickwillow, Chettisham, Stuntney, Ely Holy Trinity and Ely St Mary's. Two minor canons dominated the cathedral in the first half of the nineteenth century: John Griffiths and George Millers. Both performed their duties from 1800 to 1850, in which year they were permitted a form of semi-retirement that involved the appointment of deputies approved by the Dean.[35]

At the beginning of the period the minor canons had to rely on a patchwork of payments derived from each of their statutable offices. George Millers was the best paid, largely because he had managed to accumulate many of these offices (Plate 32c). He received £32 10s. as minor canon, £40 as divinity lecturer, £8 as epistoler, £1 6s. 8d as sacrist, £2 as librarian, £3 6s. 8d as registrar and £10 as under-master at the grammar school. He was also perpetual curate of the nearby hamlet of Chettisham. Millers held the livings of Hardwick in Cambridgeshire and Runham and Stanford in Norfolk, but he chose the busy life of a minor canon in preference to the more leisurely pace of an East Anglian vicar.[36] The other minor canons at this date obtained far less than Millers for their Cathedral duties. William Crawley Leach was the worst remunerated. He had no house, and received just £15 for his minor canonry and a paltry £2 for undertaking the responsible position of Precentor.[37] Not surprisingly, all the minor canons held livings outside Ely, in addition to their perpetual curacies in the town and its neighbouring hamlets. This method of financing the minor canonries was regarded as unsatisfactory; from the 1840s until 1855 the Dean and Chapter repeatedly pressed the Ecclesiastical Commissioners to pay the minor canons a fixed stipend of £150, believing that this was their obligation under section 45 of the Cathedral Act.[38] After 1861 new appointees were required to forsake the old statutable payments in exchange for a flat-rate annual stipend of £150, which the Dean and Chapter paid out of their own funds.[39] It was around this time that the Cathedral authorities began to give the minor canons grants to pay for assistant curates in their Ely parishes.[40] The minor canons were evidently expected to be fully occupied by their duties at the Cathedral.

In 1852 the Cathedral duties were separated from those of the grammar school. The Revd John Ingle was the first person to be appointed explicitly to teach in the grammar school, and to perform no other duty.[41] For those minor canons who had previously been involved in teaching, life had been hectic. In 1833, it had been stipulated that the fifth minor canon should teach five hours a day at the school, and that he should read the service in the choir on Sundays, surplice and saints' days, during Passion week, on Christmas day, and on other, specially appointed thanksgiving and fast days.[42] From 1843, he had also been required to preach the Sunday afternoon sermons during the summer, and to read or

---

[35] EDC 2/2A/6, p. 116, 15 June 1850.

[36] EDC 2/12/2. Information supplied to the Ecclesiastical Revenues Commission, 1832.

[37] *Ibid.* Leach was Precentor, 1827–33 (EDC 2/2A/5, pp. 247, 317); he was also Curate of St Mary's at £30 *p.a.*, and Vicar of Dilham and Honing in Norfolk. In the 1850s the precentor's stipend began to rise rapidly, reflecting the greater demands that were being made upon him. In 1866 it was raised from £200 to £250 'in consideration of his zeal and attention to the service of the church' (EDC 2/2A/7, p. 75, 26 November 1866).

[38] EDC 2/2A/6, p. 186, 29 January 1855.

[39] *Ibid.*, p. 312, 25 November 1861.

[40] *Ibid.*, pp. 305, 320, 15 October 1861 and 14 June 1862.

[41] *Ibid.*, pp. 135, 147, 9 March and 11 August 1852.

[42] EDC 2/2A/5, p. 315, 25 November 1833.

chant the litany whenever it was required. He had received an additional payment from church funds for these additional duties.[43] The arrival of a steady flow of clerical schoolmasters from 1852 evidently caused friction with the minor canons, in a way that hints at the tensions between the introspective members of the Cathedral Foundation. On 25 November 1853 the Dean and Chapter's Order Book recorded:

> The question of precedence between the Masters of the Grammar School and the Minor Canons, as well as between the Precentor and the Minor Canons, having been again brought under our notice, agreed that though by the letter of the Statutes it appears that precedence is assigned to the Upper Master, and also to the Lower Master, in case he should be M.A., and though the governance of the Church Service, assigned to the Precentor, may seem to imply a right of precedence over the other Minor Canons; on taking all the circumstances into consideration, we are of opinion that the practice which has prevailed in our Cathedral, of taking precedence according to seniority of appointment, is the best calculated to secure peace and good order and therefore recommend all the Members of our Establishment to adhere to it. We are further of the opinion that the Masters of the Grammar School are not entitled of right to any participation in the performance of the Services of the Church.[44]

Similar tensions are also hinted at by Harvey Goodwin, Dean from 1858 to 1869 (Plate 35b): 'We were not without our troubles, sometimes arising from the Minor Canons, sometimes from the School and Schoolmasters, sometimes from the Lay Clerks; but in all cases in which a matter was sufficiently serious to be brought before the Chapter, I had the Canons with me and never found myself left in the lurch'.[45]

The death in 1852 of George Millers, who had held so many of the statutable offices, acted as a catalyst for various changes, including a greater strictness about the minor canons' attendance at services.[46] The office of registrar was given to a layman, Hugh Evans, many of the traditional registration fees were abolished, and a new scale of sealing fees was established. The money raised from this was used to put the library on a sounder financial footing.[47] Millers's wealth and his goodwill towards the Cathedral that he had served for over half a century, were reflected in the fact that he left enough money to make possible the commencement of the painting of the nave ceiling.[48]

In 1881, the Dean and Chapter, acting on a recommendation from the Diocesan Conference, decided to alter dramatically the conditions of employment for minor canons.[49] They began an experiment of appointing them for fixed terms of three years,

---

[43] EDC 2/2A/6, p. 17, 7 January 1843.

[44] *Ibid.*, pp. 169–70, 25 November 1853. See also p. 284, 14 June 1860, when the matter resurfaced, and EDC 2/2A/7, p. 229, 30 April 1878. On this occasion the archdeacons raised the matter of their order of precedence in processions, apparently asserting that they should be placed immediately after the Bishop, and before the Dean and Chapter.

[45] Goodwin, *Memoir of the Life* (cit. in n. 21), p. 165.

[46] EDC 2/2A/6, p. 135, 9 March 1852.

[47] *Ibid.*, p. 137.

[48] EDC 2/2A/6, pp. 132–3. Millers left nearly £100,000, including £100 to the Cathedral, a sum which his executors augmented with another £300.

[49] Ely Diocesan Conference 1880, *Report of the Committee on 'Relations of Ely Cathedral to the Diocese'* (1880), p. 3. It recommended 'a more rapid succession' of minor canons, with the office becoming tenable for not more than seven years, with the possibility of re-election in the case of the Precentor.

advertising for suitable candidates in the High Church newspaper *The Guardian* and in the *Musical Times*. Thus in the 1880s minor canons came and went with a rapidity that must have bewildered those who remembered the old regime of fifty-year tenures. By the late 1890s the Chapter appeared to be finding that non-renewable fixed term appointments were not altogether satisfactory; perhaps they had found that they were losing good men for no very good reason. They began to appoint minor canons for three-year probationary periods, after which they would be formally appointed for a further term.[50] By the early years of the twentieth century, the Chapter returned to its policy of appointing for indefinite periods (it would adopt seven-year appointments in 1950). It also resumed another previously abandoned practice, that of requiring two of the minor canons to devote considerable time to teaching; now at the choristers' tiny school. This was an indication of the rapidly declining state of the Chapter finances, and the pressing need for fewer men to take on more tasks. Thus Seiriol Evans (Plate 49*b*), appointed in 1923 as minor canon, Precentor and sacrist on a stipend of £300, was paid a further £100 for being schoolmaster, when Edmund Boulter, the lay schoolmaster, retired.[51] In the previous year the number of minor canons had been reduced to three, and by 1929 the job appeared to have become so unattractive that it was only possible to fill a vacancy for a combined minor canonry and assistant mastership after it had been readvertised, and on condition that the appointee have voice training and singing lessons.[52] This was a far cry from thirty years earlier, when there had been considerable competition to fill the vacant post of Precentor.[53] In 1939, at a time when the number of residentiary canons was contracting to four, it was decided that the number of minor canons be reduced to two, one to act also as Precentor and headmaster of the choristers' school for a combined salary of £335, the other to be also sacrist, second master and Cathedral librarian for a combined salary of £340.[54] During the latter part of the Second World War, and again in the 1970s, the Cathedral had to manage with just one minor canon, pressing the Bishop's chaplain into service in an honorary capacity. After the war, the number was briefly increased to three, until the mid-1950s, when it was reduced to two minor canons.

About seventeen clergy lived in Ely in the second half of the nineteenth century, all dependent to some degree upon the Cathedral. The Cathedral Foundation, of course, included laymen as well as clergy, and others not on the Foundation depended on the Cathedral for their livelihood. In the 1830s there was an Organist, eight lay clerks, eight choristers, six bedesmen (Plate 45*b*), two vergers, an organ tuner, a regulator of the Cathedral clock, a bridge reeve, a purveyor, a cook, a barber and a porter. There were also four rent collectors and thirteen bailiffs, and other servants who were employed to set out seats in the Cathedral, to clean and care for the fabric and the walks, and to

[50] EDC 2/2A/8, p. 113, 14 June 1898; p. 178, 25 November 1903.

[51] EDC 2/2A/9, p. 144, 27 March 1923. Seiriol Evans later became Dean of Gloucester. He had an interesting Anglo-Catholic pedigree as the much-loved nephew of J. Arthur Price. See Frances Knight, 'Welsh Nationalism and Anglo-Catholicism: the Politics and Religion of J. Arthur Price', in Stewart J. Brown and Robert Pope (eds.), *On Naming Ourselves: Religion and National Identity in Scotland and Wales c.1730–1930* (forthcoming).

[52] EDC 2/2A/9, p. 267, 12 January 1929.

[53] EDC 2/2A/8, p. 85, 21 October 1895.

[54] EDC 2/2A/10, p. 119, 12 September 1939.

maintain the brewery.[55] The brewery was managed by one of the vergers, and operated in the lower part of the Porta. The Chapter continued to have their beer privately brewed until the late 1850s, when Dean Goodwin decided that an easier method was 'a post-card sent to Burton-on-Trent'.[56]

The Cathedral remained a major local employer well into the twentieth century, and certain Ely families were involved with it over many decades. The Kempton family supplied generations of choirboys and lay clerks. The early nineteenth-century Ely solicitor Hugh Robert Evans occupied the highly important role of chapter clerk and steward for fifty years, and was succeeded by his son of the same name. They also served as diocesan deputy Registrars and (after E.B. Sparke's death in 1879) Registrars. Evans senior lent large sums of money to the Dean and Chapter.[57] His elegant granite-topped grave in the Dean and Chapter plot at Ely Cemetery is testimony not only to his own wealth but also to the fact that the Cathedral had literally been indebted to him. Evans junior was the layman appointed registrar on the death of George Millers,[58] and after his death in 1871, the appointment, together with that of chapter clerk, passed to another family member, William Johnson Evans, who held them until 1929, when they passed to Ernest Robert Evans.[59] The Evans family's 170-year relationship with the Dean and Chapter lasted until Ernest's retirement in 1960.[60] The Bidwells were another prominent Ely family who passed the posts of Chapter surveyor, and then agent, from father to son, in an arrangement that began in 1881 and lasted until the 1960s.[61] Although the number of residentiary and minor canons shrank dramatically, in other respects the make up of the Foundation changed relatively little. In 1980 there was an Organist, an assistant organist, six (rather than eight) lay clerks, between twelve and twenty choristers, twelve King's scholars, twelve Queen's scholars (girls from the King's School), two vergers, six bedesmen, a chapter clerk, a registrar, a steward, and a high bailiff.

In 1865, Bishop Harold Browne (later Bishop of Winchester), whose episcopate at Ely was characterised by various important innovations, made a new addition to the Cathedral Foundation when he appointed Ely's first two honorary canons. He was using powers given him by the 1840 Cathedral Act, which his predecessors had disdained to use.[62] The new honorary canons were W.B. Hopkins, Vicar of St Peter's, Wisbech, and James Fendall, Vicar of Comberton, Rector of Harlton and a rural dean. Doubtless they were exemplary clergy deserving recognition for their long years of service in the diocese; the appointment of honorary canons went some way to giving a form of professional recognition to a profession that had hitherto lacked such badges.

[55] EDC 2/12/2, replies to the Ecclesiastical Duties and Revenues Commission, 30 March 1835.

[56] Harvey Goodwin, *Ely Gossip* (Ely, 1892), p. 5.

[57] EDC 2/2A/5, p. 342, 19 February 1836; p. 365, 25 February 1836; p. 378, 25 November 1837; p. 424, 15 June 1840; 2/2A/6, p. 144, 14 June 1852; p. 164, 6 July 1853.

[58] EDC 2/2A/6, p. 136, 9 March 1852.

[59] EDC 2/2A/7, p. 149, 25 November 1871; EDC 2/2A/9, p. 282, 1 November 1929.

[60] EDC 2/2A/11, p. 59, 2 January 1960. Evans's request for a pension was turned down, and he was sent £50 instead. The Dean and Chapter appeared not to recognise that this was the end of the momentous reign of the Evans family. The manager of the Ely branch of Barclay's Bank was appointed chapter clerk in his place. See also Dorothy M. Owen, *Ely Records* (Cambridge, 1971), pp. ix–x.

[61] EDC 2/2A/7, p. 273, 14 June 1881; EDC 2/2A/9, p. 138, 10 January 1923.

[62] 3 & 4 Vict. c. 113 para. 23.

Over the next few years Browne gradually increased the number of honorary canons, until there was a maximum of twenty-four (later reduced to twenty). It is not clear, however, to what extent the arrangement really benefited either the honorary canons or the Cathedral. The honorary canons were busy parochial clergy, many being also rural deans, who could devote little time to Ely, although some made useful deputies in place of sick residentiary canons.[63] The residentiaries appeared uncertain of how to regard their newly-elevated brethren, and seemed prone to forgetting to include them, or to informing them of Cathedral activities, something which continued to be a problem even after the Second World War.[64] In 1928 an arrangement was established whereby the honoraries were invited to Ely once a year to attend the St Etheldreda festival, to dine or lunch with the residentiaries, and to participate in the annual Greater or General Chapter.[65] They also received some invitations to preach at the Cathedral at other times in the year, although it was noted in 1961 that honorary canons should receive more frequent invitations.[66]

Worship at the Cathedral

At the heart of the Cathedral's life was its daily, weekly and annual cycle of worship, which changed steadily but almost imperceptibly during the 144 years under considera- tion here. In 1836, five months after his appointment, Bishop Allen expressed some dissatisfaction with the way in which the Dean and Chapter discharged their respons- ibility for worship: 'I observe that there is no sermon in the Cathedral in the afternoon [on Sunday]. I take it for granted that this is according to ancient usage. But I submit to your serious consideration, whether with a population in this City of upwards of 6000 souls, and in these times, when there is such a disposition to undervalue the established religion in general, and Cathedrals in particular, there ought not to be two sermons every Sunday in the Cathedral.'[67] Allen had further reservations about worship at Ely, disliking the atmosphere in the choir, which seemed to him more like a private chapel than a place of public worship, and also the use of 'too much modern Musick'. He wanted only words taken from the Bible or the Book of Common Prayer to be sung: 'at present some of the services, though very good in point of Musick, partake very much in terms of Mass Services; and the words are not very devotional'. His final request was that the service times remain the same, and not be altered at the whim of the canon in residence. The Dean and Chapter responded coolly to what they no doubt regarded as unwarranted interference. They informed the Bishop that additional sermons would lead to congregations becoming extremely variable, depending on the popularity of the preacher, and would interfere with the services in the two parish churches (both of which were in the immediate vicinity). Unsurprisingly, the Precentor's examination of the Cathedral music had yielded few texts that were not derived either from the Bible or

---

[63] EDC 2/2A/7, p. 293, 14 June 1883: Honorary Canon Brereton was allowed to keep residence in July 1883 during Benjamin Hall Kennedy's illness.

[64] EDC 2/2C/1, 17 October 1946: 'It was put forward that Hon. Canons would welcome being invited by the Dean to be present at services connected with the installation of new members of the Chapter'.

[65] EDC 2/2A/9, p. 255, 6 July 1928.

[66] EDC 2/2C/1, 17 October 1961. The first record of honorary canons being invited to preach is in 1908.

[67] EDC2/11/1836/1, Bishop Allen to Dean Wood, 2 November 1836.

the Prayer Book. The times of the services depended on the light levels, and varied between three and five o'clock.[68] In the following year, they did experiment with an evening sermon preached in the choir during the summer.[69] Sunday evening service with sermon continued to be a central part of the Cathedral's worship, although the time, and sometimes also the location within the Cathedral, were altered fairly frequently over the years. From time to time the Chapter experimented by holding both afternoon and evening services on Sundays, apparently in the hope of attracting different types of worshippers. Bishop Allen seems to have made no further attempts at intervention in Cathedral worship, and nor did any of his successors, until Bishop Lord Alwyne Compton tried in 1888 to prevent the choir from having a day off on Mondays.[70]

It had been the custom at Ely since at least the middle of the eighteenth century for Sunday morning prayers to be said simultaneously in the choir of the Cathedral, in the Lady Chapel (which served as the church for Holy Trinity parish until 1938) and in St Mary's church. The three congregations then joined together under the Octagon, at about eleven o'clock, to hear a sermon[71] (Colour pl. 9). The practice had ceased by Dean Goodwin's time (1858–69), but he had had it described to him: 'The worshippers from the Parish Churches, as I was told, usually arrived in the Cathedral before "College Prayers" as the service was called, were finished, and walked about the nave until the time for the sermon came . . . I gathered that the custom was a very social one, and that the news and gossip of the day were freely discussed while the Church ambulant was waiting for its spiritual food.'[72] Maria Upcher, the daughter of Canon Edward Sparke, also remembered the sermons under the Octagon in her childhood: 'When all was ready the curtain was drawn and the ladies stepped forth [from the choir]. We sat in very high narrow benches, deal, covered with shabby green baize . . . In front of us sat the clergy and the Bishop, by himself . . . Sometimes when we came out from the Choir the congregation had not settled into their places and some would be walking up and down the nave, which I have heard tell was the custom during the waiting time.'[73] For more than a century, this Sunday morning meeting of the three congregations had been the climax of each week's worship in the Cathedral. Its abandonment may have been linked to the introduction of lengthier choral services, which would have made it harder to synchronise timings between the three congregations, or it may have been due to a feeling that the old custom had become more social than devotional. Whatever the reason, the change must have affected all of Ely's Anglican worshippers, distancing the St Mary's congregation in particular from the Cathedral. By 1855, the Sunday morning sermon was preached under the Octagon only during the summer months, and it is not clear whether the other congregations attended.[74] In the same year, Dean Peacock informed the Cathedrals Commission that Sunday morning service was at half past ten and evening service was at four, both with sermon. The weekday services were at the

[68] EDC 2/11/1836/2, Dean Wood to Bishop Allen, 30 November 1836.
[69] EDC 2/2A/5, p. 371, 14 June 1837.
[70] EDC 2/2A/7, p. 348, 6 April 1888.
[71] Edmund Carter, *The History of the County of Cambridge, from the Earliest Account to the Present Time* (Cambridge, 1753), p. 62.
[72] Harvey Goodwin, *Ely Gossip*, p. 55.
[73] EDC 14/30, Maria Upcher, 'Reminiscences of Ely', 1893.
[74] EDC 2/2A/6, p. 194, 14 June 1855.

same hours, and all the services were fully choral. Holy Communion was administered at the three great festivals, and on the third Sunday of every month, as had been the custom for at least seventy years. Peacock made it clear that he would be happy to countenance a weekly communion with sermon and Litany, but only if that service were separated from morning prayers. Rolling all into one produced an intolerably long two and a half hours of choral liturgy, 'much too great for persons not in robust health'.[75]

Dean Peacock seemed to adopt a fairly pragmatic approach to the changes in cathedral worship associated with the mid-nineteenth century. Since the 1730s the minor canons had read, rather than sung, the service. In the 1840s, newly appointed minor canons were expected to sing it.[76] No one had thought of assessing the singing ability of minor canons until 1840. In the mid 1850s, the three senior minor canons (John Griffith, Solomon Smith and William Clay) read the service, but it was intoned by the more musical and recently appointed James Henderson (the Precentor) and George Hall. As has already been stated, it was the minor canons who were responsible for the day-to-day performance of services. The Dean and Chapter oversaw the arrangements, and preached sermons if they felt so disposed. If they were unwilling or unable to preach, a minor canon would do so in their place, usually for a fee of a guinea. Every Friday the Precentor had to submit 'to a member of Chapter the combination paper', detailing the music to be sung at the services in the week following, and after it had been approved by him no changes could be made.[77] According to Maria Upcher, this system was introduced because 'it was considered most arbitrary when Mr Henderson had abrogated to himself the entire right of choice, though he was always ready to put down any specially desired anthem'.[78] Thus the Dean and Chapter maintained control over worship in the Cathedral, without the necessity for direct involvement, although there seems to have been an expectation that the Canon in residence would normally be present at most services. At least two of the minor canons were required always to be present.[79]

Liturgical change came gradually to Ely. In 1870, the pattern was Mattins with sermon at half past ten, the psalms sung to Anglican chants. Evensong without sermon was at four o'clock, and at half past six a 'parochial service' was held, organised by the vicar of Holy Trinity. Holy Communion was administered every Sunday, at an early hour. Thirty years later, at the turn of the century, the pattern had changed little, although on Sunday afternoons a service comprising the Litany, hymns and anthems took place at four o'clock, and Evensong with sermon was at half past six.[80] Holy Communion was also now celebrated on holy days, Thursdays, and the first Friday of each month, all at a quarter past eight in the morning. By 1930, Sunday Holy Communion was celebrated both at an early service and again at eleven, when it was linked with Mattins and a sermon. Evensong and sermon were still at half past six, but the four o'clock service had disappeared, the Litany having been moved to eight in the morning.[81]

With the exception of those Canons who acted also as Principal of Ely Theological

---

[75] *Answers from the Dean and Chapter of Ely to the Cathedral Commission* (1855), p. 166.
[76] W.E. Dickson, *Fifty Years of Church Music* (Ely, 1894), pp. 64–5.
[77] EDC 2/2A/6, p. 169, 25 November 1853.
[78] EDC 14/30, Maria Upcher, 'Reminiscences'.
[79] EDC 2/2A/6, p. 149, 1 October 1852.
[80] This change took place in 1888.
[81] This change took place in 1924. The weekly rendition of the Litany was discontinued in 1970.

College (opened in 1876, closed in 1964), which was a distinctly Anglo-Catholic institution, most members of the Chapter seem to have been conservative in liturgical matters. Those who wished to move the Cathedral in a higher direction made gifts of vestments, in the hope that they would be used, but such items were seldom adopted straight away. Bishop Lord Alwyne Compton presented a cope when he retired in 1905, but in 1913 the Dean and Chapter were still unresolved as to whether or not they should wear it. In that year they did, however, decide to permit lights on the altar at choral eucharists, at early celebrations and at Evensong on Saturdays, Sundays, festivals and the eves of festivals.[82] The question of copes was settled in 1921, when it was decided that they should be worn by celebrant, epistoler and gospeller at Communion services held in the choir, and by the celebrant alone at services held in the side chapels.[83] This decision was prompted by a gift of three copes from a minor canon, Herbert Campion.

At this date, when Anglo-Catholicism was reaching its high point, the adoption of Catholic practices proved deeply problematic for some members of the Chapter. In October 1925 Canon Professor Kennett tried to prevent the singing of Latin anthems, and the Chapter was moved to put the issue to a vote, something which it almost never did. As a compromise, it was decided that Latin should only be sung on weekdays.[84] Next month detailed instructions were issued concerning the level of ritual permitted at celebrations of Holy Communion in the side chapels, with the injunction that the same level of ceremonial should be used there as at the high altar, and the warning that there should be no kissing of stoles, altars or books, or genuflecting during the prayer of consecration.[85] It would seem that the minor canons, who were usually responsible for the early services in the side chapels, were trying to shift the tone of worship at Ely in ways unacceptable to at least some among the Dean and Chapter.

The range of churchmanship within the 1920s Chapter was wide, and tensions were probably real. At the Low Church end of the spectrum were Professor Robert Kennett, George Evans (who was to vote against the Cathedral being used for a service to mark the centenary of the Oxford Movement)[86] and Professor John Martin Creed, who was remembered for being hostile to what he perceived as the theological students' veneration of the Virgin Mary[87] (Plate 51b). At the High Church end was Berkeley William Randolph, who had been Principal of Ely Theological College, and before that domestic chaplain to Edward King, the prosecuted ritualist Bishop of Lincoln. Under Randolph's leadership, the devotional ethos of the Theological College had become very different from that of the Cathedral. He had introduced vestments back in 1905, cunningly taking advantage of the interregnum before Bishop Chase was appointed. In the 1920s, the College day was constructed around the Roman offices, beginning with prime at seven o'clock and ending with compline at half past nine. Randolph's two successors at the College, Henry Leighton Goudge and Charles John Smith, were also High Church members of the 1920s Chapter. It seems that the Ely Chapter, which had

---

[82] EDC 2/2A/8, p. 327, 25 November 1913.
[83] EDC 2/2A/9, p. 104, 5 January 1921.
[84] *Ibid.*, p. 196, 30 October 1925. This issue resurfaced in 1969, when the Precentor was formally reminded that only English was acceptable on Saturdays, Sundays and festivals (EDC 2/2A/12, p. 26, 25 January 1969).
[85] EDC 2/2A/9, p. 201, 25 November 1925.
[86] *Ibid.*, p. 348, 25 November 1932.
[87] *Tribute to Ely Theological College* (cit. in n. 30), p. 30.

apparently been untroubled by matters of churchmanship during the nineteenth century, was to deal with disagreements in this area fairly regularly throughout the twentieth. In 1936, they were forced to take another vote, this time on the sensitive issue of using communion wafers in place of ordinary bread. Professors Creed and Raven dissented from the majority view by voting in favour of retaining the bread.[88]

Other changes in the ethos of the Cathedral's worship were gradually introduced. 1873 was the year in which the festival in honour of St Etheldreda was revived, as part of the celebration of the twelve-hundredth anniversary of the foundation[89] (Plate 45a). It developed into a twice-yearly event, on 23 June and 17 October, of considerable significance in the life of the Cathedral. The Revised Version of the Bible, which was a very limited revision of the Authorised Version, published in the 1880s, was adopted at Ely in 1908, and the Revised Standard Version in 1969.[90] The *New Cathedral Psalter* made an appearance in 1918[91] and the revised lectionary in 1922.[92] The Precentor made an unsuccessful attempt to persuade the Dean and Chapter to replace *Hymns Ancient and Modern* with the more liturgically comprehensive *English Hymnal* in 1924, but the latter hymnbook was not adopted until 1948.[93] Copies of *100 Hymns for Today* were purchased in 1973.[94] In 1937 it was agreed to relegate the Athanasian Creed to use on Trinity Sunday only, and to omit the controversial verses about unbelievers perishing in everlasting fire.[95] It is intriguing that it should have taken the Cathedral so long to respond to disquiet about the Athanasian Creed. More than sixty year earlier, in 1873, Bishop Browne had framed a question in his Ely diocesan visitation articles explicitly about dislike of the Athanasian creed, and the answers revealed that a small but nevertheless significant proportion of the diocese's churchgoers, particularly in the larger Bedfordshire parishes, did indeed object to the creed being used. Some parishes had stopped using it, as for example St John's, Bedford.[96]

Under the leadership of Lionel Blackburne (Dean, 1936–51) the voice of cautious low churchmanship remained in the ascendant at Ely (Plate 52a–b). Vestments for the Lady Chapel were turned down, because 'we did not wish to alter our present practice'.[97] The Dean himself would never wear vestments in any circumstances. Bishop Wynn's offer of a new altar service book was also turned down, because he was offering the 1928 Prayer Book with its High Church revisions, rather than the authorised 1662 version.[98] In 1947 the Dean and Chapter dispensed with the long-standing tradition of choral Mattins on weekdays, a decision based not on liturgical considerations, but on post-war educational attitudes, which were no longer sympathetic to the notion of choir boys missing school. The boys were no longer local lads who were indentured to apprenticeships

[88] EDC 2/2A/10, p. 66, 3 October 1936.
[89] Charles Merivale, *St Etheldreda Festival. Summary of Proceedings with Sermons and Addresses at the Bissexcentenary Festival of St Etheldreda at Ely, October 1873* (Ely, 1873).
[90] EDC 2/2A/8, p. 259, 25 November 1908; 2/2A/12, p. 26, 25 January 1969.
[91] EDC 2/2A/9, p. 44, 14 March 1918.
[92] *Ibid.*, p. 129, 20 September 1922.
[93] *Ibid.*, p. 159, 8 January 1924, & 2/2A/10, p. 235, 28 August 1948.
[94] EDC 2/2A/12, p. 95, 13 January 1973.
[95] EDC 2/2A/10, p. 75, 23 February 1937.
[96] EDR C3/40, Ely visitation articles, 1873.
[97] EDC 2/2A/10, p. 114, 18 July 1939.
[98] *Ibid.*, p. 149, 22 December 1941.

when their voices broke; they had been transformed into public schoolboys whose education had to be put above the demands of singing. The scrapping of choral Mattins also coincided with the incorporation of the choristers' school into the King's School. At the same time, weekday Evensong was moved from four o'clock to half past five, in order to permit the lay clerks to take on full-time work.[99] This was a frank admission that the lay clerks could no longer be expected to live on their Cathedral stipends, which had barely increased over the decades.[100] Post-war Sunday congregations were small; sometimes they were outnumbered by the clergy and choir.[101]

In early 1951 Patrick Hankey arrived as Dean (Plate 58a). He was a rigorous Anglo-Catholic, previously Vicar of Little St Mary's in Cambridge, and his arrival marked an immediate change in the Cathedral's worship, for he had no qualms about imposing the observances he valued. The Sunday morning schedule became exacting. A Communion service was said at a quarter past eight; Mattins was sung at half past ten, and a choral Eucharist followed at half past eleven, sung throughout including the collects, epistle and gospel as well as the Creed. Full Catholic ceremonial was adopted; the priest at the altar was attended by deacon and subdeacon, all fully vested. Some second-hand vestments were obtained from St Mary's, Bourne Street, a well-known centre of London Anglo-Catholicism. The servers, who during term time were students from the Theological College, wore Roman-style cottas with broad lace edgings. Victorian anthems, which had previously been favoured, gave place to sixteenth- and seventeenth-century settings. Hankey's aim was a dignified act of worship in the medieval tradition; the numbers who attended from the town continued to be small. For the ordinands, however, the arrival of Dean Hankey signalled a welcome change. For the first time, Cathedral and College were moving liturgically in the same direction. Indeed, Hankey relied on the students to encourage other members of the congregation in ceremonial matters, on one occasion pinning up a notice requesting that students attending the Good Friday three-hour service should give a lead by coming forward to kiss the cross at the newly-introduced ceremony of Veneration of the Cross. Hankey smiled on the newly stirring liturgical movement, and from 1951 he allowed the students to celebrate the Easter vigil in the Cathedral, kindling the new fire under the west tower (to the evident anxiety of the head verger). The darkness and coldness of the Cathedral, the faintly detectable incense, the echoing sound of the plainsong propers and the flames of the new fire made a lasting impression on some students. In the early 1950s this ancient ritual was a major innovation in the Church of England, being at that date otherwise observed only by the Community of the Resurrection at Mirfield.[102]

During the 1950s Ely Cathedral moved in a progressively Anglo-Catholic direction. In September 1951, the Hon. Mrs de Saumarez presented a statue of the Blessed Virgin Mary, and the gift, rather than being sent back to the donor, as would surely have happened a year or so earlier, was set up in the vestibule of the Lady Chapel, though it

[99] EDC 2/2C/1, 17 October 1947.
[100] In 1963, the lay clerks' stipends were increased from £200 to £250. In 1967 they were raised to £300, and in 1973 to £400.
[101] Recollection supplied by Pamela Blakeman.
[102] This paragraph is based on recollections supplied by Christopher Stead, Reg Macklin, Victor de Waal and John Bone.

was later moved to the south choir aisle.[103] In 1953, the Dean and Chapter introduced a chrism mass for Maundy Thursday, and made plans for the sacrament to be permanently reserved in the Cathedral. Another event in 1953, the service to mark the coronation of Elizabeth II, was the first recorded example of the Dean and Chapter inviting Ely's Free Church ministers to join them in the Cathedral. Next to the minute of this decision someone has written in pencil '? RC priest'. It is not clear whether Ely's Roman Catholic priest was invited, but it seems likely that the Dean and Chapter would have welcomed him. Roman Catholic and Orthodox priests from Europe (particularly France) were frequent visitors to the Theological College at this period, which was then flourishing (for the last time as it turned out) under its principal Henry Balmforth. An Orthodox liturgy was celebrated in the Lady Chapel in 1958. It was said that even the future Pope Paul VI visited Ely at this time, as a guest of Balmforth. Catholic-Anglican relations remained good and deepened in 1978, when the local Catholic parish were permitted to hold services in the Lady Chapel, when their own church was undergoing repair.[104] By the 1970s, the Cathedral was being regularly used by the Free Churches for various events, from Salvation Army Band concerts to Baptist retreats. Patrick Hankey remained Dean of Ely until 1969, and was succeeded in the following year by Michael Carey, who had previously been Archdeacon of Ely and Rector of St Botolph's, Cambridge (Plate 58b). Carey, although a moderate Anglo-Catholic, was, as one of his contemporaries in the Chapter put it, 'able to distinguish between the type of worship which he himself preferred, and that which he considered best for the Cathedral in its diocesan setting'.[105] He knew that the Free Churches were strong in the city of Ely, and that Evangelicalism was strong in the diocese, particularly in Cambridge. He wanted to make the Cathedral a place where different types of worshippers – the high and the low – could feel at home. Under Carey's influence the Cathedral moved towards a more central style of churchmanship. The Series 1 and 2 Revised Communion Service became the main Sunday service, with the collects, lessons and Creed said, rather than sung. The more modern Series 3 was used on selected weekdays. The Eucharist now took place in the Octagon, which was equipped with altar and choir stalls designed by George Pace. Lady members of the congregation were invited to read the lessons for the first time in 1975. The celebrant was simply attended by the Precentor acting as server, and incense was restricted to midnight Mass on Christmas Eve. Sunday Mattins was discontinued. Carey is remembered as the Dean who opened the Cathedral to the people of Ely. He introduced coffee after the main service, and for the first time, regular worshippers began to regard the Cathedral as a place in which to feel comfortable, and the clergy as friends. Carey and his wife also hosted enormous Boxing Day sherry parties for the citizens of Ely at the deanery. Before his time, communication between clergy and congregation was strictly limited.[106] The celebration of the thirteen-hundredth anniversary of the foundation, in 1973, provided a perfect opportunity to invite the city to take a greater interest in the Cathedral; it was estimated that the number directly

[103] EDC 2/12/10, p. 280, 8 September 1951.
[104] EDC 2/2A/12, p. 268, 4 March 1978.
[105] Recollection supplied by Christopher Stead.
[106] Recollection supplied by Pamela Blakeman.

involved in the celebrations, including children, ran into tens of thousands[107] (Plate 61*a*). In the 1970s, in defiance of national trends, the size of the congregation began to increase, and there was a particularly dramatic increase in the number of children attending the Cathedral. Carey responded by forming a Sunday Club for them, which provided activities for the first forty or so minutes of the service, before they rejoined their parents for the Communion.[108]

Chapter finances

In the early decades of the nineteenth century, anyone fortunate enough to be collated to a prebend at Ely would have known that financial worries were a thing of the past. The Dean and Chapter of Ely were substantial landowners, and they used the income derived from their land and property to maintain both the Cathedral and themselves. They owned different types of property, some of it in Ely, some of it much further afield. In Ely, they owned the substantial houses in which they lived during their periods of residence, and other houses, in which Cathedral staff lived. They owned the buildings occupied by the King's School, cottages and closes in Broad Street and elsewhere in the town, and the Crown and the Club public houses. They possessed estates and farms all over East Anglia, and various tenements in London.

The Dean and Chapter's income was generated partly from rents, but chiefly through fines imposed on tenants for the renewal of leases, at seven, twenty-one or in some cases, forty-year intervals. Annual revenues fluctuated wildly from year to year, depending on how many of the leases were up for renewal. Capitular incomes therefore need to be considered over at least a seven-year cycle. The Ecclesiastical Revenues and Duties Commission investigated both the annual average based on the previous three years' income, up to the end of 1831, and the amounts received and spent over the previous seven years. Calculated on the basis of the previous three years, the Ely Dean and Chapter's gross annual income was declared in 1832 to be £8,625 6*s.* 10*d*, of which £5,684 15*s.* 2*d* had come from fines on the renewal of leases. This latter figure is important because the whole of it, together with some smaller dividends, entered what was known as the onus account, and from there went directly into the pockets of the Dean and Chapter. They divided it into ten, one share to each of the eight prebendaries, and a double share to the Dean. Only the money raised from rents and legacies was paid into the domus or church account, and this was used for paying stipends and for repairs to the Cathedral and College buildings. Calculated over the same three-year period, their annual expenditure (the dividend they paid to themselves together with their expenditure on stipends and repairs) was declared to be £8,882 12*s.* 7*d*.[109] If further sums were required for maintaining the fabric, they either borrowed it, usually from Mr Evans, the chapter clerk, or they transferred a sum from the onus to the domus account, a practice that became more common as they felt it necessary to spend more on maintenance. Their declaration of expenditure over the previous seven years reveals the extent of the fluctuations inherent in the dependence on fines for renewals of leases.

---

[107] *Friends of Ely Cathedral Year Book*, 30th Annual Report (1973), p. 11.
[108] Recollection supplied by Denis A. Adams.
[109] EDC 2/12/2, p. 18. Replies to the Articles of Enquiry from the Ecclesiastical Revenues Commission, 1832.

From the Dean and Chapter's point of view, the best year was 1831, when the Dean took £1,932 from the onus account, and each prebendary took £966. The worst year was 1830, when the Dean took £429 and the prebendaries £214. Spending on maintenance varied hugely, from £298 in 1829, to a massive £2,390 in 1833, most of which went on a new iron bridge over the river Ouse. The Dean and Chapter were expected to pay for major civic projects in Ely at the beginning of the nineteenth century. As the years went on, they began to withdraw from this type of activity, although it was not until 1907, when the bridge had become unsafe and dilapidated, that negotiations for its take-over were completed with Ely Urban District Council.[110] Leaving aside the year in which they financed the bridge, average annual spending on the fabric in the early 1830s was about £450, rather less than individual chapter members could expect to take for themselves.

It was apparent from the Ecclesiastical Duties and Revenues Report that the greatest drain on Ely's revenues was the maintenance of the capitular body itself. It was this recognition that led to the passing of the Cathedral Act in 1840, the reduction in the size of cathedral chapters, and the redirection of their finances. Cathedral reform and capitular finances were therefore closely related. Although the 1840 Act gave the Ecclesiastical Commissioners a share of Ely's capitular wealth through the transfer of funds from suppressed prebends, it did not restrict the canons' activities as landowners, and they continued to manage their estates as before. They continued to rely on fines paid for lease renewals, and their incomes continued to fluctuate, often by as much as a thousand pounds; fat years were worth about £1,400, lean ones only around £400.[111] It needs to be remembered that payments from the Dean and Chapter's onus account represented only one portion of the annual incomes of this generation of Chapter members. All had significant income from other sources, and the Sparke brothers in particular were very wealthy indeed. A little glimpse of the scale of J.H. Sparke's household may be had from the 1851 Census return. He happened to be in residence at Ely at the time when the census was taken, together with his wife, daughter, German governess, butler, footman, groom and six female servants, all of whom came from Norfolk, and were presumably usually based with the rest of the household on the Gunthorpe estate.

By the 1850s there was a growing feeling that this annual lottery of fluctuating income was not the best way for the Dean and Chapter to manage their personal finances. In his submission to the 1855 Cathedrals Commission, Dean Peacock recommended the introduction of fixed stipends for existing and future members of the Chapter, as long as provision was made for 'great changes in the value of money'.[112] This important transition came in 1869. Under the terms of the Ecclesiastical Commission Act passed in the previous year, the Dean and Chapter negotiated the commutation of most of their estates.[113] The Act abolished the old system of fines for the renewal of leases, and the bulk of Chapter estates were transferred to the Commissioners, who swiftly re-endowed the Chapter with estates whose income was calculated to be adequate to their statutory

---

[110] EDC 2/2A/8, p. 209, 25 November 1905; p. 236, 7 November 1907.
[111] This observation is based on the sums paid to William Selwyn and Edward Bowyer Sparke over the period 1836–70. See EDC 3/15/4, Dean and Prebendaries private accounts.
[112] *The Cathedral Commission: Remarks of the Dean and Chapter of Ely* (1855), p. 649.
[113] EDC 2/2A/7, p. 111, 14 June 1869.

needs.[114] It was a bargain, struck for the mutual benefit of both parties.[115] By the autumn of 1869, the Ecclesiastical Commissioners had transferred to the Dean and Chapter estates in the parishes of Ely St Mary, Witchford, West Lynn (Norfolk), and Fleet and Gedney (both in Lincolnshire). The Dean and Chapter also retained a further fourteen pieces of land, most of which were in the Isle of Ely or Cambridgeshire.[116] When Dean Merivale arrived at Ely in 1870, Hugh Robert Evans (the younger) drew up a document to help him understand the Chapter finances. Evans explained that the property of the Dean and Chapter now consisted of the Cathedral precincts, certain estates held on beneficial leases that would become rack rent estates when the existing leases expired, estates already let at rack rents, tithe rent charges, stock investments, certain small annual payments, a temporary annual payment of £5,200 from the Ecclesiastical Commissioners and ecclesiastical patronage.[117] Thus the Dean and Chapter continued to be involved with land and property for some years to come, although the amount of time that they devoted to their management was far less than it had been earlier in the century, when discussion of such matters was the most time-consuming item at Chapter meetings. Most of the remaining estates were sold off in 1915, and the proceeds were invested by the Ecclesiastical Commissioners in government war loan stock.

The annual fixed payment agreed under the terms of the 1868 Act set the income of each canon at £800, with £1,600 to the Dean and £760 to be paid into a reserve fund, to be used for contingencies.[118] This was a generous remuneration for the day, but the sum remained substantially unchanged for the next hundred years, and sometimes capitular revenues were insufficient to meet even the statutory minimum. In 1930, the canons' gross income was only £776 each, reduced to £607 after tax.[119] In 1933, the Chapter began negotiation with the Ecclesiastical Commission for the transfer of the residue of their estates; the Commissioners offered them an annuity of £1,248 in exchange.[120] It was not until 1963 that the Church Commissioners (as they now were) took direct responsibility for paying the salaries of the Dean and two residentiaries.[121] From the late nineteenth century, the Dean and Chapter slid from opulent gentility to genteel poverty. They still lived in their fine medieval houses, but they became increasingly reliant on their own resources for household repairs.[122]

[114] G.F.A. Best, *Temporal Pillars: Queen Anne's Bounty, the Ecclesiastical Commissioners, and the Church of England* (Cambridge, 1964), p. 459.

[115] Lewis T. Dibdin and Stanford Edwin Downing, *The Ecclesiastical Commission: A Sketch of its History and Work* (London, 1919), pp. 40–1.

[116] EDC 8A/12, commutation papers – 'Ely Chapter Estates Commutation: plans . . . dated 7 October 1869.'

[117] EDC 8B/1/1, *An Account of the Estates and other Property of the Dean and Chapter of Ely prepared for the Information and Use of the Very Reverend Dr Merivale on his appointment to the Deanery of Ely, and of his Successors, by H.R. Evans, Chapter Clerk and Receiver, January 1870.*

[118] EDC 2/2A/7, p. 112, 14 June 1869.

[119] EDC 3/6B/9.

[120] EDC 2/2A/10, p. 5, 4 April 1933; p. 20, 17 March 1934; p. 26, 14 May 1934.

[121] EDC 2/2A/11, p. 232, 17 August 1963.

[122] EDC 2/2A/8, p. 34, 15 June 1891. It was agreed that no more than £5 from Chapter funds could be spent on any one house in any year.

Continuity and change at Ely Cathedral

The life of the Cathedral changed slowly, but steadily, between 1836 and 1980. There were at least six distinctly different generations of the Dean and Chapter, and a sketch of the characteristics of each is a good way to summarise the change that occurred. The first one was the generation of Dean Peacock, the Sparkes, Fardell, Jenyns and William Selwyn: nine wealthy men who resided at Ely periodically, but who were regarded as of significance in the Church, at a time when the Church was regarded as of significance in society. They had to cope with the threat posed by the Ecclesiastical Commission, as well as with the physical transformation of the Cathedral fabric which took place from the 1840s onwards. Some of the younger members of this first set – Selwyn and the Sparke brothers in particular – lived until the 1870s, when they were replaced by a distinctive second generation, that of Dean Merivale (Plate 43*a*), Herbert Luckock (the Theological College's first principal), Edward Clarke Lowe, William Emery (Plate 46*a*) and Frank Chapman. This generation lived entirely at Ely, and their interests were much more centred upon it. Having lost much of the influence that their predecessors had enjoyed in the wider world, they turned in more on the Cathedral and the diocese. Emery, having taken part in the first Church Congress in 1861, also played a leading role in the campaign for a diocesan assembly. Chapter meetings, increasingly free of estate management, became much briefer, and the meetings themselves more frequent. On the whole, these high Victorian years were a confident time (Plate 50*a*). The Cathedral had itself in order, and the institution seemed robust. In 1879, in what was a moment of great satisfaction for those present, Dean Merivale announced that the construction of the Cathedral was finished. 'The Dean reported to the Chapter that yesterday morning the last stone of the pinnacles of the octagon was laid by his eldest daughter Mary Sophia Merivale, and the great work of Alan de Walsingham was pronounced to be complete.'[123]

In the years before the First World War, the third generation embarked on what was to be another lengthy period of continuity within the membership of the Chapter. Dean Kirkpatrick[124] presided from 1906 to 1936, in the earlier period in the company of Michael Glazebrook, Berkeley Randolph, Henry Goudge, George Hodges, and Professors Vincent Stanton and Robert Kennett. As has been shown, these men did not all share a common style of churchmanship, and tensions hitherto not seen at Ely came to the surface. The fourth generation, still with Kirkpatrick at the helm, emerged in the mid-1920s, and included John Martin Creed, George Evans, Charles Smith and Horace McCartie Eyre Price, one of a number of former colonial bishops who returned to Ely to serve as assistant bishop in the diocese. This interwar Chapter was the last to enjoy a relatively leisurely life at Ely; tennis parties were a regular feature of Chapter life.[125] Smith, the Theological College Principal, was also remembered for his fast driving. Requests for permission to build garages and fit bathrooms began to feature in

---

[123] EDC 2/2A/7, p. 247, 18 October 1879.

[124] Alexander Francis Kirkpatrick (1849–1940) was a Fellow of Trinity College, Cambridge, 1871–82; Regius Professor of Hebrew and Canon of Ely, 1882–1903; Master of Selwyn College, Cambridge, 1898–1907; Lady Margaret's Professor of Divinity, 1903–6; and Dean of Ely, 1906–36.

[125] This phase was over by 1951, when the Chapter tennis court reverted to the Park. EDC 2/2A/10, p. 273, 27 March 1951.

Chapter discussions. In view of the straitened state of the Chapter finances, at least some members would appear to have had adequate private means for these projects. Electricity came to the houses in the college in 1928 but was installed in the Cathedral much later, between 1938 and 1946.

The arrival of the fifth generation coincided roughly with the Second World War. The suspension of canonries in 1938 and 1940 put the remaining members under greater pressure. Shortage of manpower, firewatching, the vulnerability of Ely's exposed position and the need to accommodate evacuees in Chapter properties caused a greater disruption to the rhythm of the Cathedral's life than the First World War had done. Presided over by Dean Blackburne, the dominating personalities were Gordon Walsh, formerly Bishop of Hokkaido, who was at Ely from 1942 to 1967, Henry Balmforth, at Ely from 1942 to 1956, and Edward Ratcliff, Ely Professor of Divinity from 1947 to 1958. For the first time, a layman played a significant role in the management of the cathedral. He was Sir Will Spens, former Master of Corpus Christi College, Cambridge and a relation by marriage of the Selwyns. In retirement he became the tenant of the Old Sacristy, and was given the title of Chapter Steward, with a brief to advise on financial matters. He was allocated his own stall in the Choir, and in processions took his place after the honorary canons and before the Headmaster of the King's School.

It was during the 1950s that the Cathedral began to come to the attention of a wider world. It was used for television and radio broadcasts from 1952, and in 1956 the Argo Record Company discovered the delights of recording in the beautiful acoustic of the Lady Chapel. The Cathedral shop had its origin in this period, when the SPCK asked for permission to set up a tract table to sell literature during the summer months of 1952; the shop was put on a commercial footing in 1968, when a trading company was formed.

The sixth and final distinctive generation coincided with the 1960s. It consisted of Dean Hankey, Professor Geoffrey Lampe (who favoured ecumenical co-operation and the ordination of women), Bernard Pawley (who was often away, as the Archbishop of Canterbury's representative at the Second Vatican Council) and Robert Martineau, the Bishop of Huntingdon. The 1960s generation gave more attention to the needs of visitors, and the concept of the Cathedral as a destination for modern pilgrims emerged for the first time. In 1961, the Dean prepared 'experimental material' for use with pilgrimage groups.[126]

The 1960s were a decade of change for the Cathedral, just as they were for society at large. Aspects of Cathedral life that had endured for centuries seemed to lapse quite suddenly. The night watchman, for example, was given one month's notice in 1965, on account of the need to save money and because 'present day conditions did not call for the services of a night watchman'.[127] The decades-long involvement of the Evans and Bidwell families also ceased at this time. In 1966 the large, hand-written calf-bound Chapter order books gave way to a typewriter and a loose-leaf ledger. In the late sixties, the Cathedral developed quite rapidly into one of East Anglia's major concert venues: performances were given by internationally acclaimed artists, and it was used as an outpost of the Aldeburgh Festival. Increasingly, requests to hold events in the Cathedral had to be turned away, simply because of lack of space in the diary.

---

[126] EDC 2/2A/11, p. 124, 29 March 1961.
[127] Ibid., p. 297, 5 April 1965.

The 1970s, by contrast, were a period of uncertainty for the Cathedral, as it grappled with the implications of Britain's worsening economic crisis. The Dean and Chapter went deeper into their overdraft, and began to undertake only urgent repairs. Money that had been raised from the sale of part of the Cathedral library, supposedly to finance choral scholarships, was diverted instead into emergency work on the west tower. In 1975 they debated the possibility of introducing admission charges, thus calling into question what had long been a deeply cherished principle at Ely, that access to the Cathedral must always be free. Unable to reach a decision one way or the other, the matter was deferred, and it was decided instead to have notices printed asking visitors to donate 'at least 20p'.[128] The sum was raised to 30p in 1979. The very low level of remuneration that the Cathedral offered meant that by the late 1970s staff resignations were becoming an increasing problem. Yet despite the economic pressures, the Dean and Chapter threw themselves into preparations for the enthronement of their new bishop, Peter Knight Walker, in 1977. It appears to have been the most complicated and carefully organised service that they had ever held, with a congregation of 2,500, extra microphones, car parking labels, rehearsals, and arrangements to ensure that the Cathedral was free of suspect packages.[129] The contrast with the workaday events of August 1836, when Canon Jenyns went through the installation and enthronement ceremony as the proxy of Bishop Allen, could not be more striking.[130]

At what point did Ely come closest to the vision that George Augustus Selwyn had had for it in 1838? The answer must be 1913. If Selwyn had returned to Ely then, he would have found much that he had dreamt of in place. He would have seen the boys of an enlarged and well-equipped King's School living in the shadow of the Cathedral. He would have met the ordinands of the Theological College, which was flourishing under Canon Randolph. He would have approved of the Dean and Canons of the 'third generation'; all resident, and most in robust mid-life. Dean Kirkpatrick (previously Master of Selwyn College) and Professors Kennett and Stanton were all three deeply engaged with theological scholarship. Canon Hodges was drawing on his recent experience as archdeacon to take a continued interest in the diocese. Canon Goudge was concerned with the running of the Cathedral, and Canon Glazebrook with its finances. Relations with Bishop Chase were perhaps not as warm as Selwyn would have wished, but undoubtedly he would have recognised Ely as the place for which he had provided the blueprint seventy-five years earlier.

---

[128] EDC 2/2A/12, p. 151, 7 March 1975.
[129] *Ibid.*, pp. 252–3, 1 October and 2 November 1977.
[130] EDC 2/2A/5, p. 360, 24 August 1836.

Cathedral Restoration:
Fabric and Furnishings 1836–1980

PETER MEADOWS

'Disgraceful irrepair and disfigurement'

In November 1834 Bishop Sparke announced a gift of £2000 to provide stained glass for the east window of the Cathedral. 'As some time must necessarily elapse before any glass suitable for this purpose can be procured I shall invest the money in the names of my sons and desire them to undertake the management for me.'[1] Bishop Sparke's gift was gratefully received at the November Chapter,[2] and Dean Wood returned a gracious reply, saying 'We have long been desirous of seeing this object accomplished, it being the only requisite for the completion of the interior of the cathedral', and acknowledging the renewed liberality of the Bishop.[3] Sparke had already paid for much ochre wash applied to the walls, stonework and roofs, and for the chocolate-brown staining of the medieval choir stalls.[4]

Despite Dean Wood's identification of the east window glass as 'the only requisite', several commentators had pointed out the serious state of disrepair into which the Cathedral had fallen by 1834. George Millers, author in 1807 of *A Description of the Cathedral Church of Ely*, criticised the south-west transept, used as a workshop, 'now blocked up with stud and plaster work' and 'much defaced, by being propped, cramped, screwed, and tied together in every part, and in various modes'.[5] Of the nave roof he wrote: 'few persons will . . . think it a beauty and an excellence. It is, in truth, a very great blemish. All is open and visible'; the stone vaulting-shafts supported 'nothing

---

[1] EDC 2/2A/5, p. 236, copy letter, Bishop Sparke to Dean Wood, 24 November 1834. An account book of the trustees of Bishop Sparke's fund is in Norwich, NRO, UPC 310.

[2] Neither of the Bishop's sons was present.

[3] *Ibid.*, p. 327, copy letter, Dean Wood to Bishop Sparke, November 1834.

[4] John Bacon's book, EDC 4/6/2, fos. 4–5. Bernasconi painted the walls in 1823, 'in bad taste and in such a way that it cost more to take it off than it did to put on'.

[5] George Millers, *A Description of the Cathedral Church of Ely* (Ely, 1807), pp. 46–8. Millers (1776–1852) was a minor canon of Ely, 1800–52 (Plate 32c). As well as serving at various times in many of the offices attached to the minor canonries, he was Vicar of Stanford (Norfolk), 1808–45, Vicar of Runham (Norfolk), 1811–52 and Rector of Hardwick (Cambs.), 1825–52. He ran a private school in Ely for many years, and in the late 1840s inherited the Duddon Grove estate near Ulverston from his nephew. At his death his personal wealth was sworn for probate at £100,000 (Prerogative Court of Canterbury, 24 January 1852, *ex inf.* Timothy Cockerill).

more seemingly ponderous . . . than a set of rafters'. Millers suggested, but without much hope, 'a plain vaulted stone roof'.[6] He recognised that Chapter funds should be spent on repairs, to counteract 'the injuries of time', to prevent 'further decay' and to improve what stood 'in a mean, squalid and neglected state'.[7] An example of the mean and squalid could be seen in the south transept, 'lumbered with benches', which were brought out at sermon time.[8]

Millers approved of the removal of the choir from the Octagon that had been effected in 1769, 'so desirable an alteration',[9] and he commended Essex's careful repair of the medieval stalls. He could not however praise Essex's reredos. 'It is to be wished, that the old work had been as well studied and as successfully imitated . . .[in] . . . the altar-screen . . . an eye accustomed to the examination of ancient workmanship, will easily detect some forms which could not have existed in a real work of the age intended to be imitated. Some of the arched facings applied to the pannels, are positively semicircular . . . why was there any screen at all? Probably the stone-work of the east end is ornamented below the windows.'[10] The paint covering the Purbeck marble shafts was deplorable. 'It is really wonderful, that such a monstrous depravity of taste should have existed in our days. This abomination must have been committed when the choir was removed . . . that all might be spruce and trim, and fit to be seen.'[11]

The third edition of Millers's *Description* appeared in 1834, the year of Bishop Sparke's benefaction. In 1830, William Cobbett visited Ely and 'walked round the beautiful Cathedral, that honour to our Catholic forefathers and that standing disgrace to our Protestant selves . . . [it] is in a state of disgraceful irrepair and disfigurement. The great and magnificent windows to the east have been shortened at the bottom, and the space plastered up with brick and mortar . . . for the purpose of saving the expense of restoring the glass in repair. Great numbers of the windows . . . have been partly closed up in the same manner and others quite closed up'.[12]

Bishop Sparke – or his sons, for it is doubtful whether the Bishop was capable of vigorous intellectual thought by 1834[13] – might have read Cobbett, and would undoubtedly have known Millers's work; and the east window, with its incomplete stained glass scheme, would have seemed a suitable object for his benefaction. There is little evidence that his elder son John Henry Sparke, a canon since 1818, had artistic or antiquarian leanings. His younger son Edward Sparke, appointed to a canonry in 1829, had a greater impact on the Cathedral, and poured money into its restoration for forty years. In the mid 1830s, however, both brothers were much absent from Ely, serving as domestic chaplains to their father in his declining years at Ely House in London.

When 'T.C.' visited Ely in 1843, he was struck by the evidence of neglect everywhere. As he reported in *The Athenaeum* in 1845, 'I could not help lamenting the serious dilapidations, which the cathedral was daily undergoing, and the worse than useless

---

[6] Millers, *A Description of the Cathedral Church of Ely*, pp. 50–1.
[7] *Ibid.*, pp. 54–5.
[8] *Ibid.*, p. 62.
[9] *Ibid.*, pp. 70–1.
[10] *Ibid.*, pp. 78–9.
[11] *Ibid.*, p. 87.
[12] William Cobbett, *Rural Rides*, 2 vols. (London, 1830), II, pp. 229–30.
[13] Doubts were raised about Sparke's mental state in 1831, when the Archbishop of Canterbury had to testify to Sparke's lucidity in the House of Lords (see p. 212, n. 127).

repairs which in several places evinced a feeble attempt to arrest them. Every part of this edifice . . . has from time to time, fallen under the degraded taste of ignorant economy; and, instead of repairs accomplished in the spirit of architecture, we have brickwork in place of stonework, pointed tracery under Roman arches, and Italian doorways inserted side by side with windows filled with zig-zag mouldings . . .'[14]

Nothing was done about the fabric before Dean Wood died in 1839.[15] Bishop Sparke died in 1836, and was buried in a vault in Bishop West's Chapel. There in 1838 his family erected a Gothic altar-tomb at the east end as a monument, carved by Humphrey Hopper, 'a perfect imitation of that of the Black Prince in Canterbury Cathedral, and the canopy of Bishop Mitford's, in Salisbury Cathedral';[16] and above it a stained glass window by David Evans of Shrewsbury depicting the Evangelists and St John the Baptist. The window, supposedly of surpassing awfulness, was replaced in 1938 with glass by Sir Ninian Comper (Plate 54a).

Dean Peacock

George Peacock, appointed Dean in 1839, was the driving force behind the restoration which affected every part of the Cathedral after 1840 (Plate 35a). After many years Ely had a Dean who had neither parish (though he accepted the Chapter living of Wentworth in 1847) nor the headship of a Cambridge college, and Peacock made Ely his permanent home. In university administration Peacock was a reformer (although he held his professorship virtually as a sinecure), and he numbered among his Cambridge friends Professor Robert Willis, a noted antiquary and expert on the structure of buildings (Plate 36a). Peacock had a highly developed artistic and archaeological sense; he and Willis did much investigative probing in the Cathedral before restoration started.[17]

Peacock's papers have not survived, but his letters reveal aspects of his thinking.[18] Certainly he was passionately interested in, and knowledgeable about, architecture. Sir Gilbert Scott recalled that, when he was appointed architect at Ely in 1847, Dean Peacock had extolled to him the beauties of Amiens Cathedral, which he had recently visited, and inspired Scott to see for himself – when, as he wrote, 'My eyes were at once opened. What I had always conceived to be German architecture I now found to be French.'[19]

[14] *The Athenaeum*, 1845, p. 571. The identity of T.C. is not known.

[15] James Wood (1760–1839) was Master of St John's College, Cambridge, 1815–39, and was a generous benefactor to his college.

[16] *Cambridge Chronicle*, 30 June 1838, which adds 'A superb monument . . . in memory of our late benevolent Bishop . . . it is of excellent workmanship . . . and worthy of admiration.' I am indebted to Pamela Blakeman for this reference. Humphrey Hopper (1767–c.1842), 'a competent, indeed occasionally a very good, sculptor', failed in his large-scale works; but some of his smaller monuments 'have charm and distinction and well-carved reliefs, although the majority of his later tablets are unfortunately poor works in spiky "Gothic".' Rupert Gunnis, *Dictionary of British Sculptors, 1660–1851*, revised edn (London, 1968).

[17] George Peacock (1791–1858) was a Fellow of Trinity College, Cambridge, from 1814 and Lowndean Professor of Astronomy and Geometry 1837–58. Robert Willis (1800–75) was Jacksonian Professor of Natural and Experimental Philosophy 1837–75; for an analysis of his writings, see N. Pevsner, *Some Architectural Writers of the Nineteenth Century* (Oxford, 1972), pp. 52–61.

[18] About 160 letters survive from Peacock to Edward Sparke, mostly about stained glass but also referring to the restoration of the Cathedral generally. Norwich, NRO, UPC 301.

[19] Sir George Gilbert Scott, *Personal and Professional Recollections*, revised edn by Gavin Stamp (Stamford, 1995), p. 146.

Much had been achieved in the Cathedral, and more was in hand, before Scott's appointment. Peacock and Willis were studying the structure and decoration of the Cathedral, and were poring over the muniments, in particular the account rolls, which revealed much about the surviving medieval fabric.[20] They were considerably assisted by David Stewart, a disciple of Willis, who evinced a great ability to read the rolls and to sketch architectural details, and who published an architectural history of the Cathedral in 1868[21] (Plate 37a). Stewart's drawings increased in competence as time went on, and he tried his hand at design also, being largely responsible for the restoration of Prior Crauden's Chapel in 1848, and suggesting the form of pinnacles for the Cathedral's east gable (one only of two was built, to Edward Blore's design and with Alexander Beresford Hope's money, in 1846)[22] (Plate 37b–c).

In November 1843 Edward Sparke offered £200 for the opening up and restoring of the south-west transept, 'the workshop', a donation accepted by the Chapter as 'this signal mark of his affection for our church'.[23] Sparke was to obtain plans and estimates, and although there was talk of employing Blore, Robert Willis, from his 'profound knowledge of the principles and details of ecclesiastical architecture',[24] was able to supply the designs for repairing the Norman window openings, arches and blank arcading, which time and rough treatment had damaged or hacked away. A flat, panelled ceiling was installed, covering the fir roof of 1790,[25] and was painted with a simple pattern of lozenges (overpainted by Gambier Parry in 1878).[26] The effect of the reopened transept was much praised by the *Illustrated London News*, which published an engraving of it in 1845[27] (Plate 5a).

'T.C.' reported in *The Athenaeum* in June 1845 that the transept was 'literally crammed with masons at their labours'; and in the choir 'a chaffern-fire was burning,

---

20   See CUL, MS Add. 5026, fos. 24–30, letters from Peacock to Willis, n.d. (*c.*1844), for a flavour of this collaboration.

21   David James Stewart (1814–98), of Trinity College, Cambridge, was a minor canon of Ely and also curate of Adderbury (Oxon.), 1843–8. He was one of H.M. Inspectors of Schools, 1851–91. His book, *On the Architectural History of Ely Cathedral* (London, 1868), is a mine of information, and might as well be described as a 'documentary' as an 'architectural' history, thus bearing witness to Stewart's proficiency in reading and interpreting the archival evidence.

22   Stewart's drawings are EDC 14/36, and his papers are EDC 14/37. Evidence for his involvement in the pinnacle project, and other works of restoration in the Cathedral, is found in a letter from Willis to Stewart, *c.*1844, CUL, MS Add. 5103/I/47–48, 'I send you a tracing of all that I have relating to the east gable . . . P.S. As to the canopies over Luxemburgh, pray *clean* them and leave them alone.' Drawings by Stewart, showing the effect of the east end with both turrets added, are EDC 14/36/2/24–5. The turrets are very similar to the one executed by Blore in 1846. Scott considered the design not quite right: 'finding that it did not accord with existing evidences, I made many fruitless attempts to design one which would': *Ely Diocesan Conference . . . July 22, 23, 1874 . . . General Summary of Proceedings* (Ely, 1874), p. 28. Is it fanciful to suppose that Stewart hoped to become Cathedral architect, and to recreate the golden age of the priest-architect as evinced by Alan de Walsingham?

23   EDC 2/2A/6, p. 26.

24   John Bacon's book, EDC 4/6/2, fo. 31. Bacon (d.1888) was clerk of works 1845–88, having succeeded his father, who was clerk of works for 27 years. Bacon designed the church at Prickwillow, and restored such churches as Witchford, Sutton, Lakenheath and Thetford, of which the Dean & Chapter were patrons.

25   This was Blore's work. *Cf.* his account book, CUL, MS Add. 3955, fo. 14v, 2 June 1844, 'Journey to Ely to arrange new roof for South West transept . . . Drawings sent for the same excluding estimate and specifications.'

26   Possibly not completed. The *Handbook to the Cathedral Church of Ely* (Ely, 1852), p. 17, states: 'The painting of some of the panels in the ceiling is for experiment only'. Designs for this ceiling survive in EDC 4/5/165–7 (Colour pl. 24a) and CUL, MS Add. 5103.

27   *Illustrated London News*, 27 September 1845, pp. 197–8.

tall scaffold frames were standing near, and three or four workmen were rubbing and polishing pillars of Purbeck marble, while others were stopping the holes and gaps which had been perhaps wantonly hacked upon them.' The Cathedral 'from the western porch to the east windows . . . is covered with one universal coat of stone-coloured wash, if we except the six pillars of the ante-choir. These are of light-coloured Madrapore marble, and support some of the richest arch-work conceivable, all blunted and discoloured with ochrey wash.' But 'when the degrading lime-wash, under which the sharpness and character of the choir at Ely is lost, shall be removed it may be readily conceived how admirable the colour as well as the clearness and design of this part of the cathedral will appear. The mouldings, foliage and ribs have been so drenched by the brush and lime-pail that they appear as if they had emanated from a worn-up mould, whereas originally they must have presented the sharpest lines and finest contrasts.'[28]

Jesus College offered in 1844 to repair the chapel of Bishop Alcock (their founder), the soft stonework of which had been badly worn or mutilated through time.[29] This was renewed where necessary but figures too thoroughly mutilated were not restored. The north window was filled with fragments of medieval glass from Jesus College, and Minton encaustic tiles made their first appearance in the Cathedral, in the chapel's pavement. A carved oak door on the north side was presented by Edward Sparke, 'the work of a Feltwell youth', otherwise unrecorded.[30]

In 1844 Peacock and Willis resolved to tear down the reredos, which John Bacon described as Essex's 'unmeaning lath-and-plaster screen . . . indifferent in its design and incorrect in its immitation [sic] of the Gothic'. Everything was washed, repaired and decorated. The Purbeck marble columns were carefully gritted and polished.[31] Corbels and roof bosses were coloured and gilded, St Peter over the original high altar, and St Etheldreda over the site of her shrine, and shields were painted heraldically. In 1845 the choir stalls were dismantled, and Bishop Sparke's dark graining was painstakingly removed.[32]

Work went on in other parts of the cathedral. In 1844 Bishop Joseph Allen gave a set of communion plate and two altar chairs, the latter designed by Robert Willis and executed by Ollett[33] (Plate 36b–c). In 1844 also the east window of the west tower octagon, which had been blocked with brick and rubble to shore up the unstable fabric,

---

[28] T.C., 'Ely Cathedral' (cit. in n. 14), p. 571.

[29] William French (1786–1849), Canon of Ely since 1831, was Master of Jesus College. John Bacon was executant and clerk of works. There is no sign of involvement by Pugin, who was then restoring Jesus College chapel, so it is likely that architectural direction for Alcock's Chapel was by Willis and Stewart. I am grateful to Frances Wilmoth for searching the Jesus College archives.

[30] Details from John Bacon's book, EDC 4/6/2, fos. 135–6. The design of the door is derived from the late medieval door from the south transept into the canons' vestry, which had been brought from Landbeach by Henry Fardell in 1840.

[31] John Bacon described the process in intricate detail in EDC 4/6/2, fo. 96. Willis made designs for stone arcading and an altar under the east window (EDC 14/36/1/15–17).

[32] John Bacon's book, EDC 4/6/2, fos. 97–8. Men had to be trained specially in the technique of Purbeck marble polishing.

[33] Ollett: a Cambridge carpenter? CUL, MS Add. 5026, fo. 28, Peacock to Willis, 24 December [c.1843–4], 'The chairs are admirably executed and are very effective and beautiful: the sides with the arms are particularly beautiful.' The chairs are now in the Almonry restaurant; designs for them are EDC 14/36/1/2–6. Willis designed also a simpler Gothic chair, 'frequently copied', of which at least one was made, in deal.

was opened, restored and reglazed.[34] In 1845 Hugh Evans, Chapter clerk, gave £100 for Cathedral restoration, which was used to continue the strengthening of the west tower. A lath-and-plaster vault, erected in 1802 above the tower arches, was removed, revealing the rich arcading above. The clock and bells were moved up higher, and much old stone, brick and rubble 'strengthening', which had perilously increased the weight of the tower, was removed, and a system of iron ties and supports was devised. During this work George Basevi, architect of the Fitzwilliam Museum in Cambridge and Parsons's almshouses in Ely, was invited by Dean Peacock to ascend the tower with him and inspect the improvements.[35] On 16 October 1845 Basevi tripped in the belfry and fell through a hole in the floor, 36 feet on to the plaster vault, and was killed instantly. He was buried in the north choir aisle at the Chapter's expense.[36]

With the altar screen removed and the presbytery scraped, washed, and polished, the project to reposition the choir could go forward. No one pressed for its retention at the east end; but there was considerable debate, in *The Ecclesiologist* and other architectural and antiquarian publications, about where it should go. Some writers urged that the pre-1775 arrangement of the choir stalls, across the Octagon, should be recreated; however the weight of opinion favoured an open vista in the Octagon and a position for the stalls at the west end of the choir, with a screen across the opening from the Octagon. This would allow the formation of a retrochoir and ambulatory at the east end.[37]

Prior Crauden's Chapel was Stewart's particular responsibility. It had long been subdivided into rooms for the Eighth Canonry, which was held from 1800 by George Jenyns. Willis made some investigations in 1839, when he found mason's marks on a stone which enabled him to project the form of the destroyed ceiling vault. Jenyns fell ill and was excused residence and Chapter attendance after 1840;[38] and the opportunity seems to have been taken to begin the Chapel's restoration, for in 1842 the domestic partitions were removed, and the Chapel was revealed, in John Bacon's words, to be 'a mutilated wreck' with 'some portions left to bear testimony of its former beauty'.[39] With Willis's advice, and funding provided by J.B. Sharpe, Dean Peacock was able to begin restoration in 1846, when Stewart was sufficiently skilled to be allowed to direct it.[40] The south side of the Chapel was relatively unscathed, and provided a model for the matching but much damaged north side. The east window was restored with little difficulty, but the west window had been mostly cleared away, and its design had to be reconstructed from fragments. The vault was reconstructed in wood, not stone; and the

---

[34] The blocking crashed to the floor in high winds in November 1844, after Willis had removed some of the blocks (CUL, MS Add. 5026, fo. 27).

[35] Basevi had previously surveyed the tower (EDC 14/37B/1, D.J. Stewart's draft essay on the Cathedral in the 18th and 19th centuries).

[36] Details from John Bacon's book, EDC 4/6/2, fo. 18. The earliest account is in the *Cambridge Chronicle*, 18 October 1845.

[37] *The Ecclesiologist*, viii (1847), pp. 58–9. J.W. Hewett, *A Brief History . . . of Ely* (Ely, 1848), p. 11, favoured a return of the stalls to the Octagon.

[38] EDC 2/2A/5, p. 407.

[39] EDC 4/6/3, John Bacon's book 'The College', fo. 56.

[40] Stewart, *Ely*, pp. 245–8, gives full details of the restoration. According to Stewart, in EDC 14/37B/1 (cit.in n. 35), Sharpe's motive in funding the restoration was that he intended the building as a chapel for a theological college which he hoped to found there.

medieval tiled pavement was carefully restored. Sharpe's sister Lady Smart bought five Italian stained glass panels of apostles for the east window, designed a light of the Holy Ghost descending as a dove, and commissioned Ward and Nixon to fill the tracery lights (Colour pl. 13*d*). When the Chapel was completed in 1850 it was assigned to the Cathedral School for services.

Stewart took great pride in his restoration, and prepared a volume of lithographs, tracings and photographs in which he claimed that the work had been done 'entirely under my direction'.[41] A monograph was intended, and Day & Hague prepared the lithographs, but the plan failed (Plate 37*c*). To save money in the restoration, the Chapter insisted on the use of clunch for all stonework. This soft stone was ideal for delicate interior carvings, but was useless for external work, and by 1875 the window-tracery had to be renewed in more durable stone. Further repairs, and new furnishings, were provided in the mid-1880s, funded by G. Winkfield and designed by G.F. Bodley.[42]

Sir Gilbert Scott

The need for a professional architect was now felt. Late in 1847 Peacock wrote to George Gilbert Scott offering him the commission for the choir work.[43] Scott was at the beginning of his successful career, and Ely was his first cathedral (Plate 39*a*). If the Chapter had wanted experience, Edward Blore, who had worked at various cathedrals and had been involved in minor works at Ely since 1840, might have been a safe choice.[44] The decision to employ Scott was, however, never seriously regretted. Peacock had occasional misgivings;[45] and when in 1848 Edward Sparke ventured to suggest changes to Scott's screen design, including the use of stone instead of wood, he was slapped down by Scott in a magisterial letter.[46] Thereafter Sparke was left in charge of

[41] EDC 14/36/3.
[42] EDC 4/5/148–150.
[43] He was not the automatic first choice. Sketches by Willis (EDC 14/36/1/18–41) show that he was working on the positioning of the choir stalls, the provision of western return seats for the Dean and Bishop, and a screen. He also made designs for an organ on the north side, east of the stalls, not above them, and for a Gothic-style pulpit. Stewart also made sketches for the repositioning of the choir and its furnishings: he wished to place the organ two bays east of the stalls (EDC 14/36/2/39–45). In summer 1847 Edward Sparke sounded out A.W.N. Pugin, the Roman Catholic architect and controversialist, who was then restoring Jesus College Chapel. Pugin said that he would be surprised but delighted to receive the commission, but the negotiations came to nothing (Norwich, NRO, UPC 301/17).
[44] Edward Blore (1787–1879) refitted the choirs at Peterborough 1828–32, and Ripon 1829–31, and was refitting the choir at Westminster Abbey 1843–48, of which building he was surveyor 1827–49. His account book, CUL, MS Add. 3955, fo. 14ᵛ, records journeys to Ely, on 19 August 1840 'to make a survey of the cathedral with reference to the stability of certain parts and general improvements contemplated', and 5 May 1841 'to meet the Dean relative to various contemplated improvements'. Blore's survey, if it was ever presented, has not survived.
[45] *E.g.* Norwich, NRO, UPC 301/90, Peacock to Sparke, 22 March 1851, 'I by no means feel myself bound to think Mr. Scott's taste perfect: far from it: I feel there are many imperfections in his work . . . but I have no entire faith in any architect: Pugin would probably have done better, if we durst have employed him: but he would probably have led us into greater difficulties than Mr. Scott.' Also UPC 306/27 (bundle, 13), Peacock to Sparke, 17 December 1857, Scott 'seems to me doubly unfortunate: nothing which he does pleases others, and nothing which others do pleases him.'
[46] Norwich, NRO, UPC 306/48 (bundle, [33]), Scott to Sparke, 13 July 1848. Scott had met Peacock, Willis and Sparke to discuss the screen, and had 'in many respects disapproved' Stewart's lithographed plan for the choir (EDC 14/36/2/49). 'As regards the screen I was left entirely unbiased excepting that it was to be open and I

the stained glass window scheme alone. Scott was eventually held in great respect and affection at Ely, and was eulogised by the Chapter on his death in 1878.[47]

The moving of the choir was considered in Chapter in November 1846, but it was deferred until funds were judged sufficient. The expense would exceed the Cathedral's resources, and an appeal would have to be made. Evidently this had gone sufficiently well for Scott to be summoned the following year. Scott examined the whole building and speedily reported on the state of the fabric and the restoration needed.[48] He prepared plans for moving the stalls and providing necessary furniture, including a new screen; and in August 1848 the tender of James Rattee (of the Cambridge firm of Rattee & Kett, then just established) of £3230 was accepted by the Chapter.[49]

Scott re-used most of the medieval stalls and designed new sub-stalls and benches. The oak screen was entirely his design, and incorporated, on its eastern side, identical stalls for the dean and bishop, with extravagant pinnacled tabernacles which outdid the cresting of the medieval stalls,[50] and brass gates by Hardman of Birmingham (Plate 41a). The screen was openwork, to preserve the vista to the east end, so there was no possibility of positioning the organ on it, as had been done in Essex's time.[51] Scott placed the organ in the north triforium, over the stalls, a position suggested by the example of Strasbourg Cathedral[52] (Colour pl. 13b). Scott's new case was Gothic and opulent, and in the north choir aisle he designed an elaborate openwork stone stair to the console, based on continental precedent[53] (Plate 40a–b). The Chapter accepted the tender of £580 by organ-builders Hill & Co. in November 1849. The case was carved by James Rattee and painted and gilded by Castell of London.

---

think not too heavy . . . I do not think stone was mentioned at all.' Scott resolved the problem "What is the best manner in which an open screen can be arranged for a cathedral without removing the Dean's stall from its proper place facing east?", submitted plans to the Chapter for approval and was directed to prepare working drawings. He 'went over expressly to Amiens because the Dean and yourself had spoken so strongly upon the stalls there', and was so sure that his plans were fixed that he showed a view of them at the (Royal Academy) exhibition. He was 'surprised and disappointed' when he found that Sparke was unhappy about them, and refused to countenance Sparke's suggestions, which would be 'half way between a close and an open screen'. If stone had to be used, Scott would use 'Purbeck marble for all uprights . . . which . . . would be expensive. I have a great horror of a glaring light colored screen.'

[47] EDC 2/2A/7, p. 228. The sole order at this meeting was 'That the Chapter deeply regretting the death of their architect Sir George Gilbert Scott desire to express their sincere condolence with the Family . . .' Canons and deans were not usually commemorated in this way. For an account of Scott's career see David Cole, *The Work of Sir Gilbert Scott* (London, 1980).

[48] Scott's report has not survived.

[49] EDC 2/2A/6, p. 95.

[50] Scott thought the effect from the nave would be 'rather accidental, like a spire or lofty pinnacle shewing from behind the roof of a church', but from the east the stalls would seem 'part and parcel of the screen . . . very effective and symetrical [*sic*]'. Norwich, NRO, UPC 306/48 (bundle, no. [4]), Scott to Sparke, 28 June 1848. See Kate Fearn, 'Medieval and Later Woodwork from the Choir in Ely Cathedral', *JBAA*, cxlix (1996), pp. 59–76.

[51] Essex's old organ case was sold to M. Talbot of Canterbury for £12 in March 1934 (EDC 2/2A/10, p. 22), and removed from the Cathedral in November 1934 (Reginald Gibbon, 'John Lambe, Dean of Ely, 1693–1708', *Church Quarterly Review*, cxix (1934–5), p. 228).

[52] Norwich, NRO, UPC 306/48 (bundle, 1), Scott to Peacock, 3 November 1848, 'I do not know whether I mentioned to you having seen the organ at Strasbourg which is a most magnificent one . . . I had known it pretty well from prints but had no idea of its beauty till I saw it.'

[53] EDC 4/8/8. 'Possibly inspired by the form of the organ staircase in St. Maclou at Rouen and the piercing of the early library staircase in Rouen Cathedral': Gerald Cobb, *English Cathedrals. The Forgotten Centuries* (London, 1980), p. 81.

During the reconstruction, services were held first in the south-west transept, then in the Lady Chapel, but by March 1852 the choir was sufficiently completed to allow services to resume there. On completion of the work ,the owners of the array of pews which had been placed in the Octagon for the Sunday sermon took them away, and open benches of ash and other English woods[54] were provided in the Octagon. Gas lighting was introduced, with two clusters of 29 burners, and six iron standards holding 11 burners each.[55] William Selwyn[56] proposed making seats for Chapter wives by taking away part of the boarded backs of the stalls, but the plan was roundly condemned, not least by *The Ecclesiologist*, which called the idea 'barbarous and reactionary'.[57]

Peacock had turned his restorer's eye on to the Lady Chapel in 1848, when he removed the oak panelling and pedimented reredos (said by Bacon, without any evidence, to have been by Wren)[58] from the east wall, and made sanctuary steps of Ancaster stone and Minton tiles. He contemplated but abandoned a restoration of the mutilated stonework of the east wall by a craftsman named Bostock.[59] The congregation of Holy Trinity opposed any further efforts at reordering the church at this stage.

In 1849–50 the ruined apsidal chapel off the south-west transept was rebuilt in Norman style, to designs by Robert Willis.[60] The writer of the *Cathedral Handbook*, 1852, remarked, 'The restorations, which have been for some years in progress, have been executed throughout with the most scrupulous care, preserving every portion of uninjured surface, and reproducing what is mutilated or destroyed as nearly as possible in exact conformity with . . . the ancient work'[61] (Plate 5c–d). In 1849 the south transept roof, which had fallen into deplorable disrepair, was patched with oak from the west tower and from a dismantled watermill in the fens. The roof was painted in white and colours on a black ground, the bosses were gilded and the angels repaired and coloured (Colour pl. 12a). The similar north transept ceiling was painted and gilded in 1857, also by Pashler, paid for by tradesmen and others connected with the Cathedral.[62]

In 1853 the west tower was found to be unsafe again.William Burns, engineer, was asked to report on its condition and suggest remedial action, his scheme to be submitted to Scott for approval.[63] Burns declared that the western octagon and its

---

[54] Bacon gives full details: EDC 4/6/2, fo. 66.

[55] Details in Bacon's book, EDC 4/6/2, fo. 67.

[56] William Selwyn (1806–75), Canon of Ely 1833–75, was Lady Margaret Professor of Divinity at Cambridge, 1855–75.

[57] EDC 2/2A/6, p. 168; *The Ecclesiologist*, xiv (1853), p. 370.

[58] Bacon's book, EDC 4/6/2, fo. 177.

[59] Norwich, NRO, UPC 306/48, Peacock to Sparke, 4 November 1848, 'We are modelling in clay a restoration of the tabernacle work of the altar of the Lady chapel with a view to its restoration . . . [but] . . . I fear the work is too fine for Bostock.'

[60] Plans for the chapel, in the RIBA Drawings Collection, are annotated by Willis as his own design.

[61] *Handbook to the Cathedral Church of Ely*, 1st edn (Ely, 1852), p. 17, quoting from the *Archaeological Guide*. John Bacon adds further details. The chapel was mostly rebuilt with old stone in store, and some new Casterton stone. The entrance arch was a close copy of the great arch at Barfreston church, Kent. The roof was of old oak, from the sale in 1829 of two old watermills which had drained the Littleport and Downham district. The floor, designed by Scott, combined Minton tiles, Purbeck marble and Portland stone (EDC 4/6/2, fos. 32–3).

[62] Details from Bacon's book, EDC 4/6/2, fos. 85–6 (south), 92 (north). John Storey was carver for the south transept, and carved 19 angels, 9 large wings and 3 small wings. William Pashler was an Ely painter and general craftsman much employed in and about the Cathedral.

[63] William Burns was Surveyor to Ely Local Board of Health.

turrets would fall within twelve years. Beams introduced previously to strengthen the roof increased the cracks by their added weight. Burns recommended a system of iron hoops encircling the octagon, the removal of other weighty beams and iron ties, and the replacement of most of the roof, put in when the spire was taken down in 1803, and now rotten.[64]

In the same year William Selwyn gave a font for the restored south west transept. It was designed by Scott, in the Early English style, of Aubigny stone, with Purbeck marble columns for its base, foursquare and heavy, with the emblems of the Evangelists carved on the sides. Dean Spencer's font of 1693 was loaned to the new church at Prickwillow, just outside Ely, where it still remains[65] (Plate 24c)

Scott now turned to the reredos, for which John Dunn Gardner, a landowner of Chatteris, gave money in 1850, in memory of his late wife. It was to be elaborate and striking. Scott was able to indulge to the full his love for highly detailed, ornate confections of sculpture, materials and motifs. The result was magnificent; the total cost was £4000. The reredos was alabaster and the screens were Derbyshire spar, and mosaic work in various marbles and lapis lazuli was employed, with gilding and colouring. It was featured in the *Illustrated London News* in 1854.[66] Rattee and Kett carved the stone framework, flanking screens and altar steps, the reredos sculpture was by John Phillip, mosaics were by Field, and it was coloured by Octavius Hudson.[67] The five main panels were scenes from Christ's Passion; on the many gables above stood figures of Prophets, Fathers of the Church, Evangelists, Virtues, the Annunciation and the Transfiguration (Colour pl. 11c). Peacock and Dunn Gardner took great interest in the details, though Scott was responsible for the actual design. The work, with its surrounding decoration, was not completed until 1868. Peacock would happily have countenanced screens at the sides of the presbytery, but Scott was adamant that the medieval monuments should not be moved.

Scott's Octagon pulpit was not completed until the late 1860s. It was provided by a legacy from a daughter of Bishop Allen who died in 1866. It is of Ancaster stone on Purbeck marble columns, with figures of SS Peter and Paul in alabaster by James Redfern.[68] For a few years Groves's neo-Norman pulpit of 1803 stood in splendid incongruity with Scott's screen. The eventual fate of Groves's pulpit is unknown[69] (Plate 41a–b).

---

[64] Scott had to do further strengthening in 1870–71. His report is EDC 4/5/84.

[65] The carved oak cover remained in the Cathedral for several years: it is mentioned in John Bacon's inventory of stone and woodwork as being in the north nave gallery in 1870 (EDC 4/6/4, fo. 6).

[66] *Illustrated London News*, 4 July 1854; EDC 4/5/119.

[67] Hudson continued painting and gilding the reredos for several years after 1858. For an account of his character and method of working, see Harvey Goodwin, *Ely Gossip* (Ely, 1892), pp. 66–8.

[68] Scott's first design was not approved: the Chapter thought it 'too much of a repetition of the pulpit in the nave of Westminster Abbey', Goodwin, *Ely Gossip*, p. 58. Dean Goodwin and Archdeacon Yorke suggested that the pulpit might be 'a repetition, mutatis mutandis, of the corbel above it; Sir Gilbert Scott caught the idea, approved it, and said he would try what could be made of it': *Memoir of the Life of Harvey Goodwin ... Written by Himself and Printed for Private Circulation only* (Cambridge, 1880), p. 153.

[69] Goodwin, *Ely Gossip*, p. 55, says 'I forget what became of this pulpit when it was superseded by the new one.' It stood for some years in the north triforium, and is listed and illustrated in John Bacon's MS *Gleanings from Ely Cathedral* (1887): EDC 4/6/7, p. 43.

Painted ceilings

The painting of the timber roofs and ceilings of the Cathedral started before Scott's employment and continued mostly independently, though his advice and opinion were sought for each stage of work. That the work was conceived and carried out so effectively was due to a remarkable amateur, Henry Styleman Le Strange of Hunstanton Hall (Norfolk), landowner, ecclesiologist and artist.[70] He was a friend of the Sparke brothers, Peacock, and after him Harvey Goodwin, who wrote, 'Mr. L'Estrange staid with us much of his time, and was a most agreeable inmate at the Deanery: he was unusually free from self-conceit, always ready to give advice upon any point which might turn up in connection with the Cathedral . . . and though most zealous in his work, quite devoid of artistic cant.'[71] In 1855 Hugh Evans gave money for Cathedral restoration. Goodwin recalled that during one of Le Strange's visits some ancient decoration was 'brought to light upon the vaulting of the South aisle of the Nave by the removal of whitewash . . . Le Strange . . . was much interested in the discovery and made some drawings. Dean Peacock, who was ever awake to possible advantages for his dear Cathedral, proposed to Le Strange that he should turn his skill and experience to good practical account by executing some kind of decoration.'[72] It was proposed to paint the ceiling of the west tower. Le Strange offered to design it and do most of the painting at his own expense. Boards were provided from the flooring of Essex's former high altar, 'good, dry and full of turpentine'.[73] Working on a scaffolding, Le Strange executed his first painting, the Holy Trinity, surrounded by the inscription 'Thou art worthy, O Lord, to receive glory and honor and power; for thou hast created all things, and for thy pleasure they are, and were created.'

Shortly afterwards the audacious plan to board and paint the nave roof was made. The old roof, an open structure of beams and rafters, was unattractive, and had always looked unfinished.[74] Le Strange's success with the west tower ceiling encouraged the Chapter to approve the greater project. For a boarded ceiling the Chapter had to look only to Peterborough Cathedral. The scheme devised for the decoration, God's dealings with Man in the Old and New Testaments, probably resulted from discusions between Le Strange, Peacock and the Sparkes. Scott claimed the credit for suggesting the medieval painted ceiling of St Michael's, Hildesheim as a model, but Peacock, Willis, and perhaps Le Strange, knew about that painted scheme.[75]

---

[70] Henry Styleman Le Strange (1815–62) 'delighted in all Christian art . . . He felt especially that there was something to be worked out for painting in connection with architecture, which had scarcely ever been consistently done, and he hoped to unite the two arts in a real harmony of principle'. William Butterfield in *The Guardian*, 6 August 1862, p. 748.

[71] Goodwin, *Memoir*, pp. 151–2.

[72] Goodwin, *Ely Gossip*, p. 30.

[73] Bacon's book, EDC 4/6/2, fo. 26.

[74] When George Millers died in 1852 he left money for Cathedral works at the discretion of his trustees: William Selwyn suggested panelling and painting the nave roof 'in fulfilment of Mr. M.'s aspiration in his book' (Norwich, NRO, UPC 301/62, Peacock to Sparke, 13 January 1852).

[75] Sir George Gilbert Scott, *Personal and Professional Recollections*, ed. Gavin Stamp (Stamford, 1995), p. 282: 'Under my suggestion, and with my co-operation, the ceiling . . . was painted . . . I suggested to Mr. Le Strange the ceiling . . . at Hildesheim as a model'; but Goodwin, *Ely Gossip*, p. 39, says of Le Strange: 'Some persons have imagined that Mr. le Strange's design for painting the ceiling . . . was suggested by, or modified from, the painted ceiling at Hildesheim . . . There are no doubt some striking resemblances; but Mr. le Strange himself

Le Strange's work was executed in stages between 1858 and 1862.[76] His death in 1862 left the ceiling unfinished. Fortunately, his friend, fellow artist and antiquary, Thomas Gambier Parry, stepped in to complete the scheme (Colour pl. 8*b*).

Le Strange, a Tractarian disciple, was a friend and ally of the architect William Butterfield, who from the late 1840s was restoring Hunstanton and other churches on Le Strange's estate. Butterfield in turn consulted Le Strange about his designs for All Saints, Margaret Street, London. To Butterfield, Le Strange was a pioneer in Christian art, who had studied closely religious paintings in the British Museum, the Bodleian in Oxford, and Cambridge University Library. He was fascinated by the art of the eleventh to thirteenth centuries. As Butterfield put it in 1862, 'Whatever he undertook in life he did patiently and thoroughly, always aiming at perfection.'[77] Le Strange frequently talked over with Butterfield his design for the ceiling. When in 1854 he showed it to Edward Sparke, the latter was 'delighted', and Peacock was 'entirely satisfied'. By July 1856 Peacock wanted designs from Le Strange for the ceilings of St Catherine's chapel and the nave, and Le Strange was soon drawing assiduously for the Ely ceilings. It was not, it seems, until October 1857 that Le Strange consulted Scott about the nave ceiling. In the summers of 1858, 1859 and 1860 Le Strange was hard at work on the ceiling, starting at the west end, with intervening visits to Gambier Parry at Highnam Court, Gloucestershire. By May 1861 the six western bays of the ceiling were completed.[78]

Stained glass

In 1857 the great east lancets of the Cathedral were filled with stained glass by William Wailes of Newcastle. The stained glass project was largely Edward Sparke's, with Dean Peacock's encouragement and constructive criticism at every stage. Sparke's project ran from 1845 into the 1870s. By his determination, by cultivation and sometimes cajoling of patrons, and by the generous and sustained benefactions of himself and his family, Sparke oversaw the filling of virtually all the windows of the choir and aisles, Octagon, transepts and nave aisles in the space of thirty years. There were windows by many of the mid nineteenth-century English designers, and some Frenchmen. There were a few losses, but the wholesale removal of most of the windows, which was to be recommended by Milner-White in the 1930s, did not take place.[79]

The stained glass project grew out of the east window scheme, where the difficulty lay in finding an artist capable of filling so large a space. Pearson's incomplete eighteenth-century scheme was a warning of the dangers of over-confidence. It took Edward Sparke fifteen years to commission an artist, and the window was not completed until

---

told me that when he conceived his design he had not seen the Hildesheim ceiling. I think he subsequently visited it.' Le Strange might not have seen the ceiling, but he might easily have seen Robert Willis's watercolour sketch (V & A Museum, Prints and Drawings, E1164–1930), which is undated but on paper watermarked 1846, and was presented by T.D. Atkinson 'from Willis's Coll[ectio]n'.

[76] Goodwin, *Ely Gossip*, pp. 35–7, describes the processes of designing and making cartoons, transferring them to the ceiling, and painting the ceiling boards.

[77] William Butterfield in *The Guardian*, 6 August 1862, p. 748.

[78] For details of the ceiling scheme, and an assessment of Le Strange's personality and career, see W.M. Jacob, 'Henry Styleman Le Strange: Tractarian, Artist, Squire', in Diana Wood (ed.), *The Church and the Arts*, Studies in Church History, 28 (Oxford, 1992), pp. 393–403.

[79] For details of the artists and firms involved, see M. Harrison, *Victorian Stained Glass* (London, 1980).

1857. By then about thirty of the Cathedral's windows had been filled with stained glass, by various artists. To some extent the smaller windows were trial pieces for the east window.

Sparke's first choice, in 1836, was David Evans of Shrewsbury. Sparke had been impressed by some of Evans's windows. In 1837–8 Evans worked hard on designs for the east window, and hired a London artist to draw the cartoons. Sketch plans reveal large narrative panels of scenes from Christ's life. The design did not win Sparke's approval – perhaps he was too much shocked by Evans's window over Bishop Sparke's monument in West's Chapel.[80]

Peacock gave Sparke strong encouragement from the start. He was a knowledgeable observer, and in 1841 he visited the recently established glass painter William Wailes in Newcastle. Wailes's work at Westminster Abbey had been commended to Peacock by Edward Blore and others. Peacock praised Wailes's colours and figure work: 'a perfect enthusiast in his art and a very intelligent man';[81] being newly established, Wailes charged reasonable prices.

Nothing was done about the east window until 1844 when Sparke invited tenders from selected artists. Thomas Willement declined grandly: he never entered competitions. The entrants were Evans, Thomas Ward, Ballantyne and Allan of Edinburgh, and William Warrington. The competition produced no result. It was then that Sparke seems to have hit upon the idea of inducing donors to pay for the smaller windows and to try the work of different artists. The plan was a runaway success, and money flowed in from Sparke, his family and friends, individuals and groups, and bequests; and there were gifts of glass by the artists themselves.

Such an excess of generosity brought problems, in that several artists were needed to keep the scheme going. There were differences of style, clashes of colour, and variations in quality, and Sparke and Peacock had to work hard to keep the artists up to the mark.[82] That the result was not worse was largely due to Sparke's guidance and overall control of the scheme; and Peacock, despite protestations that he left everything to Sparke, constantly monitored, prodded and sometimes agonised over the windows as they were installed one by one (Colour pl. 15a–c).

Wailes presented a window of Bede in 1848 (possibly a reject from Durham Cathedral) for the nave south aisle, but it became a glaring anomaly when that aisle was dedicated to Old Testament subjects, and was removed to the Canons' vestry. In 1849 Wailes made two windows for the south-west transept, on the theme of marriage;[83] and his first Octagon window was put up, to the south-east, featuring Ely founders and

---

[80] The work of David Evans (1793–1861), of which much survives in Shropshire, can be characterised by its vivid colouring and robust, sometimes comical, figure work. He was however quite highly regarded in the 1820s and 1830s, and was the Sparkes' first choice for the east window. Shortly after the Bishop's death, Edward Sparke, who had been examining Evans's windows in Hornsey church and the chapels of Winchester College and Wadham College, Oxford, invited Evans to tender for the window. Negotiations went on for a year or so, and Evans prepared several elaborate designs, but the Sparkes did not proceed to a firm commission. Evans's window in Bishop West's Chapel might have been in the nature of a trial piece, which swung the Sparkes away from a commission for the greater work. *Cf.* letters between Evans and Sparke, Norwich, NRO, UPC 302.

[81] Norfolk CRO, UPC 302/6, Peacock to Sparke, 12 September 1841.

[82] Norwich, NRO, UPC 306/13, Peacock to Sparke, 13 October [1852], 'I think we are approaching a state where we must reject all inferior work.'

[83] One provided by Peacock, who had married Canon William Selwyn's sister in 1847.

early benefactors. Meanwhile the south transept windows, which were to feature Old Testament patriarchs, were entrusted to the Frenchman Henri Gérente, and after his death, to his brother Alfred.[84]

The eleven nave south aisle windows were filled between 1848 and 1853. Edward Sparke was the driving force behind the Normanising of the Perpendicular openings;[85] Scott acquiesced, but Peacock, showing real antiquarian feeling, insisted that one window be left as an indication of what had been removed.[86] The Gérentes provided three windows, Howe and Wailes two each. Warrington and Gibbs presented one each, as did the Revd Arthur Moore, Rector of Walpole St Peter, a notable amateur artist for whom Peacock and Sparke entertained a high regard. One window was designed by Pugin and executed by Hardman of Birmingham. On the whole the windows showed a satisfying congruity, with subjects in roundels, rich borders and backgrounds, a style inspired by the medieval glass of Canterbury Cathedral.[87]

The north aisle windows remained Perpendicular, and continued the Old Testament theme. The glass was installed between 1853 and 1867. The larger surface of these windows allowed a greater freedom of design, colour and figure-work, and the effects were not always pleasing. Wailes designed four windows, one was by N.J. Cottingham, two were by Frederick Preedy, and two by Ward or the partnership of Ward and Nixon. One, outstanding, was by Oliphant, after a design by William Dyce (the choristers' window), one by Hedgeland, and one by the Frenchman Antoine Lusson.[88]

The north transept glass, devoted to the story of St Paul, was mostly paid for by Sparke, and, surprisingly perhaps, it was the most discordant area of the Cathedral. Three of the four main windows were by Wailes, the fourth by Arthur Moore. The

---

[84] Henri Gérente (1814–49) died of cholera after his third visit to England, and was succeeded by Alfred (1821–68), a sculptor. They took an early interest in medieval glass and in 'deliberately antiquating techniques'.

[85] Only one or two Norman windows remained in 1848.

[86] Norwich, NRO, UPC 306/28 (bundle, 40), Peacock to Sparke, 27 May [1849]: 'the alteration of the window . . . would be denounced as a barbarism . . . I have heard the strongest criticisms passed on the Deans of Durham and Norwich for authorizing the Normanizing of windows . . . a wish has always been expressed that this window at least should be saved: it is a window of so much beauty, with very correct decorated mouldings . . .'.

[87] John G. Howe (1825–78) worked as a freelance artist and also with Frederick Preedy, Heaton Butler & Payne, and James Powell. His *Tower of Babel* window was shown at the Great Exhibition, 1851, where it won an 'honourable mention'.William Warrington (1796–1869) was practising from c.1838. His window caused fierce controversy, on account of its white glass, unusual in 1850. Alexander Gibbs (1832–86) succeeded his father Isaac Alexander Gibbs (1802–51): it is likely that the son designed the south aisle window. Arthur Moore died suddenly in 1852. John Hardman (1811–67) of Birmingham executed metalwork as well as glass; A.W.N. Pugin frequently drew for him.

[88] Nockalls Johnson Cottingham (1823–54), architect and glass painter, died in the wreck of the steamer *Arctic* on his way to New York. Frederick Preedy (1820–98), a friend of Le Strange and through him of the Sparkes, started as a stained glass artist c.1852. Thomas Ward (1808–70) was in partnership with James Nixon (1802–57) until the early 1850s, then worked alone, and in 1857 went into partnership with Henry Hughes (1822–83). Francis William Oliphant (1818–59) was chief designer for Wailes, and then Pugin, before working alone. Hedgeland was either John Pike Hedgeland (1792–1873), notorious for his 'restoration' of the glass in King's College Chapel, Cambridge, or his son George Hedgeland, who sold his London premises to Preedy in 1860 and emigrated to Australia. Peacock fought a losing battle against Hedgeland: Norwich, NRO, UPC 306/17 (bundle, 16), Peacock to Sparke 21 October [1857], 'Mr Hedgland has a reputation which may entitle his work to a place in our Museum of Painted Glass, though I am not an admirer of his works.' Also UPC 306/27 (bundle, 7), Peacock to Sparke, 22 February 1858, 'Mr. Hedgland was settled against my wishes but as he has a certain character with some people as a glass painter I could not with any propriety tell Dr. Steggall that I thought him incompetent.' Antoine Lusson made his own windows and also made glass for others, *e.g.* Gérente, in the 1840s.

colours clashed badly; and the upper window, by Ward and Hughes, clashed with the work of both Wailes and Moore. The western aisle windows had Moore's last window, the *Prodigal Son* (1852), and two by Lusson (one in memory of Moore), while the east side had two early works by Clayton and Bell (one removed to the north transept tribune in 1922). In the vestries in the south transept was another window by Lusson and one by Coffretier of Paris, 'accurately copied from the celebrated ancient glass' in Bourges Cathedral.[89]

In St Catherine's Chapel Thomas Wilmshurst put in (much to Peacock's horror) two windows in anachronistic 'pictorial' style, based on paintings by Bassano and Overbeck (Colour pl. 14*a*); while Clutterbuck more or less successfully completed the sixteenth-century windows installed over the west entrance in 1808.[90]

The choir aisle windows were mostly provided by the Sparke family, and featured New Testament themes. On the south side the earliest was by N.J. Cottingham; three were by Clayton and Bell (four, after Lusson's 1856 window was moved to the north side in 1871). The north side had two windows by Ward and Hughes, and two by Clayton and Bell.

The four great Octagon windows were filled by Wailes between 1849 and 1871, and depicted founders and benefactors of Ely. The south-west window mixed old bene-factors with new, and the figures of Queen Victoria, Prince Albert, Bishop Turton and Dean Peacock were given by their respective subjects. Wailes made the choir clerestory windows; and the east window of 1857, a Tree of Jesse, in rich reds and blues, and featuring the donor Bishop Sparke in prayer at bottom left, was his masterpiece (Colour pl. 28*c*).

Already, in 1853, in answer to the Cathedral Commission's questions, Peacock paid tribute to Sparke's efforts. Before listing the donors of glass he wrote: 'Nearly thirty windows in the Cathedral have been filled with painted glass, chiefly by the unceasing exertions of the Rev. E.B. Sparke, who has been by far the most considerable benefactor to them; his expenditure upon them, in addition to many other gifts to the church, having exceeded 1,200l.'[91] The Chapter's part in the undertaking, Peacock explained, was not inconsiderable. They generally bore the cost of installing 'the windows, the ironwork and guards', at a total cost by 1853 of some £3000.[92]

Edward Sparke's benefactions and energies were not confined to the stained glass. The medieval choir stalls were surmounted by canopies incorporating niches, which prints show to have been filled with armorial panels. These armorials were removed when the

[89] EDC 2/2A/6, p. 236.

[90] Thomas Wilmshurst (1806–80) persisted with the pre-revival style, copying from paintings, but had closed his business by 1861. He was however capable of designing in a more up-to-date style, as is shown in a design for a baptistery window of 1850, with roundels illustrating the life of John the Baptist set in a rich mosaic–like background (EDC 4/8/53) (Colour pl. 14*e*). Charles Clutterbuck (1806–61), a miniaturist, turned to glass painting *c.*1844.

[91] Norwich, NRO, UPC 301/165, Peacock to Sparke, 31 May 1849, 'I must consider the painted glass as entirely your work, for it is to your liberality and public spirit that we are indebted for it'; and UPC 306/27, Peacock to Sparke, 17 February 1858, 'I have myself told him [Hedgeland], what he is indeed sure to know from all quarters, that the windows at Ely are your particular province.'

[92] Printed reply to the Cathedral Commission, in *First Report of Her Majesty's Commissioners, appointed . . . 1852, to inquire into the State and Condition of the Cathedral and Collegiate Churches in England and Wales* (London, 1854), pp. 155–81.

stalls were moved and restored. Sparke conceived a cycle of carved panels, Old Testament scenes on the south side, and New Testament scenes on the north. John Phillip provided a model, the Nativity, but Sparke found that he could obtain equally well carved but less expensive panels from the woodcarver Michel Abeloos (1828–81) of Louvain, Belgium. The 'Choir Panel Fund' was begun in 1857 when £25 was diverted from each canon's dividend for the panel above his stall. Panels were easier to afford than stained glass, and between 1857 and 1869 Sparke was able to complete the cycle in 50 panels, by attracting funds from other donors, including his daughter Maria (Plate 40c–e).

The Peacock Memorial

Dean Peacock's death in 1858 was universally lamented, not least because of his devotion to the Cathedral and its restoration. The Chapter tried hard for permission to bury him in the Cathedral, but the Burials Act (1853) forbade intra-mural interment in most circumstances. Peacock was laid to rest in a recently acquired plot in Ely Cemetery. The Chapter resolved to carry on the restoration of the Cathedral in memory of his 'unceasing zeal and care for the improvement of the Fabric', and decided on an appeal for the Octagon and Lantern as his special memorial, to return them to something approaching their medieval form.[93]

A statement prepared earlier by Peacock was revised and printed, and the Peacock Memorial Committee composed of 'men advanced in the knowledge of architecture, and of great taste and skill', met on 30th December 1858. Scott was asked to prepare plans for the stone Octagon and the wooden Lantern,[94] which he did with great enthusiasm, and combined engineering skill in strengthening and renewing the structure, with antiquarian researches of his own, and Peacock's, in determining the ancient form of the Lantern from archaeological evidence and published sources. Some committee members proposed a wooden spire or flèche,[95] and Scott prepared an enticing sketch, based on *The Ecclesiologist's* engraving of his proposed restoration, showing the effect of a crocketed flèche;[96] but on examining the Lantern roof, and its principal timbers, Scott proved that no spire had been built or projected[97] (Plate 39b–c). The Chapter resolved in October 1860 to begin work on the Octagon, without the spire, and that 'the question of such erection be reserved until an application on that subject is made by the Peacock Memorial Committee'.[98]

---

[93] EDC 2/2A/6, p. 249.

[94] No record seems to have been made of the first meeting, but a book of minutes and accounts (EDC 4/7/1) reveals the evolution of the scheme. The committee of honour was large, but those who attended the 10 June 1859 meeting were the Marquess of Bristol (in the chair), Alexander Beresford Hope, John Dunn Gardner, Henry Styleman Le Strange, the Revd G. Williams, Dean Goodwin, the Sparke brothers, and Scott. Scott's report, dated 10 June 1859, is EDC 4/5/156.

[95] EDC 4/7/1. At the meeting on 13 March 1860 Benjamin Webb, John Willis Clark and Canons Selwyn and W.H. Thompson were present in addition to those named in note 77; Beresford Hope proposed and Edward Sparke seconded a motion for 'a pyramidal capping or spire', which was carried by a large majority. At a meeting on 8 April 1862, however, the question of a spire was no longer raised.

[96] *The Ecclesiologist*, xx (1859), p. 328. The engraving and sketch are EDC 4/5/79–80.

[97] *The Ecclesiologist*, xxi (1860), pp. 77–8.

[98] EDC 2/2A/6, p. 289. For a fuller account of the Octagon work, see Phillip Lindley, '"Carpenter's Gothic" and Gothic Carpentry. Contrasting Attitudes to the Restoration of the Octagon and Removals of the Choir at Ely Cathedral', *Architectural History*, 30 (1987), pp. 84–112.

Freeman's of Ely won the contract for the carpenter's work. The Chapter had already bought oak for the project,[99] and it had been seasoned. The work was done in 1862–3. Essex's Lantern looked flimsy but it concealed a strong system of wooden supports inserted by him. The Lantern windows were now enlarged, and filled with wooden tracery designed by Scott, who claimed to have been guided by slight traces that he had found of Alan of Walsingham's work (Plate 39d). The Lantern turrets were restored to their original form, and eight flying buttresses that had been removed by Essex were replaced. Then the whole Lantern was encased in lead. After considerable discussion the Committee decided to abandon plans for a spire. The restoration of the Lantern cost £5453, leaving the Chapter with a shortfall of some £1300, which was not paid off until the mid-1870s.

Gambier Parry

Peacock's successor as Dean, Harvey Goodwin, was equally zealous for the restoration of the Cathedral[100] (Plate 35b). He was respectful of Scott, but not uncritical, and he later wrote 'My own experience taught me that with all his conscientious excellence, Scott was not a man to be followed blindly and without careful examination of his schemes, and I cannot doubt that the early work in the Ely restoration profited much by the keen intellect of Dean Peacock, and probably by the counsel of Professor Willis in the background.'[101]

In 1863 a restoration of the Lady Chapel was ordered. Holy Trinity parish was responsible for the furnishings, the Chapter for the fabric. Scott prepared plans for the intricately carved and badly decayed east and west fronts.

When Le Strange died in 1862, with the nave ceiling half finished, the Chapter was faced with the difficulty of completing the work. Some Canons looked for a professional artist, but Goodwin proposed Thomas Gambier Parry, and this was agreed unanimously[102] (Plate 42b). Like his friend Le Strange, Gambier Parry was an ecclesiologist, chiefly interested in stained glass and mural painting. As he told Lincoln Architectural Society in 1868, 'The use of art is justified in sacred buildings by its power of religious and reverential impression'.[103]

Gambier Parry agreed to complete Le Strange's project – 'a carefully studied Epitome of the Sacred History of Man, as recorded in Holy Scripture'[104] – as a mark of respect for his old friend (Plate 42a). Le Strange had conceived of the ceiling as a Tree of Jesse. Gambier Parry abandoned this idea in favour of scenes increasing in richness and interest as they progressed eastward – the sleeping Jesse, King David, the Annunciation, the Nativity, the Adoration of the Shepherds and Magi, and Christ in glory (Plate 42c).

---

[99] From Gateley (Norfolk), Soham (Cambs.), Erpingham (Rutland) and Inxworth (Herts.).

[100] Goodwin, *Ely Gossip*, p. 21: 'I threw myself warmly into the scheme' (for the Peacock Memorial). Goodwin (1818–91), a Fellow of Gonville & Caius College, 1841–5, was a good mathematical tutor and a popular preacher. He was Chaplain of St Edward's, Cambridge, 1848–58, Dean of Ely, 1858–69, and Bishop of Carlisle, 1869–91.

[101] *Ibid.*

[102] *Ibid.*, p. 40.

[103] For Gambier Parry (1815–88) see Dennis Farr (ed.), *Thomas Gambier Parry (1816–1888) as Artist and Collector* (London: Courtauld Institute Galleries, 1993).

[104] John Bacon's book, EDC 4/6/2, fo. 48.

Both men's method was to immerse themselves in the art and architecture of their chosen period 'and then to work out our own ideas as far as possible in harmony with it . . . without for a moment designing to conceal that ours was the work of the nineteenth century'. His colours, though continuing Le Strange's carefully subdued scheme, were a little brighter and clearer.[105]

Two assistants, Clay and Davies, worked with Le Strange and Gambier Parry. The medium was oil paint modified with copal and gold size. Gambier Parry coated his part with fine wax and resin. The ceiling was painted *in situ*. It was hard work, 'lying on one's back, in a painfully bad light'. The scaffolding precluded a distant view while the work was in progress. They both wanted to paint the nave walls and arches; instead, the ochre wash applied by Bernasconi in 1823 was removed carefully, for signs of medieval colouring.[106]

The ceiling was finished in 1865, and Gambier Parry wrote that since the style of Le Strange's work was 'unavoidably peculiar, understood or cared for by very few . . . under any circumstances it must have been done for love, and not for money . . . Mr. Le Strange had desired to harmonize his work with the Architecture, and had therefore followed rigidly a peculiar form of Norman art', that of *c*.1180.[107]

Next, in 1865, Gambier Parry offered to paint the Octagon.[108] This was evidently not accepted, since a scheme by C.E. Kempe was considered in 1868–9[109] (Colour pl. 10a). The Chapter were undecided whether to attempt to recreate the old colour scheme, traces of which were discovered everywhere when the ochre wash was removed from the Octagon woodwork in 1850.[110] A printed statement by Peacock states that one section was restored, experimentally, in 1850.[111] Kempe's scheme would have retained the light-and-dark theme, with further colours and the depiction of angels.[112] Gambier Parry's scheme was executed in 1873–5, but to widespread regret he covered up the medieval remains. His scheme was based on Psalm 140, and had, around the lower panels of the Lantern a band of 32 angels playing musical instruments. The work pleased Dean Merivale, who wrote to the Master of Trinity in October 1874: 'Gambier Parry . . . has made a beautiful dome, and decorated the tracery of the windows with great effect: with what is called enamelling he has toned down the rawness of the windows, and reduced them to a fair harmony with the general design. He is preparing a series of angels . . . these angelic panels will be fixed in the course of the present year . . . The ground will be a dusky

---

[105] This was especially discernible after the ceiling was cleaned of a century of dirt and grime by Hirst Conservation in 1987.

[106] *Ibid.*, pp. 50, 52.

[107] Gambier Parry's report is transcribed in John Bacon's book, EDC 4/6/2, fos. 40–9.

[108] EDC 4/5/65.

[109] Octavius Hudson reported on the traces of old decoration in July 1868 (EDC 4/5/68), Frederick Sutton advised Dean Goodwin on 31 Dec. 1868 that 'with a man like Mr. Kempe superintending the actual work at Ely – we ought to make a fine thing of the colouring' (EDC 4/5/161), and C.E. Kempe prepared his design in June 1869. A trial of Kempe's plan was about to be made when Goodwin left Ely to be Bishop of Carlisle in 1869, as he explained in a letter to Dean Merivale, 5 August 1874 (EDC 4/5/143).

[110] *The Ecclesiologist*, xi (1850), p. 158. 'The bosses and ribs were gilt, and the spaces between . . . were covered with . . . quatrefoils in white upon a green ground . . . the whole effect of this design is to suggest raised tracery work. All this is being literally reproduced.' (Plate 10e).

[111] EDC 4/5/60. But Norwich, NRO, UPC 301/123, Peacock to Sparke, 6 July 1850: 'We have been making experiments upon the colouring of the lantern which are very unsuccessful . . . the ancient work was very roughly done . . .'

[112] EDC 4/5/83.

green. I only hope the tone will not be too deep. Parry swears *not*. It is meant to harmonize with the tone of the nave ceiling, where . . . Parry and Lestrange's work now agree extremely well, except that some of Lestrange's darker colours have turned rather black, from the gas, some say, from too economical colours, say others'[113] (Colour pl. 10*b*).

To complete the decoration of the Octagon, the twelve niches under the four great windows were in 1868–69 and 1874–76 given statues of the Apostles by James Redfern[114] (Plate 10*b*).

North-west transept project

In 1873 the twelve-hundredth anniversary of the founding of the Abbey by St Etheldreda was celebrated in a week-long festival (Plate 45*a*). Scott gave a lecture on the architectural history of the Cathedral, and Dean Merivale spoke about the restoration and what remained to be done. His list was long, and much was workaday but expensive, such as repaving the aisles, Octagon and transepts, or replacing Purbeck marble shafts; but he mentioned the rebuilding of the north-west transept as 'a work much to be desired, perhaps hardly to be anticipated, yet surely not to be despaired of'.[115]

The next year, the Diocesan Conference debated the restoration of the Cathedral, and it was strongly in favour of a bold campaign to rebuild the lost transept.[116] Merivale stressed the role of the Cathedral as the parish church of the diocese, pointed out how much had already been achieved in its restoration, and urged that they were now within sight of the completion of the whole work. Of all the works which Scott still hoped to complete at Ely (including the missing north-east pinnacle and a wooden spire or 'open crown' for the Lantern), the transept was his priority, 'but I dread to name this, as the cost would be so great'.[117] Merivale then produced statistics on national spending on cathedral restoration in recent years, mostly by voluntary subscriptions. Ely itself had spent 'at least £70,000 from its own and its neighbourhood's resources'. Merivale skilfully conveyed the message that the Chapter's resources were exhausted, and that they now looked to the diocese to provide the funding, or to make the effort to raise it nationally. Merivale and the Chapter must have been pleasantly surprised to find how warmly the Conference endorsed his 'appeal' and how enthusiastically they started the fund-raising process.[118]

---

[113] Judith Anne Merivale (ed.), *Autobiography and Letters of Charles Merivale Dean of Ely* (Oxford, 1898), p. 415, Merivale to the Master of Trinity, 2 October 1874.

[114] James Redfern (1838–76) carved many statues for Salisbury Cathedral and Westminster Abbey, and reredos figures for Gloucester. Goodwin, *Ely Gossip*, pp. 62–5, says of Redfern, 'the very promising sculptor', that he deduced that the medieval statues, the subjects of which were unknown, had been seated figures, and guessed the twelve Apostles. Redfern, the son of a workman killed in an accident, was a protégé of Alexander Beresford Hope, and Hope 'perceiving his talent gave him an art education . . . Redfern was a genuine artist . . . a man of bright intellect and strong artistic instinct.'

[115] Charles Merivale, *St. Etheldreda Festival. Summary of Proceedings, with Sermons and Addresses . . . Ely, October, 1873* (Ely, [*c.*1874]). Scott's lecture, which was read by his son George Gilbert Scott, is at pp. 47–70; Merivale's statement is at pp. 100–1.

[116] *Ely Diocesan Conference, Eleventh Year . . . 1874 . . . Report, Resolutions and General Summary of Proceedings* (Ely, 1874), pp. 25–34, 'The Restoration of the Cathedral'.

[117] *Ibid.*, p. 28.

[118] Merivale wrote 'I asked only twelve thousand pounds to restore the lantern and octagon . . . but the people went in enthusiastically for rebuilidng the fallen transept, at an unknown expense.' *Autobiography of Charles Merivale* (cit. in n. 113), p. 412, Merivale to his sister Louisa, 24 July 1874.

Bishop Woodford, though preferring interior restoration of the Cathedral, nevertheless urged 'a bold plunge by going to the country generally for the transept'. G. Bower, a businessman, offered £100 immediately. Canon Lowe supported rebuilding: 'St. Catherine's Chapel showed how skilfully we could now rebuild the masonry of Norman architecture', and suggested that the transept might hold a chapter house, which the Cathedral lacked, and the library. Colonel Higgins proposed a 'Diocesan Committee of Clergy and Laity, with Branch Committees in each Archdeaconry', and Merivale announced the setting up of the Committee, composed of the Bishop, Chancellor, the four archdeacons, and a number of prominent laymen in the diocese, to seek plans and estimates, and to send out circulars requesting aid.[119]

In October 1874 Merivale, still publicly enthusiastic about the plan,[120] told George Gabriel Stokes, a committee member, that he had recruited 'ten or twelve more eminent personages for the Committee'. Bishop Woodford had proposed a meeting in Cambridge, and Canon Jarrett, Professor of Hebrew, promised his rooms in Trinity.[121] The only discouragement had come with the refusal of the Master of Trinity, William Hepworth Thompson, to join the Committee: 'he declines on aesthetic grounds'. Scott's estimates led Merivale to think that £30,000 might be needed – 'Will this frighten our friends?' – and he proposed to canvass the whole diocese by small sub-committees.[122]

The Peacock Memorial minute book was brought into use again. There is no record of the 1874 meeting, but in July 1875 a meeting resolved on a 'renewed effort for completion of the Peacock memorial and general restoration of the Cathedral.'[123] The appeal to the diocese and country built up very slowly, and it must have become evident that the £30,000 needed for the transept was not going to be raised. The Chapter decided late in 1875 that it could not commit any Cathedral money to the transept, but rather to the completion of the Octagon and Lantern, 'while they commend the rebuilding of the North-west transept to the munificence of any admirers of church architecture in general'.[124] In May 1876 it was decided to construct the Octagon parapet and turret pinnacles, according to Scott's design.[125] No more was heard of the north-west transept project.

Monuments

The nineteenth-century funerary monuments were few and relatively undistinguished. Monuments were privately funded, and in the period 1840–80, benefactions tended to be made for the restoration or embellishment of the Cathedral. Thus the Octagon and Lantern were Dean Peacock's memorial, and he was otherwise commemorated only in a

[119] *Ely Diocesan Conference . . . 1874*, pp. 25–34.
[120] But privately sceptical. He wrote 'I do not myself believe in this work being accomplished; but there seems every reason to believe that some very large undertakings will be set on foot, and I shall probably have the chief part in directing them, an occupation for the rest of my life'. Same letter as quoted in n. 118.
[121] Thomas Jarrett (1805–82), Professor of Arabic at Cambridge 1831–54, Regius Professor of Hebrew and Canon of Ely 1854–82, Rector of Trunch (Norfolk), 1832–82, linguist.
[122] CUL, MS Add. 7656/M480, 2 October 1874.
[123] EDC 4/7/1.
[124] EDC 4/5/158, Charles Merivale, *Restoration of Ely Cathedral*, printed statement, 1 December 1875.
[125] EDC 4/5/159.

small tablet in the south choir aisle. Edward Sparke's memorial was the stained glass scheme.[126]

Bishop Joseph Allen died in 1845 and was buried in a vault at the east end of the choir (soon to become the retrochoir). Over the vault in 1857 his son placed an intricate slab designed by Scott, of porphyry, malachite, other coloured stones and mosaics, including some left-over pieces from Napoleon's tomb in Les Invalides[127] (Colour pl. 24c). The unprotected slab had its inlay dislodged by the feet of visitors standing on it to survey the east window, and was expensively repaired in the 1880s and guarded by rails.[128] Nevertheless it continued to deteriorate and was removed in 1953.[129] Bishop Allen's monument, in the south choir aisle, was a costly affair in white marble, with a semi-reclining effigy of the bishop (said to be a good likeness) by James Legrew[130] (Colour pl. 16c).

George Basevi, tragically killed by his fall from the west tower in 1845, was commemorated in 1850 with a brass by John and Lionel Waller, given by Basevi's family[131] (Plate 44a).

Canon William Hodge Mill, Professor of Hebrew, died in 1853 and was buried in the retrochoir. He had been principal of Bishop's College, Calcutta, and his monument,[132] designed by Scott and executed by J.B. Phillip, was paid for by his former pupils. It featured a recumbent effigy of Mill, in electro-plated copper, with kneeling figures of an Indian student and a Cambridge undergraduate, on a tomb-chest of alabaster and serpentine, ornamented with marble mosaic and coloured stones[133] (Plate 44b).

The Burials Act (1853) forbade burials in churches, except in pre-existing vaults. When Canon William Selwyn died in 1875, he was buried in the Chapter plot in Ely Cemetery, close to Dean Peacock. He was Lady Margaret Professor of Divinity at Cambridge, and before that had been at Eton, and many Old Etonians subscribed towards his monument. The fine white marble recumbent figure, on a tomb-chest, was by Thomas Nicholls, and was installed in a recess in the south choir aisle in 1879.

Bishop James Russell Woodford died in 1885, and an empty vault was found in Bishop West's chapel – the last burial in the Cathedral. He had founded Ely Theological College, and old students subscribed towards his monument, by G.F. Bodley: a

---

[126] Sparke died on 28 June 1879 and was buried in the Chapter plot in Ely Cemetery, next to Peacock. *Cambridge Chronicle*, 5 July 1879. There is no funerary monument to him in the Cathedral.

[127] Goodwin, *Ely Gossip*, p. 57. Norwich, NRO, UPC 306/27 (bundle, 20), Peacock to Sparke, 10 October 1857, 'A Frenchman, as deaf as a post, not knowing a syllable of English and speaking most indistinctly and hardly able to read, has come from Paris to put down Allen's slab' – someone was found who spoke French – 'the work . . . is badly put together and the slab is not strong enough to cohere if unsupported'.

[128] EDC 4/5/146–147, G.F. Allen to Dean Merivale, 23 January and 21 March 1882, on repairs to the slab. Scott's design was taken from 'an ancient Florentine mosaick'.

[129] EDC 2/2A/10, p. 312: 25 April 1953. An anonymous watercolour, sent to the Revd John Taylor Allen, Vicar of Stradbroke, postmarked Ely, 27 March 1858, is the only known illustration (EDC 4/5/370).

[130] James Legrew (1804–57), a pupil of Sir Francis Chantrey, was a regular exhibitor at the Royal Academy. His style was purely classical. The Gothic architectural surround to the figure was designed by Edward Blore (Norwich, NRO, UPC 301/97, Peacock to Edward Sparke, 3 November 1850).

[131] David Meara, *Victorian Memorial Brasses* (London, 1983), pp. 18–19.

[132] Formerly over his vault, but removed in the 1950s to the nave north aisle.

[133] Goodwin, *Ely Gossip*, p. 69, 'one of the very earliest examples of the application of the Electrotype process to purposes of high art'.

recumbent figure on a tomb-chest, backed by an elaborate Gothic canopy. This was placed in the nave north aisle, breaching an old Chapter rule against erecting monuments in the nave[134] (Plate 44c).

Many of the old monuments, mostly removed to the choir aisles by Bentham and Essex, were moved again after 1850, to make use of the stone screens behind the choir stalls.[135]

Surveyors and architects 1880–1980

The Dean and Chapter maintained the practice of employing a surveyor for the maintenance and repair of the Cathedral and College buildings, and commissioning a distinguished architect or designer for any substantial addition or decorative change, until the mid-twentieth century. Thus the surveyors left scarcely any visible trace of their stewardship of the Cathedral (though in invisible works their contribution was considerable); but they used their knowledge of the Cathedral's structure, and their researches in the archives, in publications devoted to the building history of Ely.

Richard Reynolds Rowe[136] used the scaffolding erected for Gambier Parry in the Octagon in 1873 to make full measured drawings of the structure, and he published a paper on it in 1876.[137] T.D. Atkinson did much research on the monastic buildings, and published his findings in a handsome edition of 1933.[138] Inskip Ladds similarly studied the medieval monastery, and his smaller volume appeared in 1930.[139] Richard Barwell was surveyor, 1950–60, and was followed by Donovan Purcell, 1960–73, and Peter Miller, a partner in Purcell's practice (Purcell Miller & Tritton), 1973–94.[140]

In the 1880s Scott's work, largely on the Lady Chapel, was continued by his son John Oldrid Scott, who prepared designs for doors, windows and so forth. He also did structural work in securing the south wall of the south transept, and extended the lean-to choir vestries on the south side of the nave. Little more was done before Sir Guy Dawber's work in the north transept in the 1920s.

---

[134] EDC 2/2A/5, p. 260.

[135] John Bacon, EDC 4/6/2, fos. 133–4, gives details.

[136] Richard Reynolds Rowe (1824–99), appointed surveyor in 1873, was also surveyor to the diocese and the archdeaconry of Ely, and county surveyor for the Isle of Ely; he designed the Corn Exchange in Cambridge. He restored and extended three of the canonry houses between 1870 and 1883 (EDR G3/39, MGA/111, 145, 183). Richard Norman Shaw restored the 2nd Canonry in 1872 for Bishop McDougall. The work of J. Arthur Reeve for V.H. Stanton at the 3rd Canonry (Black Hostelry) is illustrated in a typescript volume, illustrated with plans and photographs (EDC 8B/12/1).

[137] Richard R. Rowe, 'The Octagon and Lantern of Ely Cathedral', *RIBA Sessional Papers*, 1 (1875–6), pp. 69–85.

[138] Thomas Dinham Atkinson (1864–1948), pupil of Sir Arthur Blomfield, partner of the Cambridge architect W.M. Fawcett, and consultant architect to the Cambridge Antiquarian Society, was appointed surveyor in 1900. In 1918 he moved to Winchester. His monograph was *An Architectural History of the Benedictine Monastery of Saint Etheldreda at Ely* (Cambridge, 1933).

[139] Sidney Inskip Ladds (1867–1950), a pupil of his father John Ladds, moved to Huntingdon in 1903 and completed designs for the Norris Library and Museum, St. Ives; he was Surveyor 1918–48. His work was *The Monastery of Ely* (Ely, 1930). His papers are EDC 14/22.

[140] Donovan Purcell (1913–73), an authority on stonework, was based in Norwich and restored such great Norfolk houses as Felbrigg, Oxburgh and Holkham. He was the first Roman Catholic to be surveyor. He wrote *The Stones of Ely Cathedral* (Cambridge, 1965).

Twentieth-century furnishings, glass, monuments

Bishop Woodford's was the last substantial funerary monument in the Cathedral. In the twentieth century, memorials were mostly wall tablets of stone, brass, bronze or marble, set up in the choir aisles and presbytery, and a few in the nave aisles and south transept. Most were unambitious, their effect depending on the beauty of their lettering. Some had their inscriptions designed and cut by David Kindersley, including the tablet to Canon Professor John Martin Creed. A few tablets incorporated a profile portrait, such as that of Harvey Goodwin (in copper), Charles Merivale (in white marble), or the most ambitious, that of Canon Michael Glazebrook and his wife (both died in 1926), in grey-green Westmorland slate, by Arthur Walker (1861–1939).

To commemorate Queen Victoria's Diamond Jubilee the Dean and Chapter wives and other ladies commissioned the 'desk of the six queens' as a lectern for the Octagon. This rather ponderous piece of furniture by Philip Thicknesse was of carved oak on a marble base, and incorporated statues of six queens: Etheldreda, Sexburga and Ermenilda (the first three abbesses), Matilda, wife of King Henry I, Philippa, wife of Edward III, and Queen Victoria. It was installed in 1905 and was removed in the 1960s, during the Octagon reorganisation scheme.[141]

A few windows remained to be filled with stained glass. In 1893 a window designed by Henry Holiday and made by Powell's of Whitefriars, was installed in the south choir aisle in memory of Dr John Marshall, a local benefactor. Its theme was 'Christ the Healer'.[142] In 1900 Clayton and Bell designed the east window in Bishop Alcock's Chapel, showing four bishops of Ely flanking Alcock, the figures drawn by George Daniels. This glass, made thirty years after the firm's windows in the choir aisles, is much quieter in tone and lighter in colour.[143]

The chapels in the north transept remained to be fitted up, and in 1898 Canon Vincent Stanton gave an altar, reredos and furnishings for the south-east chapel, St Edmund's.[144] This was formerly the lay clerks' vestry. The adjoining chapel was dedicated in 1919 as St George's, or the Cambridgeshire Regimental War Memorial Chapel, with furnishings designed in 1920–1 by Sir Guy Dawber, and a stained glass window of 1922 by Powell's.[145]

In 1930 another south choir aisle window received stained glass, in memory of Sir George Fardell.[146] The glass, again by Powell's of Whitefriars, was a new departure for Ely, being roundels of stained glass in clear glass surrounds.

The stained glass was, in fact, about to undergo the hardest-hitting attack since the days of the iconoclasts. In the first *Report* of the Friends of Ely Cathedral was an account of the windows by Eric Milner-White.[147] Milner-White had been asked to

---

[141] The prospectus, including a sketch, is EDC 4/5/34. The desk is now in store in the nave north triforium.

[142] Correspondence on this window is EDC 4/5/250–268.

[143] The window was given by Bishop Lord Alwyne Compton.

[144] The leaflet for this scheme is EDC 4/5/35.

[145] Sir (Edward) Guy Dawber (1861–1938), architect especially of country houses, was Vice-President and Chairman of the Council for the Preservation of Rural England, 1926–38. The previous window, by Clayton & Bell, was moved to the north transept west tribune.

[146] Grandson of Canon Henry Fardell.

[147] Eric Milner-White (1884–1963) was Dean of King's College, Cambridge, 1918–41, and Dean of York, 1941–63.

examine the nineteenth-century stained glass and to make recommendations. The result was a plea for most of the glass to be removed. It was 'a problem which is Ely's above that of any other Cathedral except Worcester, the poor quality of the modern glass which, to its grave detriment, fills the windows.' The report was well researched, and filled with carefully considered aesthetic assessments of the windows. He accepted that they were a 'national gallery' of nineteenth-century stained glass design. 'But the interest is historical rather than artistic.'[148]

By and large, it was the historical *curiosi* which Milner-White recommended to be kept, including the Wilmshurst windows in St Catherine's Chapel. ('Both are the negation of good glass . . . [but] . . . We shall never again see glass of this type, and there is next to none of it in existence'). Most of the nave aisle windows should be removed, though anything by Arthur Moore might be kept 'because he belongs, so to speak, to the Diocese'. He approved of the south transept windows. 'Of its kind, this wall of windows may be counted successful. The glass tones in uniformly.' Wailes's Octagon scheme seemed uneven in character, but on the whole the windows had 'a certain quality, and glow'. The Wailes windows in the north transept should be removed, the Moore window relocated, 'thus setting all four lights free for a new carefully planned scheme'. Whatever else of Wailes's glass was destroyed 'and most of his huge output should be', his great east window should remain. David Evans's window in West's Chapel had to go, 'not only for its own badness, but still more because it darkens and conceals the marvellous beauty of the chantry', though the figures might be reset in the nave triforium. In the north choir aisle, windows by Ward and Hughes ('execrable') and Lusson ('so shocking that it should be removed and destroyed') could be replaced with three by Clayton and Bell from the other side. The other south windows could be removed, save for Holiday's of 1893, which would 'thus set free almost the whole range of the southern windows for a future scheme of wholly different character and superior merit'.

Two factors probably saved the Ely windows from Milner-White's root-and-branch reforms: the need to reintegrate the Lady Chapel into the Cathedral, and the outbreak of war in 1939.

Dean Blackburne

In 1936 the Friends of Ely Cathedral were formed. In 1937 Lionel Blackburne became Dean[149] (Plate 52*a–b*). Stirred partly by the prospect of funds, he began to plan for the beautification of the Cathedral. The impending hand-over of the Lady Chapel by Holy Trinity parish required thought about its new use and furnishings. First, however, some former students of Ely Theological College who had enrolled as Friends offered to refurnish Bishop West's Chapel, in memory of their College's founder, Bishop Woodford, who lay there. Plans were commissioned from Sir Ninian Comper in 1938.[150] The

---

[148] Eric Milner-White, 'Report on the Windows of Ely Cathedral', *Friends of Ely Cathedral, 1st Annual Report*, 1937, pp. 10–19.

[149] Lionel Edward Blackburne (1874–1951) was Vicar of St Mark's, Portsmouth 1909–23, Archdeacon of Surrey 1922–36, Canon of Winchester 1922–30, and Canon of Guildford 1930–6.

[150] Sir (John) Ninian Comper (1864–1960), church architect and ecclesiologist, a pupil of G.F. Bodley and T. Garner, has been described as 'the last rose of the summer of the Gothic Revival' (*DNB*).

Sparke monument was cleared out and the Evans window removed.[151] In their place Comper set an 'English' altar, with riddel-posts and hangings, and above it, one of his typically pale windows. The funds of the theological students were limited and the window was installed panel by panel between 1938 and 1947, when the Chapter agreed to bear the remaining costs[152] (Plate 54).

In the Friends' first *Report* Bishop White-Thomson issued almost a manifesto: 'We have only to look at the font, at most of the stained glass, or even at the pulpit . . . to realise that we have already some articles of "furniture" which ought not to have been admitted into the Cathedral.' Blackburne consulted Sir Charles Peers on various aspects of the arrangement of the Cathedral, and Peers advised him to clear the Octagon of its benches and stalls 'and to use the nave for congregational worship'.[153]

The *Reports* give useful accounts of the restoration and redecoration in the Cathedral, and the aspirations and frustrations of successive deans. In the second *Report* (1938) Blackburne announced the abandonment of plans to use the nave for services until a second organ could be placed there. He redecorated St Catherine's Chapel, which was darkened by Wilmshurst's windows. One was removed, and the east window was moved aside, and replaced by a new east window by Hugh Easton, a rather stiff representation of Christ reigning from the Tree, a bright green cross of living wood. The window's plain glass surrounds succeeded in letting in more light. Sir Charles Peers designed a lectern of oak, the gift of the Mothers' Union.[154]

In the third *Report* (1939) good progress was reported in the Lady Chapel's restoration by H.C. Hughes of Cambridge. The delicate carvings were cleaned with a vacuum cleaner, and the wall monuments, barely supported by rusted iron-work, were moved to the lobby linking the chapel to the north transept. The vaulting-ribs needed much restoration, and the roof-bosses were cleaned, but not recoloured or regilded[155] (Plate 53).

Then war came, work on the Cathedral was suspended, and meetings of the Friends ceased until 1946. The fourth *Report* (1947) brought news of renewed activity in the Lady Chapel. Stephen Dykes Bower[156] was designing an altar and east end furnishings, and Martin Travers,[157] stained glass for the east window. During the war Lord Fairhaven and his brother, of Anglesey Abbey, Cambridgeshire, gave plate and furnishings for the High Altar and Lady Chapel, including two Italian gilt elbow chairs and four gilt seventeenth-century Spanish candlesticks. The fifth and sixth *Reports* (1948 and 1949) told of Lady Waechter de Grimston's work in recolouring

---

[151] It was at first suggested that the monument might be re-erected in the western aisle of the north transept, and the window might find a place in the nave north gallery, next to the Pearson window.

[152] The Friends' leaflet on the scheme is EDC 4/5/181; letters from Comper on the scheme, 1936–7, are EDC 4/5/174–180.

[153] Sir Charles Reed Peers (1868–1952), antiquary, was a pupil of Sir Thomas Jackson, architect. In 1903 he became architectural editor of the Victoria County History, and was chief inspector of monuments at the Office of Works, 1913–33.

[154] Made by Laurence Turner. EDC 4/5/182, receipt, 17 December 1937.

[155] See EDC 4/5/186–198 for correspondence and reports.

[156] Stephen Ernest Dykes Bower (1903–94) was Surveyor of the Fabric of Westminster Abbey, 1951–73, and architect for the enlargement of St Edmundsbury Cathedral, and worked in many cathedrals and churches.

[157] (Howard) Martin (Otho) Travers (1886–1948), a pupil of Sir Ninian Comper, was instructor in stained glass at the Royal College of Art, 1925–48.

Robert Steward's, William Lynne's and Sir Mark Steward's monuments, and the coats of arms on Bishop Allen's, Heton's, Greene's and Moore's monuments.[158]

In 1949 Dykes Bower's Lady Chapel work was completed, with riddel posts, altar hangings, a frontal and silver cross and tall standard candlesticks, illustrated in the seventh *Report* (1950), but Martin Travers's window 'had not altogether satisfied the Dean and Chapter' and the cost – £8000 – was thought prohibitive.

Dean Hankey

Dean Blackburne retired in 1950 and was succeeded by Patrick Hankey[159] (Plate 58*a*). In the early 1950s the programme of embellishment came to an abrupt halt when a survey of the Cathedral's roofs revealed shocking evidence of rot and infestation by death watch beetle. The 1952 *Report* estimated that £60,000 was needed for the Octagon alone.[160] A brochure *Ely in Peril* featured a stark cover photograph showing the scaffolding erected against possible collapse of the Lantern (Plate 56*a*). An appeal was launched for funds to cover a five-year campaign of eradication and repair. Stephen Dykes Bower, the architect, wrote about the Lantern's history, and previous efforts to restore or strengthen it, explaining that 'on the upper side of some of the great arched members of the vault, the wood has been eaten away almost down to the boarding of the painted ceiling', and the huge oak corner posts had been similarly ravaged. He then described the remedial action needed in the other wooden roofs, ending by saying 'there is much else to do. If further deterioration is to be avoided . . . its accomplishment is vital and urgent.'[161] By 1953 three of the eight huge Lantern beams had been repaired,[162] and work went on steadily throughout the 1950s. £60,000 had been raised by 1958, and releading of the Lantern was almost complete.

Dykes Bower was further employed in designing a County War Memorial Chapel in the presbytery behind the high altar. The *Friends' Year Book* observed that 'it will be a great pleasure to have that untidy and shapeless area restored to beauty and to use',[163] containing as it did Bishop Allen's mosaic tomb-slab, Canon Hodge Mill's monument, and incised stones over Canon Fardell's grave and possibly the eighteenth-century bishops buried there. These were cleared out, and Dykes Bower paved the area with polished Purbeck marble. Only the position of Bishop Allen's grave was marked by an inscription in the marble. The east wall ('the present discoloured stone wall') was panelled in oak, with pilasters and Corinthian capitals – not, as the *Year Book* stated, part of the old organ case, but rather woodwork removed from the east end of Holy

---

[158] Armatrude (1890–1982), daughter of Bertie Hobart and Mrs Hobart Grimston of Grimston Garth, Yorkshire, married Sir Max Waechter (1837–1924) as his second wife in 1912.

[159] Cyril Patrick Hankey (1886–1973) was Vicar of Little St Mary's, Cambridge, 1925–38, Vicar of Aldenham (Bedfordshire), 1941–6, and Vicar of St Paul's, Bedford, 1946–51.

[160] *Friends of Ely Cathedral, 9th Annual Report*, 1952, p. 7.

[161] 'The Architect Explains', in *Ely in Peril*, brochure, [1953], EDC 4/5/363. There was also a supplementary brochure, 'The Death-watch Beetle is at Work!', with monstrous bugs superimposed on an aerial view of the Cathedral, and a humorous account, 'The Tragic History of the Death-watch Beetle (Communicated, and, in the main, correct. C.P. Hankey)' (EDC 4/5/364) (Plate 56*c*).

[162] *Friends of Ely Cathedral, 10th Annual Report*, 1953, p. 7.

[163] *Friends of Ely Cathedral, 9th Annual Report*, 1952, p. 9.

Trinity church in the Lady Chapel about 1850.[164] An altar was installed, and the chapel was dedicated in 1954 as St Etheldreda's Chapel.

In 1958 a Blessed Sacrament Chapel, dedicated to SS Æthelwold and Dunstan, was formed in the south-east corner of the south transept by Donovan Purcell. A bay of the library was removed and a partition made. Old tapestries were given by R.C. Briscoe for this partition, and in 1964 and 1973 fragments of glass from other parts of the Cathedral were arranged in the window by Dennis King, in memory of Sir Will Spens.[165]

In 1961 the Goldsmiths' Company offered to provide a new high altar cross, to be made by Louis Osman, with an appliqué crucifix sculpted by Graham Sutherland.[166] When it was finished in 1965 it was not accepted – either on aesthetic grounds or because it had cost more than anticipated and could not be afforded.[167] A happier fate awaited David Wynne's bronze of Christ and Mary Magdalene, which found a place in the south transept in 1967[168] (Plate 64a).

The west tower once more gave cause for concern. Jacques Heyman reported that, in addition to serious decay and instability, some of Scott's strengthening works now needed replacement.[169] With other works the total amount needed was £200,000. The professional fundraisers Hooker Craigmyle and Co. were employed for this appeal,[170] which ran through the 1970s – a period of steep inflation – and had raised £365,000 by 1977. In 1974 Heyman devised a system for binding the west tower with a concrete ring reinforced with steel, at the top of the Lantern and linked to the turrets by the existing masonry bridges. 'This made one solid piece of immense strength holding the entire structure together ... It was felt that if the problem had not now been solved, it was insoluble'[171] (Plate 57a).

Octagon furnishings

In 1967 Mowbray Smith, an honorary canon,[172] offered £2000 for an altar in the Octagon and other beautification of the Cathedral. Dean Carey proposed to re-order the Octagon in the light of the liturgical movement's emphasis on the centrality of the eucharist in the life of the Church and the move towards celebration westwards, facing the congregation, and thus realising the full potential of Ely's great central space, which since the mid nineteenth century had been mostly filled with benches.[173]

Continuing their old policy, the Chapter did not turn to the Surveyor, Donovan Purcell, but to George Pace,[174] an architect with a distinguished career in Cathedral

---

164 A drawing of the panelling in John Bacon's 'Gleanings from Ely Cathedral and Monastery', EDC 4/6/7, p. 48, confirms this. The question remains whether this panelling was re-used in the Lady Chapel from the late 17th-century panelling around the old high altar of the Cathedral.

165 Sir Will Spens (1882–1962) was Master of Corpus Christi College, Cambridge, 1927–52, and afterwards Steward to the Dean & Chapter of Ely, 1952–62.

166 *Friends of Ely Cathedral Year Book (18th Annual Report)*, (1961), pp. 5–6.

167 It was eventually sold to a private collector in France. Correspondence on the scheme is EDC 4/5/400–45.

168 *Friends of Ely Cathedral Year Book (24th Annual Report)*, (1967), p. 16.

169 Jacques Heyman (b. 1925) was Professor of Engineering at Cambridge, 1971–92.

170 They had raised funds for Winchester, Salisbury, York, Chester and Worcester.

171 *Friends of Ely Cathedral Year Book (31st Annual Report)*, (1974), p. 8.

172 Vicar of Wisbech, 1919–60. Correspondence on this benefaction is EDC 4/5/446–448.

173 An oak altar, on castors, had been given for the nave in 1960 *(Friends' Year Book (17th Annual Report)*, (1960), and the following year it was reported as being almost permanently in place.

174 George Pace (1915–75) of York reconstructed Llandaff Cathedral after wartime bomb damage and provided

architecture and furnishing. In 1969 Pace produced a 'Feasibility Study for Liturgical Reordering of the Octagon'.[175] In this he wrote that 'Cathedrals are live buildings, and as and when the demands of worship and use require it, liturgical re-ordering is a legitimate exercise. In the past re-ordering has always been carried out naturally in the architectural manner of the time . . . Since the breakdown of organic culture it is necessary to give very special thought to re-ordering and new works in Cathedrals to make sure that whilst the works are of the age in which they are done they, at the same time, integrate with the works of previous ages. This is no longer automatic and requires the greatest care, skill, inspiration and, above all, self-discipline of the architect.'

Pace insisted that all new furniture must be 'utterly simple, self-disciplined and designed so as to integrate naturally into the total setting of the Cathedral and yet, at the same time . . . be utterly subordinate'. It must also be movable, capable of being stored when not needed, and even removed altogether 'in the future if alteration in liturgical use required this'. Pace provided three schemes, positioning the altar at the centre of the Octagon, at the entrance to the nave, or against Scott's screen, but the central location was never seriously in doubt. This was Pace's preferred scheme. As the project unfolded, modifications were made. Pace had proposed still to fill the Octagon with blocks of seating, ignoring the logic of the eight sides; and to leave the choir in their stalls east of the screen.

The altar was installed first, in 1970, a simple wooden structure raised on a dais, in light oak, without any altar cloth or frontal (Plate 59a). Behind it were simple oak seats for the celebrant and two assistants. In 1972 interlocking chairs, also in light oak, were purchased in Denmark and arranged in the nave, transepts and western part of the Octagon. It proved impracticable, and undesirable, to leave the choristers in the choir, and in 1975 two ranks of stalls, open metal platforms with oak seats, were placed obliquely in the east of the Octagon, near, but not obscuring, Scott's screen. Finally in 1978 new ranks of stalls for the bishop and the dean and canons, in style matching the celebrants' seats, were placed at the north-east and south-east angles of the Octagon (Plate 59b).

Pace's requirements, of recognising the Octagon as the focal point of the Cathedral, and of providing a set of furnishings which looked solid and permanent, yet could be easily moved as required, were fully realised in the Octagon scheme. In December 1968 this shift in emphasis was reinforced when Mattins ceased to be sung on Sundays in the choir, and the Cathedral eucharist, at 10.30 a.m., became the central act of worship, in the Octagon.

---

nave furnishings and the King George VI Memorial Chapel at Windsor. Correspondence on the Octagon scheme is at EDC 4/5/449–587.
[175] EDC 4/5/451.

Music 1836–1980

Nicholas Thistlethwaite

Robert Janes (1806–66) had been articled to Zechariah Buck, Organist of Norwich Cathedral. Buck was a celebrated, if eccentric, trainer of boys' voices,[1] and by appointing the pupil, the Dean and Chapter perhaps hoped to acquire some of the master's skills. Initially, they were not disappointed. W.E. Dickson (later Precentor) visited the Cathedral whilst an undergraduate in the 1840s. He commented on the proficiency of the eight choristers – 'big lads of thirteen or fourteen years of age' – and was assured that 'the efficient execution of treble solos was seldom or never marred by the absence of a leading boy'.[2] The new organist also improved the 'slovenly' standard of chanting inherited from the Skeats era.[3] He prepared a pointed psalter which was published in 1837.[4] Before this, cathedral singers had been left to their own devices to marry words and music using the 'rule of three and five' (*i.e.* changing note on the third or fifth syllable from the end of each half-verse) with results that can be imagined.[5] Janes's efforts to reintroduce sung versicles and responses, discontinued since 1730, encountered greater resistance. The minor canons accused him of trying to lengthen the service, and Janes was forced to retreat, having completed only a harmonisation of the General Confession.[6]

That episode illustrates the limitations of reform during the 1830s. Habits were slow to change. The canon in residence would still occasionally send one of the choristers to the organist during the morning service to tell him to omit the anthem, and the lay clerks' attendance was said to be 'very irregular'; a later generation remembered them as 'thirsty subjects', who 'used to go about drinking from place to place, and were often in an unfit state to attend afternoon service'[7] – charges which are lent some substance by a Chapter order of 1837 that every lay clerk should be required to sign an undertaking not

---

[1] F.G. Kitton, *Zechariah Buck: A Centenary Memoir* (London, 1899), *passim.*

[2] W.E. Dickson, *Fifty Years of Church Music* (Ely, 1894), pp. 53–4.

[3] Basil Harwood's reminiscences of Ely music, EDC 14/26, p. 3.

[4] *The Psalter; or, Psalms of David, carefully Marked and Pointed, by Robert Janes* (Ely, 1837). The Cathedral purchased fifty copies in 1837, presumably for the use of the choir and clergy (EDC 3/1/9, *Expensae Necessariae*, 1837–8).

[5] B.J.G. Rainbow, *The Choral Revival in the Anglican Church, 1839–72* (London, 1970), p. 83.

[6] This became known as the 'Ely Confession' and continued in use at the Cathedral until the end of the nineteenth century: see Dickson, *Fifty Years*, pp. 64–5; EDC 14/26, p. 3.

[7] Charles Johnson, *Cathedral Lay Clerks* (Ely, 1897), pp. 13–14.

to 'keep any Public Inn or house for the Sale of Beer, nor engage in any business which would interfere with his regular attendance in the Choir'.[8]

The arrival of Dean Peacock in 1839 marked the beginning of an era of reform which touched all aspects of the Cathedral's life. Under Peacock's leadership, the choir was re-ordered, a Choristers' School was founded, and efforts were made to improve both the quality and the remuneration of the lay clerks. The chanting of the service was also gradually resumed.

The Precentor

On the occasion of his first visit in 1842, Dickson had been 'much impressed by the quiet dignity and gravity of the service'. Whether standards had indeed improved radically since Peacock's arrival three years earlier may be doubted, but Dickson was encouraged to observe the new Dean and the canon in residence following the day's music in a bass part book. Certainly the means to improvement were at hand. There were daily music lessons for the choristers during the hour before Mattins, and in 1842 rehearsals on Monday and Friday evenings for the full choir were introduced.[9] Dickson described these evening rehearsals as he experienced them in the late 1850s:

> Twice in each week . . . the whole choir was brought together at the school-room; Mr Janes or his pupil sate at the piano-forte; selections from the music appointed for the week were carefully sung. It was soon found at the second rehearsal in each week [that] ample leisure was afforded for the practice of compositions other than those appointed for the weekly lists . . . [The boys] became exceedingly expert readers at sight, not easily stopped by difficulties . . . Hearing that Palestrina's celebrated 'Missa Papae Marcelli' had been sung in London . . . we sent for copies . . . I doubt if any mistake worth notice was made in rendering this great mass at sight without the pianoforte.[10]

By the time of Dickson's appointment as Precentor (1858) Janes had largely withdrawn from his duties, 'having become completely independent of professional earnings'.[11] Like Hawkins before him, he had a large teaching connection in Norfolk and Suffolk, and undertook long journeys on horseback, with 'a pair of lamps, attached to his saddle like pistol-holders, to light his lonely road at night through the fen country'. His reward was a four-figure income.[12] Articled pupils were responsible for most of the duties at Ely, although nominated lay clerks also assisted with the training of the younger boys.[13]

In 1858, Janes resigned as *Magister Choristarum*, retaining the duties and stipend (£110 a year) of Organist.[14] In his place, the Chapter appointed Frederick Helmore to

---

[8] EDC 2/2A/5, p. 377, 25 November 1837.

[9] According to Dickson, *Fifty Years*, p. 60, this occurred in 1842; the earliest reference in the Order Book is dated 25 November 1843, when Janes was given an extra £10 for his trouble in superintending the twice-weekly rehearsals: EDC 2/2A/6, p. 26.

[10] Dickson, *Fifty Years*, p. 60.

[11] *Ibid.*, p. 59.

[12] *Ibid.*, p. 54.

[13] In 1849 the 'allowance of £20' that had been paid to Robert Macro (a lay clerk and former chorister) 'for assisting Mr Janes in preparing the younger Boys' was discontinued. Macro's duties were assigned to S. Stevens, newly-appointed probationer lay clerk (EDC 2/2A/6, p. 110, 26 November 1849).

[14] *Ibid.*, p. 255, 30 December 1858.

have 'the entire charge of the teaching (musical and general) . . . of the Choristers', thus formalising an arrangement which seems to have begun in April 1857. He was to receive the statutable salary of £10, augmented to £80 a year, and was also confirmed as a lay clerk. Helmore ('the Musical Missionary') was an important figure in the Victorian choral revival.[15] He spent much of his life travelling through England and Scotland, recruiting and training parish choirs, to whom he taught plainsong and polyphony. Characteristically, he did not stay long at Ely: his resignation was noted in May 1860.[16] Dickson was thereupon appointed *Magister Choristarum*, undertaking the duties with evident satisfaction until the arrival of Janes's successor in 1867.[17]

Janes's last years were overshadowed by ill health. In 1861, he was allowed £20 to retain the services of an assistant, Walter Scott, 'Mr Janes being at present incapacitated by illness', and Scott continued to be paid gratuities up to and including the interregnum that followed Janes's death on 10 June 1866.[18]

The incapacity of the Organist increased the power of the Precentor to direct the musical life of the Cathedral. An earlier attempt by the Precentor to do so was by no means successful.[19] James Henderson (1819–79) was appointed in 1848, and in May 1849 Dean Peacock wrote to Edward Sparke: 'The choir is greatly improved but the merit of it is Mr. Henderson's and not Mr. Janes'.'[20] Henderson was already issuing weekly music lists or combination papers 'in accordance with the *accustomed practice of this and other Cathedral churches*'.[21] Not only did Henderson select the music, but he assigned the various (solo) parts to particular singers. This pre-empted the Organist's choice, and, since copies of Henderson's lists were placed in the Dean's and Canons' stalls, it also usurped their customary right to a say in the choice of music. Soon, Peacock was writing to Sparke, 'I hope to bring about a lasting peace with Mr. Janes and Mr. H. . . . I am doing my best to effect it.'[22] An uneasy truce seems to have lasted until 1851, though Peacock hinted at further trouble in 1850, in a letter to Sparke: 'I am disturbed by a correspondence with Mr. Henderson: his head is somewhat turned with his dignity as Precentor: I am very sorry for it, for though not a judicious man, he is a very likeable person.'[23]

In August 1851 Henderson drew up three combination papers and went on holiday. On his return, Janes told him that Peacock had ordered the lists to be disregarded and had issued his own lists. Furthermore, Peacock said that he intended to continue to select music. Henderson petitioned him that such action was contrary to the Statutes and brought the Precentor's office into contempt. The final straw came in October 1852, when the Chapter ordered Henderson to submit his combination papers to the Dean or

[15] Rainbow, *Choral Revival* (cit. in n. 5), pp. 115–39.

[16] EDC 2/2A/6, p. 282, 25 May 1860.

[17] *Ibid.*, p. 296, 26 November 1860.

[18] *Ibid.*, p. 311, 25 November 1861; EDC 2/2A/7, p. 28, 25 November 1865; EDC 3/1/10, 28 November 1865, 11 October 1866, 1 January 1867. Scott was a former Ely chorister who had been articled to Janes in 1853: see EDC 3/1/9, 12 December 1853.

[19] The account of James Henderson's period as Precentor is added by Peter Meadows.

[20] NRO, UPC 301/163, 18 May 1849.

[21] Appeal petition to the Bishop as Visitor, 1852, EDC 10/1C/1, from which many of the following details are derived. There are no surviving combination papers from this period at Ely.

[22] NRO, UPC 301/165, 31 May 1849.

[23] NRO, UPC 301/124, 26 June 1850.

Canon in residence before they were issued.[24] Henderson at once appealed to the Bishop. Peacock confided to Sparke 'I showed the Statutes to Charles Selwyn who as a lawyer says he could have no case.'[25] That a state of crisis continued for some time is suggested by another letter from Peacock to Sparke: 'Mr. Henderson refuses to do any additional duty . . . unless he is paid for it: this is taking high ground.'[26]

There is a copy of Henderson's petition in the Dean and Chapter archives, and in November 1852 Peacock was preparing a response to it.[27] Bishop Turton was anxious to adjudicate, and Peacock was inclined to accept the Bishop's visitatorial decision,[28] but details are lacking in the Diocesan records. Turton presumably upheld the Chapter's October 1852 order: and Peacock wrote to Sparke in February 1853: 'I wish he could find some other position, for he never can act harmoniously with us, after what has occurred.'[29] Shortly afterwards Henderson resigned as Precentor.[30] Somehow, however, matters were arranged, and in November 1853 Henderson was reappointed, subject to the Chapter order of October 1852.[31] In 1855 Henderson was appointed Curate of Holy Trinity, Ely, but even at this remove he managed to annoy Peacock, who objected to the placing of an organ in the Lady Chapel: 'I said all that I could against it and I told him that as long as it was retained I would resist the expenditure of a single shilling upon the chapel.'[32]

In the absence of further documents, correspondence, or examples of the combination papers[33] it is difficult to say where precisely the fault lay. It is probable that Henderson's idea of the role of the Precentor, advanced for its day (at Ely at least), combined with an unsubtlety of character and approach, led to the crisis of 1852 and an unsettled state of affairs for as long as Henderson continued in office.

Precentors were key figures in the reform of cathedral music in the nineteenth century. After a brief interlude when Henry Wray succeeded Henderson, before leaving in 1858 to become Precentor of Winchester, the next Precentor, William Edward Dickson (1823–1910), wielded considerable influence. He was to be paid £200 a year on the following terms:

> That he be required to superintend the performance of daily Morning and Evening Service in the Cathedral, to intone the prayers on Sundays, and also on all other days in alternate weeks, to preside at the practice of the Choir and to exercise a general superintendance over the musical and other studies of the Choristers . . .

> That he submit the weekly Combination papers of the Services and Anthems to the Dean or in his absence to the Canon in residence for his approval.[34]

---

[24] EDC 2/2A/6, p. 150, 1 October 1852.
[25] NRO, UPC 306/11, 9 October 1852.
[26] NRO, UPC 306/14, 14 October [1852].
[27] NRO, UPC 306/18, 20 November 1852.
[28] NRO, UPC 301/30, 30 December 1852.
[29] NRO, UPC 301/27, 24 February [1853].
[30] EDC 2/2A/6, p. 157, 18 March 1853.
[31] *Ibid.*, p. 169, 25 November 1853. Henderson was also required to 'take such a seat in the choir as may be deemed most convenient for the superintendence of the performance of the choral service.'
[32] NRO, UPC 306/27 (bundle, 3), 16 March 1858.
[33] They were presumably hand-written.
[34] EDC 2/2A/6, p. 244, 24 August 1858.

Dickson was to serve the Cathedral for thirty-seven years. To him, the Cathedral was indebted 'for the care and orderliness which marked the daily services throughout his term of office'. Harwood described him as 'a most excellent friend to the Cathedral Choristers', recalling his 'tall, upright figure, in his long-sleeved surplice, marshalling the boys in the Choir Vestry before each Service'.[35] Like Trollope's Septimus Harding, Dickson possessed a violoncello, whilst his mechanical skills were deployed in constructing model engines and organs.[36] The strain of serving as *Magister Choristarum* during Janes's decline took its toll, and he was given leave of absence for three months in 1864.[37] Thirty years later, on his retirement in 1895, the Chapter granted him a pension of £75 *p.a.* and the use (rent free) of the Precentor's house, where he died on Christmas Day 1910.

The Choristers' School

Dickson's concern for the welfare of the choristers was not only the consequence of personal inclination. It also reflected the Chapter's growing sense of responsibility for the formation of the boys who sang daily in the Cathedral.

There had been little evidence of this in the 1830s. Only one chorister (Thomas Kempton) appears in the list of King's Scholars at the Grammar School during that decade; and so low was the state of the school that Kempton was the sole Scholar by 1838.[38] A year or two later, attempts were made, possibly at the instigation of Dean Peacock, to set matters on a better footing. In 1842, six choristers are recorded as 'grammar boys', and in the following year, John McLochlin, one of the lay clerks, was paid as 'Teacher of the Choristers' and then (from 1844) usher.[39] Clearly, the Chapter was endeavouring to provide for the choristers' education, either on the Foundation or alongside it.

This arrangement did not commend itself to John Ingle, appointed schoolmaster in 1852 with a brief to modernise the school. In his response to the Cathedral Commissioners (1854) he noted that of the existing thirty-nine pupils, eleven were choristers, eight of whom were on the Foundation.[40] He proposed the creation of 'a commercial department, or middle school', and suggested that it would probably be found beneficial 'to draught off most of the choristers into this department'. The presence of all the choristers in the grammar school was a 'serious evil':

> From the fact of their musical and cathedral duties occupying seldom less, and sometimes more, than six hours a day, it is obvious that they cannot keep pace with the work of a grammar school. They attend during a part only of each day . . . as their ages vary from seven to seventeen, it is necessary, small as is their number, to arrange them in three classes. This greatly increases our labour, making in fact two schools instead of one; and is a fruitful source of irregularity and confusion.[41]

---

[35] EDC 14/26, p. 3.
[36] *Ibid.*
[37] EDC 2/2A/7, p. 36, 14 June 1864.
[38] EDC 3/8/3.
[39] EDC 3/1/10, 11 October 1843; 1 January 1844.
[40] Owen and Thurley, *King's School*, p. 121.
[41] *Ibid.*, p. 124.

The Chapter were unable or unwilling to accede to Ingle's views, though later that year they augmented his salary by £30 'in consideration of the free Education of 10 of the Chorister Boys'.[42] However, Precentor Wray was also unhappy with the choristers' attendance at the grammar school, and in 1857 it was agreed

> That the Boys in the Choir, who are not on the foundation of the Grammar School, be placed . . . under the instruction of Mr. Helmore and that the Dean and canon in residence be authorized . . . to fit up a Room or Rooms . . . as a temporary Schoolroom.[43]

Two years later, the Chapter created a site for a new Choristers' School by the demolition of a cottage, some stables and a coach house on land adjoining the Sacrist's Gate. There was a house for the schoolmaster, a small playground, and two classrooms – one of them a large room on the first floor, to which the twice-weekly full rehearsals were now transferred from the Organist's house.[44]

The Precentor superintended the school but the teaching was in the hands of a 'certificated master'. This was Henry Jackman, who had come from the choir school maintained jointly by Trinity and St John's Colleges in Cambridge.[45] He took up his duties in September 1860 and was paid £75 *p.a.* with occupation of the schoolmaster's house, free of rent, rates and taxes.[46] In 1876, his stipend was increased to £100 *p.a.*, 'and a further sum of £20 a year, this last sum to be dependent on the result of an annual Examination'; for this he was to educate twenty-four scholars 'on condition that they may become Choristers if found efficient'; vacancies were to be advertised as they became available and candidates admitted following a musical test.[47] Eight years later (1884) Jackman retired and was succeeded by Edmund Sergeant Boulter.[48]

Although the Chapter passed an order in 1864 that former choristers should be regarded as admissible to the Grammar School provided they were of sufficient proficiency to take their place in the second form,[49] there is little evidence of this happening. The choristers were boys from the town (the sons of small tradesmen and artisans) whose education now focused exclusively on the Chorister School; the grammar school was intended to be for the sons of gentlemen and the professional classes.

The number of choristers had been increased from the statutory eight to twelve, sometime between Dickson's visit in 1842 and the report of the Commissioners in 1854. Dickson himself seems to have added a further eight (including four probationers) while *Magister Choristarum.*[50] By 1870, the eight senior choristers were paid £7, and eight juniors received £2.[51] The £20 apprenticeship fee was invested in a Savings Bank to be

---

[42] EDC 2/2A/6, p. 183, 25 November 1854.

[43] *Ibid.*, p. 231, 15 June 1857. There were fears also that Ingle was introducing Tractarian or Romanising practices in the grammar school at this time, which might have strengthened the Dean and Chapter in their resolve to remove the choirboys: see a pamphlet *Tractarianism and Ely Cathedral Grammar School. Report of Public Meeting, Ely, held December 2, 1858*, 2nd edn (Ely, [1858]), of which there is a copy in EDC 11.

[44] EDC 4/6/3: p. 144; Goodwin, *Ely Gossip*, p. 12; Dickson, *Fifty Years* (cit. in n. 2), p. 59.

[45] Owen and Thurley, *King's School*, p. 140.

[46] EDC 3/1/11, 8 February 1861; EDC 10/5, Choir School papers.

[47] EDC 2/2A/6, p. 209, 25 November 1876.

[48] *Ibid.*, p. 305, 28 July 1884; p. 309, 25 November 1884.

[49] *Ibid.*, p. 18, 19 February 1864.

[50] *Ibid.*

[51] EDC 3/8/5, 1870.

applied for the benefit of the former chorister 'at the discretion of the Dean & Chapter'.[52] Two, for example, went on to train as school teachers.[53]

The lay clerks

The Chapter had risen to the challenge of providing an adequate education for the choristers. They were less successful in improving the lot of the lay clerks.

Few of the men were of local origin after 1830. Vacancies were advertised in the London musical press and in provincial newspapers (Yorkshire was regarded as a fruitful source of singers), and most of the men appointed during Janes's time came from elsewhere. Some stayed upwards of thirty years; others moved to other cathedrals. Supernumeraries first appeared in 1855,[54] and by 1861 there were three of them.[55]

Like their predecessors, the lay clerks were concerned about the irregularity of their income, most of which was still derived from their agricultural estate. The income varied from year to year, depending upon factors largely outside their control, and they protested that it was in any case inadequate. They also began to agitate for proper holidays.

In 1859 the Chapter agreed that each lay clerk should have a fortnight's leave of absence in the course of the year, and this was extended to three weeks from 1870.[56] The timing was to be agreed with the precentor, 'in such manner as not to interfere with the orderly Performance of Divine Service'.[57] Reducing the number of weekly choral services was more problematic. When in 1888 the lay clerks petitioned the Chapter for a day's holiday each week, and the Chapter responded by introducing a said Evensong on Mondays, the Bishop (Lord Alwyne Compton) objected and the choral service was reinstated. As poor compensation, Wednesday's Evensong was moved to 7.30 p.m. Not until 1908 did Monday's Evensong cease to be choral.[58]

In 1841 the Chapter augmented the lay clerks' salaries by £12 a year, introducing at the same time a new scale of fines for non-attendance.[59] This meant that each lay clerk enjoyed an income of approximately £80 a year from the Cathedral. Five years later (1846) the lay clerks expended £300 on the improvement of their Stuntney estate. They borrowed £100 from the Chapter, and this had to be repaid in subsequent years, diminishing the return on their land and consequently their incomes.[60] The management of the estates was a heavy burden on the lay clerks, who were ill-equipped for such a task. In 1860 they asked the Chapter to assume responsibility for the estates, granting them in return fixed stipends. The Chapter compromised by agreeing to advance quarterly payments which could then be repaid when the farm income came in, and they also gave £100 towards drainage at Stuntney. The lay clerks, however, demonstrated their dissatisfaction by boycotting the Audit Dinner in November (they were never invited

---

[52] EDC 2/2A/6, p. 25, 25 November 1843.
[53] *Ibid.*, p. 85, 8 September 1847; p. 123, 14 June 1851.
[54] EDC 2/2A/6, p. 196, 14 June 1855.
[55] EDC 3/1/11, January 1861.
[56] Johnson, *Lay Clerks* (cit. in n. 7), p. 29.
[57] EDC 2/2A/6, p. 268, 14 June 1859.
[58] EDC 2/2A/7, p. 345, 4 April 1888; pp. 347–50, 14 June 1888; EDC 2/2A/8, p. 12, 25 November 1890; p. 251, 15 June 1908.
[59] EDC 2/2A/6, p. 2, 25 November 1841.
[60] *Ibid.*, pp. 76–7, 25 November 1846.

again).[61] Five years later, when 'the prevalence of the Cattle Plague' made it impossible for the lay clerks to let their washland for grazing, the Chapter granted them £80.[62] In 1869, salaries were augmented by £10 as an interim measure until the Ecclesiastical Commissioners should make 'permanent arrangements' for the men's support.[63]

Another of the lay clerks' grievances was the lack of provision for retirement. In the past, the Chapter had occasionally made *ex gratia* payments to infirm singers – in 1849 James Barrett was allowed to retire, retaining his salary, on condition that he paid £30 each year to a substitute.[64] The earliest formal provision seems to have been in 1870 when Jesse Skelding retired on a pension of £52.[65]

A further petition from the lay clerks in 1876 finally obliged the Chapter to address the outstanding issues, and a Scheme was issued in 1877 'for regulating the Position and Emoluments of Lay-Clerks'.[66] The Chapter assumed the management of the estates on the understanding that the income would be applied to the maintenance of the lay clerks.[67] They were divided into two classes on fixed stipends of, respectively, £100 and £80 a year. Those who retired due to failure of the voice were entitled to a pension of not less than half their stipend, provided they had held office for fifteen years.[68] Shorter terms of service would be rewarded at the discretion of the Dean and Chapter. There would be four lay clerks in each division, but promotion from the second to the first class was not automatic.[69]

The lay clerks had attained two of their objectives (fixed stipends and pensions) but individual stipends were inadequate and remained so. Petitions for increases in 1903, 1913 and 1914 were turned down, and it was not until 1919 that a modest pay rise was agreed (£120, and £110 for second class)[70] (Plate 47c).

Organists and organ

In the later Victorian years, Ely attracted the services of several notable musicians. Edmund Chipp (1823–86), who succeeded Janes in 1867, was a fine player, who had made a name for himself as a concert organist in London and Belfast (Plate 47a). He was one of the first English organists to play Mendelssohn's organ sonatas.[71] Dickson disapproved of his discontinuing the second weekly choir rehearsal[72] but he seems to have given general satisfaction. He lived in a house on Palace Green, declining the new

---

[61] Johnson, *Lay Clerks*, p. 18.

[62] EDC 2/2A/6, p. 295, 26 November 1860; p. 300, 29 January 1861, p. 300; EDC 2/2A/7, p. 60, 14 June 1866.

[63] EDC 2/2A/7, p. 114, 25 November 1869.

[64] EDC 2/2A/6, p. 110, 26 November 1849.

[65] EDC 2/2A/7, p. 137, 25 November 1870.

[66] *Ibid.*, p. 215, 14 June 1877.

[67] In fact, the income more than halved between 1880 and 1900 on account of the agricultural depression; see EDC 10/3A/4, lay clerks' estate, accounts.

[68] These provisions were modified to one-third of the stipend, and twenty years' tenure in 1883; see EDC 10/3G/1, *Rules and Regulations for Lay Clerks and Probationers*.

[69] *Ibid.*

[70] EDC 10/8b (1903 petition); EDC 2/2A/8, p. 327, 25 November 1913; p. 334, 15 June 1914; EDC 2/2A/9, p. 71, 23 June 1919.

[71] Obituary notice of Chipp, *Musical Times*, vol. 28 (1887), pp. 100–1. See also 'A Visit to Ely Cathedral', *ibid.*, vol. 43 (1902), pp. 155–61, for additional information.

[72] Dickson, *Fifty Years*, p. 61.

Organist's house on the north side of the Cathedral,[73] and was given salary increases in 1870 (to £200), 1873 (£220) and 1885 (£230).[74] From 1880 he was allowed an assistant to whom the Chapter paid £20 a year.[75] Dean Goodwin recalled Chipp's playing:

> On a summer's evening, full moon by choice, he would invite us to listen to a little music in the Cathedral. The effect was thrilling . . . Beethoven's (so-called) *Moonlight Sonata*, Schubert's *Ave Maria*, and some of Bach's Fugues, rise to my memory with special delight.[76]

He was a minor composer, chiefly of piano, organ and choral pieces, but he also wrote oratorios and odes, and a number of services and settings for Ely.

Chipp's successor was Basil Harwood (1859–1949) (Plate 47b). He was 'required to preside at the Organ at all services on Week days and Sundays throughout the year . . . and also to train the men and boys for the singing in the Cathedral'.[77] He stayed only briefly at Ely (1887–92) before returning to Oxford as Organist of Christ Church Cathedral.[78] Nor did Harwood's immediate successors stay much longer. Thomas Tertius Noble (1867–1953) had been C.V. Stanford's assistant at Trinity College, Cambridge (Plate 47b). He was at Ely for six years (1892–8) before moving to York Minster. Hugh Percy Allen (1869–1946) moved to Ely from St Asaph's Cathedral. Two years later (1900) he was appointed to New College, Oxford, eventually becoming Professor of Music and Director of the Royal College of Music. His successor, Archibald Wayett Wilson (1869–1950), also arrived at Ely from St Asaph. He remained until 1919 when he moved to Manchester Cathedral[79] (Plate 50b).

The organ at which Chipp and his successors 'presided' was located on the north side of the Choir. It incorporated the new instrument provided by Elliot & Hill in 1831 at a cost of £615.[80] This stood within the old cases on Essex's screen and was the first Ely organ to possess pedals. Scott's plan to move the choir westwards necessitated the removal of the organ. William Hill, the organ-builder, proposed a new site above the north stalls, and this was accepted. He also suggested certain alterations and improvements, both to overcome the acoustical disadvantages of the new location (much of the organ was buried in the triforium) and to reflect the radical changes in organ design which he had pioneered during the 1840s.[81] The site was a tricky one. Scott's contribution was a magnificent 'hanging' case, based on the fifteenth-century example in Strasbourg Cathedral (Colour pl. 13b); this at least enabled the Choir and Great Organs to be bracketed out over the stalls. However, the Organist found himself in a loft beneath the vault of the north choir aisle from which he could neither communicate with his choir nor hear his instrument properly.[82] Because of the cost of adapting the

[73] EDC 2/2A/7, p. 99, 28 October 1868.
[74] *Ibid.*, p. 129, 14 June 1870; p. 170, 14 June 1873; p. 318, 25 November 1885.
[75] EDC 3/12, half-yearly accounts; see, for example, 1879–80.
[76] Goodwin, *Ely Gossip*, pp. 73–4.
[77] EDC 2/2A/7, p. 330, 21 February 1887.
[78] Shaw, *Succession of Organists*, p. 215.
[79] *Ibid.*, pp. 104–5, 190, 393–4.
[80] EDC 2/2A/5, p. 284, 4 March 1831; EDC 3/1/8, 1830–1.
[81] EDC 2/2A/6, p. 110, 26 November 1849; British Organ Archive, Birmingham, William Hill Letter Book (1838–61), pp. 248, 277.
[82] EDC 14/26, p. 4 (Harwood's reminiscences).

organ to its new situation (£665), most of the tonal alterations had to be postponed; they were finally undertaken in 1867, when the Swell was greatly enlarged, the missing pedal stops installed, and the instrument tuned to equal temperament.[83] The inhabitants of Ely subscribed towards the addition of a 32-foot sub-bass stop.[84]

In 1884, Hill & Son pneumaticised part of the action.[85] However, by 1906 the organ's age was beginning to tell. The mechanism was described as 'not only cumbrous and noisy but so nearly worn out as to threaten a collapse', and the tonal scheme as 'deficient in range and variety of stops'.[86] An appeal for £2000 was launched. When the reconstructed organ was opened in October 1908 it proved to be a landmark, providing a pattern for cathedral organs for the next fifty years. Even so, it was not complete. The builders (Harrison & Harrison) returned in 1910 to install the Solo Organ, donated by a Mr Harlock who gave a further two stops in 1913.[87]

Music

The choral repertoire evolved rather than changed radically during the years between 1830 and 1914. Most of the music was still sung from manuscript part books until the 1860s, when Dean Goodwin authorised their replacement with printed copies. The old part books were repaired and Dickson prepared a catalogue.[88]

Janes's taste is hard to establish. In 1838, and again in 1840, he was allowed to purchase copies of Purcell's anthems. The accounts also record the acquisition of music by S.S. Wesley (1854, 1862), Best (1860) and Ouseley (1861), as well as unspecified items from Novello's, the music publishers.[89] The Precentor's book notes that Janes reintroduced some earlier settings discarded by Skeats, and an organ book of the 1830s reveals additions by Jackson, Bridgewater, and Janes himself.[90] Possibly it was his sensational setting of the Nicene Creed, with a pedal part and clusters of chords, that provoked Bishop Allen's complaint about 'too much modern Musick' (above, p. 292).

Combination papers were printed from at least 1853.[91] They survive from December 1868 onwards.[92] Throughout Dickson's years, nineteenth-century composers were prominent – T.A. Walmisley, J. Clarke-Whitfeld, Sir John Goss, S.S. Wesley and T. Attwood from an earlier generation, with Sir Joseph Barnby, Sir Arthur Sullivan, Sir George Smart, Sir John Stainer, Sir Frederick Gore-Ouseley and E.J. Hopkins among regular contemporaries. Local composers still appeared occasionally: Hawkins and Kempton, Skeats and Chipp. The earlier repertoire (post-1660) was not neglected, and

[83] 'The Organ in Ely Cath.', *Choir and Musical Record*, vol. 5 (1866–7), p. 385; Hill & Son Order Book, vol. 2, pp. 30–1.

[84] EDC 2/2A/7, p. 85, 14 June 1867.

[85] EDC 2/2A/7, p. 303, 14 June 1884; p. 309, 25 November 1884.

[86] EDC 4/5/32 (organ appeal leaflet).

[87] EDC 2/2A/8, p. 281, 14 June 1910; p. 327, 25 November 1913; p. 335, 15 June 1914.

[88] W.E. Dickson, *Catalogue of Ancient Choral Services and Anthems, preserved among the Manuscript Scores and Part-Books in the Cathedral Church of Ely* (Cambridge and London, 1861); Dickson, *Fifty Years*, pp. 62–3; Goodwin, *Ely Gossip*, p. 87.

[89] EDC 2/2A/5, p. 387, 14 June 1838. EDC 3/1/9–11, *passim*.

[90] EDC 10/1A/5; EDC 10/7/54.

[91] EDC 3/1/10, 24 January 1853.

[92] EDC 10/8.

Handel's oratorio choruses featured regularly, but few pre-Commonwealth composers appeared apart from Gibbons and Tallis.

Attempts were made to mark the passage of the the Church's year. The organ was not used on Ash Wednesday, Fridays during Lent, or Holy Week. In 1879, on Wednesdays during Advent, there was 'Sermon and Music' including excerpts from Spohr's *Last Judgment.* A similar service was held on Wednesdays in Lent, beginning in the following year with Gounod's *Daughters of Jerusalem*, and continuing in subsequent years with Haydn's *Seven Last Words*, Stainer's *Miserere*, and unspecified Mozart. On Christmas Eve 1881, the choir sang a carol in the Octagon after Evensong, and this custom continued at the Christmas services in future years. From 1882, Evensong on Easter Eve was observed as a festival, with organ, festal responses, an Easter anthem (for example, the 'Hallelujah' chorus), and processional and recessional hymns. Dickson had a partiality for processions: Harwood later recalled 'the beauty of the Processional Hymns sung unaccompanied on great Festivals, when the Choir met the Bishop at the West Door . . .'.[93]

The music lists from 1894–5 (Dickson's final year as Precentor) reveal a modest number of contemporary pieces – services by Sir Hubert Parry, C.V. Stanford, T.T. Noble, Basil Harwood and Lloyd, for example – but the choice was predominantly mid-Victorian, with rather less 'early' music than in the 1860s.

Under Dickson's successor, John Hawke Crosby (Precentor, 1895–1923), a gradual modernisation of the repertoire is evident, though whether this reflects Crosby's own taste or the growing influence of the organists is unknown (Plate 50*b*). Composers from the earlier part of the nineteenth century are less well represented, and Sweelinck, Arcadelt and Eccard ('When to the Temple' was sung on the Feast of the Purification, 1904) make an appearance. On a rather different note, Stainer's seven Advent antiphons were introduced in 1898 on successive days in the week before Christmas, and Holy Week 1904 was a celebration of Victorian musical piety – Mendelssohn, Elvey, Stainer, Gounod, Ouseley and Handel (the latter, an honorary Victorian).

The confidence and energy of the Victorians transformed the life of the Cathedral. It is therefore hardly surprising that the achievements of their successors in the first half of the twentieth century seem modest by comparison, especially as these were over-shadowed by war and financial uncertainty.

The Great War took its toll on the staffing of the cathedral. Two lay clerks (Gentry and Key) enlisted, and another (Coates) was engaged in war work in Darlington. Gentry had also helped in the Choristers' School. Two minor canons became chaplains to the forces and so the order requiring the attendance of two at each service had to be suspended. Gentry was killed – the Chapter gave his widow a grant of £25 – and on Easter Day 1921 Sir Hugh Allen (as he had become) unveiled a memorial to former choristers who had died in the conflict.[94]

Dr Wilson's move to Manchester (1918), the death of Precentor Crosby (1923), and the retirements of Boulter the schoolmaster (1923) and Turner the senior lay clerk (1924) opened the way for change. When Turner went (he had been appointed in 1877),

[93] EDC 14/26, p. 4.
[94] EDC 2/2A/9, p. 6, 13 October 1915; p. 11, 25 November 1915; p. 16, 14 June 1916; p. 41, 21 September 1917; p. 53, 18 September 1918.

the number of lay clerks was reduced to six, salaries were equalised (£150) and regular holidays after Christmas, Easter, and in the summer were introduced.[95] Boulter had been in office since 1884. There is evidence that the Dean and Chapter had become uneasy about the school's educational efficiency[96] and upon his retirement they took the opportunity both to save money and to give themselves a greater say in its management. The new Precentor (Seiriol Evans) was appointed Master of the Choristers' School. One of the other minor canons (Reginald Gibbon) was already Assistant Master; he was shortly joined by another (Robert Lee).[97] This remained the pattern until the school's closure in 1948: one of the minor canons (usually, but not invariably, the Precentor) acted as Headmaster assisted by the others, although during the war years an assistant mistress was recruited.[98]

The Dean and Chapter did their best to enable the school to flourish. In 1924 they agreed that one of their number should be appointed 'Patronus', to visit the school and to be 'the normal intermediary between the Chapter and the Masters'. Later that year they decreed that Latin should be taught and that the cricket pitch in the Park should be levelled (the choristers had previously played on the Paradise Field). In 1934 they arranged for the boys to receive physical training from an ex-sergeant, now a publican.[99]

Attempts were made to attract other pupils to the school, though it is hard to see how this could have worked in view of the choristers' timetable (rehearsals at 8.30 a.m. and 2 p.m.; services at 9.15 a.m. and 4 p.m.).[100] After 1945, the Chapter tried to re-establish the school on a sound footing, retaining the services of the schoolmistress, spending money on furniture and re-decoration, and even talking of installing electric light, but the day of such small schools had passed.[101] In 1948, it was amalgamated with the King's School. Twenty-four boys were transferred to King's at the beginning of the summer term, the Chapter agreeing to pay an annual tuition fee of £50 for each chorister.[102]

One of the factors that had forced the Chapter's hand over the closure of the school was the difficulty of reconciling modern educational demands with the pattern of cathedral services. Various concessions had been made. In 1926, for example, it was agreed that Mattins on Thursdays should henceforth be said, in order 'to set the choristers free for work in the School'.[103] The 1939–45 war led to a reduction in the number of choral services, and sung Mattins on weekdays was finally abandoned in January 1947.[104] Holidays were gradually extended. The Christmas and Easter breaks were increased to ten days each in 1937, though the former still took place in mid-January, and it was not until 1960 that the choristers were allowed off duty after Evensong on Christmas Day. In the same year they were permitted to go home after the Lent Term, returning at the Chapter's expense for Holy Week.[105] Apart from the two

[95] EDC 2/2A/9, p. 165, 7 April 1924; pp. 167–8, 24 May; p. 171, 14 June; p. 175, 16 July.
[96] In 1919 they wrote to the Board of Education requesting 'an early inspection' of the school.
[97] EDC 2/2A/9, p. 121, 28 December 1921; p. 143, 27 March 1923; p. 147, 14 June 1923.
[98] EDC 2/2A/10, p. 151, 23 March 1942.
[99] EDC 2/2A/9, p. 162, 9 February 1924; p. 181, 25 November 1924; EDC 2/2A/10, p. 37, 26 November 1934.
[100] EDC 2/2A/9, pp. 186–7, 21 March 1925.
[101] EDC 2/2A/10, p. 199, 11 April 1946; p. 204, 14 June 1946; p. 207, 1 October 1946.
[102] *Ibid.*, p. 228, 31 January 1948.
[103] EDC 2/2A/9, p. 224, 25 November 1926.
[104] EDC 2/2A/10, p. 211, 30 December 1946.
[105] EDC 2/2A/9, p. 88, 25 November 1937; EDC 2/2A/10, p. 94, 10 August 1960; p. 61, 2 January 1960.

major festivals, singing terms had been brought into conformity with school terms by the end of the 1960s.

Noel Ponsonby, Director of Music at Marlborough College, succeeded Wilson as Organist in 1919.[106] He took the choristers for camping holidays in Norfolk (the camps continued after he left) and in 1925 he married the Bishop's daughter. When Ponsonby moved to Christ Church, Oxford in 1926, Hubert Middleton was appointed in his place.[107] Middleton came from Truro Cathedral, and the terms of his Ely appointment required him 'to collaborate with the Precentor in the choice of the Music' – the first time such a stipulation was made (though it was not until 1942 that the Organist's name appeared on the combination papers). Later that same year Guillaume Ormond was appointed assistant organist at an annual stipend of £20. His duties included playing the organ 'at not less than one of the Weekday Services in each week', and he was allowed one-and-a-half hours free practice time on the organ weekly.[108] The assistant's post has been regularly filled since then. Middleton moved to Trinity College, Cambridge, in 1931 and was succeeded by Dr Marmaduke Conway (1885–1961), previously Organist of Chichester Cathedral.[109] He was a notable player, but had to be admonished in 1944 for striking the boys. The Chapter sought his resignation in 1948, and Conway retired the following year.[110]

The repertoire in the early 1920s was little changed from the 1890s and it retained a Victorian flavour until the end of Conway's time. The passing of Precentor Crosby may have made a difference. During the mid 1920s, someone at Ely showed an interest in the contemporary revival of pre-Commonwealth church music, with the introduction of pieces such as Weelkes's *Hosanna*, Byrd's *Sing joyfully*, and Gibbons's *This is the Record of John*. By the 1930s, this taste had faded, and a few modern settings (*e.g.* Hull, Coleman, Dyson, Ireland and Bairstow) had been introduced to temper a mostly conservative list. The combination papers reveal much repetition of standard repertoire.

Sidney Campbell's appointment in 1949, accompanied by that of Arthur Wills as Assistant Organist, marks the beginning of the modern phase of Ely's musical history. Campbell had been sub-warden of the College of St Nicolas (the Royal School of Church Music) at Canterbury. Wills had been a student there. Their arrival, combined with the new educational arrangements for the choristers who could now be recruited from further afield because of the boarding facility, offered an opportunity to overhaul the system.[111]

By the time Campbell left for Southwark in 1953, much of the Victorian repertoire had been expunged, to be replaced largely by pre-Commonwealth services and anthems. The responses were sung either to Tudor settings or plainsong. Campbell often 'matched' the period of the setting and the anthem: the music lists for some weeks are predominantly pre-nineteenth century.

This process went further under Campbell's successor, Michael Howard (Organist, 1953–8). As director of the Renaissance Singers he had been involved in the revival of

[106] EDC 2/2A/9, p. 56, 8 November 1918.
[107] *Ibid.*, p. 209, 9 March 1926.
[108] *Ibid.*, p. 215, 14 June 1926.
[109] *Ibid.* p. 307, 19 December 1930.
[110] EDC 2/2A/10, pp. 178–9, 29 September 1944; p. 234, 21 June 1948.
[111] *Ibid.*, p. 242, 26 March 1949; p. 252, 25 November.

early music in this country. No doubt his familiarity with plainsong and the polyphonic repertoire appealed to Dean Hankey, and it certainly complemented the Dean's liturgical aims. Some of the earlier nineteenth-century repertoire continued to be sung but there was a great expansion in the use of early polyphony and unaccompanied compositions generally. The works of mainstream contemporary composers also began to find their way into the music lists – Poulenc, Vaughan Williams and Britten, for example.

Howard favoured a strong treble sound, with forceful diction and explosive consonants. The distinctive tone and innovative repertoire of the Ely choir soon became famous and they were much in demand for broadcasts, recordings and concerts. At the King's Lynn Festival they gave one of the earliest performances in this country of Duruflé's *Requiem*, and a recording of the Britten *Ceremony of Carols* was broadcast by the Home Service on Christmas Day 1956. Earlier, they had recorded two recitals of Tudor and Stuart church music for the Third Programme. Meanwhile, Howard and Wills pioneered a way of working which has since become the norm in cathedrals, with the organist directing the choir in the stalls and the assistant accompanying from the organ loft.[112]

Arthur Wills succeeded Howard in 1958. He continued as Director of Music at the King's School (1953–65), and later took on a part-time post at the Royal Academy of Music (1964)[113] (Plate 60*a*).

The 1960s and 70s presented many challenges. For financial reasons, the number of choristers was reduced to sixteen, but despite adequate bursaries, recruitment proved difficult.[114] The introduction of 'supplementary choristers' (boys who were at King's but were not full choristers) was of mixed success, perhaps because the offer of free musical tuition and expenses seemed less than generous.[115] Eventually, an increase in the value of the bursaries, coupled with the establishment of a separate boarding house for the choristers (1980s), helped to stabilise the situation (Plate 60*b*).

The organ, too, was a worry. Little had been done to it since 1908, and by the 1960s major repairs had become urgent. In 1962 the Chapter authorised the expenditure of £2500, and the work was completed the following year.[116] More however remained to be done, and an extensive programme of renovation and reconstruction was undertaken by Harrison & Harrison in 1974–5, with the objective of increasing the musical versatility of the instrument.

Liturgical change was another feature of the period. Until the mid 1960s, Sunday morning Mattins, Sermon and Communion remained a single block of liturgy; there was a hymn after the sermon to enable those who wished to leave before communion, but the choir remained in the stalls – often for two hours.[117] With the advent of Series II,[118] it was

---

[112] A fuller account of Michael Howard's years at Ely can be found in M. Howard, *'Thine Adversaries Roar'* . . . *Autobiographical Observations 1922–1999* (Leominster, 2001), pp. 66–82.

[113] Shaw, *Succession of Organists*, p. 106.

[114] EDC 2/2A/11, p. 41, 26 June 1958; p. 180, 22 June 1962; p. 193, 8 September 1962. The bursaries had been raised to £150 (boarders) and £80 (day boys) in 1961: EDC 2/2A/11, p. 159, 18 December 1961.

[115] EDC 2/2A/11, p. 66, 6 February 1960.

[116] *Ibid.*, p. 162, 20 January 1962; p. 211, 19 January 1963.

[117] *Ibid.*, p. 254, 22 February 1964.

[118] *Holy Communion. The 1967 Service.*

decided that there would be a single main service on Sunday mornings called 'The Liturgy'. This was essentially Holy Communion, but retained a few Mattins elements. So the service began with a psalm (at first to Anglican chant, later to plainsong) and some of the Mattins repertoire was kept in use by singing a canticle after the Old Testament Lesson. The new service was introduced on 28 December 1968.

It took place in the Octagon. For many years the Chapter had toyed with moving the principal service into the space in front of Scott's screen, but they had been defeated by a lack of suitable furnishings. In 1935 Sunday Mattins and Evensong were moved into the Octagon, but the experiment was short-lived.[119] The experience of holding an Ordination in the Octagon in 1957 re-awakened interest, and in 1960 the Cathedral received the gift of a movable altar. When the Liturgy was introduced, the choir transferred to the Octagon, eventually being accommodated in new stalls designed by George Pace (1976).[120] Since then the choir has used the Octagon stalls on Sunday mornings (sometimes afternoons) and for diocesan services.

The appearance of the choir changed in another way, too. Since 1887 they had worn surplices and black cassocks, the boys wearing stiff collars until the 1950s. In 1966 they were re-robed in hooded albs – an allusion, perhaps, to Ely's monastic past. They reverted to cassocks during the 1980s.

Like several of his predecessors, Arthur Wills is a noted composer. Much of his church music was conceived for Ely – pieces such as the *Missa Eliensis*, *The Praises of the Trinity* (for the enthronement of Bishop Roberts in 1964), the *Symphonia Eliensis* (first performed in 1976 during the festival celebrating the organ's rebuilding), and *Let All Men Everywhere Rejoice* (composed for the 1973 Diocesan Choirs Festival). Under Wills, the choir's repertoire broadened to embrace music of all periods. His own compositions were joined by the work of other twentieth-century composers – Herbert Howells, Herbert Sumsion, Lennox Berkeley, Kenneth Leighton and Francis Jackson – and some of the Victorian and Edwardian repertoire which had gone out of fashion in the 1950s was reinstated. Michael Howard had reintroduced music by John Amner and Christopher Tye, and his successor ensured that they had a permanent place in the Cathedral's repertoire. There was even the occasional performance of Kempton in B flat – a reminder of the continuity which has been so strong a feature of the life of this musical foundation.

---

[119] EDC 2/2A/10, p. 38, 26 November 1934; p. 53, 14 June 1935.
[120] *Friends of Ely Cathedral, 15th Annual Report* (1958), p. 18; *17th Annual Report* (1960), p. 7; *Yearbook* (1976), p. 7.

The Library and Archives 1836–2000

NIGEL RAMSAY

The anonymous author of one of the many pamphlets that were published in the 1830s in defence of the status quo in the Church of England, and in opposition to the proposals of the Commissioners of Ecclesiastical Enquiry, observed that 'Prebendaries . . . when properly selected from "clergymen distinguished for professional merit," are said to *read*: and they have in charge for the most part, I believe, excellent Cathedral libraries; to which they have been known to make very splendid additions from their own means.'[1] A cautious defence of this sort could as easily have been made for Ely as for almost any other English cathedral. Superficially at least, all was well with Ely's Chapter library. It could draw on an income of a few dozen pounds a year, from the sealing fees. Its books had been catalogued comparatively recently (1815) and were perfectly well housed in the room in the south transept. The registers of borrowings show it to have been more intensively used at about this date than ever before (or since): in 1840 there were 192 borrowings – as compared with 67 in 1821, the first full year for which details survive, and 90 in 1830.[2]

On the other hand, if library borrowings were to be taken as a gauge of the Cathedral's theological or scholarly life, it would have to be admitted that the loans registers show little evidence of really serious reading within the College. A few of the canons and minor canons took out books from the library quite frequently, but only rarely for reading-matter that can be called intellectually demanding. A considerable part of the general rise in borrowing is accounted for by the periodicals to which the Chapter now subscribed: the *Quarterly Review*, the *British Critic*, and the *British Magazine*. The five minor canons were the most frequent borrowers. Some of the canons presumably had considerable libraries of their own and preferred to bring their own books with them when they came to Ely for their terms of residence. Others, however, such as the Sparke brothers, perhaps did not have significant libraries of their own, since they – like the minor canons – were regular borrowers of such basic historical works as Bentham's and Millers's accounts of the Cathedral, as well as of Cruden's Biblical *Concordance*. The library account was also charged with certain newspaper subscriptions, including the *Cambridge Chronicle* and *Standard*, and (from the financial year 1839–40)

---

[1] Anon. ('Clericus Anglicanus'), *Ecclesiastical Legislation. Three Letters to his Grace the Lord Archbishop of Canterbury. On Church Property, Episcopacy, Cathedrals, and the Clergy* (London, 1836), p. 35.

[2] Borrowers' book, 1820–85: EDC 13/4/1.

John Bull.[3] These, presumably, were looked at in the library, which increasingly must have been taking on the atmosphere and tone of a general reading room.

In the political debates of the 1830s about the future role of cathedrals, many churchmen, of standpoints as diverse as E.B. Pusey and Henry Phillpotts, stressed the importance of having a learned clergy and some also suggested that cathedrals might in some way act as theological centres or colleges.[4] The Dean and Chapter of Ely in a *Memorial* in 1837 perhaps took their cue from Pusey in pointing out that 'a very large proportion of those works of religious learning, which are the glory of the English Church, mainly owe their origin and completion to the leisure and opportunities afforded by Cathedral and Collegiate institutions'; three canons of Ely had been among those responsible for the authorised translation of the Bible.[5] Such assertions were undoubtedly helpful for those who wished to uphold the importance of cathedral libraries. But just as the political debate caused the cathedrals' defenders to look back to an earlier age of scholarly canons (whether or not it could actually be shown that their scholarship ever flourished *at* a cathedral), so too the reformers began to look at cathedral libraries and archives – with a view to their accessibility and even their state of conservation.

Sir Frederic Madden, Keeper of Manuscripts at the British Museum, came to Ely on Sunday 1 March 1846. After the morning service, he recorded in his diary, 'I inquired for the library, which is in the south transept, but found I could not gain admittance, without application to one of the Clergymen.'[6] A few years later, after hearing of a jackdaw dropping an ancient parchment at Canterbury Cathedral, he expostulated about cathedrals: 'Is it not time, that an Act of Parliament should interfere before it is too late, and the Manuscripts and muniments [be] taken away from such ignorant and worldly wretches! They are truly *fruges consumere nati*, and for nothing else! It grieves me to the heart to hear of such things, yet it is everywhere the same!'[7]

Madden was writing his diary for himself alone, but others were expressing similar views to a wide public readership. Charles Dickens published a series of four articles on 'The Doom of English Wills' in *Household Words* in September, October and November 1850. Each piece looked at a different cathedral, drawing on Dickens's experiences at *e.g.* Rochester and York, and although the wills were actually those in diocesan will registries that happened to be housed in cathedral precincts – and thus were not cathedral records at all – such cleverly thrown mud no doubt often stuck.[8] Dickens's aim was to expose the lamentable state of neglect of English wills, which he contrasted

---

[3] Library account book, from 1836–7 to 1846–7: EDC 13/3/2.

[4] See *e.g.* E.B. Pusey, *Remarks on the Prospective and Past Benefits of Cathedral Institutions, in the Promotion of Sound Religious Knowledge . . .* (London and Oxford, 1833); [Henry Phillpotts], *Correspondence between the Lord Bishop of Exeter and Members of the Commission of Ecclesiastical Enquiry* (London, 1840), pp. 17–19.

[5] *Memorials and Communications, addressed to His Late Majesty's Commissioners of Inquiry into the State of the Established Church, from the Cathedral Churches of England and Wales, in 1836 and 1837* (London, 1838), p. 41.

[6] T.D. Rogers, *Sir Frederic Madden at Cambridge*, Cambridge Bibliographical Society Monograph no. 9 (Cambridge, 1980), p. 44.

[7] Journal of Sir Frederic Madden, 28 Jan. 1852, Bodl. MS Eng. hist. c. 165, p. 34; photostat copy in BL, MS Facs. *1012/27. Madden's tag, 'born to consume the fruits of the earth', is from Horace, *Epp.* 1, 2, 27.

[8] [C. Dickens, with W.H. Wills], 'The Doom of English Wills', *Household Words*, 28 Sept., 5 Oct., 2 Nov. and 23 Nov., 1850; nos. 1 and 2 are reprinted in *The Uncollected Writings of Charles Dickens. Household Words, 1850–1859*, ed. Harry Stone, 2 vols. (London, 1969), I, pp. 163–81; and *cf.* II, pp. 641–9, appx B. Dickens took his lead from the writings of William Downing Bruce, *e.g. An Account of the Present Deplorable State of the Ecclesiastical Courts of Record* (London, 1854).

with the exorbitant fees levied by registrars. Of one fictitious registry (an amalgam of those at Lincoln and Lichfield), his vivid tale of rot and decay concluded: 'Thus, then, are documents, involving the personal and real property of Seven English Counties, allowed to crumble to destruction; thus, is ruin brought on families by needless litigation; thus, do Registrars roll in carriages, and Proctors grow rich; thus are the historical records of the great English nation doomed – by an officer whom the nation pays the income of a prince to be their conservator – to rottenness, mildew, and dust.'[9]

At Ely, improvements to both the library and the archives began – gradually – during George Peacock's time as Dean (1839–58). Mathematician though he was *par excellence*, he had pressed for a rebuilding of the university library at Cambridge, and at Ely, as the borrowers' book shows, he twice took out on loan both Bentham's *History* and Wharton's *Anglia Sacra* in 1840.[10] Crucially, George Millers resigned the librarianship in 1847: he had held the post (worth all of £7 *p.a.*) for over forty-three years, and seems increasingly to have rested on his laurels as author of the *Description of the Cathedral Church of Ely*.[11] In 1833, as Chapter Registrar, he declared to the Commissioners for Public Records that after making 'repeated examinations' into the Chapter records he found it necessary to make only one correction to William Metcalfe's reply (itself perfunctory) to the previous Commission on Public Records; but it is hard to believe that Millers ever spent a significant amount of time on the more historic archives under his charge.[12] He had made negligible use of them for his *Description*. By contrast, almost every one of his successors as librarian, down to the 1930s, was to take a keen interest in the archives, whether or not he had any responsibility for them.

Millers's immediate successor, William Keatinge Clay, BD (Librarian, 1847–55), produced several volumes of English liturgical history, including two Parker Society editions of prayers and services from Elizabeth I's reign, and when he left Ely to become vicar of Waterbeach (Cambs.), he produced a series of very competent parish histories in which the Abbey and Cathedral of Ely make intermittent appearances.[13]

It was during Clay's tenure of office that a fresh Commission was appointed, 'to inquire into the State and Condition of the Cathedral and Collegiate Churches in England and Wales' (1852–5). Beriah Botfield in 1849 had published a volume of Dibdinesque *Notes on the Cathedral Libraries of England*.[14] It was slated by some reviewers – notably William Maskell, in *The Ecclesiologist*, who described it as a 'trumpery book', 'in typography splendid, and upon firstrate quality paper, with a sufficient margin, and initial letters', but in content 'trashy and bad'[15] – but it will have

---

9 *Uncollected Writings of Dickens*, ed. Stone, II, pp. 171–2.

10 He borrowed them from June until the end of August, and again in October: EDC 13/4/1. In 1841 he was to publish his scholarly *Observations on the Statutes of the University of Cambridge*.

11 For Millers's resignation and his successor's appointment, see Order Book, 1841–62: EDC 2/2A/6, p. 79 (14 June 1847). He inherited the Duddon Grove estate in 1847, as Peter Meadows has kindly pointed out to me.

12 *General Report to the King in Council from the Honourable Board of Commissioners on the Public Records . . .* (ordered, by the House of Commons, to be printed, 24 Feb. 1837), pp. 287–8.

13 Clay (1797–1867) was a minor canon, 1837–54, and Vicar of Waterbeach, 1854–67. His histories of the parishes of Waterbeach, Landbeach, Horningsey and Milton were published by the Cambridge Antiquarian Society as its Octavo Publications iv, vi, vii and xi (1859–69); to the last is prefaced (pp. v–vi) a short account of Clay.

14 B. Botfield, *Notes on the Cathedral Libraries of England* (London, 1849); for Ely, see pp. 124–31.

15 'The Durham Libraries and Mr Beriah Botfield', *Ecclesiologist*, x (1849–50), pp. 142–52; for Maskell's

helped further the process of putting cathedral libraries on the map. In 1849, too, the parliamentary Select Committee on Public Libraries looked at the accessibility of cathedral libraries – Ely *not* being one of the seven or more that were stated to be open to the public (if applicants brought some guarantee for their respectability).[16] The Cathedral and Collegiate Churches Commission of 1852–5 represented a more self-confident Church of England, and it took for granted that every cathedral would have a library. Each cathedral was asked about the size, accessibility and endowment or other source of income of its library, and for Ely the Commission accordingly reported that there were about 4000 volumes. 'It contains no MSS. and very few early printed books; it is rich in editions of the Greek and Latin fathers, in councils, and in the theological works of the first century after the Reformation; it contains also a considerable number of curious books and tracts relating to the nonjurors, and to many of the questions which agitated the church towards the close of the seventeenth and opening of the eighteenth century. The collection of modern books is small, and it is very deficient in classical and historical works.' As for its accessibility, the Commission observed that 'there seems no reason why it should not be made accessible once or twice a week, or more frequently, if desirable, to the clergy of the diocese generally.'[17]

In the event, however, no significant changes to the library were to occur, for a generation to come. Relatively few books were purchased, and those not of contemporary theology. In 1857 the Revd Henry Baber of the British Museum gave a copy of his type-facsimile of the Alexandrine Manuscript of the Septuagint Version of the Old Testament, printed on vellum, in six volumes (1816–28); Canon William Selwyn added to this a photographic copy (1856) of the Epistles of Clemens Romanus (thus providing the library with a facsimile of the Codex Alexandrinus in its entirety).[18] Selwyn was one of the most frequent borrowers from the library at this time, and it would no doubt have been overhauled sooner if such a capable man had taken charge of it (Plate 35*d*). One factor that mitigated against expansion of the library's stock – even when it was well funded, as at this period – was what seems to have been the unwritten rule that it was for the Dean or Chapter to select what books should be purchased. There was not yet a canon-librarian, with specific authority and responsibility for the library; in a practical sense, that would of course have been difficult to arrange in an age when the canons mostly resided at Ely only during their official terms.

Change came first to the Cathedral archives. As early as June 1859, Harvey Goodwin (Dean, 1858–69) seems to have been responsible for arranging to have a selection of sacrist's rolls from the time of Alan de Walsingham restored at the British Museum, and

---

authorship, see the copy given by him to the British Museum (now BL, 4108.e.55.(8)). Other damning reviews are in *The Theologian and Ecclesiastic*, viii (Jul.–Dec. 1849), pp. 169–80, and by 'R.G.' in *Irish Ecclesiastical Journal*, v (1848–9), pp. 312–15.

[16] *Report from the Select Committee on Public Libraries. . .* (ordered, by the House of Commons, to be printed, 23 July 1849), p. 23, and *cf.* p. 229.

[17] *First Report of Her Majesty's Commissioners, appointed November 10, A.D. 1852, to Inquire into the State and Condition of the Cathedral and Collegiate Churches in England and Wales* (London, 1854), appx., second sequence of pagination, p. 177. The medieval *Liber Eliensis* manuscript presumably was omitted as being part of the Cathedral's archive.

[18] Chapter Order Book, 1841–62: EDC 2/2A/6, p. 224 (19 Jan. 1857). Baber later gave a collection of about two hundred Biblical texts and commentaries: these are listed in EDC 13/2/2. For an account of Baber (1775–1869), see P.R. Harris, *A History of the British Museum Library, 1753–1973* (London, 1998), esp. pp. 31, 51–2.

he was also thinking of moving the library and muniments to fresh accommodation, perhaps in one of the buildings on the north side of the church.[19] In his own words:

> When I became Dean the muniment room was a portion of the Canons' Vestry. A simple wall ran across, so as to cut off a narrow room which had no ceiling to it, but was quite open to the vault of the transept aisle above. It might well be described as a dust-trap; for there was necessarily a constant influx of dust, and when a grain of dust had once got in, there was no possibility of its ever getting out again. . . . There was, however, a certain sacred character belonging to the place. For some reason it had come to be regarded as the Chapter House, and the practice was . . . to open the statutable Chapters in this Chapter House, or Muniment Room.[20]

In 1862 Chapter agreed to remove the archives to the room over the arch in the Northern Gateway; with architectural advice from Henry Styleman le Strange, this was adapted so as to make it fireproof and yet heatable by a flue from the adjacent porter's lodge.[21]

Goodwin's Chapter Note Book shows him to have had a persistent care for the library. In 1863, for instance, it was agreed in Chapter that he and the canon in residence would prepare a list of duplicates which they recommended for disposal.[22] But in 1869 he was given the bishopric of Carlisle: it was unfortunate that his departure more-or-less coincided with the cessation of sealing fees, the library's source of income, for while the deanery was vacant, the Chapter decided to merge the library account into the general chapter accounts.[23] The library was never subsequently to have any replacement for what in effect had been an independent revenue.

It is difficult to estimate the level of use of the library, let alone of the archives, at this date. The *Ely Diocesan Calendar* published the 'Rules for the Cathedral Library' in 1871, and it may be that a number of diocesan clergy came in to read, even though they could not borrow. On the other hand, H.E. Reynolds's survey of *Our Cathedral Libraries: Their History, Contents and Uses*, in 1878, states of Ely's opening times only the bleak words, 'Little use made of it' – despite the fact that its temperature was 'kept up to 50°F. in winter.'[24] Scholars wanting access to the muniments may also have been rare, but one at least made a profitable visit to Ely at this date: W. de Gray Birch, who in 1882 published the Chapter's earliest document, Edgar's grant of West Wratting, AD 974.[25]

---

[19] See Goodwin's Chapter Note Book, 1859–64, *cf.* EDC 2/2B/3, and EDC 2/2A/6, p. 269 (14 June 1859). The 'dozen or more' rolls were selected by Henry Styleman le Strange, 'chiefly with reference to the work of the Lantern, which was at the time under repair': Goodwin, *Ely Gossip*, p. 15. John Holmes, Assistant Keeper of Manuscripts at the British Museum, undertook to superintend the restoration-work.

[20] Goodwin, *Ely Gossip*, pp. 12–13.

[21] Order for archives' removal: EDC 2/2A/6, pp. 325–6 (25 Nov. 1862); for the room's adaptation (and the persistent failure of the heating system), see Goodwin, *Ely Gossip*, p. 14.

[22] EDC 2/2B/3, note 18 from General Chapter, June 1863.

[23] Chapter Order Book, 1863–88: EDC 2/2A/7, p. 115 (25 Nov. 1869). A library account book which was nevertheless maintained from 1868 to 1894, EDC 13/3/4, reveals a distinct drop in expenditure on book purchases.

[24] Herbert E. Reynolds, *Our Cathedral Libraries: Their History, Contents and Uses. A Paper read at the Second Annual Conference of the Library Association held at Oxford, October 1, 1878* (London, 1879), appx.

[25] W. de G. Birch, 'Original Documents. I. Original Anglo-Saxon Charter in Possession of the Dean and Chapter of Ely', *Journal of the British Archaeological Association*, xxxviii (1882), pp. 382–3. Birch thanked Archdeacon William Emery for enabling him to transcribe the charter; in 1848 it had been printed, less correctly, by Kemble, *Codex Diplomaticus*, VI, no. 1274. See further Simon Keynes, above, p. 5, n. 13.

On to this sleepy scene was then appointed in 1881 an unusually energetic and ambitious minor canon and librarian, Frederick Walker Joy.[26] He had been brought up in Leeds, had read theology at Oriel College, Oxford, and was about 29 years old. He was a keen collector of autograph letters, and it was presumably on the strength of his various publications of some of these in *Notes & Queries* that he was elected a Fellow of the Society of Antiquaries in 1882. He soon set about cataloguing the Cathedral library. Early in 1883 he was able to announce, in *Notes & Queries*, a distinct triumph: 'A Newly Discovered Autograph of Milton'. In a copy of Dion Chrysostom's *Orationes LXXX* (Paris, 1604), given to the Cathedral by Bishop Patrick, was the name 'John Milton', and, as Joy wrote, 'carrying in my memory several of those [autographs] which are most prized but seldom obtained by amateurs, without hesitation I attributed the hand-writing to the poet Milton'.[27] Subsequent scholarship has vindicated Joy's identification, and the book stands as one of just seven that are acknowledged to bear the poet's signature[28] (Plate 32a). Joy overreached himself, however, in believing a second book in the library also to have been Milton's: Archbishop Ussher's edition of the letters of Polycarp and Ignatius (Oxford, 1644).[29]

Clearly, Joy was not the sort of man to linger in Ely. He resigned his minor canonry in 1884, leaving to become rector of Bentham (Lancs.). In 1895 he was advanced to BD and DD at Oxford, by decree of Convocation (although he had only obtained a Fourth in Theology), and from 1901 to 1910 he held the Winchester College living of Andover with Foxcote (Hants); he ended his days as a resident of the Cathedral Close at Winchester.[30] Before his departure from Ely, he had completed his catalogue of the printed books, and this was printed in the same year; the print run presumably was small, as the cost was a modest £29 16s. 6d.[31]

Very different was Joy's successor, John Hawke Crosby – and not merely in the length of his tenure of the librarianship (1884–1923).[32] He devoted a lifetime to the study of Ely records, and a Cathedral historian can only regret that it was largely the Ely episcopal records, rather than those of the Cathedral Priory, that held his attention. His notes and transcripts (now CUL, MSS Add. 6382–95) show him to have worked his way through the catalogues of the collections of manuscripts in the British Museum and elsewhere, producing detailed calendars of documents there as

---

[26] Biographical details of Joy are taken from J. Foster, *Alumni Oxonienses, 1715–1866*, II (Oxford and London, 1888), p. 777; C.L. Shadwell, *Registrum Orielense*, II (London and New York, 1902), pp. 566–7; and relevant editions of *Crockford's Clerical Directory*. For Joy's appointment (in succession to George Simey), see EDC 2/2A/7, p. 276 (24 June 1881).

[27] F.W. Joy, *Notes & Queries*, 6th ser., vii (Jan. – June 1883), p. 23; I owe this reference to Dr Peter Lindenbaum. Joy's own collection of autograph letters was sold at Sotheby's, 27–8 May 1887: the 477 lots fetched £485 17s. 6d.

[28] The book is now in Cambridge University Library, Ely a. 272. *Cf.* Peter Beal, *Index of English Literary Manuscripts*, vol. II, *1625–1700*, pt 2, *Lee-Wycherley* (London, 1993), p. 79, Milton's Library, no. iii.

[29] Now CUL, Ely c. 281. Joy's attribution, which was on the basis of Milton's supposedly having written 'pretium 8^{s.}' on a flyleaf, has not gained scholarly acceptance.

[30] He died in 1913, and, as Frederick Preston Joy, is commemorated by a handsome mural tablet in Winchester Cathedral; for this and further information about Joy I am grateful to Miss Joan Bruce, of Andover.

[31] *Catalogue of Books contained in the Library belonging to the Dean and Chapter of . . . Ely*; *cf.* Chapter Order Book, 1863–88: EDC 2/2A/7, p. 303 (14 June 1884).

[32] Crosby was appointed librarian on 25 Nov. 1884: EDC 2/2A/7, p. 308. Born in 1849, he died on 13 Feb. 1923, having been a minor canon for 40 years, and precentor and sacrist for 28 years.

well as at Ely and Cambridge.[33] One notebook reveals him to have been on the trail of the then-lost Black Book of the see of Ely,[34] which was in the Phillipps collection until its purchase for Cambridge in 1898: Crosby found and compared excerpts from it by the eighteenth-century antiquaries Thomas Baker and William Cole, in the Harleian and Additional Manuscripts in the British Museum, from which he concluded that Baker (in *e.g.* Harl. 7032, fo. 419) had 'copied it better than Cole, and deciphered it fully: Cole has failed here and there with a word.'[35] In April 1889 the *Ely Diocesan Remembrancer* announced that Crosby had offered to produce for it every month a list of the incumbents of one parish in the diocese, using the episcopal registers and other sources.[36] Seven months later, he commenced on the rather less complicated but more useful task of calendaring the medieval and Tudor Ely episcopal registers.[37]

The reason that Crosby turned away from the Cathedral Priory records is surely that these were already being worked on by Frank Robert Chapman, Archdeacon of Sudbury (1869–1901) and Canon of Ely (1879–1909). Chapman was an East Anglian antiquary of considerable ability, an Evangelical who had the personal pain of seeing his son Henry leave the Anglican priesthood, be received into the Roman Catholic church and become a Benedictine monk; as John Chapman, the son rose to be Abbot of Downside.[38] In the early or mid 1870s, Chapman read a paper to the Dean and Chapter on 'The Liberty of S. Etheldreda in Suffolk',[39] and Crosby-like, he devoted much of his life to the Cathedral muniments. As early as 1889 Chapter expressed its gratitude to him 'for the improvements effected by him at his own expense in our Muniment Room and for the time expended and skill displayed by him in the re-arrangement of our Ancient Deeds and Documents'.[40] Twenty years later, Chapter thanked him again, for 'the singular zeal and skill with which he has brought the contents of our Muniment Room from chaos into order'.[41] In 1891 he was commended for his enthusiasm by Augustus Jessopp, who reported – all too summarily – on the medieval documents at Ely for the Royal Commission on Historical Manuscripts.[42] The modern historian's praise must be

---

[33] See *e.g.* CUL, MS Add. 6394, pp. 89–140, for a list and analysis of the 'Almack MS' (CUL, EDR G2/3), perhaps made when it was still in Almack's possession (*i.e.* prior to its purchase by Bishop Alwyne Compton in 1889): the analysis may have been made with a view to ascertaining whether it originated as a Priory or episcopal register.

[34] Now CUL, MS Add. 3468.

[35] CUL, MS Add. 6394, reversed, pp. [22]-[35], at [29]. For the Black Book, a 13th- and 14th century register of taxation lists and other miscellaneous material concerning the bishopric, see G.R.C. Davis, *Medieval Cartularies of Great Britain: A Short Catalogue* (London, *etc.*, 1958), no. 361, and D.M. Owen, 'The Records of the Bishop's Official at Ely: Specialisation in the English Episcopal Chancery of the Later Middle Ages', in D.A. Bullough and R.L. Storey (eds.), *The Study of Medieval Records. Essays in honour of Kathleen Major* (Oxford, 1971), pp. 189–205 at 197–9.

[36] *Ely Diocesan Remembrancer*, 1887–9, p. 245.

[37] A set of Crosby's calendar-entries for the years 1337–1581, excerpted from the *Ely Diocesan Remembrancer*, Nov. 1889 – Dec. 1914, is CUL, Adv. c. 116.1; this includes an MS index of parishes by W.M. Palmer.

[38] Cuthbert Butler, obituary notice of Abbot Chapman, *Downside Review*, liii (1934), pp. 1–12; contrast M.R. James's poor opinion of the son, expressed in 1883, after James had visited Chapman's parents: R.W. Pfaff, *Montague Rhodes James* (London, 1980), p. 56.

[39] Chapman transcripts, EDC 14/21/17.

[40] Chapter Order Book, 1888–1915: EDC 2/2A/8, p. 13.

[41] Chapter Minutes, 1887–1915: EDC 2/2B/4, 3 Feb. 1910; *cf.* EDC 2/2A/8, pp. 274–5.

[42] 'The Manuscripts of the Dean and Chapter of Ely', in HMC, 12th *Report*, Appx, pt ix (1891), pp. 389–96. It is surely more than mere coincidence that in this year, too, the records of the see of Ely were calendared by Alfred Gibbons, at the direction of the Bishop, Lord Alwyne Compton: *Ely Episcopal Records . . .* (privately printed,

a little muted, however, by the fact that Chapman's method – typical of his day – was to re-arrange or else follow the existing disarray of the main body of medieval charters, undoing what little remained of their medieval arrangement and identification (group by group), and instead numbering them in one consecutive sequence. Each was described and dated, on a separate wrapper or slip of paper, and the more decayed documents were fastened on to cards; no separate list of the charters was made.[43] They were then placed in tin boxes. It is possible that Chapman was also responsible for detaching many of the seals from the charters (presumably to protect the seals from wear and tear).

In 1907, three years before his retirement, Chapman published two volumes entitled *Sacrist Rolls of Ely*: these provide both an analysis and a complete transcription of the sacrist's account rolls from the time of Alan of Walsingham's tenure of that office and then of the priorship, together with a couple of earlier rolls.[44] It is a reliable and competent piece of work, and raises the question of why Chapman did not print it earlier. The reason can hardly have been that he had wished first to consider related material in other documents, for he was careful to state that 'some care has been taken in the notes of this first issue [of an edition of account rolls] not to encroach on, or to diminish the interest of, the Compotus Rolls which are to follow, either of the Sacrists, or of any other of the officers of the Monastery'.[45] Was Chapman simply over-modest about his own abilities, or is the explanation to be found – at least in part – in the fact that for a dozen years, from 1894 to 1906, Ely had a Dean who cared passionately about his Cathedral's history: Charles William Stubbs? (Plate 43*b*).

Deans were always liable at New Foundation cathedrals such as Ely to have their own schemes for such matters as publications: in 1887 Dean Merivale had proposed an edition of part of the *Liber Eliensis* or some other Ely documents, for the Rolls Series.[46] In the summer of 1902, the Cambridge medieval scholar John Willis Clark came to Ely to examine the obedientiary rolls.[47] He was met at the Muniment Room by Chapman, and the two were later joined by an enthusiastic Dean Stubbs. Clark's report on the rolls states that Stubbs 'welcomed the idea of the rolls being printed, and would facilitate the scheme by every means in his power. He seemed to think it probable that a pecuniary grant might be made by the Chapter; and I feel sure that he will himself do his best to obtain subscriptions towards the cost of the work.' Clark seems to have come in part as a representative of the Cambridge Antiquarian Society, whose imprimatur was clearly thought desirable. The Cambridge transcriber, Alfred Rogers, had copied six rolls for

Lincoln, 1891); Compton had recently had these documents removed from Ely House in London, Great St Mary's church in Cambridge and the diocesan registry at Ely, and brought together in the muniment room in his palace at Ely.

[43] Dorothy Owen, *The Library and Muniments of Ely Cathedral* (Ely, 1973), p. 15. Two or three of the card mounts, in one instance with a short description by Chapman, are shown in a set of 16 photographs of the Ely royal charters taken by H.E. Salter in 1908: Bodl., MS Top. Oxon. d.80 (*S.C.* 34112), fos. 34–49.

[44] F.R. Chapman, *Sacrist Rolls of Ely* (Cambridge, 1907); it was favourably reviewed in the *English Historical Review*, xxiii (1908), pp. 773–6, by J.N. Dalton.

[45] Chapman, *Sacrist Rolls*, I, p. viii n.1.

[46] *Cf.* letters of Lord Esher, Master of the Rolls, 16 Jan. 1887, and H.C. Maxwell Lyte, Deputy Keeper of Public Records, 29 Jan. 1887, in CUL, MS Add. 6395, fos. 37, 38.

[47] J.W. Clark, 'Report on the rolls of the Obedientiaries preserved in the Muniment Room of the Dean and Chapter', 19 Oct. 1902: EDC 14/17.

£7 10s., and 'so all 319 rolls would cost, say £390'; Clark drew attention to the Surtees Society's recently completed three volumes of Durham Cathedral Priory account rolls, edited by Canon Fowler. Stubbs said that he would gladly allow more than six to be taken out of the muniment room at a time, and that the Cambridge Antiquarian Society would be at liberty to get them copied at the British Museum or Cambridge University Library.

Did Stubbs or some other member of Chapter lack confidence in Chapman, or did he lack confidence in himself? The minutes of a Chapter meeting in November 1904 record that 'the question of printing some of the Chapter Rolls was considered – those connected with the Building of the Cathedral. Offer by Archdeacon Chapman'.[48] Tantalisingly, the last four words stand by themselves and have been deleted. The 1880s, 1890s and 1900s were a time when the Chapter took a particular interest and pleasure in the history of the Cathedral. Dean Stubbs was a keen supporter of the library,[49] and in 1898 (after the bequest of books of Bishop Allen[50]) and again in 1906 is recorded as pressing for some scheme for the library.[51] But Canons Vincent Henry Stanton (1889–1916) and Edward Clarke Lowe (1873–1912) were also devoted to the library; Lowe made a stream of gifts to it of sixteenth- and even fifteenth-century books, and bequeathed it yet more,[52] while Stanton gave some well-chosen works, such as a seventeenth-century manuscript of part of the *Liber Eliensis* (apparently that used for the Bollandists' edition of the Lives of Saints Etheldreda, Æthelwold and others, in the *Acta Sanctorum*) together with the History of the Bishops of Ely.[53] In 1896 he offered to provide memorials that would commemorate Prior Steward and Bishop Northwold.[54] In 1903 Stanton suggested that 'a manuscript record be kept of all gifts and other works in the Cathedral, with name of architect &c'.[55]; but this does not seem to have been maintained.

After Chapman's retirement there was still sufficient concern for the muniments for Chapter to declare in 1913 that 'it is desirable that a catalogue of our Muniments should be prepared by some competent person'.[56] The Revd J. Harvey Bloom's offer to do this was declined, and the more competent free-lance editor, William Paley Baildon, was instead brought in (possibly on the advice of the Public Record Office or the Historical Manuscripts Commission). He appears to have proposed an ambitious scheme, of both

---

[48] Chapter Minutes, 1887–1915: EDC 2/2B/4, 8 Nov. 1904.

[49] See the library book-borrowers' register, 1885–1969 (EDC 13/4/2), for his reading of ecclesiastical history. In 1900 Dean Kitchin's edition of some Winchester Cathedral obedientiary rolls was among the books he took out.

[50] A catalogue of the Allen bequest, 1897, comprising much literature, a little theology, and a near-complete set of the Rolls Series, is EDC 13/2/1.

[51] Stubbs expressed hopes for his scheme in the 20th edn of the *Handbook to the Cathedral Church of Ely* (Ely, [1898]), pp. 149–50; he was himself responsible for this edition. See also Chapter Minutes 1887–1915, EDC 2/2B/4, 14 June 1906.

[52] See *e.g.* 'A Note on the most Ancient Books etc. in the Lattice of the Chapter Library at Ely', by F.H. H[illiard], 1942: EDC 13/2/4 (iii).

[53] EDC 14/14; once Heber's, and then Phillipps MS 8174; given by Stanton in 1897; discussed in *Liber Eliensis* (ed. Blake), p. xxvii n.6.

[54] EDC 2/2A/8, p. 99 (25 Nov. 1896); a Memorial Brasses Committee of the Chapter accordingly arranged for a floor plate to mark Steward's burial-place and for a marble memorial to commemorate Northwold (Chapter Minutes, 1887–1915: EDC 2/2B/4, 14 Jan. 1897).

[55] EDC 2/2B/4, 25 Nov. 1903.

[56] *Ibid.*, 16 Jan. 1913.

transcribing the obedientiary rolls (at the Public Record Office), with a view to their publication by the Historical Manuscripts Commission, and of cataloguing the charters, at Ely. This was agreed to, as was the need to pay for repairs to some of the rolls.[57] Baildon duly set to work, and there survives a quantity of his transcripts, translations and summaries of the obedientiaries' rolls.[58] He counted 307 such rolls (perhaps because he omitted duplicates), while at Ely he counted 1185 charters, in nine tin boxes, together with some mutilated deeds in cupboard I and a volume of deeds in the library containing another 50 or so deeds. He also made an assessment of repairs needed, or at least of the documents' condition: the later court rolls for Sutton, Winston and Wratting, which were written on paper, he described as 'in very bad condition, hardly fit to touch'.

Why did nothing more substantial result from this? Was it just because of the War? After the War, sentiment within the Church became distinctly antipathetic to the notion of a cathedral as a community with aspirations to learning, let alone as a place where scholarship could be pursued. In debates in Convocation in 1925 and 1926, on cathedral chapters as centres of learning, Canon T.A. Lacey (Canon of Worcester, 1918–31) sharply asserted that chapters were not suitable centres of learning. They were too small, and would probably be made smaller in the very near future. New Foundation cathedrals had no such dignitary as a chancellor who was supposed to be a theologian and a pattern of learning; there was no provision in their statutes for the promotion of learning. There was no point advocating the impossible. A centre of learning needed, he said: almost unlimited leisure; access to a great library; and the companionship of men who were scholars first and foremost.[59] If not already, Lacey's views would soon have found assent at Ely – for instance, from Professor Charles Raven (Canon, 1932–8), who once exclaimed that 'Ely Cathedral is a great white elephant which feeds on the souls of men.'[60]

The Library shrank steadily further into the background of the Chapter's concerns. The minor canon Reginald Gibbon, who was librarian from after Crosby's death in 1923 until 1936, was a keen student of the Cathedral's history, and wrote some chatty but carefully prepared articles on aspects of the New Foundation establishment; but he appears not wholly to have had the confidence or support of Chapter.[61] Nothing can be said about his successors, the minor canons A.C.E. Widdicombe (1936–9), C.H. Hare (1939–41), F.H. Hilliard (1941–6) and E.H. Yates (1946–53).[62] Almost year by year,

---

[57] Chapter Order Book, 1888–1915: EDC 2/2A/8, p. 329; Chapter Minutes, 1907–28, EDC 2/2B/5, 5 Mar. 1914. Baildon's report, or scheme, is lost.

[58] EDC 14/31. Baildon died aged 64 in 1924, after several months of ill health: *Antiquaries Jnl.*, iv (1924), p. 279; he had been Vice-President of the Society of Antiquaries since 1922.

[59] *Chronicle of Convocation, being a Record of the Proceedings of the Convocation of Canterbury . . . in the Sessions of February 5, 6, [and April 28, 29, 30] 1925* (London, [1925]), pp. 29–34, at 31; *Chronicle of Convocation . . . 1926* (London, [1926]), pp. 42–55, at 44.

[60] F.W. Dillistone, *Charles Raven. Naturalist, Historian, Theologian* (London, *etc.*, 1975), p. 189.

[61] Between 1933 and 1940 Gibbon wrote six articles on the Cathedral in the 17th and 18th centuries for the *Church Quarterly Review*, vols. 115, 117, 119, 124, 127 and 130. He was Rector of the Chapter living of Witcham with Mepal (Cambs.), 1936–55.

[62] For their appointments, see Chapter Order Book 1933–55, EDC 2/2A/10, pp. 67 (3 Oct. 1936), 121–2 (25 Nov. 1939). For Gibbon's appointment, see EDC 2/2A/9, p. 148 (14 June 1923). A Note by Hilliard on some of the early printed books in the library is mentioned above, n. 52. Eric Yates was a minor canon only from 1946 to 1948, being Vicar of the Chapter living of Witchford (Cambs.) from 1948 to 1953; some of his correspondence as librarian is in EDC 13/5.

book-borrowings dropped: from 45 in 1910 (principally by Gibbon, who had been a minor canon since 1908, and Canon Stanton), to 25 in 1920 (14 of them by Gibbon), 35 in 1930 (13 by Canon Creed and 6 by Seiriol Evans) and 7 in 1940.[63] The librarian continued to be paid a nominal stipend (£10 *p.a.*, raised to £20 in 1936), and the sub-librarian £5 *p.a.*; but one senses that it was with reluctance that in 1930 a yearly grant of £5 was agreed to be made, to be at the librarian's disposal for binding and repairs.[64]

The archives fared a little better. Seiriol Evans, who had been appointed a minor canon in 1923, clearly did gain the confidence of Chapter, and not long after he had resigned his various Cathedral posts in 1928 (on becoming Rector of Christ Church, Upwell, Norf.), he offered to catalogue 'the Charters &c.'[65] The offer was accepted, and he launched himself into the work with enthusiasm. The Dean and Chapter were persuaded to become subscribing members of the British Records Association, they agreed to install heating in the Muniment Room and to provide £10 for the repair of old documents,[66] and Evans wrote about King Edgar's Wratting charter for the first annual report of the newly-founded Friends of Ely Cathedral.[67] In 1934 he was thanked for completing a calendar and abbreviated translation of the Chapter's 51 royal charters.[68] In this period, very few people can actually have come to Ely to consult the muniments; if any documents were wanted for extended study, the practice was to deposit them in Cambridge University Library. A rare visitor (who from time to time was also allowed to borrow documents) was the Cambridgeshire antiquary, Dr Willliam Palmer. He set down a description of the Muniment Room on 7 May 1925:

> There are windows at each end, one facing [the] street, the other the Cathedral. Door at N.W. corner, on left. Under window, two large chests with three locks each. On wall facing door are cupboards about twelve feet high or more, in three sections. The top section distinguished by capital [letters] A, B, C, D, E. These contain pigeon-holes, labelled, with contents. The first two are Court Rolls, the third contains the rolls of the obedientiaries, which are kept in boxes. The Elemosinarius's Register is in a box in this section. The second line of cupboards contains volumes, chiefly, such as accounts and leases, but other documents are mixed with them. The lowest series of cupboards, distinguished by small letters, also contains volumes. In 'a' are volumes of eighteenth-century court rolls.
>
> On the opposite side of the room are cupboards containing the charters, numbered 1–12; Archdeacon Chapman's abstract of some of them is admirable. In this line of cupboards are the Dean and Chapter registers, one of which I brought away. On the side of the room next the Charter cupboard are other large cupboards, containing some modern records but also much unsorted ancient documents.[69]

[63] Book-borrowers' register, 1885–1969: EDC 13/4/2.

[64] Chapter Order Book 1915–32: EDC 2/2A/9, p. 299 (3 Oct. 1930); *ibid.*, 1933–55, EDC 2/2A/10, p. 65 (7 Sept. 1936).

[65] *Ibid.*, p. 292 (4 Apl. 1930). Evans (1894–1984) was subsequently Archdeacon of Wisbech, 1945–53, and Dean of Gloucester, 1953–73.

[66] Chapter Order Book, 1933–55, EDC 2/2A/10 (30 Sept. 1933); EDC 2/2A/9, p. 316 (15 June 1931).

[67] S.J.A. Evans, 'A Saxon Charter', *Friends of Ely Cathedral, 1st Annual Report* (1937), p. 24. Evans also published an account of the Priory's acquisition of the manor and advowson of Mepal: 'The Purchase and Mortification of Mepal by the Prior and Convent of Ely, 1361', *Eng. Hist. Rev.*, li (1936), pp. 113–20.

[68] EDC 2/2A/10, p. 27 (14 May 1934). The calendar is now EDC 14/40.

[69] CUL, Palmer Papers, 48, fos. [2]–[4]. Another description of the room, as in 1948, is given [by L. Margaret

The Cathedral Statutes of 1937 made specific provision for the muniments (for the first time), requiring their charge to be committed to a keeper of the muniments.[70] Archdeacon Chapman had sometimes been called Custos Munimentorum, but now Canon J.M. Creed was formally appointed Keeper of the Chapter Muniments.[71]

Early in 1943, in what must seem like an act of despair about the future of the library, the Chapter accepted an offer of £150 from the London booksellers Davis & Orioli for one of the most valuable books in it, the mid sixteenth-century *Booke of hauking, huntyng and fysshyng* (London: William Coplande, n.d.).[72] After the War, there was some sense of a return to normality: books were occasionally purchased or repaired, and a dozen or so books were borrowed annually in the later 1940s and 1950s. Miss Margaret Hands came to Ely, as part of her series of visits to catalogue all the English cathedral libraries' earlier books. She noted that an overflow of books had lately been placed in the triforium.[73]

During the first part of Cyril Patrick Hankey's deanship (1951–69), the offices of librarian and keeper of the muniments were held by Seiriol Evans and then by Professor E.C. Ratcliff (Canon, 1947–58), but the actual work of producing documents for researchers was done by the Dean's daughter, Dr A. Teresa Hankey.[74] She was herself a medievalist, and continued the work, initiated by Seiriol Evans, of reclassifying the charters according to their later medieval classmarks (*i.e.* undoing Archdeacon Chapman's numerical arrangement). As a research student and then university lecturer, she was only in Ely at weekends and in the vacations, but there was only a handful of readers to attend to each year, and informal arrangements prevailed satisfactorily. Since the heating in the Muniment Room did not function, and the room's windows could not be opened, documents were usually brought over to the library.[75] The Chapter Order Books and related materials were still kept by the Chapter clerk, or Registrar, who for about a century and a half until the 1960s was one of successive generations of the Evans family. Dr Hankey herself was appointed Keeper of the Muniments in 1958, when Ratcliff became Regius Professor of Divinity and moved to Cambridge;[76] she remained Keeper until Dean Hankey's retirement.

Dramatic changes to both the library and the muniments came when Dean Hankey

---

Midgley] in the Pilgrim Trust's *Survey of Ecclesiastical Archives, 1946*, vol. II, *Province of Canterbury*, pt 1 (1951), § 5, Diocese of Ely, pp. 5–6. Sadly, no illustration is known of either the Muniment Room or the library in the south transept *in use*.

[70] [Order in Council, 8 June 1937:] *Scheme containing new Statutes for Ely Cathedral, submitted by the Cathedral Commissioners, under the Cathedral Measures, 1931 and 1934*, pp. 8–9, no. 6. The revised Statutes (Order in Council, 26 July 1968) removed the provision, but it was restored in the new Statutes of October 2000, which stipulate that the Keeper of the Archives is to be a member of the Cathedral Foundation.

[71] Chapter Order Book 1933–55: EDC 2/2A/10, p. 93 (4 May 1938), and see pp. 99–100 (21 Sept. 1938) for his Rules for the Muniment Room.

[72] *Ibid.*, p. 160 (13 Jan. 1943).

[73] M.S.G. Hands, 'The Cathedral Libraries Catalogue', *The Library*, 5th ser., ii (1947–8), pp. 1–13, at 10. She was first in touch with the Cathedral in 1941: Chapter Minute Book, 1928–46, 24 Nov. 1941; she worked at Ely principally in 1945. The 'overflow' comprised the bookcases that had been in the centre of the library: Chapter Minute Book, 1928–46, EDC 2/2B/6, 9 March 1940.

[74] Ratcliff was appointed Keeper of the Muniments, with Teresa Hankey as his Assistant, 28 March 1953: Chapter Order Book, 1933–55: EDC 2/2A/10, p. 310.

[75] The temporary storage of documents in the Lattice cupboard in the library had been authorised as part of the Muniment Room Rules in Sept. 1938.

[76] Information from Dr A.T. Hankey, 12 Feb. 2001.

retired. These changes were undoubtedly defensible in principle, even if in various aspects unfortunate and even regrettable. It was plainly unsatisfactory to store muniments in a location as insecure as the library, and since the diocesan archives had since 1962 been in Cambridge University Library, it was entirely logical to place the Chapter's historical archive there too. This transfer took place in 1970, being arranged in part by the diocesan archivist, Dorothy M. Owen (Mrs A.E.B. Owen), who was thereupon made its honorary archivist. But the fact that the Chapter archive was (and is) only on revocable deposit in the University Library meant that for decades it continued to decay, as neither the Chapter nor the University Library could justify the expenditure that was needed for its conservation. In 1930 Hilary Jenkinson of the Public Record Office, brought in to report on the muniments and to comment on Seiriol Evans's work, had observed that a good many of the documents were 'sadly in need of repair'.[77] Such comments gradually became a chorus. A.B. Emden in 1963 had stated that the obedientiary rolls 'are in so fragile a condition owing to damp as to make examination of them practically impossible', and in 1998 Benjamin Nilson wrote of the feretrar's and sacrist's rolls that 'tragically, all these documents are written on paper and are deteriorating. . . . In some cases I did not dare even to open a roll for fear of causing its total destruction.'[78]

In the 1960s and 1970s a few cathedrals placed their library of printed books under the charge of the local university: certain of the newer universities were delighted to have direct access to a historic collection of scholarly books. The library bequeathed to his successors by Bishop Yorke (Bishop of Ely, 1781–1808) had been deposited in Cambridge University Library by Bishop Wynn in 1952, and in 1970 the entire historic library of Peterborough Cathedral (comprising books printed before 1800) was placed in the same library by its Dean and Chapter. Ely's Dean and Chapter were thus following good precedents in sending their library, too, on 'permanent loan' to Cambridge in 1970, but it is sad that they did so with the differential twist of withholding books that the University Library staff found to be duplicated at Cambridge. Slightly fewer than 1800 books (counted by title) went to Cambridge, and the rest of the library (save for a few books on Cathedral history and local topography, retained at Ely) was consigned to the salerooms. The sale of the ill-disguised 'Property of an Ecclesiastical Library' at the Hodgson's saleroom of Sotheby's, on 9 March 1972, deservedly caused a storm, since it destroyed the library's integrity, while the sale total was only about £17,500.[79] Most to be regretted, perhaps, is the loss of so many nineteenth-century publications, since these were imperfectly represented in F.W. Joy's catalogue (which was the guide used by the staff of the University Library to determine what they would request).

These *bouleversements* came at a time when all English cathedrals were sensitive to feelings of financial pressure resulting from the soaring costs of paying for their staff

---

[77] Letter dated 20 Nov. 1930 in EDC 13/5, red box file.
[78] A.B. Emden, *Biographical Register of the University of Cambridge* (Cambridge, 1963), p. xxii; B.J. Nilson, *Cathedral Shrines of Medieval England* (Woodbridge, 1998), p. 154.
[79] *Catalogue of Valuable Printed Books . . . which will be sold by auction by Messrs. Sotheby & Co.,. . . at 115 Chancery Lane, [London]. . . Thursday, 9th March, and Friday, 10th March, 1972*, lots 21–647. See letters in *The Times*, 16, 20 and 25 March and 4 April 1972, as well as comments in *The Book Collector*, xxi (1972), pp. 259–60.

and fabric, while they had not yet generally gained a sense of the numinous appeal that their architecture might exert upon visitors. They had little wish to preserve continuity with their predecessor communities. Nor were they to know that in the 1990s governmental and then lottery funding would drastically lighten the burden of fabric maintenance. At least the more obviously rare books from the library had been kept together: by 1983 all these were catalogued and readily available as an element within a major scholarly library.[80] Conservation of the archives ultimately also began to be achieved. In 1998 the Dean and Chapter successfully seized the opportunity to apply for a Heritage Lottery Fund grant to conserve the medieval obedientiary rolls. At the start of the third millennium all that is lacking is a proper catalogue of the Cathedral archives.

---

[80] Pending computerisation of the University Library catalogue, the Ely Cathedral books can be identified in the shelf-list for the Ely classmark. All the Ely books published before 1701, whether sold or now at Cambridge, are included in *The Cathedral Libraries Catalogue*, by Margaret S.G. McLeod (née Hands), ed. and completed by Karen I. James and David J. Shaw, 2 vols in 3 pts (London, 1984–98); I am grateful to Dr Shaw for giving me a printout with the entries for Ely's 1054 Continental works, and to Dr John Hall of Cambridge University Library for other information.

Ely Cathedral 1980–2000

Michael Higgins

Renewal

On 25 June 1982 Peter Walker, the sixty-sixth Bishop of Ely, delivered a Charge to the members of the Cathedral Foundation following his Visitation of the Cathedral[1] (Colour pl. 29*a*). His vision was clear. He saw the Cathedral as facing 'a challenge and opportunity of the same order as the challenge of 1322, and not less.' Despite extensive work in the previous decade, further expenditure on the fabric costing at least £1.5 million was needed, while if urgent repairs to the medieval college buildings were not carried out, 'the properties would fall into irreversible decay in fifty years.' These grim facts had to be placed alongside tottering Cathedral finances, no reserves, and an overworked Chapter that needed a massive injection of specialist lay insight.

At the same time the Bishop was full of hope for the future. The spiritual appeal of Ely Cathedral lifts those who come to it into a new dimension. It offers a perspective that recovers a glimpse of the transcendent in the face of the trivial and the narrowly material. The Bishop had an underlying conviction that in the years ahead the Cathedral would develop its potential as never before. His Charge ended with the words: 'there have been no times quite like our own times, times of potential catastrophe for humanity and times of immense opportunity, a time for Ely to come into its own'.

Since 1982 these words have proved prophetic. Today the Cathedral fabric is in the best state it has ever been in its long history, and the same can be said for the surrounding College buildings. The Cathedral community has grown out of all recognition, and the finances put on a sound footing. Opportunities through worship, music, education and the arts have all been eagerly seized as Ely has played its part in the spiritual regeneration that has taken place over the last twenty years in most English Cathedrals.

It is an irony that this dramatic recovery of Ely's fortunes has been against the background of an ever-increasing secularisation of society, a development with considerable impact on the Cathedral's work. Great institutional acts of worship for secular bodies can now sometimes be seen as overly religious, and not appropriate in a

---

[1] *Diocese of Ely. Visitation of his Cathedral Church of the Holy and Undivided Trinity, Ely, by Peter, Bishop of the Diocese and Visitor. 1 April–25 June 1982.* A copy is EDC 2/11/1982.

pluralistic world. The National Lottery insists that grants must benefit the whole community, while many secular sponsors and donors ask for a *quid pro quo*. Harsh financial priorities have fundamentally changed the relationship of the Cathedral with both the King's School and the University of Cambridge, while vast numbers of visitors to Ely have no notion of the purpose of the great building or its furnishings. Secularisation and linked financial problems in this period have also severely affected the life of the diocese and the parishes which the Cathedral serves, with parish priests carrying increasingly heavy loads. This in turn has had some effect on the dynamic between parishes and the Cathedral, although this mutually supportive relationship continues strong. Despite advancing secularisation, many people sense a spiritual vacuum, and the Cathedral is well placed to meet this hunger of the soul.

The transformation of the life of Ely between 1980 and 2000 has also taken place alongside a diversification of the Church's ministry, with far greater emphasis on lay input, the ordination of women to the priesthood, new liturgies, and a stress on synodical government and modern management practices. These last two came together in the Cathedrals Measure 1999, which introduced the most far-reaching changes in cathedral government for 400 years. Earlier, the Care of Cathedrals Measure 1990 introduced fundamental changes in cathedral fabric management.

The 1982 Visitation Charge forms a convenient benchmark by which to chart developments in more detail. Everything in a cathedral is inter-linked. Worship is central, but there cannot be worship without a roof. Tourists provide opportunities for ministry, but they also provide income, a topic which over-arches every discussion. The strategy will therefore be to take worship first, the bedrock on which everything else rests. We then turn to an examination of how the immediate financial crisis set out by Bishop Walker was addressed, and how the financial foundations that were laid were then built on in later years. We then look at the Cathedral's human resources, and trace how they have enabled developments in fabric, music, and outreach to the parishes, visitors and the wider community.

Worship

The Visitation Charge is warm in its praise of Cathedral worship. Michael Carey (Dean, 1970–82) was a deeply spiritual and holy priest, who often spent long hours at night in the Cathedral in private prayer (Plate 58*b*). The central concern for worship which he handed on has been jealously guarded by his successors.

The daily offices

The continuous daily offering of Mattins, Eucharist and Evensong is rooted in the Benedictine tradition. Bill Patterson (Dean, 1984–90) described it as 'the engine room' of Cathedral life, while Bishop Walker commented that this unbroken rhythm of daily worship is the prime purpose of the Cathedral. The Eucharist is celebrated each morning in a different chapel, and in 1982 a midweek Thursday 11.30 a.m. celebration was added. Choral Evensong in November may have a tiny congregation, but during the summer, particularly on Saturdays, it can number over a hundred. Since 1981 the daily offices have used the *Alternative Service Book* as well as the 1662 Prayer Book, although Choral Evensong always follows the latter.

Sunday congregational worship

The main Sunday Eucharist at 10.30 a.m. was known up to 1981 as 'The Liturgy' but was renamed in that year 'Sung Eucharist'. Held in the Octagon, it then attracted about 100 communicants each week. By 1990 the average on a 'normal' Sunday had risen to 130, while in 1999 it was 180. Christmas Day communicants were 420 in 1980 and 779 in 2000. On Easter Day 1980 there were 320 communicants at all services, while in 2000 there were 656. This growth is striking during a period when Church attendances in general fell, and there is a combination of reasons for it, some local, some of wider origin.

Dean Carey, anxious that Cathedral worship should speak to all parties in the Church of England and not be unduly catholic, had introduced the practice of having one vested priest at the altar with a server. The Chapter decided in 1982 to return to a High Mass, with three vested priests at the altar. Such a High Mass provides drama and movement in a building which calls for it. The great activity in fund-raising since 1986 also attracted new worshippers. While Sunday Evensong was always carefully timed not to conflict with the Parish Church, from 1994 the worship at St Mary's became strongly evangelical and this led to a degree of migration.

Growth in Cathedral congregations has been paralleled in other places. In earlier years Cathedral worship tended to be cold, exclusive, and formal, an offering to God made regardless of whether a congregation was present. The climate gradually changed. Lay involvement was echoed in Ely, as elsewhere. Lay people began to read lessons and make intercessions. The *Alternative Service Book* encouraged this trend. Coffee after the 10.30 a.m. Sunday Service was introduced in 1985. In 1984 the Annual Congregation Meeting was established. At first this meeting was held in the Old Library, but soon the room became too small and it moved into the Cathedral. In 1986 a Worship Group came into being, a vehicle for congregational consumer research. In the same year the publication of the bi-monthly *Cathedral News* began. The Sunday School, an unusual feature in a Cathedral, began to grow and remains strong in 2000.

Frequent change in many parishes, and the absence in some places of a resident priest, has led to an appreciation of the stability of Cathedral worship. When many people are either too busy to be involved in parish organisations or lack the faith and commitment to do so, Cathedral worship makes available music, colour, movement, and drama in an inspiring setting without calling for major commitment. This is increasingly attractive in the modern world.

This growth in congregational worship sets a basic question for the Chapter. What should be the essential difference between Cathedral and parish worship? The answer affects the style and ethos of the liturgy, the musical repertoire, the pastoral expectations of the congregation, the amount of lay involvement and the number of supporting committees and organisations. The answer is still emerging, and is a concern of all cathedrals. It is pertinent to observe that the Cathedrals Measure 1999 places considerable stress on the role of the congregation.

Other Sunday services have also grown. The 8.15 a.m. said Eucharist attracted 15–20 people in 1980, rising to 25–30 in 2000. Numbers at Sunday Choral Evensong have risen consistently between 1980 and 2000, and today there are rarely less than 100 people present on a normal Sunday.

A feature over the last twenty years has been the growth of congregational special services at major festivals, with the aim of exploring the opportunities of light, space and movement that the Cathedral offers. The popular Advent Carol Service with Candlelight Procession began in 1986, along with a Sung Requiem on All Souls Day, while special liturgies for Epiphany and Candlemas followed in the next decade. Many of these new services owed much to the liturgical insights of successive Precentors and in particular to Michael Tavinor (Precentor, 1985–90). Every year, St Etheldreda's Days continue to be observed by the Cathedral Foundation in June and October, with a Choral Eucharist in the morning and a Festival Choral Evensong.[2]

The last twenty years have seen much change. The *Alternative Service Book* liturgies of 1980 were intended to be transitional, and now *Common Worship*, which draws on the experience of the *Alternative Service Book* as well as introducing new material, has been authorised for use since Advent 2000. Again, Cathedral worship will move through a period of further change, involving extensive preparation and liturgical experiment.

Diocesan worship

Three general Confirmations for the parishes have been held in the Cathedral each year for some time, along with a special Confirmation for King's School, Ely. In 1988 five candidates were confirmed at the Easter Midnight Vigil and first Eucharist of Easter, and over subsequent years the number rose to around 50 with a baptism normally being included. This return to ancient Church practice in a dramatic service on Easter Eve was much appreciated by the Diocese, but it gradually changed from an Easter Eucharist for the Cathedral congregation to more of a diocesan occasion. In 1997 it ceased to be a Eucharist and was made an Easter Vigil and Confirmation earlier on Easter Eve. It provides a good example of how it can sometimes be difficult to meet both diocesan and Cathedral needs in the same liturgy.

In recent years the main Ordination Service has always been held in Trinity season, normally in early July, although in 1994 there were two Ordinations. On 28 May, following the historic decision of the General Synod to admit women to the priesthood, 24 women deacons were ordained priests by the Bishop of Ely, Stephen Sykes, bringing joy to the heart of one lady who had petitioned the Chapter in 1983 to include a prayer in the Ordination Service for 'those who have not been able to be ordained at this time'. In 1993, a year before she was priested, Christine Farrington joined the Cathedral's Greater Chapter as one of the first women canons in the Church of England, and under Bishop Sykes the Diocese of Ely attracted a large number of women priests. In 1997 Jan McFarlane became Cathedral Chaplain, the first woman priest to serve on the Cathedral staff.

Every year laity and clergy from all over the Diocese come to the Cathedral, for Diocesan Synod Eucharists, Diocesan Church Music Festivals, Diocesan Schools Days

---

[2] St Etheldreda's death is marked on the Saturday which falls nearest to 23 June, while the translation of her body is marked on 17 October.

and Children's Services, and Mothers' Union Services. A Diocesan Millennium Service '2000 Years 2000 Lights' on 29 January 2000 saw standing room only, with over 3000 in the building. Throughout this period the Cathedral has at many times acted as a focal point for diocesan worship. One high point of such occasions is when all the diocesan clergy come together on Maundy Thursday to renew their Ordination vows, a practice which started in 1984. Bishop Sykes also used the Cathedral on a number of occasions for diocesan teaching days for both clergy and laity.

Perhaps the most significant diocesan occasions are those which mark the coming and going of Bishops. On 2 December 1989, Bishop Peter Walker retired with a great farewell in the Cathedral, and on 5 May 1990 Stephen Sykes was enthroned as the sixty-seventh Bishop (Plate 63a). Following his resignation to take up an academic post in Durham, people from all over the diocese gathered for a farewell on 5 September 1999. The enthronement of the 68th Bishop of Ely, Dr Anthony Russell (Plate 63b), translated from Dorchester, took place on 25 November 2000 (Colour pl. 31a). In 1997 the Diocese bade farewell to Bishop Gordon Roe, the Suffragan Bishop of Huntingdon, and following his death in 1999 the Cathedral was packed for his memorial service.

Special services

Through many special services each year, the Cathedral reaches out to the wider community. In 1980 there were services, for example, for Age Concern, the Cambridge-shire Regiment, the British Legion, St John's Ambulance, and even for Home Helps! Remembrance Day and Harvest Festival in particular draw large congregations. The latter event, since 1983, takes place in the context of a two-day Harvest Festival Exhibition mounted by the National Farmers Union, who usually bring live animals of various descriptions into the Cathedral. On this animal theme, the Wood Green Animal Shelter's Blessing of the Animals Service has become an annual feature since 1987. The Flower Festivals of 1987 and 1997 saw several special services, while since 1992 Rave in the Nave has allowed young people to worship in their own way, with over a thousand youngsters present with decibels that have to be heard to be believed. Services for transplant patients, charismatic worship, and a celebration of C.S. Lewis's centenary, demonstrate the variety of special worship.

Many special services mark particular national occasions, such as the anniversaries of VE and VJ Days, the Golden Wedding Anniversary of Her Majesty the Queen or the Civic Thanksgiving Service for the Millennium on 2 January 2000. Also memorable was the Act of Reflection and Dedication held at midnight on 31 December 1999. Most poignant of all was an Act of Prayer and Reflection that was rapidly organised to mark the sudden death of Diana, Princess of Wales, in 1997. Over 1800 people were present to mark this tragic event, with wreaths and flowers piled high on both sides of the Galilee Porch.

Informal worship

Taizé Worship was introduced in 1994 on Sunday evenings three times a year, and particularly attracts young people from the Diocese. On the first Sunday of each month informal Laying on of Hands for Christian Healing follows the 10.30 a.m. service, while the last three years have seen a Shoppers' Carol Service, and a Christmas Eve Crib Service for children. The Cathedral should be available to all Christian people, regardless of Church tradition, and recent years have seen worship from groups as diverse as Forward in Faith and Pentecost Praise, while Roman Catholics frequently hold Mass in the side-chapels. It is common for visiting Church tour parties to come with their priest, and permission is readily given for the Eucharist to be celebrated or a service held. Since 1992 informal worship for Cathedral visitors has been held at lunchtime on Thursdays, and particularly during the summer months is much appreciated.

Fabric, Finance and Property

Bishop Walker's Visitation Charge made it clear that financial crisis loomed. In 1984 Bill Patterson arrived as Dean, and he, assisted by the Vice-Dean, Canon Dennis Green, developed a three-pronged strategy for the Cathedral, the College, and income regeneration, a strategy continued in subsequent years (Plate 62a).

Cathedral

In 1981 Mr Jackman, Assistant Verger, retired. He had always stoked the seven cast-iron Gurney stoves with coal, taking over a week to get them going properly, a dirty business which gave uneven heat. On his going they were converted to gas. Work was carried out in the cold winter of 1981–2, and much hardship was endured by clergy and congregation. The stoves still function efficiently in 2000; but the £52,000 costs absorbed Chapter reserves, even with a grant of £20,000 from the Friends.

Dean Carey's last two years were dominated by fabric problems, as had been his earlier time. In 1980 the Galilee Porch was re-roofed, and in the same year serious slippage of lead on the south choir roof required urgent attention. Emergency repairs had to be carried out on the nave roof in 1981, and in 1982 he was talking of 'a rather critical situation' over the condition of the choir vault which necessitated further work. In this period well over £100,000 was spent on fabric, funded by the Appeal Fund. But it was merely plugging the gaps.

The Great Restoration, Phase I, 1986–91

Following Dean Carey's retirement the Chapter explored the possibility of a major fabric Appeal, while Dean Shaw in his short tenure of office in 1983 continued to pursue the idea. Dean Patterson came with a clear brief to launch an appeal, and in 1986 Compton Associates were appointed as fundraising consultants. An Appeal Committee was formed with the Bishop as President and the Lord Lieutenant, Michael Bevan, as Chairman, a brochure 'Ely Cathedral – Must Be Saved' was produced, and lay teams became active throughout the Diocese. An Appeal for £4 million was launched on 20 September 1986, under the Duke of Edinburgh's patronage, with a solid foundation of gifts already achieved, including a £10,000 donation from the Friends.

The success of the Appeal was dramatic. The £4 million were raised in just one year, and on 17 October 1987 a service of celebration was held during which parish representatives from the Diocese presented the Bishop with purses containing gifts from the parishes, bringing the final total raised to £4.6 million. 179 parishes contributed generously to the Appeal, a mark of love and affection for the Cathedral. At this service of celebration Dean Patterson launched the Twenty-First Century Fund, a capital endowment account designed to provide reliable maintenance income for the future. By 2000 the Fund contained investments worth £1.7 million.

It is difficult to do justice to the hard work and dedication that went into this Appeal, led by Dean Patterson, who was appointed CBE a few years later in recognition of his work. There were almost 3,500 individually identifiable gifts, many personal donations of overwhelming size, with local authorities, trusts, and industry being particularly generous. Further money was raised by Cathedral events, from opera performances to a concert by the Band of the Grenadier Guards, and from balloon races to the Flower Festival of 1987. The Dean christened a British Rail locomotive 'Ely Cathedral', and later the Cathedral Choir sang to the delight of crowds on the platform at Liverpool Street Station (Colour pl. 29b).

By the end of 1986 interest on the money raised amounted to £350 a day, which gave the confidence to begin the first urgent piece of work, the complete restoration of the timber and lead on the nave and north aisle roof. Schoolchildren who had raised money for the project gathered on St Cross Green to sign the new timbers before they were raised into position. The work required 85 tons of lead, 60 tons of stone, 45 tons of timber, and 18 miles of scaffolding. It began on 5 January 1987, cost £1.5 million, and was completed in October 1988. This first work was helped by Nature, for in March 1986 a fierce gale dislodged vast sections of the thin lead on the roof. The insurance claim was settled for £400,000 in May 1987, a great bonus. A large anonymous gift during the work made possible the conservation and refurbishment of the magnificent painted ceiling.

Further work followed, involving massive replacements of timber, lead, stone and glass. Restoration and re-glazing of the Lady Chapel and work on the two eastern bays of the north choir aisle and the higher levels of the east end began before the nave roof was completed, and to crown this work in 1989 the Friends of Ely Cathedral paid for a new concealed lighting system for the Lady Chapel which sets off the restored structure to dramatic effect. The west wall of the south transept was fifteen inches out of true, and urgent work was necessary in 1989–90 to head off collapse. The Normans built cavity walls filled with grout, and the movement was so severe that the fabric had to be stitched together with hundreds of stainless steel rods, a complicated operation expertly supervised by Professor Jacques Heyman, the Cathedral's Consultant Structural Engineer (Plate 62b).

The completion of the work was marked by a great Service of Thanksgiving on 17 November 1989. The Dean was now looking forward to the Cathedral being free of scaffolding for the first time in four years; but on 25 January 1990 a great fen gale blew in the windows of the Lantern and did extensive damage to the leadwork. The Cathedral's insurance had been renewed only weeks before, which provided approaching £500,000, and a similar sum was granted by the National Heritage Memorial Fund. With money remaining in the Appeal Fund the funds were sufficient for the complete restoration of the Octagon and Lantern to be undertaken, the work being finished in late 1991.

The Great Restoration, Phase II, 1992–2000

When Michael Higgins (Plate 63c) arrived as Dean in 1991 he was soon to discover that further urgent work remained. The south-west transept had the same problems as the south transept, with 'Danger Falling Masonry' signs displayed around it. There was a real risk that it would collapse like the north-west transept, its Victorian strengthening being weakened due to the pressure exerted by the tower. The eastern bays of the south choir aisle roof were decaying, there were precarious pinnacles on the north choir, and many other parts of the building were in need of immediate attention. There was a serious fundraising dilemma because the £4 million Appeal funds were now spent, the 1989 Thanksgiving Service had created a wide impression that the restoration was complete, and a further appeal was clearly not practicable. In addition, the feeling of dire urgency had left the situation.

The decision was reached to set up a permanent body with a prestigious image which would attract those wishing to give continuing financial support. In December 1992 the Order of St Etheldreda was born, and it rapidly became the Cathedral's principal fundraising arm. The Duke of Edinburgh again agreed to be Patron, and James Crowden, the Lord Lieutenant, became the Chairman of a Council drawn from all sections of life in the Diocese. By 2000 the membership was approaching five hundred, with £3 million raised for fabric and another £1 million raised for music and the improvement of visitor facilities. The members receive regular newsletters about the Order's work, and enjoy an Annual Gathering on St Etheldreda's Day in June, along with occasional social functions during the year. The Order raises funds for all Cathedral capital projects, and members indicate which area they wish to support. Membership is made available to individuals, trusts and corporate bodies, and substantial support of around £1 million has come from local authorities in the Diocese.

In the summer of 1991 the governmental agency English Heritage launched the Cathedral Grants Scheme, and Ely immediately applied for help with the south-west transept. A grant of over £700,000 was phased over two years, giving the Order time to raise the balance of £300,000. This partnership between the Order and English Heritage flourished, English Heritage contributing over £3 million to fabric work in 1992–2000 and the Order furnishing matching funds.[3] English Heritage contributions have varied from 70% to 40% of the contract costs, but in many Continental countries the State pays 100%. However, much of the vitality of English Cathedrals springs from self-help, and motivation might be sapped if the State became in effect the landlord, a move undesirable in itself. Happily, this prospect is unlikely, given the financial pressures on national government!

With funding secured, Phase II of the Restoration got under way. The Victorian steel girders strengthening the south-west transept were removed in 1993 and stainless steel

---

[3] Ely has been consistently among the top two or three cathedrals in terms of the size of the grants that it has been given, and in 1999 Sir Jocelyn Stevens, Chairman of English Heritage, commented that Ely's success was due to its ability to cap the grants and get the work done expeditiously.

rods inserted, along with major renewals of stone, glass, lead and timber. The work then moved to the South Porch and the Song School, followed by the lower south octagon, and restoration of the nine bays of the south choir in 1994–5. Similar total refurbishment was given to the north choir, the lower north Octagon and the north transept, completed by the end of 1999. The last project of the Great Restoration, the west end and the Galilee Porch, was completed in the summer of 2000, bringing to an end fourteen years of continuous work. Towards the end of the Restoration the whole Cathedral electrical system was re-wired at a cost of £250,000.

Related matters

Two recent additions to the fabric have been made. In 1994 the Prior's Door was enclosed, completely protecting this Romanesque feature from the elements. In 1999–2000 the medieval Processional Way between the Lady Chapel and the north choir aisle was recreated, the first substantial addition to the Cathedral since medieval times. The project was funded jointly by a substantial legacy to the Order of St Etheldreda and by the Friends of Ely Cathedral[4] (Colour pl. 32).

In 1972 during the west tower work, Ely Cathedral Trust had been established and registered as a charity. The trustees, chaired by the Dean, have since that time been responsible for all money raised for capital projects, by the 1986 Appeal, the Twenty-first Century Fund, and the Order of St Etheldreda (the Cathedral's machinery for fundraising, latterly incorporating the Twenty-first Century Fund). The trustees have always been drawn from those having financial and investment expertise, and their skills have served the Cathedral well.

Royal visits

A number of royal visits during the restoration campaign gave encouragement and support. As Patron of the Appeal and of the Order of St Etheldreda, the Duke of Edinburgh made a number of visits and on one occasion chaired a meeting of the Appeal Committee.[5] In 1987 the Queen distributed the Royal Maundy (Colour pl. 30*a*), and she returned in 1993 for the dedication of the restored south-west transept. The Princess of Wales opened the 1987 Flower Festival, while Princess Margaret opened a similar Festival ten years later. The Queen Mother visited in 1988 (Colour pl. 30*b*) and there were other visits by the Duchess of Kent, the Duke of Gloucester and Princess Alexandra.

College

For many years six of the fine medieval monastic buildings have been leased to the King's School. The Monastic Barn was repaired in 1966 at the School's expense and is held by it on a long lease at a nominal rent, an arrangement from which the School

---

[4] The design was the work of Jane Kennedy, Surveyor to the Fabric.
[5] On 14 July 2000 he chaired a banquet in the nave for 400 people to celebrate the restoration, and on 15 October attended a Thanksgiving Service in the Cathedral, unveiling a commemorative stone on one of the Octagon pillars.

reaps enormous benefit. Canonry, Priory, and Walsingham are boarding houses. Prior Crauden's Chapel is leased to the School for a peppercorn rent, but continues to be available to the Cathedral. The Headmaster lives in Queens' Hall. Apart from the Barn, all were in a poor state of repair by the late 1970s. With no funds available, the Chapter was powerless to act, and in the early 1980s various schemes were proposed for financing repairs out of future rents, but they came to nothing. Bishop Walker noted in his Visitation Charge that in 1981 the Historic Buildings Council had offered a grant of 60% towards the repair of Canonry House, but the Chapter was unable to fund the balance. The Bishop proposed a commission to look at the whole monastic buildings question.

No commission was appointed. In 1985 English Heritage offered a grant to repair Prior Crauden's Chapel, and this work was carried out with help from the School. In 1986 English Heritage offered phased grants for repair work costing £2.5 million on all the College properties. Protracted and painful discussions between the School and Chapter about how the balance was to be found led in 1987 to a 25-year amortisation agreement, by which the Chapter was to receive a nominal rent on all the properties for this period, and the School was to pay off the loans it raised to cap the English Heritage grants by using the rent it would have paid to the Chapter. This agreement is still in operation, although it has caused some problems. In 1994 the School felt that it had received a poor bargain because rents had not risen as expected, and asked the Chapter to transfer the freehold of two properties in compensation. The Chapter naturally felt that the agreement should continue to run undisturbed, pointing out that if rents rose steeply in future years the Chapter would be the loser. No further action was taken.

With funding now secured, a comprehensive repair programme began on all the buildings leased to the School. Starting with Canonry House, work moved on to Walsingham and Priory, with Queens' Hall being completed in 1994. During the work the School took the opportunity to make improvements at its own expense.[6]

The College buildings occupied by the Chapter – the Deanery, the Black Hostelry, and Powchers Hall – were in a serious condition, with a roof collapsing in the Black Hostelry in 1985. The north range was also in need of urgent attention. In that year the Dean and Chapter resorted to drastic measures with a scheme for building retirement housing on the Paddock east of the College to raise the much needed funds, but the scheme was unpopular and it is doubtful whether planning permission would have been given. It was finally abandoned when the J. Paul Getty Trust granted £500,000 to the Dean and Chapter on condition that a restrictive covenant was placed on the land preventing future development.

The Getty funds and continued English Heritage support allowed restoration to begin. By the end of 1988 the Old Choir House and the Goldsmiths' Tower had been completed, followed by re-roofing of most of the north range. The Black Hostelry was totally restored during 1990, and the Deanery in 1991. Work then returned to the north range, with the restoration of Sacrist's Gate house, and concluded with Powchers Hall in 1996. All the College buildings had been returned to good order.

---

[6] Kenneth Powell, 'Ely Cathedral Close, Cambs.', *Country Life*, 3 March 1994.

Professional support for the Cathedral and College

In 1985 a Fabric Advisory Group was established, with the Dean as chairman, and it met 31 times between 1985 and 1990 to give expert advice on both Cathedral and College. The Cathedrals Measure 1990 required that every Cathedral should have such a body; and the Group became the Ely Cathedral Fabric Advisory Committee, working in partnership with the central Cathedrals Fabric Commission. Denis Adams, the Cathedral's High Bailiff, became chairman. With members nominated by the Commission and the Dean and Chapter, the local Committee and the central Commission exercise a 'Faculty Jurisdiction' in relation to fabric. Chapter proposals for major work on either the College or the Cathedral need to be approved by the Commission or by the Ely Committee. As far as Ely is concerned the machinery works well, with excellent relationships between the bodies involved.

Under Dean Shaw the Surveyor began to attend Chapter regularly, reflecting the urgency of fabric matters. Later, as the Great Restoration and College work proceeded, the Surveyor spent many hours with Chapter. Peter Miller retired in 1994 after twenty years as Surveyor and was succeeded by the Assistant Surveyor, Jane Kennedy, a partner in the firm of Purcell Miller Tritton. Meticulous archaeological recording has been carried out above and below ground on both the Cathedral and the College, and the fascinating story of how Ely was built is now better understood through archaeologists' reports.[7] The Dean and Chapter, architects, quantity surveyors, archaeologists, and contractors Rattee & Kett have worked together as a close-knit team in what has been one of the most ambitious programmes in Ely's long history.

Income generation

Up to 1982 Chapter minutes do not show a great awareness of financial planning. No budgetary system was in place, and Bishop Walker's Visitation Charge called for 'a searching review of Cathedral finances.' He pointed out that while shop profits amounted to £16,000 this was more than offset by the £30,000 cost of Cathedral music.

By 1984 the situation was desperate. Work on the organ and Powchers Hall's heating system could not be undertaken, and reserves had dwindled to nil. A plan to get volunteers to clear the Cathedral gutters came to nothing. Entertaining allowances were drastically cut and in June 1985 all maintenance work was discontinued. Notices appeared in the Cathedral drawing attention to a financial crisis, and a deficit budget was prepared for 1986. It became obvious that the Dean and Chapter were facing bankruptcy unless radical action was taken quickly. The Chapter, led by the Treasurer, Dennis Green (Plate 62*a*), developed a strategy to deal with matters, which has been continued by his successors:

---

[7] Copies of the reports are kept in the Muniment Room at Ely: EDC 4/10B (Cathedral) and 4/10C (College).

i. Admission fee

After much heart-searching it was decided to charge for admission to the Cathedral from 10 a.m. to 4 p. m. every day, excluding Sundays. The decision, reluctantly taken, was unavoidable. A chapel was provided for private prayer, and no one coming to worship was asked for the £1 fee, which came into operation in March 1986. The charging system allowed the Chapter to recover 90% of VAT payments on Cathedral work, realising thousands of pounds for restoration work over the next fourteen years.

Levying charges to enter a Cathedral had been the general practice in Victorian times, and Anthony Trollope records Mr Harding paying his two pence to go into Westminster Abbey as 'a tourist'. Charging enabled Ely to balance the general account, and after paying the salaries of admissions staff and other expenses, entrance fees in 2000 brought in £200,000. An article in the *Financial Times* (26 July 1986) focussed national attention on Ely when charging began, extolling the new approach as 'The Entry Fee Miracle of Ely Cathedral' that solved the Chapter's problems. Correspondence also appeared in *The Times*. The current charge is £4, with reductions for parties, senior citizens, the unwaged, children and students, and staff are encouraged to exercise discretion in cases of hardship. Charging can remove the incentive to visit the Cathedral and run counter to the Christian ethos of the building, but it can also be seen as good Christian stewardship.

ii. Cathedral shops and catering

In 1980 Ely had a small shop in the north aisle. This was considerably extended in 1985, and has been enlarged since. Today it sells a wide variety of merchandise that is attractive to visitors, and another shop opened in the High Street in 1988. Together the shops make a contribution of about £50,000 annually to the Cathedral's budget.

Before 1980 the Parlour, in the north-west corner of the Cathedral, had served teas on an occasional basis, but from that year it was opened more frequently with the help of volunteers. In 1986 it was totally refurbished, and re-opened as the Refectory, with paid staff. It continues in much the same form today. Until 1989 the Almonry was the home of Canon MacDonald, but when he retired the opportunity was taken to convert it into a restaurant, which has flourished ever since. These catering outlets also make a significant contribution, again of about £50,000 a year, to Cathedral income.

iii. Domestic rents

Moves were taken to establish realistic rents for any College property that could be let. There were three flats in the Deanery up to 1994, as well as three flats in the Almonry and several other properties, such as Cherry Hill Cottage. The balance between letting properties to Chapter staff at subsidised rents and commercial lettings has always been a difficult one to strike in order that the best financial return can be achieved for the Chapter.

In 1999 the Chapter bought back from the Church of England Pensions Board four bungalows in Dean's Meadow which had been built on land sold to the Board in 1958 to provide retired clergy housing. This reclaimed a part of the Precinct, and produced commercial rents for the Chapter.

iv. High Street rents

When the Old Choir House was restored in 1988 four shops were established in the High Street, and Ely Museum rented premises on the first floor. A little later two further shops were created out of part of the Precentor's House, and the Organist narrowly avoided having his front room turned into a shop ! The shops all provided income, but the decline in retail trade at the end of the century places a question mark over their long term future.

v. Diocese

For several years the Cathedral had been making a contribution to diocesan expenses, which since 1984 had been fixed by Chapter at £2,000 each year. However, in 1990 it was recognised that the Cathedral bore heavy expenses in mounting frequent Diocesan events and services, and from this date the Dean and Chapter ceased to make such contributions.

vi. Congregational giving

A stewardship scheme was introduced in 1995, increasing congregational giving from £6,000 a year to £35,000 a year. This figure is still low in comparison with parochial giving, but reflects the fact that many members of the congregation also support local parishes.

vii. Other income

One of Canon Green's major triumphs was to extract £17,500 from a film company for use of the Precincts in the filming of *Revolution*, and every opportunity is now taken to charge fees for use of the Cathedral for non-liturgical events. Octagon and west tower tours provide additional income, as does the use of the west tower for carefully controlled use of aerials for radio transmissions.

Canon James Rone took over as Treasurer in 1993, and soon after he left, in 1995, a Bursar was appointed. Gradually, in all these diverse ways the finances of the Cathedral have been put on a sound footing. In recent years a small surplus has been made, and with shrewd investment there is now capital in the General Account with a market value of over £2 million. It is still small in comparison to most Cathedrals.

Behind the Scenes

Staff, structures, management, and Cathedral government

At the heart of Cathedral life are the Dean and Chapter. Bishop Walker commented in his Charge that the Dean and three Canons had served in Ely Diocese as parish priests, and in 1990 this was true of the whole Chapter. By 2000 all the members of Chapter had been appointed from outside the Diocese, in the case of the Canons by interview after advertisement, illustrating a trend in Cathedral life to recruit the best priests to undertake specific briefs. However, Ely had one of the smallest chapters in England. In 1980 it numbered five, one holding the Ely Professorship of Divinity in the University of Cambridge and another being Suffragan Bishop, neither paid from Cathedral funds. In 2000 there was a Chapter of three, all engaged exclusively in Cathedral duties. In 1980 Chapter meetings lasted for half a day each month; today they are three times as long, and have spawned subsidiary committees. The only way of increasing the clerical membership of Chapter is to have Canons who also hold diocesan offices. Bishop Walker rejected this approach, although it is adopted in other Dioceses. He was clear that the Canons of Ely should be involved exclusively in Cathedral work, and this view has prevailed.

In addition to the Chapter there is a Precentor who is a minor canon. For many years this office was linked with the small parish of Stuntney, close to Ely, which helped with the Precentor's stipend. Economic pressure on the Diocese led to this arrangement finishing in 1995, and the present Precentor is full-time. From 1997 to 2000 there was a second full-time minor canon, the Cathedral Chaplain, but such appointments depend on the state of the budget. The Chaplain of the King's School is a minor canon, and although employed directly by the School is able to give valuable liturgical assistance in the Cathedral.

The Visitation Charge called for an injection of lay skill and expertise. A 1977 revision to the statutes allowed for lay canons, but neither Bishop Walker nor Bishop Sykes used the provision. It was never clear how such canons could be geared into Cathedral life, what their status might be, or what tasks they would perform. Instead, the statutory offices of High Bailiff and Chapter Steward were filled by active laymen able to give advice and practical help in the day-to-day running of the Cathedral. Six advisory groups were set up in 1986 to advise the Chapter on worship, fabric, education, music, marketing, and communications, with lay people serving alongside the clergy. Large numbers of lay people also gave their skills to fundraising through the Appeal Committee and the Order of St Etheldreda. At the same time, as the work of the Cathedral grew rapidly the stipendiary lay staff also expanded. In 1980 it was tiny, but by 2000 there were 25 full-time staff and as many part-time staff. The Chapter Clerk, the Director of Music, the Visitors' Manager, the Finance Manager, the Administrator of the Order of St Etheldreda, the Education Officer, the Head Verger, the Shop Manager and the Catering Managers all head significant departments. Since 1996 there has been a lay Cathedral Bursar, who is in effect the executive officer of the Dean and Chapter, implementing Chapter decisions, although not being a voting member of Chapter. In 1980 there were few lay volunteers, but over the last twenty years the number has grown massively. There are over 400 guides, welcomers, flower arrangers, gift shop assistants, stewards, bedesmen, servers, and those who assist with cleaning and conservation work. Without this vast army of lay helpers the modern Cathedral could not function as it does.

In 1980 two rooms that were formerly part of the Black Hostelry housed the whole offices including the Friends Office. In 1981 the Chapter planned a move to larger offices in the Old Choir House in the north range; financial exigencies made this impossible, but by 1985 pressure on space had become severe. Dean Patterson decided in 1986 to move out of the Deanery to Whitgift House in the Precinct and the former Deanery became the Cathedral's administrative centre, incorporating several flats and an office rented to the Surveyor. In 1994 Dean Higgins moved back into the main rooms of the Deanery, and part of the house became a home again. In 2000 a large room in the Black Hostelry was annexed to the offices as a new Chapter Room. Relationships with Press, TV, and the media are well developed, ensuring that the work of the Cathedral has a high profile both in the Church and with the general public.

The Cathedrals Measure 1999

Between 1980 and 2000 several cathedrals experienced severe tensions, and the Deans and Provosts asked for an Archbishops' Commission on the working of cathedrals. The Commission, under the chairmanship of Lady Howe, began work in 1993 and made detailed visits to all Cathedrals. The Howe Report (1994)[8] contained the most comprehensive survey of Cathedral life undertaken this century, and after exhaustive debate in the General Synod, the Cathedrals Measure 1999 was passed by Parliament.

The main thrust of the Howe Report was concerned with five main areas of Cathedral government.

The Bishop

The Commission wished to increase the place and powers of the bishop in cathedral life. This proposal gave rise to much debate about the theological basis of Church government, an area where the report was clearly weak. Many held to the traditional Anglican view of dispersed authority, while others wished to see a more centralised approach with the bishops at the apex of it. Much discussion turned on the significance of a cathedral taking its name from the fact that the bishop's seat is within it, and in the event a compromise was reached by the General Synod. The 1999 Measure strengthened the bishop's powers in his cathedral but rejected the Report's central proposal that the bishop should be chairman of the new Cathedral Council. He may attend the Council, but not vote. In general, relationships between the Bishops of Ely and the Cathedral in recent years have been good. Bishop Walker, in particular, had a warm feeling for his Cathedral, which he did much to support.

---

[8] Elspeth, Lady Howe (Chairman), *Heritage and Renewal. The Report of the Archbishops' Commission on Cathedrals* (London, 1994).

Accountability

The Howe Report felt that a dean and chapter should not have total autonomy and unfettered powers, and so recommended that each cathedral be required to set up a Cathedral Council to which the Dean and Chapter are accountable. The exact relationship of the Council with the Chapter is not defined in the Measure, but will evolve with experience of the new system. It is intended that the Chapter will continue as the executive body of the Cathedral, while the Greater Chapter becomes the 'College of Canons'. The Chairman of the Council and several of its members are appointed by the Bishop.

The Measure retains the powers of the bishop as visitor, parallel with the supervisory role of the Council. The relationship of the two is not clear, although the Council, under the Measure, may ask the bishop to undertake a visitation.

Lay involvement

Alongside accountability, one of the aims of the new Cathedral Council is to give lay people in the diocese a constitutional place in cathedral government. Since 1980 lay people have played an increasingly important role in cathedral management but have not had any place in government, and the Measure corrects this situation. For Ely, it provides that the Chapter must have three additional members, two of whom must be lay. They are likely to be appointed as lay canons.

Management

The Howe Report laid great stress on the importance of modern management techniques in cathedrals, and the Measure introduced new systems of accounting and financial procedures. It is now mandatory for every cathedral to have a lay administrator.[9]

Constitution and Statutes

The constitutional documents of many cathedrals in 2000 were deemed out of date, as reflecting the conditions and ethos of earlier years. At Ely all canonries were freehold, and short-term appointments could not be made. The Precentor was a minor canon and could not be a full member of the Chapter. Neither the Surveyor to the Fabric nor the Cathedral Administrator were members of the Foundation, the Cathedral's constitutional family. The Cathedrals Measure provides greater flexibility in these areas.

Under the Measure each Cathedral was required to set up a Transitional Council, chaired by the Dean, to draft a new Constitution and Statutes embodying provisions of the Measure, with a good deal of local discretion being allowed. The task was arduous and took up many meetings in 1999, and in 2000 the new Ely Statutes were approved by the Archbishops of Canterbury and York. They came into force on 17 October 2000, St Etheldreda's Day.[10]

---

[9] The administrator can be chapter clerk, receiver general, chief executive, and so forth; at Ely the office is held by the Bursar.

[10] At the Eucharist on that day Lady Hughes, a solicitor, Susan Pope, Bursar of Trinity Hall, Cambridge, and Canon Brian Watchorn, Dean of Pembroke College, Cambridge, were installed as additional members of Chapter under the Measure.

Christian Ministry

Bishop Walker was in no doubt that if a text could be selected for the Cathedral it would be the words of Jesus: 'I am among you as one who serves.' Cathedral worship alongside a sound fabric and solid financial base provided a firm foundation from which to serve the wider community

Relationships

Parish links

The magnificence of the Cathedral can stimulate false feelings of grandeur in those who serve it, and may make it look formidable to those on the outside. To parishes the Cathedral can seem remote from the realities of everyday existence, and in the last twenty years financial pressures and the sheer size of the parochial workload have not helped. In 1982 Bishop Walker referred to 'a certain reticence' in some parishes towards the Cathedral, commenting that 'there was work to do to place the Cathedral in the mind and the affections of the Diocese'.

Dean Carey placed great emphasis on building strong Cathedral-parish links, and started inviting parish parties to enjoy evening pilgrimages after the building was closed to the public. This has been much developed since, and during 1999 over 100 parishes took advantage of this opportunity. The many diocesan services and events already mentioned helped to cement the relationship, as does the fact that the parishes are prayed for in rotation at Cathedral Evensong. Clergy and laity from the parishes involved are encouraged to join the worship on 'their evening' and often respond to the invitation. In addition, the Cathedral clergy take every opportunity to preach in the parishes and to speak to Deanery Synods and Clergy Chapters, while the Honorary Canons see themselves as 'ambassadors' for the Cathedral in their deaneries.

Over the years the Cathedral has naturally enjoyed a close relationship with St Mary's parish church, while there are also links with the other Ely churches,[11] and events connected with a major interdenominational Mission to Ely (Diocese) in 2000 were held in the Cathedral. International links were developed in the mid-1990s with Zanzibar and Schleswig Cathedrals, and Kreis Viersen in Germany, which the Choir visited in 1981. The people of Kreis Viersen gave generously to the Cathedral appeal, and a stone in St Etheldreda's Chapel marks this gift. The Cathedral is twinned with Hackney Parish Church, and regular visits and contacts take place in both directions. The Dean and Chapter have the patronage of a number of livings, although the recent episcopal practice of suspending patronage has deprived the Chapter of the support it had given to the parishes in previous years.

---

[11] St Etheldreda's Roman Catholic Church; Ely Methodist Church; the Countess of Huntingdon's Connexion Church; Ely Christian Fellowship; and the Olive Tree Fellowship.

The Friends of Ely Cathedral

An outstanding vehicle for fostering relationships with both the Church and the wider community has proved to be the Friends of Ely Cathedral. Founded in 1935, the Friends have a membership which includes many parishes in the Diocese, and in 1998 corporate membership for schools was introduced. During 1980, a recruitment drive brought 1000 members for the first time, in the following year it rose to 1,700, and in 2000 it was around 2500. There is an active programme of events and social gatherings, including an annual Friends' Day in September, and the Friends can thus develop a closer link with the Cathedral, learn more about its work, and support its life. They are managed by a Council chaired by the Dean. Generous legacies have been left by members, and every year the annual meeting receives proposals from the Dean and Chapter for help with Cathedral projects. It would be hard to stress too strongly the great debt the Chapter owes to the Friends in this respect. In the dark days of the early 1980s the Friends gave valuable support to fabric work and general repairs, particularly the Galilee Porch, and in the following years their help was directed to embellishments of many kinds. Choir robes, altar linen, hassocks, and copes and vestments were donated along with two handsome vestment chests. In 1986 substantial sums were given for the establishment of the Refectory, and new lighting systems in the Lady Chapel, the Octagon, and then the entire Cathedral followed. The west tower clock was refurbished, the Canons' Vestry remodelled, a Faith Exhibition funded, and new signs were introduced throughout the Cathedral. The Friends' latest project, in 2000, has been the building of lavatories and facilities for the disabled near the Lady Chapel, at a cost of £250,000.

Secular links

Much of the Chapter's work involves close partnerships with Ely City Council, East Cambridgeshire District Council, district councils throughout the Diocese, and with the County Council. The County Lieutenancy, led by the Lord Lieutenant, has always supported the Cathedral's ministry, and there are good links with industry, commerce, the Health Service and education authorities. In 2000 the Marketing Advisory Group was given the particular task of promoting the Cathedral's facilities for corporate hospitality, while Canon Peter Sills, appointed in 2000, has responsibility for developing these growing links with the secular world. Bishop Walker's vision of the Cathedral 'on offer' to the world is gradually being realised.

The channels of ministry

Music

'As he was in the beginning, is now, and probably ever shall be, Wills without end. Amen.' So sang some choristers in 1983 to mark Arthur Wills's twenty-fifth anniversary at Ely Cathedral. An outstanding organist and prolific composer, he came to Ely in 1949 as lay clerk and Assistant Organist, and took on the post of Organist in 1958, retiring in 1990 (Plate 60a). In 1996 the Choir issued a compact disc of his music to mark his seventieth birthday. Dr Wills also taught at the Royal Academy of Music, while the Assistant Organist during his time of office was also part-time, being Director of Music at the King's School. From 1990, when Dr Wills was succeeded by Paul Trepte, of St Edmundsbury Cathedral, the post was made full-time. The assistant organist also became full-time, though continuing to teach in the School music department. These moves reflect the growing professionalism of Cathedral music in recent years.

The choristers numbered 18 until 1997, when a generous arrangement with the King's School allowed the number to rise to 22. They live in Choir House and receive scholarships of two-thirds' fees,[12] but in recent years, with increasing academic pressure at school, the life of a chorister is demanding. Many have gone on to distinguished musical careers, and in 1982 Benjamin Stainer became the third great-great grandson of Sir John Stainer to sing in the Cathedral Choir. Alongside the choristers are six lay clerks supplemented at weekends and at festivals by deputy lay clerks. Recruitment of lay clerks has long been a problem at most cathedrals because of inconvenient hours and low stipends, while housing and compatible employment are often difficult to obtain. In the late 1980s part-time posts were created on the Cathedral staff to give supplementary employment to some lay clerks, but creating posts to meet a need is not always a satisfactory device (Plate 60b).

The Ely repertoire continues to draw on traditional settings of the canticles, but since Paul Trepte's appointment as Organist there has been much emphasis on contemporary anthems and music. There have also been a number of new musical initiatives, including a Jazz Mass to the music of Duke Ellington, broadcast from Ely by the BBC in 1994. Occasional orchestral Masses were begun in 1987 and have continued since, and a Music Tour has been developed, in which the Choir moves around the building singing music contemporary with the different periods of Cathedral architecture. The many diocesan and special services also give the opportunity for substantial musical contributions, and the Choir regularly sings in the parishes: two such visits are made each term. It is often broadcast on BBC Choral Evensong, and it has made many other broadcasts and TV appearances in recent years; recordings of Church music are sold in the Cathedral shop and elsewhere. The first Choir Tour to Germany in 1981 was followed by visits to France, Italy, Holland, Belgium, Denmark, Poland, Malta, the Channel Islands and the United States.

The organ was rebuilt in 1975 under the direction of Arthur Wills. In 2000 another £400,000 rebuilding became necessary, with adjustments to restore the original tonal character as well as to add some stops. In 1998 the Cathedral acquired a new Steinway grand piano, through a legacy from a son of Dean Blackburne, and this has greatly extended the musical possibilities.

The cost of Cathedral music has always been immense, and in modern times takes almost one third of the general Chapter revenue due to the heavy cost of choral scholarships. The Dean and Chapter have always been determined to do their part in preserving the great English cathedral music tradition, and in 1985 Dean Patterson called for gifts of £10 per month from members of the congregation wishing to support the Choir. More recently the Music Guild of the Order of St Etheldreda has raised endowments for named choristerships, and this approach continues.

---

[12] Increased from one-third in 1983.

Many concerts – choral, orchestral, and instrumental – are given in the Cathedral by outside bodies, and the Cathedral Choir itself puts on Cathedral concerts each year, often with visiting artists and orchestras. A charity concert has been given at Christmas since 1997. The most ambitious concert in recent years was the BBC Millennium Concert in December 1999, involving two orchestras, the Philharmonia Chorus and the Cathedral Choir, conducted by Sir Simon Rattle.

Visual arts

In 1967 David Wynne donated a Resurrection bronze, for the south transept (Plate 64*a*), and in 1981 a generous donation made possible the bronze 'Christus' by Hans Feibusch which stands at the West End (Plate 64*b*). In 1999 Peter Ball's sculpture 'Christ in Majesty' was placed over the pulpit to mark Millennium Year (Plate 64*d*), and the Friends commissioned a cross by Jonathan Clarke for the wall of the ruined north-west transept. In 2000 a sculpture of the Virgin Mary was commissioned from David Wynne for the Lady Chapel. Exhibitions are mounted every year, usually in the south transept or Lady Chapel, and have included sculpture, icons, and paintings. In 1979 the Dean and Chapter leased the nave north triforium to the independent Stained Glass Museum, the only such museum in England, which has a comprehensive collection of glass from all over England, dating from medieval times to the present day. In 1996 it was moved to the south triforium, and in 2000 was massively refurbished with a £500,000 grant from the National Lottery.

Education

For teachers the Cathedral is an exciting visual aid, and brings education alive in a way that is difficult in the classroom. Over the last twenty years, school visits have risen dramatically in number, and early in 1986 the Education Advisory Group began to produce worksheets for children. Today there are imaginatively produced worksheets for all age groups covering such topics as the Bible, music, ministry, archaeology, and architecture. Since 1999 provision has also been made for secondary school groups, while the Cathedral facilities which were made available in the first instance to Church schools, are now extended to all schools. There is an excellent partnership with the Diocesan Education Committee (which controls Church schools), a partnership particularly seen in the Children's Festivals and Schools Days, when thousands of children come to Ely in fleets of buses.

In 1995 John Inge, a former teacher, became a Residentiary Canon with an education brief, and in 2000 a full-time Education Officer was appointed to work alongside him. There are now Sixth Form Days attracting significant speakers, and a series of Cathedral Lectures began in 1996, bringing to Ely cabinet ministers, judges, academics, and prominent leaders in every part of national life. Bishop Walker had a vision of residential weekends in the Diocesan Retreat House at Bishop Woodford House, with lay people experiencing Cathedral life for themselves and enjoying the quietness and the beauty of Ely. 'The Ely Experience' was launched in 1996, and twice a year up to forty people from all over the country come for a weekend based at the Cathedral. There is now also an Annual Cathedral Retreat for members of the congregation.

Educational work needs a base, and space in the Cathedral is limited. In 1990 Canon Rone raised resources to equip the Old Library as an Education Centre, but the premises were cramped and small. In 2000 Ely Public Library, opposite the Old Palace, became redundant and the Dean and Chapter seized the opportunity to buy it from Cambridgeshire County Council for use as an Education Centre, with the cost of over £500,000 being met mainly from a timely legacy. The Centre will also provide facilities for Cathedral meetings and gatherings, as up to the present Ely has lacked a hall or any kind of social facilities.

The King's School

The Headmaster, Chaplain, and the King's or Queen's Scholars of the School have always been members of the Foundation.[13] The School continues to use the Cathedral for worship, prize-givings – as a visitor once put it, 'there is a magnificent Chapel within the School's own grounds' – and the members of the School are a lively presence around the Cathedral during term time. However, while School and Chapter have always enjoyed strong relationships, the link has changed in nature in recent years. The Chapter faced financial problems in repairing the buildings leased to the School, resulting in the complicated amortisation agreement described earlier, while for the School competition in the modern educational world, league tables, and an ever increasing administrative load on staff have resulted in a change of ethos. In 1986 a new Constitution was drawn up for the School, effectively making it independent of the Cathedral, a move felt to be desirable on both financial and educational grounds. The Dean ceased to be Chairman of Governors, although he remains a Governor, and the Chapter nominates to two places on the Governing body. Until then the school could properly be described as 'the Cathedral School', but this is no longer the case, changing a tradition of many centuries. The School now makes a significant annual contribution to the Chapter, reflecting School use of the Cathedral.

Bishop Walker observed in 1982 that 'neither the Chapter nor the School were at all clear that they were finding the way forward together in worship in a truly constructive way'. These words are still true. Until a few years ago members of the school served at week-day Communion, while until 1990 almost all the King's and Queen's Scholars were confirmed. This is now the exception rather than the rule. A significant number of pupils from other countries and religions complicates the situation, and while day-to-day relations between Chapter and School are at present excellent, the spiritual link between the two bodies will need careful nurturing in the years ahead. A principal area of hope for the future lies in music, with close links being developed between the Cathedral musicians, the Cathedral Choir, and the School Music Department.

The University of Cambridge

Until 1979 one of the Canons was also Ely Professor of Divinity in the University of Cambridge, but this chair lapsed on the retirement of Professor Christopher Stead. However, the University statutes still provide for the possibility of a member of the

---

[13] The Chaplain represents the '*hypodidasculus*' or under-master in the Cathedral statutes of 1544.

Faculty of Divinity holding a canonry. While this move brought to an end many years of formal connection between the Cathedral and the University, informal links continue strongly.[14] College chapel choirs regularly sing Evensong in the Cathedral, the Dean and Chapter preach in college chapels, and the University Education Department and Homerton College work with the Cathedral's Education Department. University staff make their skills and expertise available to the Cathedral in many different fields.

Tourism

Tourism is now a major industry in the United Kingdom. There is a growing interest in history and heritage, and cathedrals exercise a peculiar attraction. Many come to Ely, and Bishop Walker in 1982 speaks of 300,000 visitors a year, perhaps an over-estimate, while a Tourist Board survey in 1979 speaks of 250,000.[15]

In the early 1980s there were few facilities to enrich a visit to Ely, with the vergers acting as guides, assisted by a few volunteers. A Ministry of Welcome was formed in 1986, with around thirty volunteers wearing a distinctive blue gown to welcome visitors and answer their questions. The number of guides rose from 1989. They now provide daily tours of the Cathedral, and in 2000 induction for guides involves a training course and an examination. A full-time Visitors' Manager oversees the arrangements. Facilities for visitors include the shops and catering outlets, and lavatories were built in 2000. Facilities for the disabled have been improved and there has been a Touch Tour for the Blind since 1994, and a loop system for the hard of hearing since 1990. The Visitors' Manager works in close partnership with the Tourism Officer of East Cambridgeshire District Council and other organisations concerned with tourism.

Bishop Walker speaks of how men and women 'stumble' into the Cathedral, 'not quite knowing what they are looking for'. The Dean and Chapter have always sought sensitively to stress the Christian dimension of the Cathedral without in any sense 'pushing' the faith. In many ways the glory of the building itself speaks of a God of majesty and wonder, but in a secular age many visitors have little knowledge of Christian worship, and sometimes do not realise that the building is used for worship at all. In 1994 a permanent Faith Exhibition was opened in the south-west transept, showing how the Cathedral brings alive Christian belief through its architecture, stained glass, monuments, and worship. In 1995 a video presentation was set up in the Prior's Door area, describing the Cathedral community and its work, and a 'Who's Who' board displaying photographs of all staff was introduced in 1986. For the last twenty years auxiliary chaplains, drawn from the parishes, have led prayers hourly throughout the day, and recently members of the Ministry of Welcome have been trained to speak briefly about the purpose of the building to visitors. In 2000 the Cathedral staff adopted a Mission Statement that reads 'Ely Cathedral, striving to be a Christian Community of love and care'. This is the aim, reflecting the ideal that 'Christian faith is caught, not taught.'

---

[14] A formal link still continues through the University Library, in which the Dean and Chapter Archives and the Cathedral Library are kept on permanent loan.

[15] *English Cathedrals and Tourism. Problems and Opportunities. A Report by the English Tourist Board* ([London], 1979), p. 98. No formal survey has been made for several years, but an estimate of *c.*200,000 a year is reasonable.

Postscript

Bishop Walker's Charge ends by pointing to the Hans Feibusch bust, 'Christus' at the West End. 'All that the Cathedral stands for is in fact gathered into the Christ who is there represented. But you must yourself be still, and the Cathedral must have space and stillness, keeping that dimension, if you are to see.'

Herein lies the challenge for the years ahead. Commercial and financial pressures, ever increasing activity in an already busy Cathedral, along with a Chapter who have to be business managers as well as priests, can easily militate against the peace and calm that is so necessary for the rekindling of faith. It is a danger to be faced constantly, although there is much evidence to confirm that Ely continues to have at its heart that sense of worship and of the transcendent appreciated so much by all who come.

Appendix 1

Office Holders at Ely

PETER MEADOWS

Abbesses

672	Æthelthryth (Etheldreda)
679	Seaxburh (Sexburga)
699	Eormenhild (Ermenilda)
?	Werburh (Werburga)

Abbots

970	Byrhtnoth
966 × 9	Ælfsige
1019 × 16	Leofwine
c.1022	Leofric
c.1029	Leofsige
c.1044/5	Wulfric
1066	Thurstan
1073	Theodwine
	Vacancy
1082	Simeon
1093	*Vacancy*
1100	Richard

Bishops

1109	Hervey
1133	Nigel
1174	Geoffrey Ridel
1189	William Longchamp
1198	Eustace
1220	John of Fountains
1225	Geoffrey de Burgo
1229	Hugh of Northwold
1255	William of Kilkenny
1258	Hugh Balsham
1286	John of Kirkby
1290	William of Louth (de Luda)
1299	Ralph Walpole
1303	Robert Orford
1310	John Ketton
1316	John Hotham
1337	Simon Montacute
1345	Thomas de Lisle
1362	Simon Langham *(Archbishop of Canterbury, 1366)*
1367	John Barnet
1374	Thomas Arundel *(Archbishop of York, 1388)*
1388	John Fordham
1426	Philip Morgan
1438	Lewis of Luxembourg
1444	Thomas Bourgchier *(Archbishop of Canterbury, 1454)*
1454	William Gray
1479	John Morton *(Archbishop of Canterbury, 1486)*
1486	John Alcock
1501	Richard Redman
1506	James Stanley
1515	Nicholas West
1534	Thomas Goodrich
1555	Thomas Thirlby
1559	Richard Cox
1581	*Vacancy*
1600	Martin Heton
1609	Lancelot Andrewes *(Bishop of Winchester, 1619)*
1619	Nicholas Felton
1628	John Buckeridge
1631	Francis White
1638	Matthew Wren
1667	Benjamin Laney
1675	Peter Gunning
1684	Francis Turner

1691	Simon Patrick
1707	John Moore
1714	William Fleetwood
1723	Thomas Greene
1738	Robert Butts
1748	Sir Thomas Gooch
1754	Matthias Mawson
1771	Edmund Keene
1781	James Yorke
1808	Thomas Dampier
1812	Bowyer Edward Sparke
1836	Joseph Allen
1845	Thomas Turton
1864	Edward Harold Browne *(Bishop of Winchester, 1873)*
1873	James Russell Woodford
1886	Lord Alwyne Frederick Compton
1905	Frederick Henry Chase
1924	Leonard Jauncey White-Thomson
1934	Bernard Oliver Francis Heywood
1941	Harold Edward Wynn
1957	Noel Baring Hudson
1964	Edward James Keymer Roberts
1977	Peter Knight Walker
1990	Stephen Whitefield Sykes
2000	Anthony John Russell

Priors, see Appendix 2

Deans

1541	Robert Steward *(or Wells)*
1557	Andrew Perne
1589	John Bell
1591	Humphrey Tyndall
1614	Henry Caesar
1636	William Fuller
1646	William Beale
1660	Richard Love
1661	Henry Ferne
1662	Edward Martin
1662	Francis Wilford
1667	Robert Mapletoft
1677	John Spencer
1693	John Lambe
1708	Charles Roderick
1712	Robert Moss
1729	John Frankland

1730	Peter Allix
1759	Hugh Thomas
1780	William Cooke
1797	William Pearce
1820	James Wood
1839	George Peacock
1858	Harvey Goodwin *(Bishop of Carlisle, 1869)*
1869	Charles Merivale
1894	Charles William Stubbs *(Bishop of Truro, 1906)*
1906	Alexander Francis Kirkpatrick
1936	Lionel Edward Blackburne
1951	Cyril Patrick Hankey
1970	Michael Sausmarez Carey
1982	Charles Allan Shaw
1984	William James Patterson
1991	Michael John Higgins

Canons: 1st stall

1541	Richard Cox
1554	John Boxall
1559	John Warner
1565	John Parker
1592	John Palmer
1614	Daniel Wigmore *(to 2nd stall, 1616)*
1616	John Bois *(from 2nd stall)*
1644	John Montfort
[1652	Edmund Mapletoft]
1652 (1660)	Stephen Hall
1661	John Pearson *(from 5th stall)*
1673	John Spencer *(Dean, 1677)*
1677	John Moore *(Bishop, 1707)*
1691	Charles Roderick *(Dean, 1708)*
1709	Robert Cannon
1722	Thomas Jones
1759	Henry Heaton
1777	Peploe Ward
1819	Henry Fardell
1854	*Stall suppressed*

Canons: 2nd stall

1541	Matthew Parker
1554	John Young
1560	John Porie
1563	Thomas Hill
1564	Robert Beaumont

1567	Thomas Ithell
1579	Robert Norgate
1587	Thomas Nevile
1615	John Bois *(to 1st stall, 1616)*
1616	Daniel Wigmore *(from 1st stall; d.1646)*
1660	Bernard Hale
1663	Anthony Sparrow
1668	John Lightfoot
1675	Henry Harrison
1690	Henry Finch
1692	Thomas Lovett
1699	Robert Middleton
1713	Thomas Tanner
1724	Clement Tookie
1748	John Nicols
1774	Richard Watson
1779	James Bentham
1795	Philip Yorke *(to 6th stall, 1795)*
1795	George Owen Cambridge
1841	John Ashley
1859	Henry Reginald Yorke
1871	Bishop Francis Thomas McDougall
1873	Edward Clarke Lowe
1912	George Hodges
1921	Bishop Horace McCartie Eyre Price
1942	Bishop Gordon John Walsh
1967	Peter Clement Moore
1974	Anthony John Morcom
1984	*Stall suspended*

Canons: 3rd stall

1541	William May
1560	Thomas Styward
1568	John Whitgift
1577	Hugh Boothe
1603	Robert Tinley
1630	Elizeus Burges *(d.1652)*
1652 (1660)	William Holder
1698	Thomas Richardson
1700	Drew Cressener
1718	Charles Fleetwood
1737	Thomas Greene
1780	William Cooke *(Dean, 1780)*
1780	Benjamin Underwood
1815	James Croft
1822	George Gaskin

1829	Henry Thomas Dampier
1831	William French

Regius Professor of Greek

1849	James Scholefield
1853	William Hepworth Thompson
1867	Benjamin Hall Kennedy

Ely Professor of Divinity

1889	Vincent Henry Stanton
1916	Alan England Brooke
1926	John Martin Creed
1940	John Sandwith Boys Smith
1944	William Telfer
1947	Edward Craddock Ratcliff
1958	Stanley Lawrence Greenslade
1960	Geoffrey William Hugo Lampe
1971	George Christopher Stead

Canons

1980	Dennis John Green
2000	Peter Sills

Canons: 4th stall

1541	William Lyson
1550	Richard Wilks
?1553	John Ebden
?1561	Matthew Hutton
1567	Henry Hervey
1585	Thomas Nicce
1617	Roger Andrewes
1635	John Harris *(d.1658)*
1660	Henry Brunsell
1679	William Saywell
1701	Charles Ashton
1752	Henry Goodall
1753	John Gooch
1804	Caesar Morgan
1812	John Dampier
1826	Benjamin Parke
1829	Edward Bowyer Sparke *(to 7th stall, 1831)*
1831	Benjamin Parke
1835	John Maddy
1854	*Stall suppressed*

Canons: 5th stall

1541	Giles Eyre

1549	Anthony Otway
1554	John Fuller
1560	Thomas Willett
1587	Andrew Willet
1621	Ralph Brownrigge *(d.1559)*
1660	John Pearson *(to 1st stall, 1661)*
1661	Thomas Wren
1679	Humphrey Gower
1711	John Davies
1732	Christopher Clarke
1742	Charles Hervey
1783	Thomas Du Quesne
1793	Thomas Waddington
1815	Sir Henry Bate Dudley
1824	John Henry Sparke *(from 6th stall)*
1870	William Emery
1910	Henry Leighton Goudge
1923	George William Evans
1938	*Stall suspended*
1958	Stanley Lawrence Greenslade *(not clear to which stall he was appointed)*
1959	*Stall suspended*

Canons: 6th stall

1541	John Custons *(former monk)*
1544	Thomas Bacon
1559	Andrew Deane
1565	John Bell *(Dean, 1589)*
1589	Edward Grant
1601	John Hills
1626	James Wedderburne
1636	Nehemiah Rogers
1660	Laurence Womack
1686	Francis Roper
1690	Francis Ferne
1714	Whadcock Priest
1715	Ralph Perkins
1751	John Samuel Hill
1757	Thomas D'Oyly
1770	Matthias D'Oyly
1787	Houston Radcliffe
1795	Philip Yorke *(from 2nd stall)*
1817	John Henry Browne
1818	John Henry Sparke *(to 5th stall, 1824)*
1824	William Walbanke Childers
1833	William Selwyn

1875	Herbert Mortimer Luckock
1892	Bishop William Kenneth Macrorie
1905	Michael George Glazebrook
1926	Charles John Smith
1942	Henry Balmforth
1956	Harry Saunders
1957	Edmund Lawrence Randall
1960	Douglas George Hill

Bishop of Huntingdon

1966	Robert Arnold Schürhoff Martineau
1972	Eric St Quintin Wall
1980	William Gordon Roe
1988	*Stall suspended*

Canons: 7th stall

1541	Robert Hamond *(former monk)*
1554	Thomas Ellis
1556	Thomas Peacocke
1560	Edward Gascoine
1563	John May
1582	Edmund Barwell
1609	John Duport
1618	Samuel Collins *(d.1651)*
1660	Joseph Beaumont *(to 8th stall, 1665)*
1665	Richard Ball *(from 8th stall)*
1684	John Nalson
1686	Thomas Turner
1714	Samuel Knight
1746	Eyton Butts
1754	Barnard Garrett
1768	John Warren
1779	George Downing
1810	George King
1831	Edward Bowyer Sparke *(from 4th stall)*
1879	Frank Robert Chapman
1910	Berkeley William Randolph
1925	Frederick Vincent Watson
1953	Frederick Norman Robathan
1959	Bernard Clinton Pawley
1970	George Youell
1982	Murray Somerled MacDonald
1989	James Rone
1996	John Geoffrey Inge

Canons: 8th stall

1541	John Ward *(former monk)*
1548	Edward Leeds
1584	James Taylor
1622	John Cropley
1629	William Eyre
1642	John Buckeridge *(d.1651)*
1652 (1660)	Richard Ball *(to 7th stall, 1665)*
1665	Joseph Beaumont *(from 7th stall)*
1699	William Coldwell
1702	James Smith
1715	Stephen Weston
1717	William Powell
1741	John Price
1772	Thomas Hopper
1779	Thomas Knowles
1802	George Leonard Jenyns

Regius Professor of Hebrew

1848	William Hodge Mill
1854	Thomas Jarrett
1882	Alexander Francis Kirkpatrick *(Dean, 1906)*
1903	Robert Hatch Kennett

Regius Professor of Divinity

1932	Charles Earle Raven
1940	*Stall suspended*

Appendix 2

The Priors of Ely

James Bentham's account,
abridged and annotated by Peter Meadows

The Abbey of Ely was, both by regal and papal authority, converted into an episcopal see in 1109, and Hervey Bishop of Bangor became the first Bishop of Ely. The monks had a distinct part of the Abby lands and estates assigned them for their maintenance, and the bishop had the rest of the estates, and many of the privileges, honours and authority which formerly belonged to the abbot. The immediate government of the monks devolved on the prior. He presided in Chapter, and by his office was to inspect the behaviour of the other members of the society, and to see that all performed their duty. This chief officer of the monastery was at first put in by the bishop, but afterwards came to be elected by the monks. He had a number of servants and attendants to himself, and his proper apartments called the Prior's Lodgings, where he kept hospitality, and invited the other members of the society and all strangers of rank coming to the monastery. He was usually styled Lord Prior, and in some reigns was summoned to sit in Parliament.

1. VINCENT was the first Prior of Ely. He died in the lifetime of Bishop Hervey.[1]
2. HENRY, Prior till 1133, either resigned or was displaced.[2] Bishop Nigel, on his first coming to Ely gave the priorship to
3. WILLIAM, with his predecessor, were both present 1134 as witnesses to an account taken of the treasures and ornaments of the Church.[3]
4. TOMBERT, possessed of that dignity about the year 1144, and enjoyed it about nine or ten years; during which time he improved the buildings, and added some ornaments to the Church.[4]
5. ALEXANDER, a pious and learned monk, commended for his knowledge in the Latin, French and English languages. He had in 1140 or 1141 been at Rome, after

---

The text is an abridged version of Bentham, *Ely*, pp. 215–24. The words of the text are all Bentham's, though in a few instances the order of words in a sentence has been altered. Spelling has been modernised. The footnotes are mostly derived from Joan Greatrex, *Biographical Register of the English Cathedral Priories of the Province of Canterbury c.1066 to 1540* (Oxford, 1997).

[1] VINCENT. *BRECP*, p. 452. Thought to have resigned *c*. 1128. He was witness to a charter (EDC 1/A/2, almoner's cartulary, fo. 69ᵛ).
[2] HENRY. *BRECP*, p. 416. Resigned before 5 January 1134, when, as former Prior, he witnessed an inventory of the Cathedral treasury made for Bishop Nigel (*Liber Eliensis*, ed. Blake, iii. 49: p. 288).
[3] WILLIAM. *BRECP*, p. 461. Appointed in mid or late 1133, deposed before November 1137. Probably previously sacrist (Wharton, *Anglia Sacra*, I, p. 265).
[4] TOMBERT. More probably THEINBERT or THEMBERT. *BRECP*, p. 449. Prior certainly 1144–*c*.51.

King Stephen had taken into his hands the Bishoprick of Ely, and brought back letters of Pope Innocent II, directed to the King and the rest of the bishops, to restore to the Church of Ely it's ancient liberties, and to the Bishop his possessions. He became Prior about 1154, and translated the bones of several old bishops and benefactors, from the old conventual church.[5]

6. SOLOMON, who had been precentor, occurs Prior in 1163. He was present at the consecration of Geoffrey Ridel at Canterbury, 1174, at which time happened a contest between our Prior and Richard Archdeacon of Ely, concerning the right of presenting the bishop elect to the Archbishop for consecration; the Archdeacon as the bishop's Official, and the Prior, as having the same privileges as the deans held in all cathedral churches, where the chapters consisted of canons: which claim of the Prior was confirmed by the Archbishop. In 1177 King Henry II came to Ely and held a Council on affairs of state; he promoted Solomon to the Abbey of Thorney.[6]

7. RICHARD, subprior, was made Prior in 1177. He had been at Rome in the time of Pope Eugenius III, on the business of the monastery. He wrote several books, and particularly the History of the Church of Ely.[7] He was living after 1189, but his successor

8. ROBERT LONGCHAMP occurs Prior in 1194. Brother to William Longchamp, Bishop of Ely, and by him promoted. In 1197 he was elected Abbot of St. Mary's in York. His brother dying at Poictiers in France, the See of Ely and the priory became both vacant. The King, who was then in Normandy, sent orders to proceed to an election of a bishop; the convent returned answer, that they could not elect a bishop without a prior. Whereupon Hubert Walter Archbishop of Canterbury issued a mandate to elect a prior.[8]

9. JOHN DE STRATESHETE, 1198. The first prior that came in by election. Soon after, he and some of the principal persons of the convent went over to the King in Normandy, and there elected Eustace the Chancellor for their Bishop.[9]

10. HUGH was Prior 1200; he also occurs Prior in 1206.[10]

11. ROGER DE BRIGHAM, Prior before 1215. Eustace, Bishop of Ely instituted several persons to the churches of Witcham, Hauxton, &c on the presentation of Roger and the convent. Dying in 1229, whilst the temporalities of the See were in possession of the King's officers; who laid hold to seize for the King's use the

---

Witnessed a charter of Bishop Nigel *c.*1144–5, granting Hadstock to the Priory (EDR G3/28, fo. 151; *LE*, iii. 91: p. 337). He gave an embroidered cope, four albs, and other vestments to the Priory (*LE*, iii. 50: p. 293).

[5] ALEXANDER. *BRECP*, p. 388. First occurs as Prior *c.* 1151–2, last 1158. Blake shows that his visit to Rome was not in connexion with the restitution of Bishop Nigel, but rather (probably) to attend the Second Lateran Council, 1139, on Nigel's behalf, to acquire papal confirmation of Nigel's division of the Ely estates (*LE*, iii. 64: p. 316, n. 2). The translation of relics of Ely benefactors took place in 1154 (*LE*, xlviii, n. 7). As Prior he witnessed a charter of Bishop Nigel (EDR G3/28, p. 158).

[6] SOLOMON. More usually SALOMON. *BRECP*, p. 437. Prior 1163–76, when he was made Abbot of Thorney. Precentor *c.*1151–8. Witnessed a charter of Bishop Nigel (EDR G3/28, fos. 157, 159).

[7] RICHARD. *BRECP*, p. 434. Prior *c.*1177–89. He may have been responsible for much of *Liber Eliensis* (*LE*, xlvii–xlix).

[8] ROBERT LONGCHAMP. *BRECP*, p. 422. Prior 1194–7. Probably a monk of Caen (D. Knowles *et al.*, *The Heads of Religious Houses, England and Wales 940–1216* (Cambridge, 1972), p. 46).

[9] JOHN DE STRATESHETE. *BRECP*, p. 443. Prior *c.*1198–1202; previously probably subprior (witness in BL, MS Egerton 3047, fo. 97[v]; EDC 1/B/677).

[10] HUGH. *BRECP*, p. 418. Prior *c.*1203–8.

revenues of the Priory, which had never been done before. However, the monks on making application to the King's Court, obtained a precept ordering the revenues of the Priory to be restored. About this time Pope Gregory IX (by his Bull dated June 12, 1229) confirmed all the privileges of the Prior and Convent.[11]

12. RALPH was confirmed Prior, 1229. He appears to have been Prior in the year 1235.[12]

13. WALTER occurs Prior, 1241, and was Prior when Hugh Balsham, Sub-Prior, was elected Bishop in 1257, and was witness to that Bishop's appropriation of Swaffham St. Mary to the Prior and Canons of Anglesey, 1259.[13]

14. ROBERT DE LEVERINGTON, Prior 1260, died 1271. Whereupon the King's Escheator took the Priory into the King's hands; but the monks soon obtained the King's writ, commanding him to restore it to the convent, as having been wrongfully seized. On the demise of a Prior, it was now usual for the Convent to notify the Bishop, and desire leave to proceed to an election; and after the election, to present the Elect for his confirmation.[14] In pursuance of the Bishop's licence to elect, dated 1271

15. HENRY BANKS was elected Prior, and died in 1273. This prior, and likewise his predecessor, sat in the Bishop's temporal court as justices.[15]

16. JOHN DE HEMMINGSTON, Prior 1274. The new refectory, now the Deanery, begun about the year 1270, was finished in this Prior's time. He died 1288.[16]

17. JOHN DE SHEPRETH presided but a little time.[17]

18. JOHN SALEMAN, DE MELDRETH or DE ELY occurs Prior about 1291. There is direct proof that his father's name was Solomon a goldsmith at Ely, and that he had a brother whose name was Symon, possessed of an estate in Stetchworth which was afterwards given to, or purchased by the Convent. On the death of William de Luda in 1298, he was elected Bishop, by the major part of the Convent; but another party of the monks having elected John de Langton the King's Chancellor, occasioned much dissention among them. And what added to their embarrassment, was the King's officers (who were in possession of the temporalities of the See), taking also possession of the Priory. Whereupon the Prior and Convent applied for redress, and obtained at length, by a fine of 1000 marks, the King's charter, exempting the Priory from being again seized, by reason of the vacancy either of the

---

[11] ROGER DE BERGHAM or BRIGHAM. *BRECP*, p. 391. Prior *c.*1215–28. Mentioned in two presentations to livings in Bishopp Eustace's time (EDR G3/28, fo. 167 *bis*).

[12] RALPH. *BRECP*, p. 432. Prior *c.*1229–38.

[13] WALTER. *BRECP*, p. 455. Prior *c.*1241–59.

[14] ROBERT DE LEVERINGTON. *BRECP*, p. 421. Prior 1261–71; previously witnessed a charter of Bishop Hugh Northwold about the Chantry on the Green (EDR G3/28, p. 188).

[15] HENRY BANKS. *BRECP*, p. 389. Prior 1271–3, the first to be freely elected, under the Bishop's licence..

[16] JOHN DE HEMMINGSTON. *BRECP*, p. 416. Prior 1273–88. In 1281, when ill, he sent Clement de Thetford as proctor to receive absolution from excommunication for irregularities over payment of a tenth for the Holy Land (EDC 1/B/112). At a visitation in 1285 Archbishop Pecham removed all the major obedientiaries except the Prior (*Chronica Johannis de Oxonedes*, ed. H.T. Ellis, Rolls Series, 13 (1859), p. 264). On 17 November 1286 Pecham wrote to the Bishop of Ely, ordering him to stop the Prior promoting a shortened form of monastic office, approved by the Benedictine General Chapter (*Registrum epistolarum fratris Johannis Peckham, archiepiscopi Cantuariensis*, ed. C.T. Martin, Rolls Series, 77 (1882–5), I, pp. 150–1). In 1287 the Prior wrote to the community, following a request from the precentor and almoner, giving permission for monks to spend three nights outside the Priory after bloodletting (BL, MS Cotton Vespasian A. vi, fo. 130[v]; BL, Add. MS 33381, fo. 12.

[17] JOHN DE SHEPRETH. *BRECP*, p. 438. Prior 1288–92. Died 22 April 1293. In 1281 he was one of the monks absolved on account of irregularities over payment of a tenth for the Holy Land (EDC 1/B/113).

See, or of the Priory. Pope Boniface VIII annulled the election of them both, and translated Ralph Walpole, Bishop of Norwich to Ely, and promoted the Prior of Ely to the See of Norwich. He was raised to be Lord Chancellor of England in 1319.[18] On his promotion to Norwich

19. ROBERT DE ORFORD was elected Prior in 1299; and on the death of Bishop Ralph Walpole, was by the Convent elected Bishop of Ely, 1302, but did not get possession till near a year after, being obliged to take a journey to Rome, to support his claim. Pope Boniface VIII confirmed his election.[19]

20. WILLIAM DE CLARE died after he had presided only seven weeks.[20]

21. JOHN DE FRESINGFIELD occurs Prior, 1303. He augmented the revenues of the Monastery by the purchase of estates in Ely, Wicham, Sutton, and Downham, which he appropriated to the use of his successors. He presided near 18 years; when growing somewhat infirm, he resigned the Priorship, 1321, and had a pension and apartments in the monastery assigned him for life; where he lived about 18 years, dying 1338.[21] On his resignation

22. JOHN DE CRAUDEN or CROWDEN was elected Prior. He presided twenty years, during which time there were larger and more expensive buildings undertaken than perhaps in any other equal period of time, since the foundation of the church. The Chapel of St Mary was just begun, the first stone of it being laid by Alan de Walsingham the Subprior on Lady Day 1321. Soon after this, on February 21 following, the great tower in the middle of the church suddenly falling down in the

---

[18] JOHN SALEMAN. More usually SALMON or SALOMON. *BRECP*, p. 436. Prior 1292–99, previously subprior (*The Chronicle of Bury St. Edmunds, 1212–1301*, ed. A. Gransden (London, 1964), p. 113). In 1295 he was summoned to Parliament at Westminster (F. Palgrave, *Parliamentary Writs and Writs of Military Summons* (London, 1827–34), I, 581). He witnessed the confirmation of two charters of Bishop Nigel (EDR G3/28, pp. 157, 159). On his election as Bishop, see Rose Graham, 'The Administration of the Diocese of Ely during the Vacancies of the See 1298–99 and 1302–3', *Transactions of the Royal Historical Society*, 4th series, xii (1929), pp. 49–74.

[19] ROBERT DE ORFORD. *BRECP*, p. 428. Prior 1299–1302. In 1254, with Robert de Leverington and John de Swaffham, he received royal licence to elect a bishop (*CPR, 1247–58*, p. 328), and again in 1298, with Richard de Braunford and William de Brigham (*CPR, 1292–1301*, p. 345). In 1268 he was chamberlain (EDC 1/B/107), later subprior (*CPR, 1292–1301*, p. 345). When he was elected Bishop in 1302, the Archbishop of Canterbury objected on the ground that he had insufficient learning. Orford took his appeal to Rome, where he resigned but then received papal provision (LPL, MS 448, fos. 47–9; *CPL, 1198–1304*, p. 604). Alan de Hemmingford gave a vivid record of proceedings in a letter (J. Willis Bund (ed.), *The Register of the Diocese of Worcester during the vacancy of the See*, Worcestershire Historical Society, 1893–7).

[20] WILLIAM DE CLARE. *BRECP*, p. 398. On 17 December 1300, with Peter de Reche, he was appointed a proctor for the Priory (BL, MS Egerton 3047, fo. 246ᵛ); and in 1302 was one of three monks who received licence to elect a bishop (*CPR, 1301–7*, p. 26).

[21] JOHN DE FRESINGFIELD. *BRECP*, p. 412. Prior 1303–21. In 1305, with Chapter approval, he issued ordinances for his and monks' daily life (BL, Add. MS 41612, fos. 30–3; Evans, *Ordinances*, pp. 24–8). In 1307 he was ordered by Bishop Orford, after visitation, to reduce household expenses and be kind to his brethren (Evans, *Ordinances*, p. 32). In 1312, he was one of the cathedral priors summoned to meet papal nuncios in London (F. Powicke and C. Cheney (ed.), *Councils and Synods with other Documents relating to the English Church*, II (Oxford, 1964), p. 1377). In 1316 he presided at the election of a bishop, and was given power as sole *compromissarius* by Chapter: he nominated John de Hotham (BL, Add. MS 41612, fo. 40). In 1319 he was absent when a dispute arose over the subprior's authority; on his return, he rebuked the subprior for his behaviour, commanded that there be no more rancour, and the subprior forgave and kissed his adversary, the third prior (LPL, MS 448, fos. 97ᵛ–98). He resigned on 16 February 1321 because of accumulated debts and expensive lawsuits for which he was responsible. Evidence of his mismanagement is provided by the *status prioratus*, 1325, in the time of his successor: the sum owed was said to be £835 19s. 11d. (EDC 1/F/13/*status prioratus*; CUL, MS Add. 2957, fos. 65–6).

night, demolished the choir that was under it, and so damaged the arches eastward that they were obliged to be taken down and rebuilt. The Prior built a very handsome chapel, a new hall and study adjoining his lodgings. These great works, all carried on at the same time, must have been attended with a very large expense. The Prior and Convent found assistance from others, in particular from Bishops Hotham and Montacute. The former took upon him the charge of building the three arches of the presbytery adjoining the dome and lantern, and Montacute was a most liberal benefactor to St Mary's Chapel. This Prior was a great encourager of learning in those that were under him. He purchased a house at Cambridge, and sent some of his monks to reside for their improvement in learning. On the death of Bishop Hotham in 1337, he was unanimously by the Convent elected Bishop, but failed of success. He died 1341 and was buried in the presbytery at the feet of Bishop Hotham.[22]

23. ALAN DE WALSINGHAM, Sacrist, was elected Prior 1341. His knowledge and skill in mechanical arts, seems to have given rise to that reputation he afterwards attained. The first mention of him is in 1314, by Walsingham the historian, who occasionally speaks of his skill in goldsmith's work. He was then one of the junior monks. But afterwards turning to the study of architecture, he became one of the most eminent architects of his time. In 1321, he was Sub-prior, and laid the first stone of St Mary's Chapel. Being made Sacrist, he had by this office the care of the fabrick, and the fall of the great tower afforded an ample field for the display of his genius. The idea he formed of erecting a lofty spacious octagon, crowned with a dome and lantern, was new and uncommon. He had no model to follow. His success in the undertaking is a proof of his superior skill. That he himself was the devisor [sic] of that work, and acted throughout as principal architect, is clear from the account that is given of it, and is confirmed by his epitaph; and though there is no direct proof that he gave the plans of St. Mary's Chapel, and Bishop Hotham's new building, I think it is not at all improbable but he did.

Besides the great works about the church, he was continually making improvements in the buildings of the monastery, both whilst he was Sacrist, and after he became Prior. The Sacrist's office he almost new built, in the north-west corner of which he built a square building of stone, and covered it with lead. part of this he

---

[22] JOHN DE CRAUDEN. *BRECP*, p. 401. Prior 1321–41. In 1310 he was named as an executor of Bishop Orford (CUL, MS Add. 2957, fo. 68). In 1319 he was one of the monks who formed an arbitration committee in a dispute over the authority of the subprior (LPL, MS 448, fo. 97ᵛ). In 1322 he wrote to Edward II to tell him of the collapse of the central tower (HMC, *6th Report*, Appendix, p. 295; BL, Add. MS 41612, fo. 60). In 1334 he presided at the Bishop's consistory court with three justices (EDC 1/B/1159, 1163, 1172, 1173). In 1325 the *status prioratus* on the treasurer's account lists Crauden's achievements as Prior, in paying off Fresingfield's debts, and gives details of the building programme (CUL, MS Add. 2957, fos. 65–8; EDC 1/F/13/*status prioratus*). The new building containing his chapel and study cost £138 8*s. 5d.* In 1327–8 he made frequent visits to Lakenheath and entertained guests: stock and grain consumed were listed on the grange account (EDC 7/15/ account, *Expense domini prioris*). In 1337 he was elected bishop, but Simon de Montacute was provided to the see (BL, MS Cotton Titus A. i, fo. 124). Buried 30 September 1341 (EDR G1/1, fo. 25) at the feet of Bishop Hotham, near the high altar (LPL, MS 448, fos. 59ʳ⁻ᵛ). His character and achievements are recorded *(ibid.)*: he is described as a monk of fervent spirituality who was found frequently at prayer and meditation in his chapel at night. He commissioned a beautiful missal and benedictional for his chapel, and purchased a house in Cambridge for the use of his Ely monk students (J. Greatrex, 'Rabbits and Eels at High Table: Monks of Ely at the University of Cambridge, *c.* 1337–1539', in Benjamin Thompson (ed.), *Monasteries and Society in Medieval Britain. Proceedings of the 1994 Harlaxton Symposium* (Stamford, 1999), pp. 312–28, at p. 313).

appropriated to the use of goldsmith's work. Another building was contiguous to the Infirmary, chiefly intended for the use of the *Custos* of the Infirmary. In his time bells were first put up in the great western tower. Four of the largest were cast by Master John de Glocester in 1346. The names were Mary, John, Jesus and Walsingham. Notwithstanding these great expenses in building, he made several considerable purchases of lands and estates, particularly the manor of Brame near Ely, and the manor of Mepal. On the death of Bishop Montacute [1345] the Convent unanimously elected their Prior to succeed him, but Pope Clement VI conferred it on Thomas L'Isle. He lived many years after that, and probably died 1364. By his epitaph, the place of his interment is obscurely hinted at, but the exact place is not easy to be ascertained.[23]

24. WILLIAM HATHFIELD, the immediate successor, only a little while.[24]

25. JOHN BUCTON occurs Prior in 1366, and held that office above thirty years, in the times of Bishops Langham, Barnet, Arundel and Fordham. The great gate of the monastery, Ely Porta, where the manor-court was held, was begun in this Prior's time, and was in building at the time of his death in 1397.[25]

26. WILLIAM WALPOLE, elected 1397, was in possession of that office, 1401, at which time this Church was visited by Archbishop Arundel. He resigned soon after.[26]

---

[23] ALAN DE WALSINGHAM. *BRECP*, p. 453. Prior 1341–63 (or 1364). In 1318–19 he was *custos* of the Lady Altar (CUL, MS Add. 2957, fo. 50). In 1321 he was subprior, then, 1321–41, sacrist (Chapman, *Sacrist Rolls*, II, pp. 25–110). In 1322–42 he initiated and completed the Octagon and Lantern at a total cost of £2406 6s. 11d. (LPL, MS 448, fo. 119). In 1338, with the Bishop's Official, he was appointed to receive purgation of criminous monks (EDR G1/1, fo. 42ᵛ). In 1339, with others, he was appointed to treat with Bishop Hotham's executors over terms of his will (BL, Add. MS 41612, fo. 101). In 1341 he was installed as Prior by the Bishop in person (LPL, MS 448, fo. 61; EDR G1/1, fo. 25). In 1345 he was elected bishop, but Thomas de Lisle was provided. In 1348 he was appointed, with four others, to be vicar general during the Bishop's absence abroad (EDR G1/1 (De Lisle) fo. 17; some of his *acta* are fos. 22, 23ᵛ, 24, 25, 28ᵛ, 29). In 1361 he gave £66 13s. 4d. towards purchase of the manor and advowson of Mepal (S.J.A. Evans, 'The Purchase and Mortification of Mepal by the Prior and Convent of Ely', *Eng. Hist. Rev.*, li (1936), p. 118; EDC 1/B/Box 23). Possibly resigned, and died 1364. In two writings Thomas Walsingham, monk of St Edmundsbury, reported that Alan de Walsingham as a junior monk was known as a skilled goldsmith: *Thomae Walsingham quondam monachi S. Albani, Historia Anglicana*, ed. H. Riley, Rolls Series, 28 (1863–4), I, p. 104, and *Gesta abbatum monasterii sancti Albani, a Thoma Walsingham*, ed. H. Riley, Rolls Series (1867–9), I, pp. 34–5). Phillip Lindley has concluded that though Walsingham was not an architect, he probably 'played a pivotal role' in the Octagon's conception (Cambridge PhD thesis 'The Monastic Cathedral at Ely, *c.*1320 to *c.*1350'; see also Lindley, 'The Fourteenth Century Architectural Programme at Ely', in W.M. Ormrod (ed.), *England in the Fourteenth Century: Proceedings of the 1985 Harlaxton Symposium* (Woodbridge, 1986), pp. 119–129). He is believed to be buried in the nave, between the old nave altar and pulpitum. In BL, Add. MS 33381, fo. 2, it is stated that he lies '*ante chorum*' and a list is given of his achievements, including the new building and the purchase of Mepal.

[24] WILLIAM (DE) HATHFIELD. *BRECP*, p. 415. Prior *c.*1363–4. See BL, MS Egerton 3047, fo. 218ᵛ.

[25] JOHN (DE) BUKTON. *BRECP*, p. 393. Prior 1364–96. In 1350 and 1353 he was ordained sub-deacon and priest (EDR G1/1 (De Lisle) fos. 96ᵛ, 99ᵛ). In 1359–60 he was treasurer (EDC 1/F/2/15). In 1361 he contributed 20s. to the purchase of the manor and advowson of Mepal (Evans, 'Mepal' (cit. in n. 23), p. 118; EDC 1/B/Box 23). In 1373 he was at the metropolitical visitation *sede vacante* (LPL, Reg. Abp. Wittlesey, fo. 152ᵛ). In 1375 he was at the consecration of Henry Wakefield (Worcester) by Bishop Arundel at Hatfield (EDR G1/2, fo. 10ᵛ). In 1376 he was present at the enthronement of Bishop Arundel in Ely Cathedral (*ibid.*, fo. 14ᵛ). In 1378 he was appointed vicar-general during the Bishop's absence (*ibid.*, fo. 27ᵛ). In 1379 he paid £4 at the clerical poll tax (PRO E179/23/1). In 1393 he was appointed monastic visitor of Ely and Norwich dioceses for the Benedictine General Chapter (Pantin, *Black Monk Chapters*, II, p. 94).

[26] WILLIAM DE WALPOLE. *BRECP*, p. 452. Prior 1397–1401. In 1372–6 he was chamberlain (EDC 1/F/3/19, 20; CUL, MS Add. 2957, fo. 29), in 1382 and 1386–7, hosteller (EDC 1/F/5/4, 5). In 1393 a commission was issued for his appointment as sacrist (EDR G1/3, fo. 181). In 1379 he was 22nd in order on the clerical poll tax

27. WILLIAM POWCHER had been a monk at Ely and was Sacrist in 1390, in which year he was elected Abbot of Walden, but quitted that preferment in 1401, being then elected Prior by the monks of Ely, and so returned to his old house. The pillars and arches which upport the great western tower of the church, were begun in 1405 to be repaired and strengthened by a casing of stone. This Prior in 1413 first obtained of Pope John XXIII the privilege of wearing the mitre, and the use of the pastoral staff, and other pontifical ornaments, to himself and his successors. In his time also, the controversy between the Bishop and the Prior and Convent, relating to spiritual jurisdiction, and the claims and privileges in their several manors, was finally determined.[27]

28. EDMUND WALSINGHAM occurs Prior 1418, and held that dignity in 1424.[28]

29. PETER DE ELY was elected Prior in 1425. The same year the See of Ely became vacant by the death of Bp Fordham. The Convent unanimously elected him Bishop, but Pope Martin V translated Philip Morgan, Bishop of Worcester to Ely.[29]

---

list and paid 3s. 6d. (PRO E179/23/1). In 1396–7 he was sent to the Bishop at Hatfield for licence to elect a prior; election expenses were £22 8s. 9d. (EDC 1/F/13/10). In 1401 he resigned as Prior during the metropolitical visitation (LPL, Reg. Abp Arundel, I, fo. 494; Evans, Ordinances, pp. 48–9). According to a Bury chronicle, the Archbishop declared his election to have contravened canon law. Two undated letters from Archbishop Arundel in Prior Walsingham's register (EDC 1/E/1, nos. 8 and 9; after visitation) criticise provision made for him in his retirement as inadequate, and order the monks to maintain him as befitted his former status. The manor of Wodely and its c.£20 a year income were assigned to him, £10 for his clothing, a room in the Priory and the chaplain of his choice, and food and drink for himself and servants (Thomas Arnold (ed.), Memorials of St Edmund's Abbey, Rolls Series, 96 (1890–6), III, pp. 183–4). Ely Porta was known as 'Walpole's Gate or Gatehouse': its construction was under way in 1396–97 (EDC 1/F/13/10).

[27] WILLIAM POWCHER. BRECP, p. 431. Prior 1401–c.1418. In 1388 the King nominated him unsuccessfully as Prior of Swavesey, which as an alien priory was then in royal hands (CPR, 1388–92, p. 1). He was subprior, n.d. (mentioned in an undated treasurer's account, EDC 1/F/13). In 1390, the Bishop issued a commission to remove him from the office of sacrist, following his election as Abbot of Saffron Walden (EDR G1/3, fo. 12). In 1401 he was present at the metropolitical visitation, at which Prior Walpole resigned and proposed Powcher as his successor (ibid., fos. 143ᵛ, 145). In 1405 the Bishop appointed the Prior and Chapter as collectors of the half tenth required by the King (ibid.). In 1413 he petitioned the Pope to issue a mandate to the Archdeacon of Norwich to examine the Ely constitution and ordinances, to eliminate any mutually contradictory, obscure, ambiguous or unreasonable (because out-of-date) rules (CPL, VI (1404–15), p. 394; CUL, MS Add. 2947, fos. 155–6, EDR G2/3, no 5); and received a papal bull permitting him and his successors use of the mitre and other pontifical insignia in the Cathedral and Priory churches (CUL, MS Add. 2950, fo. 23; EDR G2/3, no. 4). In 1417 Powcher and other cathedral priors were appointed by the Archbishop a committee of convocation to look into poverty of university graduates (Reg. Abp Chichele, III, p. 37). In 1417 a laudum or final agreement between Bishop and Prior and Chapter ended a costly 17-year dispute over respective jurisdictions and privileges in the Isle of Ely (Bentham, Ely, p. 167, Appx., pp. *27–*34; CPR, 1416–22, pp. 183–195). Wharton, Anglia Sacra, I, p. 684, states that he built the infirmary hall in 1417.

[28] EDMUND WALSINGHAM. BRECP, p. 454. Prior 1418–24. In 1400, 1401, 1402 he was ordained subdeacon, deacon, priest (EDR G1/3, fos. 240, 241ᵛ, 242). In 1415 he was a student at Cambridge with other monks, and licensed to preach in any church appropriated to Ely Cathedral (LPL, Reg. Abp. Chichele, IV, pp. 126–7). In 1418–20, during his absence in London, the vicar-general arbitrarily removed the subprior, John de Yaxham, leading to 6 months' dispute, in which Walsingham appealed to the Court of Arches (LPL, MS 448, fos. 85ʳ⁻ᵛ). In 1420 he made a visitation of St Edmundsbury on behalf of the Benedictine Greater Chapter (Pantin, Black Monk Chapters, III, pp. 238–9), and was present at the General Chapter at Northampton (ibid., II, p. 96), where he was named as an examiner of monk proctors, an elector of monk visitors, and an elector of the presidents for the next Chapter (ibid., II, pp. 138, 145, 152). In 1423 he visited Ramsey for the General Chapter (ibid., III, pp. 241–2; EDC 1/E/1 (Reg. Walsingham), no. 24), and he and the subprior attended the Chapter and examined proctors (Pantin, op. cit., II, pp. 137–8). In 1423 × 5 he was asked by William, Abbot of St Edmundsbury, as president of the General Chapter, to appoint a prior for the monk students at Cambridge (ibid., III, p. 102; Reg. Walsingham fos. 4 and 5ᵛ, no. 4).

[29] PETER DE ELY. BRECP, p. 408. Prior 1425–c. 1430. In 1384, 1385, 1388 he was ordained acolyte,

30. WILLIAM WELLS seems to have been elected in 1430. He enjoyed this dignity above thirty years.[30]

31. HENRY PETERBOROUGH occurs Prior, 1462, and continued till July 26, 1478, on which day he resigned, having been struck with the palsy, and rendered incapable of discharging his office. The Convent assigned him a yearly pension of 40l. for himself, his chaplain, and servants, with a chamber in the Infirmary. He lived to 1480.[31]

32. ROGER WESTMINSTER, Sacrist, was elected Prior, 1478. He continued to administer the Sacrist's office five or six years after he became Prior, having begun some great repairs about the western tower. He was Prior above 20 years.[32]

33. ROBERT COLVILE, Prior 1500, at which time Ely was visited by the Chapter of Canterbury. He appears to have been Prior, 1510, and shortly after, resigned.[33]

---

subdeacon, deacon, priest (EDR G1/2, fos. 131ᵛ, 132ᵛ, 136). In 1401 the Bishop commissioned the chancellor to install him as cellarer, but then subsequently to remove him (EDR G1/3, fos. 192, 201). In 1405 the Bishop ordered his appointment as subprior (*ibid.*, fo. 201). He was sacrist 1412–13 (CUL, MS Add. 2956, fo. 167) and feretrar 1419–20 (EDC 1/F/11/1, 1/F/10/30). In 1426 he was elected Bishop by the Chapter against the King's wishes: Philip Morgan was provided (BL, MS Cotton Titus A. i, fo. 144ᵛ; LPL, MS 448, fo. 80ᵛ). He wrote to the Prior, n.d., denying any association with the Countess of Hertford (EDC 1/E/1, no. 18).

[30] WILLIAM WELLS or MARTIN. *BRECP*, p. 459. Prior 1430–61. In 1419 he was ordained acolyte, subdeacon, deacon (EDR G1/3, fo. 272ʳ⁻ᵛ). In 1423–4 and 1428–9 he was a student at Cambridge (EDC 1/F/13/12, PRO SC6/1257/4). In 1430–1, Wells, monk of Ely (most probably William Wells), owed 40s. because he did not continue his canon law lectures after his admission to the bachelor's degree (CUL, University Archives, CU Reg. 1.2.1), presumably because he had been elected Prior. In 1435 he acted as *custos* of the bishopric, *sede vacante* (EDC 1/E/1).

[31] HENRY PETERBOROUGH or BURGH. *BRECP*, p. 430. Prior 1462–78. Precentor 1447–8 (EDC 1/F/9/11); cellarer 1460 (CUL, MS Add. 2957, fo. 6). On 9 January 1465 he was present in the Lady Chapel with the subprior and senior monks, when the Bishop examined a man accused of being a sorcerer (EDR G1/5, fo. 133). In 1466 he was cautioned by the Bishop to strive to be loved rather than feared, according to the Benedictine rule (Evans, *Ordinances*, p. 58). In 1473–4 he spent two weeks with 20 servants in Suffolk (EDC 1/F/13/14), and visited the Bishop twice at Doddington; in 1474–5 he made further similar travels in Suffolk *etc.* (*ibid.*). In 1476 he sold some distant manors in Norfolk and Suffolk, and bought others closer (EDC 1/B/176). On 14 February 1478 he was struck dumb, and appointed John Soham as co-adjutor. Resigned 26 July 1478, died 10 August 1480 (LPL, MS 448, fo. 113).

[32] ROGER WESTMINSTER. *BRECP*, p. 459. Prior 1478–99. In 1458, 1460, 1463 he was ordained subdeacon, deacon, priest (EDR G1/5, fos. 205, 208, 210ᵛ). In 1466–7 he was second treasurer and granator (PRO, SC6/1257/9). In 1470–9 he was sacrist (CUL, MS Add. 2956, fo. 168; EDR G2/3, no. 221; CUL, MS Add. 2950, fo. 80; EDC 1/F/10/35–6). In 1478 he accompanied John Soham and other monks to the Bishop to discuss arrangements for former Prior Henry Peterborough's pension (LPL, MS 448, fo. 113ʳ⁻ᵛ). On 28 July 1478 he was elected Prior in the presence of Edmund Connesburgh, Archbishop of Armagh. He was examined in the Lady Chapel *per diversa argumenta doctorum* and confirmed and installed (*ibid.*). In 1480 he took part in Bishop Morton's installation (BL, MS Harl. 3721, fo. 64). On 4 July 1493 he was commanded by the Bishop to examine and assign penance for a woman of ill repute (EDR G1/6, fos 120, 149). In 1485 and 1497 he was too ill to attend convocation (*ibid.*, fos. 120, 149). Died *c.*1499.

[33] ROBERT COLVILLE. *BRECP*, p. 398. Prior *c.*1500–10. In 1466, 1467, 1469, 1473 he was ordained acolyte, subdeacon, deacon, priest (EDR G1/5, fos. 210ᵛ, 211, 211ᵛ, 214). In 1476–7 he was treasurer (EDC 1/F/13/16), in 1479–80, *custos* of the Lady Chapel (CUL, MS Add. 2957, fo. 63); in 1483–4, precentor (EDC 1/F/9/9); in 1495, cellarer (CUL, MS Add. 2950, fo. 84). In 1465–6 payment was made by the precentor for his organ studies (EDC 1/F/9/8), and in 1473–4 a similar payment was made by the treasurer (EDC 1/F/13/14). In 1468–9 he was a student at Cambridge. In 1476 he received papal dispensation to receive and retain a benefice (*CPL*, XIII *(1471–84)*, p. 493). On 30 October 1500 he was present as Prior at the visitation by the Prior of Christ Church Canterbury, while the sees of Canterbury and Ely were both vacant. Colville reported that monastic observance and discipline were kept fully by all but aged and infirm, that there were 40 monks, and that the Priory's annual income was 1800 marks (Canterbury Cathedral Archives, Reg. R, fos. 69ᵛ, 70). In 1510 he was unable to attend convocation because of illness (CUL, MS Add. 2950, fo. 85). He resigned before 27 September 1510 (Le Neve, *Fasti*, IV, p. 17). 1516, was absent from the election of a Prior to succeed William Foliot, and was declared contumacious (EDR G1/7, fos. 55ᵛ–57).

34. WILLIAM WITLESEY occurs Prior 1510. Wharton assures us, that he was Prior in 1515.[34]

35. WILLIAM FOLIOTT was Prior in 1516, as appears from Bishop West's register, in which is inserted the whole process of election of a new Prior, on his resignation, 1516.[35]

36. JOHN COTTENHAM was elected Prior, 1516. He died before 1522.[36]

37. ROBERT WELLS, otherwise STEWARD, the last Prior. In 1536 he was nominated with William More for suffragan bishop, but the King made choice of the latter. When the King and Parliament in 1539 resolved on the suppression of monasteries, our Prior readily complied, and not only persuaded the monks of his own convent, but was very active in bringing over other abbots and priors to surrender their houses to the King. On the 18th of November that year, he surrendered the whole site of the monastery, with all goods and chattels, and all estates, rents, profits and revenues, into the hands of the King's Commissioners. The prior and monks had pensions for life, or until they were provided for by preferment of as great or greater value than their pensions. The late Prior had 120l. a year, and was made guardian of the goods, plate, ornaments and furniture left there by the Commissioners.[37]

---

[34] WILLIAM WIT[T]LESEY or FOLIOT. *BRECP*, p. 463. There was another monk called Witlesey at the same time, so some biographical details are uncertain. Prior *c.*1510–16. In 1475 and 1476 he was ordained acolyte, subdeacon (EDR G1/5, fos. 215^v, 216^v). In 1489–90 he was granator (EDC 1/F/4/49); in 1504–6 and 1509–10, sacrist (CUL, MS Add. 2956, fos. 174–176, EDC 1/F/10/42–3). In 1500 he was examined at visitation by the Prior of Christ Church, Canterbury, who reported that all was well, but the cloister door [Vine Gate] remained open to the public and the precinct wall was in a ruinous state (Canterbury Cathedral Archives, Reg. R, fo. 70). In 1515, at the Archbishop's visitation, reports were made of his maladministration (LPL, Reg. Abp Warham, II, fo. 277; Evans, *Ordinances*, pp. 65–6). After he had replied to accusations, the visitation concluded in peace (*ibid.*, fos. 277$^{r–v}$). He resigned before 22 March 1516.

[35] WILLIAM FOLIOT. *BRECP*, p. 411. Probably William Witlesey. Not in the list of priors made by Robert Wells, last Prior (LPL, MS 448, fo. 96^v). Wells was a monk in 1516 and must have known the facts.

[36] JOHN COTTENHAM. *BRECP*, p. 400. Prior 1516–22. In 1488 he was ordained acolyte, subdeacon, deacon; in 1491, priest (EDR G1/6, fos 224^v, 225$^{r–v}$, 230). In 1510 he was subprior (EDR G2/3, no. 429; CUL, MS Add. 2950, fo. 85). In 1501–2, 1505–6, he was a student at Cambridge (CUL, UA Grace Book B, I, pp. 212, 216). In 1513–14 he was granted grace to proceed to inception in theology (CUL, UA Grace Book Γ, pp. 4, 35, 36, 120, 163). In 1515 he was listed 5th on *sede vacante* visitation certificate (LPL, Reg. Abp Warham, II, fo. 277). On 29 March 1516 he was elected Prior (EDR G1/7, fo. 57^v). Died 1522.

[37] ROBERT WELLS or STEWARD. *BRECP*, p. 457. Prior 1522–39. Son of Nicholas Steward of Wells, Norfolk (J. Venn, *Biographical History of Gonville & Caius College*, 4 vols. (Cambridge, 1897), I, p. 23). In 1510–12 he was at Cambridge; the pittancer gave him 42*s.* 8*d.* (EDC 1/F/8/17), the chamberlain gave 14*d.* (EDC 1/F/10/44). BA 1516–17 (Venn, *Biographical History*, I, pp. 23–24), in 1518–*c.*1520 he was a pensioner of Gonville Hall; MA 1520. In 1515 he was 16th in order on the *sede vacante* visitation certificate (LPL, Reg. Apb Warham, II, fo. 277). In 1522 he was elected Prior (Wharton, *Anglia Sacra*, I, p. 685). In 1525–6 he was ill: the treasurer paid 62*s.* to Horwood, physician, who attended him 8 days; 60*s.* 11*d.* was paid for medicine, spices, *etc.* (EDC 1/F/13/18). In 1533–4 he went to West Derham to meet the King's commissioners, to Wisbech to see the Bishop, and to London for 5 weeks; he also made a journey to London to see Thomas Cromwell (EDC 1/F/13/–; CUL, MS Add. 2957, fo. 81). On 9 and 18 October 1533 he wrote two letters to Cromwell on the King's claim to revenues of the See during a vacancy, objecting on grounds of privileges granted to the Prior and Convent in the past, and intended to defend his claims even against a royal commission (*LP Henry VIII*, VI, pp. 1310, 1494). In 1535–6 he made two long visits to London (EDC 1/F/13/22). In 1536 the Bishop of Ely nominated him a candidate for the suffragan bishopric of Colchester (*LP Henry VIII*, XIII, pt 2, p. 612). In 1539 he resigned the Priory into the King's hands, and was awarded a pension of £120 a year (*ibid.*, p. 542).

Appendix 3

The Discovery of the Bones of
the Saxon 'Confessors'

SIMON KEYNES

William Cole's account of the discovery of the bones of
Ealdorman Byrhtnoth and others, at Ely, on 18 May 1769, and
their reburial in Bishop West's chapel on 31 July 1771

One of the most striking features of the interior of Ely Cathedral from the mid-fourteenth century to the mid-eighteenth century must have been the wall-paintings depicting the seven Anglo-Saxon 'confessors' (comprising Archbishop Wulfstan, five other bishops, and Ealdorman Byrhtnoth) whose bones had been solemnly translated from the old conventual church into the new Cathedral in 1154, and re-buried in the north wall of the new Choir, in the Octagon, in the 1320s (P. Lindley, 'The Imagery of the Octagon at Ely' (1985), reprinted in his *Gothic to Renaissance: Essays on Sculpture in England* (Stamford, 1995), pp. 113–46, at pp. 128–41). The paintings, said to be 'very antient and pretty entire', were described in a letter by Maurice Johnson read to the Society of Antiquaries on 14 May 1718 (J. Evans, *A History of the Society of Antiquaries* (Oxford, 1956), p. 65). Two of the images (of Archbishop Wulfstan and Bishop Ælfgar) were copied by William Stukeley on one of his several visits to Ely in the 1730s or 1740s ('Drawings of Religious Antiquitys before the Conquest by Wm Stukeley', Bodl., MS Top. eccles. d. 6 [*S. C.* 42334], fo. 47[v], reproduced by Lindley, fig. 63). The wall-paintings were destroyed in 1769, and are known otherwise as a group from a set of drawings made by Michael Tyson, at the instigation of the antiquary William Cole and others, shortly before their destruction (Colour pl. 22*c*). The tombs of the seven 'confessors' were opened at the same time, and two years later, in 1771, the bones were solemnly re-buried in Bishop West's chapel, where they remain.

William Cole (1714–82), 'Cole of Milton', also known as 'Cardinal Cole', was part of the network of antiquaries which flourished in England in the second half of the eighteenth century. His friend Michael Tyson (1740–80), Fellow of Corpus Christi College, Cambridge, was an accomplished draughtsman, who shared Cole's antiquarian interests. The following account of their involvement in events at Ely Cathedral in 1769 and 1771 is to be found in volume 33 of Cole's collections (BL, Add. MS 5834, fos. 15[r] + 14[v]).

Ely Saxon benefactors

May 18 1769. At the Back of the North Side of the Choir in Ely Cathedral, under the Dome or Lanthorn, was an high Brick Wall which ran from the 2 inside great Pillars: on it was painted the Figures, in a sort of Gallery, of Wolstan the 2d of that name ArchBP.

of York, with 5 other Bishops, & Brithnod Dux Northymbrynensis, in a Row: the latter (also) sitting: all of them Benefactors to the old Monastery of Ely, & Buried in the old conventual Saxon Church, & removed into this Part of the new Church, when the old one was deserted. Mr Tyson & I had been over about a Fortnight before, when that Gentleman, a complete Master of Drawing, had, at the Request of Dr Nichols, Dr Gooch, myself & by his own Inclination, taken a Copy of that very antient Picture on the Wall, which was much impaired by Time, being thought, by good Judges, to be one of the oldest Paintings in England: Mr Tyson designed it very completely in one morning, & employed the Rest of the Day, & Part of another, in copying exactly & most accurately, the different Columns, Arches, Capitals & other Ornaments of the Doors & Pillars of the old Saxon Conventual Church, now in good Part remaining, & constituting the Lodgins of several of the Prebendaries, viz: Dr Green, Dean of Salisbury, Dr Nichols Preacher of the Charter House, the Hon. & Rev. Dr Hervey, etc., being supposed to be as perfect & authentic Remains of Saxon Architecture, as any among us. Under these Pictures were 7 Arches in the Wall; under which, as I conjectured were the Remains of the 7 Benefactors aforesaid, in seperate Leaden Coffres: & as I expressed a Desire to see the Wall taken down, Dr Gooch very obligingly deferred that Part of the Work till Mr Tyson, Fellow of Benet College & myself, could come over & see it. Accordingly we came this Day, May 18, 1769, Thursday, being one of Dr Gooch's Public Days during his Presidence, & presently satisfied our Curiosities, as the Wall was pulled down to the under Part of the said 7 Arches, which stood on flat Peices of grey marble, which being removed, as I had conceived, in 7 separate Holes in the Wall, about 2 Feet long & 6 Inches broad, plaistered with Morter in the Inside, were the Bones of each Person, cheifly full to the Top; being about a Foot deep. The first that was opened was the furthest to the West, the Duke of Northumberland, who, having been beheaded by the Danes, & his Head sent away, was accordingly found with no Part of his Scull in the Place: but seemed by his Bones to have been of a most enormous Size, his Thigh Bone measuring exactly 21 Inches, & his Thigh & Leg together 3 Feet one Inch: so that Mr Tooky, an Apothecary, who dined with us, conjectured his Height to be between 6 & 7 Feet. The first to the East was ABP. Wolston, whose Scull was quite whole, but the Teeth by the Dampness, or naturally, were all rotten, & crumbled like loose Chalk. The 2nd next to him was a Swedish BP., whose Teeth were firm & good, tho' the Scull was crumbled into small Peices: the 3rd Hole was full of Bones & had been covered by a Linen Cloth. The 4th was also covered by a cloth, that was still quite whole & white, but on touching fell to Peices: it was an handsome patterned Diaper Linen: the Teeth in the Jaws perfectly sound & white. In one of these Holes was afterwards found by the Workmen, a small Bit of Cloth of Gold, which was sent to Dr Gooch's at Dinner Time. I saw nothing of that Sort in any of them, tho' //fo. 14ᵛ// possibly it might be so mouldered away among the Bones, as not easily to be distinguished: & yet it is odd I did not see any; especially as I cheifly with my own Hands emptied these Bones out of their Repositories, into seperate marked Boxes, which Dr Gooch carefully sent to his Prebendal House, there to remain, 'till a convenient Receptacle is found for them in the new Choir, now removing into the Presbytery.

Later addition

On Tuesday Noon, after Matins in St Mary's Chapel, on account of the Choir not being yet completed, July 31 1771, the Bones in 7 different Boxes were brought from Dr Gooch's Prebendal House, where they had remained ever since they had been taken out of their separate Cells in the old Choir Wall, to Bishop West's Chapel, in the Arch of which, above the Altar Tomb in the South Wall, was worked up for their Reception, a Reposi[si]tory of 7 Cells, divided by a single Brick Partition from one another, where I saw them decently reposited, in the same Order as they laid in those they were taken from, 2 years before, in the Presence of the Dean, Dr Nichols, Dr Gooch, Prebendaries, Messrs James & Jeffrey Bentham, my Name Sake the rev. Mr Wm Cole of Ely, with many other Gentlemen & Ladies, among whom were my sister Jane Cole, & Cousin Anne Gray, the Chapel being quite full. In the Front Mr Essex had contrived to put 7 old gothic Arches of Clunch, being Part, I think, of BP. Hotham's Tomb, & above them a Place for an Inscription. The Dean desired me to see that a Label of Lead, with the Name & Date of each Person might be put into its proper Cell. As Mr James Bentham stood by & heard the Dean's Request, I make no Doubt but he will see it done, as he locked the Chapel up when the Bones were deposited, & designed to see them closed up properly. I measured the Swedish BP.'s Thigh Bone, which was only 13 Inches & 3 Quarters: a vast Disproportion betwene him & Duke Brithnod!

Mr James Bentham made an ingenious Discovery, which he shewed to me this Day, of the undoubted Head of King Edward the 2nd crowned, & of his Quene Isabella, in the ornamental closing of the grand North East Arch of the Octogon Dome. In the next Arch are 2 other Heads or Bustos, one mitred, which is certainly BP. Hotham, the other most probably the Prior at the Time when the Church, at least this Part of it, was erecting: these are under the South East Arch. Those under the next or S.W. are 2 Monsters; & those under the 4th or N.W. are 2 Monks: probably Alan de Walsingham before he was Prior, & some other Brother or Sub-Prior or Cellerer. They are all well engraved, & no Doubt expressed their Likenesses. that of the King is exactly resembling Mr Vertue's Print: insomuch that I should have thought that he had taken his Face from this Busto. Duke Brithnoth's Bones were put into the most westernly Cell.

An entry in Cole's journal shows that it was on Thursday 4 May 1769 that he went to Ely with Tyson, who 'took the Draughts of the 7 Benefactors on the North Wall of the Choir behind & under the Lanthorn' (BL, Add. MS 5835, fo. 206). The demolition of the north wall of the Choir is also described in the entry for Thursday 18 May 1769 (fo. 206ᵛ). The subsequent history of Tyson's drawings of the wall-paintings at Ely can be reconstructed from Cole's papers (Cole to Horace Walpole, 6 June 1769, *The Yale Edition of Walpole's Correspondence*, ed. W.S. Lewis, 48 vols. (New Haven, 1937–83), I, pp. 159–61). Bentham intended to have the drawings engraved for his book on Ely; but nothing came of it. On 8 June 1778, when about to leave Cambridge in order to take up residence at his living at Lambourne (Essex), Tyson gave Cole 'the Drawings of the 7 Benefactors of Ely Convent, which he had obligingly, at my Request, copied on the Spot, from the Originals on the Wall' (as recorded in another addition to the note in BL, Add. MS 5834, fo. 14ᵛ). Tyson's death in 1780 prompted Cole to write an account of antiquaries associated with Corpus Christi College, including a warm appraisal of Tyson himself (BL, Add. MS 5852, fos. 105–118). In 1782 Cole offered the drawings to Richard Gough, for use in his *Sepulchral Monuments*, laying great stress on their significance (see correspondence between Cole and Gough in BL, Add. MS 5829, fos. 211^v, 212^v, 217^v, 218^v; some of Gough's letters are preserved in BL, Add. MS 5992). In one of these letters (Cole to Gough, 20 May 1782), Cole supplies crucial information which clarifies the relationship between the drawings and the original wall-paintings: 'The ornamental Arches of the first [drawing, of Archbishop Wulfstan] show what the others were: for they were all ranged in a Line, & had the same Ornaments about them. You will see on the Papers what I wrote about them at the Time: so that you cannot mistake. It is a singular Curiosity: &, to a genuine Antiquary, must please. The Arch under each Figure was the Place where each Persons Bones were deposited, as I was an Eye-Witness.' Cole died about six months after sending the drawings to Gough.

Tyson's original drawings are preserved on five folded sheets of paper among the materials for Gough's *Sepulchral Monuments* in Bodl., Gough Maps 225 (*S.C.* 17583), fos. 35^v ['Wlfstanus Archiepiscopus Eboracensis', with colour wash, and Cole's note '7 figures under similar Arches'; reproduced as Colour pl. 22*c*], 36 ['Osmundus Episcopus in Suetheda Regione'], 37^v ['Alwin Episcopus Helmamensis'], 38 ['Elfgar Episcopus Helmamensis'], 39^v ['Ednodus Episcopus Lyncolniensis', with the note 'each fig. 2 feet 5 inches $\frac{1}{4}$'], 40 ['Athelstanus Episcopus Helmamensis'], and 41^v ['Brythnodus Dux Northanymbrorum', with colour wash]. A note written by Cole on fo. 37 explains the drawings for Gough's benefit: 'These 7 Figures of so many Saxon Benefactors to the Old Convent of Ely, & painted on the Back of the North Wall of the Choir, under the Duomo of that Cathedral, were, at my Request, copied by Mr. Tyson, Fellow of Benet College, just before the Wall was taken down, & the Choir removed into the Presbytery, May 18, 1769. As he was about to leave College, to settle on his Living in Essex, he very kindly gave me the Drawings, June 18 1778 at Milton near Cambridge. Wm Cole.' He added: 'The Arch under each Person (& behind which, were Holes or Receptacles in the Wall, to contain their Bones) was fashioned in the Stone Work, & were of real stone; those above were only painted on the smooth Wall, as were the Effigies.'

William Stukeley's drawings, made *c.*1740, show Wulfstan and Ælfgar seated, whereas Tyson's drawings show Wulfstan and Byrhtnoth seated, and the five bishops (including Ælfgar) apparently standing. Stukeley is unlikely to have been mistaken; so the explanation is perhaps that the paintings had deteriorated in the meantime and that Tyson failed to notice any indication of chairs in the representations of the bishops.

Engravings based closely on Tyson's drawings were duly published in Gough's *Sepulchral Monuments in Great Britain . . .*, Part I: *Containing the Four First Centuries* (London, 1786), pl. opp. p. clvi; Gough's own copy of his book, in Bodl., Gough Maps 221 (*S.C.* 17579), contains a letter from Cole to Gough, dated 5 July 1781 (p. 92). A reduced and re-drawn version of Gough's plate was published by Stevenson, *Supplement*, pl. opp. p. 69 (reproduced as Plate 9*b*). It was on the basis of Cole's notes, therefore, that Gough was able to supply the important additional information that the seven cells containing the bones were 'under their several names and painted effigies, each figure about two feet five inches and three quarters high'. One can deduce from this information, in relation to Tyson's drawings, that the whole monument (tomb in arch, surmounted by effigy in architectural frame, with name above, multiplied by seven) would have stood over six feet high from ground level, and over 20 feet in width from left to right.

Index